EAST ASIA

EAST ASIA
IDENTITIES AND CHANGE IN THE MODERN WORLD, 1700–PRESENT

R. Keith Schoppa

Loyola College in Maryland

Upper Saddle River, New Jersey 07458

Library of Congress Cataloging-in- Publication Data

Schoppa, R. Keith
    East Asia : identities and change in the modern world, 1700-present / R. Keith Schoppa.
—1st ed.
        p. cm.
    Includes bibliographical references and index.
    ISBN-13: 978-0-13-243146-0
    ISBN-10: 0-13-243146-7
1. East Asia—History.   I. Title.
    DS514.3.S36 2007
    950'.3—dc22

2007028387

Executive Editor: Charles Cavaliere
Senior Assistant: Maureen Diana
Managing Editor: Mary Carnis
Production Liaison: Joanne Hakim
Director of Marketing: Brandy Dawson
Senior Marketing Manager: Kate Mitchell
Marketing Assistant: Jennifer Lang
Operations Specialist: Maura Zaldivar
Cover Art Director: Jayne Conte
Cover Design: Bruce Kenselaar
Cover Illustration/Photo: Jean Paul
Nacivet/eStock Photography, LLC
Director, Image Resource Center: Melinda
Patelli

Manager, Rights and Permissions: Zina
Arabia
Manager, Visual Research: Beth Brenzel
**Manager, Cover Visual Research &
Permissions:** Karen Sanatar
Image Permission Coordinator: Frances
Toepfer
Full-Service Project Management: Kelly
Ricci/Aptara
Composition: Aptara
Printer/Binder: Courier Westford
Cover Printer: Phoenix Color Corp.

Credits and acknowledgments borrowed from other sources and reproduced, with permission,
in this textbook appear on pages 545–548.

Pearson Education LTD., London
Pearson Education Singapore, Pte. Ltd
Pearson Education, Canada, Ltd
Pearson Education–Japan
Pearson Education Australia PTY, Limited

Pearson Education North Asia Ltd
Pearson Educación de Mexico, S.A. de C.V.
Pearson Education Malaysia, Pte. Ltd
Pearson Education, Upper Saddle River, New Jersey

4 5 6 7 8 9 10 V092 16 15 14 13

ISBN 13: 978-0-13-243146-0
ISBN 10:   0-13-243146-7

To Beth—with love and gratitude and in special memory of our many trips to the countries of East Asia.

Contents

 Chapter One

Basic Identities *1*

Chapter Two

Chapter Three

Chapter Four

From Tributary Younger Brother to Colony: Vietnam, 1770s–1925   78

Chapter Five

The Tokugawa Regime (1603–1830): Early Modern Japan   101

Chapter Six

 Chapter Nine

Chinese Identity in Turmoil: Reform, Revolution, and Reaction, 1901–1937 202

Chapter Thirteen

From Success to Tragedy: The Chinese Communist Revolution, 1931–1976   *311*

Chapter Fourteen

Chapter Fifteen

Chapter Sixteen

Chapter Seventeen

Socialism with a Chinese and a Vietnamese Face: 1980s to the Present   419

Chapter Eighteen

Whither Japan? From the 1970s to the Present   447

Chapter Nineteen

A "Democracy" in the South, a "Hermit Kingdom" in the North: Korea, 1980s to the Present   *471*

Chapter Twenty

Contemporary East Asian Identities: Commonalities and Differences   *493*

List of Maps

Special Features

Sources

Identities

Pronunciation Guide to Chinese, Japanese, Korean, and Vietnamese Words*

CHINESE

In writing about Chinese developments before 1949 and in the People's Republic since that time, the text follows the pinyin system of romanization in general use today. Names in pinyin are pronounced generally as written, with vowels often taking on the phonetic value of vowels in European romance languages and German. Consonants are generally pronounced as consonants in English, but there are three exceptions:

> *Q* is pronounced as *CH*—as in the name of the last Chinese dynasty, Qing, pronounced as if it were written Ching.

> *X* is pronounced as *HS*, in effect a softer version of *SH*, with the *H* producing a slight hiss—as in the name of China's late-twentieth-century reformer Deng Xiaoping.

> *C* is pronounced as *TS*—as in the name of the important cultural leader Cai Yuanpei.

Vowels, as in pinyin, generally take on the value of vowels in Spanish, Italian, and German.

JAPANESE

The five vowels are pronounced much as in Spanish (*a* as in far, *e* as in mend; *i* as in he; *o* as in cold; *u* as in n*u*de. Consonants have the sounds of English consonants. Syllables are formed from a combined consonant and vowel or from a single vowel. All syllables of a word are given equal stress unless there is a macron (a straight line over a vowel); if a vowel has a macron, it is like a long mark with that vowel drawn out or emphasized. It is standard practice to omit macrons over well-known place names. Diphthongs—vowel combinations—are run together: specifically, *ai* = *I*; *ei* = *a* as in s*a*y; *ao* as in c*ow*; *ou* = *o* as in t*ow*.

---

*Please refer to pages 537–543 for a list of phonetic spellings for Chinese, Japanese, Korean, and Vietnamese words used in this book.

KOREAN

Academic works in English use the McCune-Reischauer system to transcribe the Korean language. In this system the consonants (ch, k, p, t) are pronounced like (j, g, b, d), respectively, with the consonants romanized as (ch, k, p, t) when they occur at the start of a word and as (j, g, b, d) when they fall in the middle of a word. A second reading of these same consonants is set apart by an apostrophe (ch', k', p', t'), indicating an aspirated consonant made by releasing a puff of air after pronouncing these consonants as in English. The (s) consonant is pronounced as in English except when it comes before the vowel (i); then it is pronounced as *sh*.

Korean vowels are pronounced roughly as follows: (a), as in f*a*ther; (ae) as a shorter, lighter version of *a*pple and as l*ay* when preceded by a consonant; (e) as in *e*dge; (i) as in k*ey*; (o) as in s*oa*p; (oe) as a shortened *way*; (u) as in s*oo*n or J*u*ne; (ū) as in c*oo*k or f*oo*t; and (ūi) as in gl*ee*.

VIETNAMESE

For centuries the Vietnamese wrote in classical Chinese and in a demotic script based on Chinese characters called *Nom*. It was only in the twentieth century that the use of a romanized script, *quoc ngu*, became dominant. In this system, the consonants (c, k, q, r, t, x) roughly correspond to the English consonants (g, g, g, z, d, s), respectively. Meanwhile, the consonant combinations (ch, kh, nh, ph, th, tr) can be rendered as (j, k, ny, f, t, j), respectively. The most problematic consonant is "d," because it is written two ways in *quoc ngu*, with and without a line through it. If it has a line through it, it is pronounced like "d" in English, but if it does not, then it is pronounced like a "z." When it is written in English without this diacritical mark, there is no easy way of telling how to pronounce this consonant. The reader is therefore encouraged to consult the guide to phonetic spellings on pages 537–543.

Vowels pose another difficulty, as diacritical marks are added to vowels in *quoc ngu* to indicate different variations in pronunciation. For instance, the vowel "a" can be pronounced in different ways, depending on which diacritical mark is attached to it, such as like the "a" in "father" or like the "u" in "but." Rather than detailing every possibility here, the reader should understand that what looks like the same vowel in English can be altered in both sound and form in Vietnamese with the addition of diacritical marks. Here too the reader is encouraged to consult the guide to phonetic spellings on pages 537–543.

Preface

Within the past four decades, all of the countries in East Asia except North Korea have experienced the world's fastest-growing economies: Japan from the 1960s through the 1980s, South Korea and Taiwan in the 1960s and 1970s, the People's Republic of China in the 1990s and 2000s, and the Socialist Republic of Vietnam in the late 1900s and early 2000s. All of these economies were fueled by spectacular export rates and produced hugely favorable balance-of-trade ratios. Growing commercialization meant that traditional patterns of life and relationships were being challenged by expectations brought often by radio and television. One question raised by this new reality is how the society and culture of these countries might be changed in the long term. Another question posed in many quarters is how and when national economic success might be transformed into political power. In countless ways, the modern identities of these countries are being forged day by day.

The issue of identity is, of course, not only about the present and future but also about the past. Each country is evolving from its own particular historical and cultural experience. The question facing each country is how much of the past is to be used in the formation of its modern identity and in what ways. Confucianism, the common cultural base for all these countries, was once discredited because of its supposedly stultifying social hierarchy and its focus on system maintenance rather than progressive change. Yet today, in the People's Republic of China, Confucius has been rehabilitated; and there, in Taiwan, and in South Korea, social commentators find some of the secrets of economic success in other Confucian values: the emphasis on education, the focus on loyalty to the group (whether family, company, or nation), even its embedded authoritarianism, credited by some for the economic successes in South Korea. Taiwan, and Singapore. Will other traditional cultural forms continue to play crucial roles in the working out of modern identity?

This book is a study of the four countries that make up the East Asian cultural sphere (China, Japan, Korea, and Vietnam) from roughly the mid-eighteenth century, when traditional cultures and civilizations were in full play, to the present. Since the historical trajectory of each country differed, there is no single starting year. The focus, however, is on changing political, social, economic, and cultural identities in the nineteenth and twentieth centuries; the analysis considers the experiences of each nation and of the East Asian region. Chapters 1 and 20 are topical, looking, respectively, at traditional East Asian commonalities and differences and at contemporary commonalities and differences. The other chapters are chronological. All chapters except Chapter 1 include brief biographical vignettes of men and women who played significant or telling roles in their time; they range from emperor to assassin, from female political leaders to a feminist revolutionary, from rebel leaders to a Nobel Prize winner. At the end of each chapter is a timeline of key events described in the chapter, as a shorthand way of summing up major points, and a short annotated list of suggested additional readings. Finally, following the Endnotes, I have included a phonetic pronunciation glossary for the main historical figures and key geographical sites; this should make it easier to pronounce and remember East Asian names.

I offer my deep and sincere thanks to Charles Cavaliere, who has shepherded this work from the beginning; his advice and support have been invaluable. I also offer my deep thanks to Kelly Ricci, Project

Manager at Aptara, for her indefatigable and conscientious work in overseeing and managing the day-in, day-out problems of getting a book this diverse into the best form possible. I would also like to thank the readers of the draft manuscript, whose advice and suggestions were on target; I know the book is much better for their incisive critiques. They are David G. Atwill (Pennsylvania State University), James L. Huffman (Wittenberg University), John M. Flower (University of North Carolina–Charlotte), and Sue Gronewold (Kean University). Thanks also to the manuscript reviewers David L. Kenley, Elizabethtown College; Sue Fawn Chung, University of Nevada, Las Vegas; Parks Coble, University of Nebraska; John E. Van Sant, University of Alabama, Birmingham; Jeffrey Thomas, Clark College; Theodore Jun Yoo, University of Hawaii, Manoa; Mark Bender, Ohio State University; James Carter, Saint Joseph's University; Sue Gronewold, Kean University; and Victor Cunrui Xiong, Western Michigan University. Phonetic spelling help was provided by Jeff E. Long, Bloomsburg University (Korean); Jeffrey Dym, California State University, Sacramento (Japanese); and Liam Kelley, University of Hawaii (Vietnamese). In the end, any infelicities in the text are my responsibility. Finally, I would like to offer special thanks to Beth, who has always offered her support in so many ways.

Baltimore, Maryland
January 2007

About the Author

R. Keith Schoppa is the Edward and Catherine Doehler Chair in Asian History at Loyola College in Maryland. He is the author of numerous articles and books, including *Blood Road: The Mystery of Shen Dingyi in Revolutionary China* (University of California Press), for which he won the Joseph Levenson Prize for the best book on twentieth-century China in 1997, and *Revolution and Its Past: Identities and Change in Modern Chinese History* (Prentice Hall). He has held many fellowships from the John Simon Guggenheim Memorial Foundation, the National Endowment for the Humanities, and the American Council of Learned Societies. In 1994 he was named the Indiana Professor of the Year by the Carnegie Foundation for the Advancement of Teaching and the Council for the Advancement and Support of Education.

CHAPTER ONE

Basic Identities

Like the identities of individuals, the identities of cultures and nations are derived both from their nature and from the way others perceive them. Snapshot-like images of such things as landscapes, wildlife, products, food, and politics create superficial identities of particular nations in East Asia—China, Japan, Korea, and Vietnam. Geishas, the bullet train, sushi, and samurai conjure up Japan. Giant pandas, the Great Wall, moo shu pork, and Tiananmen Square quickly bring to mind China. Kim chi (hot, garlicky fermented cabbage), bulgogi (grilled sesame steak), the hanbok (traditional dress), and a divided peninsula immediately suggest Korea. For many in the United States, the image of Vietnam unfortunately remains rather monolithic, an association with the war that occurred in the third quarter of the twentieth century. As that war fades further into memory, it may well be replaced by the ao dai (women's traditional dress), phobo (Vietnamese beef noodles), the cyclo (a pedicab form of transportation), and Halong Bay (a tourist site of 2,000 islands in 1,500 square kilometers northeast of Hanoi). These shorthand ways of conjuring up the nations' identities tell us little more than meets the eye or tongue. Yet they suggest the countries' divergent identities—among them geography and location, language, social structure, food and aspects of daily life, and, most important, unique historical experiences.

If we begin to probe for the deeper meaning behind what it means to be Chinese/Japanese/Korean/Vietnamese, we find that these nations share broad cultural elements that contributed to the shaping of an East Asian identity. These include Confucian ethics and family values, the agricultural ethos of the world of rice, attitudes toward nature and the world, and basic ways of thought and religion.

One of the best ways to begin understanding traditional East Asian culture is by comparing its key aspects to cultural configurations in the modern West. When the West came to East Asia, it was a

Halong Bay, Vietnam   Almost 2,000 precipitous islands and islets jut out from the Gulf of Tonkin to present a spectacular seascape. This 1,500-square-kilometer area was denoted a UNESCO World Heritage site in 1994. The bay's Vietnamese name means "Bay of the Descending Dragon."

modernizing and modern West meeting a largely traditional East Asia. There are several things to keep in mind before beginning this exercise. First, the modern West was not a monolith. There were many different Western countries and cultures; and within each country and culture, there were many different historical actors, worldviews, and approaches. Therefore, our generalizations will of necessity cover up millions of specificities. Second, this comparative process should not be taken to mean that there is a monolithic traditional East Asia; though Japan, Korea, and Vietnam borrowed deeply from Chinese culture, each developed its own cultural approaches and emphases. Third, in no sense were the modern West and traditional East Asia unchanging or static: they were "two vast, ever-changing, highly problematic areas of human experience."[1] Each nation, East and West, had its own direction and pace of development: each saw major changes in the years leading up to their initial confrontation. Finally, culture does not determine history. *People make history;* sometimes they adhere to cultural norms, but at other times they break out of cultural molds. So the discussion that follows should be approached with more than a grain of salt. In skeletal outline, it sets forth broad cultural differences in huge brush strokes. The exercise of comparing the main cultural aspects of Western and East Asian countries is worth undertaking because it can provide a glimpse of the general cultural chasm that served as context for the monumental and ugly confrontation that took place when modern trends, outlooks, and approaches clashed with vibrant and evolving traditional identities.

Indeed, *identity crisis* is an appropriate description for what occurred as a result of this confrontation. During the past two centuries, the countries of East Asia have all experienced identity crises of major proportions. Because of different historical contexts and varying contemporary social and political patterns, these identity crises took various forms in each country, but invariably they produced roller coaster rides for the people. Specifically, the clashes between Chinese, Japanese, Koreans, and Vietnamese cultures and Western proponents of the modern led, among other things, to social and economic disruption, revolution, and war in the national arena and to bewilderment, resistance, and shattered lives for individuals.

THE CHASM BETWEEN THE CULTURES OF TRADITIONAL EAST ASIA AND THE MODERN WEST

Anthropologist Edward T. Hall has theorized that cultures differ according to how human activity relates to context, by which he means "the interrelated environmental, social, and cultural conditions in which individuals, organizations, and communities exist."[2] Cultures, he suggests, can be placed on a scale of high to low context. Five cultures where context is least important are the Western cultures of Switzerland, Germany, the Scandinavian countries, the United States, and Canada. In decision making, these cultures pay most attention to the words being spoken and the facts; making decisions generally takes a relatively short time. Japan and China, on the other hand, are two cultures where context is most important. There social setting, history, class, education, age, gender, sexual orientation, appearance, social status, gestures, and tone are considered crucial. These East Asian cultures pay attention to the surroundings in the fullest sense; communication there takes substantially more time. To be sure, this categorization must also be taken with more than the proverbial grain of salt. It is obvious that there are people in all cultures who would be described as high context or low context and that the two might be reflected differently based on variables like gender, race, and age. Hall's theory therefore only *suggests* the very different cultural approaches, ideals, and priorities chosen by these large cultural blocs.

Recent research reported in the August 2005 *Proceedings of the National Academy of Sciences* seemed to bear out Hall's hypotheses. When twenty-five European Americans and twenty-seven native Chinese were shown a photograph, researchers tracked their eye movements. The European Americans focused on the object in the foreground, while the Chinese "spent more time studying the background and taking in the whole scene." One of the researchers noted pointedly, "They literally are seeing the world differently."[3] Now for more specifics.

Senses of Time and Space

Start with the basics: sense of time and sense of space. In the modern West, the sense of time has been shaped in large part by the Idea of Progress that originated in Enlightenment thought. This idea posited that humans are moving forward in time, ever progressing, using their intelligence and relying on science and technology to better their world. The concept pointed humans toward the future, moving inexorably away from a past that was less modern, less sophisticated, and less convenient. In Confucian East Asia, in contrast, the golden age was in the past and the story of humans was one of cyclical decline from those halcyon days. The eighteenth-century Japanese political philosopher Motoori Norinaga put it this way: "Even things that are profitable, if they are of a new form, are customarily to be considered troublesome; and for this reason, things that are traditional, even though containing slight elements of harm, for the most part should remain where they are."[4] People looked to the past with a view to trying to restore it, though with the sense that this would never be possible. Trumping the power of the past was that it was the domain of ancestors, who, in this family-oriented culture, were revered and honored.

The sense of space in the modern West is outward-looking. Europe is only a small peninsula on the great Eurasian landmass, yet it was the leader in colonizing the world. This outward drive was fueled by a modernizing capitalism, a missionizing Christianity, and empire-building governments. Infusing the Western approach were a willingness to leave home to seek fortunes and, more importantly, a missionary ethos that drove Westerners beyond their borders to try to reshape the world in their own image. In the United States, this looking outward or beyond focused, until the last years of the nineteenth century, on the western frontier and was perhaps encapsulated best in the term *manifest destiny*. Traditional East Asians, in contrast, saw their native place—where their ancestors had lived and were buried—as a perpetual home base. While many East Asians did travel, even roam—merchants, pirates, Japanese *rōnin* (masterless samurai), and others—the native place was a crucial part of family and individual identity. In addition, there were practical reasons for most East Asians to remain sedentary. Eighty percent or more of the population were farmers, an occupation that rarely involved much spatial mobility.

Basic Social Unit

It is common to say that the basic social unit in the modern West is the individual, who is celebrated as one who can make his own choices in order to shape his life. It is the individual for whom law offers legal protection even as it protects his social and political rights.

But for the East Asian, the reality is sharply different, a difference that can be dramatized by an anecdote. In a conversation at a social gathering, the American philosopher John Dewey (who spent two years in China in the early 1920s) was asked by a friend, "John, don't those two men standing over there look alike?" Dewey gazed at them thoughtfully for a moment and then replied, "Yes, they do. Especially the one on the right."[5] This was, of course, a patently ridiculous thing to say, for to look alike there must be more than one person. This requirement is similar to the sense of the individual in East Asia: "the traditional Confucian idea of a person is not an isolated entity [as in the West], but a self in relation to others."[6] Traditional East Asians found their identity chiefly in relation to others in society. Given the East Asian worldview, "any one thing can only be appreciated by appeal to its relations. Persons are known by the quality of relations that locate them within family and community."[7] A scholar of Vietnam put it this way: "Traditional Vietnamese were not socialized to strive for individual independence. They did learn to handle, and to prize, relationships characterized by nurturance, dependency, and mutual obligation."[8]

It is when one is asked to describe the group in each society that one further sees a fundamentally different definition of both the individual and the group in these two cultures. In the modern West, it is accurate

Source: "The Good Deeds of the Seven Brothers," A Korean Folktale

Every East Asian country has many stories about filial piety and its presumed benefits, both immediate and (as here) deferred. In Korea an elderly man is called a grandfather, *so the shoe seller was not a family relative; the constellation referred to is Ursa Major or the Great Bear. What brother takes the initiative in the story? What does that say about male siblings in a family with Confucian values?*

Long ago in a certain village, there was a widow who had seven sons. The sons had a fervent filial piety. If there was work to do for their mother, whatever work it was, they would do it without sparing themselves. In order that their mother could live in a warm room, they would go to the mountain, cut wood, and kindle a fire [in the hypocaust, an underground heating system]. However, their mother always said that she was cold. Even when they kindled the fire to be [really] hot, she would say she was cold. Her sons didn't know the reason [why this should be so]. One night, the eldest son awoke and saw that his mother was gone. When it was dawn, she came back to her place quietly so that her sons would not know and lay down. The next night, the eldest son pretended to be asleep, and went out and followed his mother. Mother went to the house of the home of the grandfather who sold shoes in the next village. It seemed as if the son could understand his mother's thoughts. If she went to the next village, she had to cross over a brook. She had to cross over by taking off her shoes and going through the cold water of the stream. The eldest son went home, brought back his younger brothers, and built a bridge in the middle of the night. When it became the dawn of the next day, their mother was really grateful when returning home now that she could cross the stream without taking off her shoes because of the bridge which hadn't been there in the evening. The mother looked at the heavens and prayed, "As the hearts of the people who built this bridge are really kind, please make them the stars of the north pole or the south pole." Heaven heard these words. When the seven brothers finally died, it is said that they became the Seven North Stars.

Source: James Huntley Grayson, comp., Myths and Legends from Korea *(London: Curzon Press, 2001), 301.*

to say that—other than in the family—the individual precedes the group; but in traditional East Asia, the group preceded the individual. Put another way, in the West individuals make up a group; in East Asia a group is composed of individuals. Because in the West individuals make up a group, they can also, as independent actors, freely make demands on the group or even leave the group. In East Asia, because the group has precedence over its individual members, maintaining the group and its harmony is of primary concern. The group constrains individuals, for they cannot make claims of individual rights without threatening the group's identity and cohesion. As in the West, individuals can leave the group, but in the process the East Asians will tear or break the net, and social and personal damage can be severe. In this sense, traditional East Asian individuals were much less independent actors than individuals in the West.

The most important group was the family. Confucius, who taught in the fourth and fifth centuries BCE, emphasized family relationships, at the heart of which was filial piety. Sons and daughters—especially sons—had to meet the physical and emotional needs of their parents; keep their bodies, gifts from their parents, safe and unsullied; and have children themselves so that the family line could continue, producing descendants to remember and revere their ancestors. Examples abound. In Korea's most exemplary

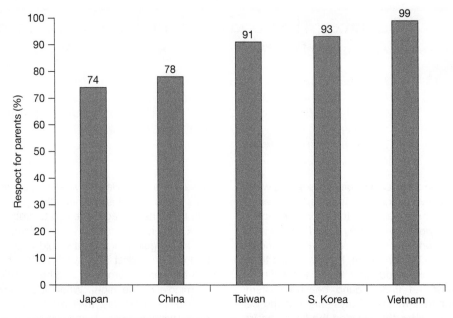

Figure 1-1: Comparative Filial Piety   This result of surveys taken by social scientists around the world shows that filial piety remained highest in Vietnam. The World Values Survey, taken periodically since 1981, is administered via detailed questionnaires in face-to-face interviews, with between 1,000 and 3,500 interviewees in each country. The World Values Survey Secretariat is located in Stockholm, Sweden. How might the relatively low percentage of filiality in Japan be explained? *Source: For Vietnam, the 2001 World Values Survey; for the other nations, the same survey from 1995 to 1998. See www.worldvaluesurvey. org/Upload/5_viet.pdf.*

story of filial piety, a teenage daughter sacrificed her life in order to provide her father with money to purchase rice that, when donated to a temple, would heal his blindness, selling herself to sailors who wanted a maiden to sacrifice to the seas. In Vietnam, "the parent-child relationship was at the very core of Vietnamese culture, dominating everything else."[9] In Japan, the Chinese *Classic of Filial Piety* was part of the school curriculum by the end of the eighth century.[10]

Chinese tales of filial piety (many from that same *Classic of Filial Piety*) are numerous. In one, the father of a desperately poor family decided that there were too many mouths to feed and that he would kill his son so that the father's mother might survive. But when he dug the grave for his son he uncovered buried treasure, which allowed him to spare his son's life: practicing filial piety, the moral went, will bring happiness and prosperity in the end. Confucius left little doubt of the importance of filiality compared to other social obligations. The following is from the *Analects,* the collection of Confucius's sayings:

> *The Governor of She declared to Confucius: "Among my people, there is a man of unbending integrity: when his father stole a sheep, he denounced him." Confucius said: "Among my people, men of integrity do things differently: a father covers up for his son, a son covers up for his father—and there is integrity in what they do."[11]*

In all East Asian countries, a family ideal was the lineage or clan, the descendants of one ancestral patriarch. In some areas, villages were made up of a single clan. In Korea of the 1930s, for example, there were around fifteen thousand villages inhabited by only one lineage. Though the strength of the lineage varied in each country from place to place, many lineages published their genealogies as an expression of family pride. Some held land, from which the proceeds of the harvests might provide a safety net for members or revenue to undertake special projects.

Social Hierarchy

In the modern West, moral principles are ideally applied universally, leading people to see social equality as the norm. But for East Asians that is not the case: family and society at large were always structured hierarchically. The Chinese philosopher Mencius put it this way: "That things are unequal is part of their nature . . . . If you reduce them to the same level, it will only bring confusion to the empire."[12] Similarly about Vietnam, one scholar noted that "[t]rue equality was perceived to be destabilizing, to be contrary to the natural order of the world."[13] Both the Korean and Japanese languages have verb endings that reflect one's place in the social hierarchy.

Confucius had talked of five social bonds that were crucial in framing society and structuring daily life; as a whole, they placed the highest premium on maleness and age. The most important bond was father-son, already touched on above; the two other familial bonds were husband-wife and elder brother-younger brother. In the Confucian system women were subordinated to men—to their father, then to their husband, and (after their husband's death) to their sons. The prevailing sense was that to have a daughter was a losing proposition, since she would have to be fed and cared for by her birth family until she married;

Confucius   The teachings of Confucius, written down by his disciples in the *Analects,* were the most important philosophical source shaping the social, political, and cultural values of all four East Asian countries.

then she was sent off to her husband's home, perhaps never to see her birth parents again. Two Vietnamese proverbs underscore the reality: "One boy, that's something; ten girls, that's nothing" and "A hundred girls aren't worth a single testicle."[14]

But it is important to see that in early Japan and Korea, before they came under Confucian influence, women were not subordinated. In Japan there were a number of female emperors. Early in Japanese history, women also had social choices: after a woman married, she could continue to live with her natal family; her husband might move in with her family or only visit her there; or the husband and wife could live in their own home together. In Korea's Koryŏ dynasty (918–1392), where society was more influenced by Buddhism than by Confucianism, a matrilineal system existed, where on marriage, the husband lived with his wife's family and where women shared inheritance rights with their brothers.

Social Goals and Patterns

The historian Benjamin Schwartz, in his study of the Chinese scholar-translator Yan Fu, noted the *Faustian-Promethean* aspects of modern Western development: "the exaltation of energy and power both over non-human nature and within human society," so that economic and social institutions are at one and the same time harnessed, energized, and given direction.[15] It is a world that is often defined most elementally by dynamism and bold initiative; it is surging, uneven, without bounds or limits. A word of cultural caution: obviously, not all people in Western cultures were bold or boundless. As elsewhere in this chapter, I am dealing with general cultural tendencies rather than cultural certainties.

For the largely agricultural population of the countries of East Asia, sedentary and bounded by the world of their ancestors, an individual's bold and surging initiative would not only have been out of place but also downright destructive of the social goals valued most: order and harmony. To attain order and harmony, Confucius emphasized ritual, education, and social order based on a strict hierarchy. Social harmony is most easily achieved when one follows what is called the *rectification of names,* that is, when one's actions match one's name: let the son truly act like a son (showing filial piety); let the father truly act like a father (shouldering responsibility for his family); let the ruler truly act like a ruler (ruling out of benevolence for the people). Such values tended to give rise to profoundly conservative societies in which bold change was often shunned and where most change could proceed only with reference to and precedence in the past.

Basic social identity comes not only from one's family and one's place in it, but also from social connections and the networks that develop from them. As one writer has said about the Chinese, "[They] instinctively divide people into those with whom they already have a fixed relationship, a connection, what the Chinese call *guanxi,* and those that they don't. These connections operate like a series of invisible threads, tying Chinese to each other with far greater tensile strength than mere friendship in the West would do."[16] Certainly social connections are important in every culture. But East Asian cultures have developed connections to the utmost, and their peoples have used them to get what they want or need. The report of the World Values Survey on Vietnam in 2001 noted that development or modernizing "does not lead away from traditional family networks, and may actually increase the density of these networks . . . which help form [Vietnamese] social and political identities."[17] The person who uses connections to gain certain ends spends social capital and builds up social debts to the one who dispenses favors or facilitates actions. His repaying those debts through reciprocal actions further nurtures the connection they share, making its *tensile strength* very great indeed. The contemporary Chinese poet Bei Dao ended his poem "Notes from the City of the Sun" with the line "Living: A net": it is almost as if traditional East Asians were linked to others by invisible threads that tied them into nets. Connections and networks thus help to shape the fundamental structure and processes of East Asian societies. Networks may encompass many people. Their basic structure, however, is dyadic, based on the connections of two people, and then two others, and so on. The strength of any two connections varies. Similarly, individuals may be part of several networks, and the strength of the personal connections to people in each network also varies.

Source: Floods and Rituals (1801)

The extent to which the emperor conceived of his responsibility for maintaining the unity of Heaven, earth, and humanity through ritual is made clear in this edict by the Jiaqing emperor at the beginning of the nineteenth century. A xun *was a ten-day period; the* huidian *was the collection of dynastic regulations. What is the ultimate reason this emperor is "beset with anxiety" and having mounting fears?*

From the first *xun* of the sixth month, the capital district has had steady rain. It has rained continuously for two *xun* and still it has not cleared.

The Yongding River has overflowed and caused damage, and the waters do not recede. I am beset with anxiety and my fear mounts. I have consulted the *huidian* but it only has the ritual praying for rain in the Altar of Land and Grain. There is no prayer for clearing, but floods and droughts are both disasters, and ought to be treated in the same way . . . on the twenty-sixth day of this month [August 5] I will go to the Altar of Land and Grain to pray for clearing. Earlier on the twenty-second I will enter the Palace of Abstinence. I will observe the three days of abstinence from the twenty-third . . . the twenty-seventh, twenty-eighth, and twenty-ninth are days of abstinence for the autumn sacrifice. On the first [August 9], after the ritual is completed, if the skies have cleared and the mud has dried I will return to reside in the Yuanmingyuan. If at that time there is still no clearing, I must remain inside the Palace of Abstinence for several days until the weather clears.[1]

[1] *In a memorial dated Jiaqing 6/6/19 (July 29, 1807) in the First Historical Archive in Beijing, 557-5-66-4/ 3778.*

Source: Evelyn Rawski, The Last Emperors: A Social History of Qing Imperial Institutions *(Berkeley: University of California Press, 1998), 228–29.*

This situation has definite ethical implications. Fei Xiaotong, China's most famous twentieth-century sociologist, notes that Chinese society is structured as "webs woven out of countless personal relationships" and that "[t]o each knot in these webs is attached a specific ethical principle." In this society, "general [ethical] standards [do not apply]. The first thing to do is to understand the specific context: Who is the important figure, and what kind of relationship is appropriate with that figure? Only then can one decide the ethical standards to be applied in that context."[18] Thus, there is no universal ethic to be applied to all people and in all situations. Ethics in East Asia were traditionally determined by connections; they varied with particular people and situations.

State and Government

In the modern West, the state has mostly political functions as it legislates and administers programs and policies; its actions are framed and delimited by law. In traditional East Asia, although the state had an obvious political role, its primary function was ritual. The Chinese character for *king* is three stepped horizontal lines connected by a vertical line; it denotes three component parts of the universe, Heaven, earth, and humans, interconnected by the actions of the king. A primary function of the king was to create that connection through rituals. As long as he did so, there would be harmony and order. But if he did not, then—since all three realms were linked—earthquakes or other natural disasters would occur, signs that Heaven's mandate to the ruler was in jeopardy. The saying "heaven sees as the people see; heaven hears as the people hear" essentially means that people are the agents of Heaven's will, and part of that will was legitimately overthrowing the ruler if he did not rule benevolently for the people.

Korea and Vietnam both based their concepts of governance on the Chinese Confucian foundation with its centrality of ritual and education. The Vietnamese king, for instance, led four ritual cults: "of Heaven, of his own ancestors, of Confucius, and of agriculture. His kingly role emphasized ritual leadership over executive and legislative functions."[19] In Korea, where "society [was] governed by a thousand ritual observances," the state at times across the centuries performed shamanistic, Buddhist, and Confucian rituals.[20] Japan, though it borrowed heavily from China, never adopted the Mandate of Heaven concept. Its head of state was the emperor, conceived as a direct descendant of the Sun Goddess (Amaterasu). But as in the other three East Asian states, ritual played a key role, so much so that it can be said that the *form* itself became *substance*. The earliest word for government in Japan was *matsurigoto,* meaning "religious observances."

A further difference in matters of governance concerns processes or ways of getting things done. Modern Western countries emphasize programs, policies, and institutions regulated and limited by law. Cherishing law was a hallmark of Western traditions, law having first been given by God on Mount Sinai. In East Asia, though administrative and penal law was utilized, there was no profession of law and no lawyers. Civil law was not esteemed, for resorting to it meant that one was somehow unable to conduct one's life based on the moral ideals that inhere in humanity. Yet Chinese "did use the magistrates' courts in serious disagreements over real estate, inheritances, and other economic matters."[21] East Asian governments were not of law but of men, and most often worked through social connections.

A simple analogy can offer a greater sense of the differences between East and West in this regard. It has been said that the West with its system of laws is like the oak tree, deeply rooted, with trunk and branches firm and unyielding; but its stolidity can be dangerous, for it does not bend and can be toppled in a storm. In contrast, a symbol for East Asian cultures is the bamboo, flexible and bending before whatever force is exerted upon it and very difficult to break. Thus, situations in state and society play out with considerable social fluidity, depending on the context and on the specific relationships between the actors.

Ways of Thinking about Life and the World

In every culture there are what one writer has called *fundamental categories,* that is, ways of thinking that people take for granted and may not recognize even if they are pointed out. Two fundamental categories have already been mentioned. One is the emphasis on context and social hierarchy in East Asian thought and life in comparison to the focus on the particular and social equality in the modern West. Another is thinking in terms of dualities: male-female, light-dark, summer-winter, hot-cold, square-round, active-passive, good-evil, north-south. The difference between traditional East Asian cultures and the modern West is that the latter cultures tend to see these categories as polar opposites. Something is *either* this *or* that. This way of thinking probably grew out of the Aristotelian penchant for categorizing through analysis, perhaps from the dualities of Manicheanism, which found its way into Christian thought and perhaps even into Western religions—Christianity, Islam, and Judaism, which assert an exclusivity that makes each religion the only true faith, with all others false.

In contrast, when East Asians see dualities, they see not opposites but elements that are complementary. The model East Asian duality is yin-yang, two forces whose interactions create the changes in the world. Often depicted as a whole circle, yang is greatest where yin is least and vice versa. Yang is the male force, while yin is female. Because dualities are complementary, the East Asian fundamental category is not *either-or* but *both . . . and,* notably inclusive rather than exclusive. In terms of religious thought, this means that East Asians can choose more than one religion. When I asked my graduate school roommate from Taiwan what his religion was, he quickly responded, "Buddhist, Confucian, and Daoist." The key approach here is pragmatic: individuals can choose whatever religious ideas are appropriate for their needs from any number of religious systems.

Source: A Cultural Misunderstanding

Vietnam specialist Neil Jamieson witnessed the incident that he describes here. He too was affected; he writes, ". . . while I had not been involved in the conversation, the two men—both acquaintances of mine—each looked to me for some sympathetic response. Although I did later and separately try to explain to each of them what had happened, neither felt that my response . . . was satisfactory. Meanwhile, I . . . [was] irritated with both of them, . . . [feeling] that I too had been judged unfairly and found wanting. . . ." In your opinion, how should this situation have been handled for a better cultural understanding?

I once saw an American point out to a Vietnamese employee that he had made a rather serious error. The American explained the situation earnestly and with great patience. The Vietnamese listened intently. When the American finished, the Vietnamese grinned from ear to ear and did not say a word. For a moment the American stared at him in amazement, then abruptly lost his temper. "Look at that son-of-a-bitch! He thinks it's funny!" The smile had indicated embarrassment; the silence, agreement and acceptance of fault. The employee had understood the explanation, accepted responsibility for the problem, and would probably have corrected the deficiency at the earliest possible moment. But the American had expected some verbal response: an explanation, a denial, an apology, or even an argument. He interpreted the silence as disinterest and the smile as impertinence.

Actually this Vietnamese employee had respected the American employer until he lost his temper and gave vent to such an emotional outburst. Then the man actually did become sullen and resentful, because the American had not treated him with respect. Ironically, when the man signaled his compliance and respect to the American, it had been viewed as insolence. Each man felt the other had acted in a rude and disrespectful manner, and never again did these two men have the effective working relationship they had enjoyed before this unfortunate exchange.

Source: Neil L. Jamieson, Understanding Vietnam *(Berkeley: University of California Press, 1993), 75–76.*

Another fundamental category of thought is one's conception of the nature of life and the world. Aristotelian thought and the development of modern science have contributed to thinking of things in the modern West in terms of classes and categories, putting them into compartments. All cultures compartmentalize, but Westerners frequently compartmentalize their lives so that their ideas and actions in one arena do not necessarily carry over into other arenas or so that different sets of values may be chosen and followed in different arenas of action. For example, about two-thirds of Bucknell University female students in a 2004 survey about religion and risk taking said that "religion and their beliefs did not play a role in influencing their decisions about sex, drugs, and alcohol."[22] Religion was placed in one compartment and sexual activity and/or risk taking in another, with the former having very little influence on the latter.

In East Asia, in contrast, because of the view that everything in the universe is connected, holism is an important concept. It is not surprising that the idea of holistic medicine, a practice becoming popular in the modern West, grew naturally out of the Chinese worldview. As a Chinese scholar put it, "The genuine Chinese cosmogony [an explanation of how the universe came into being] is that of organismic process, meaning that all parts of the entire cosmos belong to one organic whole and that they all interact as participants in one spontaneously self-generating life process."[23] In contrast, the Western model in this regard is cause and effect: something caused the universe to be created. The Chinese are not worried about cause:

indeed, they had no creation myth until the eighth century CE, thousands of years after Chinese civilization developed. The gulf between thinking causally or synchronically is obviously great.

A third fundamental category was the view of destiny. At least since the Enlightenment, many people in the modern West, operating almost from a personal Idea of Progress, have relied on themselves to better themselves. Using willpower, they believe they can change their world and their place in it. In the United States the concept was encapsulated in two myths—the log cabin to White House myth and the Horatio Alger myth. For the traditional East Asian, the dominating feature of life was fate. Fated to be born male or female, to be born to rich or poor parents, to have a strong or a sickly disposition, to be married well or ill, to die young or old—all had to accept their fate, most of the time because social harmony depended on it.

At first glance, one last fundamental category initially seems odd. It involves the concept of *sincerity*. In Western cultures, sincerity primarily means being true to one's feelings; one's words and actions convey what one truly feels. Though East Asians certainly have a similar quality in their personal relationships, in traditional East Asia sincerity meant being true to one's social role. Thus, in traditional China and Vietnam and in Neo-Confucian Korea and Japan, a daughter was sincere if she married whomever her parents betrothed her to, no matter how distasteful the match was, for she was playing her social role as a daughter. A Japanese warrior (samurai) was sincere if he followed his lord into death by committing ritual suicide (*seppuku*). During the U.S.-Vietnam war (1961–1973), a Vietnamese was sincere whenever he told Americans to whom he was subordinate what they wanted to hear—whether it was true or not. In many ways, this fundamental category is at the heart of the culture clash between East and West. In relationships, the different understanding of sincerity can lead to situations where the Westerner comes to believe that the East Asian is not being truthful and covering up his own feelings, while the East Asian sees the Westerner as embarrassingly frank and unconcerned about how his openness affects their relationship.

To sum up, the following chart reveals the vast gulf between traditional East Asian cultural ideals and those of the modern West. Again, a number of cautionary notes are in order. Traditional East Asian countries or their peoples do not appear as a result of some cultural "cookie cutter," producing clone-like identities; the same is true of modern Western countries or peoples. Further, the chart and the discussion above make broad generalizations to which there are many exceptions. But if one talks about the cultural ideals that gave *East Asia* and *East Asians* its/their commonality and identity, then the chart sets forth key aspects of that cultural core; I would argue that it does the same for the modern West and its peoples.

Chasm between Cultural Ideals—East and West

	Traditional East Asian Cultures	Modern Western Cultures
Sense of Time	cyclical decline from a past golden age	progress to the future
Sense of Space	limited; based on native place	outward-looking
Basic Social Unit	group	individual
Ethic	particularistic	universalistic
Nature of Society	hierarchical	egalitarian
Social Goals	harmony	dynamism
Key Role of Government	ritualistic	political
Concept of Dualities	complementary	polar opposites
Worldview	holistic	compartmentalized
View of Destiny	fate	human willpower
Sincerity	true to one's social role	true to one's feelings

Source: "Where Does Rice Come From?" A Chinese Folktale

Since rice is the main staple in most of the regions of East Asia, its cultivation has defined the rhythms of life and has been the subject of essays, poetry, and (as here) folk tales. What does the tale suggest was the likely existential problem that prompted Kuan Yin's actions (i.e., rice plants were there but with empty ears)? What does the tale say about relations between the gods and human beings?

Long, long ago man had no rice with which to still the pangs of hunger, but had to live from fruits and the flesh of wild beasts. It is true that the rice plant was there, but at this time the ears were empty, and naturally no food could be had from them.

One day the goddess Kuan Yin saw how difficult men's lives were and how they were always hungry. Her compassionate heart was touched, and she decided to help them. One evening she secretly slipped down to the fields and pressed her breast with one hand until her milk flowed into the ears of rice. She squeezed until there was no more milk left, but all the ears were not yet filled; so she pressed once more with all her might, and a mixture of blood and milk came out. Now her task was finished, and she returned home content.

From that time the ears were filled, and man had rice to eat. The white grains are those that were made from her milk, and the ruddy red ones are those that were formed out of the mixture of her milk and blood.

Source: Wolfram Eberhard, ed., Folktales of China *(Chicago: University of Chicago Press, 1965), 9.*

RICE CULTURE: THE WORLD OF EAST ASIAN AGRICULTURE

The staple food in Vietnam, South China, Korea, and Japan is rice. Though in North China today it is wheat, in ancient China rice was also cultivated. Rice is so important that a common way of asking "How are you?" is "Have you eaten rice [today]?" Rice agriculture likely originated in Vietnam and then spread to China. In the past, archeologists believed that rice planting began in China some three thousand to four thousand years ago. But this estimate may have to be revised: in late 2004, a rice kernel found in Hunan province was confirmed to be twelve thousand years old.

The importance of rice for East Asian society and culture cannot be overemphasized. One Japanese writer contended that "next to the Emperor, rice is the most sacred of all things on earth. Money can be squandered and the wastrel forgiven, but there is no forgiveness for wasting rice."[24] Rice is unique among cereal crops in that it grows in water. The paddy cultivation process is arduous. Paddies were small plots of land, generally twenty square yards or less. Their soil first has to be plowed. Then huge amounts of water are required to give the plowed land the consistency of a thick paste before rice plants that have been cultivated in special moist beds for about six weeks can be transplanted; once the seedlings are transplanted, they should stand in several inches of water until several days before the crop is harvested. Mastering and perfecting irrigation methods are thus crucial. Before the invention of power-driven pumps, farmers used a variety of water sources: rainwater confined in fields, reservoirs, and/or tanks; streams channeled to the site; or canals bringing water from rivers or lakes. In the process of preparing the paddies, farmers had to flood and at least partially drain one paddy after another. Because the paddy land had to be ready and sufficient water at hand, the time for transplanting seedlings in a particular paddy was limited. Transplanting was backbreaking work performed mainly by women; and because of

Terraced Rice Fields   With space at a premium in all the mountainous countries of East Asia, terraced rice fields with their striking chartreuse sheen are a common sight. Maintaining the proper amount of water for the rice plants was necessary for a good harvest.

the time crunch, the labor of lineages and local communities was mobilized. For cultures already knit together in groups, paddy agriculture only underscored the necessity of social cooperation. A Vietnamese song describes the thoughts of a farmer plowing the paddy land and, by extension, the whole strenuous rice-growing process:

> *In the heat of midday, I plough my field.*
> *My sweat falls drop by drop like rain in the ploughed earth.*
> *Oh, you who hold a full rice bowl in your hands*
> *Remember how much burning bitterness there is*
> *In each tender and fragrant grain in your mouth.*[25]

Since rice was grown in the same paddies year in and year out, with perhaps two or three crops per year in southern regions, fertilizing the paddies was a key part of rice agriculture. Until chemical fertilizers were available, human and animal excrement, called *night soil,* was essential. Together with such materials as weeds plowed into the paddies before they were flooded and sludge from the bottom of ponds and canals, night soil helped keep the soil fertile. But its use came at a cost: it carried potentially lethal parasites—hookworm, liver fluke, and blood fluke. If night soil was not properly fermented to kill the worms, they could pierce the skin of a farmer's leg as he walked in the paddy, travel to his intestinal wall, and live there sucking his blood, perhaps with many other of the half-inch-long worms. They could suck up to half a pint of the farmer's blood every day, leading to anemia and perhaps death. The hard, cold fact was that almost a quarter of all deaths in traditional China were due to these parasites.[26]

Women Transplanting Rice
Traditionally, women performed the backbreaking work of transplanting rice seedlings in flooded paddies. This particular paddy is near Kyoto, the imperial capital of Japan from the ninth to the nineteenth century.

The rhythms of daily life in rural East Asia were the rhythms of rice agriculture; at its most basic, that meant plowing in late winter and spring, planting in spring, weeding in summer, and harvesting in autumn. It was a life-work cycle that was repeated every year; it is little wonder that the cycle and a sense of the cyclical infused much East Asian thinking.

The other marker of daily life was festivals whose ceremonies, rituals, and foods offered brief respites from the world of work. In most if not all cases, eating rice in various forms was a central part of the festival. The following chart shows several traditional holidays in Korea and China with their prescribed dishes.

	Korea	China
New Year	rice cakes	glutinous rice cakes
fifteenth day, first lunar month	sweet steamed rice	rice dumplings
Cold Food Day/Qingming (China)	cold rice offered at ancestral tombs	meats, vegetables, fruits offered
fifth day, fifth lunar month	wormwood rice cakes	glutinous rice cakes
ninth day, ninth lunar month (China)		"Double Nine" festival rice cakes
Harvest Moon	half-moon-shaped rice cakes	moon cakes
eighth day, twelfth lunar month (China)		rice porridge

In traditional Japan, the central component in the marriage rites was the acceptance by the bride and groom of small rice cakes on the third night of their marriage. There the rice-growing cycle came to be closely associated with rituals carrying religious overtones. After the seedbed was prepared, rice and rice wine were sacrificed at the site where water entered the paddy. Transplanting the seedlings in some areas was the occasion for a festival, where Shinto priests blessed the seedlings at a temporary field altar. At harvest time, a bundle of rice ears was set aside to be sacrificed to the *year god* or the *field god* on the New Year. At the end of the rice cycle, there was a festive meal featuring white rice cakes.[27] Rice wine was also associated with rituals in all East Asian countries.

Almost all Japanese imperial rituals were based upon rice cultivation, from planting to harvesting. Until the end of World War II, the Japanese emperors were viewed as direct descendants of the gods. The early Japanese myth-histories, the *Kojiki* (712) and the *Nihonshoki* (720), attest to the central role of rice in Japan among the gods.

> *In one version in the* Kojiki, *the Sun Goddess (Amaterasu) is the mother of a grain soul whose name bears reference to rice stalks. The legendary . . . "first" emperor, is the son of the grain soul or the grandson of the Sun Goddess, who sends him to rule the earth. At the time of his descent, the Sun Goddess gives her grandson the original rice grains that she has grown in two fields in Heaven from the seeds . . . given to her by the Deity in charge of food (Ukemochi no Kami). The grandson's mission was to transform the Japanese archipelago from a wilderness into a land of succulent ears of rice* (mizuho) *nurtured by the rays of the Sun Goddess.*
>   *In other words, the rice grain embodies the Japanese deity.*[28]

It is interesting, in light of this connection, that the traditional deity for the rice harvest has been transformed in modern times into the deity for corporate success.

THREE WAYS OF THOUGHT IN TRADITIONAL EAST ASIA

Besides the culture of rice cultivation, the East Asian cultural world has been connected by three philosophical-religious systems of thought. Two are native to East Asia, specifically to China: Confucianism and Daoism; and the other, Buddhism, was an import into East Asia from South Asia. One other religious tradition found in Northeast Asia, shamanism, is discussed in Chapter 8.

Confucianism[29]

As with all classical Chinese philosophers, the chief concerns of Confucius (Kong Fuzi, ca. 552–ca. 479 BCE) were practical: how to order Chinese society so that it functioned harmoniously and how to create ethical harmony between human beings. What were the essential elements in ordering society? While Western culture conceives of society as composed of separate individuals, each with inalienable rights, the Chinese traditionally saw society "as being the source for circumscribing characteristics of the individual. Consequently, society becomes a repository of values and . . . individuals become concrete exemplars of value," worthy of emulation.[30] At the heart of Confucius's teaching was an emphasis on rites or ritual propriety: *li*, a word that has religious overtones. *Li* regulates the patterns of human relationships; in that sense, *li* brings order and coherence to society. Because rites have been handed down from the past as the proper way, Confucius taught that when a man practices them properly, he "extends himself into the matrix of tradition." Such a man is the "exemplary man" (*junzi*) who serves as a social model.

> *The Master said: Lead the people with administrative injunctions and keep them orderly with penal law, and they will avoid punishments but will be without a sense of shame. Lead them with excellence and keep them orderly through observing ritual propriety* (li) *and they will develop a sense of shame, and, moreover, will order themselves.*

Indeed, people will follow the exemplary man without coercion.

The cardinal Confucian virtue is *ren,* a difficult word to translate. Often rendered as "human heart-edness," *ren* means "to become an authentic human being."[31] If *li* tells us what should be done, *ren* is the spirit with which we practice *li.* Confucius refused to consider himself a man who possessed *ren,* making it clear that achieving it was an ongoing process. But the coming together of *ren* and *li* produces the exemplary man. "The Master said: Wherein do the exemplary persons who would abandon human heart-edness (*ren*) warrant that name? Exemplary persons do not take leave of their human-heartedness even for the space of a meal." Acting appropriately and morally, they set an example for others by living according to the Way (*dao*), the word Confucius used for his teaching. Exemplary persons—both wise and virtuous—can transform society, ruling benevolently through high principles, a profound sense of morality, and complete empathy with the people.

For Confucius, education was the key to developing sages who could so rule the state. Historically he was important as a teacher, instructing his disciples, who wrote down his social and ethical guidelines in the *Analects.* For his emphasis on teaching and his tenet that all classes of people (not just exemplary persons) can be educated, Confucius's birthday (September 28) is celebrated annually in the Republic of China on Taiwan as National Teachers Day. In 2004, the People's Republic of China sponsored its first commemoration of Confucius's birth. Though Confucius did not initiate the extraordinarily important civil service examination, it is perhaps his biggest monument: the examination made education the heart of state and society, and his teachings and collateral works were its subject matter.

Confucianism was introduced into Vietnam during China's millennium of control of the country (111 BCE–939 CE). It became the philosophy of state and the basis for education; the Vietnamese also adopted the civil service examination system and the Chinese writing system. With the end of Chinese rule, and perhaps in reaction against things Chinese, Confucianism went into a temporary decline, displaced by Buddhism. But with the rise of the Le dynasty in the fifteenth century, the state became thoroughly Confucian. Historians note that the Confucian philosophy had a number of impacts on Vietnamese society, among them eroding the power of the landed elites (through the rise of merit-based political and social systems); eroding drastically the considerable power of women in society at the time; and replacing "relatively informal social mores ... by a more hierarchical and inflexible system of human relationships."[32]

Confucianism entered Korea in the fourth century CE and found Buddhism already a powerful force. Like Vietnam, Korea, by the beginning of the Chosŏn dynasty in 1392, made Confucianism the state philosophy, and adopted both the Chinese script and the civil service examination system. Korea borrowed most heavily what was called Neo-Confucianism, a philosophy developed in China's Song dynasty. To the ethical teachings of Confucius, philosophers added a metaphysical overlay that reflected the impact on Confucian thinking of two other ways of thought, Daoism and Buddhism. In the end, as one historian puts it, "Korea became more Confucian than Confucian China as its influence permeated every aspect of the life of the nation."[33]

Confucianism first came to Japan in the sixth century via the Korean kingdom of Paekche. A contender for Japanese allegiance to Buddhism, Confucianism was well enough valued that by 604, in the famous constitution of Prince Shōtoku detailing concepts of government, the first article set forth the importance of harmony as seen in Confucianism. Prince Shōtoku initiated direct relations with China; from 604 to 618 Japan sent four missions to China and began to borrow many of its political and cultural elements, including the Chinese script, governmental administrative structures, and the layout of the Chinese capital for building the Japanese capital of Nara (710–784). The last military regime in Japan, the Tokugawa shogunate, made Neo-Confucianism the state ideology. What is today Tokyo National University was founded in the late 1600s as a Confucian academy. Although Buddhism remained a strong competitor and often prevailed, Confucianism continued to be an important source of Japanese values. As one writer put it, "At no time did Confucianism have the field to itself. On the other hand, there has been no time since its introduction when Confucianism has not been an active player in the shaping of Japanese politics, intellect, and behavior."[34]

Daoism

While Confucianism required the training of the wise and virtuous to lead society, Daoism called for acquiring a certain psychic, intellectual, and emotional state and then retiring from the world. The goal is to attain a mystical harmony with the *dao,* the dynamic force or flow that undergirds reality; that goal is attained by emptying oneself of desire and attachment through non-action (*wu-wei*). Non-action is not laziness; it is purposeful. The crucial Daoist imperative is "Do nothing and nothing will be not done." When one has attained one-ness with the dao, one is like an uncarved block of wood and in a state where there is no need to plot and scheme to satisfy desires and in the process threaten others. The extravagant, the excessive, and the extreme are to be put away, replaced by rustic pleasures and simple needs. The cause of disorder in the world is civilization itself. The *Daodejing,* the central Daoist text, states: "[D]ao is eternal, nameless. Though the uncarved block seems small, it may be subordinated to nothing in the world. . . . Once the block is cut [that is, when civilization begins], names appear. When names begin to appear, know then that there is a time to stop. It is by this knowledge that danger may be avoided."[35]

While for the Confucians knowledge is a chief goal, for the Daoists it should be shunned, for it is knowledge that enables people to know more about objects of desire and so causes discontentment. "A sage rules his people thus: He empties their minds and fills their bellies; he weakens their ambition and strengthens their bones."[36] "The central Daoist thesis . . . is not a plea for a return to an anarchic state of nature, but better the quiet, rural, little country than the big, efficient, warlike state."[37] From the *Daodejing:*

> *Let there be a small country with a few inhabitants. Though there be labor-saving contrivances, the people would not use them. . . . Though there be boats and carriages, there would be no occasion to ride in them. Though there would be armor and weapons, there would be no occasion to use them. Though there be a neighboring country in sight, and the people hear each other's cocks crowing and dogs barking, they would grow old and die without having anything to do with each other.*[38]

Daoism became the yin to the Confucians' yang. Committed Confucians who served the state as officials also often adopted the Daoist ideal of retreat to the world of nature—taking sabbaticals to escape the hubbub of bureaucratic pressures for periods of time in mountain recesses and the bucolic countryside.

Daoist concepts contributed to other aspects of Chinese and East Asian culture. The Daoist principle of yin-yang, the two forces whose interaction produced all things, had an immense impact on East Asian thought. For China, the concept came to be linked to health and food. Illness stemmed from unbalanced yin and yang forces in the body. Since all foods had either yin or yang properties, illnesses could be cured at least in part by eating the proper food. When illness was caused by too much yang, health was restored by eating foods that provided yin. All things, including particular places, had yin-yang properties. When it came time to bury one's parents or construct a home, it was important to find the auspicious site where yin and yang were joined most favorably; this site might be determined, for example, by its distance from mountains (yang) and water (yin). Yin-yang specialists practiced the pseudoscience of geomancy (*fengshui*— literally, "wind-water") to find the best sites. In early Japan, during a period when the Japanese were borrowing heavily from China, a Bureau of Yin and Yang was established in the government; it was in charge of the calendar, fortune-telling, and setting auspicious days for court ceremonies and for travel. Geomancy was also practiced in Korea and Vietnam.

The yin-yang concept was also significant in aesthetics. Balance between the active (yang) and the passive (yin) was the name of the game, whether in painting, garden landscaping, or literature. Landscape

Yin-Yang Symbol   The Daoist concept of yin-yang as the complementary forces whose interaction produces everything pervaded all East Asian cultures. Yin was the female force, yang the male. The symbol adorns the flag of the Republic of Korea.

painting often showed scenes with mountains balanced by what seemed to be empty spaces. Planned gardens contained "man-made buildings . . . deliberately interspersed with natural features; rock formations ('mountains') stood juxtaposed to water ('rivers'); light areas alternated with dark; rounded lines with angular ones; empty spaces with solids."[39] In 1933, the Japanese novelist Tanizaki Jun'ichiro wrote a long essay, "In Praise of Shadows," where he explained the Japanese aesthetic through the yin-yang of darkness and light:

> *We find beauty not in the thing itself but in the patterns of shadows, the light and darkness, that one thing against another creates.*
> *A phosphorescent jewel gives off its glow and color in the dark and loses its beauty in the light of day. Were it not for shadows, there would be no beauty.*[40]

One other area of East Asian culture where the regressive and passive nature of the Daoist message comes into play is martial arts, where feints, speed, and pliable flexibility can overpower brute strength and aggressiveness.

Though philosophical Daoism (*daojia*) (apart from thinking in terms of yin-yang) did not play a major role in Japan, Vietnam, and Korea, religious Daoism (*daojiao*) did. The mystical quality of Daoism gave rise to religious impulses, in China focusing on meditation, longevity, and a search for the elixir of life to bring immortality. Over time, a pantheon of gods and spirits was constructed, with the Jade Emperor at the pinnacle and local gods (in many cases merging with already existing folk gods) at the bottom of this spiritual bureaucracy. Daoist gods were assimilated with local gods when Japan, Korea, and Vietnam began to borrow and adopt things Chinese.

Buddhism

In many ways, it is almost miraculous that the one religion imported from India into all four East Asian countries, Buddhism, survived at all, much less prospered. Cultural values in India and East Asia could hardly have been more different. Whereas East Asian cultures focused on the relationship between the individual and others, Indian culture had a highly developed science of psychological analysis and emphasized the relationship of the individual to the self. East Asian cultures focused on the family and particularistic ethics; the Indians stressed a universalistic ethic and a doctrine of salvation outside the family. East

Asian cultures subordinated women to a greater or lesser degree; in the Buddhist framework, women held a relatively high position. Whereas East Asian cultures saw time as finite, conceived of in life spans, generations, or reigns, the Indians more likely thought in terms of cosmic eons rather than units of life on earth. The outlook on life for the East Asians was this-worldly and focused on the present; Buddhism was *other-worldly*, with the ultimate hope of escaping the present life of suffering. Whereas a central idea in East Asian culture is *belonging* to groups and networks and life in the here and now, one of Buddhism's most important ideas is nonattachment to the things or people of this world. But despite all these differences, Buddhism became a potent force in all four countries.

The historical Buddha, Gautama Siddhartha (also known as Sakyamuni), was a contemporary of Confucius, living in the foothills of the Himalayas in what is today Nepal. Deeply affected by human suffering, he set out on a spiritual quest to seek the Truth about life, using both fasting and meditation. After considerable time, a flash of insight struck him and he attained Absolute Truth, becoming known as the Buddha, the *enlightened one*. He then taught the Four Noble Truths: the essence of life is suffering; the cause of suffering is desire; it is therefore necessary to end desire; and the way to end it is to live according to the Eight-fold Path (which could also be called the Eight "Rights"): Right Understanding, Resolve, Speech, Action, Livelihood, Effort, Mindfulness, and Meditation. The Four Noble Truths and the Eight-fold Path made up the Buddhist Way (*dharma*). Buddhism sprang from the Hindu tradition and thus incorporated some of its elements. Reincarnation was assumed, that is, one was reborn after the present life. The acts of a person in his or her previous life (*karma*, Sanskrit for "deed") determined what he or she was reborn as in the next life. The goal was not to be born into a better life or a higher caste; rather, since all life was suffering and impermanent, the goal was to end the cycles of life and reach *nirvana* (Sanskrit for "snuffing out"), never to be born again.

Early Buddhism (Theravada, "Way of the Elders") taught simply that *nirvana* is reached by following the Way set forth by the historical Buddha; the key is self-discipline. There are no prayers, invocations, offerings, or worship. The Buddha is not a god, but a man who has attained perfection. Some Theravada influence may have affected the Khmer peoples living in the southern part of Vietnam very early. But the main school of Buddhism that flourished in East Asia was Mahayana ("Greater Vehicle")—and it was completely unlike Theravada. The emphasis in Mahayana is on salvation through the strength of others with the primary condition of faith. Mahayana transformed the historical Buddha into a god to be prayed to. In addition, the sects in this school have many deities or *bodhisattvas* ("beings of enlightenment"). A *bodhisattva* qualified to enter *nirvana* but has chosen to stay in the world and to help others attain *nirvana*. With comforting gods for all needs, Mahayana is a compassionate religion. One of the most famous, widely known, and popular *bodhisattvas* is the Pure Land Sect's Amida. Charity and good works are important, with less emphasis on celibacy, monasticism, and asceticism than in Theravada. Mahayana is syncretic, incorporating various religious ideas and cults in the regions to which it spread; it tolerates contradictory ideas, considering them degrees of relative truth.

The first Buddhist scriptures (sutras) translated into Chinese were Theravada texts; but some Mahayana texts were translated by the second century CE, and most translation after the fifth century involved Mahayana sutras. Translation itself was a tricky problem: Buddhist ideas had to be translated into terms that the Chinese could understand. The Chinese worldview focused primarily on the here and now, not on the mystical or transcendental concerns addressed in Buddhism. In Daoism, of course, the Chinese had dealt with these kinds of issues. So translators turned to the Daoist term *wu-wei* to indicate *nirvana; dao* (the Way), used both by Confucius and by the Daoists, was a natural choice for *dharma*. But translation problems went well beyond words. Indian culture has often been seen as more physically sensual than East Asian culture. Until recent years in East Asia, physical displays of affection were frowned on; hand holding and kissing in public were almost taboo. Some sutra passages contained words like *kiss* and *embrace;* these had to be eliminated so as not to offend Chinese sensibilities. Similarly, the relatively high position of women in the Buddhist framework meant that statements like "The husband supports his wife" had to be changed to "The husband controls his wife."

The reactions to and roles of Buddhism in the East Asian countries tell us much about the culture of each country and its reaction to the *Other* in the form of this religion. The Chinese had heard of Buddhism through their trading in Central Asia in the second century BCE. A Han dynasty emperor who reigned from 58 to 76 CE sent an embassy to India to bring back Buddhist sutras; on the return of the mission, he ordered the building of a Buddhist temple at the capital. But Buddhism was a curiosity and had to struggle to succeed in China, given the Central Country's feeling of cultural superiority; Buddhism bore the stigma of its foreign origin, judged by many to be alien to Chinese character and values. Buddhism probably would have had a more difficult time had there been strong political regimes in China when Buddhist influence began to grow. But with the fall of the Han dynasty, the rise of multiple states and invasions by *barbarians* from the northern steppe caused widespread social and political disarray and the shattering of people's accustomed lives. In such a chaotic and uncertain time, Buddhism found a ready audience amid elites and commoners alike; in addition, many heads of state patronized the Buddhist establishment. The glory days of Buddhism in China were roughly from 300 to 800, when it gained substantial economic power; in the 840s the state began to persecute the Buddhist establishment, not for religious reasons but out of fear that its economic power might be transformed into political power. After the ninth century, Buddhism never regained the great power of its five-century heyday. However, it remained popular among the people as a primary religion; and it contributed much to popular culture and thought, providing gods of folk religion, festivals, and popular notions of *karma* and the afterlife.

Incense Sticks at a Buddhist Temple   At this Buddhist temple in Jinan, China, believers place sticks of incense in containers before entering the temple to worship and pray.

Buddhism made its way into Vietnam from China early in China's millennium of control. From the tenth to the fifteenth century Buddhism played a crucial role, serving as the state religion. Many kings of the Ly dynasty (1009–1225) were committed to Buddhism, spending years in a monastery; the court's ideology was thoroughly Buddhist. But Neo-Confucianism began to reassert the Confucian framework strongly in the fifteenth century. In the nineteenth century the Nguyen dynasty (1802–1945) tried to gain greater control over the Buddhist establishment and, in the words of one writer, "strenuously sought to make Neo-Confucianism the foundation of the national culture."[41] The many *bodhisattvas* of the Mahayana sects were quickly adopted by commoners, who blended them into their personal pantheons of animistic and Daoist deities. Vietnam's experience with Buddhism is similar to China's in that it continued to play religious and social roles after a lengthy early period of power and state sponsorship.

Korea's Buddhist experience is also similar. Again Buddhism was an import from China, arriving first in the 370s–380s CE in the three kingdoms that comprised Korea at the time. By the 550s, the rulers of the kingdoms were active patrons of the Buddhist establishment. Since Korea had the fastest cultural pipeline to China of any East Asian nation, the influential ideas in China inevitably came quickly to Korea. As the power of the Buddhist establishment began to wane in ninth-century China, Confucianism rebounded in the form of Neo-Confucianism. In Korea too, Neo-Confucianism emerged as a force for Buddhism to reckon with. When the Chosŏn dynasty was established in 1392, it put all its eggs in the basket of Neo-Confucianism, which held such sway that one historian calls the result a "complete Confucianization of Korea."[42] For all that, commitment to Buddhism continued to be strong among commoners and especially women.

For Japan, Buddhism was an import from Korea. The king of the Korean kingdom of Paekche (in southwest Korea) sent an image of the Buddha with sutras in 552, in the process recommending this new religion. Early on, some Japanese opposed Buddhism, arguing that worshiping a foreign god would bring the wrath of Japanese deities. When powerful elites began to serve as patrons of Buddhism, however, it gained a foothold. More Korean missions in the late sixth century helped solidify the Buddhists' position. In Prince Shōtoku's constitution of 604, the second article called for revering the Three Precious Things of Buddhism: the Buddha, the law (*dharma*), and the priesthood (*sangha*)—a sign of how deeply Buddhism was making its mark. Japan's native religion was Shinto, a form of nature worship. In many ways it is hard to imagine any two religions more different than Shinto, which celebrated life and for which death was abominable, and Buddhism, which saw life as suffering and aimed to end the cycle of death and rebirth. The ability of Mahayana to assimilate with other religions created easier relations between the two religions than might have been expected.

The Japanese state's patronage of Buddhism helped it to flourish. Monasteries, many built on mountains ringing the capital of Heian-kyō, grew so economically and politically powerful that they became a threat to the state. Records show that between the eighth and tenth centuries, bands of monks raided Heian-kyō, and rival monasteries fought pitched battles, with tens of thousands of men in the streets of the capital. Though such aggressive military power did not continue indefinitely, the Buddhist establishment in Japan was more powerful for a longer period than in the other East Asian states (from the eighth to almost the end of the sixteenth century). Over time the character of Buddhism changed. Early in the period of the shogunates (roughly 1200 to 1600), Zen Buddhism, with its emphasis on enlightenment brought about by master-pupil relationships and meditation, almost became a state religion. With its austerity and simplicity, it became a favorite with the elite warrior class (samurai). The Zen establishment became a political power, with its members serving as advisors to the shoguns, and an economic power in charge of all the trade with China.

It was only in the last such regime, the Tokugawa shogunate, that Buddhism's bugaboo in China, Vietnam, and Korea—Neo-Confucianism—became more powerful than the Indian religion. The Tokugawa shoguns made Neo-Confucianism the state ideology as they tried to keep the powerful Buddhists in check. All in all, the patterns of Buddhism in each culture, despite commonalities, were unique. It is to the history of these cultures that we now turn in continuing to explore both the common and unique experiences that shaped the modern identities of the countries of East Asia.

Suggested Readings

Fei Xiaotong. *From the Soil: The Foundations of Chinese Society*. Translated by Gary G. Hamilton and Wang Zheng. Berkeley: University of California Press, 1992. This must-read 1947 work by China's most famous sociologist is key in understanding aspects of East Asian culture.

Jamieson, Neil L. *Understanding Vietnam*. Berkeley: University of California Press, 1993. This well-written and insightful work is an excellent introduction to Vietnamese culture.

Leys, Simon, trans. *The Analects of Confucius*. New York: W. W. Norton, 1997. A basic translation of the teachings of the most important philosopher in East Asian history.

Ohnuki-Tierney, Emiko. *Rice as Self: Japanese Identities through Time*. Princeton, NJ: Princeton University Press, 1994. An exploration of the Japanese sense of self and the link to the sacredness of rice agriculture.

Rozman, Gilbert, ed. *The East Asian Region: Confucian Heritage and Its Modern Adaptation*. Princeton, NJ: Princeton University Press, 1991. An important collection of essays focusing on how Confucian values spread in China, Japan, and Korea and how they were transformed in the modern world.

CHAPTER TWO

From Multicultural Empire to Semicolony:
The Qing Dynasty, 1750–1870

China: the geographic bare bones. All important rivers within the Great Wall—the Yangzi, Yellow, and Pearl—flow from west to east. The major dividing line between largely geographically produced cultural zones lay between the Yangzi and Yellow rivers. North of that line was an arid area, cold in winter, marked by dry-land farming, with donkeys, even camels, used as beasts of burden. The staple foods were wheat and millet. Buildings and family homes were made of adobe. The growing season was shorter than that in the south. South of that line, water was generally sufficient for irrigation and paddy agriculture. Water buffalo and oxen were used to prepare fields for rice. Homes and buildings were often made of bamboo with thatched roofs. A man-made waterway, the Grand Canal, linked the rice basket of the Yangzi basin to North China. Powerful lineages tended to be found in the south. In both the North and South (except for the province of Sichuan, where they lived in houses on their farms), farmers lived in villages or hamlets and went out to their farms in the surrounding countryside. The land area is 43 percent mountainous, with only 11 to 15 percent arable.

In the period when we begin, China was divided administratively into provinces, similar in size to U.S. states or some European countries. In the Qing dynasty, some provinces were grouped with others and headed by a governor-general. Provinces were subdivided generally into prefectures and prefectures into counties (roughly the size of U.S. counties). Counties were broken into townships, just as in parts of the United States. Heads of the units, moving from largest to smallest, were governors-general (sometimes called *viceroys*), governors, prefects, magistrates, and heads (of townships—local leaders not appointed by the government).

THE MANCHUS

When the Outsiders from the northeast, the Manchus, took power in China in 1644 and established the Qing dynasty, it was not the first time that non-Chinese had seized the Dragon Throne. From early in China's history, there had been continual relationships between Chinese within the wall and those outside, the peoples of the steppe—Mongols, Turks, Manchus. Almost four centuries before the Manchu conquest, all of China had fallen to the great Mongol conquerors Genghis Khan and Kublai Khan. Though the Mongols' Yuan dynasty controlled China for only eighty-nine years (1279–1368), Mongols from the north and west sporadically threatened the Chinese political order during the Ming dynasty (1368–1644). Outnumbered by about one hundred to one, the Manchus won the kingdom, as the cliché put it, "on horseback." But establishing successful long-term rule was tricky because it required the precarious balancing act of keeping enough distance from the Chinese to preserve their own cultural identity while adopting enough aspects of Chinese culture to be acceptable to the Chinese majority.

At the heart of a person's identity are the cultural values by which he or she lives. The Manchus stressed martial values, horsemanship and archery, an ethos in sharp contrast to Chinese civilian values. The first Manchu leaders were ever fearful that "hereafter our sons and grandsons will forget the old regulations and do away with horseback riding and archery in order to copy Han customs."[1] But if the fear of loss of native identity was strong, so was the certainty that they could not rule without Chinese assistance.

Probably the greatest emperor of the dynasty and perhaps in all of imperial China, the Kangxi emperor (1662–1722), grappled with this dilemma. He was a role model in upholding Manchu identity, preserving the martial vigor and skills that had made the conquest possible. He commanded the final military campaigns that ended Ming resistance and personally led military expeditions against Mongol and Tibetan forces. He preserved the Manchu military identity symbolically through hunting expeditions he led north of the wall. But he also reached out to Chinese, many embittered by Manchu brutality during the conquest, offering them a special examination as an enticement to join the Manchu regime. He made it a point of showing his concern for people's welfare by visiting flooded areas and sites where dikes were being repaired.

One way to uphold martial identity was to maintain the vehicles of Manchu military success: the banner forces, bureaucratic units used to mobilize the population under various colored flags or banners. The Manchus also preserved the Ming army as the Army of the Green Standard, a constabulary force five hundred thousand strong, assigned to garrisons throughout the country. Another strategy for maintaining martial values was to set aside Manchuria as a permanent Manchu homeland. This policy meant that Manchuria would always remain a place where military values could be revived and rejuvenated if they were eroded by life among the Han Chinese.

The Manchus also continued to maintain and promote their native shamanism, a practice that clearly set them apart from Chinese culture. A shaman was thought to have had a spiritual death and rebirth; thus, he or she could move easily to the world of the supernatural and influence events. Using spirit poles (specially prepared poles used in rituals) to symbolically connect Heaven and earth in order to communicate with clan spirits, Manchus conducted shamanic state rituals, processions, and dances in the Forbidden City into the twentieth century. In addition, they patronized Yellow sect Lamaism (*gelugpa*) in Mongolia and Tibet. In Mongolia this was a strategy for controlling tribes that had converted to that religion in the 1600s. By extending this role, the Manchus tried to maintain some control in Tibet as well from the 1720s on. From the late seventeenth to the late eighteenth century, the Manchu regime constructed or restored thirty-two Tibetan temples in Beijing.

The Manchus tried to prevent close association between Chinese and themselves by forbidding intermarriage and business partnerships. They stepped into the realm of customs to differentiate Manchus from Chinese physically. For example, they forbade Manchu women to bind their feet in the fashion of proper Chinese women. That custom had begun centuries earlier when admiration of a court ballerina led many young women to follow her example to attain tiny feet, no more than three inches long. Girls, roughly five to eight years old, had their feet tightly bound with cloth so that the arches were broken and pushed up. This meant that the girl could walk only on the base of her feet; running became impossible and even walking was difficult. This practice supposedly lent urbanity to its victim, making good marriages more likely. The patriarchal family system defined by male domination perpetuated the custom, though, as has been pointed out, "without the cooperation of the women concerned, footbinding could not have been perpetuated for a millennium." It has been called "a central event in the domestic women's culture," "an exclusively female affair."[2] Be that as it may, it hobbled women, keeping them from gallivanting. Though not all Chinese women bound their feet (ethnic Hakka women, for example, did not), footbinding continued into the twentieth century. The Manchus chose to differentiate their women from Chinese women in this obviously significant physical way.

The Manchus' desire to remain distinct from the Chinese coexisted with their need to assert that they were China's rulers. As a physical expression of that overlordship, they ordered all Chinese men to adopt the Manchu hairstyle: shave the front parts of their heads, let the back hair grow longer, and then plait that hair into queues or pigtails. In essence that hairstyle physically marked the Chinese as subjects of the Outsider Manchus. The order was particularly scandalous to Chinese who had been used to growing their hair long; it has been suggested that many men saw the new hairstyle as something like "tonsorial castration," a mutilation of their physical wholeness and their manhood.[3]

Politically, the Manchus gave themselves preferential treatment in the examination system, in official appointments, and in the justice system. Although their small numbers relative to the Chinese population meant that they had to work with the Chinese, government positions were appointed more or less equally to Manchus and Chinese. Although there was balance in this way, the Manchus were careful to check Chinese power. While Chinese might be appointed to serve as governors of provinces, governors-general, who oversaw two or three provinces, tended to be Manchu. The trump card, of course, was that the ultimate arbiter and decision maker—the emperor—was always Manchu.

Source: The Experience of Footbinding

Footbinding—whatever may be said today about its importance in the realm of female agency—was painful and ultimately crippling. Yet, for all the torturous pain, this woman, like most women in traditional China, was convinced of the importance of tiny feet for a good marriage. The "heavenly blossoms" the author talks about was smallpox. What ways have other cultures chosen to stimulate greater sexual attraction that had problems as well?

They did not begin to bind my feet until I was seven because I loved so much to run and play. Then I became very ill and they had to take the bindings off my feet again. I had the "heavenly blossoms" and was ill for two years and my face is very pockmarked. In my childhood everyone had the illness and few escaped some marking.

When I was nine they started to bind my feet again and they had to draw the bindings tighter than usual. My feet hurt so much that for two years I had to crawl on my hands and knees. Sometimes at night they hurt so much I could not sleep. I stuck my feet under my mother and she lay on them so they hurt less and I could sleep. But by the time I was eleven my feet did not hurt and by the time I was thirteen they were finished. The toes were turned under so that I could see them on the inner and under side of the foot. They had come up around. Two fingers could be inserted in the cleft between the front of the foot and the heel. My feet were very small indeed.

A girl's beauty and desirability were counted more by the size of her feet than by the beauty of her face. Match-makers were not asked "Is she beautiful?" but "How small are her feet?" A plain face is given by heaven but poorly bound feet are a sign of laziness.

Source: Ida Pruitt, A Daughter of Han *(Stanford, CA: Stanford University Press, 1967), 22.*

BUYING INTO CHINESE CULTURE

The Civil Service Examination

The Qing, for all their Manchu identity, accepted the heart of the Chinese political, social, and cultural system—the imperial civil service examination and the Confucianism on which it was based. Developed over many centuries, this system aimed to bring into government the best and the brightest. China's government personnel system rested not on birth but rather on merit measured through an examination based on what today we would call the humanities—Confucian philosophical texts and commentaries, history, and literature. It produced generalists, not specialists. Most of China's officials were trained in the same body of principles, rules, and norms; though this system could never produce uniformity of thought, it did provide a common base of learning with clearly understood standards for ruling. Therefore, the examination did more than simply test; the study required to pass it shaped ways of thinking about dealing with problems of governance.

Success in major examinations, offered at three levels, brought degrees, but pass rates for all examinations were roughly only 1 to 2 percent. Preceded by a preliminary exam at the county seat, the lowest-level exam was offered twice every three years in prefectural capitals. Successful candidates, most often between ages twenty and thirty, received the *shengyuan* (government student) degree. Receiving this degree did not entitle the degreeholder to an official position; however, it brought him and his family considerable status and marked him as an elite member of his community. Those passing the second-level examination, offered once every three years at the provincial capital, received the *juren* (provincial graduate) degree; the average

Source: Civil Service Examination Cells

Ambitious young Chinese men endured the rigors of the examination system, with its temporary deprivation, in the hope of achieving a life of status and prestige. This description comes from a 1906 travelogue, Oriental Rambles, *by the American doctor George W. Caldwell. His statement that the examination was "not on the sciences" is probable evidence of his Western cultural assumptions. Do you think that the structure containing the lumber for chairs and desks was literally a temple? If so, what does this say about the Chinese approach to religion?*

We passed up a stone walk covered with a roof of translucent sea shells to a central temple stacked with boards used in making seats and tables required in the examinations. From this temple, walks lead to the twelve thousand individual cells in which the students are locked up for two days and nights allocated for the completion of their essays or poems; for the examinations are on literature and not on the sciences. These cells are only about five and a half feet by four feet—rather cramped quarters in which to spend forty-eight continuous hours.

Source: L. Carrington Goodrich and Nigel Cameron, The Face of China, 1860–1912 *(New York: Aperture Foundation, 1978), 26.*

age for this accomplishment in the nineteenth century was about thirty-one. This degree provided an entrée into officialdom, not to the highest levels but to magistracies of counties, prefects of prefectures, and ad hoc appointments. The highest degree, the *jinshi* (metropolitan graduate), came from success at the imperial capital; there the written examination was followed by an oral examination at the palace administered by the emperor himself. In the nineteenth century, the average age for attaining this degree was thirty-three to thirty-six. It opened all official career doors immediately—from governorships to important imperial commissionerships to membership in the Hanlin Academy, the government's policymaking think tank.

If a Chinese family had a son with strong intellectual abilities, they might hire a tutor to oversee his preparations for the examination. This decision depended in part on the family's economic status. Poor farm families, for example, would have had less cash available for a tutor and probably would not have wanted to lose an extra farmhand to the long necessary study. In areas where strong lineages dominated, lineage estates might give precocious young men, even from poorer families, the money to study for the examination.

The exams took several days to complete. Candidates were ushered into tiny cubicles where they wrote essays and poetry to answer various questions. At different times, the examination's substance differed; for example, questions relating to practical administration were dropped in 1757 but restored in the late nineteenth century. The form of the answer was important: Essays with a prescribed length had to follow a particular format. Calligraphy was important because it was considered indicative of a person's morality. Throughout the centuries, questions were raised about how these kinds of examinations could produce men capable of handling the messy problems of day-to-day governance. Despite these concerns, the examinations remained central into the twentieth century.

Attaining any degree brought legal, economic, and social privileges. In legal cases, degreeholders could only be judged by someone educationally superior. They were legally protected from corporal punishment and insults by commoners and were freed from the official labor service required of all commoners. All degreeholders wore buttons on hats that indicated the degree held—the *jinshi* and *juren,* plain gold; the *shengyuan,* plain silver. They wore black gowns bordered in blue, and they alone were allowed to wear furs, brocades, and fancy embroidery. But despite the personal privileges and the status that a

The Emperor Supervises the Examination
The three-level imperial civil service examination system made China a meritocracy rather than an aristocracy. In the examination for the highest degree, the *jinshi*, given at the capital, the emperor was present to underscore the significance of the examination to the well-being of the state. *Source:* Bibliotheque Nationale de France.

degree brought to the successful candidate's family, he could not bequeath the honor to his son, who had to pass the examination himself if he wanted such status. At any time in the nineteenth century there were somewhat over 800,000 *shengyuan* degreeholders (roughly 1.8 to 2.4 percent of the population), 18,000 to 19,000 *juren,* and about 2,500 *jinshi* degreeholders.

Rituals, Religion, and Values

One other way for the Manchus to legitimate their status as rulers of China was to link themselves to the former Ming dynasty by continuing to perform its rituals, such as sacrifices to gods and imperial ancestors. Performing such rituals symbolically underscored the regime's support for Confucian ethical and political values. The Qing erected both their ancestral tablets for state sacrifices in Beijing and their familial tablets within the Forbidden City. The practice especially underscored the value of filial piety to which Qing emperors explicitly committed themselves. The Kangxi emperor noted, "We rule the empire with filial piety. That is why I want to exemplify this principle for my ministers and my people—and for my own descendants."[4] This central Confucian concept resonated in the actions of the most important Qing emperors, including those of the Kangxi and Qianlong emperors.

DEALING WITH THE OTHER

Themselves Other to the Chinese, the Qing regime in its policies toward China's others seemed acutely aware of the differences in those peoples. It developed two starkly different approaches to dealing with those outside the Chinese cultural realm. Even before it established its rule in China, in 1638 the Qing organized the Court of Colonial Affairs (*Lifanyuan*) to handle its relations with the Mongols. This court became the organ in charge of relations with peoples north and west of *China within the wall*—Mongols, Uighurs, Tibetans, and Russians. Mid-eighteenth-century military victories extended Chinese control in 1759 over Xinjiang with its six million square miles of grasslands, desert, and scattered oases. The Qing considered it a *strategic frontier zone* and did not allow Chinese colonization. Three interventions in Tibet

Map 2-1   The Qing empire, circa 1800.

from the 1720s to the 1750s made that state a Chinese protectorate. Total acculturation was not the goal. Qing policies brought economic, social, and cultural changes "that encouraged the growth of ethnic identities" among these peripheral peoples.[5] This fit the Qing emperors' definition of themselves as not simply the Chinese Sons of Heaven but also emperors of an Asian multiethnic, multicultural empire.

For those foreigners who did not come from the steppe, the Chinese devised a different system. Though they had no name for its various procedures, Western scholars have called it the *tributary system.* Han Chinese elites saw China as the Civilized Country, known as Everything Under Heaven (*tianxia*)— that is, everything that's worth anything—or the Central Country (*Zhongguo*)—central specifically in terms of culture. The Chinese believed that their role was to train and educate the Others, not by physically forcing them to accept the Chinese way but by acting as elder brothers to younger brothers, making it possible for them to participate in certain controlled ways in what Chinese saw as their superlative culture. The goal was to secure recognition of China's greatness. As with any types of connections, the strength of China's ties to various countries and peoples varied in intensity. Relations with the kingdoms of Korea and Vietnam, located along Chinese borders, were strongest.

Japan, a close tributary state during part of the Ming dynasty (1368–1644), serves as an example of this system of foreign control. The Board of Rites, not the Court of Colonial Affairs, managed this system, for at its core was ritual. The Ming regime accepted one Japanese tribute mission every three years. It brought tribute composed of native Japanese products—whatever the Japanese ruler deemed appropriate. The Chinese specified Ningbo on the East China Sea as the port of entry. There a Chinese delegation met the Japanese and accompanied them to Beijing via the Grand Canal. On the way, the Japanese were repeatedly honored at banquets and showered with costly gifts of silk and jade. When they reached Beijing, they had to wait until the most auspicious date to be ushered into the presence of the Chinese emperor. There they performed various rituals, the most famous being the kowtow (*ketou*), in which they prostrated themselves on the floor three times, each time knocking their heads on the floor three times. Three prostrations, nine head knockings: it was a ritual of extreme obeisance, one that, at least theoretically, every Chinese child performed before his or her parents each New Year's Day. Apart from the deep meaning of submission evident in the kowtow, this same ritual performed by children for their parents

Camel Caravan A guide leads a camel caravan over steep sand dunes in the Taklimakan Desert in Xinjiang province. It became part of the Qing's multiethnic empire, offering new opportunities as well as providing challenges. *Source:* The Art Archive. Picture Desk Inc./Kobal Collection.

connected the foreigners, the Others, with the larger Chinese "family" and its culture. After the rituals, the foreign mission could remain in Beijing and trade for a while before being accompanied back to Ningbo and the trip home. For the Others, the episode offered expensive presents, a lucrative trade opportunity, rounds of feasting and celebrations, and probably the experience of a lifetime. For the Chinese, it corroborated their view of themselves as the superior, generous, paternalistic elder brother offering the Other the opportunity, as the Chinese phrase went, "to come and be transformed [*laihua*]."

IDENTITY AND CHANGE: THE QIANLONG EMPEROR

Traditional China reached the height of its power and wealth during the reign of the Qianlong emperor (1736–1795). His successful military conquest of inner Asian frontier lands more than doubled Chinese territory. Efficient and effective government earlier in the century helped create economic well-being and abundance. The state treasury in 1736 had a surplus of 24 million taels of silver; fifty years later, the surplus had more than tripled. Probably nothing reveals the excellent fiscal situation better than the fact that the Qianlong emperor canceled the collection of annual taxes four times because they were not needed.

Tributary Missions This painting is entitled *Ten Thousand Countries Coming to Pay Tribute to the Qianlong Emperor. Ten thousand* is a stock Chinese number that really means a great many. With the large groups depicted here, the painter was clearly playing up China's self-image as the Central Country to which all were believed to want to come.

Regional trade in cash crops—cotton, tea, and tobacco—helped tie regions closer together. Foreign trade in silk, tea, and porcelain thrived with Japan, Southeast Asia, Taiwan, and European nations.

Economic growth brought many changes to Chinese society. Money became increasingly important: taxes were now usually paid in money rather than in kind; credit and transfer needs of interregional trade stimulated the development of native banks and new fiscal institutions. Economic growth also made possible a monumental increase in population. The population rose from over 177 million in 1749 to over 301 million in 1790, an increase of 70 percent in little more than forty years.[6] Why this happened is not completely clear, though New World food crops—sweet potatoes, maize, and peanuts—made possible cultivation of previously nonarable sandy or mountainous land, and techniques like double cropping helped support the increase. Other factors may have been a declining mortality rate and a rising birthrate. Population growth may be seen as both a "reflection of—and a contributor to—prosperity."[7] It contributed to prosperity, for example, by providing more field hands to increase harvest yields and more immigrants to develop regions of previously untilled or underpopulated land. The environmental and historical differences in the vast reaches of China remind us that this picture of the country at the zenith of its traditional strength obscures sharp contrasts. Despite general state prosperity, "one did not have to travel far from the commercialized cores to find abject poverty, unemployment, and disorder."[8]

Identity Crisis

The Emperor's Roles   In the last decades of his rule, the Qianlong emperor became obsessed with Manchu identity. At base, who were the Manchus? Outsiders who as leaders of a Chinese dynasty were actually becoming acculturated Chinese? Or rulers of a multiethnic empire of which the Chinese were only one part and because of which their identity as Manchus had to remain paramount?

In many ways, as we have seen, the Manchus had adopted Chinese traditions, upholding the examination system and practicing Confucianism and its rituals. Had the emperor become "more Chinese than the Chinese"? Absolutely not: in the words of one historian, he was "bent on authentic Manchuness."[9] He initiated policies to reinvigorate Manchu identity. In bannermen's garrisons all over the country he noted the general economic decline, which was increasingly lowering morale. Because the situation was serious, garrison commanders had begun to allow bannermen to live and do business in the towns. This exposed the bannermen to a dangerous urban diversity that threatened the integrity of Manchu identity. The emperor was determined to stop the trend and to restore and protect Manchu traditions: reviving the Manchu language among bannermen; establishing standard tests for military skills; rejuvenating the spiritual and cultural roles of the clans; and promoting education that stressed literacy in Manchu, knowledge of astronomy and mathematics, and skills of riding and shooting.

The Qianlong Emperor and His Empress   This portrait by the Italian artist Giuseppe Castiglione was painted shortly after the Qianlong emperor took the Dragon Throne; it is painted on a silk handscroll. The stamps on it were those of its owners. *Source:* Giuseppe Castiglione, Italian (worked in China), Chinese, 1688–1766, "Inauguration Portraits of Emperor Quianlong, The Empress, and the Eleven Imperial Consorts," 1736. Handscroll, ink and color on silk, 52.9 × 688.3 cm. © The Cleveland Museum of Art, 2003. John L. Severance Fund, 1969.31.

Identities: The Qianlong Emperor (r. 1736–1796): Imperial Identities

The fourth emperor of the Qing dynasty (personal name, Hongli) was born on September 25, 1711, and came to the throne at age twenty-five. He was a Manchu from Northeast Asia beyond the Great Wall, ruling both Chinese and ethnic groups living in Chinese territory. One theme of his sixty-year reign was his continual juggling of identities as Chinese emperor and as emperor of a multiethnic empire. Both themes played out in his personal life.

His persona as Chinese Son of Heaven could be seen in his daily routine. He rose at 6 a.m. After an 8 a.m. meal he acted as head of state, reading reports and state memorials, consulting with his ministers, and, if need be, holding audiences with newly appointed officials. At 1 p.m. he ate his second and last meal of the day, taking only drinks and some light refreshments later. Afterward he became the Chinese scholar-sage, reading, painting, and writing poetry; further, he served as patron to Chinese scholars and artists, collecting about 8,000 paintings and calligraphy. He himself was enormously productive, writing about 43,000 poems and 92 books of prose, though, as with any artist, quantity does not necessarily imply quality.

But he also lived his Manchu persona, a heritage marked by military action, the hunt, archery, and bravery. The story goes that at age twelve, when on a hunting trip with his grandfather, the Kangxi emperor, a bear suddenly attacked the imperial party. Hongli calmly stayed on his horse until the bear was killed. As emperor, he oversaw a number of military campaigns in Northwest, West, and Southwest China, boasting of "ten great" military victories (an exaggeration). As the ruler of a multiethnic empire, he married his third daughter (out of seventeen sons and ten daughters) to a Mongolian prince. He served as a conspicuous Buddhist patron to the Mongols and Tibetans. In addition, he worked continually to maintain a military spirit among the Manchus and especially within himself. He wrote at one point, "I did not go to the hunting ground this year . . . so I had deer [driven forth] to test my skills; those that I have recently killed were with one shot."[1] At age eighty-six, two years before his death, he led a hunting expedition on the imperial reserve north of the Wall.

---

[1]*Evelyn Rawski,* The Last Emperors *(Berkeley: University of California Press, 1998), 46.*

Symbolically the Qianlong emperor promoted things Manchu. He restored his grandfather's practice of autumn hunts north of the Great Wall, developing a hunting "preserve to its fullest extent."[10] He sponsored archery contests for his troops and oversaw publication of Manchu genealogies and histories of the banners and the imperial Aisin Gioro clan. In addition, he ordered that the practices of Manchu shamanism be written down and disseminated in order to preserve this traditional Manchu religion.

The emperor asserted his Manchu-ness as ruler of a multiethnic empire by continuing to champion Tibetan Buddhism, constructing Tibetan Buddhist temples in Beijing and in Chengde, site of the Summer Palace. He sponsored the translation of Buddhist sutras, to be distributed to temples and monasteries. In addition, he made a personal commitment to Buddhism, building a Buddhist chapel in the Forbidden City and meditating daily. He had himself painted by court painters as the Buddha and as a Buddhist monk. The tomb he designed for himself had Buddhist symbols and prayers carved into the ceilings and walls of the crypt. His multilingualism was also part of his effort to show himself as more than a Chinese leader. He began to learn Mongolian in 1743, Uighur in 1760, and Tibetan in 1776.

Literary Inquisition   The question of Manchu-ness and Chinese-ness became most strained and dangerous when posed in the context of the violently bloodly Manchu conquest. The Manchus were alert from the beginning to any writings that hinted at resistance or insurrection. From the time he took the throne, the Qianlong emperor was determined both to stifle anti-Manchu expressions and to reassert the Manchu-ness of his regime. In 1772 he ordered the collection of all books and manuscripts, whether in libraries or privately owned. The stated aim was to bring them to Beijing, review them, and recopy the most outstanding ones in new editions to ensure the preservation of important, valuable, and, in some cases, rare literary and historical treasures. The collection, known as the *Four Treasuries,* for the four sections in which it was grouped, was immense. Fully 3,593 works were recopied, filling 36,000 manuscript volumes; in addition, the *Four Treasuries* included an annotated catalogue of 10,680 extant titles. In initiating this vast project, the emperor was clearly displaying his Chinese persona.

Although not clear from the beginning, the project became a full-blown campaign of censorship or, as it has been called, a *literary inquisition.* In this regard, the Qianlong emperor was acting in his Manchu persona. A little more than a year after beginning the project, he became suspicious that some provincial governors had failed to send many books to the capital and wondered whether they were holding back books of a "rebellious or seditious nature."[11] From 1776 on, the project focused on an examination of books for indications of anti-Manchu thoughts or language; the censorship campaign developed its own momentum. From 1780 to 1782, the central government took firmer control of the effort, establishing censorship boards, issuing lists of banned books, and setting down criteria for determining sedition. Up to 2,400 works were destroyed in this literary inquisition; an estimated 400 to 500 were edited following the official decree. This movement reflects the almost schizophrenic government attitude toward Chinese and Manchu identities, and it clearly highlights the late-eighteenth-century identity crisis that helped shape the policies of the Qianlong emperor.

EMERGING PROBLEMS

At the end of the eighteenth century, several political, economic, and social indicators pointed to a host of emerging problems, some fraught with danger as China headed unawares toward confrontation with the West. The country experienced an increasing number of social explosions, small revolts, and rebellions in the 1770s and 1780s. The cost of putting them down began to erode the treasury. The strongest test for the Chinese military was the White Lotus Rebellion (1796–1804), a religious movement to establish a utopia on earth, which raked across North Central China. It took eight long years for the tentative and ineffective Chinese military to defeat the rebels, and to do so cost one hundred million taels (30 percent more than the government's annual revenue).

The population surge, while linked to prosperity in one view, was double-edged, for in the long run it was the greatest danger to the economy, far exceeding what could be supported by the newly cultivated crops from the Western Hemisphere. While the population tripled from about 1685 to 1780, the amount of cultivated land only doubled. The problem of too many people and not enough land was worsened by the Chinese custom of partible inheritance, whereby land was divided equally among all sons. Landholdings in China were generally tiny to begin with; in North China, for example, in the late eighteenth century the average farm was only 2.5 acres. Given that figure and a hypothetical farmer with three sons, each son would inherit only 0.83 acre of land. With the huge population increase, land per capita was shrinking dangerously; the chances of once economically viable farmers falling into bankruptcy and poverty escalated sharply.

Different regions of the country were affected in various ways by the population increase, since demographic growth occurred at different rates. Economic problems probably were more serious in remote rural areas with far fewer human and natural resources than urban areas. But the demographic situation affected the whole country to a greater or lesser degree. The larger population challenged an already fiscally weakened government to provide various services like public works and the distribution of relief grain at times of dearth. The political implications were serious. As the Son of Heaven, the Chinese emperor had to rule benevolently and carry out his proper ritual functions. If he did not, natural disasters—droughts, floods, earthquakes—occurred as portents that his Mandate was in jeopardy. Emperors seen as inattentive to the people's needs were in danger of losing the Mandate, that is, being overthrown by the people. When poor harvests spawned hunger, even starvation, partly empty relief granaries were potent evidence that the emperor was in trouble.

Some of the difficulty of the last years of the eighteenth century came from the personal decisions of the Qianlong emperor himself. The most obvious was his doting on a handsome court favorite, Heshen. Beginning in 1775, when he was sixty-five and Heshen was twenty-five, the emperor handed over much power to this man. Many think that they had a homosexual relationship. In any case, Heshen was able to parlay his ruler's patronage into extensive personal power. He held many important posts, including director of the *Four Treasuries* project. His son married the emperor's daughter. He appointed cronies to key bureaucratic posts throughout the empire; their corrupt activities brought them millions of taels. When the Jiaqing emperor, the Qianlong emperor's son, forced Heshen to commit suicide in 1799, his personal treasury equaled two years of the realm's revenue. Corruption had a way of spreading like a cancer on the body politic, metastasizing far beyond Heshen and his gang, in the end harming the people themselves.

THE EARLY WESTERN ROLE

Traditional state cultural and economic attitudes denigrated merchants and trade. Confucianism had called agriculture the root of the state. In contrast, commerce was considered parasitic profiting from what others had produced; merchants were the lowest legitimate social group, following scholars, farmers, and craftsmen. Moreover, Chinese perceived China to be *everything under Heaven*, by definition self-sufficient and needing nothing from outside. China allowed trade probably because of its traditional paternalistic attitude toward barbarians, but more likely it resulted from the government's desire to profit from trade even as it frowned on it.

In 1600 the British government granted the East India Company a monopoly on trade from the area east of Africa's Cape of Good Hope to South America's Straits of Magellan; this monopoly over all trade in the Indian and Pacific oceans lasted until 1834. Other nations had come before without such grandiose claims. In 1517 the Portuguese made a horrific start in southernmost China when they followed their African practice of kidnapping adolescents to take as slaves; the Chinese forbade them to return. The Spanish arrived in the 1570s, trading along the southeast coast and setting up a base in Taiwan. The Dutch came early in the seventeenth century, supplanting the Spanish by the 1640s. The famous Italian Jesuit missionary Matteo Ricci reached Beijing in 1601, followed by more Jesuit priests who oversaw a substantially successful mission operation; in the end, it was stopped by a papal bull in the 1740s forbidding them to allow converts to continue ancestral rituals. Other Catholic orders, jealous of Jesuit success, claimed that ancestral rituals—burning incense and presenting food offerings to the spirits of family ancestors—were idolatrous.

The Chinese opened four ports to Western traders in 1685, but much of the trade gravitated to Guangzhou (Canton). Beginning in the 1720s, Guangzhou merchants dealing with the Western traders established their own guild, the Cohong (composed of thirteen *hong* or company merchants) to monopolize trade. The government made them guarantors for the behavior of foreigners and the payment of transit fees. From 1759 to 1816, the East India Company sent three emissaries to expand trading privileges, but none was successful. In fact, after James Flint's mission in 1759, the Chinese retaliated by restricting trade to Guangzhou because he violated Chinese restrictions by sailing to northern ports and used incorrect procedures to present petitions. When Lord Macartney, sent by the East India Company to seek

Source: Lord Macartney's Observations on the State of China

This negative view of the Chinese state and society could not have been improved by Macartney's failure to liberalize trade. Some have found his evaluation prescient. "Tartar" refers to the Manchus. What are Macartney's chief criticisms of the Chinese polity? On the basis of his remarks, do you think he was politically conservative or liberal? Why does he single out "the French and the negroes" in the last sentence?

The Chinese are now recovering from the blows that had stunned them; they are awaking from the political stupor they had been thrown into by the Tartar impression, and begin to feel their native energies revive. A slight collision might elicit fire from the flint, and spread flames of revolt from one extremity of China to the other. In fact the volume of the empire is now grown too ponderous and disproportionate to be easily grasped by a single hand, be it ever so capacious and strong. It is possible, notwithstanding, that the momentum impressed on the machine by the vigor and wisdom of the present Emperor may keep it steady and entire in its orbit for a considerable time longer; but I should not be surprised if its dislocation or dismemberment were to take place before my own dissolution. Whenever such an event happens, it will probably be attended with all the horrors and atrocities from which they were delivered by the Tartar domination; but men are apt to lose the memory of former evils under the pressure of immediate suffering; and what can be expected from those who are corrupted by servitude, exasperated by despotism and maddened by despair? Their condition, however, might then become still worse than it can be at present. Like the slave who fled into the desert from his chains and was devoured by the lion, they may draw down upon themselves oppression and destruction by their very effort to avoid them, may be poisoned by their own remedies and be buried themselves in the graves which they dug for others. A sudden transition from slavery to freedom, from dependence to authority, can seldom be borne with moderation or discretion. Every change in the state of man ought to be gentle and gradual, otherwise it is commonly dangerous to himself and intolerable to others. A due preparation may be as necessary for liberty as for inoculation of the smallpox which, like liberty, is future health but without due preparation is almost certain destruction. Thus then the Chinese, if not led to emancipation by degrees, but let loose on a burst of enthusiasm would probably fall into all the excesses of folly, suffer all the paroxysms of madness, and be found as unfit for the enjoyment of freedom as the French and the negroes.

Source: Pei-kai Cheng and Michael Lestz, eds., The Search for Modern China: A Documentary Collection *(New York: W. W. Norton, 1999), 102–3.*

expanded trade privileges and to establish a diplomatic residence, was received by the emperor in 1793, he also went away empty-handed. Lord Amherst (1816) was not even received.

Over time, a procedure of trade and barbarian management called the *Guangzhou system* evolved; an attempt to fit Western merchants into the traditional tributary state framework, the system set regulations for outsiders. Purchased goods had to be paid for in cash. Foreigners could not enter the walled city of Guangzhou, could not ride in sedan chairs, could not learn the Chinese language, and could not bring weapons or women to the thirteen Western *factories,* or trading posts, located on the bank of the Pearl River outside the city walls. They could only deal with hong merchants and could attempt no direct communications with Chinese officials; any written communication with officials went first to the Cohong and had to include the character for *petition*. Finally, if a regulation was violated or if other problems developed, the Chinese halted all trade, as in the traditional tributary system, until the Outsiders came to their senses and followed Chinese directives. The Westerners were generally willing to dance to China's tributary tune and continued to purchase the tea, silk, and porcelains that their customers desired.

By the turn of the nineteenth century, tea made up 80 percent of Chinese exports to Europe; in the late 1820s, enough tea was imported into England to give every man, woman, and child two pounds a year. Western ships generally left London in the early spring for the four- to six-month voyage to Guangzhou. They usually arrived at that port in October and were out to sea again by January. The round trip from London to Guangzhou took over a year. Despite such a long haul and the hassles of the Guangzhou system, the eighteenth and early nineteenth centuries saw continual expansion of trade.

CHINA AND THE WEST: MUTUAL PERCEPTIONS

To the Chinese, Westerners coming to the east coast of the country were initially simply *eastern barbarians*. Indeed, in the 1860s, after two decades of treaty making, the Chinese still referred to the British ambassador as the *English barbarian chieftain*. There was great confusion in Chinese minds over the

Source: The Qianlong Emperor Says "No"

In this September 1793 edict, the Qianlong emperor rejected the demands of the British emissary, Lord Macartney. What reasons does he give for not granting British demands? What phrases resonate with the ideals and processes of the Chinese tributary system?

If you assert that your reverence for Our Celestial dynasty fills you with a desire to acquire our civilization, our ceremonies and code laws differ so completely from your own that, even if your Envoy were able to acquire the rudiments of our civilization, you could not possibly transplant our manners and customs to your alien soil. Therefore, however adept the Envoy might become, nothing would be gained thereby.

Swaying the wide world, I have but one aim in view, namely, to maintain a perfect governance and to fulfil the duties of the State; strange and costly objects do not interest me. If I have commanded that the tribute offerings sent by you, O King, are to be accepted, this was solely in consideration for the spirit which prompted you to dispatch them from afar. Our dynasty's majestic virtue has penetrated unto every country under Heaven, and Kings of nations have offered their costly tribute by land and sea. As your Ambassador can see for himself, we possess all things. I set no value on objects strange or ingenious, and have no use for your country's manufacturers. This then is my answer to your request to appoint a representative at my Court, a request contrary to our dynastic usage, which would only result in inconvenience to yourself. I have expounded my wishes in detail and have commanded your tribute Envoys to leave in peace on their homeward journey. It behooves you, O King, to respect my sentiments and to display even greater devotion to secure peace and prosperity for your country hereafter. Besides making gifts (of which I enclose a list) to each member of your Mission, I confer upon you, O King, valuable presents in excess of the number usually bestowed on such occasions, including silks and curios—a list of which is likewise enclosed. Do you reverently receive them and take note of my tender goodwill towards you! A special mandate.

Source: Pei-kai Cheng and Michael Lestz, eds., The Search for Modern China: A Documentary Collection *(New York: W. W. Norton, 1999), 105–6.*

Source: Chinese Perceptions of Westerners

These are the thoughts of the British interpreter Thomas Taylor Meadows. Excited by lectures on the Chinese language while studying science in Munich, Meadows prepared for the British foreign service and became in effect the chief British intelligence officer at the first British consulate in Guangzhou in 1843. Best known for his book The Chinese and Their Rebellions, *he here provides Westerners with Chinese perceptions of them. Are these Chinese views of Westerners very different from Western perceptions of Chinese? Or are they basically close to mirror images, biases, and stereotypes?*

The Chinese do habitually call and consider Europeans "barbarians"; meaning by that term "peoples in a rude, uncivilized state, morally and intellectually uncultivated". . . . Those Chinese who have had direct opportunities of learning something of our customs and culture—they may amount, taking all Five Ports, to some five or six thousand out of three hundred and sixty millions—mostly consider us beneath their nation in moral and intellectual cultivation. As to those who have had no such opportunities, I do not recollect conversing with one, and I have conversed with many, whose previous notions of us were not analogous to those we entertain of savages. They are always surprised, not to say astonished, to learn that we have surnames, and understand the family distinctions of father, brother, wife, sister, etc.; in short, that we live otherwise than as a herd of cattle.

Source: John K. Fairbank, Trade and Diplomacy on the China Coast *(Stanford, CA: Stanford University Press, 1954), 19.*

separate identities of Western countries, likely in part a reflection of Chinese inability to perceive much physical difference among Westerners. They all looked alike—with their big noses, generally light-colored eyes and hair, ruddy complexions, and hairy bodies. The last contributed to their repulsive body odor, especially after months on board ships in the tropics; it was a sickening smell that the Chinese, who have comparatively little body hair and odor, had trouble tolerating. Rumor had it that because of their light-colored eyes, Westerners could not see at night. Others said that Westerners could not bend their knees or stretch out their legs or feet, as Chinese could. This confusion and ignorance surely came from lack of contact, lack of interest, and strong repugnance—realities that also gave rise to reporting only superficial characteristics that seemed strikingly different from Chinese attributes. At best, Westerners were quaint curiosities; at worst, they were morally and intellectually inferior or even savages—foreign devils—who lived "as a herd of cattle." An important Manchu official reported on England: "This is naturally a country of barbarians, with the nature of dogs and sheep, fundamentally ignorant of rites and of modesty; how can they know the distinction between ruler and subject, and upper and lower?"[12]

Views of China in the abstract among Western intellectuals and statesmen in the late eighteenth century were positive, even enthusiastic. Things Chinese became the European rage. Europeans copied Chinese wallpaper, interior decor, and furniture; elite homeowners in Versailles and London created Chinese gardens with Chinese pavilions. European royalty and Enlightenment philosophers enthusiastically discussed the Chinese model of government, *enlightened* or *benevolent* despotism. But when merchants and then missionaries went to China to deal with Chinese on a day-to-day basis, the labor and stresses of cultural interaction began to color the views of some, though not all. For example, British Commodore George Anson's negative musings about the Chinese were published, allegedly fueling the growing anti-Chinese feeling in the West. Of the Chinese, Anson opined: "Indeed, this much may undoubtedly be asserted, that in artifice, falsehood, and an attachment to all kinds of lucre, many of the Chinese are difficult to be paralleled by any other people."[13] The inaccurate and often misguided perceptions that developed on both sides when Westerners interacted with Chinese helped to shape actions and reactions then and later, sometimes tragically so.

EARLY-NINETEENTH-CENTURY POLITICAL AND SOCIAL INSTABILITY

The problems emerging in the last years of the Qianlong reign were a sorry legacy for subsequent rulers and for Chinese society. Too many difficult problems faced policymakers, among them population pressure; marked deterioration of the banner men and the Army of the Green Standard; and widespread suffering in Central China in the wake of the White Lotus Rebellion. The bureaucracy was in a funk: demoralized by the widespread Heshen corruption case, unable to maintain important public works like the Grand Canal, parts of which had silted up, and increasingly corrupt. The government's salt monopoly had become inefficient and corrupt, with increasing salt smuggling. The number of disaffected social groups proliferated; banditry became common. In response, local elites organized militia units to fend off marauders.

Both the Jiaqing (1796–1820) and Daoguang (1821–1850) emperors were less concerned about the Manchu identity of bannermen and more concerned about keeping them in the garrison compounds and away from opium, the black market, and banditry. The word best describing Manchu life among the banner population even at the center of the Manchu world in Beijing was *decline*: dilapidated housing, general poverty, and spreading opium use. Both emperors were relatively ineffectual, but many of their problems were not of their own making. They faced depletion of the treasury, which meant an ongoing financial crisis that prevented any government attempts to act forcibly.

Recent research has shown the Daoguang emperor to have been conscientious, flexible, and even perhaps innovative. He was ready to experiment in trying to deal with the financial crisis. He repeatedly admonished bureaucrats to tighten their fiscal belts, and he set an example by cutting back on his own expenditures. In trying to find ways to finance crucial public works, he worked closely with regional and local officials, cajoling them to take the initiative and trying to achieve consensual center-local arrangements. The emperor's technique in ruling was to listen to men in the field, to compromise and work toward consensus, and to be flexible: "I manage the country as a whole and search out information from everyone. Then I select a good plan and follow it. Moreover, I do not go into the planning process beforehand with a prejudiced view."[14] This was his approach in overseeing the restoration work on the Grand Canal.

One wonders whether the Daoguang emperor ruled at a time that was more difficult than it was for his grandfather, who had a full treasury, military triumphs, and unprecedented prosperity. The Daoguang emperor's original name, Mianning, means "unbroken peace." Unfortunately, his reign would forever come to be associated with war; it was his fate "to be the first Emperor of China to be humiliated by a Western power."[15] The increasingly severe problem of his reign was the importation of opium.

THE OPIUM TRAGEDY AND WAR

Western merchants had a serious trade problem: they had nothing that the Chinese wanted to buy. At Guangzhou, stevedores unloaded cargo: from Britain, woolens and lead; and from India and Southeast Asia (in what was known as the *country trade*), camphor, tin, rattan, birds' nests, and spices. Woolens, the main British export, hardly appealed to Chinese in tropical Guangzhou and its environs. Even with the country trade, there was a severe trade imbalance. British ships arrived in Guangzhou with 90 percent of their stocks composed of bullion, mostly silver. The annual flow of silver into China soared to 16 million taels in the 1780s. But then opium came to the East India Company's rescue.

The Chinese had begun to smoke opium in the seventeenth century, first mixing it with tobacco in a regular pipe, a practice perhaps first introduced by the Dutch in Taiwan. Each pipe gave the smoker about 0.2 percent of morphine by volume. By the mid-eighteenth century, Chinese had begun to smoke pure opium by heating refined opium paste and inhaling it through a long-stemmed pipe, a method providing the smoker with 9 or 10 percent of morphine. Opium smoking made its users inert and dormant. The French writer Jean Cocteau described the drug as "the only vegetable substance that communicates the vegetable state to us."[16] Those who sought escape from stress and boredom were most attracted to the drug. Its use stretched across the social landscape from rich to poor. Most serious for China's political and social health was the reported large number of smokers in the military and in government. The first was dangerous, obviously, because inert soldiers cannot fight; the second, because secretaries and clerks were the government's *face,* which many people saw frequently.

Estimates of the number of smokers vary, though about 10 percent of the population was a commonly accepted figure; the number of addicts may have reached 3 to 5 percent of the population.[17] The personal tragedy was addiction. Without daily fixes the user experienced the hellish misery of withdrawal, with all kinds of wretched physical and psychological symptoms. The addict did whatever was necessary to get opium—from using all of his household's money to committing crimes. Addiction led to a host of social problems.

In 1800 and 1813, new imperial edicts (which followed earlier prohibitions in 1729 and 1796) forbade opium importation, production, and consumption. While the Cohong had handled the purchase of opium up to that time, the new edicts made it impossible for such aboveboard purchase. Consequently, opium importation became opium smuggling. Western ships anchored off the marshy Guangzhou delta, with its small bays and crisscrossing streams, to unload opium chests, either onto a receiving ship (resembling a floating warehouse) or onto well-armed shallow-draft Chinese boats that delivered the goods to networks in the delta and beyond. The number of chests smuggled into the country grew dramatically, from four to five thousand chests around 1820 to eighteen thousand in 1828 to forty thousand in 1839.[18] The smuggling got a huge boost when the East India Company's monopoly of trade was abolished in 1834; then individual shippers got into the act. Other countries joined in the trade; U.S. firms, for example, picked up opium in Turkey and smuggled it into China. Large numbers of Chinese and Westerners quickly became *economic addicts* of the drug, as it were. As the number of chests increased the number of Chinese smugglers grew, increasingly dependent on the trade for their living.

For the British, opium shifted their unfavorable trade balance to the Chinese side, with silver bullion flowing from China's coffers to pay for the drug. In the early 1830s the huge outflow, as much as five times that in the 1820s, destabilized the Chinese economy, which was based on a bimetallic system of silver and copper. As silver left the country, it became more expensive than copper. That did not affect daily purchases, which were made in copper, but for payment of taxes, copper coins had to be changed into silver. In the province of Shandong, far from the smuggling sites, in 1800, between 1,450 and 1,650 copper cash equaled 1 silver tael; in 1830, the rate was 2,700 to 1.[19] Thus, taxes were driven up by the outflow of silver, creating hardships for many people. The crisis of international relations and the social and cultural crises of opium thus helped create an economic crisis as well.

The Daoguang emperor issued eleven antiopium edicts from 1821 to 1839, but to no avail. Some at the court advocated legalizing the drug so that it could be traded and taxed, with the goal of taxing it so greatly that the expense might decrease the use; at the least, this policy would make up for the outflow of silver. Others argued that legalization would only worsen the social problems related to opium use. Finally, in early 1839, the emperor decided that the opium trade had to be eliminated. He had found the arguments of an official, Lin Zexu, persuasive—that the importers and distributors of the drug, rather than the users, had to be the principal targets of government action. To suppress the opium traffic, the emperor in March appointed Lin imperial commissioner. Lin had the highest credentials and a reputation for incorruptibility—for which he was known as Lin, the Blue Sky. In trying to smash the distribution system, Lin rapidly mobilized gentry and local officials to name dealers and distributors. By July, he had arrested about 1,700 Chinese and confiscated forty-four thousand pounds of opium and over seventy thousand opium pipes.

In his effort to deal with opium importation, Lin demanded that the foreigners also turn over their opium stocks. He tried to reason with the British and used shame to get them to surrender the drug. These were his plaintive words in a message to Queen Victoria: "The wealth of China is used to profit the barbarians. . . . By what right do they then in return use the poisonous drug to injure the Chinese people? Even though the barbarians may not necessarily intend to do us harm, yet in coveting profit to such an extreme, they have no regard for injuring others. Let us ask, where is your conscience?"[20] Such moral appeals had little effect: the British first ignored, then refused the order. Following the logic of the tributary system, Lin then stopped all trade and besieged the factories and their 350 foreigners. They held out for six weeks, blasting the action as a "piratical act against British lives, liberty, and property."[21] When they finally delivered over twenty-one thousand chests to Lin, he had five hundred laborers dig three immense trenches into which he put more than 1,300 tons of opium, decomposed it using salt and lime, and flushed it out to sea.

But this seeming moral victory over opium-smuggling foreigners was pyrrhic. Because the British superintendent of foreign trade had been, since 1834, a representative of the crown, the siege and the

Lin Zexu Destroying the Opium   This is a nineteenth-century Chinese rendering of Commissioner Lin destroying the British stock of opium by mixing it with salt and lime and flushing it out to sea.

seizure of opium were treated by the British as a national affront and a cause for war. Hostilities began with clashes between war junks in the fall of 1839 after incidents in the summer had ratcheted up tensions. The Daoguang emperor was not pleased by the results of Lin's policy. Lin, he said, had caused "a thousand interminable disorders" to grow.[22] As a result, he exiled Lin to Turkestan for four years. The war itself was an on-again, off-again struggle against a backdrop of negotiations between the two sides. Serious talks began in the fall of 1840, with a settlement reached in early 1841. But each side felt that the settlement was too lenient for the other side. So the fighting dragged on for another year and a half before the signing of the Treaty of Nanjing in August 1842, when the Central Country surrendered to the English barbarians.

For the Chinese the Opium War was a military disaster, underlining the reality that the imperial armed forces were desperately outmoded. The British not only had large traditional men-of-war but also steam-driven, shallow-draft crafts that could glide up inland streams. The Chinese, in stark contrast, had no navy at all. In land fighting the situation was the same. The British fought the Chinese with the latest self-firing rifles. The banner forces had matchlocks, in which the gunpowder had to be ignited by hand, but most troops had only cold weapons—knives, swords, clubs, and spears. The midcentury official Zuo Zongtang probably summed it up best: "the land troops could neither ride nor shoot and the water troops could not sail or fire a cannon."[23] That being said, we must remember that few nations, if any, could have withstood the military power of Great Britain at that time. They had humiliated the United States in the War of 1812, burning the White House to the ground in 1814.

The Opium War was the opening salvo of a century of aggression by Western nations against China, a century of conflict between very different cultures with sharply differing values; yet each clash had its

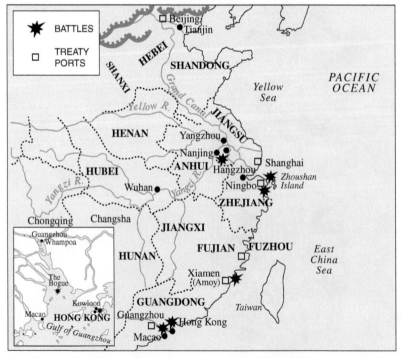

Map 2-2   The Opium War.

Opium War Sea Battle   The East India Company's steamer *Nemesis* is joined by other British ships in the destruction of Chinese war junks near Hong Kong in January 1841.

own particulars and realities. Some eventual war may have been inevitable, but it was especially tragic that this first conflict centered on questions of international morality, specifically England's claim that it had a right to smuggle opium into China no matter what the drug was doing to China or to many of its people. For a number of Chinese this pivotal first confrontation with the West marked the West as amoral, if not immoral: the plaintive question of Lin Zexu echoes—"Let us ask, where is your conscience?"

THE UNEQUAL TREATY SYSTEM

The Treaty of Nanjing (1842), which ceded Hong Kong Island to Great Britain, was the first of many treaties between China and foreign nations that were called *unequal* because China did all the giving and received nothing in return. The treaties began to erode China's sovereignty. Only over time did China realize the insidious nature of the treaties, in the beginning rationalizing its giveaways as examples of its tributary generosity. A cornerstone of the system was the application of the most-favored-nation principle, established in a supplementary treaty that Britain and China signed in 1843. It promised that each country would receive every right and privilege that every other country received even if it was not specified in their particular treaty. For example, the Treaty of Nanjing did not contain a provision for renegotiations; but because the U.S.-Chinese Treaty of Wangxia in 1844 did provide that possibility in ten years' time, the British could also claim that right.

Foreign Concessions

The series of treaties opened up more ports for trade and foreign residence. The Treaty of Nanjing opened up four new ports (Xiamen [Amoy], Fuzhou, Ningbo, and Shanghai) to join Guangzhou as sites for foreign settlements and continuous trade. Other treaties opened more ports, first along the coast, then on inland rivers, especially the Yangzi. Foreign concessions were areas carved out of existing Chinese cities where foreigners became rulers. In these areas, where many Chinese still lived, foreigners assessed taxes and collected them; foreign police and troops patrolled; and foreign law was the authority. Thus, Chinese residents of foreign concessions were uprooted from their native country without moving an inch, and Chinese sovereignty over these former citizens was ended. Yet the Chinese did not react strongly to the situation; they pointed to precedent in past dynasties when Arab traders lived under their own laws in designated parts of port cities.

The foreign population until about 1860 was made up mostly of merchants and a small number of missionaries. The most important merchant houses were two British firms, Jardine, Matheson, and Company and Dent and Company; the major American firm was the Boston-based Russell and Company. All three had been involved in the opium trade; in the new treaty ports, they still brought in opium and other goods and participated in new business interests—banks, insurance, godowns (warehouses), and shipyards. The head of a foreign firm had to rely completely on a Chinese middleman, or *comprador,* who spoke enough pidgin English (a mixture of Portuguese, Chinese, and English) to converse with the foreigner and who could conduct the business of the firm through his contacts in the Chinese community, overseeing transactions and being responsible for the firm's Chinese personnel. Many compradors became extremely wealthy.

Extraterritoriality with Consular Jurisdiction

Another treaty right established by the West was extraterritoriality with consular jurisdiction, a system by which a foreigner accused of a crime was tried not in a Chinese court but in one presided over by his national consul. The Western rationale: Chinese law was barbaric. Certainly the gulf between Western and Chinese culture over the general concept of law was wide. China had no independent profession of law and no lawyers. No independent judiciary existed. The county magistrate investigated cases, presided as court judge, and delivered judicial decisions. In criminal cases, punishments were prescribed; since extenuating circumstances were not considered, magistrates had to follow the law. Suspects were presumed guilty and were treated severely; torture and beating were expected if the suspect did not confess. In homicide cases, the Chinese system firmly upheld the "eye for an eye" policy. There was little consideration of whether the death was an accident and no possible lesser charge, as in the West, of involuntary manslaughter. If a life was taken, a life must be given. If the killer could not be found, then a family member or someone connected to the killer could be substituted.

Western experience with the Chinese legal system stretched back to the early eighteenth century, but the two most famous cases related to two ships: the British ship *Lady Hughes* in 1784 and the American ship *Emily* in 1821. Both involved Chinese who were accidentally killed through Westerners' negligence. After being handed over to Chinese authorities, the accused were executed. In thinking of crime and punishment, it is worth noting that in England burning at the stake ended only in 1789, and whipping as a punishment for men ended only in 1833. Nevertheless, because of these experiences, in subsequent incidents the British refused to turn over accused Westerners to Chinese authorities, stating that extraterritoriality was necessary until the Chinese amended their legal system.

Initially there was no strong Chinese reaction to this loss of control over foreign citizens. For one thing, it seemed advantageous to the Chinese to avoid the burden of learning all the languages of these barbarians. As with the establishment of foreign settlements, the Chinese found a precedent: they had allowed Tang dynasty Arab traders in Guangzhou to practice extraterritoriality. But problems surfaced quickly when, as in foreign settlements, some Chinese gained a measure of protection in their own courts from Westerners protected by extraterritoriality. This happened among different groups. For example, if a comprador of a Western business firm, the key to the firm's success, was accused of a crime, the officers of the firm intervened forcefully in Chinese courts to protect him. Western missionaries also offered such protection to their accused protégés, Chinese converts, intervening in Chinese court cases or prevailing on their foreign consul to do so. Thus developed a category of Chinese who were more privileged than others, a particularly galling situation for the nonprivileged.

Under the treaties, China also lost its sovereign right to set, control, and collect its own tariffs. Tariff rates were set at about 5 percent of the value of the goods, not raising a red flag in Chinese minds because they were not notably out of line with traditional tariff rates. But the times were not traditional. Unable to raise the tariff, the Chinese could not, for example, keep out unwanted items like opium. Perhaps more importantly, China's enforced paralysis concerning the tariff had serious implications for the country's efforts to industrialize. During the Opium War, China came face to face with modern technology in the form of ships and weapons; the experience was a catalyst for some Chinese, who began to think initially about buying them from the West and ultimately to consider manufacturing them themselves. But Chinese efforts to establish modern industry, both heavy and light, were hampered by their inability to raise tariffs to protect their infant industry.

Not only did China lose control of its tariff, but it also lost the right (of any sovereign state) to collect customs duties. In the 1850s, amid the turmoil of the Taiping Rebellion near Shanghai, the British began collecting customs duties to ensure their collection. This practice became institutionalized in the Chinese Maritime Customs Service. Even though the long-time director, Robert Hart, was effective and dedicated, seeing himself essentially as part of the Chinese bureaucracy, the collection of customs for one country by another was a humiliating loss of sovereignty. China would not regain control of the tariff or its collection until 1933.

Another sovereign right of a nation is control of its rivers and streams, specifically control over who can sail up waterways into its interior regions—a right critical for a country's security and defense. Yet, according to the treaties, China could not make any inland waterway off limits to foreign ships, nor could it prevent ships of any nation from using its rivers.

Foreign Ambassadorial Residence

The main structure of the treaty system was completed by the Treaty of Tianjin (1858) and its follow-up, the Convention of Beijing (1860). These agreements came during another war waged by Britain and France against China. Called the Arrow War and sometimes the Second Opium War, this struggle began with the British accusation that a Chinese ship (the *Arrow*) under British registry had been illegally searched by Chinese officers looking for a Chinese pirate. Overreactions to a series of incidents led to fighting and to British calls for upholding their honor and interests abroad. In the end, France joined the campaign, using as an excuse the murder of a French missionary in an area off limits to foreigners. It is hard to avoid the conclusion that both countries were simply spoiling for a fight to force further political and economic demands on China.

The British and French took Guangzhou in December 1857 and then sailed north, seizing in the summer of 1858 the city of Tianjin and the coastal forts protecting key cities in the capital region. Negotiations ensued, producing the treaty that bears the city's name. It expanded the treaty system, opening ten new treaty ports, four of them on the Yangzi River, and it established two more significant rights.

One of the new rights set forth in the Treaty of Tianjin was that foreign ambassadors could reside permanently in Beijing. Under the traditional tributary system, there was no ongoing presence of foreigners in the capital or anywhere else in China. Now diplomatic representatives from all barbarian nations could live near the Forbidden City. This the Chinese could not abide. Even after the treaty was signed, they continued to fight. When a British negotiating team sent to Beijing was arrested and some of its members were killed, the British commander, Lord Elgin, decided that revenge to force compliance with the treaty was the order of the day. He sent his troops to occupy Beijing; the emperor fled the capital for his hunting lodge north of the Great Wall. In October 1860, Elgin's troops marched northwest of the city to the Summer Palace (Yuan Ming Yuan), a complex of over two hundred pavilions and pagodas built during the Qianlong emperor's reign. They looted its thrones, furniture, porcelains, and robes; then they burned the whole ten-square-mile area.

Six days after the torching, the Chinese agreed in the Convention of Beijing to the permanent residence of ambassadors in the capital. What underlay the demand for permanent diplomatic residence was

The Dead at Dagu Fort   The British took the strategic Dagu Fort in May 1858, but they were repulsed by the Chinese when they tried to take it back in June 1859. Here many Chinese lie dead after the first attack.

the Western state model of equality among nations, a model with which the traditional tributary system, with its hierarchy of superior to subordinate, could never coexist. Though it would take decades for the system to die in Chinese thinking, for all practical purposes the centuries'-long tributary system was dead. While China never became a full-fledged colony, its loss of sovereignty over its own territory and people created what has been called a *semicolony,* subject to the demands and pressures of not one but many foreign nations. This was a far cry from the glory days of the multistate empire.

THE MISSIONARY AND CULTURAL IMPERIALISM

The other crucial right granted in the Treaty of Tianjin to Western nations was the guarantee that Christianity could be openly taught and practiced. Missionaries could travel anywhere, purchase property for their church and school, and spread their message freely. Christianity had been outlawed since the Yongzheng reign (1722–1736), so it had to operate underground until the Qing removed its prohibition in 1844. After 1860, the number of missionaries entering China grew quickly. By 1870, 250 Catholic and at least 350 Protestant missionaries were in China. Catholics, with a long history of mission work in the country, had about 400,000 Catholic converts compared to only about 6,000 Protestants. The Catholic mission had spread throughout China, while the Protestant effort was concentrated mostly in coastal treaty ports.

The record of the motives, approaches, and impact of nineteenth-century missionaries is complex. Yet all missionaries shared one thing: the conviction that they possessed absolute truth. Largely for this reason, the relationship between missionaries and Chinese was generally not a happy one. The political and social landscape of the Qing dynasty's last half century is marked by one episode after another of turmoil and violence touched off by the actions of missionaries in communities across China.

While a few missionaries treated the Chinese with respect and focused on social reform, most emphasized salvation. They saw the Chinese as superstitious, greedy, and materialistic. By the late 1830s, some missionaries were calling for armed invasion by the West "to break down the barriers which prevent the gospel of Christ from entering China."[24] When Opium War battles led to the slaughter of Chinese, one

Source: A Western Missionary Looks at the Chinese

In today's terms, Griffith John (1831–1912) of the British China Inland Mission would be considered a fundamentalist evangelical. He arrived in China in 1855 and served there for fifty-five years. Do you think the attitudes he expresses in this letter would have helped or hindered his mission? Why?

The people are hard as steel. They are eaten up both soul and body, by the world. They don't seem to feel that there can be reality in anything beyond the senses. To them our doctrine is foolishness, our preaching contemptible, our talk jargon, our thoughts insanity, and our hopes and fears mere brain phantoms. . . . Think of the conversion of four hundred millions of the most proud, superstitious, and godless people of the human race. Sometimes I am ready to give up in despair and think that China is doomed to destruction, that to raise it out of its state of moral and spiritual degradation is a matter of impossibility.

Source: L. Carrington Goodrich and Nigel Cameron, The Face of China, 1860–1912 *(New York: Aperture Foundation, 1978), 55.*

missionary was gleeful: "I regard such scenes . . . as the direct instruments of the Lord clearing away the rubbish which impedes the advancement of Divine Truth."[25] It is easy to see how such conceptions of the people they wanted to save affected their approach. Missionaries frequently tried to use their Western right of extraterritoriality to shelter their converts, calling on their national consul to send a gunboat as a show of force if local officials resisted their demands. The French government became a demanding protector of the Catholic mission, lobbying for the removal and execution of officials who thwarted French missionary goals.

Educated Chinese generally saw all non-Chinese and their ideas as barbarian. Whereas Chinese saw themselves as grounded in realistic pragmatism, Christian teachings like the virgin birth and a bodily resurrection seemed superstitious and fanciful. Many Chinese scholar elites found missionaries to be direct threats in their local communities. Products of the Chinese civil service examination, scholar-gentry were the locality's teachers, mediators, authorities, and charity providers. Missionaries performed those same functions for their Chinese congregations. Upset by this usurpation of their community roles, the gentry counterattacked by producing propaganda tracts that tarred missionaries with the brush of sexual immorality, traditionally an important weapon in the Chinese political arsenal. Here is a description of Christian Sunday worship from a tract first published in 1861: "The pastor takes a seat at the front and extols the virtue of Jesus. . . . The whole group mumbles through the liturgies, after which they copulate together in order to consummate their joy."[26] Such scatological tracts helped incite suspicion, anger, and fear among the Chinese populace.

A paroxysm of violence in the port city of Tianjin on June 21, 1870, underscored the cultural gulf and fragile relations between foreign missionaries and Chinese. There French Catholic nuns, who managed an orphanage, paid a small sum of money to people who brought children to the orphanage. Rumors spread that scoundrels were kidnapping children to turn them in for quick cash. Tensions escalated over rumors that nuns were killing children to harvest their body parts for making aphrodisiacs. When the French consul lost his self-control and attempted to kill two Chinese officials, a street crowd became an angry mob that killed the consul, his officer, and nineteen others, including twelve priests and nuns. Several dozen Chinese converts were also killed. France demanded and received a large sum for reparations, the punishment of the Chinese involved, and a Chinese mission of apology.

Beset by instability at home and imperialist pressure from abroad, China muddled tragically along. Having always seen itself as the Central Country, China had now been brutally decentered. And big-nosed barbarians were everywhere; merchants and businessmen in cities and missionaries in all areas. In addition, the third quarter of the nineteenth century was to produce such destructive domestic rebellions that China's very survival was at stake.

CHRONOLOGY

1600	British East India Company established
1644	Qing dynasty established
1662–1722	Reign of the Kangxi emperor
1685	Four ports opened to Western trade; by the 1720s, trade largely restricted to Guangzhou
1720s–1750s	Incorporation of Tibet and Xinjiang into the Qing empire
1736–1795	Reign of the Qianlong emperor
1740s	Papal bull ends the Jesuit mission
1749–1790	Population increases 70 percent
1772–1782	Literary inquisition
1793	Macartney mission
1796–1804	White Lotus Rebellion
1821–1839	Daoguang emperor issues eleven antiopium edicts
1834	Monopoly of the East India Company ends
1839	Mission of Lin Zexu ends in war
1839–1842	Opium War
1842	Treaty of Nanjing inaugurates the treaty port system
1859–1860	Arrow (Second Opium) War with Britain and France
1860	British destroy the Summer Palace
	Permanent ambassadors reside in Beijing
	Missionary rights established
1870	Tianjin Massacre

SUGGESTED READINGS

Crossley, Pamela K. *A Translucent Mirror: History and Identity in Qing Imperial Ideology.* Berkeley: University of California Press, 1999. This examination of the Manchu identity argues that a sense of Manchu ethnicity was not crucial in the beginning of their reign but developed over time.

Fairbank, John K. *Trade and Diplomacy on the Chinese Coast.* Cambridge, MA: Harvard University Press, 1954. Though more than a half century old, this classic study by the dean of China studies in the United States still compels our attention. Its focus is the period of the Opium and Arrow wars and the derivation of the treaty port system.

Fay, Peter. *The Opium War, 1840–1842.* New York: W. W. Norton, 1976. A well-written, thorough study of the war; reviewers often call it a classic.

Kuhn, Philip. *Soulstealers: The Chinese Sorcery Scare of 1768.* Cambridge, MA: Harvard University Press, 1990. The author uses the sorcery scare, with its social dislocation and fear, as a vehicle for analyzing the relationship of the Qianlong emperor to his bureaucracy.

Leonard, Jane Kate. *Controlling from Afar: The Daoguang Emperor's Management of the Grand Canal Crisis, 1824–1826.* Ann Arbor, MI: Center for Chinese Studies, 1996. This account reveals much about a little-studied emperor but even more about the pragmatic approaches of the Qing state in dealing with crises at the beginning of its decline.

CHAPTER THREE

Rebellion and War:
The Qing State in Decline, 1850–1901

In the second half of the nineteenth century, China seemed to be in free fall. Its sovereignty had been undermined by the unequal treaty system, and it was continually at risk from Western pressure. Its impoverished court was split over the proper policy to deal with the Western nations. Conservative reactions kept would-be reformers from making much progress from the 1860s to the 1890s. Domestically, social instability and unrest had many Chinese on edge; yet, these tensions were amorphous and unfocused. But within roughly two decades—from 1851 to 1873—China staggered under the body blows of four domestic rebellions. The largest—and, indeed, the largest in world history—was the Taiping Rebellion that ravaged Central and East-Central China. The others were the Nian Rebellion that tore through the north and two Muslim rebellions, one in the southwest, the other in the northwest. Together they challenged the very existence of the Qing state.

THE TAIPING REBELLION (1851–1864): ATTEMPTS TO REVOLUTIONIZE IDENTITY

The Taiping Rebellion was born in the Guangzhou region in the troubled years following the Opium War, caused largely by the destabilization of the region from the opium scourge and the war itself. There were also other, longer-term political and social problems in the region: contempt for the Qing and its military's pitiful performance in the war; the permanent presence of Westerners in Guangzhou after the war; the presence of many ethnic minorities and disgruntled unemployed; and the existence of secret societies—blood brotherhoods supplying mutual aid in times of peace but potential bandit groups during troubled eras. It was Hong Xiuquan and his brand of Christianity who appeared to express the deepening malaise and give it shape.

After he had his vision and came to understand its meaning, Hong Xiuquan (see Identities) converted relatives and friends, who formed the God Worshipping Society and began to proselytize. Other religious figures, mostly illiterate and poor, also emerged. Imitating Hong, many claimed to have special links to the divine. If Hong himself was the younger brother of Jesus, another claimed that when he spoke it was with the voice of God the Father, and another alleged that his voice was that of Jesus. These developments spelled future trouble: when divinity vied with divinity, who could mediate? In July 1850 the leaders called all God Worshippers, about twenty thousand strong, to Thistle Mountain, the movement's headquarters in southern Guangxi province, to form an army. The Qing government, recognizing the threat of this militarizing cult, sent the state's army, disorganized and poorly disciplined; the God Worshippers quickly defeated it in several engagements. After these victories, in January 1851 the God Worshippers declared a new dynasty, the Heavenly Kingdom of Great Peace. As a visible symbol of their anti-Manchu identity they abandoned the Manchu hairstyle, letting their hair grow long all over their heads; people called them the "long-haired rebels."

From January 1851 to March 1853, Chinese walled cities fell like lined-up dominoes. Occasionally the Taiping met defeat and suffered battlefield deaths (like that of the leader who claimed to be the voice of Jesus). But in the main, theirs was a triumphal march. When they reached Nanjing, they began to exterminate the Manchu "demons." All forty thousand Manchus who lived there and were not killed in battle were stabbed to death, drowned, or burned alive.

The Taiping Revolution

Taiping ideology and its political, social, and economic systems made the Taiping Rebellion a revolution that posed a dire threat to the regime and eventually gave rise to forces that crushed it. Underlying Taiping Christianity was the idea of the equality of human beings before God, living in a universal brotherhood-sisterhood. Certainly this idea was one of its appeals. People also joined the movement because it promised realization of a utopia or at least provided a way for dissatisfied down-and-outers to improve their impoverished lives. The Taiping world and everything in it belonged to God. There was no private ownership: according to the 1853 Taiping land system, all men *and women* received

Identities: Hong Xiuquan (1813–1864):
The Younger Brother of Jesus Christ

Born the third son of a poor farmer, Hong was a precocious youth who, despite his family's poverty, was able to study for the imperial civil service examination in Guangzhou. He failed repeatedly. On one of his trips to the city (1836), a passerby thrust a booklet of biblical passages and sermons into his hands: it asserted that moral decline was endangering Chinese society. Hong took it home. The next year, another examination failure deeply humiliated him and fueled his sense of worthlessness. Falling seriously ill, he had a vision in which he was ushered into the presence of a venerable man dressed in black robes who handed him a sword and emblems of royalty, instructing him to kill the demons. The old man ordered Hong to set out on quests that spanned the cosmos, accompanied by a middle-aged man. After Hong's illness ended, the hallucinatory vision remained in his mind.

In 1843 came another examination failure; on his return home, Hong read the Christian booklet and discovered the meaning of his vision. The venerable old man was God, and the middle-aged man was Jesus. God had addressed Hong as the heavenly younger brother; he was, in effect, God's Chinese son, instructed by God to slay the demons. A Hakka (a discriminated-against ethnic group), Hong gradually determined that the demons were the Manchus. He began organizing and mobilizing other marginal groups into a fast-growing pseudo-Christian cult. In January 1851, his movement was strong enough to announce the establishment of a new dynasty, the Heavenly Kingdom of Great Peace (*Taiping tianguo*), to oppose the existing Qing regime.

The next two years saw one Taiping military victory after another as Hong's armies reached the city of Nanjing on the Yangzi. His revolutionary message was a threat to traditional Chinese culture. However, for a host of reasons Hong's revolution failed (see the text), not the least of which was his hypocrisy: he forbade sexual intercourse even between spouses and segregated the sexes at the same time that he himself had a harem of concubines. He died shortly before Qing forces took Nanjing in the summer of 1864.

The longest-lasting impact of Hong's movement was probably the catastrophic devastation it left in its wake; in the words of one observer, "smiling fields were turned into desolate wildernesses; 'fenced cities into ruinous heaps.' The plains . . . were strewn with human skeletons; their rivers polluted with floating carcasses; wild beasts descending from their fastnesses in the mountains roamed at large over the land, and made their dens in the ruins of deserted towns."[1] Not only were foreigners besetting China, but Chinese themselves were turning productive land into moonscapes and slaughtering each other in vast numbers. In 1843, the population estimate for the Lower Yangzi macroregion alone was 67 million; a half century later, in 1893, it had fallen to 45 million.

[1] *Thomas W. Kingsmill, "Retrospect of Events in China and Japan during the Year 1865,"* Journal of the North China Branch of the Royal Asiatic Society 2 *(1865): 143.*

Source: Taiping Initiation Ritual

This initiation ceremony was for convert Tan Shuntian on April 9, 1850. The Heavenly Brother's lines were read by Xiao Chaogui, one of the Taiping kings and the so-called voice of Jesus, the Heavenly Elder Brother. Xiao was killed in battle in September 1852. Note that here only two of the Taiping leaders are named, Hong Xiuquan and Yang Xiuqing. What aspects of Taiping society and ideology emerge from this ceremony?

Heavenly Brother declared to Tan Shuntian: "Tan Shuntian, do you know who is talking to you now?"

Tan Shuntian: "You, Heavenly Brother."

Heavenly Brother; "Who is that person sitting on the bed?"

Tan: "It is Second Brother [Hong Xiuquan]."

Heavenly Brother: "Who sent him here?"

Tan: "Heavenly Father."

Heavenly Brother: "Why did Heavenly Father send him here?"

Tan: "Heavenly Father sent him to become the King of Great Peace [Taiping]."

"Heavenly Brother: "What is meant by: 'adding starlight brings the view of Holy Father'?"

Tan: "It means if we have our Second Brother [i.e., Hong Xiuquan], we will be able to see Heavenly Father."

Heavenly Brother: "Who is 'Rice King'?"

Tan: "It is Second Brother."

Heavenly Brother: "You should acknowledge him. In Heaven you should trust Heavenly Father and me; on earth you should follow his instruction; you must not be stubborn and willful, but follow him obediently."

Tan: "With all my heart I will follow Heavenly Father, Heavenly Brother, and Second Brother."

Heavenly Brother: "Who is 'Two Stars with Feet Up'?"

Tan: "It is East King [Yang Xiuqing]."

Heavenly Brother: "Who is 'Henai'?"

Tan: "It is also East King."

Heavenly Brother: "You should recognize East King since it is he who is the mouthpiece of Heavenly Father. All nations on earth should listen to him."

Tan: "Yes, I know."

Heavenly Brother: "Shuntian, at times of hardest testing do you lose your nerve or not?"

Tan: "I do not lose my nerve."

Heavenly Brother: "You should remain faithful until the end. It is just as it is with sifting rice, one watches it with one's eyes and then separates out the grains. The Taiping course is set, but caution is still essential. The basic plan must not be divulged to anyone."

Tan: "I will obey the Heavenly Command."

Source: Jonathan D. Spence, God's Chinese Son: The Taiping Heavenly Kingdom of Hong Xiuquan *(New York: W. W. Norton, 1996), 119–120.*

equal shares of land, an indication of the gender revolution that the Taiping were willing to engineer. Land grants were cultivated in common by a unit of twenty-five families, the basic social-political grouping in Taiping society. In keeping with the regime's hallmark—a primitive economic communism—all units shared a common treasury and each unit was headed by a "sergeant" who had multiple roles. He kept records of production and managed the common treasury; mediated disputes and served as judge; and directed childhood education. As the unit's military leader, he selected militiamen to defend the unit. He also oversaw church services on the Sabbath. The structure of this commune-like system came largely from a traditional Chinese work, the *Rituals of Zhou,* but since much of the ideology was based on Christian idealism, the system was clearly a hybrid.

Source: Sexual Segregation

One of the more controversial Taiping policies was sexual abstention for the masses, even between husbands and wives. By contrast, Taiping kings had well-stocked harems to provide sex at any time. What is the rationale for this policy as set forth in this Taiping text?

Moreover, as it is advisable to avoid suspicion [of improper conduct] between the inner [female] and the outer [male] and to distinguish between male and female, so men must have male quarters and women must have female quarters; only thus can we be dignified and avoid confusion. There must be no common mixing of the male and female groups, which would cause debauchery and violation of Heaven's commandments.

Although to pay respects to parents and to visit wives and children occasionally are in keeping with human nature and not prohibited, yet it is only proper to converse before the door, stand a few steps apart, and speak in a loud voice; one must not enter the sisters' camp or permit the mixing of men and women. Only thus, by complying with rules and commands, can we become sons and daughters of Heaven.

Source: Jonathan D. Spence, God's Chinese Son: The Taiping Heavenly Kingdom of Hong Xiuquan *(New York: W. W. Norton, 1996), 121–22.*

The social roles and position of women in Taiping society were markedly superior to those of women in Qing society. As part of the Hakka heritage, footbinding was not permitted. Women were allowed to take the new civil service examination based on the Bible and the various writings of Hong Xiuquan and, when successful, to hold government positions. Women were also active in military units. A revolution in gender relations seemed to be in the making.

In some areas of social policy, the puritanism of fundamentalist Christianity reinforced native Chinese puritanism. The use of alcohol, tobacco, and opium was forbidden. Taboo also were gambling, witchcraft, prostitution, and adultery. The Taiping ruled out sexual relations even between husbands and wives; chastity would preserve order and discipline until after the heavenly kingdom was firmly established. Men and women lived in segregated housing; having sex (and getting caught) meant death by execution. Not surprisingly, massive morale problems by 1855 led the Taiping leadership to abandon the policy of sexual segregation and abstinence.

The Taiping Revolution was a potent threat to the traditional Chinese Confucian system. Taiping ideology provided an all-embracing cosmology linking the three parts of the traditional Chinese universe—Heaven, Earth, and humans—in a new way. God in a Christian Heaven replaced the impersonal force of Heaven that endowed the Chinese emperor with his mandate to rule and that reflected events on Earth by the forces of nature (e.g., storms, plagues, earthquakes). Now Earth and its resources were to be shared by humans equally in a universal siblinghood—a startlingly different social arrangement from the traditional Confucian vision of a social hierarchy with dominant elites. Further, specific social and political policies of the Taiping undercut traditional Chinese norms. The centrality of the family disappeared, replaced by the twenty-five-family unit; the power of the father was taken by the sergeant, and the family lost its economic and social preeminence. Economic competition was abolished. The new state received a novel kind of legitimacy—from the Christian God—and exerted greater control over personal lives than ever before, prescribing daily economic, social, religious, and even sexual roles.

Why the Revolution Failed

During their eleven-year period in Nanjing, the Taiping tried, generally unsuccessfully, to implement their vision of politics and society even as they wreaked havoc and destruction on forays in all directions, though focused on the Lower Yangzi region. The movement's eventual collapse had many strategic reasons. Crucial was the disintegration of the central leadership, with six kings turning on each other in struggles of one-upmanship, using their alleged links to the divine as weapons. While egalitarianism was prescribed for the masses, the kings themselves had numerous perks and privileges, perhaps the most notable being heavily populated harems where they could have sex at any time. Kings expected commoners to fall on their faces in a show of obeisance whenever they passed in their sedan chairs. If they did not comply, they could become *celestial lamps* (burned alive) or be torn apart after being tied to five horses. Because political power was concentrated at the top, problems that developed among the kings had life-and-death import for the whole movement.

A second reason for the Taiping failure was its very identity and nature—a fanatical totalitarian religious movement that promised utopia but delivered nothing except hard work, strict discipline, no sex, and a harsh existence. When promises of future rewards, which had given the movement aim and direction, were not fulfilled, commitment to the regime vanished. The Taiping also failed to handle the basic issues of day-to-day governing: land reform and commune-like units were not established in many places, and where they did exist, they were administered poorly.

The Taiping also failed because of their unimaginative strategy. Instead of keeping their momentum and driving north to Beijing, they holed up in Nanjing, where the movement was eventually snuffed out. They were not adept at enlisting possible collaborators for a common drive against the Manchus. Two other significant uprisings occurred concurrently with that of the Taiping: the Nian Rebellion and the smaller Red Turban effort in South China. The Taiping frequently cooperated with the Nian, but they never pursued a long-term strategic alliance. Nor did they try to curry favor with Western nations. Initially Western missionaries were excited by the possibility of a Christian revolutionary movement seizing power, but when they visited Nanjing, they were shocked and repulsed by the substance of Taiping Christianity. Western merchants were also put off by the Taiping refusal to allow opium into their realm. Western nations, which initially might have been interested in the Taiping as a regime possibly more open to the West and its demands than the Qing, rallied instead to the Qing in order to save Shanghai from Taiping conquest. Late in the rebellion, Western-led mercenary troops, the "Ever-Victorious Army," led first by the American Frederick Townsend Ward and then by the British Charles "Chinese" Gordon, fought Taiping troops in their efforts to take the city.

The coup de grace for the Taiping was their military defeat by Chinese armies formed on orders of the Manchu emperor. Outraged by the Taiping threat to traditional culture, the important official Zeng Guofan formed his own provincial (Hunan) army. His proclamation against the Taiping in 1854 read in part: "In a single day, several thousand years of Chinese ethical principles and proper human relationships, classical books, social institutions and statutes have all been completely swept away. This is not just a crisis for our Qing dynasty, but the most extraordinary crisis of all time for the Confucian teachings. . . ."[1] Zeng recruited his army's leaders from among networks of gentry connections. Zeng's army was built on Confucian principles—"duty to one's neighbors, piety to one's family, and personal loyalty to one's commander."[2] It was largely funded by a new tax, the *lijin,* collected on shipped commercial goods at customs barriers along key routes. Zeng's protégé, Li Hongzhang, set up a counterpart army in Anhui province. Both men purchased foreign cannons and arms for their forces. These armies, not Manchu banners, played the key role in battles leading to the Taiping collapse.

In spite of its horrific death toll and destruction, the Taiping movement had great historical significance. "More than any other rebellion of their day, [the Taiping] addressed themselves directly to the

Zeng Guofan   Zeng (1811–1872) was the key Han Chinese civilian and military leader from the early 1850s until his death. Renowned as honest and upright, he kept a diary from 1839 until the day before his death in which he constantly examined his own mistakes and shortcomings in order to improve.

Li Hongzhang   Li (1823–1901) was China's most important statesman and general of the last quarter of the nineteenth century. His probity was often questioned. He was reported, for example, to have accepted large bribes from Russia to allow the passage of the Trans-Siberian Railroad through northern Manchuria.

Source: The Reality of Taiping Destruction

This memorial was sent by Li Hongzhang to the emperor on June 2, 1863. Jiangsu had been one of China's wealthiest provinces before the economic and social devastation brought by the Taiping movement. A li is a third of an English mile. Because of China's floundering economy, the government could not bear the costs of reconstruction. Why might this be a dangerous situation for the emperor and the dynasty?

The province of Jiangsu used to have a densely populated countryside, a village every half *li*, a marketplace or town every three *li*, smoking chimneys . . . everywhere, and chickens and dogs to be heard everywhere. Now we see nothing but weeds, briars, hazels obstructing the roads . . . no inhabitants for twenty or thirty *li*. Among broken walls and ruined buildings, one or two orphan children or widows survive out of hundreds of inhabitants. Their faces have no color, and they groan while waiting for death. . . . As I, your official, am holding the post of Governor, my heart grows sick when I see these terrible conditions with my own eyes."[3]

Source: L. Carrington Goodrich and Nigel Cameron, The Face of China, 1860–1912 *(New York: Aperture Foundation, 1978), 87.*

crisis of the times and offered concrete measures for resolving it. Their vision of a new system of property relations, a new mechanism of local control, and a new relationship between the individual and the state was an authentic response to the distinctive problems of the late imperial age."[3]

In the Forbidden City during the last years of the Taiping movement, the most important person dealing with the distinctive problems of the late imperial age was a woman, the Empress Dowager Cixi. From her emergence in 1861 as regent for her five-year-old son, the Tongzhi emperor, she was the most powerful figure in China until her death in 1908. For twelve years she ruled outright for him; then, in his second year of rule, he contracted smallpox and died in early 1875. Without a son or brother, the Tongzhi emperor left Cixi in the driver's seat. She chose her four-year-old nephew to become the Guangxu emperor, reigning for him until 1889. Even after that time, she maintained considerable power (see Chapter 9).

GUERRILLA WARFARE: THE NIAN REBELLION (1853–1868)

The Nian Rebellion, the only one of the four major midcentury rebellions without a religious dynamic, developed in the bleakly poor, sandy Huaibei region of North Central China along the Anhui-Henan-Jiangsu border, an area subject to severe floods and drought. In this perennially poverty-stricken area, disaffected types—White Lotus adherents, poor peasants, salt smugglers, and ruffians—joined various predatory groups engaged in banditry, smuggling, theft, plunder, kidnapping, and organized feuds. Although the origins of the word *nian* remain unclear, the term came to be applied to groups of bandits who used a blatantly Robin Hood approach. Severe floods in 1851 began the tragic shift of the Yellow River from the south to the north of the Shandong peninsula, tragic because its flooding brought death and destruction to a large area. In this case, it helped to bring bandit groups together in the Nian Rebellion. In guerrilla strikes they plundered for their livelihood as they protected and fortified their home communities. Welded into a loose federation in the early 1850s, the Nian continued to fight in small guerrilla units, notably mobile on horseback and dependent on the local populace for support. Rebels maintained fortified base communities, usually inactive in summer and winter and engaging in banditry, raiding, and plunder during spring and autumn. They adopted a scorched earth strategy in the countryside, stockpiling grain and food items in earth-walled settlements, thus depriving antirebellion government troops of subsistence.

The initial government strategy of using the Army of the Green Standard to quell the Nian went nowhere. A more aggressive policy under the Mongol prince Senggerinchin, a descendant of Genghis Khan, led to the capture of key Nian leaders. In 1864 a second phase of the rebellion began, ranging sporadically over the North China plain and fought by an increasingly expert Nian cavalry. The ambush death of Senggerinchin in May 1865 led the Qing government to appoint Zeng Guofan, the hero of the Taiping campaign, to suppress the Nian movement. He succeeded in isolating the central Nian base, invading it, "cleansing" each village, and then quarantining it from other rebels. But Nian mobility (one report noted that they moved "as freely as mercury") allowed many of the rebels to escape the base area. In late 1866, the government appointed Li Hongzhang to finish the job. The Nian's effective guerrilla activity led to two more years of fighting before Li's forces finally prevailed. Keys to victory included modern British-made guns that Li purchased and about five thousand experienced cavalrymen from Manchuria and Inner Mongolia. Despite their military prowess, the Nian, in contrast to the Taiping, did not challenge the traditional value system or cultural identity; however, they played an important role in further weakening the Manchu regime. The years of fighting drained government finances, and the Nian's scorched earth policy ruined large areas of the countryside. This destruction, together with the widespread flooding, deprived the Qing of taxes from agriculture and trade.

MUSLIMS VERSUS CHINESE: CLASHES IN ETHNIC IDENTITY

Since the time of the Tang dynasty (618–907), Muslims had settled in communities at the eastern end of the Silk Road in the northwestern provinces of Gansu and Shaanxi, and from the thirteenth century they had settled in the far southwestern province of Yunnan. There were also pockets of Muslims elsewhere. By the mid-nineteenth century, an estimated one million Muslims lived in the region of the Nian Rebellion. Though they maintained their own mosques and religious practices, Muslims saw themselves as Chinese subjects. They could take the civil service examination and receive bureaucratic posts. However, though the early Qing emperors had treated Muslims and their communities with respect, the Qianlong emperor in 1762 announced a series of anti-Muslim laws. Penalties for Muslims committing crimes, for example, became harsher than those for Han Chinese committing the same crimes. Problems also developed when Han Chinese began to move into areas where Muslims had been the majority population and controlled the region's resources. Competition between Han Chinese settlers and Hui (Han Chinese Muslims) over land and commercial opportunities led to animosity and heightened tension. Court cases over disputes relating to these issues usually found the Muslims on the losing side, discriminated against by Han Chinese and Manchu alike.

In Southwest China, the Panthay Rebellion in Yunnan province (1853–1873) grew out of a mixture of ethnic and religious tensions. Economic rivalry between Han Chinese settlers and long-time resident Muslims over copper, silver, and gold mines, long controlled by Muslims, was the root of the animosity. The rivalry escalated into feuding that led, in turn, to massacres and assassinations. The spark that ignited the rebellion was likely the Manchu government–assisted massacres of the Hui. Amid this unrest, an educated, devout Hui named Du Wenxiu established the kingdom of Panthay, covering about half of Yunnan province, claiming for himself the title of sultan. The Qing military response was weak and incompetent, but the government was able to pit opposing Muslim factions against each other. Even so, the rebellion continued until 1873, marked by siege warfare against over fifty walled cities, with most of the seizures resulting in bloody massacres by Qing troops. Du was captured and executed. Over eighty thousand Chinese Muslims were killed in the government suppression.

Source: Proclamation During the Panthay Rebellion

Written in Arabic, this proclamation was sent to the Muslim population in Lhasa, Tibet. Its purpose was to place Du Wenxiu's rebellion in the larger context of the Islamic world. What does the proclamation define as the immediate cause of the rebellion?

The cause of the dispute was that the Idolaters and their chiefs assembled together to kill the Muslims and began to insult their religion. . . . Having abandoned every hope of life, we fought with the Idolaters and God gave us victory. . . . [The ruler's] name is Sadik, otherwise called Sulieman. He has now established Islamic Law. He administers justice according to the dictates of the Qur'an and their traditions. Since we have made him our Imam we have been by the decree of God very victorious. . . . The Ministers and chiefs under our Imam are as single-hearted as Abu Bakr and as bold as Ali. No one can face them in battle. They are imperious to the Infidel but meek to the Muslim. The metropolis of Infidelity has become a city of Islam.

Source: Cited in David G. Atwill, "Blinkered Visions: Islamic Identity, Hui Ethnicity, and the Panthay Rebellion in Southwest China, 1856–1873," The Journal of Asian Studies 62, no. 4 (November 2003): 1091.

The northwestern rebellion that spread from an area near Xi'an in Shaanxi province westward into Gansu province was more serious strategically than the Panthay Rebellion. This area was the main corridor between Beijing and Xinjiang, the vast region won by conquest in the mid-eighteenth century, providing Chinese Muslims contact with the Islamic world in western Asia. Islamic currents from the west continually reinvigorated or challenged religious thought and faith. In the mid-eighteenth century a Chinese Muslim had introduced a practice from the mystical Muslim school of Sufism. Known as the New Teaching, it challenged the traditional method of "ridding the mind of all thinking except that focused on God." Muslim networks of supporters of the New Teaching became the main factor in the rebellion that erupted in 1862. Yet the New Teaching was not the root of the violence; rather, it was Muslim–Han Chinese antagonism. By 1867, all of Gansu province except for a few cities and the provincial capital was controlled by Muslims who had effectively overthrown Qing power.

In the fall of 1866 the Qing court appointed Zuo Zongtang governor-general of Shaanxi and Gansu provinces with orders to quell the rebellion. Zuo's strategy focused on taking walled urban centers for which his army (made up mostly of provincial forces with experience fighting the Taiping or the Nian) had large siege guns, including some purchased from the German firm Krupp. In approaching the Muslims, Zuo was guided by the Qing policy: "The only distinction is between the innocent and the rebellious, there is none between Han and Muslim."[4] His main target was the stronghold of the New Teaching's leader near the border between Gansu and Inner Mongolia. Zuo tightened the noose, slowly starving the walled city; by the time Muslim surrender ended the siege, the city's residents had been reduced to eating grass roots and flesh of the dead. The Muslim leader and adult males from his family were executed by slicing, and almost two thousand of his staff and troops were massacred. Zuo then continued the campaign, besieging the final walled city in October 1873. The campaign, which took five years, saw the bloody slaughter of many cities' residents. But when the fighting ended, the country was generally free of rebellion and at peace for the first time in over two decades.

All in all, the four midcentury rebellions created vast devastation, killed tens of millions of people, destroyed hundreds of towns and cities, and reflected the ballooning crisis in China. Three rebellions raised issues of identity. The Taiping championed a completely new identity for China that, if successful, would have constituted a revolution. The Muslim rebellions brought to the fore issues of ethnic identity, crucial factors in the Qing multiethnic empire with the potential to rip the fabric of state and society. Except for the Panthay Rebellion, the midcentury rebellions were suppressed by scholar-officials, civilians with advanced degrees in the civil service system. In one sense, the scholar-officials were ethnic Chinese serving and saving Manchu overlords; more accurately, they were scholar administrators imbued with Chinese culture aiding their rulers, who were also committed to that culture. They were military generalists, not professionals, who applied Confucian moral and political principles, insisted on well-trained, disciplined troops, and used some Western technology, particularly guns and ships. They were oriented both to the Chinese past—trying to save traditional culture from Taiping Christianity, the Nian plunderers, and the Muslim crusaders—and to the Chinese future, gingerly taking the first steps toward *self-strengthening,* that is, using Western technology to bolster the Chinese defense.

SELF-STRENGTHENING

Self-strengthening involved a multipronged program in the areas of diplomacy, education, technology, and the military; advances in military technology—guns, ships, and armaments—were usually considered a yardstick of successful self-strengthening, for they were most clearly related to defense. As in the defense of the realm, self-strengthening was a joint project of key men of the Qing court and scholar-officials. The three Chinese—Zeng, Li, and Zuo—who had been indispensable in quelling the rebellions led efforts to use the *means* of foreign military technology (*yong*) to protect the *end* of traditional Chinese culture or essence (*ti*). Two key Manchu figures, Prince Gong and Wenxiang, provided support and led the way in many of these efforts.

Though self-strengthening did not call for basic institutional change, emphasizing instead existing structures and policies, an important new institution, the Zongli Yamen (Office for General Management), was established in 1861, mainly at the initiative of Prince Gong. It was the general coordinating bureau for all Western affairs, including diplomacy and trade, missionary problems, and all projects and programs that involved Western matters or technology. Prince Gong headed the Zongli Yamen for twenty-seven years (1861–1884, 1894–1898).

In the area of diplomacy, the Zongli Yamen in 1862 established a school to train diplomats for the new international order. Its eight-year course of study featured a curriculum focused on languages and science. The Zongli Yamen also dispatched diplomats abroad, a huge challenge given the shame that many Chinese associated with dealing with Western barbarians. (Zongli Yamen members were frequently referred to as *devil's slaves*.) The first full-fledged Chinese ambassador did not venture out until 1877, sixteen years after foreign ambassadors were stationed in Beijing, suggesting the difficulty of changing the Chinese worldview.

Weapons for defense were at the top of China's priority list. The Zongli Yamen and the Han Chinese heroes in the wars of rebel suppression led the way in establishing arsenals, shipyards, and machine shops. In 1865 at Shanghai, Zeng and Li established the Jiangnan Arsenal, which produced ships, weapons, ammunition, and machinery. In 1866 Zuo built the Fuzhou Shipyard, operating with 3,000 craftsmen and laborers and a staff of 150 to build larger ships than those produced at Jiangnan. Attached to both shipyard and arsenal were schools of engineering and technology. Li Hongzhang also oversaw nonmilitary self-strengthening projects involving development of the Kaiping coal mines near the city of Tangshan, not far from Tianjin, and the China Merchants' Steamship Navigation Company.

Ultraconservatives, who wanted no part of anything Western, seriously hampered technological, diplomatic, and educational progress as well as the possibility of bolder initiatives, attacking self-strengtheners as traitors. For their part, self-strengtheners sought to mollify conservatives and perhaps salve their own cultural consciences by rationalizing that Western weapons and ships were simply inanimate machines— culture-neutral, as it were. They argued that foreign weapons and ships could therefore be bought or manufactured without cultural pollution. The problem with their rationalization is that means do affect ends. Foreign machines came with a host of culture-specific scientific views and worldviews. Building ships and weapons at the arsenal or shipyard required the study of engineering and technology, a task that took students into a new world where, at the least, old assumptions about the natural world would be challenged. If those students then returned to the Chinese classics, they would see those works in a broader context and ask new questions about them.

A more practical issue was, how could the arsenal and shipyard schools attract able young men to study barbarian things? The key to success remained the civil service examination. Li Hongzhang proposed introducing a new category in the examination, that of technology. But this would mean that the degree that had always been based on the classical Confucian tradition could now be obtained, at least partly, with something outside that tradition. Means, therefore, had an immense impact on ends. This logical fallacy of the self-strengtheners would begin to open China up to new, often unpredictable forces. More than a century later, when China began to use computers and high technology in the 1980s and 1990s, it seemed déjà vu: unawares, China was being transformed.

RUSSIA IN CHINA

Russia had been active in East Asia since the seventeenth century, a logical extension of its interests in Siberia. Treaties in 1689 and 1727 had established the border between Russia and China and essentially regularized relations. From the beginning, China treated Russia differently from other Western nations. Treaties were signed as between equals; the tributary system was not in play. Russia "was the only foreign country with which China maintained treaty relations, the only 'Western' state to which China sent diplomatic missions, and the only foreign power granted religious, commercial, and educational privileges" in Beijing.[5] From 1693 on, Russian merchants were permitted to come to Beijing every three years. Following the 1727 treaty, Russia was allowed to send students to learn Chinese and Manchu at a language school in Beijing; the Chinese government helped pay for travel expenses and, once students arrived at the capital for decade-long stays, it subsidized their living expenses, including providing clothing and food at no charge. All these special favors were bestowed by the Qing to ensure Russian neutrality as the Qing strengthened their hold on the northern and northwestern frontier lands, but they persisted long after those frontiers were stabilized. Russia monopolized this special status in Beijing until the 1860 Treaty of Tianjin opened the capital to general diplomatic residence.

In that treaty, the Russian ambassador helped mediate disputes between Chinese and British and French negotiators, even as he tried to further Russia's agenda in Central and Northeast Asia. From the early 1850s, the Chinese had allowed Russians to trade, build storage facilities, and set up consulates in northern Xinjiang. The Russians had also pushed into eastern Siberia, building garrisons along the Amur River. In a treaty concluded in 1860, the Russians showed themselves to be as aggressive as the Western Europeans, demanding and receiving land north of the Amur River and all land east of the Ussuri River, the latter comprising what became known as Russia's Maritime Province. Altogether these territorial gains totaled between three hundred thousand and four hundred thousand square miles. In addition, more cities in Xinjiang were opened to Russians: those chickens came home to roost when the Russians seized the northern part of Xinjiang in 1878, but negotiations led to their withdrawal and a reduction in the number of their consulates.

Russian interests in Northeast Asia did not diminish. The terminus of the Trans-Siberian Railway, begun in 1891, was to be Vladivostok on the Sea of Japan. In order to chart a less expensive route, the

Russians negotiated with the Chinese to build the railroad across northern Manchuria. With this railroad, the Chinese Eastern Railway, the Russians substantially enhanced their interests in the area.

IMPERIALISM AND CHINA'S TRIBUTARY STATES

After the rebellions, a new wave of imperialism beset China from 1874 to 1895 as foreign powers seized China's most important tributary states: the Liuqiu Islands (Ryūkyū Islands, in Japan), Vietnam, and Korea.

Loss of the Liuqiu (Ryūkyū) Islands

China had regularly received tribute missions from these islands since 1372, completely unaware that the feudal lord of the Japanese domain of Satsuma on Kyushu's southeast coast had conquered the islands in 1609; from that point on, Japan ruled the northern part of the islands directly and the rest indirectly under the titular control of the Ryūkyūan king. The islands paid tribute to Satsuma and even to the Japanese shogun in Edo. Since Satsuma wanted to trade with China, however, it ordered the Ryūkyūs to continue to participate in China's tribute system.

Late in 1871, over fifty shipwrecked Ryūkyū sailors were killed by Taiwanese natives. In 1873 the Japanese, claiming that they had the sole right to speak for the islands, sent a naval expedition to Taiwan to punish the natives. The Japanese asserted that they were acting because the natives' action clearly showed that China was not in fact sovereign in Taiwan. In the end, the British ambassador served as arbiter of the dispute. As a result, China paid five hundred thousand taels for the victims of the killings and for some Japanese barracks built in Taiwan, and promised not to condemn the Japanese expedition. For China, it was a huge mistake. In effect, okaying the expedition was a recognition of Japan's sovereignty over the Ryūkyūs, and the payment to Japan, in the words of the British ambassador to Japan, amounted to a "willingness to pay for being invaded."[6] The whole episode made China increasingly concerned about the role of the coastal region in its foreign policy. In 1879 Japan annexed the islands, which became the Okinawa prefecture.

Vietnam and French Colonialism

Vietnam, the northern part of which China had controlled directly from the Han through the Tang dynasties, was a close tributary in the Ming and Qing dynasties. Though it fought off Chinese political control, it continued in the Chinese cultural orbit, borrowing its most important political and cultural institutions. From the Chinese perspective, the tributary relationship with Vietnam was a crucial reality. The Chinese established Vietnamese emperors in office and sent troops to help their tributary younger brother put down unrest. Certainly by the 1880s, after China's experience with foreign invasion and pressures, in addition to its tributary concerns, China was also aware of the strategic importance of Vietnam for its own security. In the words of one official, "The border provinces are China's gates; the tributary states are China's walls. We build the walls to protect the gates, and protect the gates to secure the house. If the walls fall, the gates are endangered; if the gates are endangered, the house is shaken."[7]

French interest in Vietnam began with Jesuit missionaries in the seventeenth century, but the French Revolution and the Napoleonic wars put East Asian involvement on hold. At the turn of the nineteenth century the French became briefly involved, offering crucial support to Nguyen Anh in establishing the Nguyen dynasty (1802–1945; see Chapter 4). The Nguyen emperors championed Chinese cultural models; they also forbade trade and intercourse with the West and the spread of Christianity. In the late 1850s, the French began to take more concerted action to extend their interests,

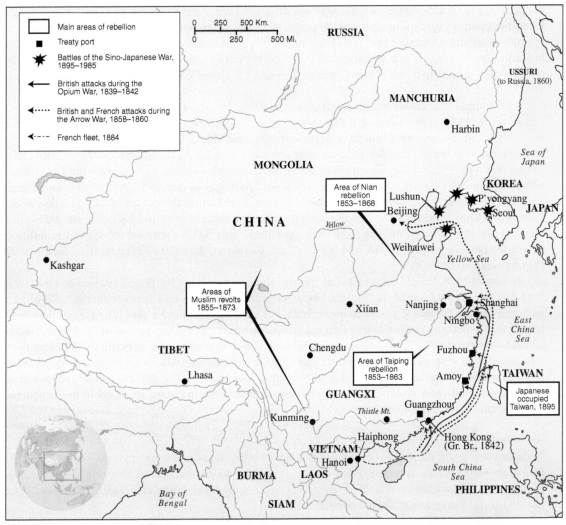

Map 3-1   Rebellions and Wars in the Nineteenth Century.

launching a military campaign in southern Vietnam in revenge for antimissionary riots. By 1862 they took Cochinchina, the three southernmost provinces of the country, and forced the Vietnamese government to cede it to them.

A treaty in 1874 further extended French influence, permitting French shipping on the Red River in the country's northernmost section, Tonkin, and allowing them to seize control of Vietnamese foreign relations. France intended this treaty to establish the independence of Vietnam from China, an obvious precondition for France to take control of Vietnam's foreign affairs. Thus, the treaty recognized "the sovereignty of the King of Annam [Vietnam] and his complete independence of all foreign powers."[8] The Chinese responded, saying that Vietnam had been a tributary state of China for centuries and that China would look into the matter, but it did not do so. Therefore, the French took Chinese nonaction as tacit acceptance of what was essentially a French protectorate. Feeling free to act, the French stepped up aggressive actions in northern Vietnam, whereupon the Vietnamese government, in the role of tributary younger brother, sent a mission to China asking for help. With the situation "as precarious as piled eggs," the Chinese sent in irregular forces—groups of former Taiping and Panthay rebels—who skirmished with French troops in 1882.[9] Regular Chinese troops were dispatched in 1883.

As the clouds thickened and then unleashed the deluge of war, Chinese policy was halting and uncertain. From 1883 to war's end in 1885, a bitter policy dispute over the proper reaction to the crisis in Vietnam raged within the Chinese government. On one side were the so-called realists like Li Hongzhang, who argued that the Chinese military was not ready to repel France. The realists called for negotiations, arguing that China could not annul the treaties France had signed with Vietnam and could not force the French to leave. Open war would only end in certain Chinese defeat and French demands on China itself. On the other side was a pro-war faction that attacked Li's position as appeasement. They argued that if China marshaled its will to fight until the French were defeated, it would deter other foreign nations from bullying China. This faction stressed the special morality of China, the bravery of the Chinese, and the idea that "battles are determined even more by men's hearts than by weapons."[10]

In August 1884, French ships sailed up the Min River to the city of Fuzhou, home port of a quarter of the Chinese navy and site of the Fuzhou Shipyard. French ships passed Chinese batteries with modern guns and cannon purchased from European firms, but none of them fired a shot. The French fleet made target practice not only of the Chinese fleet but also, disastrously, of the shipyard itself. In fifteen minutes, all but two of the twenty-three Chinese war junks and men-of-war were sunk or burning, and the shipyard was demolished. Approximately three thousand Chinese were killed. Without organization, coordination, and leadership, all the self-strengthening in the world was useless. The disastrous war ended with an agreement in mid-1885 in which China ended its centuries'-long tributary relationship by recognizing French control over Vietnam.

Struggling for Korea

In the last decades of the nineteenth century, the Japanese began to cast longing eyes on Korea. Part of this had to do with national security: in the thirteenth century, Korea had served as a bridge for would-be Mongol conquerors from the mainland. Viewing it as a potential mainland threat, Japan, in a stock phrase, contended that Korea was a "dagger pointed at its heart."

But in the first half-decade following the overthrow of Japan's Tokugawa shogunate in 1868 (see Chapter 7), some government leaders in Japan's new Meiji regime saw Korea in a new way—as an opportunity. By military action in Korea, Japan could establish itself on the continent, prevent other countries from gaining territory so close to Japan, and provide an outlet for former warriors (samurai) by turning them on Korea in retaliation for a Korean rebuff to Japanese vessels. Though that plan came to naught, Korea, located only one hundred miles across the Tsushima Strait, began to play an important role in Japan's conception of its role in Northeast Asia.

Well aware of the tributary relationship between China and Korea, Japan sent emissaries to sound out China's reactions to greater Japanese involvement in Korea. Li Hongzhang's tributary-framed answer was that "though Korea is a dependent country of China, it is not a territorial possession; hence in its domestic and foreign affairs, it is self-governing."[11] Emboldened by China's implicit permission to talk to Korea about opening trade, the Meiji government proceeded to open Korea via an unequal treaty in 1876. As to Korea's status, the treaty stated, "Korea, being an independent state, enjoys the same sovereign rights as does Japan."[12] China interpreted *independent* as *autonomous,* but it is clear from subsequent events that Japan saw things differently.

When Japan annexed the Ryūkyū Islands in 1879, China suddenly became aware of the threat that an unchallenged Japan posed in Korea. In 1880 Korean relations were shifted from the Board of Rites, which oversaw the tributary system, to Li Hongzhang, the governor-general of Zhili province, where Beijing was located. Li encouraged the Korean government to sign treaties with Western powers and to adopt a policy of using barbarians to control barbarians. The tributary elder brother acted to pull the younger brother into the international community.

Despite Li's efforts, the period saw increasing tension between China and Japan on the Korean peninsula; with both keeping some nationals in the country, the situation was tense, always on the edge of crisis. Crises in 1882 and 1884 led both countries to send troops (see Chapter 8), China in the framework of the tributary system. In the 1882 event, a mutiny in the Korean army, the Korean ruler (Queen Min) was briefly upset in a coup by a former regent, the Taewǒn'gun. Upon entering Korea, China acted as the elder brother in its tributary relationship. For his complicity in the mutiny, the Chinese arrested the Taewǒn'gun and threw him in jail in China because he had moved against the queen, whom the Chinese had recognized as the proper authority. This act, the arrest of a Korean leader by Chinese diplomats and his detention in China, dramatized the tributary mentality for the whole world. Clearly not dead, the tributary system continued to function during the seeming cultural inertia that marked China's response to change. The upshot of the crisis was that the Japanese maintained a permanent guard at their legation in Seoul; the Chinese kept three thousand soldiers in the country, sent arms and Chinese instructors to the Korean military, and posted advisors to the Korean government. These actions too were those of the elder brother.

After the 1884 crisis, a coup attempt, both China and Japan sent more forces, with the Japanese demanding an indemnity and an apology. Japanese leader Itō Hirobumi went to China to negotiate an end to the crisis with Li Hongzhang. Each country withdrew its forces and promised to notify the other if it was planning to send forces in the future. This Li-Itō convention brought a decade of peace in which the new Chinese resident general, Yuan Shikai, sought to preserve the forms of Chinese suzerainty. The agreement made Korea a virtual coprotectorate of China and Japan. The trouble was not over.

The Sino-Japanese War, 1894–1895

In the summer of 1894, Tonghak religious proponents (see Chapter 8) rebelled against the Korean regime. The Seoul government, again within the tributary framework, asked China to send troops to help end the rebellion. Following the guidelines of the Li-Itō convention, the Chinese government notified Japan of its plan to send 1,500 troops but to withdraw them as soon as the rebellion was suppressed. The Japanese response was to send about 8,000 troops. Li desperately tried to negotiate a settlement but efforts to use Britain and the United States as mediators went nowhere, so he decided that reinforcements were necessary. On July 25, the Japanese sank a British steamer that had been chartered by the Chinese, drowning 950 Chinese troops. Both countries declared war on August 1.

In the climactic naval battle off the Yalu River on September 17, of the twelve Chinese ships involved, four were sunk, four were crippled beyond repair, and four fled. All twelve of the more up-to-date Japanese ships survived without major damage. The results, in short, were the same as those in the war with France a decade earlier: complete and humiliating defeat for China on both land and sea. A nation comprised of what earlier Chinese had contemptuously dismissed as "dwarf people" had smashed the Central Country.

The settlement might have been even worse from the Chinese perspective had two unexpected developments not occurred. First, peace envoy Li Hongzhang was shot in the head by a Japanese terrorist. Though he survived, the Japanese were horrified and feared that this insane act might jeopardize their victory. They thus withdrew one of their most overweening demands: control of three cities in the Beijing area. The second event came after the conclusion of the Treaty of Shimonoseki in 1895, which ceded Taiwan and the Liaodong peninsula in southern Manchuria to Japan. Russia, Germany, and France joined in what became known as the Triple Intervention to force Japan to return the Liaodong peninsula to China. In spite of that return, China lost Taiwan and had to give up forever any tributary-related claims to Korea.

With the Sino-Japanese War, imperialism entered a far more perilous phase. The cession of Taiwan was the first major loss of Chinese territory. Japan acquired the right to build and operate factories in the treaty ports, a right that was soon taken by all the Western nations. More ominously, Japan successfully imposed a huge indemnity (230 million taels) on China to defray the costs of the war—an action that deepened China's financial crisis (its annual revenue was only about 89 million taels) and thereby further eroded the government's chances of embarking on meaningful reforms. The financial disaster also forced China to borrow money from foreign firms. From 1895 to 1898, loans were arranged from Russia, a French-Russian consortium, and an Anglo-German consortium, secured against customs revenues. From this point until the establishment of the People's Republic of China in 1949, China was continuously in debt to foreign countries.

THE SCRAMBLE FOR CONCESSIONS

One foreign policy disaster was followed by another crisis between China and the foreign powers. It was Germany that put in motion what has been called the *scramble for concessions* or the establishment of *spheres of influence* or, more graphically, *carving up the Chinese melon*. For several years Germany, desiring to establish a naval base in China, had lusted after Jiaozhou Bay on the southern coast of Shandong. All it needed was a pretext to make demands and, if need be, use force. The opportunity came in November 1897, when two German missionaries from a particularly aggressive Catholic order were hacked to death by a band of Chinese. In response, Germany occupied Jiaozhou Bay and its city, Qingdao. In March 1898, Germany forced the Chinese government to lease the port and its surrounding area for ninety-nine years; the leasehold included Germany's right to build two railroads and hold mining rights.

Driven by imperialist rivalry, the other nations followed suit. Russia used the pretext of protecting China from Germany to occupy Port Arthur and Dalian on the tip of the Liaodong peninsula in December 1897, signing a twenty-five-year lease in March 1898. As part of the leasehold, Russia also acquired the right to build a railroad from these two ports up to the Chinese Eastern Railway; it would come to be called the South Manchurian Railway and would play a crucial role in China's and Japan's subsequent history. To check the Russians, Britain countered with a twenty-five-year lease of the port of Weihaiwei directly across the Bohai Straits from Port Arthur and Dalian; in June 1898, it also leased the so-called New Territories of Hong Kong for ninety-nine years. France forced a lease of Guangzhou Bay for ninety-nine years in April 1898, thus setting up its sphere of influence in southern China. Italy, the United States, and Japan were frozen out of the carving competition: Italy's late demands were refused; the United States was interested in a particular site but was occupied with its war with Spain; Japan was focusing on its role in Korea.

After the scramble and with no sphere of influence of its own, the United States issued the Open Door notes, statements by which it hoped to ensure continuing and equal commercial opportunity. Not an altruistic policy, it was intended to ensure that countries with spheres would not freeze the United States out of treaty ports or areas of natural resources within those spheres. Though no country obligated itself to the notes, the U.S. secretary of state, John Hay, asserted that they had. In any case, the land grab ended not because of this policy but rather "because the imperialists feared rivalry and conflict among themselves. The resultant equilibrium saved the [Qing] empire from immediate collapse."[13]

At the time, of course, the Chinese were not aware that the Westerners would cease their carving competition. The establishment of treaty ports had thus escalated to the seizure of considerable territory

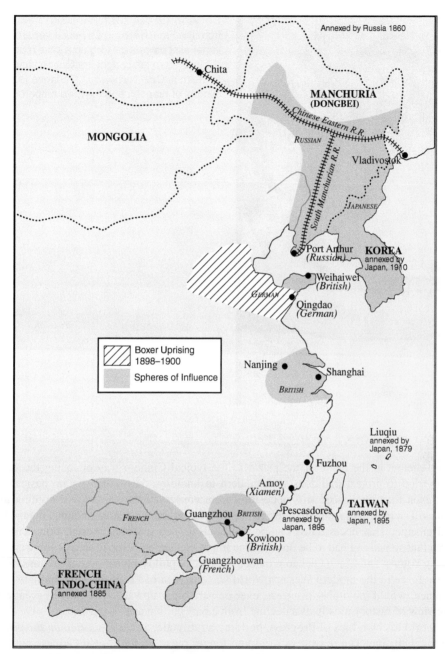

Map 3-2   Imperialism and the Boxer Uprising.

with substantial economic rights. In this scramble for more and more of China and its resources following so closely the disastrous war with Japan, imperialism had reached a far more virulent level that boded greater danger for China's future. It is not surprising that alarm about the incipient demise of the Chinese nation spread among elites all over China and gave rise to a bold reform movement.

EN CHINE
Le gâteau des Rois et... des Empereurs

Carving up the Chinese Cake   This illustration from the French tabloid *Le Petit Journal* shows the imperialist powers carving up a cake marked "China." From left to right are Queen Victoria, Kaiser Wilhelm II, Czar Nicholas II, Marianne (a national symbol of France), and the Meiji emperor of Japan.

THE REFORM MOVEMENT OF THE 1890S

Rationalizing change in the name of the past was the typical Chinese way of facing the future. Self-strengtheners tried to protect traditions with modern technology: they called for no basic institutional reforms, yet even then they faced stiff opposition from conservatives who wanted nothing to do with Western things. The reform movement of the 1890s went far beyond self-strengthening, demanding major institutional change. This necessitated compelling analysis and a strong presentation. Circumstances demonstrated that something had to be done: China might be dismembered if bold action were not taken. Scholars Kang Youwei and Liang Qichao provided the crucial philosophical rationalizations.

A motive force in the modern Western world was the Idea of Progress—that humans, using reason and science, would inevitably progress, ever onward, ever upward. This was in great contrast to the Chinese view of history mostly as a decline from a past golden age. Kang Youwei gave the Chinese intellectual world his own Idea of Progress, building a rationale, as always *based on the past,* for radical institutional change. The reformers would no longer preserve traditional Chinese culture (as the self-strengtheners would); instead, they would preserve China. Put another way, Kang moved beyond what is often called *culturalism* (loyalty to a particular culture) to the borders of a modern *nationalism* (loyalty to a particular geographic entity).

In order to build new ideological structures, Kang tried to destroy the old ones. Kang argued that the texts of Confucianism, which had been used for centuries, were forgeries. The legitimate texts were the so-called New Texts from the Han dynasty, from which he gained material to rationalize reform. The impact of Kang's arguments on the intellectual world of the 1890s was shattering. If the traditional canon was shown to be false, there was no firm intellectual ground on which to stand; indeed, there was not even a firm past on which to rationalize. Kang further argued that Confucius was not simply a transmitter of a way of thinking (which Confucius himself claimed) but an innovator to be emulated by carrying out forward-looking change. Finally, Kang presented his rationale for progress, which he found in the New Texts: history, he claimed is unilinear, moving ever onward and upward. History will progress through three ages: the Ages of Disorder, Approaching Peace, and Universal Peace. China, he argued, was stuck in the Age of Disorder, but it could progress to the Age of Approaching Peace if his reform ideas were adopted. Kang's reform proposals advocated basic institutional change, which included a constitution and representative assemblies.

Source: Kang Youwei's Three Proposals

Kang Youwei bravely called for basic institutional change to put China on a new footing in the midst of a constant barrage of problems and tragedies. In spite of the rationality of his proposals, as expressed here, Kang was seen by conservatives as a heretical "wild fox." What was to be the relation between the center and the provinces in the reform efforts? What was to happen to those who refused to participate in the reforms?

In this regard your humble servant has three proposals to make. In today's world wherein the great powers are competing for hegemony at small countries' expense, there is no way to safeguard our national survival other than the introduction and implementation of reforms. . . .

First, we should try to benefit from the experience that Russia and Japan have had in the past. Your Majesty should have the same determination as Peter the Great as far as the introduction of reforms is concerned; as for the nature and scope of these reforms he cannot be better advised than to follow the example of Japan during the Meiji Period. . . .

Second, to plan for the proposed reforms, Your majesty is requested to gather all the talented men in the government for consultation purposes. Talented men can be found not only in the Six Ministries and the Nine Secretariats but also in the Translation Bureau, the Censorate, and the Hanlin Academy, especially the last mentioned. Each of them, when summoned before Your Majesty's presence, will be asked, in a most humble manner, to express his opinion candidly on what program should be introduced, preserved, or eliminated and what program or programs should be emphasized more. When reforms are implemented in a systematic and orderly manner, good results will come about in approximately fifteen months.

Third, the governors-general and governors must be allowed to conduct reforms on their own initiative. . . .

While each province is given great latitude in introducing and carrying out new programs, the guidelines as promulgated by the central government must be nevertheless strictly followed. The archconservatives who refuse to go along with the new programs must be retired or dismissed from their respective positions; so must be all those who have sunken too deep into inertia to entertain any change to a more active role. As a general principle, each province must be given a target in terms of the number of troops to be trained by Western methods, the amount of taxes to be levied, the number of manufacturing plants to be built, the number of mines to be opened, the number of schools to be established, and the mileage of roads to be built, all to be completed in a three-year period. A new era for the nation will be then ushered in.

Source: Dun J. Li, trans. and ed., Modern China: From Mandarin to Commissar *(New York: Charles Scribner's Sons, 1978),* 90–92.

Kang's reinterpretation of Confucianism produced shock waves that were felt for decades. His thesis essentially changed Confucianism from "what so far had been the unquestioned centre of faith into an ideology, the basic character of which was problematic and debatable."[14] Once Confucianism became an ideology, for example, it could be seen as a manipulatable instrument that elevated certain social types (fathers, husbands, elder brothers) and degraded other social types (sons, wives, younger brothers). Kang's work was the revolutionary first step, however little he intended it, in deposing Confucius and his thought as the foundation of Chinese culture—the first step in dismantling traditional Chinese identities.

Liang Qichao's writings are important because many elements of his thought remained central in the discourse of change throughout much of the twentieth century. He argued that crucial political change must be based on educational reform. The spread of literacy could not be fostered through the traditional examination system. That system would have to be replaced by a new national school system that would promote intellectual development and political consciousness. A cardinal concept in Liang's thoughts about solving China's crisis was *grouping*—mobilizing the intellects and energies of China's elites to study and discuss requisite political changes. Liang's arguments implied that traditional Chinese culture, with its emphasis on individual identity and personal connections and networks, inhibited social solidarity and energetic commitment to broader goals. Further, the traditional authoritarian state limited, even repressed, the people, blocking the free flow of information. These limits had to be shattered so that Chinese political culture could develop an all-important *collective dynamism*. The new state must feature shared participation of rulers and ruled in a system of popular sovereignty. The concept of grouping thus encapsulated ideas of political community, the nation, and democracy. Liang's radical political ideas became the watchwords of subsequent Chinese reformers and revolutionaries from Sun Yixian (Mandarin pronunciation for Sun Yat-sen) to Mao Zedong.

Institutional reformers, led by Kang and Liang, began by establishing study associations to remake China by giving it a new national identity. These associations were to facilitate social integration among official and nonofficial elites and, through the study process, to educate elites and mobilize their energies. The first study societies were established in Beijing and Shanghai in the second half of 1895; they flowered in Hunan province in central China, where fourteen societies were founded in 1897 and 1898.

The scramble for concessions formed the backdrop for the Hundred Days from June to September 1898, when breakneck, breathtaking reforms promised a new China but delivered beheadings, forced flight, and imprisonment. The episode occurred after Kang won the support of the twenty-seven-year old reform-minded Guangxu emperor, whose tutor recommended Kang. At a January 1898 meeting with the emperor and key officials, Kang argued that the fate of the country depended on changing the current political and social institutions. From June 11 to September 21, the emperor, with Kang providing the agenda, issued over one hundred decrees calling for institutional reforms in almost every policy arena. They included revamping the examination system and establishing a national school system; restructuring the government and abolishing sinecure positions; modernizing the military, police, and postal systems; and setting up new institutions to promote agriculture, commerce, and industry.

The reforms threatened the status quo, specifically the empress dowager and her supporters. The empress dowager, who was openly opposed to the emperor and the reform group, brought the process to a halt. On September 21, with the help of the military under Yuan Shikai, she staged a coup d'etat, seizing power from the emperor and placing him under house arrest. Five days later, all the reform edicts were revoked. Kang escaped to Hong Kong and Liang to Japan, but six young reformers were executed.

The reform effort was put down easily, but it had great historical import. One historian argued that it "usher[ed] in a new phase of Chinese culture—the era of ideologies." The ideas of Kang and Liang, which included Western thought and dethroned Confucianism from the Way to an ideology, "raised the curtain on the cultural crises of the twentieth century."[15] The reform era led to the birth of the modern intelligentsia; unlike the old scholar-gentry, the new intelligentsia consisted of "free-floating intellectuals,"[16] not tied to localities and lacking a symbiotic relationship with the government. Unlike the old scholar

Empress Dowager   Cixi, the empress dowager, is shown with her ladies-in-waiting in a snow-covered garden in 1903.
Source: Courtesy of the Freer Gallery of Art, Smithsonian Institution, Washington, D.C.

elites, they struggled with problems of alienation from the government and, above all, of cultural identity, caught between the old and the new, East and West.

THE BOXER CATASTROPHE

The collapse of the traditional state and civilization was punctuated at century's end by an outrageous constellation of events in North China. From a culture of poverty in Shandong province came a social explosion. Led by so-called *Boxers,* a name taken from the martial art rituals, or boxing, that they performed, the movement was spearheaded mostly by young farmers, laborers, and out-of-work drifters.

Natural disasters—flood and drought—led to the rise and spread of the Boxer movement. In August 1898 floods broke the Yellow River dikes, sending torrents of water into thirty-four counties, covering over two thousand villages, and turning millions of people into refugees. The area was so devastated that crops could not even be planted the next spring. Many people received no aid because of government corruption in dispersing relief grain, intensifying antigovernment feelings.

Anti-Christian hostility was another crucial cause of the uprising. In the area where the Boxer movement began, the leaders of a stridently militant German Catholic order used aggressive and racist rhetoric to describe Chinese (e.g., "Crowds of slit-eyed Chinese swarmed about the harbor [in Shanghai] . . .).[17] This order was particularly active in interfering in their converts' lawsuits. They forbade converts to participate in or contribute to village festivals, which often featured processions following a statue of the local god, considering it idolatry. In the name of preventing that evil they ruptured the Chinese community, in effect destroying at least part of the converts' Chinese identity and offending and embittering nonconverted Chinese.

Beginning in 1898 and 1899, Boxers attacked the property and persons of Christian converts and missionaries. In the winter of 1899–1900, the movement spread beyond its Shandong origins into other northern provinces and even to inner Mongolia and Manchuria. There was no central leadership; Boxer bands would coalesce, attack Christian converts, and fade away. The movement spread quickly in part because of the dynamic of spirit possession.

> *The empowerment possession conferred made it enormously attractive to those at the bottom of the Chinese social scale, regardless of locale. Also, the possession ritual [which involved boxing, incantations, breathing through clenched teeth, and foaming at the mouth], by placing individuals in direct communication with their gods and enabling them, when in a possessed state, to in effect become gods, placed a major barrier in the way of the creation of a more centralized, structured, and perhaps durable movement."[18]*

The expansion of the Boxer movement also depended on the attitude of the officials. Governor Yuan Shikai's suppression of the Shandong Boxers contrasted sharply with Governor Yuxian's encouragement of Boxers in Shanxi.

Source: Red Lanterns

Girls who joined the Boxer movement were called Red Lanterns. *They were mainly prepubescent, ranging in the age from eleven or twelve to sixteen or seventeen. These accounts were compiled by the Department of History at Shandong University in 1980, based on interviews beginning in the 1960s. What special feats could Red Lanterns perform? Since red is the color of celebration (and of weddings in traditional China), what might red signify in the case of the Red Lanterns?*

Fenglou had the Shining Red Lantern. All the Shining Red Lanterns were women who dressed up completely in red. They waved red fans and carried red lanterns and they could get wind or rain or ride the clouds and call in the mist. Two women facing each other would wave their fans and while waving them they could ascend into the sky. That was the kind of thing they did. The elder sister of Wang San of Wangguang village was a Shining Red Lantern. This sister later got married to someone from Nanguan in the city. Before this woman was married, at the age of eighteen, she was a Shining Red Lantern. I used to go to watch the hustle and bustle. [Interview with Zhang Yuqi, age eighty-two, Ma Village, Sanlitun Commune, Renping Country, January 1966.]

Girls who joined the Boxers were called "Shining Red Lanterns." They dressed all in red. In one hand they had a little red lantern and in the other a little red fan. They carried a basket in the crook of their arm. When bullets were shot at them they waved their fans and the bullets were caught in the basket. You couldn't hit them! Some were also possessed by spirits and would say that they were Ma Guiying or Hu Jinchan. [Interview with Zhu Yunze, age eighty-two, Zhu village, Yeguantun Commune, Renping County, December 1965.]

Source: Pei-kai Cheng and Michael Lestz, The Search for Modern China: A Documentary Collection *(New York: W. W. Norton, 1999), 186.*

Perhaps the most important factor in Boxer growth was the drought that began after the Yellow River floods in late 1898, which freed many young farmers who ordinarily would have been working in the fields to join the Boxers. Psychologically the drought created a problem of hunger anxiety, of growing nervousness, restlessness, and hopelessness. The drought became linked in many Chinese minds with the presence of Westerners, particularly missionaries. Placards in villages called on people to kill "all foreigners and native Chinese contaminated by foreigner or foreign influence. Only after this . . . will the gods be appeased and permit the rains once again to fall."[19]

Western nations, frightened by the continuing attacks on missionaries, as well as by property losses, demanded that the Qing court end the uprising. Since the Boxers had championed a slogan supporting the Qing ("Revive the Qing; destroy the foreigner"), the empress dowager was reluctant to suppress them. She argued that "China is weak; the only thing we can depend upon is the hearts of the people. If we lose them, how can we maintain our country?"[20] With Western pressure on the court becoming stronger, the empress dowager threw her support behind the Boxers. The Qing sent military forces against the Boxers but undertook no concerted or sustained action to suppress them. Boxers neared Beijing in late spring, attacking railroad lines, ripping out the tracks, burning stations, and tearing down telegraph lines.

Western nations and Japan decided that they had to act to save missionaries and stop the bloodshed. On June 10, 1900, Boxers beat back a British relief force marching from Tianjin; they were eventually joined by Qing imperial troops. On June 20, the German ambassador was shot dead on the street. The next day, in a scene that conjures up the theater of the absurd, the empress dowager declared war on the eight foreign powers. Having been repeatedly defeated by one country at a time, the Qing now decided to battle all eight at once.

Slaying the Chinese Dragon   European nations and Japan vie to dismember China following the Boxer uprising. The Russian bear and the British lion are in the thick of it, while the American eagle in the background looks on.

The ambassadorial legation quarters in Beijing and the Northern Cathedral two miles northwest of the legations had become havens for missionaries and converts. In late June the Boxers besieged both sites, giving rise in the Western press to the phrase *yellow peril*. The worst Boxer violence occurred in Shanxi province, where Governor Yuxian encouraged Boxer attacks on Westerners. In early July he called forty-four missionaries and their families—men, women, and children—to the provincial capital for their "protection." On July 9, under his personal supervision, they were executed. Other missionaries in the province were also killed, along with some two thousand Christian converts.

The war was localized to the north because central and southern governors-general simply ignored the declaration of war. An eight-nation force of about twenty thousand men arrived in the capital on August 14 to lift the siege. Most Boxers disappeared into the North China countryside. Disguised and under armed guard, the empress dowager and the emperor fled in a cart to the ancient capital of Xi'an in Shaanxi province, eight hundred miles from Beijing. They remained there until January 1902.

Over the next six months, Western troops joined missionaries in raiding surrounding cities and towns, pillaging Chinese property. The missionaries were enthusiastic about revenge. For sheer outrageousness, the essay "The Ethics of Loot," written by the missionary Gilbert Reid for *Forum* magazine in 1901, wins the prize. Reid argued that "For those who have known the facts and have passed through [this] war of awful memory, the matter of loot is one of high ethics." He said he was sorry that he had not personally looted more.[21]

American Troops at the Temple of Agriculture   American soldiers march at the Temple of Agriculture after the Boxer expedition. The temple was the earthly counterpart to the Temple of Heaven, just to its east. Here the emperor came every spring to plow a furrow of soil so that a new season of sowing and planting could begin.

By late 1900, forty-five thousand foreign troops were in North China on search-and-destroy missions, trying to ferret out Boxers and kill them. But, as in any guerrilla-type action, how does one identify the enemy? The result was many innocent persons killed. One American commander noted that "it is safe to say that where one real Boxer has been killed since the capture of [Beijing], fifty harmless coolies or laborers on the farms, including not a few women and children, have been slain."[22]

The Boxer Protocol in September 1901 brought the nadir of Qing court relations with the West. Western nations, out for revenge, called for the execution and punishment of officials who had participated in the war and punished the elite class of would-be officials by forcing China to suspend the civil service examinations for five years in forty-five cities. Over two dozen forts were destroyed and a dozen railroad posts were occupied to give Western troops ready access to Beijing. The Western nations expanded the legation quarters, ordered it permanently fortified, and prohibited China's importation of arms for two years.

But the greatest disaster was an indemnity that was staggering in its immensity. For damage to foreign property and for foreign deaths, the Chinese were forced to pay 450 million taels (about $333 million in 1901), an overwhelming sum because, by this time, the complete annual Qing income was only about 250 million taels. The indemnity was to be paid annually in thirty-nine installments in gold, with interest rates that by the date of the full payment of the debt (the end of 1940) would total about 1 billion taels. For a government that could not move into the modern world in part because of lack of money, the indemnity was crushing.

The extremely harsh nature of the Boxer Protocol, the miserable showing of the Chinese military, the insane policy of attempting to use the Boxers as instruments of policy, and the mortifying flight of the country's sovereigns were on view for the whole world to see. Qing wealth and power under the Qianlong emperor had been at their height just a century earlier, yet China now entered the twentieth century in degradation, poverty, and humiliation.

An Execution   Chinese crowds watch the public execution of a Boxer leader tied to a pole. Boxer leaders of units numbering from twenty-five to one hundred or more were often chosen because of their superior boxing skills.

CHRONOLOGY

1851–1864	Taiping Rebellion
1860	Chinese territory taken by Russia; becomes Russia's Maritime Provinces
1861	Emergence of Cixi, the empress dowager
	Establishment of the Zongli Yamen
1853–1868	Nian Rebellion
1853–1873	Panthay Rebellion
1862–1873	Muslim Rebellion in the northwest
1865	Establishment of the Jiangnan Arsenal
1866	Establishment of the Fuzhou Shipyard
1876	Japan opens Korea
1879	Japan annexes the Liuqiu (Ryūkyū) islands
1883–1885	Sino-French War
1894–1895	Sino-Japanese War
1895	Treaty of Shimonoseki; Japan takes over Taiwan
	Triple Intervention takes Liaodong peninsula away from Japan
1897–1898	Scramble for concessions
1895–1898	The Reform Movement
1898	The Hundred Days
1898–1900	The Boxer uprising
1901	The Boxer Protocol

SUGGESTED READINGS

Cohen, Paul. *History in Three Keys: The Boxers as Event, Experience, and Myth.* New York: Columbia University Press, 1997. This prize-winning meditation focuses on the Boxer movement, exploring the nature of history, memory, and myth.

Cumings, Bruce. *Korea's Place in the Sun: A Modern History.* New York: W. W. Norton, 1997. This insightful and vibrantly written history puts Chinese interests and actions in Korea in perspective.

Karl, Rebecca, and Peter Zarrow, eds. *Rethinking the 1898 Reform Period: Political and Cultural Change in Late Qing China.* Cambridge, MA: Harvard University Press, 2002. This collection of wide-ranging essays sees the period 1895–1899 as laying the groundwork for the New Policy Reforms of 1901–1911.

Kuhn, Philip. *Rebellion and Its Enemies in Late Imperial China: Militarization and Social Structure, 1796–1864.* Cambridge, MA: Harvard University Press, 1970. A pathbreaking study showing how patterns of local military organization "were related to long-term political and social trends in modern China."

Spence, Jonathan. *God's Chinese Son: The Taiping Heavenly Kingdom of Hong Xiuquan.* New York: W. W. Norton, 1996. In the words of one reviewer, this is "[a] spellbinding narrative, [and] a masterpiece of careful and creative historical scholarship" on the leader of the Taiping movement and the movement itself.

CHAPTER FOUR

From Tributary Younger Brother to Colony:
Vietnam, 1770s–1925

Some people describe the geographic shape of Vietnam as a shoulder pole with rice baskets on either end. A look at a map suggests that this might be a stretch, though the rice baskets of Vietnam—the Red River or Tonkin delta in the north and the Mekong delta in the south—are in fact on either end of this generally very narrow country. The Red River, which flows out of China's Yunnan province, is crucial for irrigating the north's rice paddies, for transportation, and for hydroelectric power. But the great amount of silt deposited in the delta also piles up in the riverbed, making flood control an ongoing concern. The Mekong River, with its source in Tibet, has many branches in the delta, depositing immense amounts of silt to make it one of the world's most fertile regions. Moreover, because of the flatter terrain along the Mekong, flooding is not so much of a problem. Running along the shoulder pole, serving almost as a spine and as the border with Laos, are the Annamite Mountains that run into the Central Highlands, a region of mountains and high plateaus, whose major products include rubber, forest products, and coffee. The land area is 40 percent mountainous, 17 percent of which is arable. The central part of the country between the deltas is narrow, in the north central region, the South China Sea and Laos are only thirty miles apart in some areas. Farther south the country widens so that its breadth is about one hundred miles.

Climatically, Vietnam is in the tropical monsoon belt. Average annual high temperatures range from 74°F in Hanoi in the north to 77°F in Hue in the center to 81°F in Ho Chi Minh City (Saigon) in the south. The mountainous regions are cooler and less muggy. The rainy season runs from April to October, with rainfall varying according to place but averaging sixty inches in the country as a whole.

The population of Vietnam is ethnically diverse. Most people are ethnic Viet (likely in the beginning a mix of native Austro-Indonesia and Mongoloid peoples) who generally inhabit the deltas and the lowland along the coast. Non-Viet ethnic groups, similar to Laotians and Thais, live in the mountains. There is also a large Chinese population, descendants of immigrants who fled China at the time of the Qing takeover; historically, they have been economic leaders in commerce and banking.

PATTERNS IN VIETNAMESE HISTORY

In early Vietnamese history three important political patterns and realities emerge. First is the role that China played in Vietnam's history. China's Han dynasty (206 BCE–220 CE) took over what is today the northern part of Vietnam and ruled it directly for almost a millennium, from 111 BCE to 939 CE. During this period, Vietnamese culture became largely sinified. The Vietnamese adopted Chinese cultural values

Woman on the Mekong
This silhouette of a woman dressed in a traditional ao-dai and wearing the traditional conical hat represents an almost quintessential picture of Vietnam. Though this is just a traditional rowboat, many families lived on houseboats on the various arms of the Mekong River that enter the South China Sea.

and philosophies, artistic and literary traditions, written language, and governmental forms and structures, including a highly developed bureaucracy and a civil service examination (established in the Ly dynasty [1010–1225]). Vietnamese had always valued education. Kings from the Later Le dynasty (1428–1789) dispatched regular tribute missions to China, thus showing their admiration and respect for what they considered a higher culture.

A second pattern in Vietnamese history is an unwillingness to submit to the rule of outsiders. Almost from day one of China's overlordship, there were popular rebellions against the Chinese. Even after Chinese rule was overthrown and the Vietnamese established their own regime, the threat of Chinese intervention remained. The Vietnamese, relishing their autonomy, fought off subsequent Chinese invasions in 981, 1076, 1257, 1285, 1287, 1789, and 1979. In 1406 armies of the Ming dynasty took Hanoi, and the Chinese maintained precarious control until 1427 after the Vietnamese undertook a successful nine-year struggle for independence. Thus, it may be said that Vietnam's relationship to China was one of cultural love–political hate.

A third pattern marking Vietnamese development was southward expansion of the state. Whereas northern Vietnam had taken much of its culture from China, south and south central Vietnam had early on been most influenced by India. As the Vietnamese state pushed south, that cultural frontier provided the Vietnamese continual opportunities to incorporate non-Chinese influences into their culture. Until at least the fifteenth century, the state of Champa, with ties to India and Indonesia, controlled most of the southern two-thirds of what would become present-day Vietnam. As Vietnam expanded, there were frequent struggles with the Cham people, who were finally defeated in 1471 (fifty thousand of their descendants still live in the lowlands of central Vietnam). But lengthy conflict with ethnic Cambodians in the Mekong delta region meant that the Vietnamese did not seize the entire south as their own until about 1750.

The question of political and cultural identity was a hot potato for the Vietnamese. Who they were in relation to the Chinese was crucial, but how they stood in relation to other ethnic groups and the more Indianized cultures of the south was also of great importance. As Vietnam entered the late eighteenth century, the question of identity loomed even larger.

THE TAY SON REBELLION

Late-eighteenth-century Vietnam seems almost a harbinger of what Vietnam would experience from the 1940s through the 1970s: a three-decade cycle of dynastic wars, peasant uprisings, Chinese invasion, a war of national resistance, and a war of national unification. The Later Le dynasty, which technically existed until 1789, was a weak regime that began to lose control over the country in the 1520s. Then a family named Mac took control of the northern part of the country, ruling it from 1527 to 1592. The Chinese recognized the Mac as legitimate rulers even as they continued to recognize the more southern Le. Later two families, the Trinh in the north and the Nguyen in the south, emerged as the powers in their respective regions. Neither was able to take the other in a civil war that lasted from 1620 to 1674; the stalemate meant that the Trinh continued to rule from Hanoi and the Nguyen from Hue. Both continued to talk of Vietnamese unity as the ideal, as both continued to "recognize" the impotent Le dynasty emperors, who could at least be said to represent Vietnamese unity.

The first Westerners to live in Vietnam were Jesuit missionaries who arrived beginning in 1615. The Trinh barred them from the north, but the Nguyen allowed them in to proselytize. The small Christian community that they formed eventually participated in public affairs, and the Jesuits with their scientific knowledge were popular at court. They devised a system of romanizing the Vietnamese language: called *quoc ngu,* it became the form in which Vietnamese is written today. Early on the Vietnamese had used Chinese characters.[1] Later, they devised their own system of complicated Chinese-style characters (*chu nom*) that rendered both sound and meaning in one character. The difficulty in romanizing Vietnamese is that it has six tones whose use differentiates meaning; Jesuits devised a way of using (or of not using) diacritical marks over the main vowel in each monosyllabic word to represent the Vietnamese word. The Jesuit missionary effort was supported throughout the seventeenth century by the French government, which came to see it as a key way of enhancing France's position.

Amid the political unrest of the seventeenth and eighteenth centuries, the greatest sufferers were the peasants. Though landholding peasants did exist, historically the nobles and wealthy lords had gobbled up the land, creating vast estates. While villages traditionally held communal lands to be distributed to those in need, these lands were also being privatized by the wealthy. Peasants also suffered from excessive taxation; Pham Quy Thich, a Le loyalist, captured their plight well:

> *Last summer, harvests washed away with floods.*
> *This summer, harvest wilt with burning drought.*
> *Fields, high and low, are rigged with water scoops.*
> *At mealtime, day and night, roots sub for rice.*
> *Rainbows and clouds can't bear the Sixth-Moon frost.*
> *Men gather in the village, moaning crops:*
> *They see the tax collector—off they run.*[2]

In 1771 three brothers from the village of Tay Son in central Vietnam (who chose the surname Nguyen) dramatized the peasants' suffering in a rebellion named after their village. The Tay Son Rebellion joins the Taiping Rebellion as one of the largest peasant rebellions in pre-twentieth-century Asian history. Its roots were primarily in the peasantry and the small merchant class; one of the brothers was a minor tax collector and betel nut trader. But the rebellion had support from all levels of society. Many of its advisors had passed the highest level of the civil service examination and had been in the ruling circles of the Le dynasty and the Trinh regime.

The rebellion itself initially followed the Robin Hood model: the goal was to take from the rich and give to the poor. In areas controlled by the rebels, land was taken from landlords and redistributed, taxes were abolished, land and tax registers were burned, and food was given to the hungry from public granaries. The Tay Son brothers made quick work of defeating the Nguyen (1778) and Trinh (1786) regimes, thereby uniting the country for the first time in two centuries. They restored the Le regime, as they had promised, but that was more ceremonial than a true return to power. Dividing the country into north, center, and south, each brother became the king of one section. In 1788, the Le emperor, acting in tributary fashion, asked China for help in suppressing the rebellion; the Chinese complied, invading the country and seizing Hanoi. The king of the north, the most able of the three, proclaimed himself the Quang-trung emperor to deal with the occupying Chinese. Generally recognized today as a master military strategist, Quang-trung, in less than two weeks, led his army of one hundred thousand men and one hundred elephants to a victory over a two hundred thousand-man Chinese force. Showing his political savvy, he immediately sought to heal his relations with China by sending envoys to Beijing in a traditional tributary mission.

For all of his military and political skills, Quang-trung and his son, who followed him on the throne after his sudden death in 1792, did not introduce dramatic changes. Quang-trung did try to diminish the hold of the Chinese model in Vietnamese governmental affairs, making the military more prominent and designating Vietnamese, not Chinese, as the language of the court. When the Nguyen were defeated in the south in 1778, all were killed by the Tay Son rebels except for Nguyen Anh, the teenage nephew of the last Nguyen lord. He joined forces with a French missionary priest, Pigneau de Behaine, who was willing to

Source: Quang-trung's Speech

The most able of the three brothers who successfully executed the Tay Son Rebellion chose the imperial name Quang-trung. This speech, to rally troops to defeat Chinese invaders, was given the same month he took the throne, December 1788. What are his main arguments for resisting the Chinese?

The Qing have invaded our country; they are occupying Thanh long (Hanoi), the capital. Are you not aware of the situation?

In the universe, each constellation is assigned a specific place and, on earth, each country has its own government. The Chinese do not belong to our racial stock: therefore their intentions must be completely different from ours. From the Han dynasty to the present day, how many times have they not raided our country, massacred our population, emptied our treasuries? No one in our country could bear this humiliation, and everyone wished to drive the enemy beyond our borders. Under the Han, those were the Trung [sisters] . . . [there follows a list of freedom fighters through the centuries against the Chinese]. Those heroes could not sit silently and watch the enemy indulge in violence and cruelty toward the people. They had to comply with the aspirations of the people and raise the banner of justice. A single battle was often sufficient to overcome the Chinese and push them back into their own country. . . .

Today the Qing have retuned once again. They are determined to annex our country and to divide it into provinces and districts. How can they not be aware of what has happened to the Song, the Ming, and the Yuan? For this reason, I am assuming the leadership of the army to expel them. All of you are in complete possession of your intelligence and your capacities. Therefore, you should help me achieve this great undertaking. Should you maintain your old vice of having two hearts, I shall immediately exterminate all of you without exception.

Let this be a warning to all of you.

Source: http://www.humnet.ucla.edu/humnet/ealc/faculty/dutton/1788.html.

try to enlist French support to overthrow the Tay Son brothers. In 1787, Pigneau made it to Versailles to put Nguyen Anh's case before Louis XVI, who apparently agreed to provide some ships and men from the French outpost of Pondicherry in India. But the king later reneged. In the end, Pigneau himself scrounged up funds for supplies and two ships that he manned with deserters from the French navy. In the years after 1789, Pigneau "brought . . . a steady flow of ships, arms, and European advisers, who supervised the building of forts, shipyards, cannon foundries and bomb factories, and instructed the Vietnamese in the manufacture and use of modern armaments."[3] Nguyen Anh, helped by the French, by Tay Son regime factionalism, and by the Tay Son rulers' inability to deal effectively with a serious famine, defeated the Tay Son regime in 1802. He named himself the Gia-long emperor of the new Nguyen dynasty. All of Vietnam was again unified.

Although the Tay Son regime was brief and did not live up to its advanced billing, historians have seen the Tay Son Rebellion as a significant event in the transition to a modern Vietnam. It ended for almost a century and a half the division of Vietnam into north and south, and it saw the origins of active French involvement in Vietnamese political life. Its identity as a peasant movement served as forerunner of the peasant movement of the twentieth century.

THE NGUYEN DYNASTY

The Reigns of the Gia-long and Minh-mang Emperors

If the Quang-trung emperor tried to move away from the Chinese model, the first two emperors of the Nguyen, the Gia-long emperor (1802–1820) and the Minh-mang emperor (1820–1841), returned to it almost with a vengeance, choosing to use the Chinese names for institutions and civil service examination degrees. The Nguyen sought to replicate Beijing's Forbidden City in their capital, Hue. They copied the Chinese by setting up an executive structure of Six Boards (which China had had since the Tang dynasty), a Hanlin Academy, a Censorate, a Grand Secretariat to oversee the bureaucracy, and a Privy Council. They copied the Chinese practice of speaking of an Inner Court, comprised of the emperor, his harem, and eunuchs, and an Outer Court, basically the bureaucracy. In 1812, they copied the Qing law code verbatim. They began to offer the highest Chinese civil service degree, the *jinshi*, in 1822. Because the Qing's Kangxi emperor had issued a ten-point Sacred Edict proclaiming the significance of Confucian virtue for daily life, the Minh-mang emperor issued his own ten-point Sacred Edict. The emperors imitated these policies of the Chinese government: provinces subdivided into hierarchical units, biannual tax collections, census registration once every five years, corvee labor, and public granaries. These Nguyen leaders, who were loyal tributary vassals of China (*Zhongguo*—Central Country), mimicked China by declaring that Vietnam was also the central country and in turn made Laos their tributary state.

One problem confronting both emperors was that because the south was a relatively new part of the Vietnamese realm, this frontier region was not yet well integrated with the north and the center. Wealthy owners of large estates were separated by an economic and social chasm from a generally impoverished peasantry. Social tensions were worsened by the large number of immigrants who had poured into the region. In addition, there were not enough government officials to help regulate situations and oversee regulations. One sharp difference between the regions is that until 1860, only three people from the south had passed the civil service examination, a statistic that can be read at least two ways: education was not much valued there or was primitive, and/or the north and center were manipulating the system to keep southerners out.

Source: The Minh-mang Emperor

Known primarily for his rigid obstinacy, his high standards of service, and his aversion to the West, especially to Christianity—leading to his persecution of Christians—the Minh-mang emperor (1820–1841) appears in milder form in this description in Marcel Gaultier's 1935 biography. Nevertheless, what favorable statements in this description might be considered damning with faint praise?

Minh-mang remained, first of all, the tender literate his teachers had tried to make of him. . . . He was prepared for the vocation of a poet. . . . He was generous, ambitious, with a morbid desire to impose on everybody the fear and respect of his sovereign power. He possessed a feminine instinct in the service of a male character. . . .

The attention Minh-mang devoted to the most intimate details of the administration astonished his contemporaries. The emperor ruled directly, and the official annals show how he penetrated into every detail in regulating the existence of his subjects.

Source: Joseph Buttinger, The Smaller Dragon: A Political History of Vietnam *(New York: Frederick A. Praeger, 1958), 312–13.*

The Imperial Citadel   This tower at Hue's Imperial Citadel is part of the palace complex of the Nguyen emperors modeled on the Forbidden City in Beijing. The complex was mostly destroyed by American bombing during the American War in Vietnam.

Both emperors had to deal with the presence of Roman Catholic missionaries, the role of the pope, and the meaning of that relationship for the Confucian state they were building. They perceived that "Christian teaching demanded a loyalty incompatible with the Vietnamese state system."[4] While the Gia-long emperor maintained a "passive hostility" toward Christianity,[5] the Minh-mang emperor outlawed it in 1825 at a time when there were at least three hundred thousand Catholic converts in the country—more than in all of China. The attitudes of both emperors toward Christianity were not improved when Christian missionaries and converts supported opponents of the Nguyen regime or rebelled outright in 1833, an act that led to serious repression.

The Course of French Imperialism

From 1848 until 1860 an estimated twenty-five European and three hundred Vietnamese Catholic priests and up to thirty thousand Vietnamese Christians died in various persecutions. Ultimately it was the blood of these people that gave the French a reason or, more accurately, a pretext for forcing their way into Vietnam in colonial expansion.

The French landed troops at Danang on the central coast in 1858, their objective being the seizure of the emperor, Tu Duc. Initially, strong Vietnamese resistance kept them on the coast, unable to advance. In mid-1859, the French moved south down the coast, where larger rivers allowed them to sail into the interior. By 1861, they overwhelmed Vietnamese imperial forces. To force some action by the government, the French patrolled the rivers and coastline to prevent rice from reaching the capital, causing a severe rice shortage in Hue. Tu Duc responded by sending envoys to Saigon, which the French had seized. The Treaty of Saigon (1862) was the first step in making Vietnam a French colony. It ceded the city of Saigon, its three adjacent provinces, and the island of Poulo Condore to France; it opened three Vietnamese ports for trade; it promised free rein to missionaries; French ships could have free passage up the Mekong into Cambodia; Vietnam could not cede any territory to any other country without French permission (creating a vague but ominous protectorate); and Vietnam had to pay France an indemnity of four million piasters.

Given that one of the Vietnamese patterns discussed earlier was their repeated resistance to would-be foreign overlords, what was happening now? Coupled with the initial Vietnamese resistance along the central coast were many small insurrections against the French after 1862, but the government made no effort to mobilize widespread resistance. There is evidence that Tu Duc believed that time was on the Vietnamese side, that the tropical climate and diseases, as well as the high costs of colonialism, would undercut French dreams; Tu Duc also believed that Vietnamese resistance would come eventually.

But severe problems in Vietnam made successful resistance unlikely. The Nguyen dynasty was in serious decline. The first four emperors had championed Confucianism and the Chinese model, embracing it tightly and unwilling to look beyond it. The reaction to crisis was to dig deeper bunkers for protection, not to use initiative and think carefully about options. The government had become known for mismanagement and corruption; the officials, for inefficiency and arrogance. One historian pointed to the existence of "walls of hatred and indifference between the monarchy and the masses of the peasants."[6] The economy was in shambles; indeed, the government resorted to selling public offices as a source of revenue. The struggle with the French revealed a surprisingly weak military. It is clear that in terms of domestic politics and society, France could not have appeared in force in Vietnam at a worse time. Further, when Tu Duc should have been giving all his attention to the French threat, a northern rebellion led by a new pretender to the Le dynasty became his chief focus. Tu Duc believed that the Tonkin Rebellion was a more serious danger to the regime than the French and that the Saigon Treaty was a preferable alternative.[7] After the treaty, Tu Duc, afraid of French ire, prohibited resistance activities, and if they began, he attempted to suppress them.

In the summer of 1867, France occupied the three southernmost provinces in southern Vietnam, thus rounding out its complete control of the area it called Cochinchina; at the same time, it made Cambodia a protectorate. The French spent the next five years subduing Vietnamese resistance, organizing their administration, and focusing on Tonkin. We have seen this part of the story (see Chapter 3): the 1874 treaty that led the French to believe that China no longer maintained its tributary relationship with Vietnam; the Sino-French War; and the 1885 agreement that gave France its protectorate and nullified the tributary relationship. In essence, although not stated explicitly, it meant that the Nguyen emperors were reduced to figureheads.

The Nature of French Colonialism

As a result of French conquests, Vietnam became part of an Indochinese Union made up of five territories: the colony of Cochinchina and the protectorates of Annam, Tonkin, Laos, and Cambodia. The chief French official in Indochina was a governor-general. In each protectorate, the chief French officers were *residents superieurs;* in Cochinchina, a governor ruled. Each province in the protectorates was headed by a *resident,* one of whose jobs was to advise Vietnamese in local governments. In Annam the emperor and his bureaucracy were given a small degree of administrative authority.

The postconquest "pacification" of Vietnam, necessary before anything else could be accomplished, was not a story of sweetness and light. It was not really finished until the governor-generalship of Paul Doumer (1897–1902). When J. L. de Lanessan became governor-general in 1891, one of his goals was to win the hearts and minds of the Vietnamese.

This, he knew, could only be done if he first put an end to "the acts of incredible brutality" committed everywhere in the fight against the guerrillas. "It seemed to me," he wrote

Tomb of Emperor Tu Duc (1829–1883)   The longest-ruling Nguyen emperor, Tu Duc left four thousand poems and six hundred works of prose. He designed his tomb to blend in with the natural setting, but also had in mind creating something of a fairyland with poetic features as a proper world for his eternal life after death.

after his enemies had succeeded in having him recalled in 1894, two years before his term was up, "that the burning of villages, the mass shootings, the bayonet slaughters, and the executions of notables should be replaced by other less violent procedures."[8]

De Lanessan was especially infuriated by the common practice of beheading village chiefs who did not know or would not say in what direction bands of rebels had headed after going through their villages.

The primary French objective was economic: to exploit Indochina for its raw materials and to establish ready markets for manufactured goods. Another goal was to increase national prestige; as late-nineteenth-century European nations competed for colonies, an empire became the sine qua non of national well-being, some would even say survival. A third objective (though this could easily shade into justification and rationalization) was "'the civilizing mission' (*mission civilisatrice*)—the obligation of the advanced peoples of the world to bring the benefits of modern civilization to the primitive peoples of Asia and Africa."[9] The French colonial strategy was clearly ambivalent; generally, the civilizing mission was subordinated to economic goals. There were many difficult questions about these objectives that were never answered. If the chief goal was to exploit the land and its people, how were the interests of the colonized to be protected? If France had a "civilizing mission," what form should it take? To transform the colonized Vietnamese into Frenchmen, a possibility supported early on and known as *assimilation?* To offer choices for the colonized to pick and choose? To work with Vietnamese elites in a common endeavor, a route increasingly chosen over the years, known first as *association* and later as *collaboration?*

What responsibilities did the colonizers have to the colonized? A coherent statement of colonial goals was never developed, which likely contributed to the ultimate failure of the enterprise.

Apologists for French rule argue that the French goals were laudable: developing modernizing sectors of industry and business, building modern communications and transportation infrastructures, and raising the standard of living. These defenders of French policy aver that general economic progress did occur; they point to thriving commerce and industry in large cities—Saigon, Danang, Hanoi, and Haiphong—and smaller provincial capitals—Vinh, Qui Nhon, and My Tho—for example. The mostly light industries—paper, matches, textiles, food processing—were owned by the French. Part of the policy established by Governor-General Doumer was that France would not support the development of a Vietnamese commercial and industrial sector because it would compete with the French-owned and -controlled enterprises. Logic to the contrary, Doumer, who at one point said that the Vietnamese were "ripe for servitude," believed "that what was good for France was also good for Vietnam."[10]

One of Doumer's emphases was public works; railroads should be the focus, he argued, because they would transform Vietnam. His railroad projects, however, all suffered from insufficient and hasty planning, engineering mistakes, economic miscalculations, ballooning costs, and great loss of human lives. During the construction of the less than three hundred-mile Yunnan-Fou line in Tonkin, twenty five thousand of the eighty thousand Chinese and Vietnamese workers died. Doumer's pet project, the Trans-Indochinese Railroad running from Hanoi to Saigon, was not completed until 1936. Its placement was not carefully considered: built along the coast, it duplicated the sea route and the main highway, and it did not provide services to areas of most economic growth or greatest population. Doumer's grandiose road and bridge construction projects had many of the same problems as the railroads.

A SAÏGON

The Arrival of the French Governor-General In this engraving from the November 1902 issue of *Le Petit Journal,* Governor-General Paul Beau arrives in Saigon. During his tenure, he signed a decision creating Dong Duong University, the first modern university in Vietnam and the precursor of today's Hanoi National University.

Two other of Doumer's other policies that made the lives of peasants (over 90 percent of the population) more difficult were excessively high taxes and French monopolies on the production and sale of salt, alcohol, and opium. The tax policy had been in effect before Doumer arrived: between 1890 and 1896, taxes were doubled; in 1898, there was another 50 percent increase. Doumer's tenure saw steeper tax increase and taxation of more items, including matches, mineral oil, tobacco, stamps, cinnamon, and woodcutting. "Soon, the Vietnamese joked, there would be a tax on bowel movements."[11] These taxes and the French monopolies went to pay for Doumer's public works fiascoes. The Vietnamese were indignant about the monopolies, for the French jacked up the prices of important commodities. The monopoly on rice whiskey, an important element in the many feast days for families and villages, increased the cost of the whiskey by almost 900 percent.

THE VIETNAMESE RESPONSE TO FRENCH CONTROL

The Vietnamese response to being colonized varied from resistance to abstention to collaboration. Immediately after the Treaty of Saigon, there was an outburst of protest literature expressing contempt for the French and anyone who cooperated with them. But historians have noted that after 1867, growing numbers of Vietnamese chose to abstain, neither collaborating with nor opposing them.

After Tu Duc died in 1883, the imperial court put on a display of double-dealing and intrigue that cannot have helped its long-term image or its future. Tu Duc's successor was deposed and imprisoned after only one day on the throne. *His* successor, in turn, was compelled to commit suicide four months into his reign. *His* successor, in turn, died after half a year of his reign. Twelve-year-old Ham Nghi succeeded him. In 1885 he took refuge in the mountains of the west central region where he issued a "loyalty to the king" edict, calling on all Vietnamese to overthrow the French. People did rise up in localized actions, but they were mercilessly crushed by the new foreign overlords. Thousands died in this futile attempt for independence. In 1888, the French seized Ham Nghi and sent him into exile. One of the leaders of the loyalty to the king movement was Phan Dinh Phung, a well-known mandarin and former imperial censor, considered by many as a hero. He continued the resistance until 1896, when he died of natural causes. His army numbered about three thousand when Ham Nghi was taken, but estimates suggest that it was several times larger at its height. The French tried to make certain that subsequent emperors would be "safe" collaborators. With the court collaborating, cooperation with the French was more socially acceptable for Vietnamese elites. Many more Vietnamese came to see that French rule could be tolerated. By the first decade of the twentieth century, people were declaring openly that only by learning Western culture thoroughly could Vietnam become equal to France.

Phan Boi Chau (1867–1940) and Phan Chu Trinh (1872–1926)

Two of the most important reform and resistance leaders of their generation, Phan Boi Chau and Phan Chu Trinh shared the same surname but were not related. Chau, like the loyalty to the king leader Phan Dinh Phung and the later leader Ho Chi Minh, hailed from north central Nghe An province, known as a birthplace of rebels and heroes. He finished first on the second-level civil service examination in 1900. His concern for the fate of Vietnam had become an obsession, and in that year he proposed general guidelines for throwing out the French. First, he tried to unite former resistance leaders (with little success); then, because he wanted the new Vietnam to be headed by a renovated monarchy, he sought support from the royal family and the bureaucracy; finally, he looked for foreign support and aid, if necessary. Chau made an important contact with Cuong De, a direct descendant of the Gia-long emperor; because of his open-minded views and approaches, Chau pegged him as the right candidate for the Vietnamese throne.

As for foreign support, none came immediately. But at the turn of the twentieth century, Chau and Vietnamese intellectuals in general enthusiastically read and discussed Western works of political and social philosophy by Voltaire, Rousseau, Darwin, and Spencer. They also studied essays by the Chinese scholar-activists Kang Youwei and Liang Qichao, who were involved in similar efforts to chart the path for a modern Chinese state. In a March 1904 meeting chaired by Cuong De and attended by Chau, about twenty participants established the Modernization Society (Duy Tan Hoi) to serve as the chief organization spearheading the overthrow of the French. They agreed that dual military and civilian resistance had the best possibility of success and sought weapons for armed resistance (Chau was open to the use of violence). They also began to establish schools and business associations to serve as bases for their activities.

In 1905, Chau took his first step in attempting to gain foreign support, traveling to Japan, which had been undergoing rapid, successful modernization since the 1870s (see Chapter 7). Chau not only wanted to arrange for support but also to see for himself what Japan was doing. While he was there, Japan astonished the world with its military victory over Russia in the Russo-Japanese War, the first victory of an Asian nation over a European power. People in countries all over Asia, many of them in the hands of European imperialists, felt their hopes soar in anticipation of what might be. Chau was exhilarated at being in Japan when the victory occurred. During this and subsequent trips to Japan, the people most helpful to Chau were Chinese revolutionaries studying there, many of whom were in Sun Yixian's revolutionary organization.

The other Phan, Chu Trinh, like Chau, had studied for and passed the court level of the civil service examination in 1901. Two years later he was appointed to a prestigious post in the important Board of Rites, but he tired quickly of bureaucratic hassles and was repelled by the open corruption. He read deeply the works of the Chinese reformers and met Chau; though they had very different approaches, their common goals brought them together. Chau's openness to violent, radical change contrasted sharply with Trinh's emphasis on nonviolence, education, and gradual progress toward independence. This split was reflected in the intellectual community at large. Even members of the Modernization Society were divided as to the best strategy, agreeing only on the urgent need for Vietnamese to learn the secrets of Western wealth and power in order to save their country.

In early 1906, Chau was back in Japan with Cuong De and Trinh. While Cuong De enrolled in a military academy, Chau gave Trinh a tour of key places in the country he had come to admire greatly. Trinh was more reserved in his estimation of Japan's aims, hesitant about what Japan's two recent victories over China and Russia might mean for Japan's future goals. In order to get more Vietnamese students to study in Japan, Chau formed the Dong Du (Travel to the East) program, arranging for their admission to Japanese schools and establishing a language school where they could study Japanese before entering other schools. There were over two hundred Vietnamese students in Japan by mid-1908.

In March 1907, a new school opened in Hanoi under the leadership of Trinh. The Dong Kinh Nghia Thuc (Free School of Hanoi) was private; it had no tuition; and it accepted students of any age, male and female, rich and poor. It was funded with donations from the parents and other relatives of the students and from wealthy sympathizers. It used *quoc ngu* as a potent expression of Vietnamese national feelings. Founders of the school saw it also as the starting point for a larger mass education movement. Lecturers from the school spoke in various public forums twice a month. This initiative made the French nervous. To try to reassert their control over education, they opened a government-sponsored school in Hanoi and within less than a year closed down the Free School.

In March and April 1908, large numbers of peasants in central Vietnam rebelled. Life in the countryside was rapidly changing, unraveling the traditional peasant world. Vietnamese villages in the north and central regions were "closed and corporate communities" that, as a unit, owned land.[12] Every three years the corporate land was reallocated to the very poor or occasionally to someone as payment for a job completed for the village. Now that corporate land was being swallowed up by French companies and their Vietnamese collaborators. Most unsettling to the peasants was the expansion of a cash economy all over the country, which replaced the many traditional personal forms of social-economic interaction with a single impersonal form—money. Meanwhile, the excessive taxes levied by the French did not abate. The

Source: Letter of Phan Chu Trinh

In his 1906 letter to French Governor-General Paul Beau, the nationalist Phan Chu Trinh essentially called on the French to develop modern economic, legal, and educational institutions in Vietnam. In doing so, he pointed out how the Vietnamese perceived their treatment by the French. Is Trinh's depiction primarily racist? Or do you think any colonizer would treat colonized subjects this way?

Whether in newspapers, or letters or in conversation, . . . the French always hold us in hatred and contempt. They consider us not merely as savages, but as dogs and swine. Not only do they not treat us as equals, but to them we are something dirty and stinking, to be avoided. In this era, any mandarin who dares to object to a French administrator, no matter how well-founded his objection, is insulted scornfully.

More than a few people in the countryside have been beaten to death by Frenchmen. Everyone realizes that the French consider us as animals and brutes; eveyone is angry, but who dares to voice his anger? . . . When a Vietnamese meets a Frenchman, whether a civilian or soldier, the Vietnamese is always ready to take flight lest the Frenchmen kick or beat him.

Source: Joseph Buttinger, Vietnam: A Dragon Embattled, Vol. l, From Colonialism to the Vietminh *(New York: Frederick A. Praeger, 1967), 49.*

growing bitterness of the peasants led to the rebellion. They refused to pay taxes, pleaded for reduced corvee duty, laid siege to government offices, and seized officials. The French immediately and bloodily suppressed them; at least nine hundred peasants were summarily executed, thousands were arrested, and over one hundred were sent to the prison island of Poulo Condore, fifty miles off the southern coast. The Free School was singled out, though it had nothing to do with the episode. Chau was sentenced to death in absentia for his general revolutionary actions. Trinh was arrested and imprisoned, blamed for inciting the short-lived rebellion. After being given a "partial amnesty" in 1911, he made his way to France.

Mekong Delta Farm Scene
Vietnam's rice basket was the Mekong delta. Here a farmhome is set in the middle of lush green paddies surrounded by palm trees.

The haven of Japan was soon lost to the Vietnamese. In 1907 Japan, in exchange for a loan from France, recognized all the French holdings in Asia. Under pressure from the French, the Japanese made it clear that Vietnamese students were no longer welcome. In March 1909, Chau and Cuong De were expelled from Japan, Chau going to Siam and Cuong De to Hong Kong. In 1911 they met in Guangzhou, where a revolution was brewing. In discussions with members of Sun Yat-sen's political party, the Guomindang, Chau gave up his long-held idea of a renovated monarchy and adopted instead the goal of a democratic republic. In February 1912, he also formed a new revolutionary organization, the Association for the Restoration of Vietnam (Quang Phuc Hoi).

In 1912 and 1913, a series of terrorist attacks carried out by people loosely connected to Chau led to trouble for him. One attack was an unsuccessful assassination attempt on Governor-General Albert Sarraut. Sarraut requested that China arrest Chau; China complied, throwing Chau into prison, where he stayed until 1917. After his release, he remained in exile in China until 1925. Two more episodes of resistance in 1916 and 1917 showed that there was still a strong animus against the French in some quarters. The more famous event was the 1916 attempt of the Vietnamese emperor, Duy Tan, to lead an uprising. Its planning became known to French authorities, who immediately declared martial law in Annam and disarmed all Vietnamese soldiers. The emperor was arrested within three days and exiled to Reunion Island. In August 1917, a brief military uprising in Tonkin was quickly squelched.

Key Journalists and the Identity of a Modern Vietnam

With the scholar-patriots out of the picture (Chau in exile in China, Trinh in France), the torch of nationalism passed to a new urban generation: the wealthy, often French-educated urban upper classes, who tended to champion moderate reformism, and the working class and petit bourgeoisie, who often espoused a more radical nationalism. During and after World War I, journalists were the voice of moderate reformism. This section focuses on three of them, not only for their contributions but also as an analysis of their different responses to French control and the Vietnamese future: Nguyen Van Vinh (1882–1935), Pham Quynh (1892–1945), and Nguyen An Ninh (1900–1943).

A son of peasants in the Red River delta, Vinh was early fascinated by the West. He graduated from an interpreters' school and then worked as an interpreter for the French. Selected to attend an exposition in Marseilles in 1906, he fell madly in love with all things French; he also became excited about the possibilities of the role of journalism in Vietnam's future. On his return, he collaborated with a Frenchman who was already publishing a Chinese paper in Hanoi; they changed the format so that half of the paper was published in Chinese and half in *quoc ngu* beginning in March 1907. Vinh also translated various works, including *The Tale of Kieu* (see Identities), into *quoc ngu*, arguing that "The condition of our nation in the future, good or bad, depends on *quoc ngu*."[13] Indeed, some historians consider his promotion and popularizing of *quoc ngu* his greatest contribution.

Vinh's ideas and philosophy, about which he wrote prolifically, fill the pages of publications that he edited, including *Indochinese Review* (founded in 1913) and a number of newspapers. He was a complete Westernizer, praising everything Western, particularly French, and bad-mouthing everything Vietnamese. He disliked traditional Vietnamese society, seeing Vietnamese culture as markedly inferior to that of the French. He argued that French colonialism was better for Vietnam than traditional elite Vietnamese rule. In his essays, he pointed out faults of the Vietnamese that had to be corrected, always by adopting Western ways. Vinh was appalled by the work of Phan Boi Chau because he thought that Chau would drive a wedge between France and Vietnam. He called Chau "[a] small man, inflated with a sense of self-importance, who escapes abroad to incite people to cause trouble and sow disaster."[14] In Vinh we find an example of a Vietnamese who was willing to jettison his original identity as a Vietnamese for a new cultural identity as a Frenchman.

Pham Quynh began his career almost as enamored of the French as Vinh. After graduating from a school for translators, he worked as a librarian at the prestigious École Française D'Extreme Orient in Hanoi from

Identities: Nguyen Du (1766–1820):
Confucian Loyalty as Obsession

Nguyen Du, who produced Vietnam's literary masterpiece, *The Tale of Kieu,* was the seventh child of a former prime minister of the dying Le dynasty (1427–1786), born in north central Vietnam. At age seventeen he passed the Chinese-inspired civil service examination. But at that time Vietnam was in rebellion and civil war, and the dynasty to which Du and his family were loyal was overthrown. "Du spent much of this period as an impoverished backwoods scholar, haunted by the tragedy of a vanished 'orthodox succession' of emperors to which his family had been deeply attached, and by the whirlpool of unstable, promiscuous political affiliations which had replaced it."[1] In this largely secluded life, he spent his time reading, writing, hunting, and walking in the mountains.

The short Tay Son rebel regime was defeated in 1802 by Nguyen Anh, who established the Nguyen dynasty. Nguyen Du agreed to serve the new regime, although some sources note that he was reluctant. He served in a series of positions—as provincial prefect; in one of the imperial scholars' pavilions in Hue, the capital; as provincial registrar; and as envoy to Beijing in 1813 with a tributary mission. In none of these posts did he wield much power, and there is evidence that his obsessive loyalty to the Le dynasty colored his life with a certain bleakness. He was moody and often silent. It is said that the first Nguyen emperor, Gia Long, once asked Du why he often remained silent at court; Du's response was to dissolve into sobs and offer to resign. After he died suddenly in 1820 while preparing to serve on another tributary mission to China, the official court records described him as a "frightened man who, each time he presented himself at an imperial audience, was terrified and anxious, and could not reply."

Be that as it may, Nguyen Du's *The Tale of Kieu* is a 3,254-line epic poem on the tragic life of its heroine, Thuy Kieu. In love with a scholar named Kim, to whom she had pledged herself, Kieu instead sold herself into an arranged marriage to get money for her father, who had been thrown into prison by crooked bailiffs. But filial piety this time led to tragedy, for Kieu's husband was a brothel keeper. Kieu was forced to become a prostitute; indeed, once rescued from that plight, she was forced into it a second time. In the end she was reunited with Kim, who meanwhile had married Kieu's sister (the outcome Kieu had actually urged when she first fell into prostitution). Though Kieu agreed to marry Kim, she insisted that their relationship remain platonic since years of prostitution had made her impure. The poem's themes include the importance of *karma,* the plight of women in Confucian society, the powerful force of destiny, and a zero-sum understanding of life: "This is the law: no gain without a loss."

The bleakness of the poem's tale may reflect Nguyen Du's personal bleakness. Scholars have suggested in fact that the poem may best be seen as a political allegory. Just as Kieu remained loyal to Kim, Du was truly loyal to the Le dynasty. Just as Kim sold herself to save her father, Du believed that his serving the Nguyen emperors was selling himself from his primary duty. Just as Kieu had to endure suffering and hardship, Du suffered in serving the Nguyen regime, as suggested by his sobbing before the emperor. In both cases, their obsession was their own sense of identity as determined by their self-images and their relation to others.

---

[1]*Alexander Woodside, "The Historical Background", in Nguyen Du,* The Tale of Kieu, *trans. Huynh Sanh Thong (New York: Random House, 1973), xiii.*

Source: Nguyen Van Vinh's View of the Vietnamese

Clearly a strong Francophile, Vinh was often hypercritical of Vietnamese culture. Here he called for free conversational exchanges and for eliminating the laughter that preserved the social distance between people. Given the differences in culture and the ideas of Edward Hall discussed in Chapter 1, do you think that Vinh's suggestions were possible?

Our Vietnam has a strange habit, which is to laugh at everything. If people praise us, we laugh, but if people criticize us, we also laugh. . . . Many times our laughter is unintentionally cruel. It has a way of insolently despising people . . . it has the meaning that you self-assuredly are paying no attention to the words of other people but have already mentally slandered their thoughts beforehand; it has the meaning that you are not looking carefully at the things other people do but have already mentally criticized their work. . . .

We must understand that when people talk to us, it is in order to ask us how we are thinking. No matter who it is who speaks with us, we must reply. Following our will, if we want to express our feelings so that other people will know them, we must speak the truth. If we do not understand, we must ask them to repeat their question. But if we do not wish to speak our thoughts . . . we must subtly employ polite, elegant words to make other people understand that their questions violate our privacy a little too much.

Source: Alexander Woodside, Community and Revolution in Modern Vietnam *(Boston: Houghton Mifflin, 1976), 75.*

1908 to 1917, the year he began editing *South Wind (Nam Phong)*. Published in *quoc ngu, South Wind* was initially a pro-French journal that eventually worked to achieve a synthesis of East and West. While Pham Quynh early on had called France a "breath of fresh air" in Vietnam, he moved away from putting French culture on a pedestal. He came to see that the crucial problem facing Vietnamese was how and to what extent to adapt modern Western values and institutions to a still thoroughly traditional Vietnamese society. At stake was the very soul of Vietnam, the fundamental identity of the nation and its culture. The dilemma posed in Pham Qunyh's writings is at the heart of the cultural crisis faced by all countries and their peoples in modern East Asia. "To Pham Quynh the past, while not perfect, was preferable to certain trends he saw emerging."[15] One of the most troubling trends was individualism with its potential to destroy the family and Vietnamese society as a whole. He argued that traditional values—the essence of what it meant to be Vietnamese—must be retained but adapted to meet the demands of the modern age. Subsequent writers have faulted Pham Quynh's elitism, his failure to include society at large in his vision, and his discounting the "spirit of freedom" sweeping the early twentieth century.[16] But he hit upon the critical issue raised by the colonial experience and brought it into the arena of public thought and debate.

The position of the third journalist, Nguyen An Ninh, on the issue of a modern Vietnamese identity lay somewhere between Vinh's infatuation with French ways and Quynh's support of Vietnamese tradition. A son of a scholar, Ninh was educated at a Franco-Vietnamese school and at the School of Law in Hanoi; he received a law degree in Paris in 1920. Like Vinh and initially Quynh, Ninh admired French culture deeply. Early on he believed that the French would try to undertake meaningful reforms, but he became troubled by the fact that they did not attempt to put their ideals into action. When he returned to Vietnam, he established a French-language newspaper called *The Cracked Bell (Cloche felee)*; a charismatic figure, Ninh lectured on contemporary issues to large audiences.

Source: Pham Quynh and Modern Change

In this 1917 essay entitled "The Idea of Family," Pham Quynh pointed to a crucial problem exported to the developing world by Western civilization: the powerful ideal of individualism. What does he think is the downside of individualism? Do you think he is right?

Today modern science has progressed, the human intellect has expanded, and the human heart and the ways of the world have also very much changed with the times. Some people's hearts thirst for freedom, as if they wish to smash all the established frameworks of previous generations. The family itself is an ancient institution, dating back to the time mankind first came together in society. Can the institution of the family withstand the movement of today? Can it survive any longer? Or is the day of its destruction about to arrive?

. . . In all societies of Europe the family is passing through a crisis. It is being forced to resist the movement for freedom, for liberty. This movement seeks only advantages, prosperity, and happiness for each person, making each and every discrete human being the center of the universe. It is called, in a word, "individualism."

Most of those who are infatuated with individualism are merely followers of fashion, usually people without any foundation of their own, often lacking any moral base. Without any foundation, it is easy for them to follow the times and change. Lacking any moral base, it is easy for them to be selfish and not think about others.

But apart from those people who lead such precariously attuned lives, everyone concerned with a proper way of living knows that the family is a secluded harbor in which we may be saved from the turbulent seas of this period. Religion is now growing weaker day by day; philosophies have no evidential basis; the human heart does not know where to find a port. Without a fixed set of rules, people's hearts are perturbed, society is dangerous.

Source: Neil Jamieson, Understanding Vietnam *(Berkeley: University of California Press, 1993), 84.*

In his essays and lectures, Ninh argued that Vietnam needed "to build up the spiritual and intellectual talents of the people, in order to create a 'moral force' capable of leading the people to achieve their own salvation"; what was most needed was a "spiritual rebirth," "a revitalization of the national spirit." [17] For Ninh, retooling traditional culture, as Quynh advocated, was insufficient because traditional culture had serious problems. One was Confucianism, which, among other faults, he thought, suffocated Vietnamese creativity and thwarted the development of a natural and native Vietnamese culture. Vietnam needed such a culture on which to build a modern nation-state. For Ninh, borrowing from the West, as Vinh advocated, was necessary, but it could not be indiscriminate. Most important was to import Western science and democracy. As the 1920s wore on, Ninh became increasingly frustrated by the French failure to undertake reforms and increasingly bitter at the authorities. Here is a piece from *The Cracked Bell* in April 1925:

> *When a race is trapped to the point of having a choice only of death or slavery, to face death is the more courageous. . . .*
> *If the masses brave death rather than accept injustice and if the colonists do not want to renounce their policies of oppression and unscrupulous exploitation, it is the duty of the most courageous and devoted Annamites to dream of methods of struggle which correspond to present needs, and to organize a resistance which can combat oppression.[18]*

What is interesting about Quynh and Ninh is their evolving political and philosophical positions against the backdrop of specific experiences and episodes of French rule. Ninh was increasingly radicalized by several governors-general who began with reform agendas but who were ineffectual and whose tenures added up mostly to dashed hopes.

SCHOOLS AND EDUCATION

One of the chronic complaints of Vietnamese elites and nonelites alike was the French policies concerning schools and the few educational opportunities. This was particularly frustrating for the Vietnamese, who historically have been one of the world's most education-conscious cultures.

> *For more humble evidence of the fact that Vietnam is and always has been one of the most intensely literary civilizations on the face of the planet, Western visitors to Vietnam need only have glanced at the conical hats which peasants wear, or used to wear, in the Hue area in central Vietnam. These hats are called "poetry hats" in Vietnamese because they have poems inscribed inside their brims, and the poems can be read when the hats are held up to the sunlight.*[19]

In Annam and Tonkin, the traditional system of village Sino-Vietnamese schools existed into the 1920s, but by the late 1910s only three thousand villages out of twenty three thousand had their own school. Further, in 1919, the French began an eight-year program of closing down all village schools, and they had no plans to finance or even subsidize any alternative educational institutions. The facts are bleak. Between 1920 and 1938, only 10 percent of students who entered the first grade got beyond third grade. The literacy rate in the country was an estimated 5 percent. At the highest educational level, in Annam and Tonkin, the traditional civil service examination continued until 1918, lasting thirteen years longer than its model in China.

The French had begun to set up a public school system after their concern about the formation of the Free School of Hanoi in 1907. This Franco-Vietnamese system grew very slowly: by 1909, there were approximately 10,000 students; by 1913, about 40,000; by 1917, 75,000; and by 1921, 150,000. These figures are well below 0.5 percent of the population. Further, most of the schools were located in the large cities and provincial capitals—and most were in Cochinchina. These were primary schools (grades 4 to 6) that used *quoc ngu*. But a huge problem for those who wanted to continue their education beyond primary school was that only eleven cities and towns had upper primary schools (grades 7 to 10).[20] In 1923, in the country as a whole, there were only 83 Vietnamese students in public secondary schools (grades 11 to 13). Those Vietnamese who were able to go to France to study totaled 1,556 at nine locations throughout the country in 1930.

VIETNAMESE SOCIETY IN THE 1920s

During the years of World War I and in the 1920s, Vietnam's prosperity grew as the French established a modern economy based on the exports of rice, rubber, and mined products—lead, iron, and coal. Between 1918 and 1930 French investment shot up over 600 percent, with a tripling in the establishment of rubber plantations. The French exploited the natural resources and the people of Vietnam—for example, the workers on rubber plantations in the area north and northwest of Saigon. Rubber companies like Michelin hired recruiters to find workers in the northern part of the country, promising them the moon (rent-free houses, free schools and kindergartens) to lure them south.

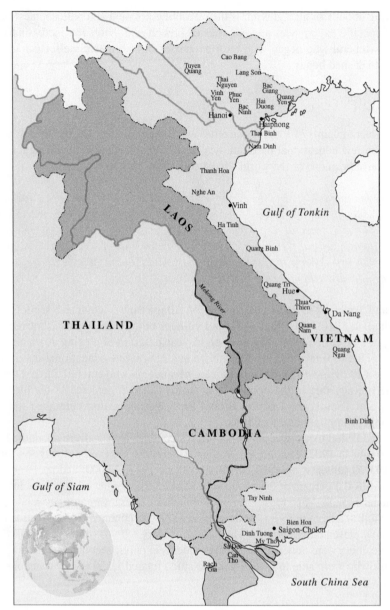

Map 4-1   French Indochina.

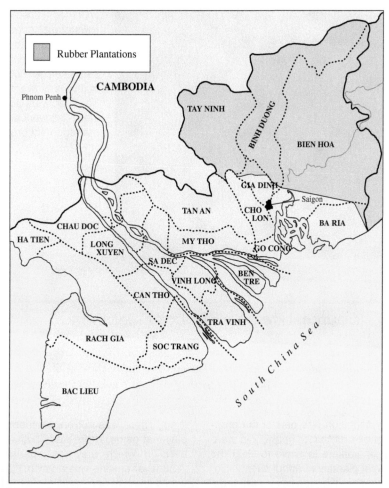

Map 4-2   Main Rubber-Producing Districts of South Vietnam, circa 1920.

But when peasants arrived at the southern plantations, they were given numbers to replace their lineage and personal names. . . . The numbers the plantations so abruptly assigned to the coolies followed a series of numbers that had begun from the day the plantation was first opened. The coolies themselves seem to have assimilated this drastic scheme completely. They even made their own informal modifications in it: they customarily abbreviated their own numbers, addressing each other by the last two numbers in each man's "number name". . . . Children who were born on the rubber plantations sometimes knew their parents only as numbers, and were not clearly acquainted with their lineage names.[21]

This practice of what might be called *cultural genocide* struck at the heart of Vietnamese culture, family identity—all to eliminate the French need to master Vietnamese names.

There were about thirty nine thousand Frenchmen in Vietnam between World Wars I and II, half of them women and children and a quarter of them soldiers and sailors. The rest, roughly ten thousand,

Rubber Plantation The neat rows of rubber trees rooted in green grass with oxen grazing in the background suggest bucolic serenity. The rubber plantations in the early twentieth century, however, were scenes of almost slave-like work and plantation management brutality.

Source: Life on a Rubber Plantation

In his memoir of a life on a rubber plantation, Tran Tu Binh underscored the brutality and almost total lack of humanity of various overseers and the manager of the plantation. A hao *is one tenth of a* dong. *Why did Vietnamese work voluntarily on the plantations?*

The Phu-rieng plantation was part of the property of the Michelin rubber company. We were the first group of workers to arrive to clear the land. It was a vast plantation, about twenty kilometers long and more than ten kilometers wide. They had set up a village about every kilometer. Since we were the first group of workers, we lived in village number one. . . .

One rainy days it flooded, and when the sun shone it was scorching. The climate in the region was oppressively hot and humid, but there were no windows in the barracks. And they had low steel roofs. We felt that we were living in ovens the whole year round. . . .

Every morning we had to get up at four o'clock to cook our food. At five-thirty we all had to form ranks in the village courtyard so the overseers could check the roll. As they did this, some of the overseers would use their batons, whacking the workers' heads as they counted them. There was not one of them who did not play that game. There was another game, however, in which they took particular delight. Whenever anyone was a few minutes late, they would fine him one *dong,* though our pay at the time was only four *hao* per workday.

After roll call, the overseers took us out to the work area from six in the morning until six in the evening. We had to toil steadily under the sun, hot as fire, except for fifteen minutes at noon to eat, drink, and relieve ourselves. . . .

The most common forms of punishment were to make the person drop his pants, then beat him on the buttocks, or beat his feet until the soles were in ribbons. After a beating, the worker would be locked up in a dark room, legs shackled, and left without food for two or three days. Some people were forgotten there until they died of thirst.

Source: Tran Tu Binh, The Red Earth *(Athens: Ohio University Center for International Studies, 1985), 23–25.*

worked in the government, the professions, and business and industry. Vietnamese living in the cities and the provincial capitals gained most from the French colonial economic surge; the upper class, made up of absentee landlords, businessmen, and officials (known as the *indigenous bourgeoisie*), totaled about 0.5 percent of the population. The petit bourgeoisie, or urban middle class, made up roughly 50 percent of the urban population; it included shopkeepers, artisans, clerks, schoolteachers, journalists, managers, and interpreters. The other emerging class was the working class; estimates suggest that in the 1920s it made up about 2 percent of the total population.

Between 93 and 95 percent of the Vietnamese lived in the countryside, where poverty was widespread. Changes in the countryside—including increasingly concentrated landlord power, more and more absentee landlords (by the 1920s, an estimated seven thousand), disappearance of communal land, and a burgeoning number of tenants and hired hands—were generally negative. About 30 percent of the rural population (seven hundred fifty thousand families) consisted of middle-level or subsistence farmers; as many as 70 percent were poor peasants, tenants, and hired hands. Both subsistence farmers and poor peasants lived precarious lives subject to extremes of weather, moneylenders whose usurious rates of interests on necessary loans could ruin a farmer and his family almost overnight, and the outrageous rates and range of taxes imposed by French authorities. Social unrest seemed to be bubbling just beneath the surface of Vietnamese society.

THE TRIAL OF PHAN BOI CHAU, 1925

In the late fall of 1925, in what in most countries might be called "the trial of the century," scholar-patriot Phan Boi Chau was put on trial for his life. We last left him in exile in China from 1917 to 1925. His jailing there from 1913 to 1917 had for all practical purposes destroyed his Restoration Society. During his exile, he played a passive role in Vietnamese developments. In June 1925, leaving Hangzhou to go to Guangzhou via Shanghai, he was arrested by French authorities in Shanghai and taken to Hanoi to stand trial for treason before the French High Criminal Commission. Originally the charges focused on the assassinations and plots of 1913. But when Chau categorically denied any involvement in these affairs, the court decided to indict his whole life, starting with his support of the loyalty to the king movement and stretching to his founding of the Restoration Society in 1912. The November 23 trial lasted from 8:25 a.m. until 8:00 p.m.

The court invited Phan Boi Chau to make a final statement. He said:

> *If the French government employs aircraft, cruisers, submarines, artillery, in short, brute force, to rule this country, according to the principle of the "big fish" swallowing the "small fish," then I am ready to die without a further word. On the other hand, if France brings civilization, justice, and law to develop better conditions for the peoples of Indochina, then truly I am innocent and should be released.*[22]

The court found him guilty on almost every count; the sentence: life imprisonment at hard labor.

The reaction of Vietnamese to Chau's seizure, trial, and sentence was outrage. Newspapers were in the forefront of popular attempts to get him released. The conservative journalist Pham Quynh reported that the political and social storm over these events reached the lower levels of Vietnamese society; he had heard a rickshaw puller say, "The French have condemned Phan because he is too patriotic."[23] Citizens sent telegrams to the new governor-general, Alexandre Varenne, pleading for a pardon. Though Varenne responded with a conditional parole, it was clear that this meant, in effect, house arrest, with no permission to engage in political activity. The widespread political reaction of the Vietnamese people is notable. As one member of the Saigon intelligentsia noted, "Vietnamese had finally joined together to protect one of their own. No longer would they be content to leave each ensnared individual to fend desperately for himself."[24]

The phase of the scholar-patriots was ending. A new generation of nationalist leaders was already on stage, beginning to stress not single episodes of protest and rebellion but organization and long-term political struggle.

CHRONOLOGY

17th century	Jesuit missionaries develop *quoc ngu*
1770s–1790s	Tay Son Rebellion
1802–1945	Nguyen dynasty
1848–1860	Christian persecutions following the 1825 outlawing of Christianity
1867	France occupies Cochinchina
1883–1885	Sino-French War leaves Vietnam in French hands
1885–1896	Anti-French loyalty to the king movement
1890	Birth of Ho Chi Minh
1890s–1920s	Reform efforts of Phan Boi Chau and Phan Chu Trinh
1904	Establishment of the anti-French Modernization Society
1907	Opening of the Free School of Hanoi
1908–1917	Series of short-lived anti-French rebellions
1919	France begins to close all village schools
1925	Trial of Phan Boi Chau

SUGGESTED READINGS

Buttinger, Joseph. *Vietnam: A Dragon Embattled, Vol. 1: From Colonialism to the Vietminh.* New York: Frederick A. Praeger, 1967. A detailed analysis of French colonialism and Vietnamese resistance.

Marr, David G. *Vietnamese Tradition on Trial, 1920–1945.* Berkeley: University of California Press, 1981. This well-written analysis tracing the rise of Vietnamese revolutionary action is organized around intellectual topics (such as "The Question of Women" and "Perceptions of the Past").

McLeod, Mark W., and Nguyen Thi Dieu. *Culture and Customs of Vietnam.* Westport, CT: Greenwood Press, 2001. An engaging overview of aspects of Vietnamese culture.

Nguyen Du. *The Tale of Kieu.* Translated by Bu Huynh Sanh Thong. New York: Random House, 1973. This is the classic Vietnamese literary work: "more than just a glorious heirloom, . . . [i]t has become a kind of continuing emotional laboratory in which all the great and timeless issues of personal morality and political obligation are tested and resolved."

Nguyen Van Huy and Laurel Kendall, eds. *Vietnam: Journeys of Body, Mind, and Spirit.* Berkeley: University of California Press, 2003. This stunning work opens the worlds of Vietnamese culture and religion with beautiful photographs and enlightening analysis by Western and Vietnamese authors.

CHAPTER FIVE

The Tokugawa Regime (1603–1830):
Early Modern Japan

The four main islands of Japan lie off continental Asia about 120 miles from the southeast coast of the Korean peninsula across the Tsushima and Korea straits and along the eastern coast of Korea up to 550 miles across the Sea of Japan. Japan's coastline is about 17,000 miles, with frequent indentations forming many natural harbors; no site in the country is more than 80 miles from the sea. The islands, moving from north to south, are Hokkaido, Honshu, Shikoku, and Kyushu; they stretch about 1,200 miles from northeast to southwest. Their land area is roughly equal to that of the state of Montana. Hokkaido, the second largest island, has 30,000 square miles; Honshu, on which Tokyo lies, has 89,000; Kyushu, the southernmost, has 16,000; and Shikoku, separated from Honshu by the Inland Sea, has 7,200. Mountains take up 70 to 75 percent of the land surface; indeed, only 25 percent of Japan's land area has slopes less than fifteen degrees. The total area of plains and basins is only about 15 percent. Arable land, then, is at a premium and every possible inch is utilized. The largest plain, the Kantō plain, totaling about 12,500 square miles, is located at the head of Tokyo Bay.

Japan's climate has been compared to that of the East Coast of the United States. The range of temperature contrasts between northern and southern sites can be clarified by comparing the growing seasons on the islands. In Hokkaido, frigid in winter and temperate in summer, the season ranges from 120 to 140 days. In Honshu's Kantō plain, it is about 215 days; and in southern Shikoku and Kyushu, it is about 260 days. Japan has over two hundred volcanoes, 10 percent of the world's total, and earthquakes are a continual danger.

ISSUES OF IDENTITY

Throughout history Japan has been almost continually aware of the issue of its identity. In part this was due to the reality of Japan's being an island nation, separated and isolated from the mainland. The identity issue also comes from the unclear origins of the Japanese people: their language, from the Altaic language family, is similar to the mainland Northeast Asian languages, Korean and Siberian; its wet method of rice culture is that of southern China and Southeast Asia; its housing structures in one Neolithic period and its creation myths seem similar to those in Southeast Asia or the South Pacific islands. The presence of the ethnic Ainu, now found on Hokkaido and considered by some to be proto-Caucasian, makes the origins of the Japanese even more mysterious.

What has become a Japanese historical pattern also raises concern among Japanese with their identity. That pattern is one of borrowing heavily from other cultures and then assimilating and/or adapting what has been borrowed. This occurred when the Japanese borrowed from cultures that Japanese considered more modern, powerful, or cultured than Japan was at the time. In the period roughly from 600 to 830 CE, China was at the height of its Tang dynasty cosmopolitanism; Japan sent mission after mission to China in these years, borrowing almost everything—from government structure to Chinese characters to political and social philosophy to the physical layout of the capital city. The prefix *kara*, meaning "Chinese," "in front of any object was invariably a mark of elegance and value, like the word 'imported' in the more expensive shops of London and New York."[1] Some of these borrowings (like the Chinese language, for example) did not fit Japanese realities at all. But the Japanese pattern was to decide which borrowed elements to retain or perhaps to adapt and transform into something Japanese. Such manic borrowing sprees (there was another in the late nineteenth century) have led some Japanese to question their identity: "Who really are we?"

Two of Japan's major historical experience patterns have also given rise to the question of identity. In the Heian period, roughly from the eighth to the eleventh centuries, the critical Japanese historical experience was the collapse of the world Japan had tried to build with its Chinese borrowings. Chinese political structures and practices did not fit Japanese realities. As that world fell apart, Japanese elites retained the culture of beauty and sophistication, of literature and ceremonies that they had borrowed even as they

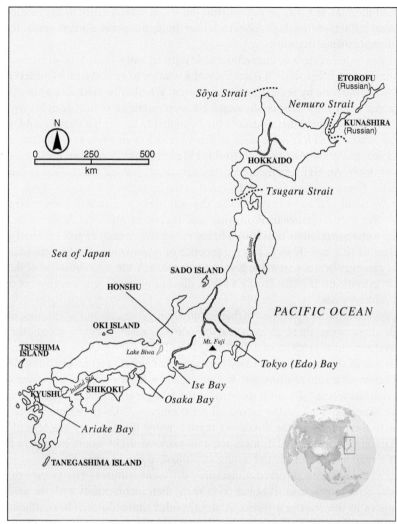

Map 5-1   Japan: Principal Features.

added distinctly Japanese elements of color and aesthetics. Japan's most famous classical novel, *The Tale of Genji*, was written by Lady Murasaki in 1000 CE. It reflected the culture of elegance and beauty that helped to shape the Japanese aesthetic and approach to life, giving rise to such activities in the warrior period as ikebana (flower arranging) and garden making.

When the Heian world slowly collapsed, it was swallowed up by a very different culture, that of the samurai, or warrior. Great lords arose as families pushed north on the Japanese frontier; as they seized extensive estates, they needed to protect them in that lawless, violent world—hence the rise of militias and then small armies. Over time a system of subinfeudation developed whereby military leaders became vassals to the great lord and those vassals had subvassals. This system centered on land given by lord to vassal; their relationship was the crucial bond. The values that gave the military ethos a higher moral meaning came to be set forth in *bushidō,* the way of the warrior—in some ways similar to the medieval Western code of chivalry. Though the word *bushidō* dates to a later time, the general ideas began to take shape when the period of the shogunates began.

At the center of this moral code was unconditional loyalty to one's lord. A twelfth-century samurai put it this way in an injunction to his son: "It is the duty of a warrior to be like a monk observing a rule. It is his business to preserve the state by protecting the sovereign. Whether he holds but a pin's point of land or rules a thousand acres, his loyalty must be the same. He must not think of his life as his own, but as offered by him to his lord."[2] It followed that a vassal's life belonged to his lord; a vassal could not decide to end his life of his own accord. Death is not a value in this system, but all roads seem to lead in that direction. It redounds to a samurai's honor to die if his lord is killed in battle. A samurai must show the utmost courage in the face of death. An eighteenth-century description of *bushidō* states: "Every morning make up thy mind how to die. Every evening freshen thy mind in the thought of death. . . . Thus will thy mind be prepared. When thy mind is always set on death, thy way through life will always be straight and simple."[3] Death was also seen as better than disgrace and shame. In medieval Japanese warfare, when prisoners of war were tortured and mutilated before being killed, the custom of self-inflicted death before capture seemed preferable to some. Thus began the practice of *seppuku* or self-disembowelment, which required the greatest courage. Besides supreme loyalty, courage, and the omnipresence of death, another aspect of *bushidō* was extreme pride in the family's name, illustrating the Confucian element of filial piety that was part of this military code.

The military system had at its apex the "barbarian-quelling generalissimo"—the shogun. From the 1180s to the 1860s there were three shogunates, or periods when shoguns ruled: the Kamakura (1185–1333), the Ashikaga (1336–1550s), and the Tokugawa (1603–1868). Other samurai values that became important elements in this historical military heritage are a simple and ascetic lifestyle, self-discipline, and scholarly habits. The values inherent in the way of the warrior often became basic values of the Japanese. One historian has noted, "To call it the Way of the Warrior is to give a wrong impression of its scope. It was a code which set high ideals before all good citizens."[4] Of the samurai code, Tokugawa Mitsukuni, grandson of the founder of the Tokugawa regime, noted that the only business of the samurai class was "to maintain *giri* (right). . . . [I]f there were no samurai, right would disappear from human society, the sense of shame would be lost, and wrong and injustice would prevail."[5]

The two historical experiences involved remarkably different cultures. The culture of beauty and elegance, of form and ceremony seems, if not at odds with, then incongruous with the austerity, hardness, and brutal choices in the warrior's world. And yet both channels—the chrysanthemum and the sword, to use a title from a World War II–era book—flowed into the river that became Japanese culture. Their presence in the Japanese character produced what might be seen as something of a bifurcated identity.

THE TOKUGAWA SYSTEM

The fifteenth and sixteenth centuries in Japan were a time of bloody civil wars. The politically weak Ashikaga shogunate (*bakufu*) had for all practical purposes collapsed by the mid-fifteenth century, and Japanese were at the mercy of great lords (*daimyō,* literally "great names") who battled each other for control all over the country. In the sixteenth century three extraordinary men—Oda Nobunaga (1534–1582), Toyotomi Hideyoshi (1536–1598), and Tokugawa Ieyasu (1542–1616)—were not only militarily victorious but also politically astute enough to lay the groundwork for another shogunate. The battle that essentially led to the establishment of the new regime came in October 1600 at Sekigahara. There Tokugawa and his allies (known as *fudai* [hereditary vassals] daimyō) faced off against powerful enemies (known as *tozama* [outside lords] daimyō). Ieyasu was formally appointed shogun in 1603.

Controlling the Daimyō

Having come to power after a century and a half of civil strife and aware of the fact that defeated daimyō were not cheerful supporters, Ieyasu set out to structure a regime in which no daimyō would remain rich enough or strong enough to be a threat. He also wanted to protect his regime from alliances of disaffected daimyō. During the Tokugawa the numbers of daimyō ranged from 240 to 295—the official definition of a daimyō being a lord whose domain's assessed production of rice was at least ten thousands koku of rice (a koku is about five bushels).

Ieyasu set down initial policies to form a *bakuhan* system that evolved over several generations (*bakuhan* from *bakufu* [the shogun's government] and *han* [domain]). Since the tozama daimyō, enemies at Sekigahara, were individually extremely wealthy and some of the most powerful vassals, he worked hard to restrict their powers. For example, only fudai daimyō could serve in the shogunate; tozama daimyō were barred. Ieyasu instituted a policy, to the extent possible, of geographical separation, creating a buffer zone of fudai daimyō domains around his capital of Edo and transferring tozama daimyō beyond it. This meant not only that mean that the tozama daimyō were physically removed from administrative or economic power, but also that if any outside lords tried something untoward, the shogun had time to prepare a defense. The shogun also gave fudai daimyō land at points of strategic importance, such as along the principal roads or at main towns. Hoping to remove surplus funds that a daimyō might use to make trouble, he required tozama daimyō to contribute great sums to public undertakings, including the construction and repair of castles and the construction of roads and harbors.

Tokugawa Ieyasu's Treasure Tower   This treasure tower is a mausoleum holding the ashes of the founder of the Tokugawa shogunate. It is located in Nikkō , about 135 kilometers from Tokyo.

Ieyasu also used some measures that applied to all daimyō, fudai included. In making certain types of decisions, daimyō were restricted. If they wanted to do the following, they needed the shogun's permission: leave their domain, repair old castles, and marry. Some things were forbidden: building new castles, constructing warships, and coining money. The shogun had detailed, accurate maps of all the castles throughout the country; he expressly forbade making any maps of the Edo castle. On major roads he set up checkpoint barriers to monitor travelers. Everyone had to carry a passport, which was examined at checkpoints. At times the regime did not build bridges in order to impede travel on the main routes to Edo.

The most famous shogunal method for keeping daimyō in check was the system of alternate attendance (*sankin kōtai*). At first applied to tozama daimyō, beginning in 1642 it applied to fudai as well. In this system the daimyō had to spend alternate years (sometimes alternate half-years) in Edo away from his own domain, but when he returned to his domain, he had to leave his wife and family in Edo as hostages. He would, in short, have to think twice about causing any trouble for the shogun. The men who manned the road checkpoints were warned to watch for "outward women and inward guns" as a sign that some daimyō might be trying to get his hostages out and weapons into Edo. In addition, the alternate attendance system was designed to weaken the daimyō financially. As befitting a great lord, the daimyō had to travel with a large retinue in great splendor on his way to Edo and back. For a daimyō from a distant domain like Karatsu in northern Kyushu, it took over thirty overnight stops to reach Edo. The outlay for shelter and food was immense. Then when he reached Edo, it was customary to have more than one mansion, perhaps up to three, which he had to maintain in a style befitting his status while continuing to maintain in fine condition the castle in his domain. Further, the cost of living was higher in Edo than at home. Senior vassals of the daimyō of Karatsu in 1782 warned, "Above all, we must economize when we are in Edo."[6] Early in the regime, it is estimated that the alternate attendance

A Traditional Marriage   The bride wore an outer silk and silk brocade kimono, usually red, decorated with scenes of flowers, cranes (a symbol of honor and loyalty), and pines or other nature motifs; her hair was adorned with golden combs. The groom wore a combination of kimono and a short *haori* overcoat over pleated *hakama* (skirt-like) pants; usually his wedding attire was black with white crests.

Source: Sumptuary Laws

The Tokugawa shogunate was careful to regulate the spending and showy tendencies of daimyō and samurai in general. In the name of encouraging frugality and preventing their vassals from falling into debt, various sumptuary regulations were issued from 1640 on. The following orders were issued in 1724. Does it seem surprising that a seventeenth-century state would insinuate itself so deeply in personal lives and choices? How does this square with other Tokugawa measures of control?

—It has been repeatedly ordered by the Shōgun that economy must be observed in all such matters as the exchange of gifts and expensive entertainments to celebrate weddings. Henceforward these rules are to be obeyed as follows:

—Women's dress has of recent years become more and more showy. Hereafter even the wives of daimyōs shall not use more than a small amount of gold-thread embroidery in their garments and shall not wear dresses made of costly fabrics. Female servants are to wear simple clothing appropriate to their position, and in every town the fixed price of these articles must be publicly announced.

—Expensive lacquer ware is not to be bought, even by daimyōs. The chairs, chests and workboxes of their wives are to be of plain black lacquer, with no more than a crest as ornament.

—Nightdresses, coverlets, mattresses, and so forth are not to be of fine embroidered fabrics.

—The number of palanquins at a wedding procession shall not exceed ten.

Source: George Sansom, A History of Japan, *Vol. III (Stanford, CA: Stanford University Press, 1958), 160–161.*

system took between 20 and 30 percent of the income of some daimyō; by the late Tokugawa period, estimates for some daimyō were about 80 percent.

Finally, the shogun limited the number of soldiers that each daimyō could have in his army and increased the number in his own. The Tokugawa maintained great wealth, controlling 25 percent of all Japanese territory and 33.3 percent of its population. No domain could equal the bakufu in this regard. The shogun established a system of inspectors (*metsuke*) in each domain who served as intelligence officers, reporting to the shogun anything that might subvert his control.

Other Measures of Control

From at least the fourth century CE, Japan had an emperor who was believed to be a direct descendant of the Sun Goddess, Amaterasu. Emperors, men and women (there were some of the latter very early on), were thus divine. Largely because of this status, Japanese emperors were kept above the political fray; while the emperor "reigned," performing essential rituals and linking Japan itself to the gods, men around him "ruled." The positions these men held varied across time. From the ninth century to the nineteenth, the seat of imperial life was Kyoto.

During the long period of shogunates, the actual Japanese ruler was the shogun, who made and executed governmental decisions. The shogun was appointed by the emperor. Relations between shogun and emperor were thus tricky. During the almost seven hundred years when shoguns ruled, the imperial court was weak and impoverished: the shogun kept the emperor in his proper place. For the truth was that an emperor, linked to the divine, could theoretically revoke the shogun's mandate to rule at any time.

It was clear that the Tokugawa shogun controlled the emperor. The shogunate kept the emperors poor: the wealth of the court was equal to that of second-class fudai daimyō (who were considerably weaker than tozama daimyō). No daimyō could directly contact the emperor or his court without approval by the Tokugawa regime. The emperor was forbidden to have any administrative function at all. No questions regarding foreign affairs could be directed to the court. The emperors, furthermore, were only allowed to marry Tokugawa family members, making the emperors Tokugawa relatives.

The Tokugawa strictly controlled the Buddhist priesthood. Since early in Japanese history, the Buddhist establishment had been not only a religious institution but also an important political and economic player on the Japanese stage. For this reason, the bakufu controlled all secular matters of the church. They attempted to weaken potential political threats, for example splitting a large Buddhist sect into two branches to diminish possible challenges in the future. The Tokugawa acted aggressively when Buddhists threatened social unrest or did not show sufficient respect. In one episode involving a theological debate, an abbot of the Nichiren sect was to have participated but could not because some Amidist sect adherents had injured him in a quarrel. He was declared the loser by default. In an emotional outburst, he said that the shogun was the greatest robber in Japan, an ignoramus who did not understand the most basic principles of governance. Ieyasu ordered the abbot's nose and ears cut off; he could not tolerate such an attack on himself and the government.

In their last dramatic effort to preserve control over the country, the Tokugawa established a national policy of excluding foreigners who might act to destabilize Tokugawa control. Having done everything to keep the lid on domestically, the Tokugawa found foreigners too unpredictable and potentially dangerous for the status quo. The first people to feel the policy's effects were Christians. Jesuit missionaries had arrived in Japan in the mid-sixteenth century and had been quite successful in converting Japanese. But Hideyoshi and Ieyasu feared what Christian missionaries and converts might do politically. They knew the pattern from the record of the Philippines: missionaries followed by merchants and then the military; Christians were, from their point of view, subversive, a potential fifth column. The basic rationale for persecuting them was set down in regulations in 1614:

> Christians seek to make Japan into "their own possession." Their religion teaches
> them to "contravene governmental regulations, traduce Shinto, calumniate the True
> Law, destroy righteousness, corrupt goodness"—in short, to subvert the native Japanese,
> the Buddhist, and the Confucian foundations of the social order. What else was this if
> not . . . the ultimate "pernicious doctrine."[7]

Christians were bloodily persecuted by methods that rivaled the horrors of the Spanish Inquisition. When, in 1637–1638, Christians openly rebelled, the shogunate repressed them brutally, killing up to thirty-seven thousand people. All foreigners were expelled except for a handful of Dutch traders who resided on a tiny island in Nagasaki harbor.

Tokugawa foreign policy on the whole, however, was not one of total isolation or seclusion. A trickle of trade continued with the Dutch. The Japanese also maintained trade relations with China, the Ryūkyū islands, and Korea, as well as diplomatic relations with the Ryūkyūs and Korea.

Tokugawa Society: The Samurai

The goal of Tokugawa political and social restrictions was essentially to freeze society, to prevent change that might endanger the regime. Society's elites were the samurai, about thirty million strong (5 or 6 percent of the population). Their right to carry a sword in public was a tangible sign of their substantial status in society.

But they were not a unified group: the samurai class was highly stratified, from wealthy daimyō at the top to impoverished warrior below. The famous late-nineteenth-century modernizer Fukuzawa Yukichi

Sacred Image   In the persecution of Christians during the early Tokugawa shogunate, one test of whether a person was a believer was to order him to walk on an image like this, which included a crucifix or the Virgin Mary. Refusal to do so would almost automatically result in the person's execution.

came from a lower-level samurai family and continually bemoaned the impenetrable barrier between upper- and lower-level samurai, which prevented social mobility. This freeze was noteworthy even in living patterns. Upper-level samurai lived close to their daimyōs' castles; lower-level ones lived farthest away. The annual rice stipend of upper-level samurai was between 100 and 250 koku; for Fukuzawa's father in the lower level, the stipend was only 14 koku. This pittance meant that the wives and children of lower-level samurai had to take on side jobs so that the family could survive. Fukuzawa noted that despite the two basic strata of samurai, "in all there were as many as a hundred minute distinctions between their social positions and official duties."[8] At a domain school for samurai in one locale, for example, boys from the highest-ranked families could go to school each day with four servants; one would watch his sandals during the day and another would hold his umbrella in the rain. The next-ranked boy could bring three servants; the next, two; and the lowest, none. Because the Japanese practiced primogeniture (in contrast to the Chinese partible inheritance), the samurai stipend went in its entirety to the eldest son. Since Fukuzawa was not the eldest, he would never receive anything.

All of this concern with hierarchy came in the name of order and stability. The irony is that the Tokugawa built its political and social structures on an elite military class during a long period of peace when the military had little reason for being: there were no long-term military problems to deal with. Over time, that reality helped to undermine the whole system. The crux of the problem was castle towns (*jōkamachi*), which literally sprang up around the daimyō's castle. They were a new urban phenomenon in Tokugawa's daimyō-based military regime (and are today the capitals in thirty-four of the forty-six prefectures). Most were built on new sites, not where established cities had been; Edo, for example, which the Tokugawa made their capital, was only a small fishing village in 1600. Castle towns were the military and administrative centers for the daimyō. It was natural for the daimyō to want to have his vassals nearby, both for service and for regular contact. As many as 50 percent of all samurai lived in the castle towns, and sometimes more: in

Source: The Model Samurai

Kumazawa Banzan (1619–1691) was a famous political philosopher. In this passage from his memoirs, he described how he disciplined himself to remain in a constant state of readiness for action. Which of his actions to attain his ends seem most drastic? What can you conclude about samurai from his description of his inkstand, paper, and books?

When I was about sixteen I had a tendency toward corpulence. I had noticed a lack of agility in other fleshy persons and thought a heavy man would not make a first class samurai. So I tried every means to keep myself agile and lean. I slept with my girdle drawn tight and stopped eating rice. I took no wine and abstained from sexual intercourse for the next ten years. While on duty at Edo, there were no hills or fields at hand where I could hunt and climb, so I exercised with spear and sword. When I was on the night watch at my master's residence in Edo, I kept a wooden sword and a pair of straw sandals in my bamboo hamper, and with these I used to put myself through military drill in the darkened court after everyone was asleep. I also practiced running about over the roofs of the out-buildings far removed from the sleeping rooms. This I did so as to be able to handle myself nimbly if a fire should break out. There were a few who noticed me at these exercises and they were reported to have said that I was probably possessed by a hobgoblin. This was before I was twenty years old. After that I hardened myself by going into the fields on hot summer days and shooting skylarks with a gun, since I did not own a falcon for hawking. In the winter months I often spent several days in the mountains taking no night clothes or bed quilt with me, and wearing only a lined jacket of cotton over a thin cotton shirt. My little hamper was almost filled by my inkstand, paper, and books, and two wadded silk kimonos. I stayed overnight in any house I came across in my rambles. In such a way I disciplined myself until I was thirty-seven or -eight years old and avoided becoming fleshy. I was fully aware of my want of talent and believed I could never hope to be of any great service to my country, so I was all the more resolved to do my best as a common samurai.

Source: Ryusaku Tsunoda, William Theodore De Bary, and Donald Keene, comps., Sources of Japanese Tradition, Vol. 1 *(New York: Columbia University Press, 1967), 378–79.*

Sendai in northern Honshu 70 percent, and in Kagoshima on the southern tip of Kyushu 80 percent. In those towns, samurai with no military duties took desk jobs as bureaucrats in the daimyō's administration.

As towns were established, merchants and artisans moved in to provide commodities and services; slowly, castle towns also became centers of economic concentration. The Japanese had borrowed the Confucian social classification: from top to bottom, samurai (in China this elite position went to the scholar-gentry), farmer, artisan, and merchant. The merchant was the lowest legitimate class, but this group became central in the development of these towns. As years of peace continued, many samurai got used to the good life in the flourishing towns, buying luxuries and enjoying various entertainments—theaters, teahouses, brothels, public baths. Over time, merchants became increasingly wealthy. More and more samurai, on the other hand, began to get into increasingly hot water financially. They lived on fixed land income at a time when prices in castle towns were rising steeply, and they lived high on the hog. Short on money and desiring to maintain their lifestyle, they borrowed money from the merchants, who owned pawnshops or were moneylenders. Merchants became creditors and samurai debtors, a relationship that placed the lowest class over the highest. The two classes began to merge. Merchants went to indebted

A Samurai   A samurai dressed in a typical kimono carries both his sword and a dagger. He stands on the traditional tatami mat floor.

samurai, promising forgiveness of their debts if the samurai married their daughters; samurai, deep in debt, sought to marry daughters of wealthy merchants to improve their own financial status. The ordered society began to be turned on its head, as these changes "had the net effect of driving the [samurai] towards a more commercialized existence and of undermining the traditional way of life of the feudal aristocracy."[9] The best-laid plans of the Tokugawa founders went shockingly awry.

THE FLOATING WORLD

The culture of the flourishing towns was often called the *floating world* (*ukiyo*: originally the word referred to the Buddhist world of change and decay, but in the late seventeenth century it meant a world of pleasure based on love and money). The quintessential period of the burgeoning urban culture was the Genroku from 1688 to 1703; but it represents a period approximately from 1675 to 1725 that also experienced a mix of glamour, indulgence, sordidness, irresponsibility, and dissolution.

> *This is the world of fugitive pleasures, of theatres and restaurants, wrestling-booths, and houses of assignation, with their permanent population of actors, dancers, singers, story-tellers, jesters, courtesans, bath-girls, and itinerant purveyors, among them mingled the profligate sons of rich merchants, dissolute samurai and naughty apprentices. It is chiefly the life of these gay quarters and their denizens that is depicted in popular novels and paintings of the day....*[10]

We can easily imagine how this world would have impacted the samurai, who were trained and inculcated with ideals of duty, frugality, diligence, and self-control.

Source: Economic Conditions, 1798

Here Honda Toshiaki (1744–1821) describes the declining economic conditions near the turn of the nineteenth century. In the measurements listed here, one hundred ryo of gold equaled three thousand koku of rice and a koku equaled about five bushels. What does Honda see as the main problems facing Japanese society at this time?

However, nowadays, it is common to see a debt incurred by a *daimyō* increasing instead of decreasing even when he continuously reduces the stipends due his retainers to pay for his debt to the merchants. There was an example of a *daimyō* with a stipend of 60,000 *koku* whose debts multiplied and finally reached an aggregate of 1,180,000 *ryō* in gold. When he was not able to repay, a public suit ensued. In this case, if the *daimyō* assigned all of his income from the 60,000 *koku* for the repayment of his debts, it would still take fifty to sixty years to complete the full payment. I doubt if all the *daimyō* are in this kind of financial difficulty. However, there is not a single *daimyō* who is not in debt with one or more merchants. How pitiful this is. In the eyes of the merchants, the *daimyō* must look like birds or fish caught by a net cast by a hunter or a fisherman. All the *daimyō* select officials who impose extra burdens on farmers in an attempt to repay their debts, but these debts do not decrease, and instead they increase year after year. Many officials are replaced for incompetence. Under their successors, farmers are again placed under enormous exactions, but the debts continue to grow. This being the case, even those of stout heart give up their positions and money to retire. Some of them feign illness and refuse to leave home, others lose their rational minds and die early. No matter how much thought they put into the matter to alleviate the difficulties, neither the *daimyō* nor their officials can find any alternatives. As the popular saying goes, when one sinks to the depth of the abyss of debts, even children and grandchildren cannot have a chance to surface. Some of them may allow the merchants to take free rein, give up their domains, place them under the merchants' control, and receive the latter's remittance to meet their official and private expenses. They can no longer give thought to keeping the functions ordained by heaven (*tenshoku*) under the grace of the deities and Buddha, and to protecting and nurturing the farmers.

Source: David J. Lu, Sources of Japanese History, Vol. 2 *(New York: McGraw-Hill, 1978), 5–6.*

Some of Japan's greatest writers and artists came from the culture of the floating world. Because sensuality was central, many works focused on the erotic. The focus of the greatest novelist of seventeenth-century Japan, Saikaku Ihara (1662–1693), is obvious in the titles of his novels: *The Man Who Spent His Life in Love, An Amorous Woman, Five Amorous Women.* He coined the term *kōshoku* ("to love life"), which "commonly meant to enjoy sex. The books were full of comedy and sex (including homosexuality)."[11] Japan's most famous playwright, Chikamatsu Monzaemon (1653–1724), wrote his plays for puppet theater (*bunraku*) so that he would not have to put up with ad-libbing actors. His plays, many of which have "Love Suicides" in their title, are tragedies in which a natural emotion or relationship, say, love or friendship collides with the claims of broader society. The poet of the most famous Japanese form of poetry, *haiku*, was Bashō Matsuo (1644–1694). Under this master, this very short poem often packed a wallop. According to Bashō, the first line of each haiku should describe a permanent element; the second, the momentary action; and the third, their intersection. Here are two gems:

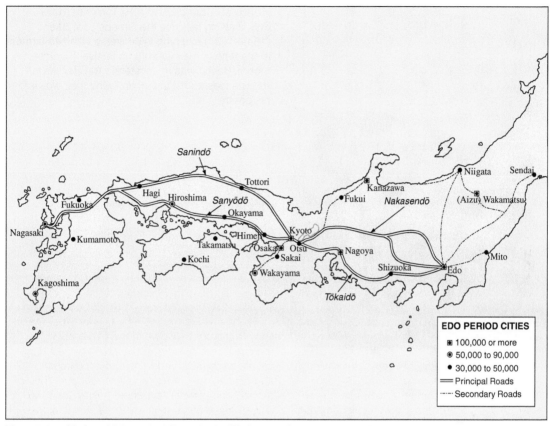

Map 5-2   Major Cities and Roads in Eighteenth-Century Japan.

Such stillness—
The cries of the cicadas
Sink into the rocks.

The sea darkens,
The cries of the seagulls
Are faintly white.

During the late seventeenth and early eighteenth centuries, one Japanese drama form, *kabuki*, was changed from what had begun as open-air dances to advertise the wares of prostitutes. As kabuki evolved, female roles began to be played by male actors, many of whom were homosexual prostitutes. Kabuki, unlike the earlier-developed *noh* drama, which is sedate and slow-moving, is filled with noise and movement, violence and posturing. The government stepped in several times to regulate kabuki's subject matter, actors, and methods of performance. Kabuki appealed especially to the samurai, perhaps giving them a vicarious experience of action, mired as they were in their desk-job doldrums; the young homosexual actor-prostitutes were also an enticement for the samurai.

Haiku Master Bashō and Two Farmers
This drawing features the famous poet Bashō (1644–1694) stopping to converse with two farmers at the time of the mid-autumn festival (harvest moon). Bashō was an inveterate traveler whose experiences and sights often found their way into his poetry.

The Japanese accepted homosexuality during this period as legitimate sexual activity. Buddhist priests had sex with other priests or young acolytes. Homosexuality among the samurai was so prevalent that it was the norm. In most inns, male prostitutes were available. "Among the samurai class, 'it was frequently proclaimed that love for a woman was an effeminate failing. In both cloister and barracks, the love of man for man was more than mere sexual gratification. Ideally, at least, it was based on a lasting relationship of loyalty and devotion.'"[12]

TOKUGAWA SOCIETY: PEASANTS

In the Confucian class categories, peasants were second only to the samurai, who, like good Confucians, admitted that agriculture was the foundation of the state. There were adages about the importance of peasants: "A farmer is worth two samurai. . . ." But the reality was very different. Tokugawa documents dealing with agriculture often began with phrases like "Since peasants are stupid people" or "Since peasants are people without sense. . . ." No less a leader than Tokugawa Ieyasu allegedly argued that "the proper way to govern was to see that farmers 'had just enough to keep alive on and no more.'"[13] Farmers were taxed heavily (in kind and in cash) and had to provide other services without pay: corvee duty (various laboring jobs) and supplying horses. Sometimes the corvee duty lasted indefinitely so that farm work could not be done. In many cases, extended corvee duty resulted in the farmer's impoverishment and loss of land.

Despite their brutalized lives, Japanese peasants never mounted a large, widespread rebellion. The Tokugawa landscape was dotted with peasant disturbances, but they tended to be local and sporadic and were not driven by more ambitious political aims. Part of the reason is that the peasants as a whole were not

A Kabuki Dancer   The colorful costume of a kabuki dancer clearly indicated the type of character he was portraying—hero or villain. Clues to the character's moral nature also came from face makeup and hairpieces (here, seemingly, insect-like). All characters were played by men.

a united social class, but instead formed a hierarchy of wealth, power, and legal rights. The peasantry was divided into those who owned land and those who did not. Landholders had public rights and duties: only their names were on village registers; only they could remit village-owed taxes and hold village offices. Landholders were also part of a hierarchical system based on how much land they owned—from the equivalent of small garden plots to large estates. Very wealthy farmers often enhanced their wealth by setting up cottage industries, like silk weaving, soy sauce production, sake brewing, and rapeseed oil manufacture.

Tenants, as in most traditional cultures, always got the short end of the stick. The percentage of tenants varied, but some estimates put it as high as 50 percent. The tenants had no public rights or duties other than the general obligation to live a law-abiding life. They were, in most cases, totally dependent on the landlord for their land, house, and work tools.

> *The personal relations of the tenant and landlord reflected the generally accepted criteria of the time for dealings between unequal parties. All relations of this kind in Tokugawa society between employer and employee, teacher and pupil, lord and vassal tended to approximate the Confucian ideal of family relationships. All had their peculiar features, but all had in common distinctions of worth between the two parties and reciprocal but different sets of obligations—obedience and loyalty on the one side and benevolence and protection on the other—that ideally obtained between father and son. To the tenant, the landlord was oyakata or "parent"; to the landlord the tenant was kokata or "child."[14]*

Source: Injunctions to Peasants

Because almost 80 percent of the Japanese population were peasants and performed a critical function, the government had a stake in enjoining peasants to work as diligently as possible and to maintain a frugal lifestyle. What attitudes toward peasants emerge in these 1649 injunctions? Would you go so far as to say that some of these injunctions were dehumanizing?

—Farm work must be done with the greatest diligence. Planting must be neat, all weeds must be removed, and on the borders of both wet and dry fields beans or similar foodstuffs are to be grown, however small the space.

—Peasants must rise early and cut grass before cultivating the fields. In the evening they are to make straw rope or straw bags, all such work to be done with great care.

—They must not buy tea or saké to drink, nor must their wives.

—Men must plant bamboo or trees round the farmhouse and must use the fallen leaves for fuel so as to save expense.

—Peasants are people without sense or forethought. Therefore they must not give rice to their wives and children at harvest time, but must save food for the future. They should eat millet, vegetables, and other coarse food instead of rice. Even the fallen leaves of plants should be saved as food against famine. . . . During the seasons of planting and harvesting, however, when the labour is arduous, the food taken may be a little better than usual.

—The husband must work in the fields, the wife must work at the loom. Both must do night work. However good-looking a wife may be, if she neglects her household duties by drinking tea or sightseeing or rambling on the hillsides, she must be divorced.

—Peasants must wear only cotton or hemp—no silk. They may not smoke tobacco. It is harmful to health, it takes up time, and costs money. It also creates a risk of fire.

Source: George Sansom, A History of Japan, *Vol. III (Stanford, CA: Stanford University Press, 1958), 99.*

Such relationships tended to involve intense personal subordination of tenants. For example, landlords demanded that the children of tenants serve as servants for the landlord family, that the tenant family prepare meals for the landlord, or that the tenants send gifts at various times to the landlord.

TOKUGAWA POLITICAL THOUGHT

The Tokugawa shogunate made Neo-Confucianism (*Shushigaku*) the state ideology; this philosophy had been set forth in China's Song dynasty by Zhu Xi (Shu Shi in Japanese). In 1633 a "Sages Hall" to commemorate Confucius was constructed with shogunal funds; it became a shogunate university in 1670. The regime's main interest in this Chinese philosophy was its social ethic, particularly its stress on subordination, filial piety, and ethical leadership. These values fit well with and reinforced the ethical elements in *bushidō*. The goal in stressing Neo-Confucian values was preservation of societal order, the purpose that had motivated the Tokugawa to set up its authoritarian state structures.

Political debate focused on two dynamics. First, there was the question hovering in the background: what was the relationship between Chinese thought and Japanese tradition? Neo-Confucianism, adopted with certainty of its appropriateness, began to be challenged in various ways by the end of the seventeenth century. Second, there was the question kept in the foreground and debated: what was the relationship between the shogun and the emperor? Both questions raised the issue of Japanese identity.

Even the writings of those who supported Confucianism undercut the role of Shushigaku. There were two schools of Neo-Confucian thought: that of Shu Shi, which emphasized enlightenment through the "investigation of things," and that of Wang Yangming (Ō Yōmei), stressing enlightenment through meditation and intuition. One late-seventeenth-century Confucian thinker championed the thought of Ō Yōmei, diminishing the importance of Shu Shi. Another, Arai Hakuseki, ("described as having eyes that flashed like lightning and a mustache stiff as spears") emphasized the importance of understanding Japanese history.[15] A third refused to accept Shu Shi's interpretation of Confucius and called for a return to pre–Shu Shi Confucianism for a purer view of Confucian thought. All three of these Neo-Confucian thinkers helped to begin to erode the state ideology and, by implication, to raise questions about the shogunate's legitimacy.

Direct reaction against Chinese thought came with the school of thought known as *National Learning (Kokugaku)*. Its goals were to use only Japanese sources to regain ethical values and spiritual direction and to reestablish the *Ancient Way* by freeing Japan from impurities that had corrupted it. Kokugaku adherents believed that the Japanese character was originally pure but had been corrupted by things Chinese. Japanese therefore had to regain a *Japanese heart (Yamato-gokoro)*. As National Learning developed, it prompted a Shinto revival because it was Shinto that celebrated the national creation myths. The more scholars thought about Shinto and the nature of Japan, the more the emperor, as a direct descendant of the Sun Goddess, became the focus and the more Japan itself was considered a *Land of the Gods*.

Two of the most important Kokugaku thinkers were Motoori Norinaga (1730–1801) and Hirata Atsutane (1776–1843). Norinaga, trained in Shushigaku and medicine, argued that the source of Japan was no less than the Way of the Gods; it was there that the Sun Goddess and her descendants were to rule until time ended. Foreign philosophies and religions such as Confucianism and Buddhism were inferior and should no longer influence the Japanese. "Our country," Norinaga argued, "is the source and fountainhead of all other countries, and in all matters it excels all the others."[16] In Norinaga's mind, the relationship of shogun to emperor was clear: the shogun was simply the emperor's deputy. Atsutane was motivated by his tremendous respect for the Japanese classics and by his hatred and disdain for Confucianism and Buddhism. His writings attempted to glorify Japan and to raise the level of Japanese national consciousness.

> [O]ur country, as a special mark of favor from the heavenly gods, was begotten by them, and there is thus so immense a difference between Japan and all the other countries of the world as to defy comparison. Ours is a splendid and blessed country, the Land of the Gods beyond any doubt, and we, down to the most humble man and woman, are the descendants of the gods.[17]

Scholars from the domain of Mito, controlled by a branch family of the shogun, set forth their ideas about the relationship between shogun and emperor (see Identities). One of the most troubling aspects of Chinese political thought for Japanese thinkers was the Mandate of Heaven; that concept allowed people to rise up and overthrow an emperor who failed to rule benevolently. In Japan, the divinity of the emperors meant that they could not be overthrown. Fulfilling obligations to the emperor, the Mito thinkers argued, was the key to restoring the Japanese way; the most important of these obligations were loyalty and duty, both of which were to be shown relative to people's status in society. In place of a heavenly mandate (as in the Chinese model) they created an imperial mandate given to the shogun by the emperor. The shogun had to show reverence to the emperor while showing benevolence to the people.

In the Shinto revival, with its glorification of the Japanese way and the Japanese, the Chinese model receded in importance. Almost ironically, some Japanese by the last third of the eighteenth century were

Identities: Rai San'yō (1780–1832):
The Historian and the Emperor's Role

Rai San'yō was the son of a scholar who had been born into a merchant family in the domain of Hiroshima. Though Rai was a poet as well, his most famous work was *The Official History of Japan* (*Nihon gaishi*), which the twentieth-century historian W. G. Beasley described as "exceedingly popular, if inaccurate."[1] Rai, on the other hand, told a friend that his history was marked by "rational observation and selection."[2]

The book was widely circulated in its Chinese original form and its Japanese translation; there were many editions. The historian Peter Duus says that it depicted Japanese history "as a narrative of the recurring downfall of successive shogunal regimes [and] was infused with regret that the emperor was no longer the undisputed ruler of the country."[3] However, it lauded historical officials and functionaries who remained loyal servants of the court. It is not surprising that Rai's work flowed into the stream of the National Learning school, which emphasized loyalty to the emperor. Indeed, Duus calls Rai's work "a bible for the antiforeign activists in the 1850s."[4]

Part of Rai's attitude about the authority figure of the shogun may have grown out of his experience with his own authority figure, his father. Described as discontented and rebellious as a youth, he incurred the wrath of his father when he left the domain of Hiroshima, a flight that angered his father and led to his disinheritance. He eked out a living in Kyoto as a private scholar and spent considerable time traveling. Many saw him as an eccentric; he saw himself as a connoisseur of fine drink and beautiful paintings.

He was a personal friend of Ōshio Heihachirō (see Identities: Ōshio Heihachirō, Chapter 6), who rebelled against the shogun in 1837. Rai admired his political determination and commitment. In a poem Rai called him a "true child of Yōmei," the Neo-Confucian who called for enlightenment through meditation followed by direct action. But Rai worried about the outcome of Ōshio's direct action: "I fear that you will bring misfortune on your extraordinary talent; I pray you sheath your sword after polishing it. . . ."[5] Apparently his own rebelliousness had also been sheathed by this point, though it is clear that Rai's writing brush would help to unsheath many swords in the years ahead.

---

[1] *W. G. Beasley,* The Meiji Restoration *(Stanford, CA: Stanford University Press, 1972), 147.*

[2] *Tetsuo Najita, "Ōshio Heihachirō (1793–1837)," in Personality in Japanese History, ed. Albert M. Craig and Donald H. Shively (Ann Arbor, MI: Center for Japanese Studies, 1995), 175.*

[3] *Peter Duus,* The Japanese Discovery of America, A Brief History with Documents *(Boston: Bedford Books, 1997), 50–51.*

[4] *Ibid., 51.*

[5] *Najita, "Ōshio Heihachirō," 175.*

---

seriously looking at Western science and technology. The Dutch, who were allowed to trade on Deshima, brought books on these topics that fascinated receptive Japanese. Translations into Japanese appeared in increasing numbers from 1750 to 1850; topics included botany, geography, math, physics, astronomy, metallurgy, ballistics, medicine, and military tactics. Study of these books and proposals on policies concerning modern technology created a school of *Dutch studies,* which grew despite official proscription. In

Source: Dutch Learning

Hirata Atsutane (1776–1843) worked to assert the supremacy of Shinto over other religions and in so doing raised the value of nationalism among the Japanese. Here, however, he praises the contribution of Dutch learning. What features of Dutch learning and of the Dutch themselves does he celebrate? Why does he take a slap at China?

With their scientific instruments the Dutch attempt to determine the properties of things. Unlike China, Holland is a splendid country where they do not rely on superficial conjectures. When the Dutch come across matters which they cannot understand no matter how much they may ponder over them, they say that these are things beyond the knowing of human beings, and belong to *Gotto* [God], and that only with divine powers could such matters be comprehended. The Dutch thus never resort to wild conjectures. Their findings, which are the result of the efforts of hundreds of people studying scientific problems for a thousand, even two thousand years, have been incorporated in books which have been presented to Japan. I have seen them and that is how I happen to be able to write of them.

The men of the countries of Europe sail at will around the globe in ships which recognize no frontiers. In Holland, one of the countries of Europe (though a small one), they consider astronomy and geography to be the most important subjects of study because unless a ship's captain is well versed in these sciences it is impossible for him to sail as he chooses to all parts of the world. Moreover, the Dutch have the excellent national characteristic of investigating matters with great patience until they can get to the very bottom. For the sake of such research they have devised surveying instruments as well as telescopes and helioscopes with which to examine the sun, moon, and stars. They have devised other instruments to ascertain the size and proximity of the heavenly bodies. It may take five or ten years or even a whole lifetime for such research to be completed; when problems cannot be solved in one lifetime, scholars write down their own findings and leave the solution for their children, grandchildren, and disciples to discover, though it may require generations.

Source: Ryusaku Tsunoda, William Theodore De Bary, and Donald Keene, comps., Sources of Japanese Tradition, Vol. 2 *(New York: Columbia University Press, 1965), 41–42.*

sum, Tokugawa political thought emphasized turning from the Chinese model both to the past, to the Ancient Way of Japan, and to the future with knowledge of scientific and technological developments brought via Dutch ships.

TRADITIONAL EDUCATION

Just as the Japanese never adopted the Chinese Mandate of Heaven, they did not adopt the Chinese civil service examination. Japanese society was aristocratic, not meritocratic. Nevertheless, education was emphasized. In the Tokugawa there were domain schools where young samurai were trained, as well as private schools, often located in Buddhist compounds, where commoners were educated. Samurai were trained to raise their ethical and moral sensibility, both to make them better administrators as they sat at castle town desks and to prepare themselves to serve their lord properly. Subjects included Chinese studies, calligraphy, arithmetic, training in formal etiquette, and military arts. Japanese studies were introduced gradually during the Shinto revival. Dutch studies were not introduced until the 1850s and 1860s.

Not all agreed that the commoners should be educated. Some thought they would get ideas above their social station and therefore erode public morality. And yet at least seventeen domain schools admitted commoners as students. Most commoners attended private schools, often taught by Buddhist monks, doctors, Shinto priests, rich farmers, or samurai who had lost their lord (*rōnin*). These schools emphasized Confucian morality and basic literacy. It is estimated that by the mid-nineteenth century, more than 40 percent of boys and about 10 percent of girls were getting some formal education outside their homes. By comparison, in England at the same time, only one child in every four or five was attending school.

What were the implications of education for Japan's modernization? Education meant that the "Japanese populace was not just a sack of potatoes": when cataclysmic change came, the Japanese could "appreciate new possibilities, make new choices," and participate more readily as citizens—reading the public notice board in the village and the newspaper.[18] That parents had sent their children to school suggests that many desired self-improvement; when the idea of self-improvement is widespread, the concept of national improvement cannot be far behind. Education spread the sense of nationalism, especially in domain schools, since by the mid-nineteenth century, most of these schools taught some Japanese history.

VALUES AND ATTITUDES IN THE WIDER SOCIETY

Though both China and Japan adopted Confucianism and its family values, they differed substantially in values related to societal goals. Chinese stressed what might be called *system maintenance* values, that is, working to attain the "relatively static ideal of harmony."[19] In contrast, Japanese values were primarily centered on *goal attainment,* with an emphasis, for example, on a focused dynamism to attain individual goals and subordination of individual members to achieve group goals. How did these ideals filter down to villages all over Japan?

Providing moral encouragement and admonition was a significant purpose of government. The Tokugawa had adopted for villages a policy called *gonin-gumi* (five-man groups); the headmen of five families served as an administrative unit that was, in effect, a mutual surveillance unit. Each member of the group observed the actions of the others and reported any malfeasance to the authorities. Because they were a group, any punishment for wrong actions was shared by all five. The men in the group often provided mutual help and support. Periodically these groups were brought together to have moral exhortations read to them: to work diligently and quickly, to pay careful attention to one's business, to be frugal. The five-man group's regulations warned about luxuries, amusements, sports, and gambling. Admonitions against luxury were especially prevalent and were supported by various sumptuary laws.

In conceiving the role of individuals in society, a key value was duty. Indeed, one's occupation was not simply what one did; it was "the fulfillment of what one owe[d] to society, it [was] the part one play[ed] which justifie[d] one's receiving the benefits of society."[20] The samurai provided the model: his devoted and selfless performance of the duties of his office fulfilled his obligations to his lord. This sense of paying back the debts owed society transcended the samurai class in the Tokugawa; peasants and merchants also had imbibed this concept.

The Hōtoku (*repayment of blessings*) movement was begun in the early nineteenth century by a farmer, Ninomiya Sontoku (1787–1856), who wanted to improve the morality of farmers and raise their level of crop production. He noted, "I began to see that even an insignificant person like myself might contribute materially to the general welfare and prosperity of his country. From that time I saw how homely daily labor, which most people think of only as a disagreeable task, might be made to have a high

Source: The "Good Life" (1816)

Here, what might be called a sumptuary policeman *recounts the evils of wearing* sendaihira *silk and eating hot soup. What social realities in the highly structured Tokugawa polity is the author really decrying?*

. . . Concerning the clothes worn by the samurai, here is a story coming from the time of the Keichō era (1596–1615) when Lord Ieyasu was still living. A samurai in attendance to Lord Ieyasu appeared before his Lordship attired in a *hakama* (divided skirt) made of *sendaihira* silk. His Lordship was angered and brandished his long sword to expel the samurai, saying that not long after the attainment of peace the man had already indulged in a taste of luxury. However, nowadays, not only those unimportant vassals but also those lower-ranking samurai, foot soldiers (*ashigaru*), merchants (*chōnin*) and farmers all wear *sendaihira* silk. The extravagance in clothing can be readily seen by this.

Concerning food and drink, when *rōju* Doi Toshikatsu (1573–1644) visited Sakai Tadakatsu (1587–1662, who later became *tairō* under Iemitsu) at the latter's home, he was treated with cold soup. In those days people had a habit of saving, and if a host invited his guests, the guests brought their own food, and the host provided the hot soup (*sirukō*). If *sake* was also added, it was considered quite a treat. Nowadays, people are so extravagant in their consumption of *sake* and food, and their pastries contain all sorts of delicacies. For example, the price of an elegant meal for one person is anywhere from two to three bags (*hyō*) to four to five bags of rice. And a pastry may cost as much as one quart (*shō*) to two or three quarts of rice. When *sake* is served, it now requires soup and other side dishes. And nowadays even those lowly people who live in insignificant town houses and back alleys refuse to eat cold soup.

Source: David J. Lu, Sources of Japanese History, Vol. 2 *(New York: McGraw-Hill, 1978), 3–4.*

meaning in it, and I determined to devote all my energies to the service of others."[21] One of his central themes was acting in life to return the blessings received. "Everyone who is, according to his heavenly gift, living within his means. . . by saving his surplus money as a fund for restoring and developing deserted wastes, paying debts, rescuing the poor, helping villages and provinces . . . until all Japan [has] become prosperous, is making return for the blessings he has received from heaven, earth, and man."[22] Through pamphlets and lectures, the founder of the Hōtoku movement spread these ideas: "work much, earn much, and spend little."

The merchant class also had its promoter and ethical spokesman, Ishida Baigan (1685–1744), who spread his message in lecture halls throughout the country. The thrust of his Shingaku (*heart learning*) movement was national and blended well with the ideas of national learning and the Shinto revival. The function of the merchant class was to help the nation: "each exhausts himself for the sake of all." Ishida argued that profit was not wrong; it was what diligent merchants received as their proper reward for services. He railed against extravagance and luxuries and emphasized honesty. He called for the merchant class to model their lives on the samurai ethic, and he emphasized the transcendent importance of the emperor. In his teachings Ishida talked repeatedly of the special nature of Japan as the land of the gods, where the Sun Goddess was the "ancestress of our heavenly ruler."[23]

Despite the efforts of the Tokugawa shoguns to freeze society so that their control could not be challenged, the nature of human relations, the passage of time, and historical developments and contingencies made it impossible to stop change that was inimical to the shogunate. As time passed, contradictions

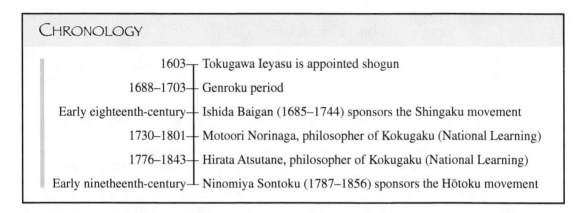

CHRONOLOGY

1603	Tokugawa Ieyasu is appointed shogun
1688–1703	Genroku period
Early eighteenth-century	Ishida Baigan (1685–1744) sponsors the Shingaku movement
1730–1801	Motoori Norinaga, philosopher of Kokugaku (National Learning)
1776–1843	Hirata Atsutane, philosopher of Kokugaku (National Learning)
Early ninetheenth-century	Ninomiya Sontoku (1787–1856) sponsors the Hōtoku movement

within politics and society became ever more serious. Despite, for example, the shoguns' attempts to isolate Japan from foreign contact, scholars by the late eighteenth century increasingly thought in terms of Japan in relation to other nations, whether in Dutch studies or in National Learning. The winds of change were readying the Japanese for a challenge from the outside, a challenge that would set in motion forces that would end the shogunate and its whole model of governing.

SUGGESTED READINGS

Bellah, Robert. *Tokugawa Religion.* New York: Free Press, 1957. Now widely considered an indispensable book, this is a study, as its subtitle puts it, of "the values of pre-industrial Japan."

Chikamatsu Monzaemon. *Four Major Plays of Chikamatsu.* Translated by Donald Keene. New York: Columbia University Press, 1969. These tragic plays reflect the daily life of late-seventeenth- and early-eighteenth-century Japan.

Chūshingura [The Treasury of Loyal Retainers]. Translated by Donald Keene. New York: Columbia University Press, 1971. This puppet play recounts the famous story of the forty-seven *rōnin*, which captures the values of the samurai class.

Perez, Louis G. *Daily Life in Early Modern Japan.* Westport, CT: Greenwood Press, 2002. This overview of Japanese life and customs covers a range of topics from food to sex, from work to amusements, from clothing to language.

Sansom, George B. *Japan, A Short Cultural History.* New York: D. Appleton-Century, 1943. This is a classic by a giant in the world of Japanese studies; despite its age, it provides a wealth of information and detail.

CHAPTER SIX

The Last Years of Feudal Japan, 1830–1868

The house that Tokugawa Ieyasu built lasted for over two and a half centuries. Its collapse in the mid-nineteenth century came, like China's nineteenth-century troubles, from a combination of foreign threats and domestic discord. In the end, however, these forces brought a very different conclusion from those at work in China.

THE TEMPŌ CRISES (1830–1844)

The Famine

The name of an era, Tempō was a period of both calamitous events and important reforms. In the beginning the chief villain was weather. The spring of 1833 was dry; the summer was inordinately rainy and cold. The rice crop and those of other staples generally failed, especially in northeastern Japan. But this was only the first of a series of bad years. In 1836, for example, it rained constantly throughout the summer and it was cold to boot: people reportedly had to wear winter capes in mid-July. The crop loss in some areas was 50 to 75 percent. Ninomiya Sontoku, the Hōtoku founder, noted that it was "the worst harvest in fifty years."[1] Records show that more than one hundred thousand died of starvation in northeastern Japan alone; the numbers elsewhere were also shockingly high. People reportedly ate weeds, leaves, and even straw. One contemporary diarist noted: "the starving and the dead were all over; some chose to stone children to death instead of letting them suffer death by starvation."[2] With such a dearth of rice and other crops, prices skyrocketed—three times higher for rice in Osaka in 1837 than in 1833 and in Edo, higher than ever before.

In the midst of starvation, want, and inflation, civil disorder abounded. A Japanese scholar has noted that the Tempō era saw "465 rural disputes, 445 peasant uprisings, and 101 urban riots, the two latter categories reaching their peak, like the Tempō famine, in 1836."[3] The rural uprisings seemed to differ from previous episodes in their scale; instead of small local disturbances, these tended to be regional disorders, as in the 1831 unrest in the domain of Chōshū and the 1836 uprisings north of Fuji, in Mikawa province, and on Sado island. They played out against a backdrop of growing social polarization between rich and poor. Many of the targets of have-nots were wealthy farmers with their stores, granaries, breweries, and pawnshops, who put down the uprisings mercilessly using torture, crucifixion, and banishment.

Three of Japan's cities were among the ten largest in the world at the time: Edo, with over a million, and Osaka and Kyoto, with almost a half million. These vast populations suffered from shortages and inflation; with so many people crowded into relatively small areas, a sense of helplessness and rumors could flare into riots that tore the social fabric. In the Tempō period, Osaka experienced eleven riots and Edo three. Ōshio Heihachirō's 1837 rebellion in Osaka (see Identities) set off shock waves around the country, giving rise to elite fears of a coming social conflagration.

The Threat from Outside

The Russians were the first foreigners to knock on Japan's doors after the early-seventeenth-century closure of the country to all but some Asian nations and the Dutch. By the middle of that century, the Russians had established themselves on the Sea of Okhotsk. During the eighteenth century, Russian and Japanese explorers and merchants encountered each other in the Kurile Islands and in the vicinity of Sakhalin Island. In 1792 and 1793, the commander of an expedition sent by Catherine the Great attempted to explore the possibility of trade with Japan; the Japanese replied that Nagasaki was the only port he could enter. Over ten years later, in 1804, a Russian envoy appeared at Nagasaki formally requesting commercial relations. When the Japanese refused, the envoy encouraged headstrong sailors to raid Japanese trading posts and garrisons in Sakhalin and the Kuriles in 1806 and 1807. In the wake of these events, the shogun ordered local authorities to drive off foreign ships from every port. It was not a particularly auspicious beginning for Japanese-Russian relations.

The English also appeared in the waters off Hokkaido in the 1790s. In 1818 a British trading ship entered Edo Bay. In 1824, there was an armed clash between British sailors and inhabitants of a small island south of

Identities: Ōshio Heihachirō (1793–1837):
The Shogun Is a "Bandit"

Ōshio Heihachirō was an Osaka police inspector and a scholar of the Chinese Neo-Confucianist Ōyōmei (who talked of the importance of taking action to right wrongs). What was wrong, according to Ōshio? Simply put, the Tokugawa shogunate and its daimyō. Outraged at the evils of the shogunate, Ōshio lectured the sons of rich farmers at a school he had established. Tokugawa rule, he charged, was decadent and arrogant, marked by bribe taking and listening to the advice of women, by living lives of pleasure and drinking expensive sake—all the while ignoring the terrible famine among the people. The daimyō cavorted with men of the theater and wicked women. They were "bandits stealing the beneficence of heaven,"[1] in cahoots with filthy rich Osaka merchants and warehouse owners, hoarding rice and sending most of it to the Tokugawa capital of Edo while shutting their eyes to the spread of famine.

The solution? In early 1837 Ōshio sent copies of a document titled "A Call to Arms" to villages in the vicinity of Osaka and called for a peasant uprising. "We must first punish the officials, who torment the people so cruelly; then we must execute the haughty and rich Osaka merchants. Then we must distribute the gold, silver, and copper stored in their cellars, and the bales of rice hidden in their storehouses."[2] The shogun, through his lack of benevolence for the people, had forfeited his right to rule. Ousting the shogun and ending the shogunate would restore the moral government of the emperor. Ōshio linked this action to the aim of restoring the Japanese emperor to his rightful position.

For all of his principled opposition, Ōshio did not spend much time thinking through a strategy that might have been successful. He arranged for about twenty men to set fires in Osaka signalling to peasants in the surrounding areas to begin the rebellion. He had roughly three-hundred supporters at the beginning. The fires were set on February 19, 1837; a two-day conflagration burned 25 percent of the city, mostly destroying the area where the poor lived. Unfortunately, though Ōshio had tried to stimulate an uprising, only a few peasants participated. The whole affair disintegrated into a looting spree—an orgy of sacking silk stores and swilling sake. So much wealth was taken from the giant merchant houses that Ōshio's rebels could not carry it all away.

The shogunate hunted Ōshio down; to avoid capture, he committed suicide. News of the failed uprising fueled other small rebellions that were, however, quickly suppressed. Significantly, Ōshio had brought up issues and concerns that would become highly significant by the 1850s and 1860s: the nature of shogunal rule, the role of the emperor, and the role of the people themselves in political issues and change.

---

[1] *David John Lu,* Sources of Japanese History, Vol. 2 *(New York: McGraw-Hill, 1978), 8.*

[2] *Harold Bolitho, "The Tempō Crisis," in* The Cambridge History of Japan, Vol. 5, The Nineteenth Century, *ed. Marius B. Jansen (Cambridge: Cambridge University Press, 1989), 123–24.*

Himeji Castle   Himeji, also known as the White Heron Castle because its wooden walls are covered with white plaster, is located in Hyogo near Osaka. Begun in 1601 by Ikeda Teramasu, the son-in-law of Tokugawa Ieyasu, it was completed in 1609. It suffered no damage during World War II. In 1993, it was registered on the UNESCO World Heritage list.

Kyushu. The Americans came too. Involved in whaling and piloting clipper ships in the great circle trade route to and from Guangzhou, American ships often came within sight of the Japanese islands. American interests in the islands were whaling ports in case of storms and better treatment of American shipwrecked sailors. Three times between 1835 and 1845, the United States tried to open negotiations with Japan but to no avail. Especially in the wake of the Opium War in China, these episodes fueled intense debates over national defense.

The tenor of the relations between Japanese and outsiders during the Tempō era is probably best shown by the episode of the *Morrison*, a private American ship, in the summer of 1837, only a few months after Ōshio's Osaka uprising. The ship, with an American businessman and some missionaries on board, was attempting to return seven Japanese castaways and anchored in Edo Bay on August 29. The next day, without warning, batteries on shore launched a volley of gunfire that drove the ship away with its Japanese castaways still on board. Clearly the Japanese were skittish about what these ships portended in the midst of the social unrest engulfing the country. When reports of the Treaty of Nanjing reached Japan in the fall of 1843, many Japanese decision makers felt something akin to panic, wondering whether Japan might be next on the outsiders' list.

The Reforms

In the wake of the famine and the inflation it induced, as well as the perceived growing dangers from abroad, Japanese leaders in the domains and in the shogunate itself responded with a wave of reforms. "They were scattered over a country of considerable economic, climactic, and topographical diversity, so that the crisis impinged on them in different ways and to different degrees."[4] The reactions in the northeast, where famine had been greatest, were different from those in the far southwest, where foreign ships had seemed the crucial threat. Coastal areas on which foreign ships had impinged were more concerned with defense issues than were domains in the interior.

The Tempō reforms relied on tried-and-true precedents. Some domains stressed the moral failings of samurai and their leadership; in this case, education was touted as one solution to the difficulties. Since much of the problem was economic, many domain governments emphasized frugality as a key to recovery. Old methods were used in trying to deal with the economic shortfalls: adopting stringent budgets, cutting samurai stipends, and simply repudiating debt. The latter two options had risks. Reducing samurai stipends had been tried before; the downside was losing samurai support or losing samurai themselves (who, with little to lose, might simply leave the domain). Debt repudiation (part of the reform in the Chōshū and Fukuoka domains) risked alienating the business community. One other traditional reform was restricting commercial development that took land out of cultivation and reduced tax revenues; this happened in the Mito, Satsuma, Chōshū, and Hizen domains.

There were, however, new initiatives, many a blend of old and new. One innovation was to encourage commercial growth—traditionally subordinated to agriculture. In Fukuoka, the town leaders focused on developing the town center, even encouraging townsmen to purchase lottery tickets and to patronize town theaters. Along with this support, in many domains there were changes in attitudes to businessmen and a readiness to cooperate with them in making local policies. Domain monopolies on production and distribution of key commodities provided many domains with the economic cushion needed in hard times. During the reforms, some monopolies were relaxed to placate people who may have wanted to trade those commodities independently (for example, in Chōshū, Usuki, and Funai). But other domains, like Mito, wanted to add new commodities to their already existing monopolies.

The domains were also compelled to deal with the foreign threat. The fact was that the Japanese military was in sad shape. Their weaponry, strategy, and tactics were mired in the seventeenth century; their weapons, for example, included swords, pikes, muskets, and dilapidated cannons. To illustrate the slackness of the years at peace and the troubling economic problems, the domain of Utsonomiya revived target practice for its samurai, having stopped it twenty-six years earlier because it was deemed too expensive. Other new policies created by daimyō would put them in good shape as the end of the shogunate approached. Mito moved samurai out of castle-town garrisons to forts along the coast and trained peasants to serve in militia units.

Satsuma, whose reforms were successful in balancing the budget and building up reserve funds, dealt with its debt crisis by stating that all loans to Osaka merchants could be repaid over the next 250 years at an interest rate of 0.5 percent, in effect canceling the debt. In addition, Satsuma's domain finances were bolstered by a trade monopoly it maintained with the Liuqiu Islands, especially in sugar cane—which it then sold in Japanese urban markets. With its wealth, Satsuma purchased arms from traders in Nagasaki and began an ambitious program of manufacturing its own artillery; it also sent men to be trained in the use of Western guns. What developed among many domains was an arms race.

The reforms often stimulated bitter disagreements; to carry them out, many daimyō had to provide strong leadership. The Tempō crisis "had shown the domains some unpalatable truths: their tenuous control over the common people, their bankruptcy, and their vulnerability to attack."[5] Domains also had to direct and control their reforms on their own with their own resources. Historians agree that most reform programs were not very effective and that only one, in the Satsuma domain, brought measurable success.

The shogun's personal domain was about six times larger than the next largest province; it was, however, scattered over forty-seven of Japan's sixty-eight provinces; thus, when reform was instituted, it was harder to administer than in other domains. The shogunate's finances had taken a beating with famine relief, tax shortages, and civil disorders, and the crisis in foreign affairs was the shogun's alone to deal with. Like most daimyō, the shogun did those things that traditionally had been part of reform: reduce taxes in famine regions, bolster food supplies for cities, send missions to check out coastal garrisons, focus on public morals, and issue sumptuary laws. The shogunate did announce a policy change regarding foreign ships. Instead of driving them away without any contact, the Japanese would supply the ships as needed—and then drive them away.

New approaches included the introduction of commodity price controls and the abolition of state-sponsored monopolies for shogunate and domain alike. This last was a major effort of the shogun to weaken those domains whose monopolies bolstered their economies. This method and others revealed that in the Tempō reforms the shogun was trying to strengthen his position vis-à-vis the daimyō: he expropriated land from some daimyō; he required daimyō north of Edo to pay large sums for the draining of a great swamp; and he required huge economic outlays from daimyō to pay for his 1843 ceremonial pilgrimage to the tomb of Tokugawa Ieyasu at Nikkō, ninety miles from Edo. Such a trip had not been made for about seventy years; now the shogun revived it at a time when it created economic hardship, but it was also a celebration of Tokugawa rule and an expression of Tokugawa authority. Over the past century or so, the political system had become in effect shogun-daimyō joint rule (the bakuhan system), whereby daimyō had generally ruled in their own domains. The shogun's attempt to reassert power displeased many daimyō. Broad, difficult problems were beginning to shatter the whole bakuhan system.

THE COMING OF PERRY AND JAPANESE REACTIONS

On July 8, 1853, four American steamships anchored in Edo Bay, a mile offshore and some thirty miles from Edo itself. Commanded by Commodore Matthew Perry, the fleet had instructions from President Millard Fillmore to seek a treaty that would allow U.S. ships coaling and provisioning stops, protect castaways, and open trade. Japanese on shore were startled by the ships, whose hulls were painted black and whose smokestacks emitted huge puffs of black smoke; some thought either that the fleet was afire or that the foreigners had harnessed the power of volcanoes.

Commodore Matthew Perry   Before opening Japan, Commodore Matthew C. Perry (1794–1858) had served in the U.S. navy all over the world—from Africa to Europe to Mexico. Perhaps his most significant contribution was his avid support for a steam-powered naval force; he was also a strong advocate of spreading U.S. naval power into the Pacific.

Source: "Dutch Ship," A Poem

This poem by Rai San'yō (see Identities in Chapter 5) was written in 1818 during a three-month stay in Nagasaki. It reveals his strongly xenophobic outlook. What negative images of the Western ship and Westerners does he use? What is his attitude to dealing with them?

In Nagasaki Bay, southwest where sky and water meet,
suddenly at heaven's edge a tiny dot appears.
The cannon of the lookout tower gives one roar
and in twenty-five watch stations bows are bared.
Through the streets on four sides the cry breaks forth:
"The redhaired Westerners are coming!"
Launches set out to meet them, we hear the drum echo,
in the distance signal flags are raised to stay alarm.
The ship enters the harbor like a ponderous turtle,
so huge that in the shallows it seems certain to ground.
Our little launches, so many strings of pearls,
tow it forward amid a clamorous din.
The barbarian hull rises a hundred feet from the surface,
sea winds sighing, flapping its pennants of felt.
Three sails stretched among ten thousand lines,
fixed to engines moving up and down like wellsweeps.
Blackskinned slaves nimble as monkeys
scale the masts, haul the lines, keeping them from tangling.
The anchor drops with shouts from the crew,
giant cannon bellow forth roar after roar.
Barbarian hearts are hard to fathom; the Throne ponders,
aware that defenses are far from complete.
Ah, the wretches, why do they come to vex our eyes,
pursuing ten thousand miles their greed for gain,
their ships pitiful leaves upon the monstrous waves,
drawn like giant ants to rancid meat?
Do we not bear ox-knives to kill a mere chicken,
trade our most precious jewels for thorns?

Source: Peter Duus, The Japanese Discovery of America, A Brief History with Documents *(New York: Bedford Books, 1997), 51.*

As in the coming of Western nations to China, each side had many misapprehensions about the other. Perry came with convictions that the Japanese were "a 'weak and semi-barbarous people,' a people 'vindictive in character' and so 'deceitful' that customary standards of diplomacy were meaningless."[6] Nor did he understand the nature of the Japanese government. He knew that the shogun existed but called him the "tycoon"; an American shipmate wrote, "The Tycoon is their king. There is another chap somewhere to the west [the emperor in Kyoto]. The Mikado. We think he is a spiritual ruler. A pope perhaps."[7] For their part, the Japanese, who had relatively sparse facial hair, were struck by the beards and mustaches of the Westerners. They also surmised that the heels on American shoes existed to compensate for the lack of a bodily heel and that barefoot, without heels, Americans could easily be shoved over.

Source: The Views of Ii Naosuke

Ii Naosuke (1815–1860) clearly believed that the old policy of seclusion could neither keep Japan safe and tranquil nor lead to a situation where the country's "courage and prestige [would] resound" around the world. The reference to Batavia concerns the Dutch East Indies colony of Java. In this response to Abe Masahiro's request in October 1853, what were his specific plans for strengthening Japan's defenses?

. . .Careful consideration of conditions as they are today . . . leads me to believe that despite the constant differences and debates into which men of patriotism and foresight have been led in recent years by their perception of the danger of foreign aggression, it is impossible in the crisis we now face to ensure the safety and tranquillity of our country merely by an insistence on the seclusion laws as we did in former times. Moreover, time is essential if we are to complete our coast defenses. Since 1609, when (large) warships . . . were forbidden, we have had no warships capable of opposing foreign attack on our coasts with heavy guns. . . . There is a saying that when one is besieged in a castle, to raise the drawbridge is to imprison oneself and make it impossible to hold out indefinitely. . . . Even though the shogun's ancestors set up seclusion laws, they left the Dutch and the Chinese to act as a bridge [to the outside world]. Might not this bridge now be of advantage to us in handling foreign affairs, providing us with the means whereby we may for a time avert the outbreak of hostilities and then, after some time has elapsed, gain a complete victory?

Then, too, there is the question of trade. Although there is a national prohibition of it, conditions are not the same as they were. The exchange of goods is a universal practice. This we should explain to the spirits of our ancestors. And we should then tell the foreigners that we mean in the future to send trading vessels to the Dutch company's factory at Batavia to engage in trade; that we will allocate some of our trading goods to America, some to Russia, and so on, using the Dutch to trade for us as our agents; but that there will be delay of one or two years because we must construct new ships for these voyages. By replying in this way we will take the Americans by surprise in offering to treat them generally in the same way as the Dutch.

We must construct new steamships, especially powerful warships, and these we will load with goods not needed in Japan. For a time we will have to employ Dutchmen as masters and mariners, but we will put on board with them Japanese of ability and integrity who must study the use of large guns, the handling of ships, and the rules of navigation. Openly these will be called merchant vessels, but they will in fact have the secret purpose of training a navy. As we increase the number of ships and our mastery of technique, Japanese will be able to sail the oceans freely and gain direct knowledge of conditions abroad without relying on the secret reports of the Dutch. Thus we will eventually complete the organization of a navy.

Moreover, we must shake off the panic and apprehensions that have beset us and abandon our habits of luxury and wasteful spending. Our defenses thus strengthened, and all being arranged at home, we can act so as to make our courage and prestige resound beyond the seas.

Source: http://web.jjay.cuny.edu/~jobrien/reference/ob105.html.

The Japanese took the Fillmore letter to consider their actions; Perry promised to return for a response. The Japanese were thus faced with a political crisis; we have seen that in the previous decade the shogun, relatively weakened vis-à-vis powerful daimyō, had tried to begin regaining some of his power; and that earlier in the century thinkers in the Mito domain had noted the essential role of the shogun in foreign affairs. What was the shogunate to do, knowing that Japan's military unpreparedness made it no match for the American navy? The shogun had died less than two months after Perry's visit, and the new shogun did not take over until late November. In this period, the senior councilor of the regime, Abe Masahiro, took an unprecedented step to deal with the dangerous predicament. To this point in the history of the regime, tozama daimyō had not been allowed to participate in government decision making; that had been the purview only of fudai daimyō.

Now, in an effort to present a united front when Perry returned, Abe decided to consult all daimyō: should the demands of the Fillmore letter be agreed to? Of the fifty-nine most important daimyō, the "votes" were as follows: Twenty-two daimyō supported some form of trade with the United States. The main argument of their chief spokesman, Ii Naosuke, a fudai daimyō, was that any victory at this point over the American navy would only be temporary. It would be better to trade in order to build up profits so that ships and armaments could be purchased—and then drive the Americans away. Eighteen daimyō called for granting just enough concessions to the Americans to give Japan more time for military preparations; the chief spokesman here was Shimazu Nariakira, daimyō of the wealthy domain of Satsuma. The third group of nineteen were hard-liners and included the powerful Tokugawa Nariaki of the Mito domain; they argued that the Americans must be driven off, with Japan making no concessions at all. This group included other powerful daimyō from the domains of Chōshū, Tosa, and Hizen.

When Perry returned in March 1854 (with eight ships, one-quarter of the U.S. navy), he threatened force; the Japanese felt compelled to accept minimum American demands. The Treaty of Kanagawa opened two ports—Hakodate on Hokkaido and Shimoda down the coast from Edo—for provisioning and some trade; shipwrecked American sailors would be well treated; a most-favored-nation clause was included; and an American consular agent could reside in Shimoda. Later treaties with Great Britain and Russia included extraterritoriality and opened the port of Nagasaki.

Perry Takes in the Local Sights   This woodblock print, perhaps by the famous printmaker Hiroshige, shows Perry riding in a carriage following a procession of musicians and led by the U.S. flag through the streets of Yokohama.

BAKUMATSU

Abe's attempt to establish some sort of national solidarity with which to meet Perry had failed miserably. With the three groups of daimyō of roughly equal size, he had no mandate whatsoever. Many historians think that Abe's precedent-breaking action and its unhappy result was the first step down the road to the fifteen-year collapse of the Tokugawa regime. The period, called *Bakumatsu* (the end of the shogunate),

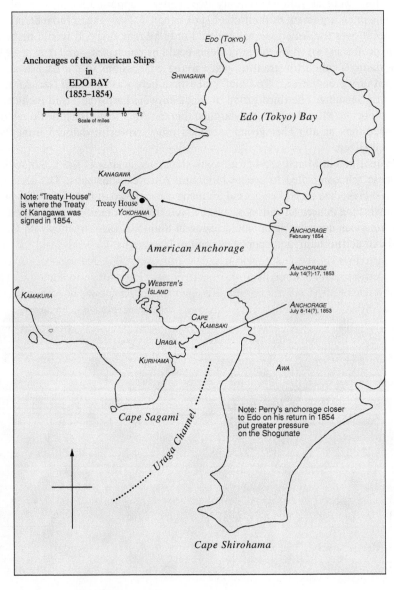

Map 6-1   Edo (Tokyo) Bay.

from 1853 to 1868, was a confusing time of countervailing political forces and actions, violence, and turmoil. It is important to understand, however, that when and after Abe chose to consult with the daimyō, the collapse of the regime was not inevitable; no one at the time could likely have even conceived of the possibility. There were too many alternatives, too many people making decisions, and the possibility of too many contingencies. Rather, it is later historians who "impose . . . a narrative line upon disparate images . . . [or] freeze the shifting phantasmagoria which is [everyone's] actual experience [into a particular meaning]."[8]

FOUR NARRATIVE STRUCTURES[9]

In the bakumatsu period, "many and different voices echoed around the land."[10] To make the historical din more understandable, historian George Wilson has suggested entering this echoing and complex world by focusing on four narratives. Though a chronological approach is clearest, I will use the historical actors of his narratives as a topical entrée into the period: Western envoys, the bakufu and daimyō, the common people, and the imperial loyalists.

First, let us consider the Western envoys: not because they were most important, but because they served as the catalyst for Japanese decision making and action. To be sure, as we have seen, there were many problems and contradictions in the Tokugawa system that people were beginning to address, but the Western threat was immediate and forced the Japanese to make rapid decisions. The goals of the ethnocentric Western diplomats were to bring Japan into the international community as the West defined it, to end what they considered Japanese barbarism, and to work toward stability in the islands. Their approach from Perry on was what might be called *forcible persuasion*.[11]

As events in the 1860s spiraled out of control on the Japanese home front, the Western presence (American, British, French, and Dutch) was never far from the public eye. Japanese who lived in the area permitting Western ships and foreigners were startled at these strange-looking and eerily frightening aliens. Popular crude prints (*kawaraban*)—depicting Perry, for example—were sold by street peddlers in Edo; one depicted Perry as a Buddhist devil. Others called for people "to drive away the 'foreign dogs'" and to "kill the barbarians using a beam of bright light."[12] From 1862 to 1868, Japanese mounted sporadic attacks, which brought fierce reprisals from the Western nations. It is clear that despite Western military power, the Western envoys did not shape Japan's history. Describing the events in 1867 and 1868, British diplomat Bertram Mitford asserted, "We began to feel that the dogs of war were loose."[13]

The goal of the shogun and most major daimyō coincided with the West's desire for stability; many were willing to return to the status quo before Perry—but not all, as the responses to Abe Masahiro reveal. Some wanted to turn the clock back to the time when the shogun was supreme in the bakuhan system. Others wanted the shogun to share even more political power with the daimyō. Still others wanted to challenge the shogun. And some toyed with establishing an alliance between shogun and emperor. The common denominator among these different opinion makers was that they accepted the reality of the bakufu and domain system and wanted to fix it. Not until the mid-1860s, after the shogunate had moved to punish the domain of Chōshū for attacking Westerners, did antishogunal forces crystallize. The heart of *bushidō*, loyalty, in this case of daimyō to shogun, was at stake as the drama played itself out.

For commoners in the 1860s there were many uncertainties. Rapid inflation had dramatically pushed up the cost of living: from 1865 to 1867, the cost of rice more than tripled; soy sauce was up 150 percent and bean paste 300 percent. Violence was frequent in many communities, and the presence of Westerners was destabilizing. The number of farmers' uprisings skyrocketed, reaching a peak in 1866. The commoners had two responses to their world in obvious flux. The first was a turn to religion that sprang out of the context of "pessimism, anxiety, and yearning."[14] New religions like Tenrikyō promised, in millennialist fashion, the coming of a world renewed in the here and now for the benefit of all.

Source: Perry Views the Japanese

Perhaps because of his own experiences in seeing other peoples and cultures, Perry's views of the Japanese seem to reflect crucial aspects of Japanese culture. What does he find to be their strong points? What does he suggest is perhaps the most difficult thing about interacting with them? Lew Chew is the Liuqiu Islands (in Japanese called Ryūkyū) lying between the southernmost Japanese island of Kyushu and the island of Taiwan.

. . . The Japanese are remarkable for their inordinate curiosity and, in the display of so many of the inventions of our ingenious countrymen; they had ample means of gratifying this propensity. They were not satisfied with the minutest examination of all these things, surpassingly strange as they must have been to them, but followed the officers and men about, seizing upon every occasion to examine every part of their garments, and showing the strongest desire to obtain one or more of their buttons. Those who were admitted on board the ships were equally inquisitive, peering into every nook and corner accessible to them, measuring this and that, and taking sketches after their manner of whatever they could lay their eyes upon, though it would be difficult to discover from their drawings what they were intended to represent.

Notwithstanding that the Japanese are themselves so fond of indulging their curiosity, they are by no means communicative when information is required of them, alleging as a reason that their laws forbid them to communicate to foreigners anything relating to their country or its institutions. We have had much better opportunities of picking up here and there, and from time to time, many interesting particulars respecting the laws, customs, and habits of these people than others who have preceded us. Yet a long time will elapse before any full and authentic account of their internal laws and regulations will be obtained; certainly not until we can establish men of intelligence in the country in the character of consular agents, merchants, or missionaries who, to enable them to make any progress, should acquire a knowledge of the language.

We found the common people more disposed to fraternize than were the mandarins or officials. It was evident that nothing but a fear of punishment deterred them from entering into free intercourse with us; but they were closely watched, and it may be inferred that the higher classes would be equally inclined to greater intimacy if they in their turn were not also watched. In truth every native has a spy set upon him in this country, as in Lew Chew. No one is entrusted with public business of any importance without having one or more associated with him, who are ever on the alert to detect and take note of the slightest suspicion of delinquency.

Source: Peter Duus, The Japanese Discovery of America, A Brief History with Documents *(New York: Bedford Books, 1997), 95–96.*

Commoners participated in religious pilgrimages to sites like the Grand Shrine at Ise, where Japanese emperors were crowned. Another response began in Nagoya and spread throughout central Japan in 1867. Called *ee ja nai ka* ("Why not!" or "What the hell!"), these social outbursts consisted of large numbers of people spontaneously and continuously dancing wildly and singing. In a kind of mass hysteria experienced in an almost carnival-like atmosphere, huge crowds paralyzed towns, highways, and whole areas. Historians have noted the links between these outbursts and the millennial thrust of the new religions, both evidence of the desperate plight of commoners. One historian argues that "these efforts to defy public norms . . . [were] tantamount to political acts of violence against the old regime."[15] In any case, they burned themselves out by 1868.

Sights at Edo's Kyobashi Bridge   This Hiroshige woodblock print suggests what early Westerners might have seen in the shogun's capital of Edo. In addition to the Kyobashi Bridge are the area's bamboo yards. The print is dated 1857. *Source:* Utagawa Hiroshige, "One Hundred Views of Edo: Bamboo Yards, Kyobashi Bridge." 1857. Color woodblock print. The Brooklyn Museum of Art.

To many elites, *ee ja nai ka* was extremely upsetting and another dangerous sign that the bakuhan system was bankrupt and ineffectual. These people, whom we can call *imperial loyalists,* came to see the emperor as the solution. The loyalists' goal was to "make Japan a proper place by relieving [the great] distress" of the nation.[16] They had a variety of motives—old grudges, empathy for the plight of commoners, self-gratification, expelling the foreigners, simple idealism. They were also divided in many cases by their samurai rank. Many from lower ranks lived in poverty or at least in straitened circumstances and had little possibility of moving up; they harbored a growing resentment against those in upper ranks. In the end, many idealistic loyalists came to see the world in black and white, in simple terms of right and wrong.

These four large social and political groups—the Western envoys, the bakufu and daimyō, the common people, and the imperial loyalists—had different perceptions of Japan's problems and were prompted by a variety of motives. But even so, the tumultuous actions of the bakumatsu period were ad hoc, with people in different groups acting often on the basis of contingencies. Each group had its own historical pattern, but each "was affected by the playing out of the other three."[17]

Revere the Emperor, Expel the Barbarian (*Sonnō-jōi*)

The most volatile group was the loyalists. The earliest was the Mito school, which emphasized the shogun's moral and political responsibility to deal with Japan's crises. Its leading teacher, Aizawa Seishisai (1781–1863), was the advisor to the influential Tokugawa Nariaki (1800–1860), the daimyō of the Mito domain, one of the three most important Tokugawa-related domains, located on the Pacific coast north of Edo. Aizawa was educated in Mito and Edo; in 1820 he opened his own lecture hall in Mito. His most important work, *Shinron* [New Theses], was written in 1825 but not published until 1857—even though copies were widely read in the 1840s and early 1850s.

Aizawa harbored a deep distrust of foreigners, recounting his bitter memories of the Russian probes in the last years of the eighteenth century. Years later, when English whalers ventured into the waters off Mito, Aizawa, thinking that they were Russian, tried to interrogate them; although he could not communicate with them, he sensed their aggressiveness. In *Shinron,* Aizawa argued that Westerners were dangerous not because of their military might but because they would corrupt "[Japanese] commoners through Christianity, cultural assimilation, and economic involvement. . . ."[18] The solution was to reform the bakufu and allow daimyō to build up their own military strength.

Aizawa was the earliest important advocate of *expulsionism,* simply expelling the West—no ifs, ands, or buts about it. His arguments emphasized the special nature of the Japanese nation and the role of the emperor in the mystical body of the state or *kokutai.* He wrote, "Our land of the gods has emerged from the sun, from which it derives it natural vitality. The successors of the sun have occupied the throne from generation to generation, from the beginnings to the very end."[19] Aizawa was a major advocate of *sonnō jōi*—"revere the emperor, expel the barbarian." While he embraced the restoration of the emperor to political control, he never talked about abandoning the shogunate or fomenting a popular movement at the local level. Indeed, Aizawa greatly mistrusted the people. They could never, he argued, be allowed to assume positions of leadership, for invariably "they would act like children and pursue profit, pleasure, and personal luxury at every opportunity."[20]

American with Japanese Courtesan   It is hard to tell from their expressions how this American man and Japanese woman feel about each other. Note the American's big nose and both beard and mustache. These were oddities for Japanese men with their smaller noses and substantial lack of facial hair. Note also the man's shoes with specifically drawn heels, recalling the Japanese belief that American men lacked actual heels and that wearing shoes with heels kept them from falling over. *Source:* American Drinking and Carousing by Utagawa Yoshitora, ca. 1850–1880, Edo period, woodblock print, ink and color on paper, overall 35.4 × 24 cm (13-15/16 × 9-7/16 in). Arthur M. Sackler Gallery, Smithsonian Institution, Washington, D.C., Gift of Ambassador and Mrs. William Leonhart, S1998.93.

Aizawa played a crucial role in Nariaki's career. On the death of the Mito daimyō in 1829, a succession dispute erupted in the absence of a male heir. Aizawa and a number of reformers favored the dead daimyō's brother, Nariaki; they persuaded the shogun of their viewpoint, and Nariaki became daimyō. Aizawa was Nariaki's advisor during the Tempō reforms. He became a general advisor in 1841 and a teacher in a school Nariaki established. Nariaki's political inclinations and policy choices were clearly affected by Aizawa's views. "Highly articulate" and "strongly opinionated," Nariaki "saw his society as being in a state of advanced decay and facing an insidious foreign menace, and he found inactivity intolerable and policy compromise abhorrent."[21] Consequently, Nariaki aggressively undertook reforms in Mito, paying particular attention to bolstering economic and military strength. In the face of Western probes he created new defenses along Mito's coastline, even melting down bells from Buddhist temples to produce cannon. He constantly insisted that the shogun allow all domains to strengthen themselves,

Source: The Views of Tokugawa Nariaki

Tokugawa Nariaki (1800–1860) clearly puts the onus of Japan's future success vis-à-vis foreigners on the shogun and his policies. His memorial shows keen awareness of the Opium War and the difficulties that had beset China. What specifically does he want the shogun to do?

It is my belief that the first and most urgent of our tasks is for the Bakufu to make its choice between peace and war, and having determined its policy to pursue it unwaveringly thereafter. When we consider the respective advantages and disadvantages of war and peace, we find that if we put our trust in war the whole country's morale will be increased and even if we sustain an initial defeat we will in the end expel the foreigner, while if we put our trust in peace, even though things may seem tranquil for a time, the morale of the country will be greatly lowered and we will come in the end to complete collapse. This has been amply demonstrated in the history of China and is a fact that men of intelligence, both past and present, have always known. . . . Now there is not the slightest chance that the feudal lords will complete military preparations, however many years may pass, unless they are set an example in military matters by the Bakufu. . . . On the arrival of the foreign ships recently, all fell into a panic. Some take matters very seriously while foreign ships are actually at anchor here, but once the ships leave and orders are given for them to revert to normal, they all relax once more into idleness and immediately disperse the military equipment which they had hurriedly assembled. It is just as if, regardless of a fire burning beneath the floor of one's house, one neglected all fire-fighting precautions. Indeed, it shows a shameful spirit, I therefore believe that if there be any sign of the Bakufu pursuing the policy of peace, morale will never rise though preparations be pressed forward daily; and the gun-batteries and other preparations made will accordingly be so much ornament, never put to effective use. But if the Bakufu, now and henceforward, shows itself resolute for expulsion, the immediate effect will be to increase ten-fold the morale of the country and to bring about the completion of military preparations without even the necessity for issuing orders. Hesitant as I am to say so, only by so doing will the Shogun be able to fulfil his 'barbarian-expelling' duty and unite the men of every province in carrying out their proper military functions.

Source: Peter Duus, The Japanese Discovery of America, A Brief History with Documents *(New York: Bedford Books, 1997), 103, 105.*

keeping up a continual drumbeat that made him what one historian called "the nation's chief complainer."[22] Because Nariaki's blunt criticism antagonized the shogun, the shogunate retired him and put him under house arrest in 1844; that did not shut him up, however, as he continued to write lengthy letters on policy to Abe Masahiro, the shogun's chief councilor. Nariaki was rehabilitated by 1852 and continued to preach about defense and holding the Western nations at bay. Until his death in 1860, he never deviated from his antiforeign position; in Abe's poll of daimyō after Perry's first visit, he strongly advocated resisting Western demands no matter how great the risk of war.

The other center of *sonnō jōi* thought in the years before Perry's coming was the domain of Chōshū. There Yoshida Shōin emerged in the same roles as Aizawa, whose *Shinron* he had read: as a teacher and proponent of both expulsionism and a strong coastal defense. Brilliant (at the age of ten, he had delivered a lecture at the domain's castle), Yoshida hungered for knowledge of the West. When Perry arrived in 1854, Yoshida rowed out to his ship, hoping to stow away to the United States to study. Taken back to land, he was arrested for trying to emigrate, though he was not executed, as was the usual practice. Perry's coming changed Yoshida's perception: he realized that expulsionism was no longer a viable approach—if it had ever been. " 'In reality,' he wrote in his characteristic shrill hysteria, 'the emergency before our eyes is the greatest illness of the last ten thousand generations.' "[23] The situation required positive action rather than holding on to a system that was becoming increasingly irrelevant. The inability of the shogun to meet the foreign threat and instead acquiesce to foreign demands was almost criminal in its negligence.

Between 1857 and 1859, Yoshida taught at an academy he established at the castle town in Chōshū. There he taught men who would become some of the key leaders of the new post-shogunate Japan: Itō Hirobumi, Yamagata Aritomo, Kido Kōin, and others. Calling for men of high purpose (*shishi*) with "the will to test new conditions by experimenting with political possibilities,"[24] he argued that Japanese must show their resolve by accepting and adopting the new military technology to meet the Western threat. In the last year of his life, he became an outspoken advocate of overthrowing the bakufu-domain system and restoring the emperor to power. He himself emerged as a man of high purpose, joining in an assassination plot against a police official of the shogun. He was captured and executed in 1859; his death for the cause he believed in made him a martyr and subsequently transformed him into an almost mythic figure.

Generally, the debate over national isolation from the 1790s to the mid-1850s had been waged without great urgency. But Perry's trip in 1854 and his apparent readiness to use force changed everything. The treaty with the United States was followed by treaties with Russia, the Netherlands, and France. The issue of how to handle Western demands had become a crisis, and the Mito solution of simple expulsionism, championed by Aizawa and Nariaki, was "outmoded."[25] Because Mito did not accommodate its position to the new reality, its importance in the arena of political decision making diminished.

Domestic Complications

The foreign crisis that dominated the middle to late 1850s was played out against a backdrop of political feuding over the shogunal succession. The twelfth Tokugawa shogun died a few months after Perry's first landing in 1853. His successor was childless, physically ill, and soon died. During the years between 1853 and his death in 1858, policymakers not only had to deal with the Western threat but also had to choose the next shogun. That job fell to the bakufu's head councilor, Hotta Masayoshi, who had succeeded Abe.

There were two main contenders. One was a twelve-year-old daimyō from the Kii domain; he was closest by blood to the main shogunal line and at an age to be manipulated by members of the state council. The other was a political hot potato, the son of Tokugawa Nariaki, called Keiki or Yoshinobu, born in 1837 and generally recognized as a man of great ability. This choice would have raised the status of

Source: Yoshida Shōin's Letter from Prison

Yoshida Shōin (1830–1859), a Chōshū scholar-samurai and teacher of some of the important leaders of the Meiji Restoration, in this 1856 letter sets forth his strong conviction that the shogun had usurped the rightful powers of the emperor. The reference to six hundred years is to the first shogun, Yoritomo, and (at least in Yoshida's eyes) his improperly assuming prerogatives of the emperor. Yao and Shun were mythical Chinese emperors noted for their wisdom and virtue; (Wang) Mang and (Cao) Cao were noted Chinese usurpers. What does Yoshida see as his own role in this period?

. . . I am a subject of the house of Mori. Therefore I bind myself day and night to the service of the house of Mori. The house of Mori is subject to the Emperor. When we are loyal to our Lord, then we are loyal to the Emperor. For over 600 years our Lords have not bound themselves completely to the service of the Emperor. This crime is evident. It is my intention to let him expiate his guilt. But because I am condemned to confinement in the house, I can neither write nor speak with him directly. I can only speak about this with my brother and my parents and I await with patience the occasion to speak about this with the samurai and the loyalists. This opportunity will occur, when—pardoned—I can freely visit those who have the same opinion as I. Then I shall undertake with them: (1) to show to the *shōgun* his crime committed during more than 600 years and to show him his actual duty; (2) to show also to our *daimyō* and all the other *daimyō* their crimes, and (3) to show to the whole bakufu all their crimes in order to make them serve the Emperor. If I am condemned to death before I can realize these things, I cannot help it. If I die in prison, after me another will execute this intention and certainly there will be an occasion for my successors to do this. I should like to write this to you with the following words:

The sincerity of one single man touches the hearts of millions. I hope that you will understand me. By nature, it is repugnant to me to speak lightly about things that touch my innermost heart, but to you alone I confide by thoughts. Observe well how I dedicate my life to it. I know only too well that the Emperor is just as Yao and Shun and that the *shōgun* is just as Mang and Cao. Because I know this, therefore I give myself up to study and cultivate my spirit in order to accomplish someday something grand. I have a reason for not speaking night and day about the crimes of the shōgun. Namely it is in vain when I accuse him, because I am imprisoned. And because I live here without speaking openly of the crimes of the shōgun, therefore I can say that—in a sense—I take part in his crimes. This is also the case with my Lord. Never—even if I should have to die for it—shall I disclose the crimes of others unless I have corrected my own fault. Therefore, until such an occasion arises—as I have told you above—I am satisfied to ponder over these things in my thoughts or to give advice to my acquaintances. If one day I explain the wrongs to my Lord and he does not listen, I shall sacrifice my life in order that he might repent.

Source: David J. Lu, Japan, A Documentary History *(Armonk, NY: M. E. Sharpe, 1996), 299–300.*

Nariaki himself and perhaps even strengthened his antiforeign and pro-emperor policy line. Hotta himself had come to one mind with Ii Naosuke, who supported the opening of Japan and trade with the Western nations. Ii was 180 degrees apart from Nariaki, so he supported the Kii alternative.

Before a decision could be made, however, foreign affairs intruded in the person of Townsend Harris, the first U.S. consul, who had come to his residence (an abandoned temple) in Shimoda in the fall of 1856.

Harris had one main objective: getting a treaty ratified that would provide for trade relations between the United States and Japan. Authorities of the shogunate kept him waiting in Shimoda until late 1857, when Hotta let Harris know that the shogunate was willing to negotiate. Harris basically wanted a treaty identical to those in China's unequal treaty system: ports opened for trade, ambassadorial residence in the capital, extraterritoriality, fixed tariffs.[26] Such a treaty would have a much greater impact on Japan than Perry's. What was Hotta to do? The crucial daimyō were still far apart in their views on how to proceed. Hotta and Ii, among others, believed that the treaty should be signed because there was no realistic alternative. There was also "now a substantial recognition, at least among those close to the centers of power, of the inevitability of foreign trade and diplomatic relations."[27]

Hoping to get the most powerful endorsement for his position, Hotta took a momentous step in the spring of 1858, visiting the emperor in Kyoto to get his approval for the treaty and his choice of shogun—momentous because it brought the emperor questions of foreign policy (which Tokugawa guidelines specifically did not allow) and of shogunal succession (reminding all that the emperor ultimately named and commanded the shogun). Much to Hotta's chagrin, the emperor did not sanction the treaty, saying that, as it was, it would not preserve Japan's national honor. In the end, what Hotta achieved was his own undoing. He lost his key position to Ii Naosuke, who became *tairō,* or regent.

To no one's surprise, Ii selected the young daimyō from Kii. But to the surprise of many, Ii decided on his own, even with the emperor's stated objection, to sign the Harris treaty. His rationale: "Better . . . to act against the Emperor's wishes than to fight a losing war. Nor must the council deny its duty: 'State policy is the responsibility of the Bakufu, which in an emergency must take such administrative action as seems expedient.'"[28] With every decision in these years, the line and the relationship between emperor and shogun became starker. Japan's foreign policy crisis had begun to bring into bold relief the fractures in Japan's political system.

Later analysts have seen Ii's actions as critical to the fate of the shogunate. Aware of the firestorm that *sonnō jōi* enthusiasts—supporters of the emperor and the antiforeign bloc—would unloose against him for his high-handed actions, Ii launched a preemptive strike against the opposition. Nariaki was put under house arrest; his son, the would-be shogun, was banned from public life; two daimyō were forced to give up the leadership of their domains; and others were arrested, exiled, or executed. This *Ansei purge* lasted into 1859. With it, Ii hoped to stabilize the shogunate, strengthening it as it eliminated or weakened its chief and loudest opponents. Some historians claim that Ii was the shogunal system's last best hope of maintaining power. For a very short time, it seemed that it might work. No less a person than the Emperor Kōmei himself in February 1859 made it clear that what was most important was "greater unity between Court and Bakufu,"[29] a position that men like Nariaki naturally found repugnant. But in the end, Ii's personal rigidity and harshness brought his personal firestorm—in the midst of a snowstorm.

On the morning of March 3, 1860, seventeen samurai from Mito and one from Satsuma attacked Ii's entourage with swords as it neared Edo castle, decapitating Ii. Their rationalization: "Ii had wielded his power willfully and in disregard of 'public opinion and morality'. . . ; it was contrary to the national interest to conclude treaties with foreigners . . . ; in short, 'too much compromise ha[d] been made at the sacrifice of national honor.'"[30] Despite Mito's leadership in the assassination, Mito's star sank quickly. Tokugawa Nariaki died little more than six months after Ii's assassination, and the Mito school of thought declined in importance as Japan moved toward civil war.

TERRORISM AND CIVIL WAR

Japan in the 1860s was drenched in blood. While some continued to hope for an alliance between bakufu and crown, others, in what turned out to be a breakdown of feudal discipline, resorted to their swords in political terror and assassination. Ii's death was the first of many such episodes. Groups of disgruntled

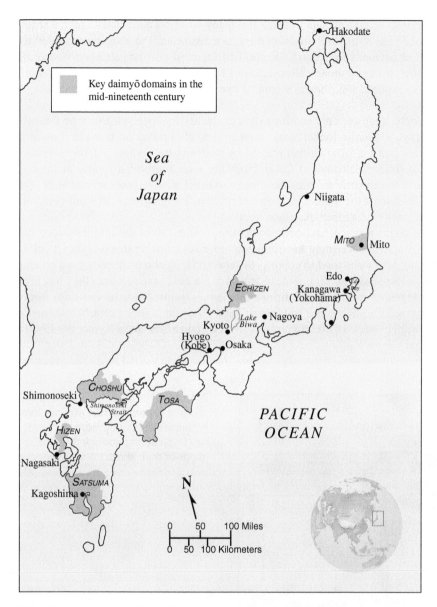

Map 6-2 Japan in the 1860s: Key Daimyō Domains.

sonnō jōi samurai, many of them middle- and low-ranking, from domains all over Japan, attacked bakufu officials and merchants who were dealing with Westerners. Apparently these samurai thought that their actions might undo the treaties. These men of high purpose attacked Westerners, killing Townsend Harris's Dutch interpreter and two diplomats at the British legation.

Many in the shogunal council believed that the violent extremists had to be controlled and a policy of bakufu and court unity pursued. A symbol of this proposed political unity was a marriage between the emperor's sister and the shogun in 1862. But many powerful daimyō felt that the arrangement would empower a council in Kyoto and diminish their own positions. The shogun responded to their fears by giving in to their demands for reform. He abolished the old alternate attendance system, which would allow the daimyō to spend money allocated for that system on military defense and preparedness instead. This also reduced the Shogun's control over the daimyō, ultimately continuing to weaken the shogun politically.

Unfortunately, these steps did nothing to halt the increasing social violence. An English merchant visiting from Shanghai, Charles Richardson, was murdered after riding his horse in front of a procession of the daimyō from Satsuma. The British reacted by bombing the domain's castle town of Kagoshima in 1863. Loyalists from the domain of Chōshū together with antiforeign figures at the imperial court in Kyoto persuaded the emperor to order the shogun to expel all foreigners immediately. The shogun traveled to Kyoto to discuss the order with the emperor, thus bringing once off-limit policy questions to the emperor and further eroding the bakuhan system.

When the shogun realized that he could not change the minds of the antiforeign court elements, he returned to Edo, implicitly accepting the expulsion order yet knowing that carrying it out was impossible. Only the domain of Chōshū tried to comply. In June 1863, its shore batteries fired on an American ship passing through the Straits of Shimonoseki, and over the next several weeks they had French and Dutch ships in their sights as well. Like the British retaliating against Satsuma, the ships from these Western countries destroyed Chōshū's shore batteries in 1864. The court, seeing clearly that foreigners could not be expelled forcibly, ordered Chōshū activists and their court allies out of Kyoto. But Chōshū would not be

Watching the Smoke-Belching Ship   On shore, a Japanese man and boy look at the American ship; early fears were that Americans had been strong enough to harness the volcanoes to power their ships.

so easily put down; its radical leaders launched another attack on Kyoto to seize the emperor and extricate him from Tokugawa control. They were defeated in January 1865 by forces from Satsuma and other domains still apparently loyal to the shogun. But soon the whole context changed.

The Bases of Chōshū's and Satsuma's Power

Foremost among the daimyō who looked ever more supportively at the emperor in the mid-1860s were the leaders of Chōshū and Satsuma. Both were tozama daimyō, defeated at Sekigahara. Chōshū had lost the most in that decisive battle; the second greatest feudal power at the time, it had been reduced from nine to two provinces. Though now more than two and a half centuries in the past, the memory of the defeat at the hands of the Tokugawa was kept alive. It is said that a particular ritual marked every New Year's Day: at dawn Chōshū officials went to the daimyō and asked whether the time had come to begin the struggle against the bakufu. The standard daimyō reply up to the 1860s had been that the time was not yet right. It was also reported that mothers in Chōshū instructed their sons to sleep with their feet to the east as an insult to the bakufu in Edo and, even as they dreamed, to never forget the humiliating defeat by the Tokugawa at Sekigahara. Satsuma also kept alive its bitterness: every year on the anniversary of the battle of Sekigahara, castle town samurai donned armor and traveled to a temple near Kagoshima to meditate on the battle. On their return to the Kagoshima, they were read an account of the battle itself.

These bitter rituals kept historical wounds raw, but the two domains had more than rancor propelling them into an antishogunate leadership. Economically, they were relatively well off. As we have seen, Satsuma fared better than other domains in the Tempō reforms by strengthening the daimyō's commercial monopolies, especially its monopoly over sugar cane, and by taxing its trade. Its trade with China also increased its economic success. In the 1860s Satsuma was the second richest domain. Chōshū benefited from an institution it set up in 1762, in essence an investment office to provide emergency funds for the domain. Chōshū was thereby able to build a surplus in its treasury to use in modernizing its military. It was the fourth or fifth richest domain in the 1860s. In addition, both Satsuma and Chōshū had larger armies than the shogun had permitted. Chōshū had eleven thousand, almost double the permitted number (the bakufu itself had only about thirty thousand). Satsuma had twenty-eight thousand, or one samurai for every three commoners; the ratio in most other domains was closer to one samurai for every seventeen commoners. This situation points to the decay of the strict bakuhan regulations from the early Tokugawa period.

One other historical reality perhaps helped prompt Chōshū to support the emperor. Even before the Tokugawa victory in the early seventeenth century, Chōshū had had special ties to the imperial court. The daimyō had originally come from the Kyoto official class. During the sixteenth century, when the financial situation of the imperial court was miserable, Chōshū contributed to it annually. Because of these pre-existing ties to the emperor, the Tokugawa permitted the Chōshū daimyō to pay his respects to the emperor in the alternate attendance trips from southwest Honshu to Edo; he was the only daimyō allowed to have such contact with the emperor.

Finally, Chōshū proved to be almost revolutionary in its approach to the dangers and opportunities of the time. In the late 1850s its leaders began to form rifle units, structuring them as joint samurai-peasant units in 1863. Peasant soldiers were unheard of in the Tokugawa system. Studies have shown that many of these units were led by young men of relatively low social status with radical ideas about the bakuhan system and Japan's political future. A number of officers in these mixed units were Yoshida Shōin's student disciples. A prime example was Itō Hirobumi, who would become a key leader in the new Japan. Itō had been born into a peasant family but was adopted by a family with the lowest samurai rank. With no stake in the existing system and potentially everything to gain from something new, he and men like him were ready to dispense with the status quo.

The End Game

The shogunate, we have seen, had bested Chōshū in the 1864 military campaign (when Satsuma sided with the shogunate). But young men like Itō were not ready to be kept in subjection by the shogunate. While the shogun's orders had included abolition of the mixed units (which had attacked Kyoto), in Chōshū these units, now outraged, began armed resistance against their daimyō. Winning a long string of military victories, they seized the domain's castle town in March 1865 and set up a new regime with a faction committed to reform. Their victory in this brief Chōshū civil war has been seen by at least one scholar as "a turning point in Japanese social and military history. Samurai of humble birth had defied with impunity their domain government, and mixed peasant and samurai forces had proved

Source: Sakamoto Ryōma's Plan for the Post-shogunate Political System

Sakamoto Ryōma (1834–1867) played a crucial role in the last days of the bakumatsu period but did not live to see the new system that he here envisioned. What is the tone of his presentation? What were the chief features of the new system, and how much did they diverge from practices under the shogunate?

1. Political power of the entire country should be returned to the Imperial Court, and all decrees should be issued by the Court.

2. There should be established an Upper and a Lower Legislative House which should participate in making decisions pertaining to all governmental policies. All governmental policies should be decided on the basis of deliberation openly arrived at.

3. Men of ability among the court nobles, *daimyō* and people at large should be appointed as councillors and receive appropriate offices and titles. Those sinecure positions of the past should be abolished.

4. In dealing with foreign countries, appropriate regulations should be newly established which would take into account broadly the deliberation openly arrived at.

5. The laws and regulations . . . of earlier times should be scrutinized [to preserve only those provisions which are still applicable], and a great new code to last forever should be promulgated.

6. The navy should be properly expanded.

7. An Imperial Guard [directly controlled by the Imperial Court, and not dependent on the *bakufu* or various *han*] should be set up to defend the capital.

8. There should be a law established to equalize the value of gold, silver and goods with those of foreign countries.

The above eight-point program is proposed after due consideration of the present state of affairs in the nation. When this is proclaimed both internally and externally to all the countries, it becomes inconceivable to think of engaging in the urgent talk of alleviating the current crisis outside of this program. If with determination these policies are carried out, the fortunes of His Majesty will be restored, national strength will increase, and it will not be difficult to attain the position of equality with all other nations. We pray that based on the enlightened and righteous reason . . . , the Imperial Government will act decisively to undertake the path of renewal and reform of the country.

Source: David J. Lu, Japan, A Documentary History (Armonk, NY: M. E. Sharpe, 1996), 301–2.

superior to its aristocratic, class army."[31] The shogunate reacted to this turn of events by sending its army to Chōshū in the late summer of 1866, in essence to teach it a lesson and bring it back into line. But this time Satsuma refused to join the shogunate's forces, and with a much weaker force, the shogunate had to sue for peace in October. The fact was that in March 1866, Chōshū and Satsuma had agreed to an alliance of sorts. What had brought these old competing forces together?

The shogunate had weakened notably after the death of Ii Naosuke. Aware of the situation, its leaders began a program of military reforms and started to discuss basic political reforms as well (including abolishing the feudal domains)—all with a view to strengthening the shogunate. The key advisor here was the French minister to Edo, Leon Roches, who hoped that the policies would redound to the benefit of France. As if this turn of events were not enough to frighten some daimyō, a new, able shogun, Nariaki's son Yoshinobu, came to power in 1866 with the goal of restructuring the shogunate into a centralized national government. The specter of a new, powerful shogunate bolstered by military and political modernization was threatening to the daimyō of Satsuma and Chōshū. Against this backdrop of perceived threat, in the spring of 1866 a samurai from the domain of Tosa on the island of Shikoku, Sakamoto Ryōma, mediated a secret agreement between Satsuma and Chōshū that promised mutual support in the event of a bakufu attack. Thus, when the shogunate's forces attacked Chōshū in 1866, Satsuma was bound by this agreement not to join Edo's army. The shogunate's defeat by Chōshū forces demonstrated that the Tokugawa regime was living on borrowed time.

But how would the final defeat come, and what would follow? Tensions among the people in central Japan in the *ee ja nai ka* movement were perhaps greatest in 1867. Though "more appropriate to festival than to fury," this popular hysteria doubtless raised in the minds of leaders and potential leaders questions about what kind of Japan was developing and who would give it shape.[32] By November 1867, Yoshinobu had already approved one plan proposed by Tosa domain's Sakamoto Ryōma. The plan's outline: the shogun would give up his post and return power and sovereignty to the emperor. In place of bakufu rule, power would lie with a bicameral council, a council of lords (court nobles and daimyō), and a council composed of lower-ranking samurai and commoners. The shogun would continue to hold his land and play an important role in the upper council.

But Satsuma and Chōshū and their allies would not hear of it. In December 1867 their armies neared Kyoto. On January 3, 1868, they seized the imperial palace and had the new Meiji emperor declare an imperial restoration. The Tokugawa shogunate was over, but the shogun and his diehard supporters fought on until the spring of 1869 in what is called the *Boshin* (the name of the year) civil war. Battles ranging from Kyoto to Hakodate on the island of Hokkaido killed between three and four thousand.

THE RESTORATION'S MEANING

What occurred in late 1860s Japan came in the name of restoring the (fictional) past, that is, a Japan controlled and administered by the emperor. In fact, however, except for a few scattered years over the last thousand, the emperor had always reigned but never ruled.[33] This restoration would be no different, with the leaders of the forces that had toppled the shogun emerging as the key power holders. Their use of the term *restoration* enabled their success by conveying a public relations sense of righting what had gone wrong with the Tokugawa. Theirs was an effort to change the present (and the future) in the name of the past. The restoration was neither a class struggle nor a mass movement; rather, it was an effort of elites, though many were in the lower echelons of the samurai, to replace those above them.

Statue of Sakamoto Ryōma   A loyalist samurai from the domain of Tosa, Sakamoto Ryōma played a pivotal part in helping to shape the alliance that overthrew the shogun. He set forth an eight-point program of principles on which a new regime should be based (see Source 6-6). A man of great promise, he was assassinated in November 1867 at the age of thirty-three.

These leaders were generally young, "men of modest rank but immodest self-assurance, who gloried in the opportunity to establish for themselves, their friends, and their domain a visibility that had been denied them" by the strict hierarchy of the bakuhan system.[34] Though acting in the name of the past, they were not tied to the past. Indeed, their relative youthfulness and their low to middle social standing made them all the more likely to act decisively and in new ways. From Chōshū, there were Itō Hirobumi (in 1868, twenty seven years old) and Kido Kōin (thirty five), both students of Yoshida Shōin; Inoue Kaoru (thirty two), a middle-ranking samurai who, with Itō, had studied in London in 1863–1864; and Yamagata Aritomo (thirty), a foot soldier ranking beneath the samurai who had risen to head Chōshū's mixed units. From Satsuma came Ōkubo Toshimichi (thirty eight) and Saigō Takamori (forty), both middle-ranking samurai who were the main leaders in the Satsuma domain from 1864 on. Men from these two domains tended to dominate the main political decision-making bodies almost until World War II.

Finally, it is important to note that the ultimate goal of these men—a strong nation that could play a proud role in the world—was also the goal of those who, at the last, had supported the Tokugawa. The contribution of the bakumatsu period to Japanese history was thus crucial. In fifteen short years, the experience changed the worldviews of the men who would lead the Meiji Revolution—from conservatives who were driven to expel the Western nations to eager learners and borrowers from the West.

Source: The American Dance, or Watching "So Many White Mice"

Muragaki Norimasa (1813–1880) was vice ambassador on the shogunate's 1860 mission to the United States. In his diary he recorded this account of a dinner dance given at the home of U.S. Secretary of State Lewis Cass. What is his reaction to what he saw? What does he note as the chief difference between Japanese and American cultures?

Upon entering Secretary Cass's residence, we found, to our great surprise, that its entrance hall, passages, and rooms were simply packed with several hundreds of ladies and gentlemen. Under chandeliers of many gas lamps, with their brilliant light reflected by innumerable mirrors and glassware, the entire place was illuminated as bright as day, being almost breath-taking. We somehow managed to make our way through the crowd to the room where Secretary of State Cass and his family stood, and were greeted by them in a most cordial manner. Even his grand-children came to shake hands with us. As we sat on the chairs, every one in the room came also to take our hands; as their greetings were not interpreted, we did not understand at all what was said, but stood there looking on this scene of confusion smilingly. . . .

. . . After dinner, we were ushered into another large room, the floor of which was covered with smooth boards. In one corner, music was played on instruments which looked like violins. Officers in uniform with epaulets and swords and ladies dressed in *robes décolletées* of light white material and wide skirts began, couple by couple, moving round the room, walking on tiptoe to the tune of the music. They went round and round as nimbly as so many white mice, on their monotonous walk, without making fluttering gestures with their hands even. I was quite amused to watch the way in which the ladies' voluminous skirts spread to an enormous proportion, as their wearers took quick turns. Upon our inquiring, we were told that this was what is called a "waltz," and that even officials of high rank and elderly ladies, as well as young people, were very fond of this pastime. The dancers went for drinks and light refreshments in the other room, and came back for another dance. This, we were told, would continue all night. We stood there gaping at this amazing sight such as we had never seen or dreamed of. . . . Although taking into consideration, the very fact that this nation attaches no importance to decorum and formalities, it seemed to me a little odd that the Prime Minister should issue an invitation to the foreign ambassadors. However, there would be no end to our getting embarrassed, should we allow ourselves to be disconcerted by minor transgressions on our sense of propriety. I felt, however, greatly comforted, when I was brought to a full realization of the fact that with this nation, the basic precept of life was drawn from neither loyalty nor etiquette, but from the very spirit of friendliness.

Source: Peter Duus, The Japanese Discovery of America, A Brief History with Documents *(New York: Bedford Books, 1997), 155–56.*

CHRONOLOGY

1790s — Russian ships in Japanese waters

1820s–1840s — British and American presence around Japan

1837 — Rebellion of Ōshio Heihachirō

1853 — Arrival of Commodore Matthew Perry

1854 — Perry returns; the Treaty of Kanagawa

1853–1868 — Bakumatsu period

1858 — Harris Treaty

1859 — Execution of Yoshida Shōin

1860 — Assassination of the accommodationist Ii Naosuke

1864 — Western ships destroy Chōshū shore batteries that had attacked them in 1863

1866 — Chōshū-Satsuma alliance

1867 — Peak of *ee ja nai ka* movement

1868 — Meiji Restoration

SUGGESTED READINGS

Duus, Peter. *The Japanese Discovery of America: A Brief History with Documents*. Boston: Bedford Books, 1997. The excellent documents in this brief book elucidate both Japanese and American viewpoints during this crucial time from the 1840s to the 1870s.

Harootunian, H. D. *Toward Restoration: The Growth of Political Consciousness in Tokugawa Japan*. Berkeley: University of California Press, 1970. A classic study of the important strains of political thought as the restoration neared.

Jansen, Marius. *Sakamoto Ryōma and the Meiji Restoration*. Stanford, CA: Stanford University Press, 1961. An important study of this man of high purpose from the domain of Tosa, who played crucial roles in the bakumatsu period.

Wakabayashi, Bob Tadashi. *Anti-Foreignism and Western Learning in Early-Modern Japan: The New Theses of 1825*. Cambridge, MA: Harvard University Council on East Asian Studies, 1986. An analysis of the context and meaning of Aizawa Seishisai's important work.

Wilson, George M. *Patriots and Redeemers in Japan: Motives in the Meiji Restoration*. Chicago: University of Chicago Press, 1992. A fresh and compelling analysis of the social and political groups who played the leading roles in the restoration drama.

CHAPTER SEVEN

Forging a New Japanese Identity:
The Meiji Revolution

The Meiji Emperor   Dressed in military uniform with epaulettes, the Meiji emperor (r. 1867–1912) took the throne at age fifteen. Yet he stands as the chief symbol of Japan's headlong rush to modernization beginning in the 1870s.

If the pivotal event in modern Japanese history is called a *restoration* (and was actually little more than a coup d'etat), what followed was nothing less than a revolution—an almost total remaking of Japanese society and a complete restructuring of the state and government. The fifteen-year-old taking power as the emperor in the renamed capital of Tokyo is best known by his posthumous name *Meiji*, celebrated during his lifetime "as the motivating force behind the transformation of Japan from an obscure oriental monarchy into a modern nation ranking as one of the great powers."[1] While historians of Japan have always downplayed the political role of the emperor (who reigned but did not rule), the Meiji emperor, while perhaps not initiating policies, played an active political role.

THE CHARTER OATH AND ITS REVOLUTIONARY IMPACT

His first act of major historical importance was his presentation of the Charter Oath on April 7, 1868, only three months after taking the throne. It set down ideals "for those who hoped to make Japan into an enlightened and modern state."[2] In a ceremony studded with Shinto symbols and rituals, the emperor read the oath, which was eventually signed by 767 people:

> *Deliberative assemblies shall be widely established and all matters decided by public discussion.*
>
> *All classes, high and low, shall unite in vigorously carrying out the administration of affairs of state.*
>
> *The common people, no less than the civil and military officials, shall each be allowed to pursue his own calling so that there may be no discontent.*
>
> *Evil customs of the past shall be broken off and everything based on the just laws of nature.*
>
> *Knowledge shall be sought throughout the world so as to strengthen the foundation of imperial rule.*[3]

Source: The Return of the Daimyōs' Domains

One of the remarkable things about the political changes in Japan in the 1860s and 1870s was the complete destruction of the old political system in the name of old traditions. Here Kido Kōin (1833–1877) spells out why the old daimyō domains had to be destroyed. What is his reasoning?

Unless we could discuss the danger inherent at that time, formulate general policies to be followed, destroy the evil customs prevailing in the past seven hundred years, and unify this imperial country, we could not possibly expect to preserve our nation and give security to its millions of people. I could not rest at ease for a moment with this perturbing prospect, and secretly started a discussion leading to the return of feudal domains and census registers. . . . I was especially anxious to clarify and rectify the way of the subjects, and in so doing guide the country to the logical solutions of this urgent issue. I also wanted to have our own Chōshū *han* take a leading role in order to maintain its own existence. However within our *han,* many difficulties were encountered. And such problems were multiplied and compounded in the entire nation, which were hard to describe.

I was aware that if we failed to take advantage of an opportune moment, the country might find itself in utter confusion. So I made up my mind and secretly had an audience with our Lord Tadamasa (Lord of Chōshū). I discussed major trends in the country and shared with him my fear of a great calamity which could take place in the near future. Lord Tadamasa agreed with me and gave me permission to enter into secret conversation with the Satsuma *han.* In this way there was a hopeful beginning. There were many indescribable difficulties in bringing about the return of feudal domains. And, without Lord Tadamasa this difficult task could not have been accomplished.

Source: David J. Lu, Japan: A Documentary History *(Armonk, NY: M. E. Sharp, 1996), 313.*

It is a remarkable statement. Historians have debated what the declaration about deliberative bodies meant. It was probably not a promise of self-government: Japan had no such tradition, though in June 1868, a "constitution" set up a bicameral legislature within a government separated into executive, legislative, and judicial branches. Perhaps an example of the Japanese infatuation with the American model at that time, this effort was abandoned the next year. Most likely the first declaration of the Charter Oath represented the authors' efforts to reassure those not in power that their voices would be heard.

Points 2 through 4 assert nothing less than a social and cultural revolution. Envisioned here is the overthrow of the high classes and officials from their pinnacles of power, with the former low classes—lower samurai, peasants, and merchants—gaining the ability to participate in government and to pursue the occupation or calling of their choice. The promise that unnamed "evil customs of the past shall be broken off" was a blank check for the regime to fill out. During the succeeding eight years, one after another of the Tokugawa institutions and social structures was tossed into history's dustbin. Early in 1869, the domain lands and population registers were returned to the emperor and the daimyō were reappointed as local governors, servants of the emperor. In 1871 the seven-hundred-year-old bakuhan system was destroyed when the daimyō domains were transformed into prefectures to be controlled from the center; feudalism, a system of decentralized government, thus was replaced by a centralized regime.

If the daimyō were eliminated, the samurai were not far behind. The end of the samurai class had its harbinger in the mixed samurai-peasant units in the Chōshū domain before the restoration. In 1869 a vice-minister (from Chōshū) in the Department of Military Affairs proposed a conscription army—a suggestion for which he was assassinated by infuriated samurai. His protégé, Yamagata Aritomo, adopted the proposal and oversaw regulations to initiate a military draft. Conscription went into effect in 1873, drafting every twenty-year-old man without regard to social rank to serve actively for three years and remain in the reserves for four more. This was a devastating blow to the elite Tokugawa class, whose raison d'être was to fight as the legitimate military class. But there was even more reason to end the samurai class and status.

An immense problem for the new government was making financial ends meet, and a huge cause of this difficulty was the need to continue paying samurai stipends. In 1874 under the leadership of Ōkubo Toshimichi, who served as finance minister and home minister, samurai were offered the option of converting their stipends into interest-bearing bonds. When few samurai responded, the conversion was made mandatory in 1876. One writer has called this action "a forced buy-out of the class, paid for by government bonds that would only come due in the future."[4] At the same time, almost adding insult to injury, the government decreed that samurai could no longer wear swords, their traditional mark of status identity. It is probably not surprising that Ōkubo, whose power in the government from 1873 to 1878 was almost supreme, was assassinated by six disgruntled samurai in May 1878.

Other customs of the past were also shucked away. As the new government began its modernization programs, it had to set budgets to support its announced goals and it had to know how much tax money would be flowing. In the Tokugawa, the land tax was based on the harvest, which could obviously vary from year to year and was completely unpredictable; it was assessed in kind (rice) on village communities. In 1873, a new land tax law changed the game: from then on, the tax was based on the value of the land, not the harvest, and taxes were paid in cash and assessed on individuals. The changes made the fiscal system rational and the individual rather than the group accountable.

Yet another dying custom was favoring males and the samurai class in schooling. During the Tokugawa, though some women and nonsamurai attended various schools, males and samurai were the expected students. In 1872 the state decreed universal compulsory elementary school education, without regard to class or gender—the first country in the world to adopt universal compulsory education.[5] The new regulations made it clear: "In no village shall there be a house without learning…, and in no house an individual without learning."[6] These changes in the five years from 1871 to 1876 were revolutionary: abruptly different state and political relationships; a military draft; the end of the samurai class; a new, rationalized tax system; and a changed rationale for and approach to education.

The fifth point of the Charter Oath—seeking knowledge throughout the world—was the key to strengthen the new Japan. Missions to the United States in 1860, to Europe in 1862, and to Europe and the United States from 1871 to 1873, ostensibly for treaty ratification and renegotiation, were really focused on finding models that the Japanese could use to modernize their country. As such, these missions emphasized the identity that the country would assume. The shogunate sponsored the 1860 trip because the Harris treaty mandated it; thus, undertaking the mission did not in the least suggest a willingness to open Japan. (To put this mission into temporal perspective, the ships sailed three weeks before Ii Naosuke was assassinated.) On board were ninety-six foreign experts working for or closely allied with the shogunate and samurai from various domains.

One member of the mission who did favor major changes in the life of the country was Fukuzawa Yukichi, a lower samurai from a small domain in northern Kyushu. As a young man, he had chafed under the feudal restrictions imposed by his low rank. At age twenty in 1855, he had enrolled in an Osaka school for Dutch studies, where he distinguished himself, so that in 1858 he was asked to head his domain's school for Dutch studies in Edo. After the Harris treaty, Fukuzawa turned his sights on the West. He was able to participate in the 1860 mission because of his "manipulation of personal associations and his utilitarian educational achievements."[7] As an observer of life in the United States, Fukuzawa was "a virtual walking antenna, eager to absorb any and all information."[8] Where he found himself at a loss in his several-month stay in San Francisco was in interpreting American culture—"matters of life and social customs and ways of thinking." An example:

*One evening our host said that some ladies and gentlemen were having a dancing
party and that they would be glad to have us attend it. We went. To our dismay we
could not make out what they were doing. The ladies and gentlemen seemed to be
hopping about the room together. As funny as it was, we knew it would be rude to
laugh, and we controlled our expressions with difficulty as the dancing went on.*[9]

In 1862, on an official tour of Europe, Fukuzawa was one of about forty Japanese observers traveling
to Paris, London, Prussia, the Netherlands, Russia, and Portugal. In his autobiography Fukuzawa noted
his approach:

*So in Europe I gave my chief attention to other more immediately interesting things
[than science and technology].*

*For instance, when I saw a hospital, I wanted to know how it was run—who
paid the running expenses; when I visited a bank, I wished to learn how money was
deposited and paid out. By similar first-hand queries, I learned something of the
postal system and the military conscription then in force in France but not in England.
A perplexing institution was representative government.*[10]

Knowledge gained through this approach provided the materials for Fukuzawa's wildly popular 1866
book *Conditions in the West (Seiyōjijō)*. Japanese snatched up over one hundred fifty thousand copies to
read Fukuzawa's descriptions of the West: its life, culture, and institutions.

Japanese Students in London   These five
young men attired in Western suits journeyed to
the United States and Europe on what could
best be called study tours, in which they imbibed
Western culture and studied Western technology.
At the top right is Itō Hirobumi (1841–1909), who
emerged as the most important civilian official in the
1880s and 1890s; at the bottom left is Inoue Kaoru
(1835–1915), who served in a number of cabinet
posts and was a leader in Japanese finance.

Identities: Tsuda Umeko (1864–1929): Educator and Philanthropist

On the Iwakura mission (1871–1873) were forty-eight members on the official delegation and fifty-nine students with ex-samurai family backgrounds; five of these students were girls, ages seven to fifteen. Seven-year-old Tsuda Umeko was born in Tokyo, the daughter of a samurai known as an agricultural specialist and a progressive thinker who had traveled to the United States in 1867 as an interpreter with an official delegation. It is said that she carried her doll with her on board the ship. The purpose of including females on the mission was to cultivate Western ways so that girls could become models of ideal womanhood and help Japan enter the modern world.

Tsuda stayed in Washington, D.C., for eleven years with the secretary of the Japanese legation, Charles Lanman, and his wife. There she asked to be baptized and became a Christian. She attended the Georgetown Collegiate Institute and the Archer Institute in Washington. Her stay in the United States at such an early, formative age had the effect of separating her from Japanese culture. On her return, Tsuda barely spoke Japanese and had difficulty adjusting to Japanese food and even tatami mats. She was especially shocked at the dependence of Japanese women on men.

Because she had been the product of Westernization (as opposed to modernization), on her return to Japan in 1882 she was bemused by the conservative turn away from Western thought and commodities. She wrote,

"A few years ago everything foreign was liked, and the cry was progress . . . . Now Japanese things are being put ahead, and everything foreign is not approved of . . . ."[1] For a while Tsuda served as the English tutor in Itō Hirobumi's household, and in 1885 she began to teach English to the daughters of former samurai at the Peeresses School. In 1889 she received a grant to study biology at Bryn Mawr College in Philadelphia, where she received her undergraduate degree. She returned to the Peeresses School on her return to Japan and taught as well at Tokyo Women's Normal School.

In 1900 she set up her own school, Tsuda's Women's College of Tokyo, with the stated goal of improving the status of women. It remained a premier institution for women's education into the twenty-first century. Tsuda was also heralded as an important philanthropist, making it possible for more women to attend college and university through fellowship funds that she founded.

Yet, for all her progressive thoughts and actions, Tsuda remained grounded in the basic Japanese cultural conservatism that was a hallmark of Meiji intellectual, social, and political leaders. Despite her desire to improve women's status, she never supported women's suffrage. She also refused to support an organization, the Bluestocking Society, that challenged patriarchal leadership in Japanese society and, in a literary journal, probed the desire of women for love and sexuality.

[1] *Peter Duus,* Modern Japan *(Boston: Houghton Mifflin, 1998), 116.*

In addition to the 1860 and 1862 missions abroad, the shogunate sponsored such missions every year from 1864 to 1868: in 1864, 1867, and 1868 to France; in 1865 to England and France; and in 1866 to Russia. All but one had the ostensible purpose of diplomatic negotiations; that one, in 1865, was designed to gain information and establish connections to open a foundry and a shipyard. All of them, however, contributed to the making of the new Japan by providing many eyewitness experiences in Western countries, thereby revealing to the Japanese modernizing possibilities and options (see Identities).

Probably the most famous mission was that led by Iwakura Tomomi, a court noble who had sided with antishogunate forces after 1858. From 1871 to 1873, he led a forty-eight-member delegation, including top-ranking government officials—Kido Kōin, Ōkubo Toshimichi, and Itō Hirobumi—to twelve countries. About 20 percent of the mission's time was spent in the United States, where the group traveled cross-country from California to the East Coast via Chicago. Its stated purpose was to renegotiate the unequal treaties with the Western nations, but its unstated primary goal was to allow the delegates to see for themselves the conditions in the West and to determine which models of modernization Japan might borrow. In addition to these official missions, by the early 1870s there were about two hundred students studying in Western countries, many on government scholarships and some on their own.

In the early years of the Meiji regime, the government and political and social elites threw themselves into studying and copying the West, trying to discover the secrets of Western power and wealth. Uncertain where those secrets lay, Japanese borrowed indiscriminately: Might those secrets lay in Western-style clothes? Or haircuts? Or umbrellas? Could they be in Western hygienic practices? The Western calendar? Eating beef? Western political forms? Western architectural styles? Ballroom dancing? Growing beards? Japanese were also convinced that they must stop doing those things that would evoke criticism from Westerners and feelings of shame: mixed bathing of the sexes, pornography, abortion, and tattooing were forbidden. In these early years, Japanese things were rejected in favor of Western things. There was even discussion about establishing an official policy of intermarriage with Caucasians in order to "better" the Japanese race.

THE SATSUMA REBELLION

A backlash against the Meiji regime came in a rebellion in 1877, led by former samurai who did not want their way of life based on *bushidō* to perish. In the early 1870s, there had been a falling out among leaders of the central government, most often called *oligarchs* in this system of joint rule. The issue at stake was Japanese policy toward Korea. When Japan tried to open Korea in 1872, Japanese envoys had been turned away and insulted. A key figure in the affair was Saigō Takamori from the Satsuma domain, who had been an important leader in overthrowing the shogunate. "Always an idealist and a man of action, he deplored the gradual degradation of the warriors as a class."[11] He was also jealous of other oligarchs, in particular Ōkubo, Kido, and Itō, all on the Iwakura mission from 1871 to 1873. Those on the mission had gotten Saigō and those remaining in Japan to promise that no important policy changes would be undertaken while the mission was abroad.

Saigō, however, now advocated an invasion of Korea to punish its insulting conduct and to hearten and benefit the dispossessed samurai by having them fight and gain land. When those on the Iwakura mission learned of the possible military action, they hurried home to get the emperor to issue an order preventing war. Enraged, Saigō withdrew from the government to his home in the former Satsuma domain. Other pro-war government officials also resigned, notably Itagaki Taisuke, whose home was the former domain of Tosa on the southern coast of Shikoku. Thus, the oligarchy that had emerged after the overthrow of the shogunate had fractured.

Statue of Saigō Takamori   Saigō Takamori (1828–1877) led the only large insurrection against the Meiji oligarchs. Upset by the overthrow of the samurai class, he was also personally disgruntled over various policies of the Tokyo government. Today he is celebrated as a national hero.

Saigō let his psychic and political wounds fester. He and his supporters resented the commutation of samurai stipends into bonds and were enraged by the government's order to samurai to stop wearing swords. They resented the power that Ōkubo (also from the former Satsuma domain) had amassed in the government. Then came the straw that broke the camel's back: the government, aware of the potential instability in the area, ordered that the military's ammunition stored in Kagoshima, the capital of the prefecture, be moved to a more secure district. Saigō, pushed by his subordinates, reacted by seizing the ammunition depots and marching fifteen thousand men to Kumamoto, where they besieged imperial troops in the garrison there. The government's reaction pointed to the seriousness of the situation. It dispatched all of its new conscript army (thirty-two thousand men) with its reserve forces (ten thousand men) to Kumamoto. Saigō and his forces held out for nine months, making the episode an expensive one for the new government. In the end, Saigō, the unyielding samurai, committed seppuku. The government suppression of the Satsuma Rebellion was a milestone in the making of modern Japan. The largest challenge to the government throughout the Meiji period, it proved that an army of draftees could beat an army of the old samurai class and it ended the samurai challenge to the new regime. Finally, it allowed the government to move on to other difficult challenges.

THE PEOPLE'S RIGHTS MOVEMENT AND THE TURN TO REPRESENTATIVE GOVERNMENT

While Saigō's disaffection had led to outright rebellion, Itagaki's took the form of political organizing, a striking departure from tradition since it was generally seen in East Asian cultures as subversive. In 1874, his newly formed political association called for the establishment of a national assembly to end government

Source: Yamagata's Letter to Saigō Takamori

In September 1877, Yamagata Aritomo (1838–1922), the architect of the modern Japanese conscript army, sent this letter to Saigō, the leader of the Satsuma Rebellion. What was the purpose of the letter even though Yamagata never spelled it out explicitly?

. . . How worthy of compassion your position is! I grieve over your misfortune all the more intensely because I have a sympathetic understanding of you . . . .

Several months have already passed since hostilities began. There have been many hundred casualties every day. Kinsmen are killing one another. Friends are fighting against one another. Never has there been fought a more bloody internecine war that is against all humanity. And no soldier on either side has any grudge against the other. His Majesty's soldiers say that they are fighting in order to fulfill their military duties, while your Satsuma men are, in their own words, fighting for the sake of Saigō . . . .

But it is evident that the Satsuma men cannot hope to accomplish their purpose, for almost all the bravest of your officers have been killed or wounded . . . . I earnestly entreat you to make the best of the sad situation yourself as early as you can, so as, on the one hand, to prove that the present disturbance is not of your original intention and, on the other, to see to it that you may put an end to the casualties on both sides immediately. If you can successfully work out remedial measures, hostilities will soon come to an end.

. . . I shall be very happy if you would enter a little into my feelings. I have written this, repressing my tears, though writing cannot express all that is in my mind.

Source: Ivan Morris, The Nobility of Failure *(New York: Farrar, Straus, and Giroux, 1988, reissue), 266.*

control by a few oligarchs. However, Itagaki, always the opportunist, was no democrat; he recommended that the national assembly have restricted powers and that the vote should go only "to the samurai and the rich farmers and merchants."[12] While those in power rejected the proposal, they did offer a commitment in the emperor's name that a national assembly would be established in due time. Many historians suggest that the oligarchs, for all their conservative bent, actually considered some form of representative government early on. Some believed that constitutional representative institutions were one source of the power of Western states and that Japan could similarly benefit by setting up its own. Some saw the establishment of a constitutional government as a worldwide trend and believed that Japan should strive to be on the crest of that global wave. Others pointed out that adopting such a government would prove to the West that Japan was a stable modernizing state for which unequal treaties were inappropriate.

The government took a huge step in moving to representative forms with the establishment in 1879 of elected prefectural assemblies. They were not perfect representative assemblies, to be sure: the franchise was limited to males who paid a certain amount of land tax; their powers were limited to certain arenas; and prefectural governors could veto their decisions and even dissolve them. But they were the first elected political assemblies in the non-Western world and were effective in helping rural elites to participate in the movement toward parliamentary government.

In the late 1870s, Itagaki and others, inspired by such recently translated Western works as Mill's *On Liberty* and Rousseau's *Social Contract,* began to call for the realization of *people's rights.* Over six hundred local political associations were organized; speakers fanned out across the country to make passionate pleas in speeches at schools and temples; and newspapers sprang up to demand popular rights. At this time, Japan was little more than a decade away from the bloody bakumatsu experience of attack and assassination. The line between legitimate political dissent and violence was still unclear. Headlines such as "Freedom Must Be Bought with Fresh Blood" or "Tyrannical Officials Must Be Assassinated" indicated to the oligarchs that danger lurked in calls for people's rights. A letter from Yamagata to Itō put it this way: "Every day we wait, the evil poison will spread more and more over the provinces, penetrate into the minds of the young, and inevitably produce unfathomable evils."[13] The oligarchy's solution was to try to keep the lid on the movement by announcing repressive press and libel laws to silence newspaper attacks (1875 and 1877) and severe restrictions on public meetings, including requiring police permission for any public gathering and outlawing the participation of policemen, soldiers, teachers, and students in any political activities (1880, 1882, and 1887). Police records show that in 1881, 131 political meetings were broken up and the next year, 282; in addition, many never occurred because the police would not give permission. Arrests (including those of journalists) from 1875 to the mid-1880s generally numbered several hundred every year.

Were the oligarchs attempting to snuff out burgeoning democratic ideas? Many historians believe that the repression stemmed not from opposition to representative institutions but rather from the oligarchs' determination to make the decisions themselves at the time of their own choosing. Believing that they knew better how to strengthen Japan and work toward parliamentary government in a disciplined and deliberate way, they thought that political agitation would lead to political chaos. The oligarchs also took some of the wind out of the sails of the People's Rights Movement by having the emperor announce in October 1881 that he would issue a constitution and establish a national assembly within ten years.

The promise was given following a governmental crisis involving a Hokkaido land development scandal. Oligarch Ōkuma Shigenobu's outrage over other oligarchs' positions on that issue led to his expulsion from the government. From the former domain of Hizen on Kyushu's northwestern coast, Ōkuma, who held various governmental positions in the 1870s and 1880s, had come to be a fervent supporter of British constitutionalism. In 1881 Ōkuma joined with Itagaki in calling for elections to be held in 1882, with the meeting of a parliament the next year and the establishment of a cabinet responsible to the parliament. "Constitutional government is party government, and the struggles between parties are the struggles of principles," Ōkuma wrote.[14] Indeed, Ōkuma's proposal explicitly challenged the domination of the government by men from the former Satsuma and Chōshū domains. Itō and the other oligarchs from those two former domains, and with a more conservative approach, decided that Ōkuma had to go, a departure made somewhat less bitter by the constitutional promise.

The years from 1881 to 1889 saw preparations for constitutional government on many levels. Itō took on the main responsibility for drafting the constitution, hoping to base it on firm Western political theory. In early 1882 he led a constitutional study commission to Europe, traveling first to Berlin, where he encountered and was most impressed by the German constitutional system and its specialists. Shorter visits to Vienna, Paris, and London followed. The actual drafting of the constitution began in 1885, the same year that the cabinet was created with regulations from the Prussian model of 1810. It was a strong executive body composed of the heads of government ministries under a prime minister who coordinated the work of the cabinet; cabinet ministers were clearly subordinated to him. Detailed regulations on the organization of the bureaucracy were also issued in 1885. In 1887 the government adopted the civil service system, also based on the German model. After Itō finished the draft of the constitution in 1888, the government created the Privy Council to study the draft and serve as its highest interpreter.

While Itō studied and wrote, the politically active elites and masses prepared in their own ways. The government's opposition forces worked at organizing political parties. Itagaki, a political activist since the mid-1870s, formed the Liberal Party in 1881; based on a French model, it advocated popular sovereignty and a constitution to be decided on at a national convention. In 1882, the ousted Ōkuma formed the Progressive Party, which championed the British parliamentary model with its focus on a powerful parliament. More moderate than the Liberal Party, the Progressive Party received support from a growing business elite. Both parties supported the emperor.[15]

Beneath the oligarchy and its major political opposition groups was a vast array of political activity. Ad hoc study groups in both urban and rural Japan discussed topics ranging from constitutionalism to agricultural modernization, from political philosophy to economic development, and debated the viability of specific political and economic policies. An especially interesting facet of this growing political activism was the drafting of constitutions by the masses—in rural villages: this truly was a People's Rights Movement, and it shows that the ethos of representative government stretched far beyond Tokyo. One such constitution, found in a farm storehouse in the late 1960s, was more radical than the positions of any of the Japanese political parties. "It included an article giving the national assembly power to 'pass judgment on and revise proposals emanating from the bureaucracy and from the Emperor.' "[16]

THE MEIJI CONSTITUTION

The Meiji Constitution was a gift from the emperor to the Japanese people in 1889. Drafted in the tumultuous years of the people's rights movement, marked as they were by the oligarchy's repression of civil rights, the document was conservative. It was shaped by the attraction of Itō and his allies to the Prussian model.

The emperor was key. The person of the emperor was "sacred and inviolable";[17] the emperor, a descendant of the Sun Goddess and a link in a dynasty unbroken since its founding, held the supreme power of the state. The emperor alone had the right to draft constitutional amendments (this was never done); he exercised all executive authority and had supreme command of the army and navy. Cabinet ministers were responsible individually to the emperor rather than as part of the cabinet.

Issuing the Meiji Constitution The constitution adopted in 1889 was a gift from the emperor to the Japanese people. This triptych woodblock print shows the ceremony for the issuance of the constitution on March 14. It was held in the State Chamber of the new palace. *Source:* Shosai Ginko (Japanese, act. 1874–1897), View of the Issuance of the State Constitution in the State Chamber of the New Imperial Palace, March 2, 1889 (Meiji 22), Ink and color on paper, 14 1/8 × 28 3/8 in. "The Metropolitan Museum of Art, Gift of Lincoln Kirstein, 1959 (JP3233-3235) Photograph © The Metropolitan Museum of Art."

Source: The Meiji Emperor

Journalist A. Morgan Young described the Meiji emperor and his wife, the empress, on their meeting with former U.S. President Ulysses S. Grant in 1879. What trait seems most striking to you? Why?

The emperor stood quite motionless, apparently unobservant or unconscious of the homage that was paid him. He is a young man, with a slender figure, taller than the average Japanese, and about the middle height according to our ideas. He has a striking face, with a mouth and lips that remind you something of the traditional mouth of the Hapsburg family. The forehead is full and narrow, the hair and the light mustache and beard intensely black. The color of the hair darkens what might pass for a swarthy counte-nance at home. The face expressed no feeling whatever, and but for the dark, glowing eye, which was bent full upon the General, you might have taken the imperial group for statues. The empress, at his side, wore the Japanese cos-tume, rich and plain. Her face was very white, and her form slender and almost childlike. Her hair was combed plainly and braided with a golden arrow. The emperor and empress have agreeable faces, the emperor's especially showing firmness and kindness.

Source: Donald Keene, Emperor of Japan: Meiji and His World, 1852–1912 *(New York: Columbia University Press, 2002), 312.*

From 1880 on, the emperor "routinely exercised his powers as emperor," signing off on proposals, attending cabinet meetings (sixty six in 1881), attending lunch meetings to discuss state business, and after 1885 offering his opinions to break cabinet deadlocks.[18] And yet, the reality was not as it appeared. The structure of the government suggests that the emperor was to be removed from the often sullying world of politics. When the cabinet was established, the man who had previously served as chancellor, Sanjō Sane-tomi, took the "lesser post of imperial household minister. The fact that this was not to carry membership in the cabinet underlined the reality of the decision to remove the emperor from an active involvement in politics."[19] Itō Hirobumi, the Meiji emperor's closest advisor, thought that the emperor should be a "symbolic leader whose presence lent authority . . . ."[20] Thus, Itō wanted the emperor to attend cabinet meetings as that symbolic presence of sovereignty. To emphasize the unique position of the emperor, Itō created certain positions that ranked above the cabinet and whose appointees would speak in the emperor's name: the Imperial Household Minister, the Lord Keeper of the Privy Seal (in a revival of an ancient post), and the Privy Council. The real day-to-day power lay with the oligarchs around the emperor. They basically decided policy, and the Meiji emperor rarely if ever opposed their decisions. One further reason Itō's constitution placed so much emphasis on the emperor's absolute power was that the oligarchs, amid powerful opponents, could maintain their extensive power and prerogatives in the emperor's name. In short, the oligarchs used the emperor to achieve their goals.

The Diet (parliament) consisted of two houses, the House of Peers (composed of nobility, imperial appointees, and some elected representatives) and the House of Representatives (elected by adult males who paid national taxes of at least fifteen yen—1.1 percent of the population). So that the Diet would not control the government, the emperor was empowered to end a Diet session at any time and to issue impe-rial ordinances when the Diet was not in session. Finally, to keep the Diet from hamstringing or extorting concessions from the government by not passing an annual budget, the constitution stipulated that if the Diet failed to pass the annual budget, the previous year's budget would automatically go into effect. This supposed government safeguard did not work, for Japan's rapid economic expansion meant that last year's

Source: The Japanese Constitution

The constitution issued in 1889, Japan's first, was a gift to the people from the emperor, who was the locus of sovereignty. Here are the Preamble and the first five articles of Chapter I, "The Emperor." What assumptions are made about the Japanese state in the Preamble? What does the constitution say explicitly about the Japanese emperor? About the role of the people?

PREAMBLE

Having, by virtue of the glories of Our Ancestors, ascended the Throne of a lineal succession unbroken for ages eternal; desiring to promote the welfare of, and to give development to the moral and intellectual faculties of Our beloved subjects, the very same that have been favoured with the benevolent care and affectionate vigilance of our Ancestors; and hoping to maintain the prosperity of the State, in concert with Our people and with their support, We hereby promulgate, in pursuance of Our Imperial Rescript of the 12th day of the 10th month of the 14th year of Meiji, a fundamental law of State, to exhibit the principles, by which We are to be guided in Our conduct, and to point out to what Our descendants and Our subjects and their descendants are forever to conform.

The rights of sovereignty of the State, We have inherited from Our Ancestors, and We shall bequeath them to Our descendants. Neither We nor they shall in future fail to wield them, in accordance with the provisions of the Constitution hereby granted.

We now declare to respect and protect the security of the rights and of the property of Our people, and to secure to them the complete enjoyment of the same, within the extent of the provisions of the present Constitution and of the law.

The Imperial Diet shall first be convoked for the 23rd year of Meiji and the time of its opening shall be the date when the present Constitution comes into force. . . .

CHAPTER I. THE EMPEROR

Article I. The Empire of Japan shall be ruled over by Emperors of the dynasty, which has reigned in an unbroken line of descent for ages past.

Article II. The succession to the throne shall devolve upon male descendants of the Imperial House, according to the provisions of the Imperial House Law.

Article III. The person of the Emperor is sacred and inviolable.

Article IV. The Emperor being the Head of the Empire the rights of sovereignty are invested in him, and the exercises them in accordance with the provisions of the present Constitution.

Article V. The Emperor exercises the legislative power with the consent of the Imperial Diet.

Source: Hugh Borton, Japan's Modern Century *(New York: Ronald Press, 1955), 490–91.*

budget was completely inadequate. The Diet was thus able to use control over the budget to wrest concessions from government executives.

One other political institution of note was the military. As Itō was building up strong civilian executive structures, Yamagata Aritomo set out to structure and strengthen the military as a reliable support for the government. As an administrator, he had taken the lead in 1870 in establishing a conscript army. In 1878 he adopted the German general staff system, in which the chiefs of staff of the army and navy were directly under the emperor's command, unmediated by the civil government or the army and navy ministers. The chiefs of staff also had direct access to the emperor, a prerogative that could (and did) lead to the claim that they were the proper interpreters of the imperial will.

Source: From "Imperial Prescripts to Soldiers and Sailors," 1882

Yamagata Aritomo formally received this rescript from the emperor, though its views were his own. What are the main values that this founder of the modern Japanese army stresses? Which is considered more valuable, unrestrained, self-giving bravery or prudence and self-control?

. . . Soldiers and Sailors, We are your supreme Commander-in-Chief. Our relations with you will be most intimate when We rely upon you as Our limbs and you look up to Us as your head. Whether We are able to guard the Empire, and so prove Ourself worthy of Heaven's blessings and repay the benevolence of Our Ancestors, depends upon the faithful discharge of your duties as soldiers and sailors. If the majesty and power of Our Empire be impaired, do you share with Us the sorrow; if the glory of Our arms shine resplendent, We will share with you the honor. If you all do your duty, and being one with Us in spirit do your utmost for the protection of the state, Our people will long enjoy the blessings of peace, and the might and dignity of Our Empire will shine in the world. As We thus expect much of you, Soldiers and Sailors, We give you the following precepts:

1. The soldier and sailor should consider loyalty their essential duty. Who that is born in this land can be wanting in the spirit of grateful service to it? No soldier or sailor, especially, can be considered efficient unless this spirit be strong within him. . . .

[The second article concerns the respect due to superiors and consideration to be shown inferiors.]

2. The soldier and the sailor should esteem valor. . . . To be incited by mere impetuosity to violent action cannot be called true valor. The soldier and the sailor should have sound discrimination of right and wrong, cultivate self-possession, and form their plans with deliberation. . . .

3. The soldier and the sailor should highly value faithfulness and righteousness. . . . Faithfulness implies the keeping of one's word, and righteousness the fulfilment of one's duty. If then you wish to be faithful and righteous in any thing, you must carefully consider at the outset whether you can accomplish it or not. . . .

4. The soldier and sailor should make simplicity their aim. If you do not make simplicity your aim, you will become effeminate and frivolous and acquire fondness for luxurious and extravagant ways; you will finally grow selfish and sordid and sink to the last degree of baseness, so that neither loyalty nor valor will avail to save you from the contempt of the world. . . .

If you, Soldiers and Sailors, in obedience to Our instruction, will observe and practice these principles and fulfil your duty of grateful service to the country, it will be a source of joy, not to Ourself alone, but to all the people of Japan.

Source: Ryusaku Tsunoda, William Theodore De Bary, and Donald Keene, comps., Sources of Japanese Tradition, Volume II *(New York: Columbia University Press, 1965), 198–200.*

One essential group was left out of the constitution: the oligarchs themselves. They were, of course, behind the scenes and around the emperor, but their continuing existence was crucial for coordinating a regime where the emperor had absolute power on paper but not much in reality; where the Diet had insufficient power to direct the government or control the military; where the military was constrained only by the emperor (really by the oligarchy); and where the officials around the emperor and speaking for him had no grounding in or specific connections to constitutional government. The Meiji Constitution was thus headless. To work, it assumed a strong political leadership that could coordinate and lead. Once the oligarchs began to die off, the political system had to grow a "head" that could direct the state.

THE EARLY YEARS OF THE JAPANESE DIET

During the last two decades of the Meiji emperor's reign, the most important political development related to the Diet was the growth of political parties. When the Diet met, the political parties formed by Itagaki and Ōkuma made their weight felt primarily through their veto power over the budget: this trump card of the oligarchs turned out to be worthless. In the first four years of the Diet (1890–1894), the budget issue often caused the oligarchs to dissolve the Diet. However, in what one historian has called the *second phase* of the evolution of Japanese parliamentary government (1895–1900)—at a time of "rapid expansion of armaments"—the oligarchs saw that they would have to accommodate some of the demands of the Diet. By the turn of the twentieth century, no less a person than Itō Hirobumi (who served as prime minister from 1892 to 1896 and in 1898, 1900, and 1901) recognized that the parties were there to stay and formed his own parliamentary party, the Seiyūkai. This promoted "mutual accommodation" between oligarchy and opposition political parties that led to a more stable basis for political and economic progress.[21] This period of greater balance lasted until 1918. In the meantime (as evidence that all the oligarchs were accepting political parties as bases for their support), a protégé of Yamagata in 1913 formed his own party, the Dōshikai. The parties were thoroughly conservative, with little grounding in grassroots politics. That situation would begin to change in the World War I years and later.

ECONOMIC DEVELOPMENT

The Meiji government did not have to start economic modernization from scratch; the first steps taken during the late Tokugawa had established a base and a direction. Western countries provided both the military challenge and the scientific knowledge (through Dutch studies) for these early modernizers. The first Japanese moves came in strategic industries, specifically the manufacture of arms and shipbuilding. By the time of the Restoration, fourteen domains had shipbuilding or ship repair facilities. To build a modernized base of strategic industries, the Meiji also adopted various patterns and methods used in the Tokugawa. This early industry was owned and managed by government (of specific domains and the shogunate). Leaders of the industrial projects supported and offered training programs to produce qualified personnel, as well as utilizing the expertise of foreign engineers and technicians. The Tokugawa legacy to Meiji modernizers also included "a spirit of enterprise, widespread entrepreneurship, commercial institutions, trading networks, capital savings, . . . financial mechanisms, and [a] responsive labor force."[22]

The Meiji regime responded to the military challenge of Western nations to build (in a key slogan of the times) a "rich country and strong military" (*fukoku kyōhei*). But the Western challenge in the Meiji period was broader than the strategic threat; it included potent economic threats. A commercial treaty between Japan and Western nations in 1866 had set Japan's tariff rate at an average of 5 percent. As waves of cheaply made Western goods flooded into the country, Japan could not raise tariffs to try to keep them out. The result was the destruction of Japan's traditional handicraft cottage industry. Many farmers who had established this industry to provide the margin on which they often lived found their livelihood destroyed.

In addition, the flood of imports led to a wildly unfavorable balance of trade, resulting in the loss of gold and silver bullion. Imports exceeded exports for all but two years from 1867 to 1880. In 1880 Japan had a debt of 135 million yen, with only 5 million yen in bullion available. The government had no choice (since it needed large sums to achieve its goals) but to print paper currency, producing an inflationary

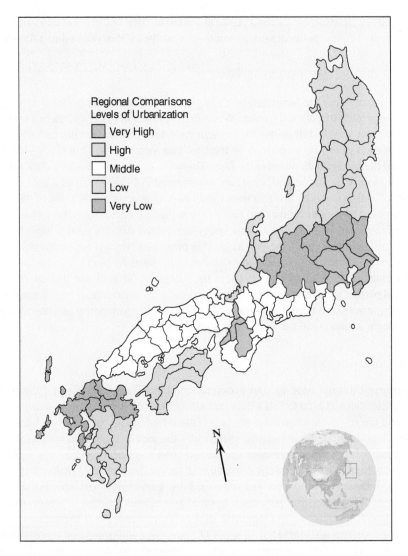

Map 7-1   Degree of Urbanization in Japan, 1875.

spiral in which the value of the currency declined. This meant loss of revenue to the government because 78 percent of that money came from the land tax that was set and remained the same annually. Finally, into the mid-1870s, inflation meant that the samurai who lived on fixed incomes had less money every year, adding to already plummeting samurai morale.

To deal with these problems, Japan had only one way to reduce the waves of imports: to produce its own goods in large enough quantities to decrease the impacts of foreign competition. This became one of the prime objectives of early Meiji industrial policy. A big question was how to accomplish what seemed a daunting task. The government did not blindly follow the government-ownership approach of the Tokugawa; they tried to encourage potential entrepreneurs through measures like extending easy credit and offering

Tokyo Railroad Terminal   For the Japanese, the railroad became the quintessential symbol of modernization in the late nineteenth century. This is the Tokyo terminus of the Tokyo-Yokohama line that was built in 1872 with the advice of foreign engineers.

subsidies and technical assistance, but they were generally unsuccessful. For example, in 1871 the government enlisted wealthy merchants to establish the Kansai Railroad Company, for which money would be raised to construct a twenty-seven-mile line. The government agreed not only to construct and operate the railroad, but also to give the investors a return of 7 percent a year. But even with these lucrative terms, the company raised only half of the capital. The upshot: the company was abolished, and the government built the railroad with government funds.

In the textile industry, private entrepreneurship was relatively successful. But analysts point out that this success came only after the government created the necessary conditions: purchasing the machinery, building model mills to work out the technical and organizational kinks, and offering long-term loans for the importation of spinning equipment. One successful entrepreneur was Shibusawa Eiichi (1840–1931), the son of a prosperous farmer with a cottage industry of indigo dyeing, who traveled to Europe with a delegation in 1867. After the Restoration, he formed a banking and trading company and emerged as an important official in the finance ministry. In 1880 he set up the Osaka Spinning Mill, larger than most mills and with the most up-to-date machines and techniques. He went on to become, in the words of one historian, "one of the nation's greatest entrepreneurs, having a hand in the creation and management of more than one hundred companies."[23]

Major government involvement in industry came in communications and transportation (telegraph and railroads), mining, shipyards, armaments, large-machine building (steam engines and boilers), and construction (girders, cement, glass, and brick). It has been estimated that about 5½ percent (35 million yen) of regular government revenue went to these industries from 1868 to 1881. The rest of its revenue went to samurai

A Foreign Mercantile Firm   This woodblock print triptych shows the busy activity in the salesroom of a foreign mercantile company in Yokohama. *Source:* Hashimoto Sadahide, 1807–1873, Japanese, Edo period, 1861. Woodblock print triptych picture of a sales room in a foreign mercantile firm in Yokohama (detail). Woodblock print; ink and color on paper. Image (assembled): 34.8 cm H × 72.8 cm W (13-11/16 in × 28-11/16 in) Origin: Japan. Freer Gallery of Art and Arthur M. Sackler Gallery, Smithsonian Institution, Washington, D.C., Gift of Ambassador and Mrs. William Leonhard, S1998.44a-c.

payments (which took 50 percent of ordinary revenue), the army and navy, and grants to prefectures. Historians note that the government could not have provided a bigger response without raising the land tax. That was impossible given the desperate financial state of farmers in these years; farmers suffered greatly in the government economic retrenchment from 1881 to 1886 (a policy applauded by businessmen) when farm prices fell drastically in a period of deflation. Indeed, between 1883 and 1890, 11 percent of all peasant landowners lost their land for not paying the land tax, and tenancy increased in general. It is perhaps not surprising that those years were marked by over two hundred peasant outbursts and uprisings. This deflationary cycle, however, produced an industrial boom: the number of cotton spindles in operation increased 100 percent between 1886 and 1890, and mileage of private railroad tracks went from 63 in 1883 to 898 in 1890.

In November 1880 the government announced that it was getting out of the industry-owning business. Although historians have debated the motives of the government decision makers, the consensus seems to be that the government unloaded these industries for financial reasons. Since 1868, the government had spent 745 million yen while taking in only 628 million. The fact was that in 1880 the government had only 7 million yen in specie but outstanding notes of 159 million. The government's prime objective was to stop inflation, that is, to restore the paper currency's value by amassing specie. The sale of government-owned industries was part of the retrenchment plan that buoyed business and industry even as it brought poverty to rural Japan. All in all, government actions in the early Meiji broke ground and provided a foundation for private entrepreneurship that would oversee the majority of Japan's industrial development.

CONSERVATIVE REACTION

The late 1870s and 1880s saw a conservative backlash against Western things and a reemphasis of traditional values. The Japanese initially turned to the U.S. model of school governance, setting up independent school boards in towns and villages; they also adopted the educational philosophy emphasizing the Western value of individual fulfillment. A conservative reaction to these policies was first apparent in an imperial rescript of

1879, which mandated a centralized Ministry of Education and championed a more traditional philosophy of education, that is, "for the sake of the country." It decreed that education's chief goal was moral training that stressed loyalty and filial piety. In 1880, under the direction of retired army officers, military drill was added to the school curriculum. Key Ministry of Education roles included listing the standard textbooks for all subjects and controlling their content. Conservative scholars argued that Western thought and philosophy had many inadequacies and asserted that Japan had to build its own moral system by "retrieving the basic Confucian spirit and updating it with appropriate maxims from Western philosophy."[24]

The oligarchy's efforts to curry favor with the West in order to end the unequal treaty system ignited the anger of conservatives. They were especially outraged by the ballroom dances regularly held at the Rokumeikan, a Victorian-style dance hall constructed in 1883. While the oligarchs had hoped that such dances would demonstrate to foreigners that Japan had made sufficient cultural progress to be treated as an equal, conservatives derided them as immoral. Here is an excerpt from one press report on a dance: A beautiful woman's "bare arms circle the man's neck, and her undulant bosom touches the man's chest, rising and falling with her breathing. Her legs intertwine with the man's like vines on a pine tree . . . with each move he presses her ever more tightly to his body."[25] Conservatives also cringed at how the wives of oligarchs, officials of the Foreign Office, the Imperial Household Ministry, and other government agencies spent time taking dancing lessons. Seen as the last straw or (alternatively) as the apex of Tokyo dance culture was the fancy dress ball held in 1887 at the prime minister's residence, where over four hundred Japanese officials and nobility joined foreign diplomats and their wives. Prime Minister "Itō and his wife. . .were attired as members of the Venetian nobility, and their daughter as an Italian peasant girl."[26] Conservatives were scandalized.

Source: The Imperial Rescript on Education, 1890

Many historians see this rescript, drafted mainly by the Confucian mentor of the emperor, as evidence of a backlash against Japan's heavy borrowing from the West. It stressed traditional Confucian values that had shaped the Japanese identity. In addition to filiality and a general social hierarchy of superiors and subordinates, what other values are especially praised?

Know ye, Our subjects:

Our Imperial Ancestors have founded Our Empire on a basis broad and everlasting, and have deeply and firmly implanted virtue; Our subjects ever united in loyalty and filial piety have from generation to generation illustrated the beauty thereof. This is the glory of the fundamental character of Our Empire, and herein also lies the source of Our education. Ye, Our subjects, be filial to your parents, affectionate to your brothers and sisters; as husbands and wives be harmonious, as friends true; bear yourselves in modesty and moderation; extend your benevolence to all; pursue learning and cultivate arts, and thereby develop intellectual faculties and perfect moral powers; furthermore advance public good and promote common interests; always respect the Constitution and observe the laws; should emergency arise, offer yourselves courageously to the State; and thus guard and maintain the prosperity of Our Imperial Throne coeval with heaven and earth. So shall ye not only be Our good and faithful subjects, but render illustrious the best traditions of your forefathers.

The Way here set forth is indeed the teaching bequeathed by Our Imperial Ancestors, to be observed alike by Their Descendants and the subjects, infallible for all ages and true in all places. It is Our wish to lay it to heart in all reverence, in common with you, Our subjects, that we may all attain to the same virtue.

Source: David J. Lu, Japan: A Documentary History *(Armonk, NY: M. E. Sharpe, 1996), 343–44.*

The conservative response to what was seen as extreme Westernization is perhaps best illustrated by the Imperial Rescript on Education in 1890. Issued by the Meiji emperor, this document stressed Confucian ethics and "loyalty to the sovereign and love of country."[27] It emphasized that among the Japanese there was a common national morality that had grown out of shared origins stretching back to the Sun Goddess. All moral and civic instruction after 1890 was based on this rescript, which hung with the emperor's picture in every schoolroom in the country. There were many reports of school administrators and teachers who risked death in order to retrieve them from burning buildings. One Japanese historian has written that "the Imperial Rescript on Education clearly decreed the end of a fervent 'turn to the West,' whose start [had been] symbolized by the Charter Oath."[28]

JAPAN'S DEALING WITH THE OUTSIDE WORLD

Preeminent among Japan's concerns with the outside world was treaty revision, the main objective of the ill-fated dance offensive. Two elements of the treaties, extraterritoriality and loss of tariff control, most wounded Japan's pride and affected its emerging international role. Early Japanese treaty revision initiatives in the 1873 Iwakura mission were turned down by Western nations—and would only be considered after Japan redrafted its laws to bring them more in line with Western models. Negotiations, which included some concessions by both sides, dragged on sporadically and unsuccessfully during the 1880s while the Japanese recodified their laws.

The issues came to bitter life in an 1886 episode in the waters off Wakayama prefecture south of Osaka. When a British ship, the *Normanton,* sank, the British captain and crew took all the lifeboats and escaped, abandoning twenty-three Japanese to drown. Under extraterritoriality, a British judge in a consular court heard the case and completely cleared the captain and crew of wrongdoing. The Japanese uproars prompted a rehearing—which led to a measly three-month sentence for the captain and no compensation for the victims' families.

By 1890, new Japanese civil commercial and civil codes had been written, and a new criminal code was already in use. Treaty revision became the focus of foreign affairs specialists in 1893 and 1894, with a former foreign minister dispatched to London in the latter year to negotiate with renewed favor. These negotiations were successful, bringing a treaty undoing extraterritoriality and giving Japan control over its tariff in 1899. Comparable treaties with other Western nations were signed in the following months. Through its rapid modernization, the revision and codification of its laws, and its efforts to mollify Western nations, Japan had won release from the unequal treaties in a relatively short forty years (in contrast, they would last almost a century in China).

The late 1880s and early 1890s saw a surge of Japanese nationalism. Japan's other idée fixe in the Meiji period was Korea. We have seen the thwarted desires of key early Meiji leaders like Saigō Takamori to become militarily involved on the Korean peninsula. The motives of those who were ogling Korea were many: to channel samurai anger into battles on another country's soil; to imitate the West's aggressive action in establishing a Japanese empire, thereby keeping out Western powers; and to carry out what some began to see as a mission of Japan, itself seen as linked to the gods, to become a leader on the Asian continent. We have also seen (Chapter 3) Japan's opening of Korea, the decade-long struggle between Japan and China for predominant power in Seoul, and the stunning victory over China in the 1894–1895 war. That victory brought Japan territory (Taiwan) and bitter frustration (when the Triple Intervention took the Liaodong peninsula, ceded to it by China).

The Triple Intervention was a humiliating experience for the Japanese. From their perspective, they had simply imitated the imperialist Joneses; then, when they had beaten China and demanded spoils, France, Germany, and Russia had treated Japan as a parent who slaps his child's hands for taking cookies from a cookie jar. Then, just three years later, adding insult to injury, one of the three—Russia—had seized the Liaodong peninsula to lease it from China in the scramble for concessions. The fact that Japanese leaders had seen themselves as members of the imperialist club made the Triple Intervention seem like diplomatic treachery. Perhaps an exaggeration, but suggestive nevertheless, is the judgment of one historian: "One can make a strong case...that the [Triple Intervention] was the most important single event in recent times which diverted Japan to a policy of nationalistic aggression....Russia, Germany, and France had sown the wind; a half century later, the United Nations were to reap the whirlwind."[29]

The Sino-Japanese war also left Japan the predominant power in Korea. Japan's relationship with Korea was marked by paradox. Though Japanese travelers to Korea noted the similarities between Koreans and Japanese ("their appearance and build," the "structure and grammar of their language," and "their ancient customs"), they argued that

> [i]f you look closely [at the Koreans], they appear to be a bit vacant, their mouths open and their eyes dull, somehow lacking . . . . In the lines of their mouths and faces, you discern a certain looseness. . . . Indeed to put it in the worst terms, one could even say that they are closer to beasts than to human beings.[30]

The openly racist language used by Japanese diplomats and travelers demonstrated their outrageous negativity and arrogant condescension. Korean life, for example, was supposedly marked by filth, squalor, and laziness. Here is a picture of Korea provided by the writer of a travel account called *Korea Behind the Mask*:

> The "defecatory habits" of the Koreans . . . ranked among the wonders of the world. The Koreans showed no reluctance to relieve themselves in the streets, in the front of house gates, in ditches and moats, even in front of the royal palace. The city of Seoul . . . was the "shit capital" of the world.[31]

Korean politics, furthermore, were allegedly steeped in corruption, passivity, and toadyism.

Another Japanese writer described Koreans as "a degenerate people full of lies, bereft of moral sense, weak in endurance and courage, who will never raise themselves up as a civilized people."[32] And here are the remarks of a Japanese newspaperman who visited Korea in 1893: "Their only aspiration, it seems, is to fulfill their animal wants and live out their lives. As long as they are able to get food and clothing and to live a peaceful life, they do not deeply question who it is that rules them."[33]

The drift of these descriptions is clear. The first one animalized and dehumanized the Koreans; once they were dehumanized, it became easier to do anything to them. The second judgment denigrated them as morally degenerate, weak, and incapable of civilizing themselves; therefore, if they were to become civilized, others had to step in to raise them up. The third asserted that they were simpleminded people who, like animals, only needed to fulfill basic needs and desires, had no aspirations, and did not care who ruled them. Such judgments offered Japanese rationalizations on which to hang their aggressive inclinations. Japan could act to change Korea because the Koreas did not care and, in any case, could not do it themselves.

But if the Sino-Japanese War had rid Japan of one competitor on the Korean peninsula, Russia quickly emerged as another. Russia's interests in Korea included timber concessions in the north, gold mines, and coaling stations on an island off Inch'ŏn on the Yellow Sea and off Pusan on the Korea Strait.

Japan was already embittered by Russia's leadership of the Triple Intervention and by its taking its slice of the Chinese melon with a leasehold on the Liaodong peninsula. An effort to stem the increasingly bitter animosity between Russia and Japan came with an agreement in 1898 pledging both countries to maintain Korean independence and promising to consult before sending advisors to Korea (a reprise of the failed Li-Itō convention of 1885). Russia pledged that it would not hamper any Japanese business interests in the country. However, when Japan followed with the request that Russia recognize Japan's paramount position in Korea in exchange for Japan's recognition of a Russian sphere in Manchuria (despite Japan's own deep interest in that area), Russia balked.

The next few years saw proposals and counterproposals between the two countries but to no avail. When Russia absolutely refused to countenance any role for Japan in Manchuria, Japan opted for war, interested as it was in the rich land, timber, mineral, and hydroelectric resources in what was practically frontier territory. Capturing Manchuria in a war would make Japan a large landholder on the Asian mainland and the main power in Northeast Asia. By and large, the Japanese people strongly supported the war and the government as it moved to war. The American ambassador in Tokyo reported that "The Japanese nation is now worked up to a high pitch of excitement, and it is no exaggeration to say that if there is no war it will be a severe disappointment to the Japanese individual of every walk of life."[34] An Imperial Conference in early February 1904 committed the country to war.

Japan declared war on February 10, one day after launching a surprise attack on the Russian naval base at Port Arthur on the tip of the Liaodong peninsula. The most famous battle of the war was the great sea battle near Tsushima Island in the Korea Strait in May 1905. There, in a two-day battle, the superior Japanese navy annihilated the Russian fleet. Bloody land battles also occurred. In the winter of 1905, seven hundred thousand men from the two armies fought a ten-day battle in the snow near Shenyang in Manchuria—the "largest land battle in world history up until that time."[35] Casualty rates were high. Among the two million Russians, approximately forty-five thousand were killed. The Japanese sent four hundred thousand military forces, of which more than eighty-five thousand were killed. Not all Japanese gloried in the victory. Here is a poem by General Nogi Maresuke, commander of the forces that took Port Arthur in a battle where, through his field glasses, he saw two of his sons killed:

> *Imperial troops, a million strong, conquered the arrogant enemy;*
> *But siege and field warfare left a mountain of corpses.*
> *Ashamed, what face can I show to old parents?*
> *How many men have returned this day of triumphal song?*[36]

After the naval victory off Tsushima, the question for Japanese military leaders was whether to continue the war in order to annihilate the Russian army as well. Because such a campaign would have meant another quarter of a million men and huge sums of money, the Japanese leaders favored a negotiated settlement; they approached U.S. President Theodore Roosevelt, who was sympathetic to Japan as the "virile" power in Asia (just as the United States, according to Roosevelt, was the virile power in the Caribbean). The president agreed to mediate the talks, held in Portsmouth, New Hampshire, that produced the Treaty of Portsmouth in September 1905. In the treaty Russia agreed to recognize the paramount position of Japan in Korea; though both countries recognized Chinese sovereignty in Manchuria, Japan took over the Russian leasehold on the Liaodong peninsula (the area involved in the 1895 Triple Intervention) and control of the Russian-built South Manchurian Railroad that ran from Harbin to Dalian and Port Arthur. That opened up southern Manchurian natural resources to the Japanese. Japan also received the southern half of Sakhalin Island north of Hokkaido, known for its oil, coal, forests, and fisheries. The Japanese negotiators had been instructed to seek a large financial indemnity from Russia, but when the issue threatened to end the talks, Roosevelt convinced the Japanese to give up their demands.

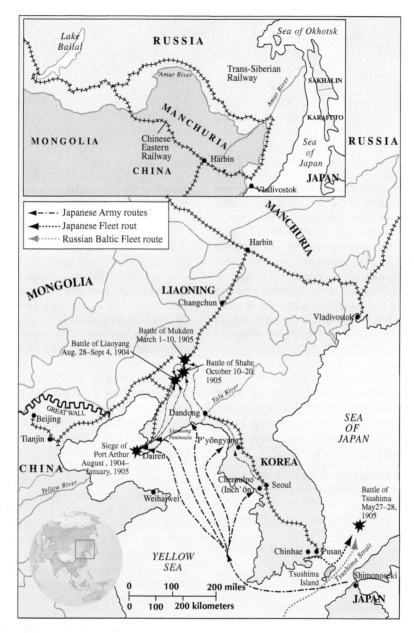

Map 7-2   Campaigns in the Russo-Japanese War.

For his mediation Roosevelt won the 1906 Nobel Peace Prize. But the Japanese were furious with him, for they had expected to be granted even more, specifically the entire island of Sakhalin and a large monetary indemnity. On the day of the signing, opponents of the treaty tried to stage a rally in Tokyo's Hibiya Park. Locked out by police, the ralliers turned into rioters. For two days up to thirty

Source: "One Soldier"

This brief excerpt from a short story by Tayama Katai called "One Soldier" shows that not all Japanese were jingoistic about Japan's involvement in the Russo-Japanese War (in which Tayama himself served). The desperate, lonely death depicted here put the bravado of military victory into somber perspective. Yet, many Japanese considered it blatantly antimilitaristic, and it was frequently published with some passages deleted. The story was written in 1908, yet the style makes it seem more recent. Why is that the case?

When he set out for war, he had dedicated himself body and soul to the service of his country and the Emperor. He had made a fine speech on the theme at his old school in the village. "I have no wish to return alive," he had said. He was in the prime of spirits and health, at that time. He had made that speech, but, of course, he had never expected to die. Beneath it all had been nothing but dreams of victory and glory. Now, for the first time, he was experiencing an uneasiness on the score of death. He really felt that he might not, after all, return alive, and the thought filled him with terror. There was this sickness, this beriberi—and even if he recovered, the war itself was nothing but a vast prison from which, no matter how he struggled and craved for freedom, there was no escape. He recalled some words which his comrade who had been killed had once used to him.

"There's no way out of this hole. We have to be ready to die, and we have to put a good face on it."

. . .

"This pain, this pain, this pain!"

He screamed the words at the top of his voice.

"This pain! Somebody . . . is there no one here?"

The powerful instinct to resist, to live, had fast dwindled, and he was not consciously calling for assistance. He was almost in a stupor. His outbursts were the rustling leaves of leaves disturbed by forces of nature, the voices of waves, the cries of humanity.

"This pain, this pain!"

His voice echoed startlingly in the silence of the room. In this room until about a month ago, officers of the Russian railway guard had lived and slept. When Japanese soldiers first entered it they had found soot-stained images of Christ nailed to the wall. Last winter those officers had looked out through this window at the incessant snowstorms sweeping across the Manchurian plain, but they had drunk vodka. Outside had stood sentries, muffled in furs. They had joked among themselves about the shortcomings of the Japanese army, and they had bragged. In this room, now, sounded the agonized sounds of a dying soldier.

He lay still a moment. The cricket was singing the same melancholy, pleasing song. The late moon had risen over the broad Manchurian plain, the surroundings had become clearer, and the moonlight already illuminated the ground outside the window. He cried again. Moaning, despairing, he writhed on the floor. The buttons on his blouse were torn away, the flesh on his neck and chest was scratched and bloody, his army cap was crushed, the strap still about his chin, and one side of his face was smeared with vomit.

. . .

At dawn, when the doctor arrived from the depot, the soldier had been dead an hour.

Source: Tayama Katai, "One Soldier," in Modern Japanese Literature, *ed. Donald Keene (New York: Grove Press, 1956), 149–50, 155–56, 157.*

At the Meeting for the Treaty of Portsmouth, 1905 Here are the principals who negotiated the Treaty of Portsmouth—the antagonists from Russia and Japan and the mediator, Theodore Roosevelt. They are, from left to right, Sergei Witte (1849–1915), Russian statesmen, finance minister, and premier; Baron Roman Rosen (1847–1922), Russian diplomat; Theodore Roosevelt (1858–1919); Baron Komura Jutarō (1855–1911), Japanese ambassador and foreign minister; and Takahira Kogoro (1854–1926), ambassador to the United States from 1900 to 1909.

thousand people staged violent demonstrations, at the end of which 70 percent of the police boxes in the capital were destroyed, seventeen people were killed, and over a thousand were injured. Disturbances also occurred in Kobe and Yokohama, and demonstrations were held for several months afterward. The toppling of Prime Minister Katsura Tarō and his cabinet in January 1906 was blamed on the treaty and Japanese reactions to it. Militarily victorious the Japanese were, but for the second major military victory in a row they felt cheated by Western nations. The writer Mori Ōgai expressed the feelings of many:

> *Win the war,*
> *And Japan will be denounced as yellow peril.*
> *Lose it,*
> *And she will branded a barbaric land.*[37]

One historian has called the military victory of Japan "electrifying." For the Asian world, it was remarkable: an Asian nation had defeated a European nation, and a nation of Mongoloid peoples had defeated a nation of Caucasians. Not only East Asians but South and Southeast Asians expressed jubilation at the turn of events and the promise of more such victories in the future. Japan would use its victory as a springboard for further action on the continent now ringed with itself and its colonies from Sakhalin in the north to the Ryūkyūs and Taiwan in the south.

CHRONOLOGY

1868	Charter Oath
1871–1873	Iwakura mission
1871	Feudal domains replaced by prefectures
1872	Establishment of universal compulsory elementary education
1873	Conscription instituted; new land tax law
1873–1878	Heyday of Ōkubo Toshimichi
1877	Satsuma Rebellion
1878	Ōkubo assassinated
1879	Establishment of prefectural assemblies
1880	Beginning of the People's Rights Movement
	Government announced that it was selling its industrial holdings
1881	Government crisis leads oligarchs to promise a constitution within a decade
1889	Meiji Constitution adopted
1890	Diet established
	Imperial Rescript on Education
1894–1895	Sino-Japanese War
1895	Triple Intervention
1904–1905	Russo-Japanese War

SUGGESTED READINGS

Duus, Peter. *The Abacus and the Sword: The Japanese Penetration of Korea, 1895–1910*. Berkeley: University of California Press, 1998. This is a compelling and frank analysis of Japan's actions and the motives and attitudes behind them.

Fukuzawa Yukichi. *The Autobiography of Fukuzawa Yukichi*. Translated by Eiichi Kiyooka. New York: Columbia University Press, 1968. This book provides important insights into the mind and life of the man who arguably was the Meiji period's most important intellectual leader and foremost advocate of modernization.

Natsume Soseki. *Kokoro*. Washington, DC: Regnery, 2000. To some critics, this novel is the best in modern Japanese fiction; it probes the nature of social relationships in the midst of modern change.

Ravina, Mark. *The Last Samurai: The Life and Battles of Saigō Takamori*. Hoboken, NJ: Wiley, 2004. Both an excellent biography that reads like a novel and a cogent study of the nineteenth-century history of the Satsuma domain and of bakumatsu period politics.

Rosenstone, Robert. *Mirror in the Shrine: American Encounters with Meiji Japan*. Cambridge, MA: Harvard University Press, 1988. A fascinating description and analysis of three American men and their experiences and reactions to living in Meiji Japan.

CHAPTER EIGHT

"A Sea in a Heavy Gale": Korea, 1724–1905

A Sea in a Heavy Gale
Mountain range after mountain range seems to produce a "wave after wave" appearance on the Korean peninsula. Here the sun rises over the Toham mountains in the southeast.

Korea's geography has dealt it an often bleak hand. For military invaders, it has functioned as a bridge to the Asian continent (in the sixteenth-century invasions of the Japanese leader Hideyoshi) and from the continent (in the thirteenth-century invasion of the Mongols). These events brought servitude and death to tens of thousands of Koreans. The title of this chapter comes from a description of the Korean topography by early Catholic missionaries. Fully 70 percent of the country's territory is mountainous, mostly "massive, rugged mountains"—five major ranges and several smaller ones.[1] The mountains have had a great impact on Korea's history: they prevented easy invasion and conquest (invasions routes were located along the plains in the western part of the peninsula); they were a large obstacle to the development of a national economy; they reduced the arable land to 20 percent of the total land area; and they shaped and maintained local cultures and customs. By the mid-twentieth century, most mountains were deforested.

Korea, shaped like the side view of a rabbit with extended ears, is as large as Michigan and Indiana combined, stretching 600 miles from north to south and 120 to 150 miles from east to west. Five of its seven major rivers flow to the west; its main cities are on those rivers or on the seacoast. Its climate is continental, with winds blowing south from Siberia and east from China. The clearest and perhaps best Korean season is fall, long called the "season of high sky and fat horses." Anthropologists think that the earliest Koreans probably migrated from the plains of Mongolia and Manchuria, the second phase of migration from their original home in Central Asia. The Korean diet emphasizes rice (grown mainly in the western part of the country or on terraced mountains) and seafood—given the peninsula's six thousand miles of coastline. Koreans tend to be taller and sturdier than other Asians.

PATTERNS IN KOREAN HISTORY

One constant influence on Korea was China, which borders Korea on the north. Over their long history, Korean life and thought were generally shaped by Chinese religions and institutions. Early in Korean history, China controlled part of the peninsula's northwest and tried unsuccessfully several centuries later to seize more of it. Korea was the closest tributary state to China. In the Chosŏn dynasty (1392–1910) and especially during China's Ming dynasty (1368–1644), Korea sent four regular tribute missions per year—at the New Year, on the emperor's and crown prince's birthdays, and at the winter solstice. Special tribute missions were sent on the death of the Chinese emperor and the crowning of his successor. From 1637 to 1881,

Korea dispatched 435 tribute missions to China. It is perhaps not surprising, given this adulation, that the phrase used by the Chosŏn kings to describe their China policy was "serving the great."

As one might expect from a state with that viewpoint, Korea borrowed heavily from China. Koreans adopted the Chinese system of written characters. The Chosŏn regime used the Qing dynasty calendar to date its official papers and documents as a sign of its submission to Beijing. Korean governments set up a civil service examination on the Chinese model, starting with Silla in 682. In the Koryŏ dynasty (918–1392), the exam was given 252 times in the years after 958. Korea imported Buddhism, Confucianism, and Daoism from China.

The indigenous Korean religion was shamanism, in which all natural objects were endowed with spirits and evil spirits caused human suffering. In this view, the human world is a middle realm between the sky where deities dwell and the kingdom of the dead below the earth. Shamans, predominantly women, served as mediums between the worlds of humans and spirits, using rituals, music, dance, and divination to connect humans to the spirit world and ultimately alleviate suffering. The path between the realms was called a *worldtree*; shamans used it to contact the deities and call them down. One could pray to the deities in a forest at a sacred tree or by using a special pole. Koreans, unlike other East Asian peoples, were monotheists, believing that one god ruled over all.

Buddhism came to Korea from China in the late fourth century CE, gaining adherents so rapidly that in both the Silla (668–892) and Koryŏ dynasties it was patronized by the kings and became the state religion. In addition to religion, Buddhism brought contributions in art and architecture. In the Koryŏ period, thousands of temples dotted the Korean landscape. Many Buddhist establishments owned vast estates and were wealthy; some even had their own military forces. Popular among the masses was the Pure Land sect in which salvation could be attained quickly and economically by chanting certain phrases. When the Son sect (Zen in Japanese) was introduced, with its emphasis on meditation and sudden enlightenment, it spread among the intellectuals.

In the Silla and Koryŏ dynasties Buddhism and Confucianism coexisted, but Buddhism had the upper hand. One aspect of society proving that Confucianism and its emphasis on patriarchy were not yet deeply embedded in the Korean social structure was the role of women. Three rulers in the Silla dynasty were queens. Though Korean society was by no means a matriarchy, it had more elements of a matrilineal system than did China. Women could own and inherit property and enjoyed equal status with men. On marriage, husbands could move in with their wives and raise a family there. That situation changed in the

Buddhist Temple, Pagoda, and Statue   Buddhism, imported from China, became Korea's dominant religion in the Silla (668–982) and Koryŏ (918–1392) dynasties; it also had great political and social power. Built in 553, this temple is located in Mount Songnisan National Park, northeast of the city of Taejŏn in central South Korea. The statue is the largest bronze statue of the Buddha in Asia. A pagoda houses relics of the Buddha.

Chosŏn dynasty, the first kings of which were Neo-Confucian ideologues who felt that Buddhism should not be the state religion. They set out to transform Korea into a Neo-Confucian state shaped by the ethos of patriarchy. All leaders in state and society were men, and men made the rules. The family and its larger configuration, the patrilineal lineage, were at the heart of society. Lineages held power and prestige, the latter partly through genealogies that they wrote periodically. The practice of primogeniture made the eldest son the heir; no longer would all siblings inherit their parents' estate. In such a system,

> *[t]he daughter did not merit a name before she was betrothed, yet she was a key link in solidifying family alliances. To send a daughter off to another house . . . was to make a strategic choice for one's own family fortunes. To send a daughter who could bring forth sons was even better, for with the birth of the son a woman achieved her designated place in the new family, and got an honored name: so-and-so's mother.*[2]

To uphold Neo-Confucian orthodoxy, laws forbade a widow to remarry after her husband's death, a sharp change from the Koryŏ period, when widows often married again. The rationale was that another marriage would make the woman unchaste to her deceased husband; further, because a marriage was a joining of two different surnames, not simply two people, the widow had to remain loyal to the lineage she married into, for that link was almost a form of property.

The virtue par excellence in Korean families, according to New-Confucianism, was filial piety. A Koryŏ king, Sŏngjong, put it this way: "in governing the country, nothing surpasses filial piety"; it is "the core of all virtues." Filial piety is owed to the older by the younger. In contemporary Korea, filial piety is still valued:

> *Newspapers sing praises of those noted for filial action, and to many South Koreans, the obligation to serve one's elderly parents on a daily basis is central to their existence. . . . Major holidays center on venerating deceased parents and grandparents.*[3]

One historian has pointed to another pattern of Korean society and culture linked to filial piety, positing that the "principle of filial piety was *hierarchy* within a web of duties and obligations" (emphasis added).[4] Indeed, the sense of hierarchy marked all of Korean culture. Familial hierarchy—male to female, old to young—was at the center of daily life. The Korean language itself is structured to reflect hierarchical positioning, with verb endings and conjugations varying according to the speaker's rank relative to that of the person addressed.

In the larger society, Confucianism had four legitimate social ranks: the elite, farmers, artisans, and merchants. The Koreans adopted this ranking, but departed from the Chinese model in two ways. Classes in Korea were hereditary. As long as at least one ancestor in the last four generations had passed the civil service examination and thereby entered the yangban class, a man would inherit the title. Therefore, whereas the system of social mobility in China was meritocratic, in Korea it was a mix—but far more aristocratic than China's. The yangban's hereditary elite status was based on property and lineage; in the late seventeenth century the yangban comprised 9 to 16 percent of the population. This elite was extraordinarily privileged: "To be a yangban male . . . was to be everything and give nothing: not military service, not [corvee] labor, not even taxes. To work with one's hands was beneath him; to possess a lot of slaves, a mark of his station in life."[5]

Peasants were second ranked. They included those who owned and farmed their own land and those who rented from landlords, paying them generally up to 50 percent of the harvest. These freeborn commoners bore the brunt of heavy taxation, including the land tax and various local taxes, as well as military service and labor (required each year for a fixed time period—theoretically not more than six days).

Rank Badge from the Chosŏn Dynasty
Even though it adopted the Chinese civil service system, Korean society was more aristocratic than meritocratic, revealing the high value placed on social status and hierarchy. In 1454 the Chosŏn court established a system of insignias of rank based on that of the Ming dynasty (1368–1644). Civil and military officials wore on the front and back of their official dress square badges showing birds and animals embroidered on silk. The system ended in 1899. Here a crane flies among the clouds; double cranes were worn by officials of the highest three ranks. *Source:* Rank Badge. Choson Dynasty. Colored silk and gold paper, thread on figured silk. 1600–1700. Victoria and albert Museum, London/ Art Resource NY.

Most tenant farmers lived in "grinding poverty."[6] Though early in the Chosŏn dynasty major enterprises were monopolistic state-run guilds, they became local private handicraft concerns following invasions in the sixteenth and seventeenth centuries. These private businesses could at times be pressed into service by the government. Similarly, merchants, at the bottom of the legitimate social order, had private shops; the government licensed some of them in Seoul with monopolies on silk, cotton cloth, thread, ramie cloth, paper goods, and fish products. There was no centralized market and no centralized economy. Villages were for all practical purposes economically self-sufficient, though peddlers existed. The economic system was so fractionalized that the circulation of goods was insufficient to provide relief for many areas in times of famine.

Beneath the legitimate social classes were the lowborn, including hereditary outcasts (*paekchŏng*), almost castelike, of butchers, tanners, beggars, and wicker workers; they were shunned by the legitimate classes, often living in separate, isolated villages. In the early Chosŏn period King Sejong granted them land to integrate them into the farming population, but they continued to practice their occupations and were never able to cast off their lowborn identity. At the bottom of the social order were slaves, who astonishingly, may have comprised up to one-third of the population. One became a slave if he was born to a slave mother, was sold into slavery by his parents, sold himself into slavery, or was an abandoned child. In the late fifteenth century in Seoul alone there were over two hundred thousand slaves, and a report in the late seventeenth century showed that perhaps 75 percent of Seoul's population were slaves. Because slavery was hereditary, the number of slaves continued to swell. There were public slaves owned by the government and private slaves; both could be bought and sold at any time. Some slaves were independent householders whose servitude was expressed in money payments rather than in labor. Scholars have suggested that Korean slavery was not as onerous as, say, African American slavery; escape from slavery and release by owners were not uncommon. The government abolished slavery in 1800, but yangban families had household slaves up to the twentieth century. It is said that even up to the 1920s, it was not surprising for a person to be called "so-and-so, slave"—without a surname.

Source: Regional Differences

This description comes from Charles Dallet's translated book Histoire de l'Église de Corée *[History of the Church in Korea], published in Paris in 1874. Dallet's analysis was based on reports of Catholic missionaries who described perceived differences in the provinces. How seriously should we take the evaluations of what we might call amateur anthropologists? Do you think that these generalizations are based on reality or primarily reflect bias? Why?*

Those of the two northern provinces, particularly of Pyongan, [the other being Hamgyong,] are stronger, more savage and more violent than the other Koreans. There are very few nobles among them, and consequently very few dignitaries. It is thought that they are the secret enemies of the dynasty, and so the government, while it humors them, watches over them closely and always dreads an insurrection on their part which would be extremely difficult to overcome. The people of Hwanghae [in the central part] have the reputation of being narrow and limited, and they are accused of great avarice and of bad faith. The populace of Kyonggi, or province of the capital, is flighty, inconstant and given to luxurious living and pleasure. It is this populace which has set the tone for the whole country, and it is particularly to it that what we have said [about] the Koreans' ambition, rapacity, prodigality and ostentation applies. Dignitaries, nobles and scholars are numerous there. The people of Chungchong [to the south of the capital] resemble those of Kyonggi in all points, and share their vices and good qualities to a lesser degree. In the [southern] province of Cholla few nobles are encountered. The inhabitants are regarded by the other Koreans as coarse, hypocritical, and rascally, seeking only their own interest and always ready to commit the most odious treason if they can profit from it. The [southeastern] province of Kyongsang has a character apart. Habits are much more simple, morals less corrupt, and the old customs more faithfully preserved. There is little luxury and few foolish expenditures, thus the tiny heritages are handed down in the same family from father to son year after year. Literary study flourishes there more than elsewhere, and often young persons are found who devote the evening and part of the night to reading after working in the fields all day long. Women of rank are not shut in as strictly as in other provinces, but go out during the day accompanied by a slave, and need fear no insult nor any lack of respect. . . . The nobles, who are quite numerous in this province, belong to the Nam-in party [or Southern faction], and since the most recent revolutions [they] have no longer any part in dignities and public offices.[24]

Source: Dallet's description is found in Lee Chong-sik, The Politics of Korean Nationalism *(Berkeley: University of California Press, 1965), 15–16.*

Education was highly prized as the route to improving the life of one's family. The civil service examination was central to the Koryŏ and Chosŏn dynasties: it was the method for selecting Korea's civil officials, providing them with a common body of knowledge (the Confucian classics and their commentaries). In the Chosŏn dynasty there were three categories of exams: civil, military, and miscellaneous. While commoners could theoretically take the exams, the yangban, for all practical purposes, monopolized them. Those who passed the civil exams, which were more prestigious than the other two categories, monopolized high and low government posts. Successful military examinees became military officials. Those who passed the miscellaneous exam (on foreign languages, astronomy, medicine, and law) were

Source: Memorial on Sŏwŏn (1738)

Though the sŏwŏn began as private institutions of higher learning, by the eighteenth and nineteenth centuries they had become havens for military deserters, sources of economic profiteering and extortion, and institutions preying on both social elites and the masses. This 1738 memorial by Pak Mun-su (1691–1756) describes the social evils of the sŏwŏn. This situation remained until the Taewŏn'gun took power and attempted to rein in some of the worst abuses. What pattern noted by Pak led to the deterioration of the sŏwŏn?

If a man becomes councillor or minister, makes his name, and leaves a couple of sons, the rich and those who want to escape military service start to build a shrine for him. Moreover, his sons build a majestic *sŏwŏn* for him, using their influence to obtain permission from the governor and magistrate. Treacherous creatures entering the *sŏwŏn,* afraid of military service, number a few hundred to each *sŏwŏn.*

They extort money from the people as though they were officials . . . And they make the *sŏwŏn* a place to steam chickens, slaughter dogs, eat, and become intoxicated. Even the magistrates are afraid of them and refrain from intervening in their affairs. The evil custom of extorting the taxes of dead men and escapees from their kinsmen and neighbors began with the *sŏwŏn.*

Source: Ching Young Choe, The Rule of the Taewŏn'gun, 1864–1873; Restoration in Yi Korea *(Cambridge, MA: East Asian Research Center, Harvard University, 1972), 72.*

technical experts hired by the appropriate government agencies. In the slightly more than five-hundred-year Chosŏn dynasty, 15,547 Korean men passed the civil service examination. In addition to the examination, there were educational institutions. A national university was established in the tenth century. Private academies (*sŏwŏn*) began to develop in the Koryŏ dynasty, but it was not until the Chosŏn that they flourished. By 1700, Korea had more academies than China, over six hundred.

THE CHOSŎN DYNASTY: THE SCOURGE OF FACTIONALISM

Probably Korea's greatest king, King Sejong (r. 1418–1450), was an enlightened monarch, promoting scholarship as he himself made various cultural and technical contributions to Korean life. He tried to strengthen the monarchy's control over the government and raise the stature of the Korean monarchy relative to that of China. But his chief claim to fame comes from his commissioning scholars to write a Korean script. The result was *han'gŭl,* "one of the world's premier alphabets for accurately representing the sounds of words."[7]

One scholar has argued that in the Chosŏn period, "Korea became more Confucian than Confucian China."[8] One unfortunate result was that Confucianization fueled an almost malignant factionalism among groups of scholars: "Factionalism was an inevitable result of the gap between the ideal pattern of personal and institutional conduct prescribed by Confucian masters and the realities of the patterns of behavior of both the monarch and scholar-officials."[9] These factional struggles were often personal and trivial, frequently thinly-disguised struggles for power. But seemingly inevitably, they took on ideological dimensions when one faction accused the other of misusing, even trashing, Confucian ideals and concepts or being wrong about court ritual. The tragedy was multiplied because factional rivalry went beyond verbal assaults. Government officials resorted to bloody purges of opposing factions. The bitterness was so deep that sometimes killing one's opponents was not enough: their corpses were dug up and mutilated. Because the struggles became ideological, there was little possibility of compromise.

Factionalism became a serious problem in the late fifteenth century. From then until the twentieth century it was an almost continual scourge; if no apparent factional feuding was occurring, its potential was just beneath the surface of society. Fundamental issues of political power were at stake: struggles between monarch and bureaucracy; rivalry among powerful yangban families for government positions and control of government bodies; and bitter animosities between long-time bureaucrats and newcomers. The destructiveness of factionalism was compounded by the fact that while battles were waged, the scholar-officials paid little or no attention to matters of day-to-day rule, ignoring the welfare of the people, economic stability, and any kind of positive change—like Nero fiddling as Rome burned.

INVASIONS: A SEA IN A HEAVY GALE

Though this chapter's title refers specifically to Korea's topography, metaphorically from 1592 on, the Chosŏn dynasty's tumultuous and tragic history resembled such a sea—rough and choppy, with waves cresting and falling into immense roiling troughs. In the forty-five years between 1592 and 1637 Korea was the victim of four invasions, two by the Japanese and two by the Manchus. The Japanese invasions in 1592 and 1597 were led by the megalomaniac Hideyoshi, who had his eyes on the prize of China. Korea, as a bridge to China, paid dearly. In 1592, about one hundred sixty thousand Japanese landed at Pusan and marched up the peninsula, meeting little Korean resistance; within three weeks they occupied Seoul. Slaves took advantage of the situation to rise in revolt and burn slave registries. The Japanese reached as far north as P'yŏngyang, at which point they proposed to the Chinese that Korea be divided, with the Japanese taking the southern part of the peninsula and China the north. In this campaign Korea was saved by the naval hero Yi Sun-shin, who destroyed Japanese shipping near the coast and cut their supply routes. The Ming dynasty, playing the role of tributary elder brother, sent forces, and over twenty thousand Koreans formed *righteous armies* to fight the Japanese in guerrilla warfare. Negotiations dragged on inconclusively until Hideyoshi launched yet another invasion in 1597, this time with one hundred forty thousand men. Admiral Yi then engineered a stunning Japanese naval defeat near the port of Mokp'o on the southwestern coast. Then suddenly Hideyoshi died. This seven-year war, ending in 1598, devastated Korea. Farmland was laid to waste, towns and villages were burned, and irrigation works were demolished. The poet Pak Il-lo's "Song of Great Peace" sums up the tragedy:

> *Higher than mountains*
> *The bones pile up in the fields.*
> *Vast cities and great towns*
> *Became the burrows of wolves and foxes.*[10]

These two invasions stirred bitter Korean enmity against the Japanese, whom Koreans (like Chinese) called "dwarfs." The Koreans temporarily broke off relations with Japan, though they renewed trade relations in 1609. In contrast with their view that their policy toward China was serving the great, they described their relations with Japan as "neighborly."

The Manchu invasions in 1627 and 1636 were meant to neutralize Korea and thereby shore up their southern flank as they went about conquering China. In 1627 their forces numbered about thirty thousand, and they quickly forced a peace treaty on Korea. But the Korean king persisted in following an anti-Manchu policy, refusing to hand over anti-Manchu Korean officials. Such "insolence" brought the 1636 invasion, this time with one hundred twenty thousand men. Early in 1637, the Manchu emperor compelled the Korean king to end Korea's relationship with the Ming dynasty and establish a tributary relationship with the Qing dynasty.

KINGS AND PRINCES: THE EIGHTEENTH CENTURY

Two of the Chosŏn dynasty's most enlightened kings dominated the eighteenth century: Yŏngjo (1724–1776) and Chŏngjo (1776–1800). Both supported equal opportunity or impartiality in appointing officials from all factions, a policy that greatly reduced factional strife. Yŏngjo overhauled the tax system, making it more rational; he revised the law codes; and he established a system of inspectors to review the performance of local government officials with a view to eliminating corruption and abuses of power. Finally, he worked to change women's hairstyles, eliminating the traditional big wigs.

Yŏngjo supported scholarship, and especially *sirhak* (practical learning), a school of thought that emerged in the seventeenth century and flowered in the eighteenth and nineteenth centuries. It was practical in the sense that its goal was to eliminate the evils of the day by carefully studying the roots and roles of contemporary political, social, and economic institutions. The validity of institutions and policies should, it was thought, be based on whether they were useful and of benefit. Yŏngjo's own continuing study of the Chinese classics made him a model Confucian monarch. For example, he was so disciplined and committed to Confucian ideals that he set aside almost two years (1725–1727) to study the works of Mencius, and later in his career he set aside another year (1763–1764) to do so.

Yŏngjo's reign was marred by his relationship with his son, Crown Prince Sado, who was lazy and immoral. Even more serious was Sado's mental illness, which Yŏngjo apparently did not recognize. The king constantly rebuked and belittled him both as a child and as an adult; even so, Sado was allowed almost free rein. He had orgies in the palace. He murdered court eunuchs by beating and decapitation and then graduated to murdering court physicians, shamans, servants, and bearers of bad tidings. Here is a diary description by his wife, Lady Hyegyŏng:

> In that month [the sixth month of 1757—when Sado was twenty two years old]
> Prince Sado began to kill. The first person he killed was Kim Hanch'ae, the eunuch
> who happened to be on duty that day. The Prince came in with the severed head and
> displayed it to the ladies-in-waiting. The bloody head, the first I ever saw, was
> simply a horrifying sight. As if he had to kill to release his rage, the Prince [also]
> harmed many ladies-in-waiting.[11]

Sado tried unsuccessfully to commit suicide several times. Enraged by Sado's actions and by what he interpreted as lack of filial piety, King Yŏngjo, in the end, ordered Sado to climb into a large rice chest in a pavilion courtyard. He was locked in under the broiling July sun until he starved to death eight days later. This action reignited with a vengeance the factionalism that had been lying dormant, one faction sympathizing with Sado and the other supporting the king.

Sado's son became King Chŏngjo, who frequently attempted to show his devotion to his father in concrete ways—in processions to Sado's tomb and in various efforts to memorialize him. In the minds of some, his own legitimacy was questionable because of his grandfather's execution of his father. "Royal and affinal relatives, powerful families, and officials were divided on the issue of Chŏngjo's acceptability and became involved in debilitating feuds."[12] Perhaps that sensitive situation spurred Chŏngjo to prove himself by being the best monarch possible. Chŏngjo clearly tried to emulate Yŏngjo. He lectured officials about properly interpreting the Confucian moral codes, imported new editions of the Confucian classics, and placed them in a new royal library. He set out to improve printing techniques to benefit scholars and banished shamans from court and capital. In addition, he established a benevolent relief program for the poor. Unfortunately, after his death, the next two kings took the throne at the ages of eleven and eight; the factionalism that had sprung up after Sado's death spread, with child kings sometimes becoming factional pawns. The early years of the nineteenth century also saw the rise to power of queens' families in Korean factional politics.

CATHOLICISM (WESTERN LEARNING)

Catholicism first reached Korea from Jesuit missionaries in China; with its teachings came the first information about Western culture. Catholicism was called *Western learning*—a label that included not only theology but also the secular learning of the Jesuits: astronomy and the calendar, geography, weaponry, and science and technology. During the reign of Chŏngjo, Catholicism spread rapidly through one of the most influential factions; the number of converts grew, based on written materials from China, producing what one scholar called "a bookish Catholicism."[13] Its initial appeal was to scholars who, like *sirhak* devotees, were seeking possible solutions to Chosŏn's political and social problems. Chŏngjo himself labeled Catholicism heresy and outlawed it in 1785, banning the importation of books from China. The court's championing of Confucianism over Western learning became clear with the 1792 execution of a yangban convert who allegedly had not performed the proper Confucian rituals after his mother's death.

Nevertheless, by century's end there were about four thousand Catholic converts on the peninsula. By this time, Catholicism itself was often a political football in the factional struggles, resulting in severe persecution of Catholics in 1801 and 1839. Korea became a Catholic diocese in 1836, but with off-again, on-again Catholic persecution into the 1860s. Whereas most of the initial converts had been yangban, beginning in the early nineteenth century most of them were commoners—peasants, craftsmen, merchants, and wage laborers—as well as urban dwellers and women. By the early 1860s, a number of French Catholic priests were proselytizing in the country, and the number of converts reached about twenty thousand.

THE STATE OF POLITICS AND SOCIETY IN MID-NINETEENTH-CENTURY KOREA

In many ways, the political and social deterioration of late Chosŏn Korea resembled a meltdown. The political and social elites—the monarchy, the queens and their relatives, and the yangban ruling class— seemed oblivious to anything but their own power. Scholars have noted the intense competition for political office (in the words of one, "convulsive and desperate"[14]), where the office itself, not what could be accomplished there, was the name of the game. Many officials, high and low, held as many as one hundred to two hundred positions during their careers. This *official roulette* meant that government became more and more superficial and less and less able to govern let alone deal with problems and crises. In this situation, power devolved to permanent local elites. The tragedy was that the local elites—powerful yangban families—had characteristics similar to those of central government yangban families. They were often factionalized, provincial, attaching supreme importance to family and personal status and power, and obsessed by the formalities and rituals of Confucianism, paying little attention to its moral core.

Because of the rapid turnover in official positions, in localities the real power lay in the hands of office clerks, who stayed on through official changes and whose positions became mostly hereditary. They were a scourge. Scholar Chang Yak-yŏng (1762–1836) stated:

> *The people cultivate the soil for a living, but the clerks exploit the people as their profession. They exploit their prey by skinning and hammering the people, reaping their harvest from the labor and grain of the people. This became their habit, and they now do it as a matter of course. Without restraining the clerks, no one can govern the people.*[15]

Chang's reference to "skinning and hammering" points to the taxes that seemed to multiply. One of the most abused levies was the interest on grain loans, which had been established early in the dynasty to provide grain to peasants in early spring before the winter barley was harvested. The loans were to be repaid after the autumn harvest at an interest rate of 10 percent. The interest, however, was raised and manipulated,

Traditional Elite Male Dress
Traditional elite male attire included baggy pants, vest, outer coat, and overcoat. There were no pockets or buttons; clothes were held together by strings, belts, and cords. Koreans were fond of white garments. On his head the Korean man wore this distinctive horsehair hat.

causing great suffering to the peasants. With the power of local families and the deterioration of central government power, the land tax became increasingly difficult to collect; easier were taxes on cloth and handicrafts that were assessed on all. Increased taxes made widespread corruption more likely. Between 1850 and 1862, about 450 provincial governors, magistrates, and military commanders were charged with corruption and dismissed. Amid a generally disintegrating economy, and subject to the taxation and whims of local power holders, peasants in the early 1860s rose in spontaneous rebellions: five of the eight provinces saw substantial unrest. The most serious one, the Chinju uprising in 1862, erupted in reaction to exploitation by a provincial army commander. Peasants armed with bamboo spears killed government officials and burned government buildings. Though the uprising was suppressed, it set off a rash of copycat outbursts.

THE TONGHAK MOVEMENT

In the 1860s two responses to the general crisis arose, the first a grassroots religious-social movement and the second a reformist regime in Seoul. The first was the Tonghak (*Eastern learning*) movement, based on the teachings of Ch'oe Che-u (1824–1864). Ch'oe's story seems similar to that of China's Hong Xiuquan, the leader of the Taiping movement. Ch'oe came from a destitute family and, like Hong, failed to pass the civil service examination. He too had visions and began to teach a syncretic religion based on Confucianism, Buddhism, Daoism, Catholicism, and shamanism. The incorporation of Catholicism seems strange because Ch'oe was particularly upset by Catholicism, fearing that the Western religion might bring a foreign invasion; indeed, the name of his teaching was directly counterposed to *Western learning*. Ch'oe based his teaching on the idea that the human spirit replicated that of God and that serving others was service to God. The key ramification of such a view is human equality. It is easy to see why this teaching appealed to many commoners, submerged as they were in castelike hereditary classes. Also appealing to the lowborn were the chanting of magical formulas and the worship of nature deities. Ch'oe wrote:

> *Only Tonghak will be able to annihilate the enemy through the use of incantation and magic. In the World of the New Creation those who have been rich and noble will become poor and lowly, and those who have been poor and lowly will become rich and noble.*[16]

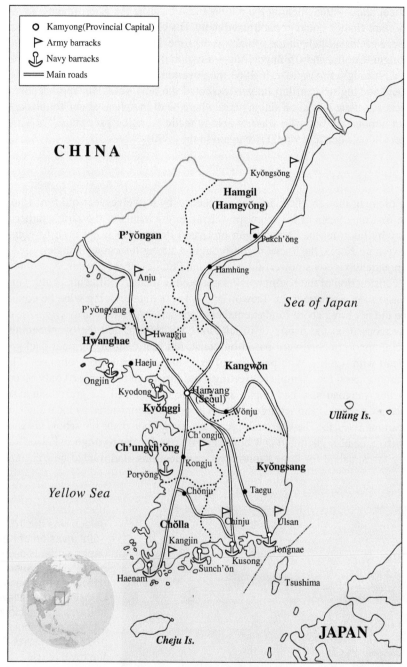

Map 8-1   Korea: Provincial Capitals, and Key Military Bases, 1392–1896.

Ch'oe had practical aims—strengthening the nation and reforming the government—as well as the conviction that important change could come immediately. His championing the nation is remarkable given the general absence of this attitude in the country at the time. He began his teaching in the three southern provinces—Kyŏngju, Chŏlla, and Ch'ŭngch'ŏng—a region that had been largely frozen out of key government positions. It caught fire rapidly. In 1863 the government sent agents to arrest Ch'oe for misleading the people and stirring up conflict; he was executed the next year. His apprehender noted that "in numerous districts . . . there was not a single place where he did not hear about Tonghak: 'There was not a shop-woman or a mountain boy who was not able to recite [Tonghak] scripture.'"[17] Though the movement fizzled after Ch'oe's death, it would rise again in the 1890s.

THE ERA OF THE TAEWŎN'GUN

When King Ch'ŏlchong died in 1864, he was succeeded by a twelve-year-old boy who became King Kojong. For the first nine years of his reign, power lay in the hands of the king's father as regent, best known in history by his title, the Taewŏn'gun or Grand Prince. He faced both foreign and domestic problems. In governing Korea, the Taewŏn'gun brought a strong reform agenda designed particularly to strengthen the monarchy vis-à-vis powerful lineages and families of the queens. A visible symbol of this effort was his reconstruction of the Kyŏngbok Palace, built in the early fifteenth century and destroyed in Hideyoshi's invasion. As a reformer the Taewŏn'gun was pragmatic, doing what he could to ameliorate problems, but he did not bring about fundamental change.

His reforms focused on the nature of officialdom, tax reform, and the overweening power of the yangbans. Official appointments were based on merit, not factional or regional background. Corrupt officials were dealt with harshly, with penalties of exile or death for serious offenses. The Taewŏn'gun also reformed various taxes, for example converting a military cloth tax imposed only on commoners into a household tax that yangban now had to pay as well. He reorganized the grain-loan system, canceling past loans that had not been paid and setting up village granaries administered by local elites, not magistrates and clerks. Concerning taxes, the Taewŏn'gun's record is mixed. Though the household tax and the grain-loan system were positive, he also instituted new commercial taxes for the Kyŏngbok Palace's reconstruction, levied temporary taxes, called for large "voluntary" contributions, and minted new currency. New taxes

Kyongbok Palace   This palace was destroyed in the 1592 invasion of Korea by Japan under Hideyoshi. It was not rebuilt because of financial difficulties and because most Chosŏn kings believed that the site was inauspicious. The Taewŏn'gun rebuilt the palace in 1867 to symbolize the dignity of the royal house.

were assessed on commodities that passed through the seven gates of Seoul and certain districts, on ginseng, and on the fishing and salt-making industries. Some of these taxes were used to fund the notoriously weak and ineffective military. A new land surtax for the military was to be paid by landlords, not tenant farmers. The Taewŏn'gun ordered closed all but forty-seven of the over six hundred academies (*sŏwŏn*), most of which owned large tax-exempt landed estates. His regime also made tax exemption on private land illegal. Coupled with the household tax, the new tax funds from these lands brought more money into government coffers. On the whole and in the short run, the Taewŏn'gun's reforms were successful in shoring up the throne's authority and bolstering the troubled economy. Confucian scholars criticized his reforms for being too concerned with outward institutional change and not enough with moral standards.

In dealing with the outside world, "the Taewŏn'gun, had a simple foreign policy: no treaties, no trade, no Catholics, no West, and no Japan."[18] He was greatly suspicious of Catholicism because it represented foreigners in Korea (and also perhaps because his wife was interested in it). In 1866 he launched an anti-Catholic campaign that ended in the deaths of 9 French missionaries and about 8,000 converts. When a French missionary persuaded the commander of a French fleet in China to punish Korea for the persecution, French sailors on seven warships seized part of the island of Kangwha on the coast west of Seoul in October 1866; but their efforts to march to the capital were stopped, and they were forced to withdraw. In response, the Taewŏn'gun strengthened coastal defenses with new gun emplacements and cannon. That same year a merchant ship, the *General Sherman,* registered to the United States but consigned to the British, sailed up the Taedong River in northern Korea with the goal of opening Korea. It ran aground; locals attacked and burned it. In 1871, an American ship sent to punish the Koreans was fired on by coastal batteries and met such heavy Korean resistance that it withdrew, but the Koreans suffered about 650 deaths. One particularly shocking episode in these first years of facing outside aggressive forces involved a German adventurer named Oppert, who tried unsuccessfully to open trade in 1866. He returned two years later with a plan to raid the grave of the Taewŏn'gun's father and to hold his bones for ransom until the Korean leader agreed to trade. This bizarre effort failed when his forces encountered Korean troops and fled. In response to these events, the Taewŏn'gun established a strict exclusionary policy, attempting to avoid the unequal treaties imposed on China and Japan.

It is ironic that the rule of the Taewŏn'gun was undone by the plotting of his son's wife, Queen Min (see Identities), and another queen dowager because one goal of his reform agenda was to diminish the power of queens and their families. In 1873 he was forced to relinquish power to his son, King Kojong. From the 1870s to the mid-1890s, the family of Queen Min took more and more power and emerged as one factional center; the Taewŏn'gun himself led the other faction. Sometimes it seemed as though policies alternated less on the basis of substance than on the position of the other faction.

THE OPENING OF KOREA

The factional pas de deux affected the Korean reaction to China and to rapidly modernizing Japan. The Taewŏn'gun viewed Japan's progressive reforms as evidence of how far it had fallen from the Chinese model. But the king and his assertive wife, Queen Min, were more open to dealing with the outside world and accepting change. Japan was ready to open Korea. In 1875, Japanese ships entered an "area that was known to be off-limits to foreign ships" to provoke the Koreans. The Koreans fired, and Japanese gunboats leveled a Korean fort on Kanghwa Island. After this inauspicious episode, Japan approached China to determine its reactions to Japanese initiatives in Korea. China's response was somewhat ambiguous but not negative, so Japan pushed ahead. As we have seen (Chapter 3), the Treaty of Kangwha, forced on Korea by Japan, did nothing to clarify Korea's status in regard to either China or its own independence.

Source: Message from General Yi Yong-hŭi to French Admiral Pierre-Gustave Rose

In 1866, a fleet of seven French ships landed on Kangwha Island off the coast west of Seoul and spent time pillaging. A Korean force of a little over two thousand men (not ten million, as the document boasts) planned to attack them but could not find enough boats to cross the channel to the island. On October 19, Yi sent the following message to Admiral Rose, describing Korea's traditional foreign policy and the rationale for the Taewŏn'gun's policy of seclusion. Several battles followed this letter; in November the French withdrew. What is the rationale for the policy of seclusion given here?

The people who betray the heavenly principle are doomed to perish. Those who violate the laws of the country must be punished. . . . From time immemorial, there has been [in all nations] an established custom according to which people from near and far lands have been treated. This is also the case with our country, which has shown much tolerance and kindness to other people. Officials of our country are ordered to receive and inquire after those who happen to drift to our boundaries, and to treat them as if they were old friends, even if we do not know the names of their countries. . . . If they are hungry and cold, they are offered food and clothes. If they are sick, they are cared for with medicine. If they want to go home, we send them home, giving them provisions to take with them.

These are the customs which we have honored generation after generation. Even to this moment we practice them. Therefore, there is no country in the whole world which does not call our country the land of civility. If there be those who infiltrate our land . . . wear our clothes, learn our language, deceive our people and country, and corrupt our customs, we . . . have a law for them. Whenever they are found, they are punished severely. This is the great law which is applied by all nations. You are behaving outrageously. Your present invasion of our cities, killing of our people, and plundering have no justification whatsoever. You betrayed heaven and are so against our laws that there is no precedent to compare with. Heaven has already rejected you, and we have reason to punish you. Furthermore, we hear that you have a desire to practice your teaching in our land. If this is true, it can never be permitted. There is no uniformity . . . and each has what each prefers. Therefore, there is no need to talk about how other people base their principles of justice and wrongdoing. We esteem what we have learned, you practice what you have learned. As a principle, each hands down the teachings of his forefathers. How can you tell us to abandon the teachings of our forefathers and accept those of others? . . . Now we can no longer bear your stubbornness, even with our outmost benevolence. Therefore, we are about to cross the sea, commanding a great army of ten million. Since it is necessary to tell you the reason for our coming to subdue you, . . . we propose that we see each other beforehand. Then . . . we shall decide who will be the victor.

Source: Ching Young Choe, The Rule of the Taewŏn'gun, 1864–1873; Restoration in Yi Korea *(Cambridge, MA: East Asian Research Center, Harvard University, 1972), 103–4.*

But it did bring the unequal treaty system that the Taewŏn'gun had feared, with all the elements of the similar systems in China and Japan. The treaty opened three ports between 1876 and 1881: Tongnae (near Pusan), Inch'ŏn, and Wŏnsan. In 1880, China advised Korea to sign treaties with the Western powers as well in order to protect itself more effectively by stirring up rivalries and preventing Japan from gaining undue power.

Identities: Queen Min (1851–1895): Tragic Enigma

Born into an aristocratic family, Queen Min lost both of her parents at the age of eight. She was chosen to marry the minor King Kojong by the wife of the king's father, the Taewŏn'gun, who ruled as regent until Kojong came of age. Min married the king in the Changdok Palace in 1866. For over five years the king was not intimate with her. She spent her time learning court procedures and protocol, reading voraciously, and suffered a staggering blow when the king fathered his first child with a palace woman. She wanted her husband to became king, but Kojong was intimidated by his father and uncertain whether he could rule. As time passed, the animosity between Min and the Taewŏn'gun grew. Finally, in 1873, the queen plotted with her own family and the king to place Kojong on the throne. Her first son died shortly after birth, but in 1874 she gave birth to a son who would become the last king of Korea and thereby solidified her position at court.

From then until the mid-1890s, Queen Min and her family took more and more control, becoming a center of political power; they struggled almost continually against the Taewŏn'gun. Under King Kojong and Queen Min, Korea was opened to trade and diplomatic relations with Japan and the Western nations. Under Queen Min (King Kojong remained too weak), Korea took the first steps toward modernization under Japan's leadership. In the 1880s, these efforts led to several clashes between China and Japan over their roles in Korea. In each episode Queen Min played a pivotal role, sometimes defeating the Taewŏn'gun and at other times being bested by him. She was a strong and astute leader. An American female missionary described her in 1888:

> *According to Korean custom, she carried a number of filigree gold ornaments decorated with long silk tassels fastened at her side. So simple, so perfectly refined were her tastes in dress, it is difficult to think of her as belonging to a nation called half civilized . . . . Slightly pale and quite thin, with somewhat sharp features and brilliant piercing eyes, she did not strike me at first sight as being beautiful, but no one could help reading force, intellect and strength of character in that face.*[1]

In the 1890s, the queen sided with China rather than Japan. Rumors abounded about her corruption and her bringing fortune-tellers and entertainers into the palace. Some people then and historians later saw her as "an embodiment of all the evils of the decaying dynasty."[2] The Tonghak Rebellion brought China and Japan into Korea, leading to war. Japanese victory brought Japanese reformers led by Lieutenant General Miura Gorō into Seoul. When the Taewŏn'gun asked the Japanese for assistance in ousting the queen, and because Miura already believed that she was thwarting his reforms, Miura plotted violent action. On October 8, Japanese soldiers with hired Japanese thugs invaded the palace. "They found the queen hiding in a side room and cut her down with their swords. Her body was then wrapped up with a silk quilt and taken to a grove of trees not far distant; wood was piled around, kerosene was poured on, and all was set on fire."[3]

Recently, the image of Queen Min has undergone substantial rehabilitation. She became the main character in a large Korean musical production, *For Whom FOXHUNT—Foxhunt* being the name of the operation to murder her. Films, television, novels, and newspapers have hailed her as a symbol of Korean nationalism and as a leading Korean figure.

---

[1] *Internet: http://www.gkn-la.net/history_resources/queen_min_tmsimbirtseva_1996.htm.*

[2] *Ibid.*

[3] *Lee Chong-sik*, The Politics of Korean Nationalism *(Berkeley: University of California Press, 1965), 45.*

When Confucian scholars, focused almost frantically on the absolute necessity of exclusion, got wind of the king's openness to this policy, they denounced it as a step toward the destruction of Korea. Scholars in every province signed a joint memorial to the king stressing the danger of such action: simply put, linking Korea to these countries would ruin Korea. To halt the outcry and because of "disrespect for the throne,"[19] King Kojong had one of the scholars, named Hong, decapitated in September 1881 to teach a bloody object lesson. An American scholar places these Confucian naysayers in their historical context:

> *What can we call people like Mr. Hong? Illogical, irrational, obscurantist, traditionalist, anachronistic, myopic, arrogant, obtuse, stubborn, backward, posterior, positively dorsal. . . . We might, however, want to call them patriots. Or conscientious scholars, men of principle, virtue, strength, vigor; they all let out learned wails for the fate of old Korea, and correctly predicted the shot that came a few years later.[20]*

Treaties with Western countries followed: with the United States in 1882, with England and Germany in 1883, with Russia and Italy in 1884, and with France in 1886. Merchants, diplomats, and visitors in general from the West brought to Korea new players with new ideas and challenges. Korean reactions to these new forces ranged from Confucian opposition to any change to openness to broad change, the latter position notably held by the king and queen, the latter the more powerful of the monarchical duo. The government dispatched missions to study Japan's modernizing policies in 1876, 1881, and 1882. Meanwhile the Taewŏn'gun was in the wings, increasingly embittered by the throne's policy of openness. The treaty-making years saw two bloody episodes that highlighted this polarized reaction to modern change.

In 1881 the government had hired Japanese military officers to train the nucleus of a modern Korean army. In the process, the regular army units were practically abandoned; by July 1882 they had not been paid for thirteen months, and when they were paid with rice, it was mixed with sand and small stones. They mutinied. The Taewŏn'gun, determined to break Queen Min's power, took advantage of the situation. As the mutineers attacked the palace and burned the Japanese legation, the Taewŏn'gun took the reins of government. Both China and Japan sent forces to "restore peace." Informed of the Taewŏn'gun's complicity in the mutiny, the Chinese performed their Confucian big brother act, hauling him to China and throwing him in jail. The result of the crisis was that the Japanese maintained a permanent guard at their legation in Seoul; the Chinese kept three thousand soldiers in the country, sent arms and instructors to the Korean military, and posted advisors to the Korean government.

In the early 1880s, a number of youthful Koreans, sons of yangban families, went to Japan and became passionately enthusiastic about the Meiji reforms. Three of the more well known—Pak Yŏng-hyo (son-in-law of the late King Ch'ŏlchong), Kim Ok-kyun, and Sŏ Chae-p'il—were part of an informal group known variously as the Independence Party or Progressive Party—advocates for reform and for nationalism. Kim had established ties with Fukuzawa Yukichi, the Japanese advocate of Western-style reforms. In 1884 the group attempted a coup against the Korean regime, where the king and queen were now solidly in the Chinese camp. The Japanese ambassador was involved in the conspiracy and had Japanese legation guards ready for action. The plan was to assassinate key Korean leaders at a large state dinner celebrating the opening of the new modern post office. Plans went awry and only one man at the dinner was wounded, but the conspirators (Korean reformers and Japanese) convinced the king that Chinese troops were attacking the city. Japanese guards rushed the palace and seized the king and queen. On December 4, the reformers, led by Kim, set up their new government. Its goals were set down later by Sŏ Chae-p'il:

> *abolition of class distinctions, such as different kinds of yangban . . . and the commoners; reorganization of the law court, the army, the tax office, and the treasury; appointment of government officials through the examination of the candidates'*

Korean Farmer with an A-Frame Carrier   Though this is a twentieth-century photo, one can imagine the same scene in the nineteenth century. Here a young farmer transporting rice in the traditional A-frame carrier stops briefly to rest on his staff while viewing rice fields, thatched huts, and the mountains in the background.

qualifications; establishment of public schools in every district; improvement of public sanitation, highways, and housing for the poor; prohibition of "devil worship" and other superstitious practices; cutting the topknot; wearing foreign style clothes; establishment of paper currency; abolition of slavery.[21]

Queen Min appealed to the Chinese military leader Yuan Shikai, who advanced on the palace, freed monarch and spouse, and suppressed the coup. The reformist regime lasted less than two days. The queen, who had been in Japan's pro-reform camp early on, now firmly backed the Chinese. Japan sent more forces and demanded an indemnity for Japanese lives lost in the coup attempt and an apology—an irony given the Japanese role of coconspirator. In 1885 the countries negotiated the Li-Itō convention, a mutual abstention pact that lasted a decade, promising no more troops until and unless each side notified the other beforehand. Pak, Kim, and Sŏ fled to Japan, and many progressives were killed in street fighting.

Things were relatively quiet into the 1890s; the Chinese, with Resident-General Yuan calling all the shots, seemed to have made Korea their protectorate, but Chinese control increasingly alienated many Koreans. Domestic problems weighed more heavily than ever. An oppressive tax burden, rampant government corruption, rice shortages after an 1889 drought and in the face of larger rice exports to Japan, and spontaneous banditry formed an explosive situation, while in Seoul relationships between Queen Min and the Taewŏn'gun (who had returned from China in 1885) deteriorated even more. In the summer of 1892, the queen had the Taewŏn'gun's home bombed twice.

Then out of the southwest came a protest that exploded into rebellion; its leaders were followers of the Tonghak religion of Ch'oe Che-u. The immediate cause was a local official's extorting money and pocketing the wages of farmers who had worked on the construction of an irrigation reservoir. When local appeals for redress were rejected, Chŏn Pong-jun, the local Tonghak leader, marshaled a thousand enraged farmers who seized the county office, destroyed the reservoir, and distributed rice to hungry peasants. The Seoul regime's reaction was to suppress the movement by arresting the leaders. This was like pouring oil on a fire: Tonghaks sprang up everywhere, distinguished by their multicolored headbands and waistbands. By April 1894 the movement had grown, with the explicit twin goals of equitable taxation and ending rice exports to Japan and the more basic twin goals of overthrowing the government and throwing the Japanese out of the country. At the end of May, the rebels took the capital of Chŏlla province. Quaking in his

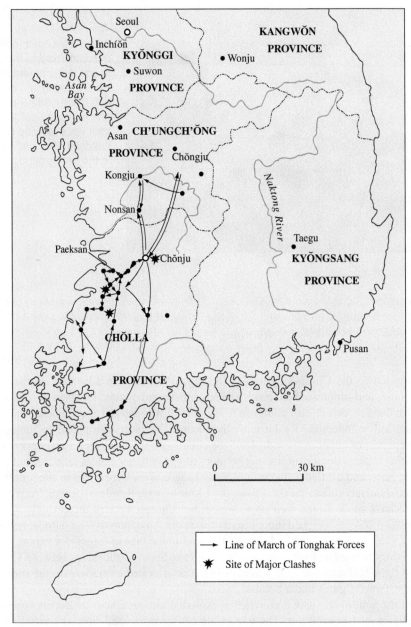

Map 8-2   Campaigns of the Tonghak Peasant Army, 1894–1895.

boots, King Kojong asked the Chinese to send troops. They did, notifying the Japanese of their plan to send 1,500 troops and fulfilling the pledge of the Li-Itō convention; the Japanese, who were ready to make their move, sent about 8,000 troops. By the time the troops arrived, the Tonghak leaders had agreed to a cease-fire, though they continued to hold Chŏlla province. This was the largest peasant uprising in Korean history and the first hint of a modern Korean nationalism; yet in the end, it was swallowed up by the

Source: Twelve-Article Reform Plan of the Tonghak Rebels

This twelve-point plan for the Tonghak government was written by an important Tonghak leader, Ŏ Chi Yong. By July 1894, a Tonghak "government" was established alongside the Korean government in all fifty-three countries and prefectures in Chŏlla province. What do these articles reveal about Tonghak objections to the Chosŏn dynasty and about their policies after taking control?

1. The [Tonghak] believers and the [government] officials should dissolve their mutual aversion and cooperate in the administration of the affairs of the state.
2. The avaricious and corrupt officials should be severely punished after proved guilty of crimes.
3. The high-handed rich men should be severely punished.
4. The depraved Confucian and yangban men should be severely punished.
5. The slave registers should be burnt.
6. The treatment of men of [the so-called] seven vile occupations should be improved and the butcher be relieved of the custom of wearing his hat [symbolic of his status].
7. The youthful widows should be allowed to remarry.
8. The nameless, miscellaneous tax assessments should not be imposed.
9. In the employment of officials the social status and the family lineage should be done away with and the men of ability be appointed.
10. Those who covertly communicate with the Japanese should be severely punished.
11. The existing public and private loans should be nullified.
12. The land should be equally distributed among those who farm and cultivated by them.

Source: Wanne J. Joe, A Cultural History of Modern Korea *(Boston: Weatherhill, 2001), 239–40.*

Sino-Japanese War. In the fall of 1894, when word reached the Tonghak leaders that the Japanese had seized the royal palace and ousted Queen Min (who had supported the Chinese), they mobilized 100,000 people to force the Japanese off the peninsula. But they met initial defeat by Korean government forces and crushing defeats by Japanese forces. Chŏn Pong-jun and three other Tonghak leaders were captured and executed in Seoul in May 1895.

The Sino-Japanese War was, as we have seen, a disaster for China and the start of Japanese expansion on the Asian mainland. In the midst of the war Inoue Kaoru, an important Meiji-era leader, was dispatched as Japanese minister to Korea. He approached Korea, in the words of one historian, as if it were "a sick man; the question is how to diagnose the disease, give medicine and bring about recovery. It did not concern him that the patient did not like the taste of the medicine."[22] Inoue believed that the proper medicine was a reform program such as the one the Japanese had undertaken; but many Koreans resisted Japanese direction, and the Tokyo government did not want to foot the bills. In September 1895 they recalled Inoue, replacing him with a military leader, Lieutenant General Miura Gorō, who had little sense of the niceties of diplomacy. Convinced that the resistance was centered in Queen Min's palace, he plotted a coup. At dawn on October 8, 1895, Japanese-trained troops and Japanese adventurer-thugs invaded the palace, grabbed Queen Min before she could flee, and stabbed her in the chest. Probably still alive, she was carried out to the garden, doused with kerosene, and set afire; she burned to death. The king, with the assistance of

Source: Regicide

Journalist Frederick A. MacKenzie (1869–1931) here records the gruesome killing of Queen Min in October 1896. Why do you think the Japanese and their hired thugs acted so brutally, cutting her down and then burning her alive as she was dying?

The Royal apartment [Konch'ong House] was of the usual one-storied type, led to by a few stone steps, and with carved wooden doors and oiled-paper windows. The Japanese made straight for it, and, when they reached the small courtyard in front, their troops paraded up before the entrance, while the *soshi* [strong men] broke down the doors and entered the rooms. Some caught hold of the King . . . . Others were pressing into the Queen's apartment. The Minister of the Household [Yi Kyong Sik] tried to stop them, but was killed [by Hirayama] on the spot. The *soshi* [Kunitomo, the editor of the *Kanjo shinpo*] seized the terrified palace ladies, who were running away, dragged them round and round by their hair, and beat them, demanding that they should tell where the Queen was. They moaned and cried and declared that they did not know. Now the men were pressing into the side-rooms, some of them hauling the palace ladies by their hair. Okamoto, who led the way, found a little woman hiding in a corner, grabbed her head, and asked her if she were the Queen. She denied it, freed herself, with a sudden jerk, and ran into the corridor shouting as she ran. Her son, who was present, heard her call his name three times, but, before she could utter more, the Japanese [Takabashi Kenji, the seller of medicine, and Nakamura, the owner of a general store] were on her and had cut her down. Some of the female attendants were dragged up, shown the dying body, and made to recognize it, and then three of them were put to the sword.

The conspirators had brought kerosene with them. They threw a bedwrap around the Queen, probably not yet dead, and carried her to a grove of trees in the deer park not far away. There they poured the oil over her, piled faggots of wood around, and set all on fire. They fed the flames with more and more kerosene, until everything was consumed, save a few bones.

Source: Cited in Wanne J. Joe, A Cultural History of Modern Korea *(Boston: Wealtherhill, 2001), 285–86.*

the Russians, who had their own political interests in Korea, fled to the Russian legation, where he remained for a year. Japan, in the face of a huge international outcry in reaction to this episode of essentially state-sponsored terrorism, recalled the general and put him and other conspirators on a show trial, where all were found innocent for lack of evidence. Miura was rewarded by being named to the Privy Council, the advisory body to the emperor, in 1910.

The period of King Kojong's retreat to the Russian legation inaugurated a new struggle over the Korean peninsula between Japan and Russia. The Russians wanted to use the presence of the king at their legation for their own advantage, but they were as pushy as the Japanese. The king returned to his palace in 1897 and took the new title of emperor.

THE INDEPENDENCE CLUB AND REFORM

While the king was at the Russian legation, a reformist movement calling for a modern, independent Korea was born. It was led by Sŏ Chae-p'il, a member of the reformist clique in 1884, who had received a medical degree in the United States and had become a naturalized U.S. citizen with the Anglicized name of Philip Jaisohn. Sŏ established the first *han'gŭl*-written newspaper, *The Independent*, to educate people about the social and political principles on which a Korean democracy could be built. Published three times a week, it had a circulation of three hundred in April 1896 that soared to three thousand by December 1898. Sŏ was also instrumental in getting reform-minded nationalists to form an Independence Club. Its founding members included Yi Sŭng-man (Syngman Rhee) and Yun Ch'i-ho, both of whom were students who had returned from the United States and converted to Christianity. Whereas the reformers of the 1880s had been enamored of Japanese modernization, those of the late 1890s were awed by Western liberal ideas. Yun's diary entry for March 30, 1889, offers his analysis of and solution for Korea's problems:

> *Our people have for several hundred years been slaves of others, possessing no wisdom or manly character, and suffering for 500 years under the oppression of an incomparably bad government; high and low, official and commoner, all seek miserably to preserve their lives through the bondage to others. How, then, given the present state of our country, can we hope for independence . . . ? The pressing need at present is to increase knowledge and experience, teach morality and reliability, and cultivate patriotism . . . .[23]*

The Independence Club had an educational agenda; it sponsored speakers and debates and served as a forum for the discussion of democratic ideals and national and individual independence. Club and newspaper goals included protecting Korean independence from aggressive imperialists, promoting reforms (modern schools, industrialization, a modern military), and initiating a democratic movement securing individual rights and allowing the people to participate in their own rule. One of the club's first actions

Source: Independence Club Agenda, 1898

The first elite response to Korea's continual harassment by other powers came from the Independence Club in the late 1890s. Technically, Korea was independent, but Japanese and Russian activities were threats that could not be ignored. These proposals are basically reformist. At a time when the foreign threat seemed most severe, why do these proposals focus almost entirely on domestic reforms?

1. That both officials and people shall determine not to rely on any foreign aid but to do their utmost to strengthen and uphold the Imperial prerogatives.
2. That all agreements with foreign nations concerning mining, timbers, railways, loans, military aid and treaties must be countersigned by all the Ministers of the State and the President of the Privy Council.
3. That all trials for felony should be open to the public, and grave offenders should be given an ample opportunity to defend themselves.
4. That all sources of revenue and methods of collecting taxes shall be under the control of the Finance Minister, and other ministries and private firms shall not be allowed to interfere, and that the annual budget and balance shall be made public.
5. That His Majesty shall appoint his ministers only with the concurrence of the majority of the Cabinet.
6. That the existing laws and regulations shall be faithfully enforced without fear or favor.

Source: Andrew C. Nahm, Korea: Tradition and Transformation: A History of the Korean People *(Elizabeth, NJ: Hollym, 199), 197.*

was to tear down a city gate that symbolized Korea's longtime subservience to China and to erect a new Independence Arch in November 1896. The club sponsored debates on women's rights, demanded the end of concubinage, and formed a society that established a school for women. In February 1898 at a mass meeting, the club's leaders demanded that the government stop granting concessions to foreigners, in this case the Russians. Government arrest of some club leaders brought daily protest marches in the streets of Seoul. In response, the government arranged for masses of peddlers to form a so-called Imperial Association with the express purpose of attacking the protesters. Bloody street fighting led to many casualties in late November 1898. In the end, the government banned the Independence Club and arrested and tortured most of its leaders. Sŏ and his wife were forced to leave for the United States. Yun went into hiding, and Rhee was tortured and imprisoned until 1904. Like the ill-fated 1898 reform in China, this Korean effort ended in crushed hopes, banishment, and imprisonment. Emperor Kojong was simply unable to stand up to the ultraconservatives in the government or to demanding foreigners. As one Korean historian put it, the king "at this time to his people, as they would say of an unmanly man, did not seem to be in possession of the [sic] testicles."[24]

THE FALL OF THE CHOSŎN DYNASTY

During the period 1900 to 1904, Japan and Russia edged closer to war over the issue of Korea, which seemed unable to save itself (see Chapter 7). The war was tragic for the Koreans. Despite Seoul's declaration of neutrality, the Japanese seized the capital on February 9, 1904, and took advantage of the war to force protocols on the Korean government that in effect made Korea a protectorate of Japan. The protocol of February 23, 1904, pledged Korea to rely on Japan for advice and for the settlement of internal troubles or problems with other nations. This might mean, the protocol stated, that Japan would have to occupy certain strategic sites in Korea. In essence, this protocol meant that the Korean government was agreeing to Japanese military occupation. The Koreans simply had no power to resist Japanese demands.

In a follow-up in August, Korean leaders signed an agreement that spelled out in detail the appointment of Japanese diplomatic and financial advisors to the Korean government. As part of this agreement, the Korean government pledged to "consult the Japanese government previous to concluding treaties or conventions with other powers, and in dealing with other important diplomatic affairs such as the granting of concessions to, or contracts with foreigners."[25] Under Japanese pressure, the government in May had already nullified all agreements with and concessions it had made to Russia.

Especially following the August accord, Japan began to expand its influence in Korea. Japanese took control of police powers and suppressed all anti-Japanese activity. They sponsored two pro-Japanese collaborationist organizations of Koreans to promote the unification of Korea with Japan. Japanese advisors pushed through financial reforms and the coinage of new money; Japanese currency also became legal tender, and the Daiichi Bank of Japan became the central bank of Korea. Eyewitness Frederick McKenzie, a British reporter, described the scene:

> Martial law was now enforced with the utmost rigidity. . . . Scores of thousands of Japanese coolies poured into the country. . . . They went through the country like a plague. If they wanted a thing, they took it. If they fancied a house, they turned the resident out. . . .
>
> The Japanese had evidently set themselves to acquire possession of as much Korean land as possible. The military authorities staked out large portions of the first sites in the country, the river lands near Seoul, the lands around Pyong'yang, great districts to the north, and fine strips all along the railway. Hundreds of thousands of acres were thus acquired.[26]

In the spring of 1905, the Japanese seized control of the postal system and of the telephone and telegraph networks. The Japanese minister to Korea, Hayashi Gonsuke, traveled to Tokyo in the early fall to consult on policy, determined to make the protectorate complete.

As the Japanese noose tightened, Emperor Kojong attempted to enlist the help of the United States. In October he dispatched a confidant, an American teacher, Homer Hulbert (also a friend of Philip Jaisohn), to Washington with a letter underscoring the friendly relationship that had existed between the two countries since the treaty of 1882 and asking for help in fending off Japanese aggression. On November 15, Hulbert tried to meet with Secretary of State Elihu Root, who refused to see him. The Korean emperor could not have known that since the early days of the century, President Theodore Roosevelt and the U.S. government had been urging Japan to seize Korea. At the outbreak of the Russo-Japanese War, William Rockhill, a Roosevelt advisor, had written to the U.S. ambassador in Korea: "The annexation of Korea to Japan . . . will be better for the Korean people and also for the peace in the Far East."[27] The memorandum of July 1905 signed by U.S. Secretary of War William Howard Taft and Japanese Prime Minister Katsura Tarō essentially gave Japan the go-ahead in Korea when Japan agreed not to go after the Philippines. In Washington, Hulbert delivered Emperor Kojong's letter to Root four days *after* the Japanese pounded the final nail into the Japanese protectorate coffin on November 17 (see below); Root's response was that nothing could be done.

To force their way into Korea, Japan sent the Meiji leader Itō Hirobumi, who came armed with the draft of an agreement that gave Japan complete control of Korea's foreign relations. All Korean legations around the world would be closed, and the Korean Ministry of Foreign Affairs would be eliminated. The Japanese ambassador would henceforth be known as the *resident-general*. The Japanese would place residents in treaty ports and other locations. And in an ironic twist that almost reaches the sardonic, Japan promised to "undertake to maintain the welfare and dignity of the Imperial House of Korea."[28] Itō applied immense pressure on the emperor, making it clear that if the Korean government did not agree, Itō could not predict what might happen. But the emperor put him off. Itō then turned to the Korean cabinet. An account of the pro-Japanese Yale University professor George Ladd states:

> *On the 17th of November, at 11 a.m., all of the Korean Ministers went to the Japanese Legation, lunched there, and conferred with Mr. Hayashi until 3 o'clock, when they adjourned to the Palace and held a meeting in the Emperor's presence. Their decision was, finally, to refuse to agree to the Convention in the form in which it had been proposed.*[29]

At 8 p.m. Itō, accompanied by a general and several mounted police, went to the palace, which was surrounded by Japanese troops. The prime minister refused to sign the convention, but five of the eight cabinet members complied after a few minor changes in wording. Itō ruled that a simple majority was sufficient to ratify the agreement. Known in Korea as the *1905 agreement* or the *five-article agreement,* it was never ratified by the Korean emperor, who was essentially under house arrest in the palace. Nominally, the emperor would not abdicate under Japanese pressure until 1907, but for all intents and purposes, the Korean throne and nation were erased.

The five cabinet ministers who signed the agreement were branded almost immediately as the *five traitors,* and became the targets of several assassination attempts. There were no major street disturbances in Seoul, for "[a]ll the Japanese troops in the district had been for days parading the streets and open places. The field-guns were out, and the men were fully armed."[30] The Korean nobleman, diplomat, reformer, and the emperor's military aide-de-camp Min Yŏng-hwan committed suicide. Other patriotically outraged officials followed suit. In Chŏlla and Ch'ŭngch'ŏng provinces in the peninsula's southwest, righteous armies fought Japanese troops. Nothing would change Japanese policy: Itô became the Japanese resident general early in 1906. Many Koreans were enraged. An editorial of November 20 by Chang Chi-yŏn, president of the *Hwangsong Sinmun*, a Seoul newspaper, states:

> *This day, we wail loudly . . . . Our so-called government ministers, who are worse than pigs and dogs, have become traitors to their country, [even if] with vacillation and apprehension. Frightened by empty threats but coveting honor and advantages for themselves, they offered to the stronger the four thousand year old country and the five hundred year old dynasty, and made the twenty million people the slaves of the stronger . . . . How sorrowful! How painful! Oh, our twenty million enslaved compatriots! Is this life? The spirit of the nation . . . perished in a single night. How painful it is! Fellow countrymen! Alas!*[31]

Chosŏn Korea had met its heaviest gale, a storm so severe that it had destroyed the dynasty and changed the country forever.

CHRONOLOGY

1392–1910	Chosŏn dynasty
1724–1776	Reign of King Yŏngjo
1762	Death of Crown Prince Sado
1776–1800	Reign of King Chŏngjo
1860s	Beginning of the Tonghak movement
1864–1873	Rule by the Taewŏn'gun
1866–1871	Western ships prowl Korea's west coast
1876	Treaty of Kangwha (with Japan)
1882–1886	Treaties with Western powers
1882	Army mutiny brought in Chinese and Japanese troops
1884	Coup attempt brought in Chinese and Japanese troops
1885–1894	Years of Chinese dominance after the Li-Itō convention
Early 1890s	Tonghak Rebellion
1894–1895	Sino-Japanese War
1895	Murder of Queen Min
1886–1898	Independence Club published a newpaper, *The Independent,* in *han'gŭl*
1904–1905	Russo-Japanese War
1905	Korea becomes a Japanese protectorate
1910	Korea becomes part of the Japanese empire; called Chōsen

Suggested Readings

Cumings, Bruce. *Korea's Place in the Sun.* New York: W. W. Norton, 2005. For a textbook, this is a gem. It is filled with strong insights and is written with rare verve—a great read.

Deuchler, Martina. *The Confucian Transformation of Korea: A Study of Society and Ideology.* Cambridge, MA: Harvard University Press, 1993. This book offers important insights into Chosŏn society and makes it clear that though Chosŏn was being Confucianized, it was not being Sinicized.

Finch, Michael. *Min Yŏng-hwan: A Political Biography.* Honolulu: University of Hawaii Press, 2002. This thought-provoking book looks at the life of Min (1861 to 1905) and probes the complexities and ambiguities in the late Chosŏn period and in colonial history.

Haboush, JaHyun Kim. *The Memoirs of Lady Hyegyŏng: The Autobiographical Writings of a Crown Princess of Eighteenth Century Korea.* Berkeley: University of California Press, 1996. Lady Hyegyŏng tells the tragic story of King Yŏngjo and Crown Prince Sado.

Haboush, JaHyun Kim, and Martina Deuchler, eds. *Culture and State in Late Chosŏn Korea.* Cambridge, MA: Harvard University Asia Center, 1999. A broad array of solid essays ranging from religion (Buddhism and Catholicism) to controversies over ritual to relationships between academies (*sŏwŏn*) and the state.

CHAPTER NINE

Chinese Identity in Turmoil:
Reform, Revolution, and Reaction, 1901–1937

After China's humiliation by Western imperialists in the Boxer uprising and the crushing Boxer Protocol, the next four decades saw violent searches for a new identity: political revolution toppled the Manchus; an intellectual-cultural revolution attempted to throw Chinese traditions into history's trash can; and a nationalism-inspired revolution apparently unified the country but in the end shriveled and died. Each effort, begun with high hopes, failed to achieve them.

THE REVOLUTIONARY MANCHUS

The empress dowager's post-Boxer exile transformed her from an obstructionist conservative into a leading reformer, initiating change in all areas that the reformers of the Hundred Days had dreamed about. The reforms focused without apology on adopting the strengths of foreign countries in order to make up for China's weaknesses. In substance they varied from mildly reformist to radical, even revolutionary. When the world of the Manchus ended with their abdication in early 1912, it was after a decade-long bang of activity rather than the whimper of those who, resigned to the forces of history, do nothing.

The Manchu reforms in the run-up to the 1911 revolution brought the first signs of a new China—from modern-style economic developments to outbursts of nationalism to the appearance of new social forces. The stirrings of the new China were spatially uneven, with cities along the coasts or important river systems exhibiting a greater degree of modern change. Variability in the rate of change tended to create different experiences, attitudes, and worldviews among the people in different areas. Cities, for example, were being paved, lighted, and policed; they were bases for wide-ranging reformist voluntary associations to deal with social problems like footbinding, opium smoking, and gambling. Cities were also centers of nationalistic sentiment expressed in public meetings and demonstrations—concerns about British threats to Tibet and Russian influence in Mongolia and Manchuria. Patriotism in Chinese coastal cities perhaps peaked in the 1905–1907 boycott against the United States for its immigration policies. In addition in this decade, a *rights recovery* movement to win control over foreign-owned mines and railroads attracted urban society as a whole. People from all social classes—gentry, merchants, students, and shopkeepers, even beggars—gave money to the movement. Some contributors, upset by foreign control, threatened to commit suicide in front of foreign embassies in Beijing. Their patriotic shout: "To die for one's country is glorious."

An important group in the rights recovery movement was overseas Chinese, particularly those in Southeast Asia, who provided financial and moral support for reformist and revolutionary causes. New in-country groups, especially youth and women, were for the first time finding public voices. Beginning in the late 1890s, China sent students to Japan, many on provincial government scholarships: in 1899, two hundred; by 1906, some thirteen thousand. Students formed associations, and some published their own newspapers. Those studying in rapidly modernizing Japan tended to become enamored of Western liberal and radical ideas and returned to China ready to reshape their world. Those in Europe and the United States tended to concentrate on more technical subjects, but they were still affected by life in these more modern states. Studies have shown that some elite women, at least in East Central China from the eighteenth century on, were educated in the classics and developed their own discussion networks of like-minded women.[1] Yet, women generally had little public voice. That situation began to change in the early twentieth century, when women organized and participated in demonstrations and revolutionary organizations. Newspapers reported the suicides of women whose mothers-in-law forbade them to unbind their feet.

Educational Reform

In its reforms, the government turned first to education. In October 1901 the empress dowager called for a national school system to run alongside and feed into the traditional examination system, serving as

Source: Questions and Topics on the 1903–1904 Jinshi Degree Examination

Throughout its long history, questions on the civil service examination varied, sometimes dealing with practical administrative issues and sometimes not. These questions show that the men who drew up this examination were concerned with China's modern development and were knowledgeable about Western models and experiences. What are the concerns of the examiners in Topics 2 and 5?

Topic 1: "Western countries attach great importance to foreign study tours. How can we define the purpose and contain the time span [of such tours] in order to obtain the maximum benefits with the least costs?"

Topic 2: "Japan Westernized its system of learning with great rapidity. In its initial rush to change, Japan invariably encountered problems from deliberately skipping over normal steps. Yet Japan can still be called a Confucian country. What are suitable goals [for Japan] that preserve strengths while rejecting weaknesses?"

Topic 3: "Chambers of Commerce and modern banks are the main features of a modern fiscal system for which budgeting and balancing accounts are fixed practices. In order to put [modern fiscal practices] into effect, the[se] fundamental components are necessary."

Topic 4: "A modern police system is closely linked to a modern political system. We should obtain foreign police codes and proceed to implement their practice."

Topic 5: "Industry, modern shipping, and railways augment military strength. All countries that have achieved wealth and power have done so using these means. Should we therefore adopt these things? What about the foundational values of a nation?"

Source: Fan Peiwei, "Qing mo guimao jiachen ke huishi shulun" (A review of the late Qing metropolitan examinations of 1904–1904), Lishi Dang'an (History archives), 3 [1993]: 105–10, trans. Douglas R. Reynolds in China: 1895–1912: State-Sponsored Reforms and China's Late-Qing Revolution (Armonk, NY: M. E. Sharpe, 1995), 94.

another route to traditional degrees. But this approach did not work; there was no incentive to choose this new route to examination success. Even more serious, there were no provisions for financing the new schools or for obtaining teachers and textbooks.

In August 1905, moving to the logical conclusion, the empress dowager accepted the advice of key officials and abolished the civil service examination. *This was the most revolutionary act of the twentieth century.* The examination was at the heart of traditional culture: it was the chief vehicle of the orthodox Chinese Way, and of recruiting political elites who manned the imperial bureaucracy and social elites, the scholar-gentry, who provided essential leadership at the local level. With the abolition of the examination, there was no way to convey official state orthodoxy—indeed, there was no longer an official state orthodoxy. There were many questions but no answers. From here on, what would give state and society its direction and its values? How would political and social leaders be recruited? What would hold China together? Once the civil service examination was gone, there was no way to stop, divert, or even slow the tides of change.

From 1906, then, China had no option but to rely on the new school system to educate its citizens. The problems remained: insufficient schools, funding, teachers, and textbooks. Local elites opened and taught in schools. The problem was that the school system in any particular locality depended on the level of economic development and the presence of interested elites. As it developed, the system remained weak at its base: elites could achieve higher salaries and greater prestige by setting up a high school rather than an elementary school, so some communities had no kindergartens or elementary schools. Nevertheless, the education system was quickly, if haphazardly, transformed. Perhaps most revolutionary were the curriculum (with both Chinese and Western studies replacing the classics) and the social impact, for instead of studying individually with a tutor, students now met in a classroom with other students as peers.

Military Reform

A well-known Chinese proverb says, "Good iron is not beaten into nails; good men are not made into soldiers." Chinese civilization had hailed and stressed the virtues of civilian rule and civil values. The early twentieth century saw a remarkable revaluation of the military and increasing militarization of Chinese politics and society. At the start of the century there were several types of military organizations—the banner forces, the Green Standard Army, and the mid-nineteenth-century regional armies—that were weak and almost useless. In the fight against Japan in the 1890s, only 60 percent of Li Hongzhang's Anhui army had guns; the rest used swords, spears, and pikes.

Two so-called New Armies, established in the mid-1890s by Zhang Zhidong and Yuan Shikai, were trained by German military officers and equipped with modern weapons. In July 1901 the Manchus transferred Zhang's army to Yuan's control, making him the key military leader in the country and the head of the united New Army. New military academies were established in Beijing and several provinces. Using Japanese instructors, they produced cadets inculcated with patriotism. Many academy graduates enrolled in Japanese academies. When they returned to China, many were filled with the anti-Manchu and revolutionary ideas of Sun Yixian and others. New Army divisions were stationed at garrisons around the country.

Constitutionalism

The Chinese interpreted Japan's victory over Russia in 1905 as that of a constitutional power overcoming an authoritarian regime and came to see constitutionalism as a possible reason for Japan's modernizing success. In addition, since much power had flowed from the center to lower levels in the state after the Taiping Rebellion (due to the center's political weakness and economic bankruptcy), Qing policymakers thought that constitutional forms might strengthen their control over localities and their elites. Study missions sent abroad in 1905–1906 favored the Japanese model to secure the throne's power. In 1906 the empress dowager endorsed that model, calling as well for a government overhaul, replacing the traditional Six Boards with modern ministries. In August 1908 she announced a nine-year calendar during which specific constitutional forms would be established, with full implementation of a constitutional system by 1917. Had she lived, the empress dowager might have instituted that new system, but her death in November 1908 and that of the Guangxu emperor a day earlier left the government in the hands of a regent, the father of the new three-year-old emperor. Inept and concerned mainly with enhancing their own power, he and other Manchu princes made decisions that increasingly alienated the Han Chinese.

Elections for the provisional provincial assemblies, the first Chinese elections ever for representative bodies, were held from February to June 1909. Educational or economic requirements for candidates and voters meant that only a tiny minority of the population could vote, averaging about 0.42 percent, barely over four people per thousnd. Yet, these were the first elections in the country and thus were very important. When the assemblies met, they were bold and demanding: representatives from sixteen provinces petitioned the Qing court to convene a national assembly immediately. Three times in 1910 similar petitions were presented, with the number of signatures increasing with each attempt—reportedly two hundred thousand signed the first and up to twenty-five million the third—but the regent refused to consider them. County-level self-government bodies—county seat, town, and township councils—were meeting in most provinces by late summer 1911. Alongside the councils were other Qing-mandated organs: chambers of commerce (1903), education associations (1906), and agriculture associations (1907). Elites saw these new bodies as ways to solidify and enhance their own political leadership.

The provisional national assembly met in Beijing on October 1, 1910. Disobeying restrictions on its deliberations, it petitioned for the immediate establishment of a full-fledged national assembly. The throne caved in on November 4, promising an assembly by 1913—a date rejected by the provisional assembly, which cried, "Now." In December, demonstrations in Tianjin before government offices called for the assembly's immediate establishment. In the face of increasing political pressure, the throne announced in May 1911 the formation of a cabinet of thirteen, but it had only four Han Chinese—which many Chinese considered a slap in the face. Given the rising anti-Manchu bitterness, the situation was volatile and dangerous. Every reform of the Qing court hastened its demise. It is no exaggeration to call the Manchus revolutionary.[2]

THE ANTI-MANCHU REVOLUTIONARY MOVEMENT

Japan, China's Other, served as the incubator of revolution against the Manchu Other. The key revolutionary organization, the Revolutionary Alliance, was formed in Tokyo in 1905 by Sun Yixian (1867–1925). By the 1890s he was devoting all his energy to throwing off Manchu rule, but his efforts to instigate revolution by organizing small-scale revolts failed. The revolutionary goals set down when he founded his Alliance (the Three Principles of the People) continued to be the watchwords of his party until his death: *nationalism*: ending Manchu rule and the presence of imperialists; *democracy*: focusing on election, initiative, referendum, and recall; and *socialism* (*people's livelihood*): focusing on equalizing land ownership and controlling capital.

Study in Japan turned many young Chinese into antigovernment revolutionaries. Three deserve mention. The most influential revolutionary work of the decade was *The Revolutionary Army,* written by eighteen-year-old Zou Rong, who argued that a revolution must sweep out Manchu "bandits" and install a constitutional republic.[3] In 1907, Qiu Jin (see Identities) joined other former students in a plot to revolt after the assassination of a Manchu governor. Before she could act, Qiu was seized and beheaded. Today she is seen as a national heroine and as the earliest feminist in China. In 1910 Wang Jingwei, a key member of the Revolutionary Alliance, tried to assassinate the prince regent. The police were tipped off; Wang was imprisoned, but he was released when the 1911 revolution broke out.

THE 1911 REVOLUTION

The revolution was shaped by timing and contingency as much as by planning. It began at the Yangzi River city of Wuchang, the site of an important New Army garrison. Two revolutionary organizations had worked to enlist the support of New Army troops for a planned revolt. When police discovered the plot, the revolutionaries, facing arrest and certain death, decided to proceed. Key commanders and the city's civilian officials fled, and the revolutionaries had no leader. Finding the New Army officer Li Yuanhong hiding in fear at a staff officer's home, they asked him to lead them, but he refused. They threatened him. With no viable options, he became the leader of the revolution.

The government wanted former military leader Yuan Shikai, whom they had dismissed in 1908, to lead their forces. Yuan put them off, wanting to see which way the winds would blow. After the rebels gained victory after victory, Yuan agreed, but only after the government consented to appoint

Identities: Qiu Jin (1875–1907):
The Autumn Wind and Rain

Qiu Jin's formative years differed from those of most Chinese women, as she received a classical education alongside her older brother. An arranged marriage produced two children, but in 1903 she left her family for education and radical discussions in Japan. Though she studied at the Aoyama Vocational Girls School in Tokyo, she was most influenced by her association with other Chinese students in revolutionary organizations. She came to see herself as a knight errant, styling herself the Heroine of Jian Lake (near her home); she posed for photographs dressed as a man, with a dagger that she frequently carried; she also studied bomb making and practiced marksmanship. An accomplished poet, she was charismatic and assertively individualistic, filled with revolutionary romanticism. "When she turned toward the revolutionary movement, [she] entered a world of dragons and tigers, clouds and raging seas, where only the brave might prevail.

> Ascending to heaven mounted on a
> white dragon,
> Crossing the hills astride a savage tiger.
> Angry shouts summon the winds and
> clouds
> And the spirit dances, flying in all
> directions.
> A great man in the world
> Must commune with heavenly spirits,
> And look after those other sons of
> pigs and dogs
> Who are beneath his company."[1]

Before returning to China for good in 1906, Qiu joined Sun Yixian's Revolutionary Alliance in August 1905 and became party head for her home province of Zhejiang. In early 1906 in Shanghai, she joined the Restoration Society, a revolutionary group founded by men from Shaoxing, Qiu's native place, becoming active in revolutionary organizing and fund-raising. In February 1907 she returned to Shaoxing, where she took over the Datong school (which functioned both as a school and as a revolutionary front), scandalizing the local community by dressing as a man and having female students participate in military drills. She became a close friend of Wang Ziyu, a degreeholder, teacher, and newspaperman. Qiu frequently visited Wang at home, discussing revolution, reciting poetry, and drinking. Both Qiu and Wang could drink huge quantities of wine, reportedly downing as many as five catties in one sitting; more than once at Wang's home, Qiu became drunk. After her death, Wang and his family were the most important promoters of her memory.

In the summer of 1907, Qiu coordinated revolutionary plans with Xu Xilin of the Restoration Society. He and several others planned to assassinate Enming, the Manchu governor of Anhui province, and at roughly the same time, Qiu was to begin an uprising in Zhejiang. Xu succeeded in killing Enming, but he was immediately arrested and executed. When authorities discovered Qiu's involvement in the plot, they sent troops from Hangzhou that stormed the Datong School and seized her. Shortly before her execution, she allegedly wrote the lines that have the ring of a epitaph: "The autumn wind and the autumn rain will make me die of sorrow." Qiu was beheaded in Shaoxing on July 15, 1907. She is renowned today for her revolutionary character and contributions, for her actions as China's first feminist, and for her poetry. She should also be remembered for her courage. Wang Ziyu remarked that dying would be difficult for any man but that Qiu Jin had gone to her execution with bravery and dignity.

---

[1] *Mary Backus Rankin*, Early Chinese Revolutionaries *(Cambridge, MA: Harvard University Press, 1971), 45–46.*

Revolution: Cutting the Queue   Chinese men were forced to wear a queue in the seventeenth century, a constant humiliating reminder of Han Chinese subjection to the Manchus. Yet, over the two and a half centuries that they had worn this hairstyle, it had become the standard and accepted custom. Cutting the queue became a visible symbol of breaking with the past, and many Chinese were unwilling to lose this part of themselves.

him premier with the right to name his own cabinet. But revolutionary events spiraled out of control. Provincial and prefectural cities across China saw New Army troops join scholar-gentry, rich merchants, and students returned from Japan to declare the beginning of the republic. By late November, fifteen provinces had seceded from the Qing dynasty. Yuan emerged as power broker in the struggle. In early December, the revolutionaries offered Yuan the presidency of the republic if he agreed to support it and bring about the emperor's abdication; Yuan leaped at the opportunity. It was a decision that the revolutionaries would come to regret. Though Yuan had been a powerful and capable dynastic official, he had had no experience with republicanism. The revolutionaries, it seems, had offered Yuan the post to stop the disorder quickly out of fear that foreign powers might take advantage of the situation. The Chinese were skittish about anything that might incur foreign wrath, retaliation, or aggressive demands.[4]

When Sun returned to China from his fund-raising trips abroad, he supported the earlier deal with Yuan, who secured the Manchu abdication on February 12, 1912. In memory of the Ming, the last Chinese dynasty, people hung white flags to symbolize the restoration of political control to the Han Chinese. The date of the revolution's beginning—the tenth day of the tenth month, or Double Ten—has since been celebrated as National Day by the Republic of China on the mainland and in Taiwan. On the whole, the winners of the revolution were already-ensconced elites and Yuan; this was no social revolution. Nevertheless, it had extraordinary implications. The abolition of the monarchy demolished the political structure in place for over two millennia and left an untried republic, as yet only a name without substance.

Source: The Qing Abdication Edict

The court called on the longtime official Yuan Shikai to put down the revolution that began in the fall of 1911. In the end, he worked to bring about the dynasty's abdication. This edict, issued by the Qing court on February 12, 1912, marked the end of two thousand years of imperial rule in China. Why, according to the edict, did the Manchus decide to abdicate? What did they call on Yuan Shikai to do?

As a consequence of the uprising of the Republican Army, to which the different provinces immediately responded, the Empire seethed like a boiling cauldron and the people were plunged into utter misery. Yuan Shikai was, therefore, especially commanded some time ago to dispatch commissioners to confer with the representatives of the Republican Army on the general situation and to discuss matters pertaining to the convening of a National Assembly for the decision of the suitable mode of settlement. . . . Separated as the South and North are by great distances, the unwillingness of either side to yield to the other can result only in the continued interruption of trade and the prolongation of hostilities, for, so long as the form of government is undecided, the Nation can have no peace. It is now evident that the hearts of the majority of the people are in favor of a republican form of government: the provinces of the South were the first to espouse the cause, and the generals of the North have since pledged their support. From the preference of the people's hearts, the Will of Heaven can be discerned. How could We then dare to oppose the will of the millions for the glory of one Family! Therefore, observing the tendencies of the age on one hand and studying the opinions of the people on the other, We and His Majesty the Emperor hereby vest the sovereignty in the People and decide in favor of a republican form of constitutional government. Thus we would gratify on the one hand the desires of the whole nation who, tired of anarchy, are desirous of peace, and on the other hand would follow in the footsteps of the Ancient Sages who regarded the Throne as the sacred trust of the Nation.

Now Yuan Shikai was elected by the provisional parliament to be the Premier. During this period of transference of government from the old to the new, there should be some means of uniting the South and the North. Let Yuan Shikai organize with full powers a provisional republican government and confer with the Republican Army as to the methods of union, thus assuring peace to the people and tranquility to the Empire, and forming to one Great Republic of China by the union as heretofore, of the five peoples, namely, Manchus, Chinese, Mongols, Mohammedans, and Tibetans together with their territory in its integrity. We and His majesty the Emperor, thus enabled to live in retirement, free from responsibilities and cares, . . . shall enjoy without interruption the courteous treatment of the Nation and see with Our own eyes the consummation of an illustrious government. Is not this highly advisable?

Source: Pei-kai Cheng and Michael Lestz, with Jonathan Spence, The Search for Modern China: A Documentary Collection *(New York: W. W. Norton, 1999), 211–12.*

THE PRESIDENCY OF YUAN SHIKAI

Yuan had built his reputation as a military reformer, but he had also overseen reforms in education, commerce, and industry. Though he had never traveled beyond Korea and knew no foreign languages, he recruited men with experience in other countries. Politically, he was devoted to order and centralized control as he set out to modernize the country. For him, the republic that he had inherited—with political parties and representative bodies—was too messy and so unpredictable that it could not serve as a realistic base for a new China. Careful management by a strong head of state was required.

Sun Yixian turned his Revolutionary Alliance into a political party, the Guomindang (the Nationalist Party), to field candidates in the December 1912 National Assembly elections. As in the late Qing assemblies, there were age, gender, educational, and economic qualifications for voting and serving. While some corruption marred the elections, they were carried out with relative smoothness. These elections were the high point of electoral democracy in the twentieth and twenty-first centuries on the Chinese mainland and in Taiwan until the late 1980s. The Guomindang won about 43 percent of the vote, a plurality among the multiple parties; they would control 45 percent of National Assembly seats. But the euphoria was short-lived. In March 1913, as he was leaving for Beijing to form the new government, the thirty-year-old party leader Song Jiaoren was shot at the Shanghai train station. Yuan was implicated in the assassination. To add insult to tragedy, Yuan, without even a nod to the National Assembly's constitutional involvement, negotiated a huge loan of about $100 million from a foreign consortium. By the summer, pro-Guomindang forces began to rebel against him. This second revolution ended in the military rout of the revolutionaries and the flight of Sun and others to Japan.

Yuan then built his dictatorship. In October he forced the National Assembly to ratify his election as president for a five-year term. In November he outlawed the Guomindang, evicting its members from the Assembly. In February 1914, he abolished all assemblies—national, provincial, and county—ending China's democratic experiment. A 1914 law tightened general press censorship. The government took greater control over often-powerful chamber of commerce organizations. Police were given the right to open mail and search luggage at train stations. However, Yuan did support some reform initiatives, blending old and new. He called for universal education for males, which meant four years of free primary school, and suppressed the domestic cultivation of opium. In advancing economic development, he was very

President Yuan Shikai   Though he had been an able military and political leader, Yuan (shown here in uniform) had never shown any commitment to republicanism. But the possibility of imperialists taking advantage of the revolution to meddle in Chinese affairs persuaded the revolutionaries to yield power to him. It turned out to be a colossal mistake.

much the self-strengthener. He reinstituted tradition in the form of Confucianism as the state religion. In schoolbooks, passages from *Mencius* replaced stories about Sun Yixian; Yuan's attempts to put old wine into new bottles seemed inappropriate.

In August 1915, Yuan launched a campaign to take the throne as "Grand Constitutional Emperor" on January 1, 1916. It was a mistake. Even though the monarchy had been gone for barely three years, people's reactions showed that Chinese political culture had already left it far behind. Military forces in Southwest China raised an army against Yuan in December 1915. As more and more provinces declared themselves independent, Yuan could not staunch the bloodletting. His June 6 death from uremia was, from a personal standpoint, a merciful ending. But for the country, it was the moment of collapse into a national nightmare that would last for more than a decade.

THE POWER OF THE GUN

As long as Yuan lived, he was able to control the New Army generals he had trained; he had been their patron and they his students. When he died, the destructive genie of military struggle was freed to wreak havoc over the land. The goal of Yuan's former generals, now transformed into *warlords,* was to seize Beijing and its government in order to be recognized as president of the Republic. The warlord wars produced one of the most tragic and chaotic periods in twentieth-century China. Though technically it ended in 1928, when the country was nominally unified, *residual warlordism* persisted into the 1940s.

The national-scale militarists were separated into two main cliques that formed around Yuan's two chief lieutenants. Between 1920 and 1926 these cliques fought 4 major wars, mainly in North China, with some shifts in the makeup of the cliques in each war. One historian has, however, counted more than 140 wars fought in the country between 1916 and 1928. These were bloody affairs that grew bloodier over the years. Though many of the officers were military professionals, the soldiers themselves were mostly recruited from rural areas. Though national regulations specified that they were to be nineteen to twenty-six years old, commanders took them at all ages. Fatalities in battle were high, a situation worsened by the lack of medical care; even light wounds could bring death.

All warlords held territories of varying size, but the name *warlord* covered many different types. Some had the abilities, character, and potential to unite the Chinese nation and become head of state. An example was North China's Feng Yuxiang, a self-taught Christian who indoctrinated his troops with Christian and traditional Chinese values and baptized them with a fire hose. A committed social and educational reformer, he established orphanages, drug rehabilitation centers, and schools. Other warlords had lesser goals, some regional, others local; some were simply thugs. One of the more notorious was Zhang Zongchang, the "Dog-Meat General." His troops (many of them ten-year-old boys) were notorious for their practice of *opening melons*—that is, splitting skulls—and for hanging strings of human heads on telegraph poles to elicit respect for their power.

Among the populace, the warlord scourge included loss of life, rapes by military victors and losers, destruction of crops and agricultural infrastructure, and widespread economic dislocation and property destruction. Troops lived off the areas they occupied or moved through, looting and pillaging. In addition, warlord armies needed money for weapons and supplies, two sources of which were opium and taxes. Aware of opium's capacity to bring in huge profits, warlords forced farmers to plant opium poppies instead of food crops. Whereas 3 percent of China's total farmland was in opium production from 1914 to 1919, in the period 1929 to 1933 it shot up to 20 percent. Taxation was another warlord scourge. Every conceivable item was taxed—from consumer goods to life situations (getting married, owning a pig, going to a brothel). Land taxes were collected as much as ten years in advance. Taxes on commodities in transit were exorbitant. Taxes reached confiscatory levels, wrecking economies and people's livelihoods. Yet another tragedy of warlordism was that many battles were made more destructive because Western

Source: The Dog-Meat General

The warlord Zhang Zongzhang was basically a thug, known for his propensity for wanton violence and brutality. Lin Yutang, one of China's most popular writers, penned this description. What is its tone? Why might Lin have adopted such a tone?

He was six feet tall, a towering giant, with a pair of squint eyes and a pair of abnormally massive hands. He was direct, forceful, terribly efficient at times: obstinate and gifted with moderate intelligence. He was patriotic according to his lights. . . . He could drink, and he was awfully fond of "dog-meat," and he could swear all he wanted to and as much as he wanted to, irrespective of his official superiors and inferiors. He made no pretence to being a gentleman, and didn't affect to send nice-sounding circular telegrams, like the rest of [the warlords]. He was ruthlessly honest, and this honesty made him much loved by all his close associates. . . . If he made orgies he didn't try to conceal them from his friends and foes. If he coveted his subordinate's wife he told him openly, and wrote no psalm of repentance about it like King David. And he always played square. If he took his subordinate's wife he made her husband the chief of police of [a major city]. And he took good care of other people's morals. He forbade girl students from entering parks in Jinan, and

protected them from the men-gorillas who stood at every corner and nook to devour them. And he was pious, and he kept a harem. . . . He was very fond of his executioner, and he was thoroughly devoted to his mother.

Once he appointed a man magistrate in a certain district in Shandong, and another day he appointed another man to the same office and started a quarrel. Both claimed that they had been personally appointed by General Dog-meat. It was agreed, therefore, that they should go and see the General to clear up the difficulty. When they arrived it was evening, and General Zhang was in bed in the midst of his orgies. "Come in," he said, with his usual candor.

The two magistrates then explained that they had both been appointed by him to the same district.

"You fools!" he said, "can't you settle such a little thing between yourselves, but must come to bother me about it?"

. . . like all Chinese robbers, he was an honest man.

Source: Edgar Snow, Living China *(Westport, CT: Hyperion, 1937), 222–25.*

nations supplied guns and ammunition. Foreign nations picked their pet warlord and aided him, hoping that he might become president and reward them with privileges.

Though some warlords aspired to unite the nation, warlordism was the antithesis of nationalism. Warlords' actions radically fragmented a state whose modern identity had not yet had time to develop. Their reliance on foreign arms and aid undercut the late Qing rights recovery movement. Further, their actions and policies seriously damaged the economy and inhibited national economic progress. Warlords contributed to the growing militarization of Chinese society, and their actions demoralized and devastated the people.

THE MAY FOURTH MOVEMENT

Lu Xun (1881–1936) was China's most important twentieth-century writer. In one of his most famous stories, "The Diary of a Madman," an official, suffering from obsessive paranoia, convinced that everyone wants to kill and eat him, discovers an old history book: " . . . scrawled over each page [of my history] are the words: 'Virtue and Morality'. . . I read intently half the night, until I began to see words between the lines, the whole book being filled with the two words—'Eat people.'"[5] This was a savage indictment of traditional Chinese society—parroting the proper Confucian pieties masking the reality that Confucian values destroyed human lives by crushing them beneath a social hierarchy of superiors: parents over children, husbands over wives.

Lu's writing contributed to what is called the *New Culture Movement*, actually a cultural revolution. It was part of a larger *May Fourth Movement*, an amorphous array of political and cultural activities usually dated from the 1915 founding of the journal *New Youth* to roughly 1924. Lu desperately believed that something had to be done to awaken the Chinese to what he saw as the destructiveness of traditional culture. He captured the danger and the opportunity in a strong metaphor:

> *Imagine an iron house without windows, absolutely indestructible, with many people fast asleep inside who will soon die of suffocation. But you know since they will die in their sleep, they will not feel the pain of death. Now if you cry aloud to wake a few of the lighter sleepers, making those unfortunate few suffer the agony of irrevocable death, do you think you are doing them a good turn? But if a few awake, you can't say there is no hope of destroying the iron house.*[6]

THE NEW CULTURE MOVEMENT

At the core of the New Culture Movement was the rejection of traditional culture and efforts to define a new cultural base and direction. The most influential forum was *New Youth,* edited by a returned student from Japan and France, Chen Duxiu. In the lead essay, "Call to Youth," Chen championed the young as China's saviors:

> *Youth is like early spring, like the rising sun, like trees and grass in bud, like a newly sharpened blade. It is the most valuable period of life. The function of youth in society is the same as that of a fresh and vital cell in a human body. In the processes of metabolism, the old and rotten are incessantly eliminated to be replaced by the fresh and living.*[7]

The traditional value most castigated was filial piety, the heart of the Confucian family system. Countless young Chinese rebelled against their fathers in particular. Student Shi Cuntong, in a 1919 essay, asserted that filial piety was the same as "the virtue required of a slave." A writer noted the widespread rebellion against the family system. "There were also people who wrote letters to their fathers saying, 'From a certain date on, I will not recognize you as my father. We are all friends, and equal.'"[8]

Women were subordinated from birth. Considered almost burdens by their natal families, girls were provided for until they were married off and then perhaps never seen again. Matchmakers arranged child betrothals to benefit families, not to satisfy the desires of individuals; sometimes the result was suicide. If a fiancé died before marriage or if a husband died early, the unmarried or widowed woman had to remain forever chaste, choosing death rather than risking intimate involvement. Parents whose daughters committed suicide might erect memorial arches to them. Suicide rates were highest among woman in their late teens and twenties—more than double the rates in Japan at the time. Liberating themselves from the family system brought women new choices. The title character in "Miss Sophie's Diary," the best-known story of China's famous twentieth-century female author Ding Ling, was a "modern girl" torn in her affections between two men.[9] The story raised issues about the roles

Source: The Role of Youth

Written by Chen Duxiu (1879–1942), this editorial appeared in the inaugural year of the most important journal of the May Fourth Movement, New Youth. *It is Chen's call to youth to change their approach to life in order to change Chinese society and culture. What does he call on youth to do?*

1. Be independent, not servile. Emancipation means freeing oneself from the bondage of slavery and achieving a completely independent and free personality. I have hands and feet, and I can earn my own living. I have a mouth and a tongue, and I can voice my own likes and dislikes. I have a mind, and I can determine my own beliefs. . . . [T]here is definitely no reason why one should blindly follow others. . . . [It should be clear that] loyalty, filial piety, chastity, and righteousness are a slavish morality.

2. Be progressive, not conservative. Now our country still has not awakened from its long dream, and isolates itself by going down the old rut. . . . All our traditional ethics, law, scholarship, rites and customs are survivals of feudalism. . . . Revering only the history of the twenty-four dynasties, and making no plans for progress and improvement, our people will be turned out of this twentieth-century world, and be lodged in the dark ditches fit only for slaves, cattle, and horses. . . . Whatever cannot skillfully change itself and progress along with the world will find itself eliminated by natural selection because of failure to adapt to the environment.

3. Be aggressive, not retiring. It is our natural obligation in life to advance in spite of numerous difficulties.

4. Be cosmopolitan, not isolationist. If at this point one still raises a particularistic theory of history and of national circumstances and hopes thereby to resist the current, then this still indicates the spirit of an isolationist country and a lack of knowledge of the world. When its citizens lack knowledge of the world, how can a nation expect to survive in it?

5. Be utilitarian, not formalistic. Though a thing is of gold or jade, if it is of no practical use, then it is of less value than coarse cloth, grain, manure, or dirt. That which brings no benefit to the practical life of an individual or of society is all empty formalism and the stuff of cheats. And even though it were bequeathed to us by our ancestors, taught by the sages, advocated by the government and worshipped by society, the stuff of cheats is still not worth one cent.

6. Be scientific, not imaginative. To explain truth by science means proving everything with fact. Although the process is slower than that of imagination and arbitrary decision, yet every step is taken on firm ground, it is different from those imaginative flights which eventually cannot advance even one inch. The amount of truth in the universe is boundless, and the fertile areas in the realm of science awaiting the pioneer are immense! Youth, take up the task.

Source: Ssu-yu Teng and John Fairbank, eds., China's Response to the West: A Documentary Survey, *1839–1923 (Cambridge, MA: Harvard University Press, 1954), 240–46.*

that modern women were to play in the new culture (Sophie was sexually aggressive) and the impacts of these roles on women's psyches. As a sign of the times in Zhejiang province, the message on an arched memorial—"Respect chaste women and filial sons"—was blotted out and replaced with a new message: "Long live women's liberation."[10] From roughly 1917 to 1921, the emphasis on individualism and achieving individual goals was greater than in any time in modern China's history. The absence of a powerful state and the wide-open search for a new social, political, and ideological Way was liberating for the young.

THE LANGUAGE REVOLUTION

Before 1917, *New Youth* was written in classical or literary Chinese, like all printed materials. Classical Chinese was difficult: it valued concision, often omitting subjects and objects; it used characters that were particles giving sentences a particular tone or turn; and it used no punctuation. These characteristics made it both difficult and ambiguous, a huge obstacle to increasing literacy. In addition, as a strong language-revolution proponent, the American-educated scholar Hu Shi, put it: "A dead language can never produce a living literature; . . . [w]e must . . . elevate this [vernacular] tool. Only [then] can we talk about . . . new ideas and new spirit."[11]

This literary revolution slowly succeeded. Literary magazines came to be published in the vernacular. In 1921 the government's Ministry of Education announced that all primary school text books would be published in the vernacular as well. The literary revolution joined the anti-Confucian cultural revolution as the two centerpieces of the May Fourth Movement. The speed of monumental change in the first years of the twentieth century was nothing short of breathtaking: within about a dozen years, the examination system and the monarchy had been dismantled, the traditional language turned into a museum piece, and traditional culture trashed.

Chen Duxiu and Hu Shi became colleagues at Beijing University (Beida), one of the centers of the New Culture Movement. The scholar Cai Yuanpei was appointed university chancellor in 1916, arguing that it should be the central laboratory for the new culture. In revamping Beida, he insisted on three points. First, its purpose was academic research with the goal of creating a new culture; such research, Cai believed, should be critical of both Western civilization and Chinese traditional civilization. Second, students had to get rid of the idea that a Beida diploma was their ticket to a job. Finally, at Beida, complete academic freedom was the sine qua non. Scholars had to express divergent ideas openly so that the new Chinese Way could be found. Cai brought scholars of all intellectual and political stripes to Beida to debate about possibilities for the new China in an atmosphere of unfettered academic freedom.

The excitement of the intellectual quest was enhanced by lecture tours of foreigners with a range of intellectual positions. Among them were the American pragmatic philosopher John Dewey, the British pacifist philosopher Bertrand Russell, and the American birth control advocate and feminist Margaret Sanger. There were loud supportive calls for two "men" whose backgrounds were in the West and whose names became watchwords at the time and a siren song in China for the twentieth century: Mr. De and Mr. Sai. Mr. De(mocracy) became the rallying cry of those angered and humiliated by the wretched situation of the Chinese state. Democracy seemed more plausible in a world that had seen the victory of the "democratic" Allied powers in World War I and the 1917 Bolshevik Revolution in Russia. Mr. Sai (Science) led the march into the modern world, banishing the darkness of ignorance and superstition. Since whatever was scientific seemed progressive, the essential route for the future of the individual and the nation was the scientific road. A few intellectuals, like Liang Qichao, condemned the West's use of science for constructing destructive weapons during World War I, but the majority of Chinese saw science as a panacea for the country's ills.

THE MAY FOURTH INCIDENT AND ITS AFTERMATH

The May Fourth Movement takes its name from a student demonstration in Beijing on May 4, 1919, an incident fueled by nationalistic fervor that changed the direction of the movement. Prompted by the Allied decision to allow the Japanese to retain control of Shandong province after taking it in World War I (see Chapter 10), the incident marked the increased politicization and political involvement of students. On May 4, about 3,000 students from thirteen universities and colleges massed at the Gate of Heavenly Peace in front of the Forbidden City. A distributed manifesto read in part, "This is the last chance for China in her life and death struggle. Today we swear two solemn oaths with all our countrymen: (1) China's territory may be conquered, but it cannot be given away; (2) the Chinese people may be massacred, but they will not surrender."[12] Students marched to the home of a Chinese official considered a Japanese collaborator and torched it. After 32 students were arrested, the demonstrators focused on getting their peers released. On May 19, the citywide Student Union (formed two weeks earlier) declared a general strike, demanding that China's president refuse to sign the Versailles Treaty and punish the three alleged pro-Japanese traitorous officials. Government policy toward the students wavered from harsh to lenient. By June 4, over 1,100 students had been arrested; the next day, over 1,000 female students from the Beijing area, in an unprecedented action, marched to the presidential palace demanding the release of the prisoners and freedom of speech.

By this time, the Beijing action was simply part of a larger nationwide protest. The Beijing Student Union served as a prototype for similar organizations in Shanghai, Wuhan, and Tianjin and ultimately for a Student Union of the Republic of China. Up to twenty thousand protested in Shanghai on May 7. Two days later, the Shanghai Student Union launched a boycott against Japanese goods. The demonstrations and boycott culminated in a general strike that began on June 5 to force the Chinese delegation at Versailles not to sign the peace treaty. The trump card of the Shanghai general strike was that the city was the economic heart of the Republic of China; a long general strike could bring an already weak economy to its knees. On June 6 industrial workers joined the strike, first printers, then textile workers, and, most important, streetcar workers, whose participation paralyzed the city. The strike continued until June 12, when word came that the three offending pro-Japanese officials had been dismissed. Protests continued until the July 2 announcement that the delegation had not signed the treaty.

Of great importance for later developments was that focused political action had brought victory. In cities, it had flowered into a mass movement of students, business and industry leaders and managers, urban professionals (journalists, teachers, doctors, lawyers, and engineers), shopkeepers, and the urban working class. Acting together, they had forced the government to change its position.

May Fourth Demonstration, 1919 Students, scholars, and others associated with colleges and universities demonstrated in traditional dress and with placards in front of the Gate of Heavenly Peace in Beijing. They called for the replacement of government officials thought to be collaborating with the Japanese. *Source:* Courtesy of the Kautz Family YMCA Archives and the YMCA of the USA.

POLITICAL CHANGE FIRST; CULTURAL CHANGE WILL FOLLOW

Two camps emerged in the May Fourth Movement that battled over the direction of the movement. Some pointed to the people's political victory in mid-1919 and argued that direct political action was key to changing China. They asserted that the political system had to be altered so that it could not jail or snuff out advocates of change and so that other modern changes could be facilitated. Direct political action (violent, if need be) had to become the main tool for revolutionary change. A leading supporter of this view was Chen Duxiu, dean of the School of Letters at Beida. Especially appealing were Marxism and, after the success of the Bolsheviks in 1917, Leninism. One of the early converts to Marxist-Leninist thought was Beida's librarian, Li Dazhao, who commemorated the anniversary of the Russian Revolution in a *New Youth* essay, "The Victory of Bolshevism"; he devoted the May 1919 issue of the journal to articles on Marxism.

The appeal of Marxism-Leninism? On a basic level, nothing succeeds like success: it had succeeded in overthrowing Russian autocracy. Chinese intellectuals were also drawn to the Soviet model after the 1919 Soviet government's Karakhan Declaration to renounce all the privileges in China that the czars had won in unequal treaties, as well as Russia's share of the Boxer indemnity. Compared to the other imperialists, who at the Versailles Conference had so recently thumbed their noses at China, the Soviet Union seemed to be a cut above. Above all, Marxism-Leninism was *scientific*. Marx's idea of historical materialism explained history and the chief dynamic of historical development: history moves through stages—from slave to feudal to capitalist to socialist to communist, propelled by classes struggling for control of the means of production. This thesis offered a vision of where a particular society stood in its revolutionary progress toward the communist utopia. Leninism explained China's plight as a semicolony of the imperialist powers, arguing that for Western capitalism to survive, Western nations had to develop empires with raw materials and cheap labor. Cut off the support from their colonies, Lenin claimed, and Western capitalism would wither. Leninism further promoted that all-important revolutionary vehicle, a tightly organized and controlled party. In the end, Marxism-Leninism's most important appeal was that it offered a sweeping, systemic solution to China's myriad problems.

CULTURAL CHANGE FIRST; POLITICAL CHANGE WILL FOLLOW

The other camp formed after the May Fourth incident contended that any meaningful political change must be preceded by and built on cultural change. Cultural change was an evolutionary effort and could not be engineered rapidly by tools like violence. One of the most important advocates of this path to change was Hu Shi, a pragmatist who saw a world of problems that needed solving. Since problems varied in different areas, among different kinds of people, in different arenas of life, each problem had to be solved through careful study. Hu argued that "[t]here is no liberation *in toto* or reconstruction *in toto*. Liberation means liberation from this or that institution, from this or that belief, for this or that individual; it is liberation bit by bit, drop by drop."[13] Hu attacked what he called *isms*—like Marxism and Leninism— as overarching creeds, systems, or *fundamental solutions* that seemed to offer a way out of China's predicament but in reality could not.

Many Chinese had difficulties with this approach. For a civilization in crisis, this solution, based on education and evolutionary change, was not intellectually or practically satisfying. It would take many years, perhaps decades, even a century or more; even then, it brought no guarantee that it could remake China before the country might disintegrate and fall completely into Western hands. For many Chinese intellectuals and students, so recently enamored of individual liberation, the emerging priority came to be the fate of the nation. Without national liberation, individual liberation would ultimately be meaningless.

THE HISTORICAL SIGNIFICANCE OF THE MAY FOURTH MOVEMENT

The May Fourth Movement marked an important split in the intellectual and cultural history of China. Scholars have called it *China's Renaissance*, in part because the vernacular first came to be used then. Western vernacular languages—French, Spanish, and Italian—as opposed to Latin, first came into use in the Western Renaissance. Scholars have also called the May Fourth Movement the *Chinese Enlightenment*, a term recalling the important role of science and experimentation and the casting off of tradition. It was also an intellectual and cultural revolution in which tradition was discarded—even trashed—and replaced by bold experimentation with new ideas and methods. It was the first of a series of twentieth-century attempts to dismantle traditional culture.

Because it discarded traditional Chinese culture, the May Fourth Movement has drawn strong reactions from various Chinese political forces. For the Nationalist regime of Jiang Jieshi (the mandarin pronunciation of Chiang Kai-shek) and his successors, the movement seemed too radical, destroying much that was good in Chinese traditions; further, in its emphasis on direct political action, it was linked too closely to the rise of Chinese Communism. The Nationalists viewed the movement with considerable distrust and suspicion. The Communists, whose party grew out of the intellectual ferment and issues of the time, have looked more kindly on the May Fourth period but have disapproved of the first phase glorifying individual aspirations and satisfactions. The Communists attacked this emphasis as *bourgeois* and accused intellectuals of being poisoned with the toxin of individualism. Thus, both major political parties have been somewhat negative about the May Fourth Movement. We must note that the time these cultural revolutionaries had to make major social and cultural changes was absurdly short. Their efforts were overtaken by the sweep of revolutionary political events. The movement for cultural renewal was swallowed whole by the movement for national salvation.

THE BIRTH OF THE COMMUNIST PARTY

A key question for Chinese nationalists was how to build national power fast enough to prevent continuing national humiliation or, even worse, dismemberment by foreign powers. A strong government was essential. That meant building political parties to serve as the engine and military forces to serve as the vehicle by which to defeat warlords and then expel or, at least, deal more effectively with the imperialists. These were the institutional components of China's 1920s revolution. Yet, a revolution is made by people who, in the process of revolution, do not know the end results; therefore, their choices and decisions are often shaped by personalities, emotions, and reactions to contingencies and day-to-day realities.

The midwife for the Communist Party's birth was the Communist International or Comintern, an organization established in Moscow to direct world revolution. In 1920 a Comintern agent met with Chinese students and intellectuals in Beijing and Shanghai. That summer, Marxist study societies—the building blocks for the Chinese Communist Party (CCP)—were formed in Shanghai, Beijing, Guangzhou, Hankou, Jinan, and Changsha (by Mao Zedong) and by Chinese students in Japan and France. In November 1920 the agent also met with Sun Yixian, who was eager for talks to determine whether a liaison might be profitable for his Guomindang. Sun had been spinning his wheels trying to get a political movement underway. Meeting him was an important development for the Comintern, which had decided that Communists in colonial countries (given their small numbers) should adopt the short-term tactic of joining bourgeois parties to work for national ends in a united front against common enemies. The Guomindang was China's largest bourgeois party. Once common enemies were defeated, the united front would end and the former allies would become enemies.

Twelve delegates attended the founding congress of the CCP, which began its meeting in the Shanghai French concession in July 1921; the party had fifty to sixty members. The delegates elected the central executive committee and chose Chen Duxiu as secretary-general. The Comintern representative at the congress urged the Communists to join Sun's Guomindang. In December 1921 the agent met Sun to discuss China's situation and its relationship to the Soviet Union. In June 1922, the CCP, feeling Comintern pressure and coming to see the Guomindang as "relatively revolutionary and democratic,"[14] indicated that it was ready to join the Guomindang in a united front against the warlords and imperialists. Sun favored letting individual CCP members join his party, forming a *bloc within* system rather than having a dual party alliance. Most Chinese Communists favored an outright alliance between the parties, fearing that a *bloc within* would reduce the CCP's independence. But the Comintern had already decided that the bloc within was more appropriate; the CCP had no choice but to concur. From the beginning, then, the decision for the united front was made primarily by Sun and the Comintern, with the CCP forced to agree.

GIVING THE GUOMINDANG A NEW IDENTITY

After lengthy talks with a Soviet diplomat in early 1923, Sun asked for assistance. The Soviet Union offered him advice and training to restructure the Guomindang and to build a party army. In late 1923, the Comintern sent Michael Borodin to help reorganize the Guomindang. A Russian Jew, Borodin had served as Comintern agent in several countries and was described as almost larger than life—a big, husky man with a magnetic personality and great intelligence. In China, Borodin's personal power expanded quickly.

As a party, the Guomindang was open, factionalized, unruly—not the kind of organization that could engineer a revolution. Borodin drafted a new party constitution, restructuring the party in Leninist fashion according to the concept of *democratic centralism*. Debate and discussion (*democracy*) occurred at each level of the party hierarchy, with recommendations passed up the chain of command. Once the top level (the Central Executive Committee) reached a decision, it had to be carried out (*centralism*). In short, there was a façade of democratic-style discussion but, in the end, centralized autocracy. Further, surveillance operatives at every hierarchical level and in every arena of party activity made it difficult to subvert. By early 1924, both of China's parties were Leninist-style organs. This development was unpopular among many Guomindang members who were jealous of what seemed to be the inordinate power of Borodin and the Communists in the party. The "united front" was marked by constant backbiting, fear, suspicion, and distrust. The Guomindang's ideology, in contrast to its structure, was more homegrown. Sun spent considerable time fleshing out his Three Principles of the People.

The other essential prerequisite for building a modern nation-state was a capable military force. As a first step, in late 1923, Sun sent a delegation led by Jiang Jieshi to learn from the Soviet Union. After attending military academies in China and Japan, Jiang had participated in the 1911 revolution in Shanghai, where he had worked in the late 1910s as a stockbroker. In 1924, under Borodin's leadership, a military academy was established at Huangpu (usually called Whampoa), ten miles downstream from Guangzhou; Jiang was named commandant.[15] Funded by Soviet government contributions and monthly subsidies from Borodin, the academy opened in June 1924 with almost five hundred seventeen- to twenty-four-year-old cadets. After completing the academy's six-month program, cadets had to serve in the army one year for every two months they were students at the academy. Faculty and administrative staff was balanced between Communists and Nationalists, with many of the former being part of the bloc within. Zhou Enlai, a pivotal member of the leadership of the People's Republic after 1949, was a political instructor at Whampoa. The cadets became fiercely loyal to Jiang, who supervised the training of the first three classes. Many became his generals in the 1930s and 1940s, and almost all became avid backers in his strongest supporting faction, the Whampoa clique.

Sun Yixian and Jiang Jieshi   This photograph of a sitting Sun (1866–1925) and a standing Jiang (1887–1975) was taken before Sun left the South for the North to negotiate with the warlord Zhang Zuolin in the fall of 1924. Sun died of liver cancer in March 1925, setting the stage for Jiang's rise to power.

THINGS FALL APART

Even though it had been restructured in the Leninist mode, the Guomindang remained a party with many factions and networks. In that sense it reflected Chinese social and political culture, which tended to give rise to factions based on personal connections—kinship, native place, alumni connections, friendship, teacher-student ties, and patron-client ties. Politically, party members varied from right to left, but the basic split between right (conservative) and left (liberal) clarifies the general elements of disagreement. The political right believed that the Soviet Union had too much power in shaping the Chinese revolution, that Borodin had become a much too powerful decision maker, and that the bloc within was basically a bad policy. The political left had positions similar to those of the Communists, offering some support for social and economic as well as political revolution, though they may have had doubts about the extensive power of Soviet advisors. In the center were men like Jiang Jieshi who made their own way, supporting Sun and his decision to work with the Soviets but capable of shifting to the right, depending on the situation. In the context of growing polarization the united front was clearly unsteady, but Sun still held it together. He was the Guomindang leader for life, and party members owed personal loyalty to him. But then, on a trip to Beijing in early 1925, he was diagnosed with liver cancer. On the day before he died (March 12), Sun signed a statement to the Soviet Union asking for continued help for the revolution.[16] Death transformed Sun into a potent symbol of patriotism and unfinished revolution. But for all its power, a symbol cannot hold parties together. The situation was worsened by the May 30 Movement, an unprecedented anti-imperialist explosion. Demonstrations following the killing of a Chinese worker by a Japanese textile mill guard in Shanghai led to the arrest of several students. On May 30, thousands of demonstrators massed before the police station to demand their release. With little warning, a British inspector gave orders to fire on the crowd; eleven were killed and at least twenty wounded. Then on June 23, British troops in Guangzhou opened fire on demonstrators protesting the May 30 deaths, killing fifty-two and wounding over one hundred more. These shootings, by British troops still in Chinese cities as part of the unequal treaty system, intensified the deepening sense of national peril; street demonstrations, strikes, and incendiary newspaper editorials, all revealing revolutionary rage and fervor, swept the country.

Sun's death and the May 30 Movement put great pressure on the parties, bringing closer the military phase of the revolution and forcing the parties to clarify their revolutionary goals. But this honing of goals drove even greater wedges between factions and networks. The second half of 1925 saw an increasingly malevolent polarization, often with violent results. In August, a leader of the Guomindang left was assassinated in Guangzhou; right-wing party members were implicated. In late 1925, some right-wingers met in the Western Hills section of Beijing to demand Borodin's dismissal, the elimination of the bloc within, and the end of any relationship with the CCP. At the second Guomindang congress in January 1926, 60 percent of the delegates were leftists or Communists and only 16 percent were rightists; the rightists decided to hold their own party congress in Shanghai in March to chart their own direction for the future. Within a year of Sun's death, the Guomindang had fallen apart.

THE BEGINNING OF MASS MOBILIZATION

Marx had argued that the engine of revolution would be the urban working class (the proletariat). However, early CCP attempts to organize the working class into unions failed, producing violence and bloodshed.[17] Developing in the 1920s was a conviction that the peasants would also become important players in the revolutionary game. By the mid-1920s the Guomindang had begun to organize both workers and peasants, primarily in the province of Guangdong, where the party and army were headquartered. Workers were embedded in local groups and could not see the advantages of being grouped in larger organizations with people they did not know. In May 1925 the CCP succeeded in forming an umbrella National General Labor Union. However, though its national membership rose to 1.2 million within a year, the most important branch in Shanghai had to go underground in late 1925.

Authorities suppressed early attempts to organize farmers in Zhejiang province in 1921 and in Guangdong province in 1922–1923. The Guomindang began organizing peasant associations in 1924, establishing a Peasants Bureau to train deputies for this difficult work. Without connections it was hard for outsiders to organize farmers, who were suspicious and uncooperative. Village elites were hostile because peasant associations were potential enemies; elites attacked organizers with local militia units or gangs of local toughs. Borodin believed that peasant associations were the key to a successful military campaign in northern Guangdong and Hunan provinces because they would provide a supportive population. Men trained at an enlarged Peasant Movement Training Institute were sent mainly to those two provinces. When formed, peasant associations focused on reducing rents paid to landlords and lowering various taxes that devastated some localities.

THE NORTHERN EXPEDITION

Guomindang and Soviet advisors disagreed over when the military campaign to unite the country should begin, with the Guomindang ready to go but the Soviets urging caution. In March 1926, learning of a plot to oust him, Jiang launched his own preemptive coup against the Communists, arresting some Soviet advisors and declaring martial law. However, though he became increasingly suspicious of Communist aims, he still agreed to work in the united front.

In July 1926, at the head of his National Revolutionary Army (NRA), Jiang began the Northern Expedition, a two-pronged campaign to reach the Yangzi River and gain South and South Central China

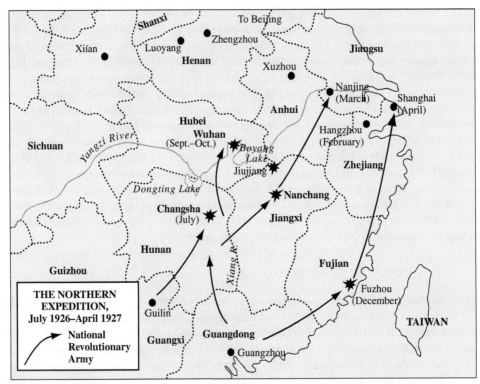

Map 9-1   **The Northern Expedition in South-Central China.**

for the Guomindang. The armies on the western route moved up through Hunan province, quickly reaching their goal, taking the key Yangzi River metropolis of Wuhan on October 10. What caused the rapid success? One reason was the army itself: trained well for two years and inculcated with patriotism, it was strictly disciplined and forbidden to loot and rape, the usual modus operandi of Chinese armies. Credit should also go to Soviet strategists and advisors.

Perhaps most important was the mass organizing that preceded and accompanied the campaign. Peasant association members served as scouts, guides, and porters; offered food and water to the troops; and assisted by harassing the enemy's rear. The Northern Expedition itself was the occasion for frenzied mass mobilization of both peasants and laborers. Before the campaign, peasant association membership in Hunan, Hubei, and Jiangxi, numbered less than 50,000, but Communist leaders claimed by the end of 1926 that there were 1.5 million organized farmers in ninety-one counties of Hunan and Hubei alone.

But this action naturally stirred up the hostility of landlords, who often retaliated with violence against tenants, eliciting violent tenant reactions in an ever-escalating struggle between the classes. Such mass mobilization raised the crucial question of where the revolution was headed: should it have social and economic goals, as the Communists desired, or should it remain primarily political in its call for ousting warlords and imperialists? Increasingly those two ideological groups became bitterly antagonistic, and relations between Borodin and Jiang became icily hostile.

As Jiang's forces made their way to Shanghai from the southwest, Communists and Guomindang leftists, who had organized and led Shanghai labor unions, revolted against the warlord controlling Shanghai. In late February 1927, workers staged a general strike to undercut the warlord's power in order to ease NRA seizure of the city. Though the six-day strike was violently broken by the warlord's troops, it mobilized hundreds of thousands of workers and revealed the strength of Communist power. It also increased the conviction of Shanghai businessmen and Guomindang right-wingers that the Communists had to be stopped. On March 21, as the NRA was nearing the city, the General Labor Union called another general strike, involving over six hundred thousand workers who cut electrical and telephone lines and occupied railway and police stations. The commander of the NRA ended the strike when the army took the city on March 24. Already suspicious about the import of peasant and worker mobilization by the left, Jiang was faced with substantial leftist and labor power in Shanghai. He now moved to crush those who had facilitated his seizure of the city. On April 12, forces loyal to Jiang attacked all union headquarters; NRA soldiers opened fire on civilians who protested. Hundreds were mowed down by machine guns; on that rainy day, the streets ran with blood. An estimated five thousand were killed; thousands more fled the city in panic. The slaughter, for some, came to signify Jiang's treachery—turning brutally on those who had helped him take the city. This tragedy was the beginning of what the left called the *White Terror,* a determined effort to destroy leftist and Communist power. The terror spread to almost all major cities of the country and continued well into 1928. The revolution was destroying its own; millions of young, idealistic Chinese were losing their heads. The battle over ideology and the direction of the Chinese revolution was fought with executioners' weapons.

The purge and its disarray forced choices on the Communists and the Guomindang left. From Moscow, Stalin continued to call for the Communists to work with the Guomindang left and to strike out at those allied with Jiang. Given the political realities of the purge, CCP General Secretary Chen Duxiu cynically remarked that those orders were "like taking a bath in a toilet."[18] For its part, the left, now doubting the intentions of the Communists, rejoined the Guomindang right. Borodin and other Soviet advisors left the country in the summer. The last months of 1927 saw several Communist efforts to establish CCP-led regimes, but they were all short-lived and ineffective. Several so-called Autumn Harvest Uprisings failed because of insufficient planning, leadership, and manpower. The bloodiest was the December Guangzhou commune, established briefly by Communists and workers, three thousand to four thousand of whom were killed in the two-day uprising. Many deaths came by execution squads that roamed the streets, often killing innocent people in an orgy of revenge—the low point of Communist fortunes.

By August 1928, Jiang and the NRA, fighting warlord resistance, reached Beijing. The Nationalist Revolution had grown out of the uneasy collaboration of the two Leninist-style parties, the CCP and the

Summary Execution in the Guangzhou Commune
The violence in the ill-fated Guangzhou Commune (December 1927) is captured in this beheading on a city street. With the suppression of the Commune, the Communist efforts to rise against Guomindang control in the late 1920s failed.

Guomindang. In the success of the Northern Expedition the CCP was vanquished, seemingly dead after a short life of six years. At least on the map, China was unified for the first time since the death of Yuan Shikai. Jiang Jieshi was now faced with immense tasks of reconstruction after years of war and of the construction of a viable Chinese state.

A Failed Revolution: The Nanjing Years

Having risen to power on a wave of nationalism, Jiang began to undo the unequal treaty system, gaining tariff autonomy in 1928–1929 and reducing the number of foreign concessions. But extraterritoriality was not abolished until 1943—and then only as a gift from the Western democracies to a wartime ally. Jiang's government had big plans for industrializing and modernizing the economy—especially the transportation and communications infrastructure. He made some gains, but in the end it was only a drop in the bucket. By 1937, China with its four to five hundred million people had less industrial production than Belgium with its eight million; it had the same number of modern highway miles as Spain, one-third of the telegraph lines of France, and less railroad mileage than the state of Illinois.

The Guomindang state established by Jiang Jieshi in 1928 faced innumerable problems. Jiang rose to power in the Northern Expedition, one aim of which had been to rid China of warlords. But the Northern Expedition coopted many warlords instead of defeating them, and they remained a thorn in Jiang's side into the late 1930s. Jiang also faced the Japanese military in Manchuria, Mongolia, and North China until open warfare erupted in 1937 (see Chapter 10). Finally, Jiang retargeted his bête noire, the Communists, whose movement was quickly revived after Jiang's purge in 1927 and 1928. For the six years beginning in October 1928, when he became head of state, Jiang was involved in military campaigns for forty-five months (62.5 percent of the time). Confronted by almost continual military challenges, he had little time to structure a modern nation-state. Coupled with military challenges was ongoing factional struggle for leadership within the party into the mid-1930s; men like Wang Jingwei gave Jiang fits.

Beset by troubles on all sides, Jiang retreated to traditional thoughts and values, resurrecting Confucianism as the state religion. He resorted to authoritarianism and flirted with fascism in dealing with growing dissent and any political challenge. His New Life Movement, begun with considerable fanfare in 1934, was an effort to reduce the ideological advantage of the Communists. But it became an object of satire with its ninety-five rules by which people were to live their lives, none of which were necessarily bad but also none of which could begin to handle China's desperate problems—for example, "If we are to have a new life that accords with [propriety, justice, honesty, and a sense of self-respect], then we must start by not spitting heedlessly. If we are to restore the nation and gain revenge for our humiliations, then we need not talk about guns and cannon, but must first talk about washing our faces in cold water."[19]

As if military and political problems were not enough, the worldwide Great Depression made modernization efforts almost impossible. Jiang had to wrestle with the same problem as the imperial state from the 1860s on: not enough money. In the end, he wrote off the land tax, the staple Chinese government tax for centuries. After all the turmoil of the warlord period and continual struggles in the 1930s, land had been abandoned and then farmed by others: a new census was necessary before the tax could be levied—and a census was time-consuming and expensive. Jiang let provinces collect that tax if they wanted to do so. Therefore, his regime had to rely primarily on tariff duties and commodities' sales taxes; both had huge downsides. High tariffs handicapped trade and industry, the modern sectors that the government wanted to develop; and the sales taxes were regressive, hitting hardest those who were least able to pay.

Jiang's writing off the countryside seems to have been his ultimate mistake. Farmers, who would emerge in the Communist Revolution as key, suffered year in, year out from natural disasters—floods, droughts, insect pests—and continually lived on the edge of financial ruin. A farmer planted his crop after borrowing money for the seeds. When natural disaster struck and his crop was wiped out, the bills

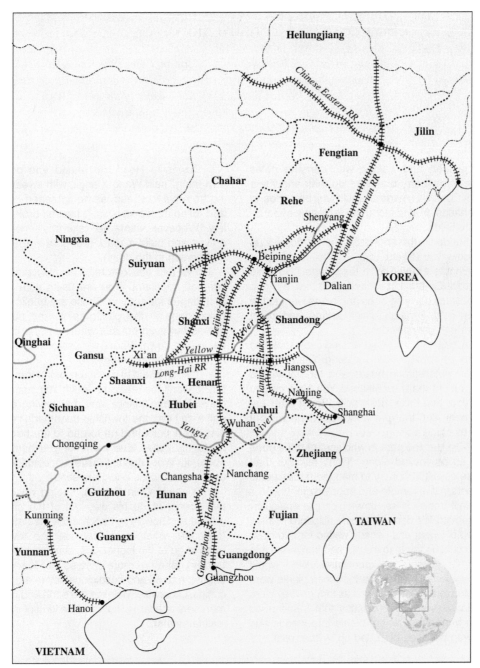

Map 9-2   Key Transportation Routes: Railroads and Rivers.

Source: Road Construction

Deciding to publish brief accounts of life in China, the Shanghai newspaper Shenbao *solicited descriptions of what people were doing and how they were living on May 21, 1936. This piece, by Kang Yimin of the city of Wuxi in Jiangsu province, describes road construction. The "ten household heads" refers to the heads of the traditional mutual surveillance units called* baojia. *What effects did this road construction have on people's lives?*

Village men and women with carrying poles made of mulberry branches on their shoulders or with baskets made of mulberry branches in their hands, trotted along the footpaths separating the fields. . . .

Suddenly the sound of a gong floated up and down the streets. . . .

Shouts erupted from the village, "Go build the road! Go build the road!" After that, a group of peasants carrying hoes and rakes went to the wheat field, through which a line had been drawn with gray powder.

A peasant who had arrived late spoke to the person who sounded the gong: "Qian Erguan, all you watch-group heads and ten-household heads must really be pleased. You have only to use your mouth to make assignment after assignment, and the real work gets done without your touching a thing. . . ."

"Old He," the person who sounded the gong said as he walked along, "Don't talk like that! These days it isn't easy to manage public works projects in this remote and poor village. . . ."

In the end it is we common people who suffer a bitter fate. We conscientiously, diligently planted a crop of wheat and eagerly waited for it to ripen so it could be taken to market and converted into cash for household expenditures. Who would have expected that just as the green plants were about to form kernels, it was as though they were suddenly struck by a disease that transformed them from green wheat plants into weeds and required that they be pulled up by the roots. . . ."

"Township Head, go ahead and do your own thing," said Wang Xiangji, with sweat pouring from his forehead, as he tightened his fists and rolled up his sleeves. "I haven't broken any law. Whoever wants to take my ancestors' graves and build a road through them, I'll fight that person to the death."

"I've told you before." The township head seemed impatient. "You are using your mouth and tongue for nothing. These are public affairs being done in the public spirit, and not only graves but even houses where people live are being torn down. What's the use of your fighting to the death against me!"

"I'm not afraid of my house being torn down, but it won't be easy to touch my ancestors' graves!" Wang Xiangji saw that having argued half a day with the township head hadn't scored him half a point and he turned to the people to plead his case: "Every one of you here think about it. Who doesn't have ancestors? Who doesn't want sons and grandsons?. . ."

"Xiangji." Qian Erguan, seeing no end to this scene, made his way out of the circle of people and sought to become the mediator. . . . "I wonder whether we can ask the township head to go to the higher-ups, clear matters up a bit, and get a few more days so that Xiangji can choose a good and auspicious day to dig up the coffins. Otherwise, violating the earth and making members of a family suffer some kind of disaster isn't fair either."

Source: Sherman Cochran, Andrew C. K. Hsieh, and Janis Cochran, eds., One Day in China: May 21, 1936 *(New Haven, CT: Yale University Press, 1983), 101–4.*

for seeds and other expenses still had to be paid. This meant a trip to the pawnbroker—if he had anything to pawn. If natural disasters came in twos or threes, he could easily lose everything, especially his land. Even if his crop were harvested, if he was a tenant he had outstanding debts and rent, often massive, to the landlord as well. Because partible inheritance was the practice (with land distributed equally to sons), each succeeding generation had less and less land to farm, making earning a livelihood increasingly precarious.

Jiang's government established regulations in the Land Law of 1930 limiting rent to 37.5 percent of the harvest (it often ran 60 to 70 percent). But it was not implemented; the government was fearful about upsetting rural elites. The government developed programs to increase agricultural production, funding and sponsoring research on new varieties of seeds and on fertilizers and pesticides. In some areas the infrastructure of agricultural production began to be renovated—some rivers were dredged and some irrigation systems constructed. Rural reconstruction efforts were undertaken privately, underwritten partly by the government, attempting to reform a limited area (generally a county or less) holistically, focusing especially on economic and educational transformation. The success of these efforts varied, but all of them were destroyed in the war with Japan. There were, in addition, efforts to establish rural production, marketing, and credit cooperatives to assist farmers. Making credit available to farmers on reasonable terms through cooperatives was a hopeful attempt. But as with many hopeful beginnings in early-twentieth-century China, less than 3 percent of the money loaned to farmers came from cooperatives even at the height of the Nanjing government's cooperative fever; over 97 percent came from traditional usurious sources.

During his rule, Jiang came increasingly to see himself and China as one and the same, and believed that anyone who opposed him was treasonously betraying China. Even the most remarkable man could probably not have succeeded given the times and their challenges, but Jiang, a thin-skinned, aloof man with a fiery temper and traditional inclinations, never really had a chance. In the end, he provided a succinct judgment on the impact of his leadership: "The Chinese revolution has failed."[20]

Ritual Burning This elaborate paper Model A Ford and its chauffeur were designed to be burned at a graveside for use in the deceased's afterlife.

CHRONOLOGY

1905	Abolition of the civil service examination system
	Sun Yixian organized the Revolutionary Alliance in Tokyo
1908	Empress dowager announced a constitutional schedule
	Death of the empress dowager (November) a day after the emperor's death
1911	Local self-government assemblies and councils began to meet in the summer
	Revolution to overthrow the dynasty breaks out on October 10 in Wuchang
1912	Abdiction of the Qing dynasty
1915	Publication of *New Youth*, the most important journal of the New Culture Movement
1916	Death of President Yuan Shikai
	Cai Yuanpei named chancellor of Beijing University
1916–1928	Warlord era
1919	May Fourth Movement
1921	Founding congress of the Chinese Communist Party
1923–1924	Comintern agent Michael Borodin restructures Sun's Guomindang
1924	Opening of the Whampoa Military Academy headed by Jiang Jieshi
1925	Sun died (Mar. 12)
	May 30 Movement
1926–1928	Northern Expedition
1927–1928	Jiang's White Terror
1928–1937	Nanjing decade

SUGGESTED READINGS

Eastman, Lloyd. *The Abortive Revolution: China under Nationalist Rule, 1927–1937.* Cambridge, MA: Harvard University Press, 1974. A discussion of the mostly failed policies of the Nationalist government, which acted as if the revolution was over and its only goal was to remain in power.

Lu Xun, *Selected Stories of Lu Xun.* Beijing: Foreign Languages Press, 2000. This anthology of Lu's most famous stories includes the preface of his collection *Call to Arms*.

Rhoads, Edward J. M. *Manchus and Han: Ethnic Relations and Political Power in Late Qing and Early Republican China, 1861–1928.* Seattle: University of Washington Press, 2000. This prize-winning book analyzes the 1911 revolution not from the perspective of the revolutionaries but from that of the

Manchu court; the author's interpretation of Manchu identity has contributed to an ongoing debate on the issue.

Schoppa, R. Keith. *Blood Road: The Mystery of Shen Dingyi in Revolutionary China.* Berkeley: University of California Press, 1995. Written as a murder mystery, this prize-winning book suggests new ways of approaching and understanding the Chinese revolution of the 1920s.

Wilbur, C. Martin, and Julie Lien-ying How. *Missionaries of Revolution: Soviet Advisers and Nationalist China, 1920–1927.* Cambridge, MA: Harvard University Press, 1989. Encyclopedic in scope, with fascinating documents, narrative, and analysis of the Nationalist Revolution.

CHAPTER TEN

"Grown, But Not Grown Up":
Japan, 1912–1937

The dizzying pace of change in Meiji Japan left many Japanese uncertain not only about the nation's future direction but also about the meaning of the present. Novelist Nagai Kafū wrote, "We have arrived at a moment when we must seek to understand what this 'period' is in which we are living."[1] The title of this chapter comes from the writings of the novelist, pacifist, and Christian socialist Tokutomi Roka, who questioned whether Japan and the Japanese "were any better off" in the early twentieth century than during the late Tokugawa.[2] During the period from the Meiji emperor's death in 1912 to the beginning of the full-scale war with China in 1937, both at home and abroad Japan faced questions about its identity.

THE TAISHŌ-ERA POLITICAL SYSTEM

The new government established in 1890 under the Meiji constitution was hydra-headed. We have seen (Chapter 7) that the oligarchs viewed themselves as indispensable in guiding the Japanese nation. But as they began to age, retire, and die, it became obvious that the constitutional structure had no institution to coordinate and direct the government as the oligarchs had done. The emperor was at the heart of the constitution, but the oligarchs intended that under the new system, as under the old, the emperor would reign but not rule. The energetic Meiji emperor may have become a political force if he had so wanted. But his son, the Taishō emperor (r. 1912–1926), was physically weak and mentally affected after an attack of meningitis early in life. A famous story revealed his mental deficiency: At the opening of the Diet in 1913, he rolled up his prepared speech and peered at the Diet members through it. With the emperor out of commission (he performed no public duties after 1919), other groups had to fill the vacuum. Contenders for power emerged: political parties, the bureaucracy, the army and navy, institutions around the emperor, and the *zaibatsu,* powerful business combines; in the 1910s and 1920s they all jockeyed for political leadership.

Political parties became increasingly important. By the 1910s two parties, the government Seiyūkai and its main opposition party (called the Dōshikai from 1913 to 1916, the Kenseikai from 1916 to 1925, and the Minseitō after 1925), dominated politics. Historians point to the period 1918 (the end of World War I) to 1932 as an era of party dominance; a gambler looking at Japan in the mid-1920s would likely have bet heavily that Japan was evolving into a full-fledged democracy.

The bureaucracy was a counterweight and a contender with the political parties for political and government control. There was, of course, no monolithic bureaucratic world. The "bureaucracy" ranged from the prime minister and the cabinet, to men who staffed the cabinet ministries, to conductors on the state railway lines.

The army and navy, as contenders for power, had great constitutional advantages. They had the right to speak directly to the emperor on their own, with no control by or interference from any other government institution. Moreover, the two chiefs of staff were directly responsible to the emperor, meaning essentially that in their command they were not answerable to anyone—even the cabinet. The army and navy could operate independently. As long as the oligarchs were around, they could rein in these two military forces, but by the 1920s many oligarchs were dead. Trouble was in the offing.

A fourth group of contenders for government power consisted of several institutions close to the emperor, whose prominence and potential power grew from their link to this descendant of the Sun Goddess. The Privy Council, established in 1889 to approve the constitution, came to be composed of fourteen retired ex-ministers appointed for life by the emperor. It advised the emperor and was ultraconservative, often opposed to and successfully beating back some party cabinet decisions. The House of Peers, one of the two houses in the Diet, was "a bastion of emperor-centered authoritarian politics."[3] Like the Privy Council, it obstructed certain legislation. From the 1890s through World War II, a key informal body was the *genrō* (elder statesmen), who advised the emperor on policy and personnel. There was substantial overlap in the membership of these three bodies.

Finally, there were the *zaibatsu,* big business conglomerates: their very name, meaning "financial clique," was pejorative. Existing outside the government, they wielded yen power, putting pressure on various government institutions to obtain their objectives. Unlike American monopolies and trusts, which tended to focus on one particular business, like oil or steel, zaibatsu included firms that covered the manufacturing process from raw material to finished product. Each company, for example, had its own mines, transportation lines, factories, shipping firms, and banks. In 1930, the national share of major industries of the three major zaibatsu—Mitsubishi, Mitsui, Sumitomo—amounted to over 63 percent of mining, 54 percent of iron and steel, 64 percent of transportation and communications, and 51 percent of finance and banking.[4]

Political parties, the bureaucracy, the army and navy, emperor-related bodies, and zaibatsu did not work as self-contained units; rather, there were horizontal groups that cut across these rivals for political power. For example, the Home Ministry, in charge of the police, might have special ties and arrangements with one of the parties, perhaps the army, and maybe a company like Mitsubishi.

THE HEYDAY OF POLITICAL PARTIES

What accounts for the success of political parties in the 1910s and 1920s in a country that had no experience with representative government? Part of the answer was that oligarchs and their opponents alike saw the parties as powerful tools to attain their goals. When party cabinets emerged in the government bureaucracy, the spoils system—giving jobs to party colleagues—and the pork barrel—providing money for local projects—became important in building party power. Prime Minister Hara Kei (1918–1921), whose background was in journalism and business (a most unusual route at the time), was a master at using spoils and the pork barrel to bolster the Seiyūkai.

But other forces also bolstered democracy's stock in general. For a nation always attentive to world trends, the victory of the Allies in the world war trumpeted democracy in the defeat of autocratic regimes. The Bolshevik Revolution in 1917 also suggested that democracy was the political rage. In addition, there was a growing sense among the people that the government might be helpful in dealing with problems. In August 1918 the Rice Riots erupted all over the country, protesting sharp increases in the price of rice. It is estimated that more than seven hundred thousand citizens participated, hoping that their actions would bring government intervention. A growing number of labor disputes, the consequent growth of urban labor unions, and the rise of tenant unions in rural areas all demonstrated that *people power* might make a difference in individuals' lives. The founding of the Japanese Communist Party in 1922 was also an expression of this populist thrust.

There was much discussion of how people power embodied in some form of democracy might fit with the strong monarchy envisioned in the Meiji Constitution. A term coined to deal with the apparent discrepancy and to express democracy in the Japanese setting was *minponshugi,* literally "politics based on the people" or "politics for the people." One of the best-known proponents of the term was Yoshino Sakuzō, a professor at Tokyo Imperial University, who believed that a full-fledged democracy with popular sovereignty was incompatible with the Japanese system. Rule by the people, he thought, was too volatile and potentially dangerous. What he preferred was "government on behalf of the people."[5] Be that as it may, there was a growing rush for universal manhood suffrage, a goal reached with a 1925 law that effectively quadrupled the electorate.

Party leaders remained conservative, governing within a well-defined consensus. They were heavily committed to satisfying their major interest groups—landlords and business elites. Party leaders quaked in their boots over liberalizing trends, fearful that leftist activists would destroy what party leaders and the government had built. A sign of their political wariness was almost a coupling of the Universal Manhood Suffrage Law with a Peace Preservation Law that outlawed groups that advocated abolishing the system

Source: The Rice Riots as Described in the Diary of Hara Kei

Caused by rising inflation, the Rice Riots in the closing months of World War I swept across Japan, necessitating martial law. Some historians have interpreted them as an indication that the people began to see that they might play a more direct political role in the new Japan. What does Hara Kei (1856–1921), who served as prime minister from 1918 to 1921, see as the major cause of the riots?

. . . There has been a number of riots in different parts of the country resulting from a sharp rise in the price of rice, and some of them have required the sending of troops. In view of this, I sent a telegram [from my home in Morioka] to the Seiyūkai's branch office in Sapporo indicating my desire to proceed with the Northeast regional meeting of the Seiyūkai scheduled to be held in Sapporo on the 18th, but also suggesting that festivities and banquets must be canceled. A telegram of similar content was also sent to the party headquarters. However, a telegram from Mr. Yokota [Sennosuke, 1870–1925], the party secretary general, requested that I reconsider the matter, citing that disturbances in the Kyoto-Kobe area were getting worse. There were also other telegrams. Martial law was declared in Osaka, and Tokyo did not escape riots, which were followed by the dispatch of troops. In other areas there were major and minor disturbances. The Imperial Household graciously donated three million yen, and Mitsui and Mitsubishi each donated one million yen. The national treasury also appropriated ten million yen for the relief effort. People were restive, and last night the government suppressed all news publications relating to riots. With these in mind, I became convinced that it was not appropriate to hold the projected regional meeting even though its site, Hokkaido, remained calm. Thus I sent another telegram to the Sapporo branch office canceling my previous telegram. I noted that the riots related to the rising rice price were getting much worse and troops were being dispatched to guard against further disturbances. It would not be appropriate at this time to hold the projected meeting, and it ought to be postponed. I also sent telegrams to the same effect to Secretary General Yokota and other parties.

Since last year, the agriculture minister worked diligently to adjust the price of rice, but every step he took failed and instead stimulated further rise in the price of rice. Finally, the great riot occurred. However, the government seems intent on finding a scapegoat without admitting its own mistake. At present, we do not have a shortage of rice in local areas. Yet we have riots reminiscent of the times of poor harvest. This is caused by the misrule of the government who has erroneously believed in the power of laws and regulations through which it has sought to lower the price of rice. . . .

Source: David J. Lu, Japan: A Documentary History *(Armonk, NY: M. E. Sharpe, 1996), 386–87.*

of private ownership or changing the country's national polity. Penalties ranged up to ten years in prison for belonging to such groups.

Party leaders' skittishness may have come in part from memories of the events of autumn 1923. A powerful earthquake on September 1 struck the Kantō Plain (the site of cities like Tokyo and Yokohama), killing over 130,000 people and causing immense devastation. Even worse was what happened in the quake's aftermath. Rumors spread that Korean residents in Japan were poisoning wells and that radical groups were taking advantage of the disaster to carry out sinister plots. Vigilantes murdered Koreans (an estimated 2,500 to 6,000); police rounded up suspected Communists and radicals and shot them to death. Political elites enjoyed their power, wealth, and prestige, but their world seemed ringed by danger, disorder, and crisis.

Source: Universal Manhood Suffrage

Opposed by many Japanese, who feared that it would lead to greater political turmoil and place too much power in the hands of nonelites, letting all men vote was a controversial idea. Under the administration of Katō Komei (1860–1926), this bill, Articles 5 and 6 of which are presented here, became law in 1925. Do you find any of the reasons why some men do not have the right to vote unusual? Which one(s) and why?

CHAPTER II. THE RIGHT TO VOTE AND ELIGIBILITY FOR ELECTION

ARTICLE 5. A Japanese male citizen, twenty-five years of age or older, shall have the right to vote.

A Japanese male citizen, thirty years of age or older, shall be eligible for election to the House of Representatives.

ARTICLE 6. Those who come under one of the following categories shall not have the right to vote or be eligible for election:

1. A person adjudged incompetent or a quasi-incompetent person.

2. A bankrupt person who is not rehabilitated.

3. A person, on account of poverty, who requires relief or assistance from public or private sources.

4. A person who does not have a place of residence.

5. A person who has been sentenced to penalties heavier than six years of penal servitude or imprisonment.

[6 and 7 omitted.]

Source: David J. Lu, Japan: A Documentary History *(Armonk, NY: M. E. Sharpe, 1996), 395.*

TAISHŌ SOCIETY

From the 1910s to the 1930s, Japan was in the so-called take-off period of industrialization, an era of transition to heavy industry from agriculture and light industry and to an industrial workforce from a mostly agricultural one. The years of World War I were boom years, with the real gross national product soaring by 40 percent. However, living standards did not rise markedly because a large proportion of this increase came from exports. The output of heavy industry and machinery from 1915 to 1919 shot up by 72 percent, and employment in those industries rose by 42 percent. However, the end of the war brought a financial panic and a deflationary slump that lasted for much of the 1920s.

Cities during this period saw the development of a consumer culture, which had begun in the last fifteen years of the Meiji era. The population in urban centers of over ten thousand rose dramatically, from 12 percent in 1895 to over 45 percent by the mid-1930s. Cities were centers of Japan's modern transformation; once that transformation began, it seemed to pick up speed. Superficial changes included Western-style buildings, horse-drawn streetcars, new schools and colleges, and gas lamps. Cultural changes also occurred as living standards rose. People with more money stopped at a bar for a beer, bought the latest weekly magazine, saw a movie, and went to a dance hall. Western imports were the rage. The word *modan* (modern) meant "stylish": *modan garu* was shortened to *moga* (modern girl) and *modan boi* or *mobo* (modern boy). Mobo and moga strolled the streets of the Ginza, watching Western movies and eating in Western-style restaurants. They scandalized their parents by

Source: Articles of the Peace Preservation Law

Almost as a balance to the Universal Manhood Suffrage Law, the Diet about two weeks earlier had passed the Peace Preservation Law, which curtailed civil liberties. What were the main offenses under this bill, and how were they to be punished?

ARTICLE 1. Anyone who organizes a group for the purpose of changing the national polity (*kokutai*) or of denying the private property system, or anyone who knowingly participates in said group, shall be sentenced to penal servitude or imprisonment not exceeding ten years. An offense not actually carried out shall also be subject to punishment.

ARTICLE 2. Anyone who consults with another person on matters relating to the implementation of these objectives described in clause 1 of the preceding article shall be sentenced to penal servitude or imprisonment not exceeding seven years.

ARTICLE 3. Anyone who instigates others for the purpose of implementing those objectives described in clause 1, article 1, shall be sentenced to penal servitude or imprisonment not exceeding seven years.

ARTICLE 4. Anyone who instigates others to engage in rioting or assault or other crimes inflicting harm on life, person, or property for the purpose of attaining the objectives of clause 1, article 1, shall be sentenced to penal servitude or imprisonment not exceeding ten years.

ARTICLE 5. Anyone who, for the purpose of committing those crimes described in clause 1, article 1, and in the preceding three articles, provides money and goods or other financial advantages for others, or makes an offer or commitment for same, shall be sentenced to penal servitude or imprisonment not exceeding five years. Anyone who knowingly receives such considerations, or makes demand or commitment for same, shall be punished in a similar manner.

ARTICLE 6. Anyone who has committed the crimes described in the three preceding articles and has surrendered himself voluntarily to authorities shall have his sentence reduced or be granted immunity from prosecution.

ARTICLE 7. This law shall be made applicable to anyone who commits crimes described in this law outside of the jurisdiction in which this law is in effect.

Source: David J. Lu, Japan: A Documentary History *(Armonk, NY: M. E. Sharpe, 1996), 397.*

openly flaunting their interest in "the *surii-esu,* the three s's: sex (*sekkusu*), cinema (*shimena*), and sports."[6] Western sports were the name of the game—first and foremost baseball but also including tennis, bowling, and skiing.

But then there was the Japanese countryside, where the masses lived in poverty and degradation. Read the account of a doctor's assistant in northern Japan:

There is no one as miserable as a peasant, especially the impoverished peasants of northern Japan. The peasants there wear rags, eat coarse cereals, and have many children. They are as black as their dirt walls and lead grubby lives that can be compared to those of insects that crawl along the ground and stay alive by licking the dirt. They may walk upright, but most of the time their spirit crawls along the ground. . . .
[E]verytime I come in contact with their musty, smelly, dull, miserable existence, I feel a sense of displeasure and distaste grounded on a hatred of ugly things.[7]

Devastation from the Great Kantō Earthquake   About noon on September 1, 1923, one of history's strongest earthquakes (estimated to have been between 7.9 and 8.4 on the Richter scale) hit the Kantō plain, on which Tokyo and other cities are located. Pictured is a destroyed retail district. An estimated one hundred thirty thousand people were killed. In the aftermath, rumors spread that Koreans and others were poisoning the water supply; in response, Japanese resorted to vigilante "justice," killing Koreans and political radicals.

Farmers lived in a hierarchical world, with the main division being between landowners and tenants. Tenants' lives were little better than those of stereotypical medieval serfs, who "were at the beck and call of their landlords to perform chores in the landlords' fields or in the landlords' home even if this meant delaying vital chores of their own." The result was often deep resentment verging on "seething fury."[8] It is little wonder that thousands of landlord-tenant disputes dotted the 1920s and early 1930s or that as many as 10 percent of all tenant families joined tenant unions during that time.

Another part of the underclass, factory workers, suffered as they have in industrializing countries around the world. A female worker in a silk textile mill noted that "from morning while it was still dark we worked in the lamp lit factory till ten at night. When we worked late into the night, they occasionally gave us a yam. . . . There was no heat even in the winter, and so we had to sleep huddled together."[9] The attitude of government leaders was demonstrated in factory legislation in 1916 that set an eleven-hour workday for women and children and a minimum work age of twelve years. In 1926 the workday was set at ten hours and the minimum age at fourteen—though there was generally weak enforcement of these limits.

The worst conditions were probably found in coal mines, source of the fuel that played a central role in Japan's modernization. Women who joined men in the underground mines were paid half of what men received. Notoriously unsafe working conditions killed and injured thousands each year. One of the more infamous mines was the Mitsubishi coal mine, dubbed *Battleship Mountain,* an island four miles off the coast of Nagasaki. There poor farmers, prisoners, and outcasts—men and women— worked nearly naked in shafts with temperatures of up to 130°F and walls so low that miners had to crawl rather than walk upright. Whole families lived in tiny, dark cells called *octopus dens.* If people were caught trying to escape, they were killed.

The first trade union, the Yūaikai (Friendly Society), was founded in 1912, with a membership rising to 19,190 in 1917; the members were mostly factory workers in modern industries. The organization was so moderate that it garnered the support of company officials. In 1921 it became the Sōdōmei (Japan Federation of Labor) at a time when labor strikes had become common and the labor leaders more militant. The number of labor disputes in 1919 was five times higher (at 2,388) than in 1918. By 1921 almost three hundred labor unions had been formed, many associated with the Japan Federation of Labor.

JAPAN AND THE WIDER WORLD, 1912–1928

In the Meiji period, Japan had repeatedly used its military power unilaterally: against Korea in 1882, 1884, 1894, and 1905–1910 (for the last, see Chapter 11); against China in 1894–1895; and against Russia in 1904–1905. After Japan sucked Korea into its empire from 1905 to 1910, the nation entered a new period, becoming more active in international affairs. This change probably resulted in part from a feeling of greater self-confidence. Not only had Japan enjoyed several overwhelming military victories, but, like the United States and several European countries, it had built an empire, stretching from Sakhalin Island to Taiwan, controlling Korea, and having predominant interests in southern Manchuria. Its unequal treaty relationships had ended by 1898. In 1902, it had signed a treaty of alliance with Great Britain, an act one historian called "a symbol of one of the most remarkable transformations in modern times," signifying "not only that Japan had come of age as a modern nation but [also] that its manhood, its vitality, and its potentialities . . . had been recognized . . . by one of the strongest nations in the world."[10]

Japan's period of international cooperation, especially in the 1920s, has come to be known as the era of *Shidehara diplomacy*—named for Shidehara Kijūrō, vice-minister of foreign affairs during World War I, ambassador to the United States from 1919 to 1922, and foreign minister from 1924 to 1927 and from 1929 to 1931. When World War I erupted in August 1914, Great Britain asked Japan to seize German men-of-war on the Chinese coast. Japan took advantage of this request to launch a military campaign seizing German-held territory in China's Shandong province and islands in the Pacific (the Marianas, Caroline, and Marshall). Shandong and the defenseless islands were in Japan's hands by November. Involved in no other military action during the war, Japan spent the war years trying to make imperial hay while the European war's sun shone. As the Japanese government put it, "Japan must take the chance of a millennium" to "establish its rights and interests in Asia."[11]

Its first step, in January 1915, was to approach China with a list of demands for mostly economic concessions in North and Central China, many aimed at increasing the Japanese presence in Manchuria and Mongolia and getting control of Germany's former leasehold in Shandong. One group of demands was, however, particularly upsetting to the government of Yuan Shikai. They demanded, among other things that would have expanded Japan's power within China, the right to appoint advisors to the Chinese government. China refused even to countenance this group of demands, which would have gone far to make China a Japanese protectorate. The Japanese finally tired of Yuan's stalling in making a decision; they issued an ultimatum in early May, dropping the controversial group of demands but ordering Yuan to sign the other demands within forty-eight hours. Yuan signed, and Japan's feet were planted ever more firmly on the Asian continent.

During the rest of the war, Japan worked to solidify its control over the former German-held territory by signing secret treaties with the European powers recognizing Japan's control of the areas. Even the United States, always vigilant about its Open Door policy toward China, in conversations with the Japanese government recognized Japan's "special interests in Manchuria" and concurred that Japan had "special and close relations, political as well as economic," with China.[12]

The Allied victory over the Central Powers in the war made Japan one of the victors in the international tragedy. The postwar peace conference at Versailles was the first such conference Japan had ever attended: it was a grand step onto the world stage, a coming of age as an international power. Japan had two goals at Versailles: to get open international agreement of Japan's right to control the former German territories and to have a racial equality clause written into the covenant of the proposed League of Nations, the brainchild of U.S. President Woodrow Wilson. The racial equality clause was considered first. It read: "The equality of nations being a basic principle of the League of Nations, the high contracting parties agree to accord . . . to all alien nationals of state members of the League equal and just treatment in very respect, making no distinction in law or in fact, on account of their race and nationality." Japan was acutely sensitive about maltreatment of Japanese abroad. Racial problems between Japanese and Caucasians on the West Coast of the United States had cropped up repeatedly in the early years of the twentieth century, and Japanese immigration was stopped in 1908; other countries also had halted or restricted immigration. Now faced with the equality clause, countries in the British Empire, led by Australia, opposed it, arguing that it would hamper state sovereignty. Wilson, who chaired the session when the vote was taken, ruled that the vote had to be unanimous, even though 65 percent of the committee (eleven of seventeen) voted for it. Japan did join the League of Nations.

The defeat of the racial equality clause made the Japanese more determined than ever to hold on to the territory they had won during the war. When they threatened to walk out of the conference (as the Italians had just done) if they did not get their way, the specter of a conference collapse was too great for Wilson and others. Though China argued that their ceding control of Shandong was coerced in the Twenty-One Demands, the conference left Shandong in Japanese hands—a decision that had huge repercussions in China (see Chapter 9).

One event in the era of international cooperation that should have served as a red flag was Japan's involvement in the Allied powers' intervention in the Russian civil war between the Whites and the Reds following the Bolshevik Revolution. Russia had ended its war with the Central Powers in March 1918, a withdrawal that caused the eastern front to collapse and allowed German troops there to move to the western front in France. The Allies hoped to fight the Reds and perhaps reopen the eastern front. Japan was interested in Siberia for economic reasons: it had invested much in Russian companies through government bonds and had considerable trade with Vladivostok. When the Communists took that city in April 1918, they seized Allied military supplies and attacked several Japanese. Therefore, Japan had another reason to participate: the Red danger to Japanese subjects. In summer 1918 Wilson asked each Allied nation to send seven thousand men with arms to be shared equally; all did except Japan, which sent seventy-two thousand. In approving the expedition, the Japanese government had been split between those who favored large-scale intervention and those who wanted a limited one. The large-scale group, led by Yamagata Aritomo, won; once the troops were sent, the general staff insisted on its autonomy of command, so the civilian government had little, if anything, to say. It was an ominous development and a harbinger of what would come in the 1930s and 1940s: the first clear case in modern Japan of autonomous action by the military. When the war ended in November 1918, all the Allies except Japan withdrew their forces. Japanese troops stayed until 1922.

From November 1921 to February 1922, Japan participated in the Washington Conference to stabilize the status quo in China and to deal with a naval battleship race. In the latter, Japan, allowed to have three ships for every five held by the United States and Great Britain, felt that its security was nevertheless strengthened. Naval strategists argued that war against Japan could be waged successfully only with double force, that is, by a country that had the equivalent of six ships for Japan's three; this agreement thus protected Japan from attack by a single power. At the conference, Japan also agreed to return Shandong to China, although it retained economic interests on the peninsula.

THE WANING OF PARTY DOMINANCE

Apart from the brief military action in World War I and the Siberian expedition, the years from 1912 to the mid-1920s were a time of peace and active internationalism. In this context, political parties seemed firmly in control and the military's star sank. As part of a broader retrenchment effort, in which the civilian bureaucracy eliminated twenty thousand jobs, the army minister agreed to cut army manpower by four divisions (totaling thirty-five thousand men). The navy's construction program was cut back and naval personnel were reduced. The military budget, which in 1922 had been 42 percent of the national budget, was cut to 29 percent in 1925 and to 28 percent in 1927. It is said that the prestige of the army had fallen so low that off-duty officers dared not wear their uniforms, donning civilian clothes instead.

But by the late 1920s significant changes were underway. Out of South China came Jiang Jieshi's army, driven by the potent ideas of Chinese nationalism: China for the Chinese, not for the imperialist land and privilege grabbers. Suddenly Japan, a relative latecomer to the feast that was China, felt that what it had gained in China might be lost. Twice, in 1927 and again in 1928, Japan sent forces to "protect"

Japanese citizens in Shandong province. In 1928, they blew up a train and killed Zhang Zuolin, their collaborating Manchurian warlord, because they could not trust the kind of deal he might make with Jiang. The Japanese military was keenly and warily watching the continental thunderclouds.

But it was not only the danger to Japanese interests in China that began to destabilize the domestic political power scene. Events and actions of the Japanese political parties themselves quickly destroyed party power and success. A financial panic and crisis hit Japan in 1927 when a number of bank failures caused a run on banks, which the government then closed for twenty days. Between the end of 1926 and the end of 1932, 41 percent of Japanese banks closed (1,575 reduced to 651). In essence, when the Great Depression hit in 1929, Japan had already fallen into economic doldrums. The experience of the silk industry shows the devastating impacts of the Depression. While silk exports had fueled Japan's industrial modernization, these exports all but stopped by 1930, when the price of silk cocoons dropped 80 percent from the 1925 price; this had a devastating impact on the 2.22 million farm families that relied on sericulture to supplement their agricultural incomes. A sixty-year-old farmer from Aomori prefecture was blunt about his desperate situation in 1931:

> *My only son is in Manchuria as a soldier. I wrote him a letter the other day telling him to fight bravely for the sake of the country and die in battle. Then I would get some grant from the government that would enable me and my wife to survive this winter. A father who has a daughter could sell her [into prostitution], but I have only a son and I am thinking of selling him.*[13]

As in any political regime, those in power receive kudos when thing go well but blame when things go poorly—even if they have little control over the situation. In this case, the political parties were blamed. Then they shot themselves in the foot or, more accurately for its effect, in the head. Political mudslinging in the elections of 1928 and 1930 was worse than Japan had ever seen. It has been suggested, given Japan's Confucian background, that the Japanese may expect greater probity in elections and electioneering. Whatever the case, the mudslinging and accusations of corruption sullied the parties in the minds of many. Finally, the parties came to be seen as reducing the stature of the country. At the London Naval Conference in 1930, in another round of disarmament, the civilian prime minister, Hamaguchi Osachi, went further in accepting naval cuts (this time in cruisers) than had previous administrations, cuts that even U.S. naval strategists said were unfavorable to Japan. Hamaguchi was shot by a nineteen-year-old rightist in November 1930 and died nine months later.

MANCHURIA

The tribulations of the political parties allowed other institutions to take center stage. All of their difficulties tended to enhance the military. Then came Manchuria, offering land for emigration, a source of raw materials, abundant arable land, and a base for further actions on the mainland. After 1912, Japan encouraged Koreans, now Japanese subjects, to emigrate there to make Japan's presence more secure. In Manchuria's 1930 population of thirty million, one million were Japanese subjects, about eight hundred thousand being Korean; foreign investment was 75 percent Japanese, and of Japan's trade with China, 40 percent was with Manchuria. These were Japan's interests, now threatened by China.

Zhang Zuolin, blown up in the train in 1928, was succeeded by his son, Zhang Xueliang, who agreed to continue to work with the Japanese in friendly fashion. In June 1929, Japan formally recognized Jiang's government, which set out immediately to establish a greater Chinese presence in Manchuria. Guomindang party branches were organized everywhere. Jiang worked to undercut Japan's economic position, setting up competing railroads that, using techniques like rebates, began to eat into Japanese railroad profits. The years from 1928 to 1931 saw tensions ratcheted up by railroad "wars" and skirmishes between Korean settlers and Chinese over property and irrigation disputes. In the summer of 1931 two incidents—one a dispute over irrigation issues and the other the killing of a Japanese military officer suspected of being a spy by Chinese troops—angered Japanese and Koreans.

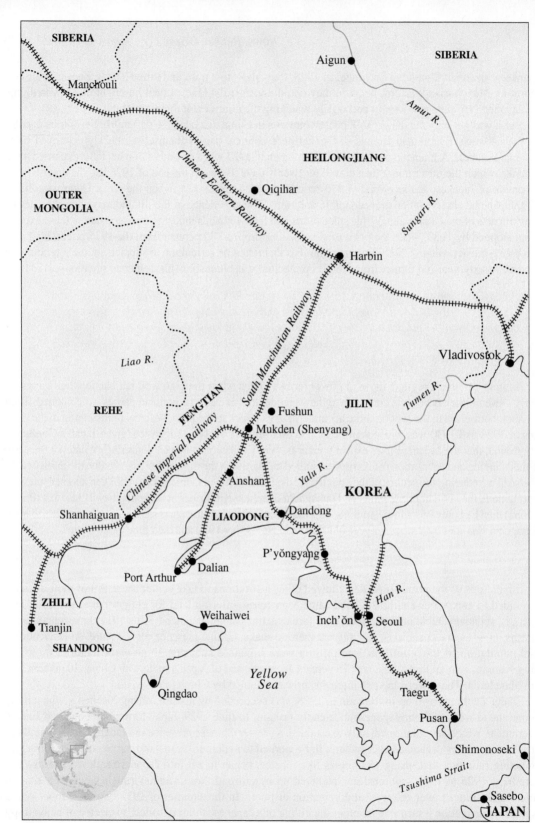

Map 10-1 Northeast Asia with Key Rail Routes.

Japanese Troops Entering Manchuria   Japanese troops here enter a town in Manchuria after the September 18, 1931, incident at Mukden. This action is part of a military campaign that by early 1932 had given rise to the puppet state of Manchukuo.

The Japanese military in the field saw these things close up and magnified them into a towering threat to Japan's position. Field officers in Manchuria, without the knowledge of Tokyo military authorities or the government, plotted to secure Japan's position by taking over Manchuria. On September 18, 1931, they blew up one length of track on the South Manchurian Railroad, just to the north of Mukden near a large barracks housing Chinese troops. The destruction was not even bad enough to prevent the next train from passing. Nevertheless, the Japanese army blamed Chinese for the bombing and used the incident to launch a military campaign. Tokyo repeatedly declared that the military action would be halted, only to find that it had to eat its words as the campaign continued. Japanese military officers in the field made policy autonomously; they were loose cannons, as it were, with no one controlling them.

The Guomindang military's action in Manchuria amounted to nonresistance; military commanders ordered men to lay down their arms and surrender. Patriotic Chinese were outraged that Jiang had come to power under the banner of nationalism but that his military decisions now seemed cowardly and even treasonous. When the Manchurian *incident*—as the Japanese called it—occurred, Jiang's military was in the middle of a campaign against a reborn Communist threat. But Jiang appeased the Japanese largely because he believed that his army was not strong enough to fight two wars at one time—against both Japan and the Chinese Communists. The Communists must be defeated first, he insisted, comparing them to a serious heart problem that must be healed before tackling the Japanese, whose aggression he compared to a skin disease. It was perhaps not illogical, unless, of course, the skin disease was melanoma, not a bad analogy given Japan's malevolent actions.

By early 1932, the Japanese had completed their conquest of Manchuria. Instead of seizing it outright, as they had Korea in 1910 (see Chapter 11), the Japanese set up a puppet state under Manchu leadership to help tone down the negative foreign reaction. In the fall, the Japanese recognized the independent state of Manchukuo (meaning "country of the Manchus") under the leadership of the last Qing emperor, Henry Puyi. When war erupted in China in 1937, and especially after the beginning of

Source: Jiang Jieshi on the CCP and Japan

With Japanese aggression on the Asian mainland in Manchuria in 1931 and continuing into the mid-1930s, Jiang's reaction was appeasement. He was obsessed with the threat of the Chinese Communists, and he felt that the Chinese army was not yet strong enough to battle both forces successfully. In this speech Jiang delivered to senior officers in May 1933, what did he argue caused the Japanese invasion at this time?

Most of you have been in Jiangxi fighting the Communist bandits for three years; some of you have been here only one year. During this difficult, bloody struggle, more than ten thousand of our brave men have perished, including colonels and generals. Yet, despite this enormous sacrifice, the Communist bandits have not been exterminated and the country remains ununified. Taking advantage of this situation, the Japanese imperialists have continued to advance and persist in their aggression.

Today we are facing dangers from within as well as without. Domestically the brutal, violent bandits are burning and killing every day, and across the sea come the Japanese imperialists who take over one piece of territory after another. These imperialists will not be satisfied until they exterminate China as a nation.

Why do the Japanese imperialists choose this particular time to attack us?

They, like other imperialists, relish other people's misfortunes and bully those who are too weak to resist. They attack us because we have this bandit rebellion that prevents our country from being unified. In other words, it is this internal rebellion that invites aggression from abroad. We have no hope at all to resist this aggression as long as the bandits persist in their violent activities and as long as China remains ununified. To resist aggression at this time would mean the subjection of China to simultaneous attacks by both the Communist bandits and the Japanese imperialists. Attacked from within as well as without, China would certainly be defeated. In the name of saving our country by resisting Japanese aggression, we might send her to an early end. . . .

The Japanese aggression comes from without and can be compared to a disease of the skin, while the bandit rebellion, working from within, is really a disease of the heart. We must cure a disease of the heart before proceeding with the cure of a disease of the skin, because the heart disease, if not cured, will kill the patient, while the skin disease will not. Once the Communist bandits are exterminated and the country is pacified, I firmly believe that the Japanese imperialists will not dare attack China again. If they do, they will be destroyed. Therefore, as revolutionary soldiers, we must have the right sense of priority, namely, the precedence of internal pacification over external war.

Once we realize how important this sense of priority is, we will not envy the glamour that is associated with the resistance to Japanese aggression. We must know that only by crushing the bandit rebellion can we carry out the Three Principles of the People and thus assure our country's everlasting existence. I cannot find any task more honorable than this one.

Source: Quoted in R. Keith Schoppa, Twentieth Century: A History in Documents *(New York: Oxford University Press, 2004), 85, 87.*

Henry Puyi   Puyi came to the Dragon Throne in Beijing's Forbidden City at the age of three and was deposed at age six. Between 1912 and 1932 he lived a pampered life—in the Forbidden City until 1924 and afterward in Tianjin. Though he desired to rule in his Manchurian homeland, he was never more than a Japanese puppet.

the Pacific war in 1941, the independence of Manchukuo was shown to be the sham it was. When the League of Nations in early 1933 adopted a committee report stating that Japan was guilty of military aggression in Manchuria, Japan thumbed its nose at the world and stalked out. International condemnation united Japanese public opinion, creating an even more dangerous, chauvinistically charged atmosphere.

THE MILITARY AND THE REVOLUTIONARY RIGHT

The early 1930s saw not only expanding Japanese aggression on the Asian mainland but also terrorism from the revolutionary right inside Japan. Dubbed *government by assassination* by a journalist of the day, this period mixed ultranationalism, alienation, and resentment to produce a combustible situation that threatened the stability, indeed the very existence, of the Japanese government.

Modern Japanese nationalism had been born in the late Tokugawa and Meiji periods, stimulated by both the imperialist threat and example. The new institutions and approaches of the modernization effort were legitimated at least in part by constantly pointing to the nation, to national goals, and to the unique Japanese polity (*kokutai*). The last included the mystical relations between the fatherlike emperor, linked to the divine, and the people—all of whom formed one great *national family*. Traditional virtues were continually appealed to: the subject's loyalty to the emperor; duties to family and community; respect for and adherence to traditional values, behavior, and culture. And yet, there was an increasing dualism in Japanese society between the haves, who pretty much monopolized the fruits of modernization—the newly wealthy, absentee landlords, party politicians—and the have-nots or alienated, whom the advantages of modernization had generally passed by. The latter perceived the former as selfish and concerned only with their self-aggrandizement, certainly caring nothing for the Japanese family—the nation—as a whole. Nationalism became a way of criticizing "contemporary leadership. It demanded a reaffirmation of what used to be and a call to Japanese leadership to go back to it. This involved [among other things] a return to the kind of ambitions overseas and the same kind of imperialist policies in pursuit of them as had developed in the Meiji era."[14]

In many ways, the nationalism of the revolutionary right was a reprise of the teachings of Norinaga's and Atsutane's eighteenth-century kokugaku, which saw Japan as incomparably special. Atsutane had put it this way: "[O]ur country, as a special mark of favor from the heavenly gods, was begotten by them, and there is thus so immense a difference between Japan and all the other countries of the world as to defy comparison. Ours is a splendid and blessed country, the Land of the Gods beyond any doubt, and we, down to the most humble man and woman, are the descendants of the gods."[15]

This view's foremost spokesman in the 1920s and 1930s was Kita Ikki, whose book, *A Plan for the Reorganization of Japan,* set forth a vision of radical reform at home that would assist mainland Asia in throwing off the imperialist yoke. Kita presented his argument in terms of a generous Pan-Asianism, masking the brutal seizure of power in Asia to create Japan's New Order (announced by Prime Minister Konoe Fumimaro in 1938) or the euphemistic Greater East Asia Co-Prosperity Sphere. Because of Japan's special polity (combining the divine with the human), Japan's actions abroad were always, to this way of thinking, purely motivated and consistently moral. Konoe patronized a Shōwa Association that framed the arguments rationalizing the New Order:

> It [was not] desirable that Asian peoples should be allowed to equate Japanese imperialism with Western imperialism . . . because . . . Western imperialism, they said. . . was self-seeking, was tyranny (hado). By contrast, Japanese expansion, which sought to free Asia from the West, was just. Its object was partnership. For practical reasons, this must be a partnership in which Japan led, resting on an ethic in Japanese form: on Japan's "national polity" (kokutai), manifested in Japan's "imperial way" (kōdō).[16]

For many advocates of aggressive Japanese expansion, the skies were seemingly the limit. One of them, Utsunomiya Tarō, on his deathbed, had a captain "draw a red line [on a map on the wall] around all of Siberia, India, Southeast Asia, Australia, and New Zealand. With his dying breath, he asserted 'That all belongs to Japan.'"[17]

Japan's problems, according to the revolutionary right, resulted from the evil advisors around the throne who had forgotten or deliberately forsaken Japanese-ness in favor of the blight of Western values and modernization. The solution, as set forth by Nishida Mitsugu in 1922: "In order to . . . rectify the evils of the past fifty years, ordinary measures are not enough. What we need is a thorough destruction of the existing order. . . . To save Japan from disaster, we must cut away all rotten parts, and our scalpel shall be the sword and bomb."[18] Just as a Meiji restoration had destroyed the shogunate, with its apparent inability to fend off the Western threat, now what was needed to free Japan from capitalist politicians was a Shōwa restoration (Shōwa was the reign name of Hirohito, who became emperor in 1926). This idea had been introduced by the assassin of the head of the Yasuda zaibatsu in 1921; in his call for a new restoration, he advised, "Do not get excited, and do not be conspicuous. You must be quiet and simply stab, stick, cut, and shoot. There is no need to meet or to organize. Just sacrifice your life."[19]

The emerging leaders of this radical right diagnosis of and prescription for Japan's "illness" were young army and navy officers often linked to civilian superpatriotic societies; many of these officers were

Source: Advice on Beginning a Taishō Restoration

Ultranationalist Asahi Heigo committed the first murder of a capitalist when he assassinated the head of the Yasuda zaibastsu in September 1921. He called for a restoration of the emperor to his proper place. From his statement in the early 1920s, what is his platform for the new Japan?

My fellow young idealists! Your mission is to bring about a Taishō Restoration. These are the steps you must take:

1. Bury the traitorous millionaires.
2. Crush the present political parties.
3. Bury the high officials and nobility.
4. Bring about a universal suffrage.
5. Abolish provisions for inheritance of rank and wealth.
6. Nationalize the land and bring relief to tenant farmers.
7. Confiscate all fortunes above 100,000 yen.
8. Nationalize big business.
9. Reduce military service to one year.

These are initial steps. But the punishment of the traitorous millionaires is the most urgent of all these, and there is no way of doing this except to assassinate them resolutely.

Finally, I want to say a word to my colleagues. I hope that you will live up to my principles. Do not speak, do not get excited, and do not be conspicuous. You must be quiet and simply stab, stick, cut, and shoot. There is no need to meet or to organize. Just sacrifice your life. And work out your own way of doing this. In this way you will prepare the way for the revolution. The flames will start here and there, and our fellow idealists will band together instantly. So forget about self-interest, and do not think about your own name or fame. Just die, just sleep. Never seek wisdom, but take the road of ignorance and come to know the height of great folly.

Source: Ryusaku Tsunoda, William Theodore de Bary, and Donald Keene, comps., Sources of Japanese Tradition, Volume II *(New York: Columbia University Press, 1965), 261–62.*

from rural areas. Brutal conditions in the countryside, when contrasted to the urban world of relative plenty and comparative ease, tended to give rise to rural disgruntlement and bitter hostility to the urban milieu, capitalism, and Western ways. It is no surprise that as the Depression wore on, the membership of ultranationalist associations doubled, from three hundred thousand in 1932 to six hundred thousand in 1936.

For these young officers, occupational and personal dynamics were also at work in the origins of their political position. The military was factionalized. Ever since the Meiji Restoration, the army had been in the hands of men from Chōshū (and their chosen allies), who had worked closely with political parties and were seen by some as part of the establishment. They were opposed by men outside the Chōshū clique—many of them in the young officers' group. In addition, a split developed between those who went onto the War College after graduation from the Military Academy and those whose training stopped. War College graduates were the elite: they received the top assignments abroad, were well paid, and could wear special insignia. In contrast, the young officers were the have-nots of the military. They were restricted in the rank to which they could rise (colonel), were often assigned to uninteresting tours of duty, and led austere lives with low pay. Generally they resented, even hated, the Chōshū clique and what was called the *Control faction*—the two of which had considerable overlap in membership.

In the early 1930s, the Young Officers' Movement took off when it began to advocate ideological training and indoctrination as the key to military success; central, they averred, was adherence to the *Imperial Way* (*Kōdō*). "The Shōwa Restoration was meant to restore a moral order in which all parts of society were believed to be members of one family, with the Emperor as its head."[20] *Kō* as a prefix for many terms (*imperial army* and *imperial country*) was introduced into daily army speech by Araki Sadao, who became war minister in 1931. The young officers were pitting themselves against the Control faction, which generally espoused mechanization, air power, and mobilization as the keys to military victory. One of the leading spokesmen for this position was Nagata Tetsuzan, a War College graduate who had been an army researcher in Europe during World War I and advocated strategic planning and total war.

The political and military landscape from 1931 to 1936 is studded with assassinations and coup attempts created by the military dynamics of the time. The coup attempt of March 1931 was planned by higher-ranking officers to end the power of the Chōshū clique; developed in conjunction with a secret military Cherry Society (Sakurakai), civilian patriotic societies, and men in the navy, its goal was to topple the political parties and institute national reform. After the coup occurred, power was to go to the current war minister, Ugaki Kazushige, who, on learning of the plot, refused to cooperate; the coup never proceeded. Another planned coup attempt in October 1931—this one involving young officers and targeting government officials, police, newspaper staff, financial magnates, and palace advisors—was uncovered before it could occur.

It was a different story on May 15, 1932: navy officers led a coup that resulted in the assassination of Prime Minister Inukai Tsuyoshi, a longtime party activist, and attacks on party headquarters, the Mitsubishi bank, and Tokyo's power transformers. The officers distributed a flier that called for revolution by "farmers, workers, and all the people." As an indication of the attitude of military brass at the time (controlled by the darling of the young officers, General Araki), those who were arrested for the crimes "were not handcuffed and were offered refreshments at their interrogation." Here is Araki's revealing, if rather shocking, reaction:

Members of a Superpatriotic Society, 1925 Superpatriotic societies burgeoned in the military and the countryside in the late 1920s and the 1930s. Jingoistic and militaristic, they helped fuel the ultranationalism that formed the mindset of the Japanese as they moved to war. These men are attired in samurai dress with flags, helmets, and weapons.

We cannot restrain our tears when we consider the mentality expressed in the actions
of these pure and naïve young men. They are not actions for fame, or personal gain,
nor are they traitorous. They were performed in the sincere belief that they were for the
benefit of Imperial Japan. Therefore in dealing with this incident, it will not do to dis-
pose of it in a routine manner according to shortsighted conceptions.[21]

Party cabinets in Japan until after World War II died with Inukai; the last genrō, Prince Saionji, named a former admiral to the post of prime minister, warned as he was that the military chiefs would not support any more party cabinets. There was also the belief that only military men could control the impetuous young followers of the Imperial Way.

As the prefix *Kō* (imperial) was much bandied about, early 1935 saw a debate about the meaning of the emperor's function. Since early in the century, accepted political theory, as set forth in the works of Minobe Tatsukichi, a leading scholar at Tokyo Imperial University, was that the emperor was an organ of the state. His works on the Meiji Constitution served as textbooks in many universities. The revolutionary right contended that the emperor was in a mystical way the embodiment of the state. They charged that Minobe's organ theory, which posited that the emperor was one organ among many, was an offense violating the emperor's dignity and sovereignty. Minobe was attacked mercilessly, even after the emperor announced that he supported Minobe's view. He was forced to resign from the House of Peers and Tokyo Imperial University, and his books were not allowed to be used as textbooks; in the words of one historian, he was "singled out for spectacular humiliation."[22]

At about the time of the Minobe uproar, the two highest-ranking supporters of the Young Officers' Movement were removed from their posts. The young officers blamed the Control faction's Nagata Tetsuzan for the transfers. They had already intensely disliked him, seeing him as an ideological and political threat to their position. In August 1935, a longtime participant in the Young Officers' Movement named Aizawa Saburō burst into Nagata's office and slashed him to death (see Identities). The loss of Nagata, probably the most brilliant and savvy planner and spokesman for the Control faction, was significant—not only for Japan's military future but also because he was an influential moderate in a world careening ever more dangerously to the right. Aizawa was put on trial, which became "a circus of ultranationalist hysteria."[23] His military counsel declared at the trial, "Murdering a senior officer is, of course a crime. But the defendant's sincere motive in doing so can make up for the criminality of the method he employed."[24]

While Aizawa's trial was still underway, the last and most dangerous of the coup attempts erupted; it was the "greatest insurrection in modern Japan."[25] On the snowy morning of February 26, 1936, more than 1,400 Imperial Way faction troops, who dubbed themselves the *Righteous Army of Restoration,* set out to restore the emperor to his "proper position." Armed with the slogan "Revere the emperor and destroy the wicked," they murdered key civilian and military officials and seriously wounded others. Then they occupied a large area containing key government buildings that police fenced off from the rest of Tokyo, holding it for four days while they waited for a response from civilian and military authorities. The army was uncertain: "Was it a rebellion, or should army leaders bless the young officers and use the opportunity in order to seize power for themselves?"[26] When the emperor expressed displeasure with the troops' actions, the army labeled it a rebellion. They declared martial law, which lasted into July; the emperor ordered the mutineers to surrender. There were no show trials; the rebellion had substantially altered the political atmosphere. Nineteen of the rebellion's leaders were put on trial and executed quickly and in secret. Aizawa also found that the episode had changed the context for his trial; he was found guilty of killing Nagata and executed. The upshot of the rebellion was that the Control faction solidified its power over the army and used the episode to argue that greater army control was necessary to forestall any similar action in the future. One of the leaders of this group was Tōjō Hideki, who would emerge as a key leader in World War II.

Identities: Aizawa Saburō (1889–1936), Assassin:

"In an Absolute Sphere"

Aizawa Saburō was born in Iwate prefecture in the northeast of Honshu. In 1917 he studied in Sendai with the Soto Zen master Fukusada Mugai, one of the most outstanding Zen priests of the twentieth century. Aizawa was a member of the Young Officers' Movement after 1927 and a close friend of Nishida Mitsugu, one of the leading firebrands of the revolutionary right, often staying at Nishida's house when he came to Tokyo (Aizawa was based in Fukuyama). At the Military Academy in the mid-1920s, one of his instructors was Mazaki Jinzaburō, inspector general of military education; they had remained friends. Mazaki and Araki Sadao were key officers who supported the Imperial Way faction that promoted spiritual training and indoctrination over modernization as the key to military success. A leading proponent of modernization was Nagata Tetsuzan, who in the mid-1930s was director of the Military Affairs Bureau and a leader of the Control faction. He was heartily disliked by soldiers in the Young Officers' Movement. In turn, he was bitterly critical of the Young Officers' Movement, calling for the "obliteration of that illegal reform ideology."[1]

In July 1935 Mazaki was transferred from his important military position; Nagata was blamed for the transfer. For Aizawa it was a hard pill to swallow. Not only was Mazaki a Young Officers' spokesman, he was Lieutenant Colonel Aizawa's teacher and friend. On July 19, in an appointment with Nagata, Aizawa brazenly advised him to resign because of Mazaki's transfer. Nagata did not give him the time of day; shortly thereafter, Aizawa found that he himself was being transferred to Taiwan.

In Tokyo in early August on his way to his new assignment, Aizawa went to the War Ministry, barged into Nagata's office where Nagata was meeting the chief of the Tokyo Military Police, and slashed at and wounded Nagata with his officer's sword. As the police chief tried to intervene, Nagata attemped to leave. Aizawa followed him and slashed him in the back, killing him. Aizawa was arrested in the building; he made no attempt to flee; indeed, he stopped to talk to acquaintances. One major general thanked him for what he had done.

In the beginning, his trial was a show trial as supporters and members of the Young Officers' Movement painted a picture of Aizawa as acting through pure motives and sincerity in upholding the emperor and the Imperial Way. When asked by the judge which of the Zen teachings had influenced him most, he replied without thinking, "Reverence for the emperor is absolute." Another time Aizawa reportedly said, "I was in an absolute sphere, so there was neither affirmation nor negation, neither good nor evil."[2] Indeed, the young officers, with their radical right thinking, were sure that their sphere of action and thought was absolute; nothing else mattered. Aizawa's former Zen master, Fukusada, saw Aizawa's actions as consistent with Zen practice to "destroy the false and establish the true. . . . For my part, I fully understand why he acted as he did."[3]

After the February 26 incident, the political climate in the capital changed. Aizawa was found guilty and executed July 12, 1936. His ashes were interred together with those of twenty-two officers of the February 26 incident in the Soto Zen temple of Kensoji in Tokyo. Ironically, his actions helped bring the Control faction, which he hated, absolute control of the military.

---

[1] Ben-Ami Shillony, Revolt in Japan *(Princeton, NJ: Princeton University Press, 1973), 44.*

[2] *Internet. http://www.jbe.gold.ac.uk/11/loy.html.*

[3] *Internet. http://www.cimabue1.home.mindspring.com/zen_war_stories.htm.*

POLITICS AND SOCIETY IN THE 1930s

The early 1930s had remained relatively open and tolerant. Popular culture was cosmopolitan: many Japanese flocked to Hollywood films, and Western jazz reverberated in major cities and remote prefectural towns. Professional baseball teams began to play in 1934, the year that Babe Ruth and an American team played eighteen exhibition games in twelve Japanese cities, with tens of thousands of spectators. By 1941, over 45 percent of Japanese homes had radios (Japan ranked fourth in the world in radio ownership), and the number of homes with telephones was almost one million in 1937. Buses, taxis, and some private automobiles crowded city streets. By 1933, Tokyo and Osaka could boast of subway lines.

And there was open dissent as the *Manchurian incident* mushroomed into the *China incident.* Yanaihara Tadao, a Tokyo University professor who specialized in colonial policy, published an article in the journal *Reconstruction* (*Kaizō*) in April 1932 that condemned Japanese actions in Manchuria, calling them "self-defeating" and predicting that they would ultimately fail because of the emerging Chinese nationalism.[27] But as Japan moved to war in China in 1936 and 1937, what was viewed as orthodox political thought became ever more narrow and inflexible. Minobe was not alone in being attacked for his views; in 1937 Yanaihara was forced to resign for his criticism of Japan's China policy. Other university professors suffered as well. Several religious groups were accused of crimes and disbanded after a 1939 Diet law gave the government the authority to break up "any religious organization whose teachings did not conform to the 'Imperial Way.'"[28]

There were frequent round-ups of Communists. The Ministry of Education issued a manifesto in 1937 to all schools—"Fundamentals of Our National Polity"—that "blamed Japan's social and ideological crisis on Western beliefs ranging from individualism to communism."[29] It specified that the basic principle of Japanese life should be serving the emperor and the family while exhibiting loyalty and the proper military spirit. Students were required to participate in martial arts, primarily judo and kendo. It became increasingly difficult for dissidents to speak out. Even general mainstream women's magazines were filled with articles that supported military expansion and glorified war. "After 1933 it was difficult to find on corner newsstands an alternative to the official view that Japan was acting in self-defense to protect its legitimate rights and interests in northern Asia."[30]

As the China war began and then bogged down, jazz was displaced by patriotic and war-related music; in October 1940 the government banned the performance of jazz and shut down dance halls in Tokyo as it moved to increase its power over and control of all aspects of Japanese life. On January 1, 1936, it set up a wire service, the Domei News Agency, to distribute all national and international news to radio stations and newspapers in the country.

Following the coming of the Great Depression, the Manchurian incident, and political terrorism, senior statesmen believed that party cabinets could not deal with Japan's serious problems. Throughout the 1930s, the Seiyūkai and Minseitō continued to function; they dominated the Diet, which regularly met, deliberated, and legislated. But the parties experienced continual decline vis-à-vis the bureaucracy. In the period 1924 to 1932 there were seven cabinets, all having a prime minister from a political party, with an average of 8.7 of 12 cabinet ministers from political parties. In contrast, from 1932 to 1940, there were eight cabinets, none with a prime minister from a political party and an average of 9.9 of 13 cabinet ministers from the government bureaucracy. They were the new bureaucrats, convinced that political parties were morally weak and that the bureaucracy had to be in control to put the economy on a war footing. As the 1940s and the Pacific war approached, parties generally became supporters of the military.

As war neared and then became a reality, the government moved to make Japan a *national defense state* that tightly managed the economy so that it could wage war effectively. This meant organizing and integrating the Japanese colonies to achieve as much economic self-sufficiency as possible and then centralizing all economic decision making. In 1938 a cabinet-level agency, the Cabinet Planning Board, was formed. It set up a Ministry of Health and Welfare to administer health care and social welfare programs;

Emperor Hirohito The Shōwa emperor (1901–1989) is pictured here in uniform on horseback. According to the Meiji Constitution, he was all-powerful and the "locus of sovereignty" in the state. His exact role in the militarism of the 1930s and 1940s is still debated.

it nationalized the power industry; and it drafted a national mobilization bill that gave the government the power to apportion labor according to the needs of key industries and to organize all industries into cartels to carry out government directives. In this national defense state, the key elements were "central planning, wage and price controls, and the rationing of raw materials and consumer goods."[31] The zaibatsu continued to play key roles, but they were attacked by ultranationalists who roundly condemned capitalism. However, the 1930s also saw the emergence of new zaibatsu—Nissan, Nakajima Aircraft, and Nitchitsu—conglomerates that were not family-based, emerged in the manufacturing industries, and were willing to cooperate with the military.

JAPANESE AGGRESSION ON THE MARCH

One of the key conspirators planning the *Manchurian incident* was Ishiwara Kanji, recognized as "the army's leading theorist on strategy and military history."[32] He believed that Japan was fated to destroy Marxism and other perverted ideologies through a series of colossal wars with the Soviet Union, Britain, and, last and biggest, the United States. These gargantuan struggles would involve whole populations and the use of all of their resources, at the end of which Japan would "stand as the champion of Asia and the embodiment of Confucian righteousness."[33] The first step in this forced march was Manchuria. As we have seen, success came quickly for the Guandong army conspirators. By March 1932, Manchukuo was a done deal; just two months later, Prime Minister Inukai was assassinated. (See the chart for a timeline of events in Japan and developments on the continent.) Japan rationalized that it could act in China because, as it announced when it left the League of Nations, "in its present condition, China could not be regarded as 'an organized state.' Therefore 'the general principles of international law . . . had to be considered modified in their operation as far as China is concerned.' "[34]

In part, Japan's Manchurian victory came because Jiang Jieshi refused to resist, choosing instead to eat humble pie. But the Chinese people struck back at Japan through an effective boycott in the autumn of

Source: "Fundamentals of Our National Polity"

These hallmark positions of the Japanese government as it lunged toward war appear in a book with the same title as this source's name. Published by the Ministry of Education in 1937, it eventually sold over two million copies. What does the writer see as the fundamental characteristics of the Japanese spirit?

Our country is established with the emperor, who is a descendant of Amaterasu Ōmikami, as her center, and our ancestors as well as we ourselves constantly have beheld in the emperor the fountainhead of her life and activities. For this reason, to serve the emperor and to receive the emperor's great august Will as one's own is the rationale of making our historical "life" live in the present; and on this is based the morality of the people.

Loyalty means to reverence the emperor as [our] pivot and to follow him implicitly. By implicit obedience is meant casting ourselves aside and serving the emperor intently. To walk this Way of loyalty is the sole Way in which we subjects may "live," and the fountainhead of all energy. Hence, offering our lives for the sake of the emperor does not mean so-called self-sacrifice, but the casting aside of our little selves to live under his august grace and the enhancing of the genuine life of the people of a State. The relationship between the emperor and the subjects is not an artificial relationship [which means] bowing down to authority, nor a relationship such as [exists] between master and servant as is seen in feudal morals. . . . The ideology which interprets the relationship between the emperor and his subjects as being a reciprocal relationship such as merely [involves] obedience to authority or rights and duties, rests on individualistic ideologies, and is a rationalistic way of thinking that looks on everything as being in equal personal relationships. An individual is an existence belonging to a State and her history which forms the basis of his origin, and is fundamentally one body with it. . . .

In our country filial piety is a Way of the highest importance. Filial piety originates with one's family as its basis, and in its larger sense has the nation for its foundation. Filial piety directly has for its object one's parents, but in its relationship toward the emperor finds a place within loyalty.

Source: Ryusaku Tsunoda, William Theodore de Bary, and Donald Keene, comps., Sources of Japanese Tradition, *Volume II (New York: Columbia University Press, 1965), 280–81.*

1931—slashing the sale of Japanese products in China by two thirds. Tensions were especially high in Shanghai, with its population of thirty thousand Japanese citizens, many of whom called for the military to end the boycott. The military did its part, declaring the boycott an act of aggression. With goading by Japanese ultranationalists who cried, in essence, "Teach the Chinese a lesson," the Japanese navy (wanting to share some patriotic glory with the Manchurian Guandong army) bombed northern Shanghai. Japan sent seventy thousand troops, who dropped firebombs and shelled civilian areas with tanks and artillery. The Chinese Nineteenth Route Army, against Jiang's will, resisted valiantly. The bitter fighting led to over four thousand Chinese and almost eight hundred Japanese deaths. This undeclared war raged for six weeks (January–March 1932) and ended when both sides agreed to an armistice. Clearly, Japan had decided not to push further at this time.

Furious that the Nineteenth Route Army had resisted, fearing that it might ignite a full-scale war that would endanger his own position, Jiang transferred the army to out-of-the-way Fujian province. But for many Chinese the Nineteenth Route Army became instant heroes, the names of its leaders appearing as brand names for cigarettes and other goods. As one historian put it, "The Chinese people, who had been gagging on never-ending humiliations and pusillanimous compromises, took the Nineteenth Route Army to their hearts."[35] The Shanghai incident only increased the polarization between the government and

A Comparison of Japanese Foreign and Domestic Actions in the 1930s

Japan on the Continent	Terrorism at Home
September 1931—Manchurian incident	Sept. 1930—Sakurakai coup plot
Jan.–Mar. 1932—Shanghai war	Mar. 1931—Planned coup plot thwarted
Jan. 1933—Seizure of Shanhaiguan	Oct. 1931—Planned coup plot thwarted
Feb.-Mar. 1933—Seizure of Rehe	May 15, 1932—Conspiracy plot successful—end
May 1933—Tanggu Truce	of party government
Aug. 1933—Eastern Chahar province falls	Summer 1935—Attack on Minobe
April 1934—Amau Doctrine	Aug. 1935—Nagata killed
June 1935—He-Umezu agreement	Feb. 26, 1936—Mutiny and terror
Qin-Doihara agreement	
Sept . 1935—Autonomy demand	
Dec. 1935—Hebei-Chahar council	
Dec. 1936—Xi'an incident	
July 7, 1937—War begins	

those calling for resistance against this imperialist threat. Jiang's response was to suppress the protesters, a policy that only escalated the animosity.

The years from 1933 to 1937 saw the patterns repeated again and again: Japanese aggression, Jiang's appeasement, mass Chinese reaction, Jiang's suppression of the protesters. In early January 1933 Japanese forces seized Shanhaiguan, the pass between the Great Wall and the Gulf of Liaodong. Its fall was of great symbolic value, because it was through this pass 289 years earlier that the Manchus had marched on their way to conquering China. A shock wave washed over and unnerved thinking Chinese: might this be the start of another conquest of China? Jiang sent no reinforcements to assist his forces, which fought well but were no match for the Japanese. In late February and early March 1933, the Japanese took the easternmost province of Inner Mongolia, Rehe—a territory as large as Virginia, Maryland, and West Virginia combined. Jiang dispatched no planes, sent no guns, and ordered the poorest and most politically unreliable troops to fight; most of them melted away before the Japanese attacks. The popular reaction was disbelief and chagrin.

The Tanggu Truce in May 1933 created a demilitarized zone between the Great Wall and Beiping (the name by which Beijing was known from 1928 to 1949) the size of the state of Connecticut. Jiang negotiated it to stop the Japanese advance and the certain seizure of Beiping (Japanese troops were only thirteen miles from the city). Although Chinese troops were not allowed in the demilitarized zone, Japanese troops had a right to remain under specifications of the Boxer Protocol. The words *surrender* and *defeat* were used in newspapers to describe the truce, while Jiang and other government figures were called traitors. Jiang struck back at his opponents, sponsoring the assassination of the head of the League for the Protection of Civil Rights—organized in reaction to Jiang's suppression of anti-Japanese activity.

Territorial dominoes continued to fall: in August 1933, Japanese forces took Inner Mongolia's eastern Chahar province, a territory slightly larger than the state of Connecticut. In this episode, Jiang took actions that actually helped the Japanese retake an area they had held early on but then lost. The following April, the Japanese Foreign Ministry asserted the Amau Doctrine, under which Japan gained control of all aid and development programs that China might establish with Western nations. Chinese questioned whether this was the first move toward the establishment of a Japanese protectorate. Two "agreements" in June

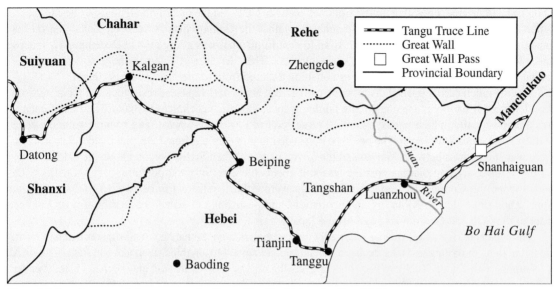

Map 10-2   Arena of Japanese Action: North China in the 1930s.

1935 further tightened Japan's grip on northern China. The He-Umezu agreement removed all Guomindang institutions, Nanjing government bodies, and army troops from Hebei province (where Beiping was located). The Qin-Doihara agreement gave Japan a free hand in the province of Chahar, stipulating that Chinese could not interfere with any activities undertaken there by Japan or Manchukuo. In response, a Tianjin paper blasted the "traitorous Kuomintang [Guomindang] [who are] . . . selling the nation's territory and the people's rights. Whatever Japan wants the Kuomintang gives them."[36]

In September 1935 Japan, interested in structuring an economic bloc consisting of itself, Manchukuo, and northern China, made its most aggressive demand to date, insisting that the five northern provinces of China be made autonomous, a demand that shocked even Jiang.[37] If he had agreed, these provinces would have become independent. He did not give in: this was the only domino that did not fall. Three months later, at the end of the year, eastern Hebei province came under Japanese control with the establishment of a collaborationist council with Chahar. This act gave rise to a campaign of student protests and the proliferation of units of the National Salvation Association, which called for the removal of Japanese troops and puppet regimes in Manchukuo and East Hebei. Jiang attacked them as "tools of the Communists."

By summer 1936, however, Jiang was well aware of the nation's restiveness and gave the first indication that he might consider some resistance to Japan's aggression, saying specifically that appeasement had its limits. But he still suppressed protesters, arresting seven National Salvation Association leaders, to the outrage of millions across the country. This was an example of what would become known late in the century as *human rights* problems. Even Western intellectuals—Albert Einstein and John Dewey, for example—cabled Jiang's government asking for the leaders' release. At home the arrests only stimulated anti-Japanese activity.

THE XI'AN INCIDENT

Out of this context came one of the most sensational and still mysterious episodes in twentieth-century China. After the Communists reached Yan'an in late 1935 (see Chapter 13), Jiang used many troops to blockade their base. They were commanded by Zhang Xueliang, former military leader of Manchuria, who had been ousted in the 1931–1932 Japanese victory there and was frustrated by his assignment to fight other Chinese rather than the Japanese. In April 1936, Zhang had met with the Communist leader

Zhou Enlai to discuss a possible united front between the CCP and the Guomindang to fight the Japanese. When Jiang ordered Zhang to begin a campaign against the Communists in October, Zhang sat on his hands. In early December, Jiang flew to Xi'an to determine what was going on. On December 12, troops under Zhang's direction attacked Jiang's headquarters. They seized and detained the president and presented a number of demands, including establishing a united front to meet the Japanese threat.

Having much earlier opened discussions with Zhang about anti-Japanese resistance, the Communists, headquartered little more than one hundred miles away at Yan'an, had choices to make. Their chief enemy was now practically in their hands; should he be seized and killed? Or would Jiang be more valuable alive in the present crisis with Japan if he could be persuaded to join a united front? Despite rocky relationships, there was still contact between Yan'an and the Soviet capital. When Stalin weighed in on the side of keeping Jiang alive, arguing that his prestige was still a valuable asset of great potential use in a nationwide united front, the Communist leadership in Yan'an were either confirmed in or swayed to that position. Thus, Zhou Enlai flew to Xi'an to join negotiations and push Jiang to accept leadership of a new united front of the CCP and Guomindang against the Japanese.

His captors released him after he reportedly gave verbal assurances that he would support a united front. He put nothing in writing and later declared that he had not agreed to anything. In any event, Jiang flew back to Nanjing, with Zhang Xueliang now his captive. Zhang was court-martialed and kept in custody under Jiang's control. Moved to Taiwan when the Guomindang lost the civil war in the late 1940s, Zhang remained under house arrest at least until 1991. He left Taiwan in December 1993 and settled in Hawaii, where he died in October 2001. Jiang emerged from the affair as a national hero. Approximately four hundred thousand people watched his motorcade from the Nanjing airport on his return; spontaneous celebrations of joy and relief erupted in cities around the country, with many people apparently willing to forget Jiang's extended period of appeasement and his harsh repression of thousands of Chinese civilians. Almost immediately there was a cease-fire between Nanjing's forces and the Red Army, and within little more than eight months a united front was established. Jiang had come to realize that he could no longer appease Japan.

THE MARCO POLO BRIDGE INCIDENT

During night maneuvers of Japanese troops near the Marco Polo Bridge, fifteen kilometers west-southwest of Beiping, on July 7, 1937, one soldier turned up missing. The Japanese demanded the right to search a nearby town. Although the missing soldier returned less than half an hour after he disappeared, his commanders did not know this. In the meantime, when Chinese troops refused to allow the Japanese to search the town, Japanese troops opened fire and a battle ensued. Though negotiations brought a settlement by July 11, tensions remained high. Fighting broke out again near the end of July, this time with thousands of Chinese casualties. Within days the Japanese seized control of the whole region around Beiping. On July 27, Japanese Prime Minister Konoe announced that he would seek a "fundamental solution of Sino–Japanese relations." Three days later, Jiang asserted that "the only course open to us now is to lead the masses of the nation, under a single national plan, to struggle to the last."[38]

Was full-scale war inevitable? While nothing in history is inevitable, by late summer 1937 neither country would compromise. In Japan's view, it had given too much to the continental struggle to back down. Even though the relationship between the two nations during the 1930s was one long string of Chinese capitulations to Japanese demands, appeasement never satisfied Japan's territorial and political appetites. Japan's attitude seemed to be that capitulation at every turn was not enough: China also had to show respect to Japan. In the summer of 1937, a Japanese commander in North China bluntly asserted that he would lead "a punitive expedition against Chinese troops, who have been taking acts derogatory to the prestige of the Empire of Japan."[39] With such attitudes and with Japan's long history of involvement, Japan would not likely back down or compromise.

On the Chinese side, there could also be no compromise. The tension and drama of the Xi'an incident and Jiang's mysterious escape had made him popular. The perception, whether it matched reality or not, was that he had committed himself to resistance against the Japanese. It would have been politically suicidal for Jiang to return to a policy of appeasement. He could not backtrack. Thus, in any crisis he had to avoid even the appearance of caving in to Japanese threats or attacks. This meant, as Jiang himself said, that China had only one route if Japan persisted: "to struggle to the last."

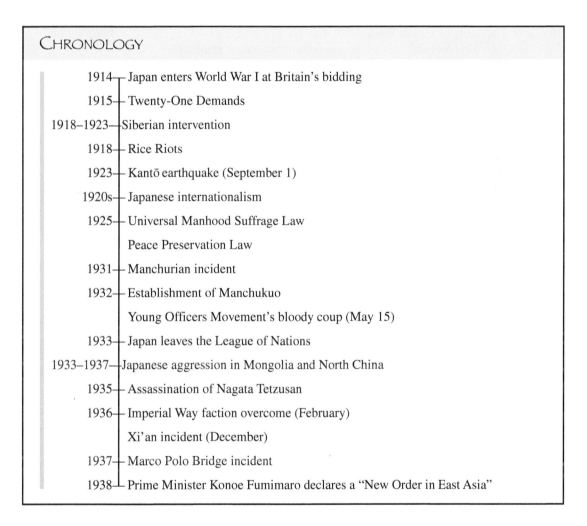

CHRONOLOGY

1914	Japan enters World War I at Britain's bidding
1915	Twenty-One Demands
1918–1923	Siberian intervention
1918	Rice Riots
1923	Kantō earthquake (September 1)
1920s	Japanese internationalism
1925	Universal Manhood Suffrage Law
	Peace Preservation Law
1931	Manchurian incident
1932	Establishment of Manchukuo
	Young Officers Movement's bloody coup (May 15)
1933	Japan leaves the League of Nations
1933–1937	Japanese aggression in Mongolia and North China
1935	Assassination of Nagata Tetzusan
1936	Imperial Way faction overcome (February)
	Xi'an incident (December)
1937	Marco Polo Bridge incident
1938	Prime Minister Konoe Fumimaro declares a "New Order in East Asia"

SUGGESTED READINGS

Coble, Parks. *Facing Japan: Chinese Politics and Japanese Imperialism, 1931–1937*. Cambridge, MA: Harvard University Press, 1991. A rich, balanced, and insightful study of Chinese domestic politics and its interaction with an aggressively expanding Japan.

Duus, Peter. *Party Rivalry and Political Change in Taishō Japan*. Cambridge, MA: Harvard University Press, 1968. A well-written account of the process by which a two-party system emerged and of the gap between party and people.

Duus, Peter, Ramon H. Myers, and Mark R. Peattie, eds. *The Japanese Informal Empire in China, 1895–1937*. Princeton, NJ: Princeton University Press, 1989. This excellent collection of essays probes many facets of the relations between China and Japan.

Lewis, Michael. *Becoming Apart: National Power and Local Politics in Toyama, 1868–1945*. Cambridge: Cambridge University Press, 2000. An interesting study about the intersection of national power and local politics in an outlying prefecture.

Minichiello, Sharon, ed. *Japan's Competing Modernities: Issues in Culture and Democracy, 1900–1930*. Honolulu: University of Hawaii Press, 1998. This book of essays moves beyond identifying Taishō Japan as a nation in crisis and focuses on questions of nation and ethnicity.

CHAPTER ELEVEN

Under the Imperialist Gun:
Vietnam, Korea, and Taiwan

In the early twentieth century, Vietnamese, ruled by the French, and Koreans and Taiwanese, ruled by the Japanese, were continually confronted with questions of their national, political, and cultural (and, in the case of Vietnamese, racial) identity. A nagging question in the face of control by outsiders—who had different cultural values and superior technological power—was what to do with native traditions and culture that appeared to be weaker and perhaps less valuable than the ways of their overlords.

VIETNAM: FRANCE'S COLONY

The Beginning of the Revolution, 1925–1941

Leaders of every colonial power must be aware, if only in the deep recesses of their minds, how uneasily the imperialist crown rests on their heads. During the 1920s, France conducted "an intense colonial campaign to convince Vietnamese that French rule was not only inevitable but just and beneficial as well."[1] Schoolchildren's assignments included essays that praised and exalted the French occupation. One school primer began with the announcement that "Franco-Vietnamese collaboration is the road to a paradise of advantages," and another asserted that "France is treating us better than our own fathers and mothers."[2] Yet, there was no personal freedom. Before a Vietnamese could travel, begin a new job, form an organization, or start a newspaper, there were always the necessary loyalty checks.

How did the Vietnamese respond to such pressures of identity? As we have seen with Nguyen Van Vinh and Pham Quynh, some Vietnamese glorified everything French (Vinh), while others championed things Vietnamese (Quynh). These almost diametrically opposed reactions continued throughout the colonial period. The "I long to be French and despise my Vietnamese identity" attitude appeared openly in the remarks of a landowner's grandson:

> *The more deeply I entered the French world, the more frustrated I became at the*
> *Vietnamese world in which I was forced to participate, the more I could see only the*
> *coarse yokel uglinesses of people with yellow skin and flat noses, to whom I used to*
> *feel I was connected because I also had a flat nose and yellow skin.*[3]

At the opposite end of the identity spectrum was the Vietnamese poet The Lu, who wrote in the 1930s. His "Remembering the Jungle," subtitled "The Word of the Tiger in the Zoo," is seen by one scholar as "one of the . . . most powerful statements of Vietnamese nationalism and ethnic identity." In these excerpts, The Lu rued the deleterious impact of French control on traditional Vietnamese nobility and glory, seen symbolically as the indigenous jungle:

> *Growing upon our resentment, we stretch out in an iron cage,*
> *Watching the slow passage of days and months.*
> *How we despise the insolent crowd outside,*
> *Standing there foolishly, with tiny eyes bulging,*
> *As they mock the stately spirit of the deep jungle.*
>
> . . .
>
> *We sustain ourselves with fond memories of days long past,*
> *A time of freedom and assertiveness.*
>
> . . .
>
> *We now embrace the rancor of a thousand autumns,*
> *Hating these never-changing scenes.*
> *Scenes that are altered, commonplace, and false.*

. . .

O stately soul, heroic land,
Vast domain where yesteryear we freely roamed,
We see you no more.
But do you know that during our days of frustration
We follow a great dream, letting our souls race to be near you,
O formidable jungle of ours.[4]

Both examples reflect the psychological costs of colonialism. The 1930s and 1940s were marked by political efforts to reassert Vietnamese political identity and toss off the yoke of colonialism. The French overlords fought Vietnamese efforts every step of the way. (See Chapter 4 for a description of how the government functioned in Vietnam.)

The French patronized all Vietnamese ("treating them as inferiors or as children"), foreshadowing American attitudes three decades later.[5] Political freedoms—assembly, association, and the press—did not exist for the Vietnamese. French rule embittered Vietnamese with its monopolies over opium, alcohol, and salt; the imposition of soaring regressive taxes; abominable working conditions in factories; and brutal practices of labor recruitment for rubber plantations. The Great Depression brought hunger, malnutrition, and even starvation to the countryside and bankruptcy and staggering unemployment to the cities.

In 1927, Nguyen Thai Hoc, of peasant stock, formed the Vietnamese Nationalist Party (VNQDD). Originally interested in moderate tactics, Hoc turned to armed revolt when the French government censured a party publication. He used the model of Sun Yixian's Nationalist Party and appealed to students, soldiers, lower-level government functionaries, women, the urban petit bourgeoisie, and some landlords and wealthy peasants. In 1929, French secret police estimated a membership of 1,500 in 120 cells, especially in provinces in the northern Red River delta. That year the French authorities blamed the VNQDD for the killing of a French labor contractor and used it as a pretext to crack down on the party, an action that led to 400 arrests and prison terms of up to twenty years for almost 80 party members. In response, Nguyen Thai Hoc, who had escaped arrest, called for uprisings at four Red River delta military posts in early February 1930. The plan called for breaking into the posts with the hope that local troops would forsake their French officers and join the rebels. The largest post, at Yen Bay (which gave its name to the whole effort), was breached, but the troops went to the defense of the French, who quickly restored order and seized the rebels. All the uprisings failed disastrously, dealing the VNQDD a staggering blow; though ragtag groups of party members remained, for all practical purposes for the rest of the 1930s the party was moribund. Instead of making precision attacks on party sites, the French used a sledgehammer approach, bombing and leveling eleven villages from the air. All prisoners were ordered killed, a terrorist tactic "to scare the population."[6] From June 1930 through 1933, the government executed 527 and sent almost 9,000 to hard labor and to concentration camps, including the notorious one on Poulo Condore island, where many were given life sentences.

The VNQDD had primarily been composed of and directed by urban intellectuals who had attended French schools and, unlike the anticolonial resisters of Phan Boi Chau and his followers, were post-Confucian. But, as one historian pointed out, they shared some of the negative qualities that marked Chau's efforts: "an inability to avoid . . . reckless impetuosity that was so characteristic of early [Vietnamese] nationalism . . . , a lack of understanding of how to involve the masses in the struggle for independence, and an insufficient realization of the economic basis of discontent in Vietnam."[7]

In the early 1930s there was a flurry of hope that France might at last undertake crucial economic reforms—lower the rice export tax, make agricultural credit more available, and halt the imprisonment of debtors. The visit of French Minister of Colonies Paul Reynaud in 1931 brought petitioners out of the

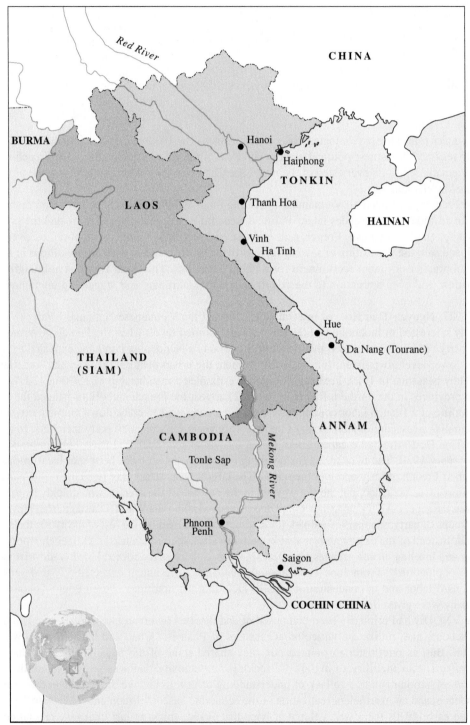

Map 11-1   Early-Twentieth-Century Vietnam and Its Neighbors.

Emperor Khai Dinh (1885–1925) Taking the throne in 1916, Khai Dinh, rumored to be a drug addict, was a close collaborator with the French. He authorized the French to raise taxes on the peasants, antagonizing many Vietnamese, and signed orders for the arrest of the nationalist Phan Boi Chau. *Source:* The Art Archive. Picture Desk Inc./Kobal Collection.

woodwork, including Pham Quynh, now a professor at a French *lycée* in Hanoi, who called for a Vietnamese constitutional monarchy that would allow the Vietnamese "to develop their own personality as a nation and to assure them a national life dignified of the name within the body of the French Empire."[8] It was at this time that the nineteen-year-old Crown Prince Bao Dai, who had been studying in France, returned to take the throne at the death of his father, Emperor Khai Dinh, in 1925. He named Pham to head a joint Franco-Vietnamese commission to oversee the economic reforms; the secretary of the commission was Ngo Dinh Diem, a thirty-five-year-old former province chief. In the end, nothing ever came of the reforms.

Searching for New Communities in a Period of Malaise

A major development in the 1930s was the formation of two syncretic religious-political movements, Cao Dai and Hoa Hao, that some have seen as the products of popular unrest under French domination and the inability of Vietnamese to effect any sort of change. Both sects were regional, not national; and they were able to function because the French allowed the formation of political party–like organizations only in Cochinchina. Cao Dai, whose key symbol was the Heavenly Eye, was organized in 1926 as a highly eclectic mix of three East Asian religions—Confucianism, Buddhism, and Daoism—as well as Christianity and folk religions. It embraced spiritism as a way to recover social harmony and equilibrium, which had been lost. Practically, that meant reforming personal habits and improving personal relations. The "Caodaist pantheon was a gloriously motley collection of gods and saints which included, amidst Chinese [Sun Yixian] and Vietnamese figures, Victor Hugo, Jesus Christ, Shakespeare, and Joan of Arc, all of whom had claimed to be in direct communion with the Supreme Being."[9] Whereas the

Cao Dai Temple   Located in Tay Ninh near the Cambodian border, this temple was the main seat of the religion born in the 1920s. Combining Asian religions with Asian and Western secular figures, it had an array of saints ranging from Confucius, the Buddha, and Sun Yixian to Joan of Arc and Victor Hugo.

VNQDD and early nationalist reformers had attracted mostly urban dwellers, Cao Dai's appeal was to small farmers and small-town dwellers, though its leadership came from large landholders and relatively well-off businessmen and officials. Both leaders and followers "prided themselves ... on their receptivity to modern ideas, but they were also anxious to find within their own culture some spiritual equivalence with the West."[10] Their movement gave evidence of a "search for new forms of organized communities" at this time of political and cultural confusion in Vietnam.[11] Based in Tay Ninh province, northwest of Saigon along the Cambodian border, its Holy See (which many took as Cao Dai's Vatican) was near the provincial capital.

The Hoa Hao sect, an offshoot of Buddhism, was founded by an extraordinarily popular healer, Huynh Phu So, who believed he was the reincarnation of the Buddha Master of Western Peace. Highly charismatic, "he was a handsome youth [at age twenty—in 1939] with an emaciated face framed by his shoulder-length hair. His distinctive feature was his burning gaze. ..."[12] By 1939, he had attracted over ten thousand followers, many of whom were devoted, even fanatical, in their personal commitment. His base was Can Tho, southwest of Saigon in the Mekong delta. With the potential to attract such support came political potential as well. In addition to his popularity was his message—one that spoke of the coming of a utopian society born in revolutionary action. An example:

> *Cataclysm is about to come*
> *Sun and moon will change places in the sky, smoke will envelope the earth.*
> *No house, no tree, no blade of grass will be left.*
> *And then, there will be peace and perfect tranquility.*[13]

Since Hoa Hao attracted mainly peasants and poor daily laborers, authorities were nervous about the possibility of the sect's producing rural violence.

The Communist Movement in the 1930s: Like a Yo-Yo

One other force in the search for new social forms that became increasingly significant in the 1930s and 1940s was the Communist movement, whose central figure was Ho Chi Minh (born Nguyen That Thanh in 1890 in Nghe An province in central Vietnam). Son of an anti-French Confucian gentry father, Ho left Vietnam in 1911, eventually making his way to France after working in several other countries, including the United States. In Paris, he took the pseudonym Nguyen Ai Quoc (Nguyen the patriot). As the representative of a group of overseas Vietnamese, he penned a number of demands—including Vietnamese autonomy and equal rights between French and Vietnamese—that he wanted to present to the Versailles Conference that ended World War I. Like other spokesmen for colonized nations, he was refused a hearing at this conference dominated by U.S. President Woodrow Wilson, who had championed the self-determination of peoples in the abstract.

Ho became active in French politics and was a founding member of the French Communist Party. In 1923 the Comintern beckoned him to Moscow, where he studied Marxism and was a delegate to a Comintern congress. In 1924, as part of Michael Borodin's mission, he traveled to Guangzhou, China, where in June 1925 he formed the Revolutionary Youth League of Vietnam, the first Marxist organ in Indochina. Its goal was educative: to cultivate a body of committed revolutionaries for overthrowing the French and achieving Vietnamese independence. In late 1925, Ho wrote *The Road to Revolution (Duong Cach Menh)*, essentially a training manual aimed at an audience in Vietnam emphasizing the roles of both the peasants and the proletariat in the coming revolution, a stance that echoed the position of Mao Zedong. The League's journal, *Thanh Nien* (Youth), which was published from July 1925 to April 1927, had to be smuggled into Vietnam. Its message was "half nationalist and half watered-down Marxism as it attempted to inculcate a sense of Vietnamese identity and to introduce new Marxist terminology and theory."[14] Unlike the united front in China, there were no efforts to establish any united front between the leftist Revolutionary Youth League and the more moderate VNQDD. These were rocky years for the League. Even though its membership had risen to over one thousand by 1929, different short-term goals had split the organization: some wanted the immediate establishment of a full-fledged Communist party; some indeed accused League members of not being truly revolutionary.

In February 1930, Ho opened a unity conference in Guangzhou that established the Indochina Communist Party (ICP). The conference came in the midst of the greatest uprising against the French thus far in the century. Earlier in the year, the failed VNQDD uprisings had, in a sense, kicked into action several waves of violence. The number of labor strikes shot up from twenty-four involving about 6,000 workers in 1929 to ninety-eight with almost 32,000 workers in 1930. Strikes grew in intensity and violence.

Ho Chi Minh in France, December 1920   Ho Chi Minh (then called Nguyen Ai Quoc) is shown at the annual congress of the French Socialist Party, at which part of the party broke away to form the French Communist Party. Ho was a founding member. *Source:* Bibliotheque Nationale, Paris, France/The Bridgeman Art Library.

In May 1930, 3,000 peasants in Nghe An province rioted, leaving destruction in their path as they seized grain and property. Their demands were both economic and political, calling, for example, for reduced taxes and the freeing of political prisoners. In late August, peasants and workers again in Nghe An province exploded in violence, destroying official property and forcing local government officials to flee. The French, fearful of the role of Communism in precipitating this popular uprising, picked up where they had left off seven months earlier in crushing the Yen Bay uprising. They strafed and bombed demonstrating Vietnamese on September 12, killing 174 and injuring hundreds more.

But the Vietnamese were not easily cowed. That same day, encouraged by a Communist committee and taking advantage of the power vacuum left by fleeing government officials, a village in Nghe An established a soviet (council) to serve as a new revolutionary government. Soon, like the proverbial "bamboo shoots after a spring rain," soviets sprouted up all over the province and in neighboring Ha Tinh. These autonomous bodies, essentially peasant associations, set up militias for defense; advocated seizing communal, though not individually owned, land; and organized classes to teach *quoc ngu*. The ICP tried to take advantage of the movement to foster its own efforts; leaflets were smuggled into the country with such messages as "Workers-Peasants-Soldiers! Your wives and children, sisters and brothers are hungry and ill-clothed because of the imperialist, feudalist system of the royal court. Join together to wipe out those who suck the blood of your relatives."[15] But the ICP was not yet organizationally mature enough to direct and guide the movement.

The soviets were a Communist challenge the French could not abide. The French authorities were supported by the Catholic Church, which feared and was obsessed with the threat of Communism. As rioting continued, authorities declared martial law and sent in Foreign Legionnaires to crush the movement. Using search-and-destroy tactics, they used unchecked brutality, killing 90 percent of the men and women they captured. They also used the Vietnamese government to enlist local lineage or clan leaders and teachers, making them responsible for keeping local order. In the end, the Nghe-Tinh soviets were mostly undone by a serious famine in the area when French authorities issued free food only to those with identity cards indicating their loyalty to the regime. The last soviet ended in August 1931, with almost all leaders of the movement dead or in prison. The same fate befell many of the Communists; even Ho was arrested by British intelligence officers in Hong Kong, though he was released in 1932. The Nghe-Tinh soviets brought the young ICP to one of its lowest points.

But the rebound was rapid. Communist candidates ran in municipal elections in 1933 and 1935, and an ICP congress was held in Macao in 1935 to rebuild the party. The party's situation in Vietnam was much improved with a government change in Paris. The Popular Front government, with socialist Leon Blum as premier, set out to better the political situation in Vietnam: political parties were allowed to be formed in Cochinchina, restrictions on the press were relaxed, and political prisoners were freed. For the ICP the new policies meant, among other things, open publication of its journals and newspapers and the ability to operate legally and openly. In 1936, ICP membership grew by 400 percent. In the same vein as the French Popular Front and with World War II in the offing, the ICP central committee called for the establishment of an Indochinese Democratic Front—a multiparty multiclass union to fight fascism and reactionary policies.

In the economy, new labor laws, on paper at least, improved the lives of workers—a six-day workweek, working hours reduced to eight per day, women forbidden to work at night in mines and factories, and paid vacations extended to ten days per year. Unfortunately, living conditions did not markedly improve since salaries remained very low and working conditions in mines and factories and on plantations continued to be bleak and often dangerous.

Also, unfortunately, the decline of the French Popular Front led to the erosion of recent gains in political liberalization and increasing repression. With the German attack on Poland in September 1939 and the coming of World War II, France ordered general mobilization in its colonies. All parties in Vietnam were declared illegal. The ICP became a special target after the Nazi-Soviet Non-Aggression Pact in

August 1939 made Communists even more distrusted. Two thousand party members were arrested in 1939, the ICP's publications were again forbidden, and its urban leaders were arrested or fled to the countryside.

Japan had been at war with China since 1937; it lustfully eyed the mainland and the island nations of Southeast Asia, with their rich natural resources. But before Japan began its march to the south through Vietnam, it had to deal with the government in Paris. However, when France fell to Nazi armies in June 1940 and a collaborative government was established at Vichy, Japanese demands became more palatable. In summer 1940, Japan demanded of the new Vichy-controlled colonial regime the right to transport troops across northern Vietnam, to construct airports, and to post six thousand troops there. The French authorities acceded in September, the same month Japan joined Germany and Italy in the Tripartite Pact. In July 1941, French authorities gave Japan the same troop, transport, and airbase rights in the south as in the north. By December 1941, when Japan attacked Pearl Harbor, Japanese troops were based throughout Vietnam. Vietnam thus faced two foreign overlords, France and Japan. Vietnam was the only European colony taken by Japan during the war that allowed its European colonizer to remain as ruler until 1945.

In 1940 there were two Vietnamese uprisings, one in the north near the Chinese border by a minority group angered by Japan's moving troops into the region; ICP agents had done spade work with the group and were briefly able to direct this initially spontaneous effort. They used guerrilla warfare successfully and established some governing committees, but the French quashed the uprising handily. Late in the year, what was essentially a military mutiny set off a series of uprisings led by Communists in the Mekong delta; the French crushed it as well, capturing some five thousand rebels. One crucial weakness of the Communist movement up to this point was its inability to plan and coordinate actions in the country as a whole.

Source: Resolution Establishing the Viet Minh

This excerpt from the resolution setting up the Viet Minh was adopted at the Eighth Plenum of the ICP in May 1941. How does it handle the problem of whether the Viet Minh was primarily a nationalist or a Communist organization?

The landlords, rich peasants, native bourgeoisie, have all greatly changed their attitude. Before, they had an antipathy to the revolution and wanted to destroy it or were indifferent. Now it is different, and with the exception of a few running dogs who flatter and fawn on the Japanese enemy, the majority have sympathy with the revolution. . . . If previously the landlords and the native bourgeoisie were the reserve forces of the antirevolutionary imperialists, they have now become the reserve army of the revolution. With these changes, our strength is on the rise and the reserves of the enemy are dwindling rapidly.

[This does not mean] that our party is abandoning the concept of class struggle in the Indochinese revolution. No, the problem of class struggle will continue to exist. But in the present stage, nation is above all; thus, all demands of the party which would be beneficial to a particular class but would be harmful to the nation should be postponed in order to be resolved at a later date. At this moment, the interests of a particular class must be subordinated to the survival of the nation and race. At this moment, if we do not resolve the problem of national liberation, and do not demand independence and freedom for the entire people, then not only will the entire people of our nation continue to live as beasts, but also the particular interests of individual classes will not be achieved for thousands of years either.

Source: William J. Duiker, The Rise of Nationalism in Vietnam, 1900–1941 *(Ithaca, NY: Cornell University Press, 1976), 275–76.*

In 1940 Communist leaders began to plan methodically for more concerted action. In May two important figures, Vo Nguyen Giap (1912–) and Pham Van Dong (1906–2000), went to meet with Ho Chi Minh in Kunming, in China's Yunnan province, where Ho was recruiting and training soldiers to penetrate northern Vietnam to fight the Japanese. Giap had joined a short-lived revolutionary party in the mid-1920s; he was arrested in 1930 and imprisoned for two years. From 1932 to 1937, having studied law, he taught history at the Thanh Long School in Hanoi. He became a member of the ICP. While he was in Kunming with Ho, French police captured his wife and her sister. His sister-in-law was almost immediately executed, and his wife died of torture in prison. Dong, the son of a Confucian gentry family, studied at a famous Hanoi school built by the French. He went to China in 1925 to be trained by Ho. When he returned to Hanoi, he was kicked out of college for organizing student strikes during the funeral of Phan Chu Trinh. In 1929 he was arrested in Saigon and served a seven-year sentence on the prison island of Poulo Condore.

On May 10, 1941, Ho Chi Minh convened a party meeting at Pac Bo, just inside Vietnam's border with China in Cao Bang province. It was a momentous meeting, for it established a new front organization, the League for the Independence of Vietnam, or, as it is usually known from part of its Vietnamese name, the Viet Minh, which would launch the successful Vietnamese revolution. The goal was the establishment of a united front of all nationalists, and the method was a guerrilla strategy. Two revolutionary bases were set up in far northern Vietnam and were increasingly strengthened throughout 1941.

Source: Vietnamese National Anthem

This anthem, "March to the Front," was written by Nguyen Van Cao (1923–1995) for the Viet Minh and adopted by that organization in 1946. It became the national anthem in 1976 at the establishment of the Socialist Republic of Vietnam. What themes dominate its words?

Soldiers of Vietnam, we go forward,
With the one will to save our Fatherland,
Our hurried steps are sounding
On the long and arduous road.
Our flag, red with the blood of victory,
Bears the spirit of our country.
The distant rumbling of the guns mingles with our marching song.
The path to glory passes over the bodies of our foes.
Overcoming all hardships, together we build our resistance bases.
Ceaselessly for the people's cause let us struggle,
Let us hasten to the battlefield!
Forward! All together advancing!
Our Vietnam is strong, eternal.

Soldiers of Vietnam, we go forward!
The gold star of our flag in the wind
Leading our people, our native land,
Out of misery and suffering.
Let us join our efforts in the fight.
For the building of a new life.
Let us stand up and break our chains. For too long have we swallowed our hatred.
Let us keep ready for all sacrifices and our life will be radiant.
Ceaselessly for the people's cause let us struggle,
Let us hasten to the battlefield!
Forward! All together advancing!
Our Vietnam is strong, eternal.

Source: http://www.coombs.anu.edu.au/~vern/van_kien/anthem.html.

KOREA: JAPAN'S COLONY

The Elimination of a Nation: Korea Becomes Chōsen

The shock and humiliation of the Japanese protectorate and occupation in 1905 were more than difficult for patriotic Koreans. But they did not "go gentle" into the night of national disappearance. After King Kojong's failure to obtain intervention by an unsympathetic United States before the agreement of 1905, he tried once more to save his country, agreeing to the suggestion that a mission be sent to the second International Peace Conference at the Hague in 1907 to plead Korea's case. The three emissaries were allowed to speak with the help of the Russian envoy, who was happy to support action against Russia's recent military adversary. The Koreans accused the Japanese of violating international law and coercing the protectorate agreement, arguing that the world community should find the agreement null and void and that Korean independence should be restored by the powers represented at the conference. Japan objected vociferously, arguing that since Korea had given Japan all its diplomatic rights, Korea had no right to speak through a separate delegation. In reaction, one of the Korean representatives committed suicide.

The Japanese were outraged at what King Kojong had done. Resident-General Itō Hirobumi, who felt personally humiliated, wrote to the Japanese prime minister, ". . . this kind of event happens because the protectorate convention transferred the power only over diplomacy. In order to prevent further nuisance, Japan must control the internal administration of Korea as well."[16] The Japanese forced Kojong to abdicate (getting the pro-Japanese Korean cabinet to ask him to step down) in favor of his young son. The *Convention Concerning the Administration of Korea* in late July 1907 placed all decision making in the hands of the Japanese resident-general, who had to give preliminary approval to all laws, appointments, and removals. Japanese officials were installed as second-in-command in each government ministry; since the Japanese were calling all the shots, this amounted essentially to government by vice-minister. Dominoes fell one by one. In August the Japanese disbanded the Korean army; that same year the Oriental Development Company was chartered (it would eventually own 20 percent of all arable land on the peninsula); in July 1909, all judicial power was handed over to Japanese courts; in June 1910, Japanese took over all police powers; and in August 1910, Korea became a part of the Japanese empire, called by its Japanese name, Chōsen.

If Kojong had resisted Japanese demands, so did the Korean people in the face of their nation's elimination. In the eyes of many Koreans, Itō got his comeuppance in October 1909, when an outraged Korean nationalist assassinated him at the Harbin train station in Manchuria. The Korean prime minister, who had been one of the five cabinet ministers supporting the 1905 protectorate agreement, now signed the Treaty of Annexation. He was roundly denounced; rumor had it that he was a sushi and sake pal of Itō and his successor, General Terauchi Hisaichi, almost adding insult to injury. Angered Koreans burned his house down, and a young Korean attempted to assassinate him.

In addition to these individual revenge attacks, large-scale resistance fighting rocked the country as a whole, an explosive expression of rising nationalism. In the last years of the nineteenth century, a practice stretching back to the sixteenth century was revived: the formation of guerrilla forces called *righteous armies (uibyŏng)*. They had emerged in the wake of Queen Min's assassination in 1895, but with the protectorate treaty they received "a new injection of energy as more men joined their forces."[17] Composed of demobilized soldiers, nationalistic elites, and peasants and appearing in all the more populous areas, these "armies" were generally small, though in 1907 an army of 10,000 neared Seoul before Japanese forces beat it back. The Japanese reported almost 1,500 violent engagements in 1908, 900 in 1909, and about 150 in 1910. About 17,600 Koreans were killed in these battles.

One of the more famous righteous army leaders was seventy-three-year-old Ch'oe Ik-hyŏn, a former provincial governor. Motivated by hatred for the Japanese, Ch'oe put together a force of several hundred in Chŏlla province in far southwestern Korea in early 1906. He wrote, "The four oceans have been filled with foul-smelling barbarians. Nevertheless only our country . . . could preserve a superior, pure land. . . . Who would have reckoned that inferior, icy element would now make its way and overwhelm the superior, Pure land."[18] His army was defeated handily and Ch'oe was imprisoned on Tsushima Island, where he died of starvation later that year.

> When his body was brought to Pusan, wailing multitudes came to the pier and thousands of people followed his coffin to the north, the number of mourners increasing in snowball fashion, so that the procession moved less than three miles a day. Fearing mob action, the Japanese Army first attempted to disperse the crowds. . . . An automobile was finally called for faster transportation, but it still took ten days to move Choe's body the seventy-five miles to his burial place. Street wailing was observed everywhere in the country.[19]

Like the righteous armies, this vast outpouring of emotion suggests the rapid development of national sentiment.

The Japanese dealt with the righteous armies through what would later become known in Vietnam as *search-and-destroy* tactics. The Korean insurgents were sought out and killed and their villages burned. Furthermore, since the Japanese forces did not discriminate between guerrillas and the Korean populace in general, many nonguerrilla Koreans were killed as well. A British observer described what he witnessed and presciently predicted its impact:

> What struck me most . . . was . . . the futility of the proceedings from the Japanese point of view. In place of pacifying a people, they were turning hundreds of quiet families into rebels. During the next few days I was to see at least one town and many scores of villages treated as this one [i.e., burned]. To what end? The villagers were certainly not the people fighting the Japanese. All they wanted to do was to look quietly after their own affairs. Japan professed a desire to conciliate Korea and to win the affection

A Korean Amid Poverty
This grizzled, elderly Korean man is shown in front of shacks along the Han River. *Source:* UN/DPI Photo/Photographer.

and support of her people. In one province at least the policy of houseburning had
reduced a prosperous community to ruin, increased the rebel forces, and sown a crop
of bitter hatred, which it would take generations to root out.[20]

Under the Black Umbrella[21]

The Japanese occupation of Korea remains controversial. For most Koreans, it was a time of "national subjugation, shame and betrayal, political authoritarianism and violence, and profound human suffering."[22] The author prefaces this verdict, however, by noting that this period also saw "enlightenment and progress" in industrialization; the construction of roads, railroads, and harbors; the development of modern schools; and the origins of capitalism. The following comes from an announcement in 1941 from Japanese Governor-General Minami Jirō:

> *The benevolence of our Imperial Family has reached throughout Korea and bestowed*
> *upon the Korean people a peaceful life. Why is it that the government of Korea has pros-*
> *pered so in only thirty years? It is because each succeeding governor general devoted*
> *himself wholeheartedly to the task of disseminating the spirit of equality. Agriculture*
> *and mining have made notable progress, and manufacturing industries have developed*
> *remarkably. Business and commerce prosper and the volume of trade is expanding*
> *each year.*[23]

This was not the viewpoint of most Koreans, for whom Japanese control had the effect of blocking the sun with the black umbrella—or, as another historian described this period in a similar metaphor, the "eclipse."[24] Historians have found three different phases of Japanese rule over the peninsula: the dark age of subjugation and suppression (1910–1919), a more relaxed period of cultural accommodation (1920–1931), and a midnight black period of cultural assimilation, even Japanization (1931–1945).

National Subjugation: The Dark Age.   Japan's chief aim in Korea was "to exploit human and natural resources in order to aid the economic development of Japan."[25] A list of what Koreans lost in the first phase of colonial rule points to the tragedy that befell them. All Korean political organizations were abolished, all meetings and public speeches were forbidden, all Korean newspapers were closed, and Korean ownership of guns and other weapons was outlawed. Korean-written school textbooks were banned. All industrial and commercial companies were required to have Japanese on their managerial staff or participating as joint investors. The numbers of Japanese emigrants to Korea soared: 171,543 in 1910; 424,700 in 1925; and up to 650,100 in 1939, with roughly 45,000 of these owning their own land. From 1910 to 1923, Japanese-owned land almost quadrupled to 820,750 acres, almost 1,300 square miles. All of the top government positions went to Japanese, as did all posts above the level of clerk in national and local governments; none of these men, at least in the beginning, spoke Korean. Rough estimates suggest that Japanese men held over 80 percent of high-ranking posts, 60 percent of middle-ranking positions, and up to 50 percent of clerical positions.[26] As a measure of the difference in colonial experiences, by the late 1930s there were about 246,000 Japanese government administrators ruling roughly 21 million Koreans (1 Japanese for every 85 Koreans), while in Vietnam about 14,000 civil and military personnel ruled 17 million Vietnamese (1 Frenchman for every 1,214 Vietnamese).

But the brutal reality of Japanese power went well beyond this array of statistics. In the face of the resistance of Korean righteous armies, Japanese authorities purposefully adopted an overbearing military policy: "even classroom teachers wore uniforms and carried swords."[27] Every governor-general in the period of Japanese rule was a military man, all but one being a general on active duty. Then there were specific Japanese reactions to perceived threats. In December 1910 and January 1911, between 600 and

700 Koreans were arrested for involvement in a purported plot to kill Resident-General Terauchi (many were Christian nationalists); of these, 105 were prosecuted and imprisoned for five to ten years. The reaction of the Japanese reflected their belief that Christian converts and missionaries, especially Presbyterians and Methodists, who were especially supportive of Korean nationalism, were subverting Japanese control. More generally, between late 1910 and 1918, more than 200,000 Koreans were arrested and tortured after being charged with having "rebellious" tendencies.

Thousands of Koreans, unwilling to live in their subjugated homeland, fled to exile in China, Japan, the United States, Siberia, and Manchuria, where they set up various organizations that expressed both Korean nationalism and openness to world developments. Korean groups in the United States, for example, formed the Korean National Association in 1905 to facilitate nationalism; it had branches in Manchuria and Siberia. In 1918 the New Korea Youth Association was formed in Shanghai. A group of Korean exiles in Japan debated "the problems of independence in radical terms and [asserted] that one must sacrifice one's life for the cause."[28] These groups became excited by U.S. President Wilson's Fourteen Points extolling the self-determination of subject peoples in early 1919. The Korean National Association sent two members (Syngman Rhee and Chŏng Han-gyŏng) to Paris to plead Korea's case for self-determination and independence, as did Shanghai's New Korea Youth Association, which sent American-educated Kim Kyu-sik. The Western democracies meeting at Versailles refused to hear the Korean case. Young nationalists in Korea received news of these efforts and decided that they too should become involved. Their commitment was intensified on the death of former King Kojung in January 1919. Action was supported by Ch'ŏndogyo (Teaching of the Way of Heaven), the religious teaching of the Tonghak movement; its leader reportedly said, "At a time when young students are carrying out this kind of righteous action, we cannot just sit and watch."[29] The organization contributed two hundred thousand yen to help meet the movement's expenses.

With the former monarch's funeral set for March 3, nationalist leaders in Korea, among them Hyŏn Sang-yun (see Identities), planned to take advantage of the symbolism of their dead national ruler to oppose rule by outsiders. On March 1, 1919, a declaration of independence was read in Seoul and at over six hundred sites in every province. It stated in part:

> *"We herewith proclaim the independence of Korea and the liberty of the Korean people. We tell it to the world in witness of the equality of all nations and we pass it on to our posterity as their inherent right. . . .*
>
> *[W]e have come . . . to experience the agony of ten years of foreign [oppression], with every loss to the right to live, every restriction of the freedom of thought, every damage done to the dignity of life, every opportunity lost for a share in the intelligent advance of the age in which we live. . . .*
>
> *The result of annexation, brought about without any conference with the Korean people, is that the Japanese, indifferent to us, use every kind of partiality for their own, and by false . . . figures show a profit and loss account between us two peoples most untrue, digging a trench of everlasting resentment deeper and deeper the farther they go. . .*
>
> *[This] is the day of the restoration of all things on the full tide of which we set forth, without delay or fear.*[30]

One to two million participants shouted in response, "Long live Korean independence." About the statement, Hyŏn Sang-yun later wrote, "At this time we did not believe that Korean independence would be immediately realized . . . [b]ut we seriously felt that we must express the desires of the people before the world, as a beginning stage of the independence movement."[31] In the effort, religious groups (led by Ch'ŏndogyo, Presbyterians, and Methodists) and students played major organizational roles, but of the

Identities: Hyŏn Sang-yun (1893–1950):
Korean Nationalist, Confucian, Educator, Victim

Hyŏn Sang-yun was seventeen when Japan swallowed his country whole. We do not have his reaction at the time, though we know his viewpoint from his later actions. In the following decade he studied at Waseda University in Tokyo. In early 1919 he was one of a small group of nationalist strategists for the March First demonstration in Seoul, setting down plans and methods for the protest. He was also one of the thirty-three signers of the Independence Declaration. For that he was imprisoned for two years by the Japanese, perhaps tortured, almost certainly flogged.

Hyŏn emerged as an important academic figure in the cultural renaissance of the early 1920s, the first person to earn a doctoral degree in Korea. As in all East Asian countries beset by Western cultural forces, Korean intellectuals were faced by questions of tradition and modernity. According to Hyŏn, Korean traditions were "rotten" and "deficient."[1] In a 1922 essay, "Let's Be Reborn" [*Kodum naja*], published in *Kaebyŏk* [The Dawn], a major intellectual journal much like *New Youth* in China, Hyŏn argued that for the rebirth of Korean society, the first step had to be the character reform of the individual. For Hyŏn the individual was of prime importance, but in line with traditional values, the individual had to harmonize his or her needs with those of the group. In the end, though he called for a complete renovation of Korean culture, he was deeply committed to Confucian values.

Hyŏn served as principal of Chung-Ang High School in Seoul for many years. In August 1946 he became the first president of Korea University, the former Bosung College, established in 1905. He was serving in this position when the Korean War erupted in June 1950.

In a cruel twist of fate, Hyŏn was kidnapped by North Korean agents that summer as one of more than seven thousand public figures seized for propaganda purposes.[2] He was wounded in an American bombing attack on North Korea and died at Suhung on September 15, 1950. He was buried at the cemetery at Sinmi-ri near P'yŏngyang.

---

[1] *Michael Edson Robinson,* Cultural Nationalism in Colonial Korea, 1920–1925 *(Seattle: University of Washington Press, 1988), 60.*

[2] *See the account in* Chosun Ilbo, *January 23, 2001, at http://hpe60.ibl.co.kr/dprk/ReadBoard.asp?DBname= 3&tCode=123&cFile=20010123160647&page=28.*

19,525 arrested, 10,864 (56 percent) were farmers.[32] Those arrested were beaten, flogged, and tortured; 2,656 were imprisoned. The number of Koreans reportedly killed varied from 553 (Japanese sources) to 7,645 (Korean sources); the number injured, from 1,409 to 45,562. Whole villages were burned to the ground; in one case, demonstrators were locked in a church that the Japanese then set ablaze. The world leaders in Paris, including President Wilson, had no response.

One month later, in Shanghai, the Korean Provisional Government was established. Most of its leadership was composed of prestigious nationalists, among them Syngman Rhee (with a Ph.D. from Princeton University), An Ch'ang-ho (California resident from 1902 to 1919 and head of the Korean National Association), Kim Kyu-sik (a graduate of Roanoke College), and Yi Tong-hwi (a radical nationalist reformer). Most of the leaders were not in Shanghai, but their names gave this government in exile greater

Source: Remembering the March First Movement

These are the memories of Pak Chun'gi, a housewife in Kyŏnggi province. Born in 1914, she was a small child at the time. What particular experiences and scenes stand out in her memory?

I remember March First. I was only six, but I remember vividly that along the back wall of our yard, we had a lot of persimmon trees. Because of how the branches grew, we often had fun climbing them. That day, everyone said, "Let's go demonstrate," but Grandmother said, "Why can't we shout *mansei* from our own house?"

So we all climbed on the persimmon trees and shouted over the wall at the top of our lungs, "*Mansei, mansei.*"

Even I climbed up, it was so easy, but I had mixed emotions. In order to shout *mansei,* you know, you have to raise both arms in the air. I was afraid I might fall, so I stood up very timidly.

While we were doing all that, we noticed that people came out from the other houses shouting and waving flags. I remember dogs barking and Japanese soldiers with their long swords, beating people down right and left.

Since we were the first to shout, Grandmother and I trembled with fear, for we thought the soldiers were coming to get us. We went into an inner room and hid ourselves. I cried, and Grandmother held me tightly.

Policemen came by, making great noises, stamping their feet, but they passed our house and did not come in. We were spared. They went after the young men. Those young men were beaten and speared, slashed with the sabers, and I've seen it—they cut off some men's legs. It was just a gory scene. I heard crying and screaming.

My uncle, Mother's brother, was taken to prison. My maternal grandfather also went to prison because of independence activities, and for some reason, he stayed in prison ten years.

Source: Hildi Kang, Under the Black Umbrella: Voices from Colonial Korea, 1910–1945 *(Ithaca, NY: Cornell University Press, 2001), 21.*

status. Unfortunately, though they were all staunch nationalists, nothing else held them together. As had happened far too often in Korean government circles throughout the years, this provisional regime split into three groups over the strategy to attain their common goal, independence. One faction, led by Rhee, contended that the best option was using diplomacy to build support for Koreans independence. Another, headed by Yi Tong-hwi, argued that military action should be launched against Japan immediately; this was a position he had espoused in 1910. (In 1911, he had collaborated with other Koreans in forming a military school in Manchuria, and in 1914 he had established a military unit there—the Korean Restoration Army.) The third faction, whose spokesman was An Ch'ang-ho, favored a gradual route to independence, eschewing violence. The Korean Provisional Government ceased functioning in 1921 with the resignations of Yi and An and because of Rhee's prickly personality. The range of nationalists found in the Shanghai regime would never be replicated, nor would these men ever work together again.

Cultural Accommodation. Because of the Korean resistance and some international backlash over their handling of the March First Movement, the Japanese shifted their policy, moving from oppression and violence as methods of control to a *cultural policy* of training Koreans for independence in some indeterminate future. Some of the new conciliatory policy was window dressing; behind the scenes, the authorities maintained as much of a stranglehold as ever. But there were substantial changes. The Japanese relaxed some of their restrictions on freedom of speech, the press, and assembly. They allowed the publication of

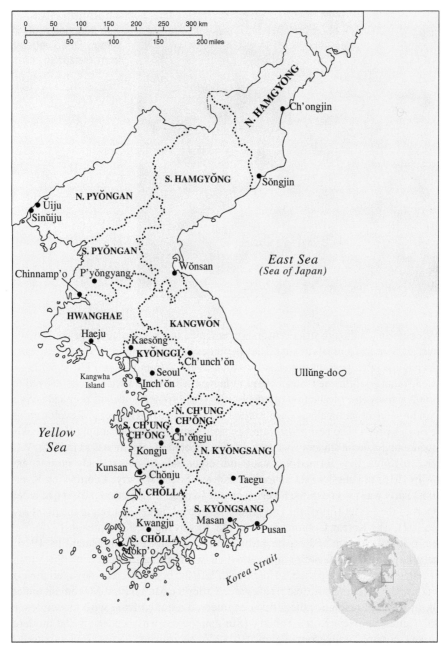

Map 11-2   Korean Provinces, Early Twentieth Century.

Thatched Huts   Farmhouses with thatched roofs in a Korean village. Dried vegetables hang from horizontal poles.

Korean newspapers and, although strict censorship remained in force, hundreds of new popular magazines and intellectual and political journals as well. They permitted "a mushrooming of youth, religious, educational, academic, social, and labor/peasant organizations after 1920"—from 985 in 1920 to 5,728 in late 1922.[33] Koreans took advantage of this new atmosphere to launch what some writers have referred to as a renaissance in cultural activity (the production of novels, plays, and films) as well as political activity.

Many young Korean nationalists were excited about the 1917 Bolshevik Revolution and the emergence of the Soviet Union. The new possibilities of state socialism spread among Korean exiles in Siberia and China and among Korean students in Japan, who numbered several thousand in 1922. When these students returned to Korea, they formed various youth organizations, leftist study groups, and tenant and labor unions. In 1918, Yi Tong-hwi set up the first Korean Socialist Party; a competing Korean section of the Communist Party was formed in the Siberian city of Irkutsk. Like factions striving to receive the blessing and support of the Soviet Union, the two groups competed fiercely—even to the point of outright violence in June 1921. The Korean Communist Party (KCP) was founded in Korea in 1925.

The rise of leftist thought and organizations split the nationalist movement by 1925. The leftists attacked the gradualist cultural nationalists for their willingness to work with the Japanese, putting them on the defensive. Japanese police, suspicious of leftists, began to crack down on their organizations and publications. By 1926, the political rights gained after the March First Movement ended in renewed suppression. In 1927, in response, the leftists engineered a united front with moderates, radicals, and Communists. Called the New Korea Society (Sin'ganhoe), it was headed by the moderates, thereby neutralizing any possible police opposition. By 1930, there were almost four hundred branches all over the country with about seventy-seven thousand members. The New Korea Society created networks of subsidiary youth, intellectuals, workers, and peasant organizations, and it gave the KCP considerable room to act. It survived until 1931, when the Comintern's position on a united front with bourgeois nationalists and reformers was discarded in favor of emphasizing a *united front from below*. With Japan moving aggressively in Manchuria, Korea's Japanese overlords began to tighten their grip ever more tenaciously. Because of the policy change, open political opposition occurred primarily among Korean exiles.

Assimilation.   The third phase of colonial rule began in 1931 (when Japan took Manchuria) with efforts to assimilate Korea more aggressively into the Japanese empire. This policy had great cultural and economic impacts. In the words of one historian, "Korean culture was simply squashed" in the Japanese program of assimilation.[34] That, indeed, was Japan's goal: to transform Koreans into Japanese. Beginning in 1934, the educational curriculum was revised to include more hours of Japanese language instruction, as well as the teaching of ethics and history from the Japanese point of view; the study of Korean language and history was eliminated. Further, all teaching was to be done in Japanese. In 1938, using the Korean language was forbidden in all public offices. In the 1940s, all banks and businesses were required to maintain their records only in Japanese.

Starting in 1937, all Koreans were required to recite the Pledge for Imperial Subjects at all public gatherings: "We are the subjects of the great empire of Japan. We shall serve the Emperor with united hearts. We shall endure hardships and train ourselves to become good and strong subjects of the Emperor."[35] The Japanese governor-general ordered all students, government officials, and workers to attend ceremonies at Shinto shrines, varying from once a week to several times a month. This policy embittered many, especially Korean Christians. Police used all sorts of pressure to enforce compliance. One Korean housewife noted, "Of course we had to go up to the shrine on Namsan. The head of our neighborhood group was Japanese; that's why we had to do everything he said. If we didn't go, we didn't get any food ration."[36] Another noted, "Those opposed going to the shrine expected prison and torture."[37]

After Japan invaded China in 1937, the Japanese regime in Korea moved even more forcefully to assimilate Korea. This occurred under the tongue-in-cheek Japanese rationalization that it was bringing its gift of modernity to Korea. The governor-general abolished all Korean organizations and set up mass organizations—of youths, intellectuals, tenant farmers, laborers, fishermen—to mobilize the populace. Every Korean by the 1940s was a member of one of these bodies, which were used "to facilitate labor and military recruitment (the Japanese army began to accept Korean volunteers in 1938), to collect cash and in-kind contributions to the war effort, and for the staging of patriotic rallies."[38] The most flagrantly objectionable policy, announced in 1939, was that all Koreans had to adopt Japanese names—give up their personal and family identity and culture to become Japanese. While some refused to do so, eventually 84 percent of Koreans chose a Japanese name to replace their Korean one. Farmer/fisherman Pak Sŏng-p'il was one who tried to refuse:

> I got beaten up many times by the Japanese because I resisted changing my name to Japanese. Everybody around me changed theirs, but I had lost my grandfather and then my father, and had taken over the responsibility for my eldest son. That is why I tried not to change my name. But I got tired of being so badly beaten. . . . I held out awhile longer, but I couldn't stand any more persecution. I finally changed my name to Otake.[39]

Even if people changed their names, they greatly resented this policy, since the family name was a gift received from one's ancestors and passed on to one's descendants as the main mark of identity. "[Sixty years] after liberation [in 1945], the memory of this policy remains burned in the consciousness of Koreans, and the psychological trauma it engendered is embedded in literature and song."[40]

The question of economic development during the Japanese occupation remains controversial. Scholars have noted that Korea's industrial revolution took off between 1935 and 1945, when Japan constructed factories for heavy industry. These primarily served Japanese interests, as available investment capital remained predominantly in the hands of Japanese banks, corporations, and bureaucrats who made the crucial planning decisions and allocations. Because the Japanese controlled this earliest phase of industrial development, few opportunities remained for the formation of a Korean managerial class.

Source: Suffering Japanese Torture

U Ch'an'gu, who became a railway worker, was born in 1916 in North Ch'ungch'ŏng province. His memoir begins when he was eighteen years old and a student in the agricultural high school. He was arrested and imprisoned without any announced charges. Since prisoners could be detained for only twenty-nine days, he was released and immediately rearrested. This happened several times. His account picks up at this point.

In the third prison, torture began. They had gotten wind of a plot to have a nationwide student uprising, and they thought we were part of it. They feared it might be a repeat of the Kwangju student uprising that swept the country. They wanted to nip it in the bud.

I found out later that a fourth-year Korean student in our group of eight, named Sin, was a contact point in our school for the uprising. The police really tried to learn things from him—signals, codes, people's names. I insisted that I had no knowledge at all about the plot.

So they tortured me. With my hands tied behind my back, they beat my cheeks, slapped my face, then with a long rod like a baseball bat, they hit me everywhere. The most painful thing was being tied on a long bench, on my back, and then they poured water on my face. When I couldn't breathe, I fainted. Then they revived me. I kept saying I didn't know anything, and they poured it again and it started all over. It lasted two or three hours, and then they started over again.

Some of the others were tortured in different ways—one awful one they called the airplane torture. They take a rope hanging from the ceiling and tie your hands behind your back. Then you stand on a chair, the rope is tied to your hands behind your back and the chair is removed. You are left hanging in the air, and your arms gradually go up and up and up, giving you excruciating pain in your shoulders. I escaped this, but all the others suffered it. After so much of this, time after time, Sin, the leader, finally confessed. Then one by one, the rest of us broke down and confessed. I admitted being part of the network of planning in our school. They detained us about two more months, the eight of us. I was one of three who were not indicted but were released on probation for three years. I was released on June 5, 1934. Six months of my life spent in prison. When I tried to get back into the school, they would not let me in. They told me, however, that since I was a good student, I should try other schools.

Source: Hildi Kang, Under the Black Umbrella: Voices from Colonial Korea, 1910–1945 *(Ithaca, NY: Cornell University Press, 2001), 47–48.*

The main Japanese goal was to integrate Japan, Manchuria, and Korea into a solid Northeast Asia economic bloc. To that end, the Japanese built trains through the peninsula, "hastening the commercialization of agriculture and replacing the A-frame carrier [which men carried on their backs and shoulders], oxcart, and meandering path with the most up-to-date conveyances."[41] By the early 1930s, six thousand kilometers of track in Korea were linked to ten thousand in Manchuria. To further strengthen the transportation infrastructure, the Japanese oversaw the construction of fifty-three thousand kilometers of roads and highways by 1945, creating in Korea a better transportation and communications system than existed in any country in East Asia except Japan itself. Vietnam, in contrast, had only one main railroad line from Hanoi to Saigon. In addition, the Japanese built dams for flood control and related hydroelectric power plants.

Though Korean textile mills existed, the emphasis was on heavy industry: machines, both electric and nonelectric, heavy vehicles, mining tools (for oil, coal, magnesium, zinc, and aluminum), steel mills, and auto plants. The second largest chemical plant in the world was established during these years, along with chemical fertilizer plants. This industrialization had a tremendous social impact on the Korean population. Peasants left farms and headed to cities for work in new factories, increasing the class of workers and greatly boosting urbanization. The following table shows the rise of the proletariat on the peninsula.

Koreans Employed in Industry within Korea, 1923–1943[42]		
Year	Number of Persons	Index of Increase
1932	384,951	100
1936	594,739	154
1940	702,868	183
1943	1,321,713	343

Though the Japanese occupiers built an industrial base, most Koreans did not benefit at the time. The uprooting of Koreans, either by choice from farm to city or by forced labor, was traumatic for many. Estimates suggest that up to 40 percent of the Korean people moved or were moved. The countryside in the 1930s was mired in poverty. As more and more rice was produced, the lion's share was sent to Japan. Whereas in 1914 annual per capita rice consumption was 124 liters, by 1929 it had fallen to 77 liters. In Japan by the latter date, it was 198 liters. Tenancy grew as peasants lost their land because they were unable to pay the rent or had their land bought by wealthy Japanese landlords.

Street Market Though this photograph dates from the 1950s, it is typical of what would have been seen in earlier times. Cabbages are sold in this outdoor street market. Cabbage was a crucial ingredient in kim chee, the hot, garlicky, fermented, pickle-like national dish.

TAIWAN: JAPAN'S COLONY

Taiwan and the Penghu Islands (Pescadores) became part of the Japanese empire through the Treaty of Shimonoseki, which ended the first Sino-Japanese War in 1895. Originally inhabited by Malayo-Polynesian natives, Taiwan saw Han Chinese settlement begin in the late Ming dynasty. It was brought under Chinese control in 1683, when the Manchus finally ended the last Ming resistance. Taiwan was ruled as a prefecture of Fujian province from that time until 1887, when it became a separate Chinese province. Eight years later, the Taiwanese found themselves Japanese subjects.

Resistance and Suppression

For many Taiwanese it was an unhappy reality. Initial panic at the exodus of Qing officials was followed by armed resistance across the island, five months of sustained fighting, and seven more years of sporadic attacks. Resistance came from some Qing military hangers-on, local volunteers, and even remnants of Black Flag forces who had fought in the Sino-French War of the 1880s. They raided Japanese military

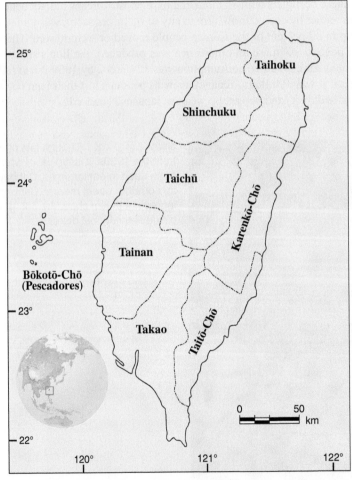

Map 11-3   Taiwan in the Colonial Period.

installations, police stations, and other public sites. The Japanese reacted brutally. In June 1896, for example, in the so-called Yunlin massacre, six thousand Taiwanese were killed. Between 1898 and 1902, twelve thousand more were slain. In the fear and panic of the time, many fled to the central mountainous area, inhabited mostly by the native peoples, or across the Taiwan Strait to the Chinese mainland; it is said that most of the upper-degreed gentry sailed the ninety miles to China.

From the beginning, there was much Japanese discussion and disagreement about the status of Taiwan. Assimilation became a key issue: should the Taiwanese be integrated into the Japanese empire, equal to the residents of the Japanese islands themselves, should they remain subordinate islander inhabitants, or should their status be somewhere in between? The answer to this question varied according to the time period and the nature of the rule from Tokyo, as well as with the particular governor-general, the supreme power in the colony. Whatever the stance on assimilation, there was always a strong overlay of the idea that the Japanese were "bearers of a superior culture to be imparted" to the Chinese.[43]

The Beginning of Modernization

From 1898 to 1915 the Japanese moderated their rule: the power of the military was lessened, and the governor-general allowed domestic affairs to be carried out by his chief of civil administration, from 1898 to 1906 the rather enlightened colonial reformer Gotō Shimpei. During this time, Gotō established the base for substantial economic development. A railroad was built from Taibei (Taipei) in the north to the seaport of Gaoxiong (Kaohsiung) in the south, and an important harbor was dredged and prepared at the northern port of Jilong (Keelung). These years also saw the tripling of the number of miles of primary and secondary roads, the expansion of postal and telegraph facilities, the beginning of telephone service, the construction of a hydroelectric plant, the first modern newspaper, the establishment of a banking system, the construction of a public hospital and a medical college, and work in the areas of public health and sanitation. During this modernizing process, Taiwan became economically tightly connected to Japan, sending exports of rice, sugar, and camphor to the "mother country" and after 1902 importing the majority of its goods from Japan.

But the sporadic violence that had punctuated Japan's control over the island continued: there were six armed insurrections from 1907 to 1915. Further, there was a particularly nasty episode when the Japanese decided to open the mountains, home to the natives, to logging. This required subjugation of the natives, which included attacks from the air and naval bombardment from off the island's east coast. After this spate of revolts and violence abated, the domestic situation calmed down.

A More Liberal Colonialism

From 1915 through the 1920s, the Japanese seemed to moderate their colonial harshness. In part this shift reflected changes in Japan. The idealism of President Wilson, which resonated in many countries around the world, did so in Japan as well. The success of democracy, or at least party government, in Japan from 1918 to the late 1920s suggested a more tolerant attitude from Tokyo. In 1918 and 1919, the Japanese government adopted an assimilation policy that treated Taiwan "as an extension of Japan proper," a change that "moved from high-handed police control and differential treatment of the Taiwanese to a more enlightened self-governance, emphasis on education, and cultivation of a more congenial relationship between Japanese and Taiwanese."[44] Thus, direct involvement of police in local administrations decreased; law codes were rewritten to make them less draconian; government reorganization led to considerable decentralization and more community control; and elements of self-government were introduced.

Perhaps most important, there was a more liberal public climate, with tolerance of ideas that earlier might have been considered subversive. A Taiwanese New Culture Movement that paralleled the May Fourth Movement in China began in 1920 when Taiwanese students in Tokyo organized the New People Association and the Taiwanese Youth Association. That same year they began to publish *Taiwan Youth*, like *New Youth* in China an effort to stir progressive thinking and to discuss the state of affairs on the island; by

1927, its publication site had been relocated to Taiwan. The 1920s saw the development of a feminist movement, the organization of the Taiwan Communist Party, and the establishment of a Taiwan Farmers' Union.

Probably most interesting in light of early-twenty-first-century talk of Taiwan's independence were efforts in the 1920s and 1930s to assert Taiwan's separateness. The New People Association rejected both integration with Japan and restoration to China, calling for home rule and a Taiwan parliament. A new organization, the League for the Establishment of a Taiwan Parliament, carried the ball on the latter from its founding in 1923 until its demise in 1934. Throughout those years, it sent a number of petitions to the Japanese Diet asking for a parliament. The 1926 petition had two thousand signatures, indicating no small support, but the Diet saw none of them. In 1931 and 1932, Taiwanese consciousness appeared in debates to create a more Taiwan-centered literature written in Taiwanese. In the words of one scholar, this debate "revealed the anxieties and ambivalent feelings of a colonized people in their attempts to develop a national language. . . . [It also] functioned to sever the Taiwanese intellectuals' emotional ties to China."[45]

Finally, in the first half of the 1930s, some Taiwanese leaders established the Taiwan League for Local Self-Government to work for greater power and influence on the island. These men argued that Taiwanese leaders were best prepared to deal with internal developments and problems, that they had the education and experience to do so, and that it was proper that they lead. This effort at home rule was suppressed during World War II, but it reemerged after 1945.

Colonial Policies During the War (1937–1945)

As war with China neared, Japan's governor-general instituted policies of industrialization and imperialization to place Taiwan on a war footing—militarily able and with an industrial base that would help Japan. Japan indeed helped to lay modern Taiwan's industrial base. By the late 1930s, in addition to agriculture-related industries like chemical fertilizers and food processing and canning, Taiwan was producing steel, aluminum, cement, chemicals, and petroleum. The number of factory workers rose almost 600 percent from 1914 to 1941—from 21,800 to 127,700; the number of miners soared over 800 percent—from 6,500 to 53,700. A hydroelectric power plant on the west coast supplied one hundred thousand megawatts. Several industrial complexes were built, like the Japan Aluminum Company plants in Hualian (Hualien) on the east coast and Gaoxiong on the southwest coast, which by 1940 were supplying Japan with one-sixth of its imported aluminum.

Imperialization was an ominous development, especially in the context of the more liberal 1920s and early 1930s; it was an effort to transform Taiwan into the model of Japan as the empire moved to war. In April 1937, for example, newspapers were ordered to stop publishing Chinese language sections, and elementary schools were ordered to stop teaching classical Chinese. Later that year, colonial authorities began to discourage the use of Chinese for any reason. In the early 1940s, as in Korea, the Japanese overlords ordered all Chinese, as well as Taiwanese natives, to change their family and personal names to Japanese names. Given the importance of surnames for cultural identity, this was nothing less than an attempt to destroy traditional identity and replace it with a new subordinate colonial identity. Records indicate that only about 7 percent of the Han Chinese had complied with this order by the end of the war. There were other attempts to replace elements of Chinese culture with Japanese culture. The Japanese banned traditional Chinese operas and puppet plays, likely because they could become subversive. Chinese marriage and funeral ceremonies were forbidden and replaced by Japanese ceremonies. The Japanese attempted to force Shintoism on the Taiwanese, building public shrines and decreeing that each home must have its own Shinto shrine for household worship. Scholars have judged that on the whole the policy of imperialization was not very effective, but the effort was a form of cultural terrorism.

While Japan's colonialism in Korea and Taiwan had more tolerant liberal phases, it also had repressive and assimilative phases, especially as Japan moved to war. Yet, on the whole, Japanese control in Taiwan offered more political initiative and flexibility than Korea was allowed. Even expressions of the desire for Taiwan independence were tolerated. French control of Vietnam was iron-fisted; any sign of rebellion or resistance was met with a massive response. Unfortunately, for both Korea and Taiwan, the coming war would bring not long-sought liberation but new overlords.

CHRONOLOGY

Vietnam

1925 — Ho Chi Minh forms the Revolutionary Youth League of Vietnam in Guangzhou

1925–1927 — League publishes *Thanh Nien* (Youth)

1927 — Establishment of the VNQDD

1930 — Establishment of the ICP (February)

Yen Bay uprising (February)

1930–1931 — Establishment of Nghe Tinh soviets

1941 — Formation of the League for the Independence of Vietnam (*Viet Minh*)

Korea

1907–1910 — Righteous armies struggle against Japan

1910 — Korea assimilated into the Japanese empire as Chōsen

1918 — Establishment of the Korean Socialist Party

1919 — March First Movement

Establishment of the Korean Provisional Government in Shanghai

1925 — Formation of the KCP

1927 — Formation of the New Korea Society, a united front organization

1930s — Japan forces Korea's cultural submersion

Taiwan

1896–1902 — Eighteen thousand Taiwanese killed in massacres

1907–1915 — Six armed insurrections

1920 — Taiwanese New Culture Movement

1920s–1930s — Talk of Taiwanese separateness and independence

1930s — Taiwan League for Local Self-Govern

Late 1930s–1940s — Japan's policy of imperialization

SUGGESTED READINGS

Duiker, William J. *The Rise of Nationalism in Vietnam, 1900–1941*. Ithaca, NY: Cornell University Press, 1976. A thoughtful analysis of these crucial years for the Vietnamese Revolution.

Kang, Hildi. *Under the Black Umbrella: Voices from Colonial Korea, 1910–1945*. Ithaca, NY: Cornell University Press, 2001. This interesting collection of interviews shows that the reactions of Koreans to the Japanese occupation were both positive and negative.

Rubinstein, Murray, ed. *Taiwan: A New History*. Armonk, NY: M. E. Sharpe, 1999. An especially rich collection of essays covering the period from the late Ming to the present, as well as topics like aborigines, religion, and literature.

Schmid, Andre. *Korea between Empires, 1895–1919*. New York: Columbia University Press, 2002. A rich, subtle analysis of the evolution of Korean nationalism as Korea was caught, in the words of one reviewer, "between the empires of declining China and metamorphosing Japan."

Tran, Tu Binh. *The Red Earth: A Vietnamese Memoir of Life on a Colonial Rubber Plantation*. Athens: Ohio University Center for International Studies, 1985. A chilling and graphic account of the terrible conditions on a Michelin rubber plantation.

CHAPTER TWELVE

Cataclysm:
East Asia in World War II

These are the memories of Japanese soldier Inoue Hitoshi:

> *I was also sent to the Chinese front in 1939. We were told that we were to give up our lives for our country and not expect to return. I was attached to a unit full of veterans. They had taken part in many engagements in various places since their unit had landed in Shanghai in the face of the enemy. The following three points were immediately impressed on our minds: (1) if we don't kill, we will be killed; (2) the lives we have today we may not have tomorrow; (3) even if we can eat today we may starve tomorrow. . . .*
>
> *Although there may have been some differences due to an individual's rationality and nature, I think this way of thinking was held in common by all soldiers. No one dressed it up as a holy war for peace in Asia. It was a place where impulsive acts and massacres were committed. It was only natural that the propaganda directed at the homeland, which glorified militarism, was in sharp variance to the reality of military forces invading another country. War itself is most brutal and wretched.*[1]

In this account, the three points impressed on Japanese soldiers' minds would not have caused concern about Chinese life, livelihood, and humanity. Put that mindset into an equation with the words of Major General Sakai Ryu, chief of staff of Japanese forces in North China—"The Chinese people are bacteria infesting world civilization"—or the thoughts of a Japanese war correspondent—"To us Japanese, they [the Chinese] were a pitiful, spineless people."[2] The results were a tragedy of cataclysmic proportions: an estimated twenty million Chinese dead, twenty million refugees, the use of biological (bubonic plague–infested "bombs" that started deadly epidemics) and chemical (poison gas) warfare, and episodes like the notorious rape of Nanjing and the aptly named *kill all, burn all, loot all* three-year campaign in North China.

Japanese military deaths numbered about 1.5 million. Civilian deaths, mostly from American fire and atomic bombs, totaled about 300,000, with another 170,000 civilians dying in Manchuria and China after the war. Approximately 60,000 Koreans were killed, at least 10,000 of them in the atomic bomb blasts at Hiroshima and Nagasaki—where they had been sent as forced laborers by their Japanese overlords.

THE COURSE OF THE WAR IN CHINA

Japanese strategists expected a short, easy war. One general assured the Japanese emperor in July 1937 that the war would be over "within a month or so."[3] First of all, they did not see China as a *main enemy,* a term most often applied by the army to the Soviet Union. But even more was Jiang Jieshi's shameful unwillingness to defend against Japanese attacks in Manchuria, Mongolia, and North China. China, according to the Japanese, would be bested by threats of force and some local, handily winnable battles. But the Chinese fought back doggedly, so much so that by the end of 1937, Japan had to commit to the struggle "700,000 men, approximately the strength of the entire standing army."[4] Japan's largest territorial gains of the war were won in its first year; after that, Japanese forces bogged down in what was mostly a stalemate, with Chinese forces relying on a war of attrition. At its high point, Japanese troop strength in China reached 850,000 before it was necessary to transfer forces to the Pacific theater after the attack on Pearl Harbor.

The War in Central China

Though the fighting began in the North, the main battleground in the first sixteen months of the war was the Yangzi River valley, from Shanghai to Yichang at the mouth of the Yangzi gorges. The destruction in the three-month struggle for the Chinese and Japanese sectors of Shanghai, beginning in mid-August, was horrific; Japanese gunships killed civilians and military alike in a point-blank barrage. Jiang lost 60 percent (270,000) of the modernized core of his army; the Japanese, more than 40,000. In early November

Japanese Soldiers in the Shanghai War Zone   A road in the Shanghai war zone, shelled mercilessly during the attack on the important railroad junction, is choked with infantry and supply carts as the Japanese army advances.

the Japanese undertook an initiative to settle things; but Jiang did not respond until early December, at which point his forces were in full retreat and the Japanese, sensing a rout and a victory, retracted their proposal to negotiate. Jiang's policy, to trade space for time, meant giving up territory to the advancing Japanese, thereby pulling them farther inland, away from their resources. Jiang believed that preindustrial western China could hold out indefinitely and that time would ultimately be on his side.

When the Japanese reached Jiang's capital, Nanjing, in December, they committed one of the twentieth century's most notorious war crimes. From the Tokyo War Crimes trial, here are only two horrific examples:

> *[On December 15], 2,000 of the city's police force, having been captured by the Japanese army, were marched toward an area . . . where they were systematically machine-gunned. Those who were wounded were subsequently buried alive. . . .*
>
> *[On the next day], 5,000 refugees who had gathered in the Overseas Chinese Reception Center . . . were systematically machine-gunned and their bodies thrown into the river.*[5]

To their families, troops sent photographs of beaming soldiers alongside naked women they were about to rape or had raped and of smiling soldiers holding severed heads.

"Foreign observers at the time estimated the number of dead at around 40,000, later histories revised that figure upward to 200,000, and the memorial to the massacre in today's Nanjing speaks of tens of thousands of rapes and a total of 300,000 dead."[6] Whatever the number (and even the lower estimates are shocking), this terror likely had a constellation of reasons: Japanese vengeance for the unexpected Chinese resistance; the nature of Japanese troops, many of whom were "poor farmers, industrial workers, and criminals" who were physically abused by their officers; and an army filled with lurid propaganda laced with racial slurs about the moral depravity of the Chinese.[7] Once in Nanjing, their officers gave them free rein to revel in crimes against the Chinese. Japanese commanders apparently wrongly believed that this calculated terror would bring an end to further Chinese resistance.

By late 1938, most of the major industrialized cities had been taken by Japan as Jiang's forces retreated upriver to Chongqing in Sichuan province. Japanese predictions that they would win within three years went the way of earlier wrong forecasts. Throughout the stalemated war, Japanese atrocities seemed part of their military repertoire. In Zhejiang province, the Japanese used biological warfare against three cities in 1940 and poison gas against at least one other. Less well known than the infamous activities of Unit 731, which conducted bacterial warfare research on people in Manchuria, this strategy was a resort to terror as policy.[8]

The War in North China

The Japanese quickly built up their army to two hundred thousand after the Marco Polo Bridge incident, taking Beiping and Tianjin and then moving out along railroad lines to the south. Dependence on train transport for troops and supplies meant that they had to hold on to three thousand miles of rail lines and occupy urban centers on those lines. Maps of Japanese occupation by mid-1938 show not large chunks of occupied territory but rather a "network of points and lines."[9] Japan's first major defeat came in April 1938 at Taierzhuang near the Shandong-Jiangsu border as the Japanese moved to take an important railroad center. Chinese sources assert that thirty thousand Japanese were killed; however, China's lack of military coordination prevented it from following up on the victory. In June 1938, in an effort to slow down Japan, Jiang's forces blasted open the Yellow River dikes, a drastic action that stopped the Japanese advance for only three months. But the Chinese people in the flooded area were not warned. An estimated three hundred thousand were drowned; the inundation of four thousand to five thousand villages left over two million homeless.

The Communists spent the early years of the war establishing base areas across the north (see Chapter 13 for an account of the Communist revival in the 1930s). By 1939, Jiang, ignoring the united front, ordered one hundred fifty thousand to five hundred thousand of his best troops to reinstitute a military and economic blockade of the base area led by Mao Zedong. Late that same year, the Japanese set out to consolidate their control by clearing areas of anti-Japanese guerrillas and forming puppet governments, policies that began to undo the Communists' success in organizing peasants. In response, in August 1940 the Communists' Eighth Route Army launched its largest action of the war, the Hundred Regiments Campaign. Eventually 104 regiments (about one hundred ninety thousand men) challenged the Japanese policy of consolidation by attacking all major rail lines and roads, cutting them in many places; they destroyed bridges, bombed switching yards, and attacked Japanese blockhouselike strong points. By December 1940, however, the campaign ended with no strategic success.

The viciousness of the Japanese response prompted some Communist leaders to question the wisdom of their campaign. Responding with furious revenge, the Japanese launched the kill all, burn all, loot all campaign in July 1941, in effect, declaring open season on all Chinese: anyone and anything alive was fair game. This practice of indiscriminate violence—in a word, terrorism—continued through November 1944. Most small towns and villages in the path of the Japanese troops had their atrocity tales. These so-called mopping-up campaigns were accompanied by other "pacification" policies, like the construction of blockade lines and fortified outposts. By 1942, the Japanese had set almost 7,500 miles of blockade lines and had built about 8,000 fortified outposts. In addition, they dug ditches-turned-moats and set up palisades to restrict the mobility of Communist guerrillas. Except for Mao's Shaan-Gan-Ning base area, all Communist base areas were so disrupted that they were essentially reduced to small guerrilla bases.

Keeping the Pressure on Jiang

As the war in Central China stalemated in late 1938, the main Japanese strategy was to apply enough pressure on Jiang's Chongqing government, in the form of bombing attacks, to make it collapse. Though part of Chongqing's attraction as a wartime capital was that fog frequently shrouded it in fall and winter, providing some protection from bombers, many raids were successful. From 1939 to 1941, Chongqing suffered 268 bombing raids that destroyed much of the city and killed thousands. The air war was an effort to demoralize not only Chongqing residents but those of other cities as well—Xi'an, Kunming, and Guilin.

The Japanese hoped to apply additional pressure with an economic blockade in Central China, but it leaked like a sieve. More effective were Japanese battle victories that deprived Jiang's *Free China* (as the Guomindang territory was called) of supplies, arms, and ammunition to carry on sustained military action. Guangzhou's fall in 1938 and Japan's control of the Guangzhou-Hankou Railroad prevented supplies from reaching Sichuan and Yunnan provinces from Hong Kong or Guangzhou. Another rail route for shipping those supplies from Hanoi in northern Vietnam to Kunming in Yunnan was closed as well when the Japanese took northern Vietnam in September 1940. The sole route left open at that point was the Burma Road, completed in late 1938, a 715-mile mud-surface route connecting Mandalay in Burma with Kunming. Even though a truck convoy on this road was dangerous, with slippery roads over high mountain passes, one-lane sections, rickety bridges, and landslides, it was a crucial lifeline for Jiang until it, too, was closed when the Japanese seized Burma in early 1942. The only alternative left was an airlift, which could transport only a fraction of the supplies that had come over the Burma Road.

During the stalemate in Central China through 1942, the Japanese undertook several campaigns with limited objectives. To make the economic blockade more effective, in June 1940 they seized Yichang at the mouth of the Yangzi gorges to stop the hemorrhaging of trade up through the gorges to Chongqing. In the late spring and summer of 1942, the Japanese launched an offensive in Zhejiang and Jiangxi provinces aimed at destroying air bases that might be used to bomb the Japanese islands. These bases had been the intended landing sites for planes involved in America's Doolittle Raid over Tokyo in April 1942, an act that enraged and embarrassed the Japanese military leadership.

The Ichigō Offensive

The war's face changed dramatically with the Japanese attack on Pearl Harbor on December 7, 1941. Japan's troops were stretched thinner than ever because more and more troops had to be deployed to Southeast Asia and the Pacific, perpetuating the stalemate in China. The United States and the other Allied powers became allies of China, and the U.S. military role in China (see below) changed the nature of the China war.

The main Japanese offensive in the latter part of the war was the 1944 *Ichigō* (Number One) offensive, with goals similar to those of the 1942 Zhejiang-Jiangxi offensive—to destroy air bases in South Central China. Under the leadership of General Claire Chennault, American pilots had used the bases to launch punishingly effective bombing attacks on Japanese bases in China and on Japanese shipping along the coast. The U.S. chief of Jiang's allied staff, General Joseph Stilwell, had warned that such action might bring Japanese retaliation, and it came in the form of the Ichigō offensive. But the offensive was not only aimed at the South Central air bases. Beginning in the north, it had the additional purpose of creating a north-south route from Mukden in Manchuria to Hanoi that could serve as an alternative to sea routes.

The offensive was a rout; in only one battle, for the city of Hengyang in Hunan province, did the Chinese put up any sustained resistance. The Japanese seized previously unoccupied major cities and destroyed all the bases that Chennault's pilots had used. When the Japanese turned west toward Chongqing in what seemed an imminent attack, British and U.S. civilians were evacuated from the city. But then the Japanese suddenly stopped. Losing the war against American forces in the Pacific made simple survival their main goal in China, not delivering a death blow to Jiang. But the Ichigō offensive had a dire impact on China: almost half a million soldiers killed or wounded; immense property damage; destruction of 25 percent of the factories contributing to Free China's economy; and loss of almost all the 1944 grain crop, making the dearth of rice nothing short of desperate for masses of people.

THE EXODUS

When fighting erupted in and around Shanghai in August 1937, millions of Chinese fled. Leaving one's native place with no specific destination (except for staying out of the way of the enemy) was naturally

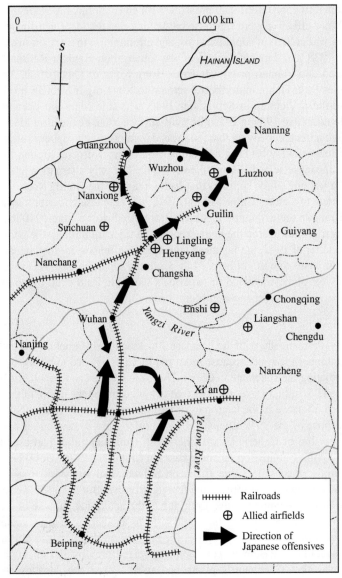

Map 12-1   The Ichigō Offensive, 1944.

traumatic. In a culture where individual identity was largely determined by personal connections, becoming a refugee meant giving up that known and comfortable world to sojourn with strangers. Travel itself was undependable and dangerous, but life would now be lived in a dangerously unpredictable world. Fleeing was not a decision to take lightly, but it was often taken out of the sheer panic of being caught in the brutal grip and bloody warfare of the enemy.

There were many different kinds of refugees in the exodus out of the Yangzi Valley. Millions were individuals and their families. Though most (several million) traveled west, following the government up through the Yangzi gorges, some from the Lower Yangzi went south into Zhejiang or Fujian, while others fled to Jiangxi and points southwest. On arriving in Chongqing, refugees experienced culture shock. Many who had been used to prosperity and a modern urban lifestyle moved into a city that the modern

A Refugee Casualty
Chinese stand and gawk at this young man, who has fallen from a jammed refugee train in the massive flight from eastern China and is seriously injured. His mother weeps.

world had scarcely touched. Refugees were caught in a time warp, moving back from the late 1930s to the time of the Qing dynasty. Sichuan and Yunnan had never even been under Jiang Jieshi's control. Many refugees viewed the locals with sneers and condescension; locals resented these intruders and charged them more for items that locals could purchase more cheaply.

There were also institutional refugees. Workers dismantled machines and equipment, packing whole factories on barges to be sent upstream and reconstructed. These included military-related facilities like arsenals and airplane plants, as well as private industrial plants. The government, desperate for wartime necessities, offered incentives for the latter to move, including low-interest loans, free factory sites, and a guaranteed profit of 5 to 10 percent for five to seven years. In the end, 639 private industries moved, 75 percent of which returned to production. Yet this was only a small portion of the prewar industrial facilities and was never able to provide all that was needed. At risk for wartime damage in China, most industries relocated to Hong Kong or the International Settlement in Shanghai, a site no longer feasible after Pearl Harbor, when the International Settlement fell to Japan.

Whole schools and colleges were also moved. Laboratory equipment and libraries, like factory parts, were packed on barges and transported inland. Since educators and students had been in the forefront of anti-Japanese activities during the 1930s, Japanese singled them out as special targets. Tianjin's Nankai University, for example, was bombed, shelled with artillery, and set afire with kerosene. Universities in Shanghai, Wuhan, and Nanjing were bombed repeatedly. The staff and students of over fifty educational institutions fled into the interior; twenty-five retreated to Hong Kong or the foreign concession area of a treaty port. Some universities joined together in their straitened wartime exile to pool their resources: the most famous, the Southwest Associated University in Kunming, brought together the three prestigious universities of Beijing, Qinghua (China's equivalent of MIT), and Nankai.

SOLDIERS AND THE MILITARY

The Nationalist army was a coalition of armies, numbering around 3.5 million, most of its units descendants of warlord armies. The core or Central Army numbered about 300,000 in 1941, rising to 650,000 by the end of the war. Most of its officers had been trained by German instructors in the 1930s at the Central Military Academy in Nanjing. It had the best training, equipment, and military expertise in the coalition of armies.

The military capability, leadership quality, and even loyalty of many of the armies varied widely. Some former warlord armies remained more loyal to their erstwhile warlord leaders than to Jiang. Many non–Central Army commanders defected with their troops to the Japanese; no fewer than sixty-nine generals defected between 1941 and 1943. In 1944 a coalition of militarists even plotted a coup against Jiang's government.

The army's rank-and-file in the early twentieth century consisted of volunteers and those who were commandeered. Conscription (the draft) of men ages eighteen to forty-five became universal at the outbreak of the war. However, for all practical purposes, it had collapsed by 1941 and, even though revived, it remained seriously flawed. Chongqing assigned quotas to each province, which, in turn, decided quotas for counties where party cadres managed the draft. Though one to two months' training of draftees was supposedly provided, fewer than three thousand men between 1936 and 1946 had any training at all. Local officials made up or falsified records, sold exemptions, stole government money intended to support the families of draftees, and drafted those who were officially exempt: underage children and sole sons of families. The rich were not drafted, but the poor, who had no money to buy their way out, were taken. If local draftees were insufficient to fill the quota, passersby were snatched up. An American GI reported that streets in Shanghai were roped off: all men of draft age caught there were simply sent to the front.

Even the sick were drafted; in 1942, only 28.9 percent of the draftees from Sichuan province met Chinese health standards. Most were in no shape to fight. Draftees were forced to march many, perhaps hundreds, of miles to reach their units. Over a million men died on their way to their units, "doomed men," in the words of American journalists Theodore White and Annalee Jacoby:[10]

> *Frequently the recruits were tied together with ropes around their necks. At night they might be stripped of their clothing to prevent them from slipping away. For food, they received only small quantities of rice . . . . For water, they might have to drink from puddles by the roadside—a common cause of diarrhoea . . . . Medical treatment was unavailable, however, because the recruits were not regarded as part of the army until they had joined their assigned units.*[11]

Once with their units, the men were poorly and lightly fed, mostly rice with a few beans or turnips. White and Jacoby note that

> *American soldiers used to laugh when they saw Chinese troops carrying dead dogs slung from poles; they cursed when a pet puppy disappeared from their barracks. The Chinese troops stole dogs and ate them because they were starving and because the fat pets the Americans kept ate more meat in a week than a Chinese soldier saw in a month.*[12]

A poor diet and lack of sanitation sent contagious diseases—dysentery, tuberculosis, influenza, typhus—racing through units, joining malaria and a host of vitamin-deficiency diseases as killers.

Wounds received in battle would not bring automatic death, but this was a strong possibility. If soldiers were lucky, they might make it to a primitive hospital four days to a week after being shot or otherwise injured. "An abdominal or head wound meant certain death; an infected gash meant gangrene."[13] Large numbers were killed on the battlefield. Even though a military stalemate had generally been reached by 1939, many Chinese soldiers continued to die in battle. Altogether in the war, Chinese figures put casualties at 3,211,419 and deaths at 1,319,958.

COLLABORATION

With such horrific carnage caused ultimately by the Japanese, it is not surprising that any Chinese who worked with the Japanese would have been viewed as traitors. Millions of people, however, lived in areas

Source: Burning Alive a Chinese Collaborator

Japanese private Matsugatani Toshio remembers this episode, in which a Japanese sergeant turned on his personal Chinese interpreter and killed him out of seemingly misplaced suspicion. Why might the sergeant have reacted so brutally?

In 1941 our platoon was stationed in a village called Fuzhuang Zhen in Hebei Province in China. I was a second-year private at that time. The platoon leader, Sergeant "A," was using as his personal interpreter a Chinese named Chen. Chen had previously worked in Osaka as an electrician and was good at speaking the Osaka dialect. Small of stature and round of face, Chen made a good impression.

With the outbreak of the Greater East Asia War, army personnel were pulled out of various posts to form a mixed company. This unit was sent out to occupy the British concession in Tianjin. One night when the defenses were thin, our barracks was attacked with trench mortars and machine guns by the Communist Eighth Route Army. The flashes of explosives bursting in the dark were terrifying. With the coming of dawn, the Communist enemy abandoned the attack and retreated.

Around eight o'clock, interpreter Chen came to work as usual. Sergeant "A" called Chen to his office. Binding Chen's hands behind his back, he repeatedly tortured him, insisting that the previous night's attack was due to Chen's passing information to the enemy. The sergeant paid no heed to Chen's protestations that he had been home with his two children. Chen's face rapidly turned purple and swelled up. The sergeant calmly ate his breakfast in front of his disfigured prisoner.

Chen was dragged out to the open space next to the barracks. The local people, worried, watched from a distance. Ordered to guard him, I stood there, bayonet fixed. The sergeant shouted at the peasants, ordering them to gather around. He made an announcement: in reprisal for last night's attack and Chen's betrayal, Chen would be burned at the stake.

The sergeant always carried his revolver in his right hand. Any attempt at escape and he would shoot. Chen was at his mercy. His ankles were tied with rope and he was hung upside down from a log portal. Beneath his head some wood was piled and kerosene was poured on to it. The sergeant ordered soldiers to set fire. Chen hung there, his head and arms dangling down.

As the flames rose, his body twisted and his arms danced like grilled squid legs. That lasted for about thirty seconds. The local people's eyes seemed to be burning with rage at the barbarity of the sight, as Chen's blackened body hung in the smoke. The peasants wept as they placed his body on a plank and carried it away.

In those days the Chinese thought of the Japanese forces as "fearful Eastern devils" [*Dongyang kuizi*]. I heard later from the locals that Chen's two sons had lost their mother as well. They became orphans.

Source: Frank Gibney, ed., Senso: The Japanese Remember the Pacific War *(Armonk, NY: M. E. Sharpe, 1995), 65–66.*

controlled by Japan, which had insufficient manpower to govern directly and thus sought out Chinese collaborators. *Collaboration* may be defined as actions that had the effect of maintaining Japanese power, attaining Japanese ends, or making Japanese control tolerable. Later Chinese, carrying the torch of Chinese nationalism, condemned collaborators as morally reprehensible traitors. But there were many reasons to collaborate: a sincere belief that it was the best way to protect oneself and one's property; previous experience in Japan or connections to the Japanese; previous experience in governing and a desire to serve the people; being coerced to do so; or a desire to profit economically, politically, or socially. The type and extent of collaboration varied markedly across the occupied territory. A collaborator might act

Poster of Wang Jingwei   A poster of Wang Jingwei, head of the Nationalist collaborationist government in Nanjing, is hung beyond the barbed wire that divides British- and Japanese-held territory in Hong Kong.

under Japanese direction, with Japanese participation, or with tacit Japanese approval. The range of collaborative actions was thus broad. Some collaborators worked directly in Japanese institutions; others worked at the command of the occupiers; some worked for the Japanese for a time and then resisted; others simply assented to Japanese rule by not actively resisting.

Whatever the form of collaboration, all collaborators adopted a new identity. Since motive and intent were crucial factors in choosing to collaborate, the choice was a complex, even ambiguous phenomenon involving individual histories, social circumstances, economic self-interest, personal and family safety, and individual inclination. Individual motive and intent generally cannot be gauged given the nature of the sources; further, even if collaborators had set down their reasons, the issue in retrospect is so emotionally charged that those public reasons would be highly suspect.

In the beginning of the occupation, there were two main collaborative governments. A *provisional government* in Beiping was established in December 1937, and in Nanjing the Japanese established the *Reformed Government* in March 1938. Both governments were headed by former warlord associates and thus did not rank high on the prestige lists of most Chinese. Ideally, Japan wanted to find someone with name recognition and prestige to rival even Jiang Jieshi and thereby possibly compel Jiang to start negotiations. In 1939 they hit the jackpot—Wang Jingwei, longtime Guomindang leader, former close ally of Sun Yixian and rival of Jiang (see Identities). Negotiations led to the March 30, 1940, establishment of a new government in Nanjing, recognized by both heads of the preliminary collaborative regimes. Wang, who had been the golden boy of nationalism following his 1910 attempt to assassinate the Qing regime's prince regent, thirty years later betrayed Chinese nationalism to a foreign power. But Wang had his reasons. Apparently he was convinced that peaceful accommodation with Japan was the only realistic way for China to maintain its national interests and unity. He argued that his government, not Jiang's, was the legitimate national government and that he was Sun Yixian's rightful heir.

The Japanese tried to invest Wang's government with the appearance of independence and equality. In early 1943, they gave up their concession areas in China and their right of extraterritoriality; Nanjing responded by following Japanese bidding and declared war on the United States and Great Britain. Nanjing also took over the International Settlement and the French concession in Shanghai.

Identities: Wang Jingwei (1883–1944): "Nationalism's Golden Boy" and Collaborator with the Japanese

The youngest of ten children, Wang received the traditional *juren* degree in 1903 and a degree from Tokyo Law College in 1906. He became a leader in Sun Yixian's Revolutionary Alliance, an editor of the *Min Bao*, and a confidant of Sun. In 1910 he attempted to assassinate the prince regent; he was arrested and imprisoned but released after the beginning of the 1911 revolution. He spent the years of World War I in France.

From 1917 to 1924 Wang was a member of Sun Yixian's personal entourage, emerging as Sun's most senior and trusted leader. Elected the second-ranking member of the Guomindang's Central Executive Committee in 1924, he drafted Sun's final political testament. In the mid-1920s, he was the presumptive successor to Sun, especially after the left-wing party leader Liao Zhongkai was assassinated in August 1925. Rising to challenge Wang, the leader of the Guomindang's left wing, was Jiang Jieshi, who rode to power with the Northern Expedition. Wang continued to work with the Communists until the summer of 1927, when he became suspicious of Soviet aims and Jiang began his White Terror.

From 1928 to 1931, Wang headed the Reorganizationist clique, which attempted to form anti-Jiang coalitions. However, from 1931 to 1935, Wang reconciled with Jiang and worked in his government as head of the most powerful branch, the Executive Yuan, which managed the bureaucracy. Required to deal with the Japanese after their seizure of Manchuria, Wang received much of the blame for Jiang's policy of appeasement. On November 1, 1935, he was seriously wounded in an assassination attempt; following failed surgery in Shanghai, he sought treatment abroad after resigning his government posts.

Once all-out war with Japan began and the enemy piled up victory on victory, Wang was frustrated and upset. Chinese scorched earth policies, which led to the torching of the city of Changsha in November 1938, repelled him. The next month, he asked Jiang to halt the fighting and work for peace. In March 1939, Guomindang secret agents entered his residence in Hanoi, where he had been staying, and attempted to kill him; instead, they killed a close friend. Wang was outraged at Jiang's government.

By the following March, he had established a collaborationist regime at Nanjing, which was recognized by Tokyo in November 1940. Attempting to get the Japanese to treat his regime as an equal, Wang persuaded Japan to give up its concessions in China, including extraterritoriality. He conceived of himself as Sun Yixian's legitimate successor. His goals were to achieve peace, oppose Communism, and rebuild the country. Still ailing from the 1935 attack, he sought treatment in Japan and died in Nagoya on November 10, 1944.

> On 13 November, Wang's coffin draped with the [Guomindang] "blue-sky white-sun" flag was returned to Nanjing. Ten days later . . . the body was buried on a small hill located to the right of Sun Yixian's shrine, a burial spot believed to have been chosen by Wang personally to show his wish to follow [Sun] and complete the revolution even after he departed from this world.[1]

At her own trial for treason, his wife, Chen Bijun, emphasized that Wang's motives in collaborating were patriotic and sincere; he believed, she said, that the only realistic way to protect China's national interests was to work out an arrangement with the Japanese.

---

[1] *Andrew Cheung,* "Slogans, Symbols, and Legitimacy: The Case of Wang Jingwei's Nanjing Regime"; *Internet: http://www.indiana.edu/~easc/resources/working_paper/noframe_6a_sloga.htm.*

A treaty in October 1943 stipulated that Tokyo and Nanjing would cooperate "as equal and independent neighbors in the establishment of Greater East Asia." Wang thus seemed to have adopted the Japanese idea of a pan-Asian and anti-Western bloc. From this point on, Japanese overtures to Jiang stressed that if Jiang collaborated with Nanjing, they could finally break the back of the Communist movement. This idea swayed a number of Jiang's conservative supporters but it did not sufficiently move Jiang.

For millions of Chinese in East Central China, Wang was accepted as head of state, and his government, patterned administratively on Jiang's government in Chongqing, provided some protection for the people. As it turned out, Wang's reason for collaborating—that it was the only way to save China—was wrong. Wang did not live to see the end, however; he died in Japan, where he had gone for medical treatment in late 1944. The main collaborators in Wang's government and the two earlier preliminary regimes were tried for treason after the war ended. Many were executed.

WARTIME GUOMINDANG CHINA

During the war, various cancers ate at the innards of the Guomindang state. Though it and the Communist troops tied down a million Japanese troops for eight years, the effectiveness of the Nationalist army by 1942 was practically nil—an ominous development for a state whose political power was based on the army. Deepening the military tragedy was the destruction of the meager accomplishments of Jiang's Nanjing decade—new highways, railroads, industry, bridges, and roads. The tragedy was intensified because the

---

Source: The New Order in East Asia

Prime Minister Konoe Fumimaru (1891–1945) sets forth Japan's vision of the future when Japan becomes the acknowledged leader in East Asia. What are the main details of his vision?

Inspired by His majesty's power and might, the land and sea forces of the Empire of Japan have now captured the cities of Canton and Wuhan and pacified many important regions in China. . . . [W]e shall proceed with our effort in the establishment of a New Order that guarantees permanent peace in all of East Asia. The establishment of a New Order in East Asia is the final goal of our military operations.

By the establishment of a New Order in East Asia we mean mutual assistance and cooperation between Japan, China, and Manchukuo in political, economic, and cultural matters. Eventually a new form of internationalism will prevail between these three countries in the sense that we shall build a common defense, create a new culture, and cooperate fully in economic matters. An East Asia thus stabilized will contribute materially to world progress. China's willingness to shoulder her share of the responsibility in establishing this New Order is what the Empire of Japan actively seeks. All Chinese must understand the constructive nature of this New Order, given the present situation in East Asia. What the Empire of Japan can and will do for China is certainly more beneficial than any aid offered by her traditional allies.

Source: Quoted in R. Keith Schoppa, Twentieth Century China: A History in Documents *(New York: Oxford University Press, 2004), 110.*

Source: Wang Jingwei's Tokyo Radio Address

In this radio address on June 24, 1941, Wang recalls his student days in Japan in the early years of the century, likening the people of Japan to his old teachers and classmates. Why does Wang believe that a "new order in East Asia" should be established?

I am deeply moved as I speak to you today in Tokyo, the capital of your great country. I studied in your country thirty-eight years ago. My stay then was short, and due particularly to my limited abilities I could not master your language and learning. However, if, fortunately, I know something, I owe it to my old teachers and classmates. I can never forget what they have done for me. To have been able to come to your great country again and meet you, the people of Japan, is like meeting my old teachers and classmates and I am filled with the warm feeling.

When the slogan of "the construction of a new order in East Asia" was heard in your country, our people found a gleam of hope in the darkness. . . . The significance of the construction of a new order in East Asia lies, on the one hand, in endeavoring to eliminate from East Asia the evils of Western economic imperialism and, on the other, in checking the rising tide of Communism which has been threatening our prosperity for these twenty years. Japan was the only country in the East who could shoulder the responsibility for such undertakings single-handedly. Although we have Dr. Sun Yat-sen's Pan-Asianism, his followers and compatriots have failed to make united efforts for the attainment of that ideal.

There may be causes for the recent unfortunate conflict between our two countries. If, however, we examine ourselves as to why we have failed in our efforts to purge the country of the evils of Western economic imperialism and to check the rise of Communism, thereby leaving the country to deteriorate into a semi-colonial status and the people in the deepest distress, we cannot but blame ourselves. When we heard of the slogan of the construction of a new order in East Asia put forth by Japan, we immediately opened our eyes to the fact that it was not time for quarreling among ourselves, and realized that we should revert to our essential character founded upon the moral principles of the East, breaking down the old order consisting of a chain of pressures brought to bear upon us by economic imperialism and Communism, and establish a new order based on independence, freedom, co-existence, and co-prosperity. . . .

Source: Quoted in R. Keith Schoppa, Twentieth Century China: A History in Documents *(New York: Oxford University Press, 2004), 112–13.*

Chinese themselves destroyed much in scorched earth actions designed to deny the Japanese the use of these facilities. The blowing up of the Yellow River dikes is but one of many depressingly numerous examples. A bi-level bridge across the Qiantang River flowing into Hangzhou Bay, a great engineering feat four years in the making, was finished with great fanfare in September 1937. Three months later, the Chinese blew it up to keep the Japanese from using it. Further, 20 percent of newly constructed highways in Zhejiang province were destroyed. In neighboring Zhejiang and Jiangxi provinces, 62,000 workers were requisitioned to destroy railroad tracks, highways, and even small mountain and village roads in a frantic and futile effort to stop the Japanese. The Japanese made the Zhe-Gan Railroad inoperable when they blew up its railroad bridges; why, in addition, did forced laborers rip the train tracks out of the ground? The destruction reveals panic and, more important, a tragic loss of perspective and sense of reality on the part of military and civil authorities.

The most virulent cancer attacking the body politic was inflation. While prices rose approximately 40 percent during the war's first year, from the time of Pearl Harbor in 1941, prices increased more than 100 percent each year. The average price index, pegged at 1.04 in July 1937, soared to 2,647 at war's end. Thus, a trinket that cost 1.04 yuan at the start of the war cost 2,647 yuan in August 1945.[14] Nothing guts popular political support for a government faster than soaring inflation. Produced by simply printing more money when there was an insufficient supply, it resulted in hoarding of commodities, scarcities, and higher prices; corruption; and ravaged lives of officials, soldiers, intellectuals, people on fixed incomes, and students. For sowing inflation through irresponsible economic practices, Jiang would reap the whirlwind.

Perhaps the most critical effect of the eight-year-long war, military ineffectiveness, scorched earth devastation, and cruel inflation was rampant demoralization. Did the government of Jiang Jieshi really care about the needs of the Chinese people under its control? One clue might be its response to a natural disaster of immense proportions, a famine that ravaged Henan province in 1942 and 1943. Though reports of the famine reached Chongqing by October 1942, the government sent no emissaries until November. They reported the situation desperate. The government then sent two hundred million yuan in inflated paper currency rather than relief grain. By March 1943, half a year after the situation had already become tragic, only eighty million yuan had arrived, worth only about twenty-four million because of inflation. But worse: "It was left to lie in provincial bank accounts, drawing interest, while government officials . . . bickered as to how it might best be used. In some places, when money was distributed to starving farmsteads, the amount of current taxes the peasants owed was deducted by local authorities from the sums they received; even the national banks took a cut of the relief funds as profit." Up to the beginning of March 1943, the government provided money for the equivalent of a pound of rice per person for the "10,000,000 people who had been starving since autumn."[15] An estimated two to three million died of starvation. An American journalist perceived "a fury, as cold and relentless as death itself, in the bosom of the peasants of Henan [and] that their loyalty had been hollowed out to nothingness by the [inactions] of their government."[16]

THE UNITED STATES AND CHINA DURING THE WAR

Early in the war, the Soviet Union, driven by the common aim of defeating a Japan it saw as fascist, was Jiang's biggest supplier of foreign aid. From 1937 to 1939, it sent airplanes, artillery, munitions, and gasoline. It also provided low-interest loans, volunteer pilots, and about five hundred military advisors. Decreased after 1939, when World War II erupted, the aid stopped with the German invasion of the Soviet Union in 1941.

In contrast, at the Sino-Japanese War's beginning, Great Britain and the United States did very little to assist China out of fear of angering Japan, though the United States, at least, was sympathetic to China's plight. By 1940, the United States began to supply more aid; in 1941, China, like other allies, began to receive assistance under lend-lease, a policy that essentially provided free arms and materiel to countries fighting the Axis aggressors. After Pearl Harbor made them allies, the U.S. goal was to build up Jiang's forces until they were strong enough to retake eastern China, which could be used as an air base from which to attack the Japanese islands. Sufficient arms and supplies were necessary for such a rebuilding program, but, as we have seen, after the Burma Road was cut in 1942, the only way to get them to Jiang and his forces was the airlift over northern Burma's mountainous Hump. The airlifted tonnage into China did not equal the Burma Road's 1941 tonnage until 1944; only a figurative pound of aid reached Jiang when a ton was needed. The situation was complicated by the Europe First priority of the Allies. China, as part of the China-Burma-India (CBI) war theater, was low on the aid totem pole. Of the total lend-lease aid given by the United States, China received a paltry 1.5 percent in 1941 and 1942, 0.5 percent in 1943 and 1944, and only 4 percent in 1945. Because of U.S. strategic policy and the constraints of the airlift, the United States had little chance of achieving its policy objective of building Jiang's army.

. Other problems also bedeviled the relationship between China and the United States. The commander of the CBI theater and the chief of Jiang Jieshi's allied staff was General Joseph Stilwell. Stilwell looked like the perfect man for the job on paper. He spoke Chinese, having studied it in Beijing during the May Fourth period; he therefore had some knowledge of Chinese society and culture. But he did not get along with Jiang at all; their personalities clashed bitterly. Stilwell, whose appropriate nickname was "Vinegar Joe," was direct, frank, tactless, and unwilling to put up with bureaucratic hassles and ritualistic procedures. He was not a man to stroke other men's egos, and unfortunately, Jiang, indirect, proud, taciturn, and deeply aware of status, often needed his stroked. Stilwell did not hide his disdain for Jiang. "The trouble

Source: President Jiang and General Stilwell

This work is from a summary of notes of conversations between U.S. Vice-President Henry Wallace and President Jiang on June 22, 1944. The relationship between Jiang and General Joseph Stilwell was notoriously bad; here Jiang suggests why and reacts to the bad press his army received in American newspapers. What is the gist of the "minor incident" he describes? Do you think he was justified in being rankled? T.V. Soong and Wang Shih-chieh were members of the Chinese government; John Carter Vincent was a U.S. foreign service officer.

President Chiang then discussed his relations with the American Army in China. He said that American army officers clearly indicated their lack of confidence in China but that he, President Chiang, "continued to have full confidence in his army." He asked Mr. Wallace to report this to President Roosevelt and to tell him that, in spite of the attitude of the American Army, he would be guided by the advice of President Roosevelt. President Chiang, somewhat apologetically, (but with obvious intent to get across a point) mentioned what he described as a minor incident involving General Stilwell. He said that in the early stages of the Honan [Henan] campaign he had asked General Stillwell for diversion to his air force of 1,000 tons of gasolene [sic], but that General Stilwell had very abruptly refused the request, saying that the Chinese Army could get the gasolene [sic] from its own "over the hump" supplies. President Chiang indicated that it was difficult for him to operate in the face of such an uncooperative attitude. In response to Mr. Wallace's query, President Chiang said that he lacked confidence in General Stilwell's judgment. He went on to say that critical comment in the American press of the Chinese Army and the attitude of the American Army in China had adverse effects on Chinese morale but that he retained the confidence of his army and confidence in his army. Mr. Wallace commented upon the remarkable degree of faith which China had in the Generalissimo. At this point (5 p.m.) President Chiang, Mr. Wallace, Dr. Soong, Dr. Wang Shih-chieh, and Mr. Vincent went into the drawing room to continue the discussion, which lasted until 7:30 p.m.

Source: The China White Paper, 1949, Volume II (Stanford, CA: Stanford University Press, 1967), 552.

in China," he asserted, "is simple: we are allied to an ignorant, illiterate, superstitious peasant son of a bitch." Stilwell's code name for Jiang in communications was "Peanut." He once mused on Jiang: "Why can't sudden death for once strike in the proper place?"[17]

Stilwell and Jiang also had substantive policy differences. The most basic one was that Stilwell saw Japan as the enemy against which all military strategy and strength should be brought to bear. In Jiang's estimation, the Communists were a more crucial enemy than the Japanese; he continued to blockade Communist areas with his best troops. Part of Stilwell's goal was to increase the U.S. supplies and equipment for Jiang's army in order to strengthen it to retake eastern China. Sole reliance on the airlift made this impossible; Stilwell thus wanted to take retake Burma to reopen the Burma Road. Jiang thought this was asinine: why send Chinese soldiers to Burma when they might be fighting to take eastern China? Instead, Jiang argued, it made more sense to use air power to take out Japanese bases and shipping in East China. Hoping to break the deadlock, Roosevelt demanded that Jiang put Stilwell "in unrestricted command of all [his] forces." Given the long history of China's subordination to foreign powers, the demand that Jiang turn over his army to a foreigner was flagrantly imperialistic. In the end, Jiang's refusal to work with Stilwell forced Roosevelt to fire his general. By that time, the original goal of using eastern China to bomb Japan had been shelved in favor of an island-hopping campaign (see below).

JAPAN'S GREATER EAST ASIA CO-PROSPERITY SPHERE

Japan's assumptions about its national needs, the world, and the war shaped its policies. Its goal in East Asia was to seize an area, make it economically self-sufficient, and defend it—the Greater East Asia Co-Prosperity Sphere. Early in the war Japan believed that Germany would be victorious, England would be defeated, and Japan itself would prevail in China. If war came with the United States, it would, Japanese leaders posited, be a one-on-one struggle; Japan hoped to be able to fight the United States to a standoff. Visions of the postwar world were a rather vague division into four territorial spheres headed by Japan, the Soviet Union, Germany, and the United States.

Japan's envisioned Greater East Asia Co-Prosperity Sphere extended beyond China (for all of its centrality in Japan's plans); it included Northeast, Southeast, and ultimately South Asia as well. Northeast Asia (Korea and Manchuria) by 1932 was already part of the Japanese empire. Eventually, the Sphere included Burma, Thailand, occupied China under Wang Jingwei, Manchukuo, and the Philippines. But it never became the force the Japanese had hoped for because the bottom dropped out of Japanese wartime fortunes so rapidly. The nations met only once—in November 1943. The rhetoric lambasted Western imperialism and proclaimed Pan-Asianism. Here is its (read: Japan's) sense of why war had come:

> *The United States of America and the British Empire have in seeking their own prosperity oppressed other nations and peoples. Especially in East Asia they indulged in insatiable aggression and exploitation and sought to satisfy their inordinate ambition of enslaving the entire region, and finally they came to menace seriously the stability of East Asia. Herein lies the cause of the present war.*[18]

THE PACIFIC WAR

War between Japan and the United States was not inevitable. Even with a natural inclination because of Japan's policies regarding the fascist governments of Germany and Italy, there were periods from 1939 to 1941 when some in the Japanese government leaned toward a rapprochement with the United States and Great Britain. For many Japanese, the Soviet Union remained the bogeyman that ultimately would have to be confronted. Three battles with the Soviet Union from 1937 to 1939 did nothing to reduce Japan's fears. Though the first two were inconsequential, the battles at Nomonhan on the west Manchurian frontier with Outer Mongolia from May to September 1939 were of major importance: Japan lost the battles and eighteen thousand men. In dealing with its China quagmire, the Japanese military continually had to consider the number of troops to station at the Manchurian frontier.

German actions did not make Japan's position with regard to the Soviet Union any easier. Just as pro-German sentiment was growing among Japanese policymakers with thoughts of a Japanese-German alliance against the Soviet Union, in August 1939 Germany signed a nonaggression pact with the Soviet Union. This perceived double-cross encouraged some exploration of better relationships with the United States and Great Britain. The stumbling block in negotiations between the United States and Japan was Japan's actions in China: the United States would not budge from its position that Japan had to withdraw. The early 1940 Nazi blitzkrieg victories in Northern Europe and what seemed the imminent fall of Great Britain confirmed for many Japanese that Germany was emerging as the victor and that Japan would do well to link itself to the Nazi juggernaut. In September 1940, that goal was accomplished when Japan joined Germany and Italy in the Tripartite Pact, pledging to go to war against any country (not already at war) attacking one of the three. One of Japan's objectives was to use Germany's good graces to mediate a neutrality treaty with the Soviet Union—accomplished in April 1941; the other was to isolate the United States, ostensibly the targeted country in the pact itself.

Chagrined by Japan's role in China, the Roosevelt administration in July 1939 imposed an embargo on aviation fuel and on high grades of iron and steel against Japan. The Tripartite Pact alarmed American leaders, who also winced in September 1940 when Japan got permission from the French collaborationist colonial government in Indochina to open bases and station troops in northern Vietnam. In July 1941, after Japan moved into southern Vietnam, the United States froze Japanese assets in the United States and established a total embargo. If the United States had intended this action to be a wake-up call to Japanese leaders, who would respond with a "thanks-I-needed-that" pullback from China, it was sadly mistaken. What the embargo did was to push Japan faster into more overt aggression. Japanese oil imports were cut by about 90 percent, raising the possibility that Japan's industry and war machine might come to a grinding halt if it did not seize oil-rich territory. For this reason, and because it felt secure on its northern continental border after its neutrality pact with the Soviet Union, Japan decided to move south to take over Dutch territories in island Southeast Asia and the British holdings on the mainland.

On September 6, 1941, the attendees at an Imperial Conference decided to go to war with the United States while continuing to pursue diplomatic efforts to solve the oil problem. Several deadlines were set and eventually were pushed back to early December. In October, the hard-liner Tōjō Hideki, who had served as head of the military police in Manchuria and, with the assassinated Nagata Tetsuzan, was a leader of the Control faction in the 1930s, became prime minister. The final deadline passed in November when the United States rejected a Japanese compromise to turn the clock back to July (and withdraw from southern Vietnam) in exchange for oil. With that decision, the plans for the attack on Pearl Harbor, which had been rehearsed for months, went forward automatically.

The December 7 attack sank or seriously damaged eighteen ships, including eight battleships, killing 2,433 Americans and wounding 1,178. While Westerners had praised Japan's surprise attack on Port Arthur in the Russo-Japanese War, Americans, now the victims, saw the Japanese as sneaky, underhanded, and immoral. The Japanese struck the Philippines hours after the attack in Hawaii. In April, when the Japanese took the Bataan peninsula, they captured 76,000 Americans and Filipinos. "With supplies and a transport system barely capable of sustaining their own forces, the Japanese ordered their dehydrated and starving captors on a sixty-five-mile forced march in the blazing sun. Almost 7,000, including 2,300 Americans did not survive the ordeal"; death came from exhaustion and being shot, bayoneted, or buried alive.[19]

Source: American Demands on Japanese, November 26, 1941

U.S. Secretary of State Cordell Hull presented this document to Japanese Ambassador Nomura describing America's vision of how peace could be established in East Asia ten days before the attack on Pearl Harbor. In your opinion, was this a reasonable document for attaining peace? Why or why not?

The Government of the United States and the Government of Japan propose to take steps as follows:

1. The Government of the United States and the Government of Japan will endeavor to conclude a multilateral non-aggression pact among the British Empire, China, Japan, the Netherlands, the Soviet Union, Thailand and the United States.
2. Both Governments will endeavor to conclude among the American, British, Chinese, Japanese, the Netherland and Thai Governments an agreement whereunder each of the Governments would pledge itself to respect the territorial integrity of French Indochina and, in the event that there should develop a threat to the territorial integrity of Indochina, to enter into immediate consultation with a view of taking such measures as may be deemed necessary and advisable to meet the threat in question.
3. The Government of Japan will withdraw all military, naval, air and police forces from China and from Indochina.
4. The Government of the United States and the Government of Japan will not support—

militarily, politically, economically—any government or regime in China other than the National Government of the Republic of China with capital temporarily at Chungking.
5. Both Governments will give up all extraterritorial rights in China, including rights and interests in and with regard to international settlements and concessions, and rights under the Boxer Protocol of 1901.
6. The Government of the United States and the Government of Japan will, respectively, remove the freezing restrictions on Japanese funds in the United States and on American funds in Japan.
7. Both Governments will agree upon a plan for the stabilization of the dollar-yen rate, with the allocation of funds adequate for this purpose, half to be supplied by Japan and half by the United States.
8. Both Governments will agree that no agreement which either has concluded with any third power or powers shall be interpreted by it in such a way as to conflict with the fundamental purpose of this agreement, the establishment and preservation of peace throughout the Pacific area.

Source: The China White Paper, 1949, Volume I *(Stanford, CA: Stanford University Press, 1967), 465–66.*

For six months Japan put together an exhilarating catalog of victories after its more than four-year quagmire in China: Guam, Wake Island, Hong Kong, Singapore, the Philippines, and Burma all fell by May 1942; sea victories brought Japan naval control of the southwest Pacific. The first hint of a turning tide came with the Battle of the Coral Sea on May 8; the Japanese won a tactical victory by destroying more U.S. ships, but the United States stopped them from seizing Port Moresby in New Guinea. *The* turning point came on June 4 at the Battle of Midway when four Japanese aircraft carriers were sunk. From then on, it was almost all downhill for Japanese war goals and plans. Nearly six months of bloody battles from August 1942 to February 1943 in the Solomon Islands northeast of Australia inaugurated the *island-hopping* campaign in the central Pacific, with the goal of securing islands far enough north to reach Japan

Pearl Harbor The U.S.S. *Shaw* explodes spectacularly after being hit by Japanese bombs on December 7, 1941.

with bombers. A second island-hopping force moved north from the southwest Pacific, with retaking the Philippines one of its main goals—achieved from January to June 1944. The battles in the central Pacific campaign for many tiny islands or atolls were incredibly blood-drenched as the campaign moved through the Gilbert Islands in late 1943, the Marshalls in early 1944, and the Marianas in the summer of 1944. Once Saipan in the Marianas was reached on July 9, U.S. bombers could reach the Japanese islands 1,500 miles to the north. An historian has noted that "the war was essentially lost at this point."[20]

When U.S. forces reached Saipan, Tōjō resigned his posts in the government. The cascade of military defeats destroyed support for him in the army and navy and among civilian leaders as well. Talk among those leaders turned secretly to some sort of negotiated ending to the war, now clearly a national disaster. They were opposed by the army, which feared the United States and what it might do to the emperor. Army strategy continued to prevail into early 1945. For that reason, after Saipan was taken, it was another year before peace came, a year almost literally one of hell for the Japanese islands and their people.

THE JAPANESE HOME FRONT

The key power holder in the Japanese government from the fall of 1941 until the summer of 1944 was General Tōjō Hideki, who served as prime minister and concurrently held other cabinet posts. Because of the Japanese general staff system, wherein the military chiefs of staff were responsible only to the emperor, not the prime minister or the cabinet, Tōjō, though a military figure, was sometimes out of the loop. Though he functioned as commander-in-chief, he did not have the authority to take part in operational planning or decision making. The most shocking example of his position vis-à-vis the military was that the navy chief of staff did not tell Tōjō about the critical Japanese defeat at Midway for a month after it happened. As one historian put it, "Tōjō wielded authority within the military establishment, but he did not dominate it."[21]

Though the Diet met regularly during the war, it had very little influence. A quasi-government political party, the Imperial Rule Assistance Association (IRAA), was established in October 1940, called by one scholar "a sort of political cheerleading squad."[22] Its founders, admiring what the Nazis had done, believed that liberal democracy was outmoded and that the IRAA would eventually displace the Diet. Those who were enamored of fascism hoped that the IRAA would become the chief vehicle for instituting it in

The Mighty Axis from Japan's Perspective
This wartime poster shows a mighty Japan, symbolized by a giant samurai. With the flags of the Axis powers waving behind him, the samurai destroys Allied ships with his sword.

Japan. Indeed, the two major political parties dissolved themselves two months before the IRAA was formed. But the autumn it came into being, it was taken over by the Home Ministry; in effect, it was swallowed by the bureaucracy. For all the hoopla surrounding its establishment, in the end it was stillborn.

The military draft took 2.4 million men by 1941 and 7.2 million by the end of the war. Because conscription took so many men out of the work force, the government instituted a draft for labor service as well; though both men (ages sixteen to forty) and women (ages sixteen to twenty-five) were required to register for the draft, women were not drafted. From mid-1944 on, middle school boys were drafted for labor service. At the end of the war, almost 20 percent of all industrial workers were under twenty years old. Other wartime workers included fifty thousand prisoners of war, thirty thousand Chinese contract workers, and from six hundred thousand to one million Koreans, many of whom worked in coal mines.

Many Japanese were relatively prosperous during the 1930s, but troubles increasingly appeared after 1937, when double-digit inflation and large tax increases beset the economy each year. From 1934 to the end of the war, real wages sank by 60 percent and standards of living fell through the floor. By 1938, 75 percent of the national budget went to the military. As war continued and worsened for the Japanese, personal freedom was reduced, wages fell even further, and changing jobs was forbidden. The availability of consumer goods shrank drastically as the war dragged on. Whereas in 1941 consumer goods made up 40 percent of the gross national product, in 1945 they were only 17 percent. Clothing was rationed, and food shortages abounded. Firewood for heating was expensive; families faced frigid winters with no or little heat. As firebomb raids became a fact of Japanese life, students were evacuated to mountainous rural areas; adults also began to flee the cities.

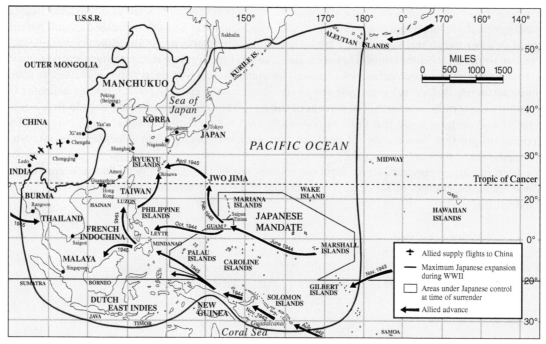

Map 12-2   The Japanese Empire During World War II.

The government used tightly controlled central planning of the economy, authoritarian political rule, and heavy-handed social control. In 1938 the Diet passed a bill that gave the bureaucracy the right during times of national emergency to "issue any orders necessary—without Diet approval—'to control material and human resources." [23] Prime Minister Konoe invoked that right a month later. Under the mobilization law, the government established Control Associations for every industry, which had the right to control and direct all industrial and manufacturing activity. All labor unions were dissolved and folded into a Federation for Patriotic Industrial Service.

The government maintained strict censorship. For example, the Japan Publishing Association was charged with overseeing and controlling books and magazines. In the summer of 1943, it refused to give paper to *The Central Review* (*Chūō kōron*) to publish part of Tanizaki Jun'ichirō's now classic novel *The Makioka Sisters* because it was "irrelevant" to and did not contribute to the war effort. The government worked to establish patriotic mass associations throughout the nation incorporating almost everyone. Throughout the war, things Western (American and British films, jazz, beauty parlors and permanents, baseball) were outlawed. As the war ground on, antiwar feeling was just below the surface. Graffiti appeared on walls: "Kill the Emperor," "Overthrow the Government," "End the War." [24] But no antiwar movement occurred.

WARTIME EXPERIENCES IN KOREA AND TAIWAN

To fight the war, Japan had to mobilize its own population and those of its colonies. First, the colonies. Japan's needs for manpower of various sorts were staggering. To protect its prime war-related industries from bombing, Japan relocated munitions and ordnance plants, the chemical industry, and the tool and machine industries to northern Korea and Manchuria; some textile mills were also relocated. Koreans were moved from southern to northern Korea and into Manchuria to work in factories there. An ordinance in 1944 transformed all Korean students into half-time workers. Many Koreans were taken to Japan to work in dangerous mines. They were also taken to China, where many labored to build airfields. Between one hundred thousand and two hundred thousand Korean women were taken as *comfort women* (more accurately, sex slaves) to provide sexual services for Japanese soldiers. It has been estimated that as many as four million Koreans (16 percent of the population) lived and worked outside Korea at this time. Historians have noted that these migrations "raised the political and social consciousness of the population" and that "beneath the accumulated psychological trauma lurked a deepening resentment of the Japanese and their collaborators."[25]

Establishing *comfort stations* for Japanese soldiers was tantamount to giving them a license to rape. These are the experiences of Kim Pok Tong, daughter of a once prosperous farm family that had become impoverished:

> *Pok Tong was then taken to a comfort station [in China]. . . . She was expected to provide service from her second day there. On resisting, she was beaten and denied food, so she yielded. The usual daily total of men was fifteen, rising to fifty or more over weekends. All bought condoms and tickets, which were handed over nightly to the Japanese manager. The women received no money, being told that they would be paid when Japan won the war . . . .*[26]

Deepening the tragedy was that the Japanese relied on local Korean leaders to select the men and women for labor conscription and to serve as comfort women. As one historian has noted, "to open up inquiry on this sexual slavery would be to find that many women were mobilized by Korean men. Japan fractured the Korean national psyche, pitting Korean against Korean with consequences that continue down to our time."[27]

During the war Taiwanese were recruited for military service, a change in Japanese policy, which before 1937 did not allow colonial subjects to serve. Over two hundred thousand Taiwanese served in the Japanese army or navy during the war, and over thirty thousand died. Many more were drafted to labor in military-related industries. Significantly, there were no major Taiwanese resistance or sabotage efforts during the war. Taiwan itself became an important staging and supply area for the attack on Guangzhou in the fall of 1938 and for the naval seizure of the island of Hainan in late winter 1939. By 1940 the Japanese navy controlled the Taiwan Strait and the coastline of Fujian province. The sudden end of the war surprised everyone on the island. Controlled for fifty years by a now totally defeated Japan, Taiwan now also had to face a new world.

The Firebombings

Deadly firebombings of Japanese cities began in November 1944 and intensified into 1945; from February 1945 on, the U.S. bomb of choice was napalm, a jellied gasoline, which burned with intense heat. Japanese buildings and homes were constructed mostly of wood; firebombs turned cities into raging infernos. This was deliberate, indiscriminate bombing of the civilian population, the main purpose of which was to break Japan's will to continue the war. Decades later, Robert McNamara, who had been involved in the planning and execution of the bombing, stated that if the United States had lost the war, those involved in the bombing would have been convicted of war crimes.[28]

The most destructive of the firebomb raids—indeed, according to an official history of the war, "the most destructive single bombing raid in history"—came on the night of March 9, 1945 in Tokyo. Estimates of the casualties vary, but most suggest that about one hundred thousand were killed and another two hundred thousand injured—with sixteen square miles of the city burned to the ground. French journalist Robert Guillain was an eyewitness:

> *As they fell, cylinders scattered a kind of flaming dew [napalm] that skittered along the roofs, setting fire to everything it splashed and spreading a wash of dancing flames everywhere. . . . Roofs collapsed under the bombs' impact and within minutes the frail houses of wood and paper were aflame, lighted from the inside like paper lanterns. The hurricane-force wind [roaring in from all directions to feed the flames] puffed up great clots of flame and sent burning planks planing through the air to fell people and set fire to what they touched.*[29]

Guillain also noted more tragic scenes, as paraphrased by a historian:

> *Those who could make it fled in the direction of the wide Sumida River which flows through the center of the city. There are many steel bridges across the river, but they offered no safety for . . . the flames were so fierce that they leaped across the river and bridges, leaving the bridge clogged with the bodies of those who were trapped there. The river itself was partially evaporated, and even in areas where the flames did not reach, people were choked to death in boats because all of the oxygen over the river was consumed by the heat. In some parts of the city, the 1,800 [degree] heat from the inferno was enough to boil water in canals. . . . The burning city could be seen from 150 miles out to sea.*[30]

In evaluating the meaning of this and countless similar bombings in cities across Japan in comparison to the atomic bombings, the historian stated that "if any 'moral frontier' was crossed [in these events], it occurred with the Tokyo fire-bomb raid of March 9–10."[31]

Devastation This picture shows the remains not of Hiroshima or Nagasaki, victims of atomic bomb attack, but of Tokyo, which the United States made an inferno in firebomb attacks, a catastrophe that flattened much of the city and killed over one hundred thousand on the night of March 9, 1945.

By the spring of 1945 Japan was dying. Most of its cargo ships were at the bottom of the Pacific and therefore could not transport food supplies, equipment, and raw materials. In addition, to knock out ships that still sailed, the United States dropped twelve thousand magnetic and acoustic mines by parachute into all Japan's important ports and shipping channels. Artificial gasoline was now made from the roots of pine trees. The railroads broke down. Airplane production fell sharply; because of a dearth of metal, planes were now constructed of wood and bamboo. Bombing knocked out electricity for weeks, even months. Half of Japan's telephones were not working. The Tokyo clothing ration in the winter of 1944–1945 was one pair of socks for every four people By the summer of 1945 the sweet potato was the main staple, with the government instructing its citizens to eat various weeds, leaves, and thistles when those ran out. It is estimated that the actual caloric intake was less than 1,500 per day.

THE END GAME

Early to mid-1945 saw bloody battles and horrific human losses as U.S. forces neared Japan. In February and March, on the eight-square-mile island of Iwo Jima, Japanese dead totaled 22,500 and Americans 6,821. From April to June, the Battle of Okinawa killed 110,000 Japanese soldiers, 100,000 Okinawan civilians, 7,374 U.S. soldiers (with almost 32,000 wounded), and 5,000 U.S. sailors in *kamikaze* attacks. In those attacks, 30 U.S. ships were sunk and 368 were damaged. Named for the typhoon (*kamikaze* or "divine wind") that had saved the Japanese of the thirteenth century from the threatening Mongols, these suicide planes were designed for only one purpose—to slam into enemy ships and destroy them. Their use in the closing months of the war shows both the desperation of the Japanese and the vain hope that the courageous actions of the young pilots (most were in their late teens or early twenties) might save Japan, just as the typhoon had centuries earlier. The statistics show their ability to wreak serious destruction.

In the last months of the war, the Supreme Council for the Direction of the War (SCDW) was the chief policymaking body. It was composed of six men: the prime minister, the foreign minister, the army and navy ministers, and the army and navy chiefs of staff. Their decisions could be ratified at

Kamikaze Pilots   Soon after this photograph was taken, these six soldiers climbed into bomb-laden planes and deliberately slammed into American warships. These suicide missions—called *kamikaze attacks* after the *kamikaze* (divine wind) that blew Mongol ships to destruction in the thirteenth century—were Japan's dying gasp. These airmen have already tied on the honorary ribbons they wore on their mission.

Source: Kamikaze Pilots' Letters to Parents

These two letters were drafted by kamikaze *pilots on the night before their mission; both died the next day. What is the tone of each letter? If these letters reveal the moral priorities of each man, what would you say they were?*

"My dear parents, [tomorrow morning] 29th June 1945, at seven o'clock I shall be leaving this earth for ever. Your immense love for me fills my entire being, down to my last hair. And that is what makes this so hard to accept the idea that with the disappearance of my body this tenderness will also vanish. But I am impelled by my duty. I sincerely beg you to forgive me for not having been able to fulfil all my family obligations."

"Please convey my thanks to all those who have shown me friendship and goodness. Dear sisters, farewell. Now that our parents will no longer have a son, you must show them all possible consideration as long as they live. Always remain kind and worthy of being Japanese women."

I should have liked to go on writing endlessly, but instead I simply signed my name and added the date "10 p.m. on 28th June 1945." I put my Will, together with the paper containing my lock of hair and nail parings, into an enve-lope. After I had sealed it. I realized that everything was finished.

Dear Parents:

Please congratulate me. I have been given a splendid opportunity to die. This is my last day. This destiny of our homeland hinges on the decisive battle in the seas to the south where I shall fall like a blossom from a radiant cherry tree. . . .

How I appreciate this chance to die like a man! I am grateful from the depths of my heart to the parents who have reared me with their constant prayers and tender love. And I am grateful as well to my squadron leader and superior officers who have looked after me as if I were their own son and given me such careful training.

Thank you, my parents, for the twenty-three years during which you have cared for me and inspired me. I hope that my present deed will in some small way repay what you have done for me. . . .

Source: Ivan Morris, The Nobility of Failure *(New York: Farrar, Straus, Giroux, 1988), 291, 311.*

Imperial Conferences when the SCDW requested the attendance of the emperor. In May, during the Battle of Okinawa, the SCDW met to discuss Japan's relationship to the Soviet Union. Neutrality between the two countries had continued since 1941, but after the surrender of Germany on May 8, 1945, Moscow announced an end to this policy. Japanese leaders favoring a brokered peace with the United States wanted to stay on good terms with the Soviet Union; they spent the early summer getting the emperor to take the initiative in opening talks with Moscow, fearful always of igniting the military diehards into using violence against them. They were unaware that at the Allies' Yalta conference in February 1945, Stalin had promised that he would enter the Pacific war within three months after the end of the war in Europe. Former Prime Minister Konoe Fumimaro was sent to the Soviet Union while the Allies were meeting at Potsdam in late July. It was far too late, for at Potsdam the decision was made to use the atomic bomb if Japan did not surrender. The Potsdam Declaration, issued July 26, called on Japan to surrender and ended with a chilling but vague warning: "The alternative for Japan is prompt and utter destruction."[32]

When the official Japanese response was to press ahead, the decision to use the bomb went into effect automatically. On the clear morning of August 6, 1945, an atomic bomb with the equivalent force of twenty thousand tons of TNT, obliterated Hiroshima. A scientific investigatory commission described the power of the bomb: "the epicenter instantaneously reached a maximum temperature of several million degrees and an atmospheric pressure of several 100,000 bars. . . ."[33] About eighty thousand people perished that day, and tens of thousands more were burned; an untold number would die of radiation sickness in later years. Before the government could compose itself to deal with what it thought was just a super-firebomb, word came that Soviet troops were crossing the border into Manchuria. This was an even more stupendous blow than the Hiroshima bomb because there was no way that Japan could stop it. The government had to decide whether to agree to the Potsdam Declaration with or without reservations.

The SCDW met on August 9, Prime Minister Suzuki Kantaro already having obtained the emperor's support for immediate acceptance of the declaration. But the SCDW deadlocked, with the prime minister, foreign minister, and navy minister supporting acceptance but the hard-liners, the army minister and the chiefs of staff, supporting the stipulation of conditions, including no Allied occupation, Japanese control of military demobilization, and no change in the status of the emperor. While they were deliberating, word came that a second bomb had destroyed Nagasaki; that news did not change the opinions of any of the hard-liners. But in the pre-dawn hours of August 10 the SCDW agreed to surrender, with the emperor stating his support but with the provision that the status of the emperor would not be affected. The Allied response was that after surrender the emperor too would be under the power of occupation forces. The ball was back in the SCDW court. On August 15, the council again deadlocked, three-three. The prime minister asked for the emperor's opinion. When he supported surrender with no reservation, the diehards relented. In a sense, they used the emperor as cover for their humiliating surrender—as if, in the traditional military system, they had followed the will of their lord. The war was over.

The role of Emperor Hirohito in the war is still debated. Some historians argue that he played a significant role in the decision to go to war, and in the war itself, and that he could have acted earlier to move toward peace. Others contend that throughout the last thousand years the Japanese emperor has reigned but not ruled, that actual rule has rested in nonimperial hands. They suggest that the emperor could not interfere for peace in, say, the September 1941 Imperial Conference because the members of the conference were of one mind. In August 1945, however, the decision makers were deadlocked, giving the emperor's words much more power than they would have ordinarily had. It was a bitter defeat. In his Imperial Rescript on Surrender, the emperor stated:

> The thought of those officers and men as well as others who have fallen in the fields of battle, those who died at their posts of duty, and those who met with death and all their bereaved families pains our heart night and day.
>
> The welfare of the wounded and the war sufferers, and of those who have lost their homes and livelihood is the object of our profound solicitude. The hardships and sufferings to which our nation is to be subjected hereafter will be certainly great.
>
> We are keenly aware of the inmost feelings of all you, our subjects. However, it is according to the dictates of time and fate that we have resolved to pave the way for a grand peace for all the generations to come by enduring the unendurable and suffering what is insufferable. Having been able to save and maintain the structure of the Imperial State, we are always with you, our good and loyal subjects, relying upon your sincerity and integrity.[34]

CHRONOLOGY

1937 — Marco Polo Bridge incident (July)

Nanjing Massacre (December 1937–January 1938)

1939 — Russia and Japan battle at Nomonhan (May–September)

1940 — Establishment of Wang Jingwei's collaborationist Guomindang government (March)

Hundred Regiments' Campaign (August–December)

Tripartite Pact (September)

1941–1944 — Japan's kill all, burn all, loot all policy in North China

1941 — Japanese Neutrality Pact with the Soviet Union (April)

United States declares total embargo on Japan and freezes Japanese assets in the United States (July)

Japanese Imperial Conference (September)

Attack on Pearl Harbor (December)

1942 — Burma Road cut (May)

Battle of Midway, war's turning point (June)

1942–1945 — Island-hopping campaign

1944 — Ichigō offensive (April–December)

United States takes Saipan, using it to bomb the Japanese islands (July)

1944–1945 — U.S. firebombing of Japan

1945 — War ends in Europe (May)

Atomic bombings of Japan (August)

Japan's formal surrender (September)

SUGGESTED READINGS

Brook, Timothy. *Collaboration: Japanese Agents and Local Elites in Wartime China.* Cambridge, MA: Harvard University Press, 2005. An important study of the controversial phenomenon of collaboration.

Fogel, Joshua, ed. *The Nanjing Massacre in History and Historiography.* Berkeley: University of California Press, 2000. Essays in this important book look at what happened in Nanjing in late 1937 and early 1938, how Chinese and Japanese historians see it, and the interpretive challenges posed by the event.

Hogan, Michael J., ed. *Hiroshima in History and Memory.* Cambridge: Cambridge University Press, 1996. These insightful essays survey the crucial issues involved in dropping the atomic bomb; the book ends with an essay on the 1994 controversy surrounding the Smithsonian Institution's *Enola Gay* exhibit.

White, Theodore H., and Annalee Jacoby. *Thunder Out of China.* New York: William Sloane, 1946. The authors create a vivid picture of wartime China; it well deserves its reputation as a classic.

Young, Louise. *Japan's Total Empire: Manchuria and the Culture of Wartime Imperialism.* Berkeley: University of California Press, 1998. A cogent analysis of how different Japanese institutions and groups shaped Manchuria as part of the Japanese empire.

CHAPTER THIRTEEN

From Success to Tragedy:
The Chinese Communist Revolution, 1931–1976

YEARS IN THE WILDERNESS: INCIPIENT REVOLUTION

Jiang's purge of the late 1920s had seemed final and fatal at the time to the CCP. Yet, though the Central Committee of the party remained underground in Shanghai until 1933, a new party was shaping up in rural Southeast China under the leadership of Mao Zedong (see Identities). Mao and others came to see that a Communist movement based mainly on the proletariat would never be successful; instead, the peasants (80 to 85 percent of the population) would be the heart of China's Communist revolution. Mao worked with Zhu De, a former officer under Jiang Jieshi, who organized and expanded the new Red Army. Mao organized peasants and began to establish soviets (councils) to govern. Mao's Jiangxi Soviet was not alone. By 1931, over a dozen soviets were located in parts of some three hundred counties, mostly in the foothills of Central China, between the plains to the north and east and the higher mountains to the south and west.

In November 1931 in his soviet, Mao and others established the Chinese Soviet Republic, a national regime that was in effect a state within the state, called the *democratic dictatorship of the proletariat and peasantry*. As an independent state, it began to experiment with social revolution. The heart of that revolution was class struggle that would lead to the confiscation of the land of "feudal landlords, village bosses, gentry, militarists, and other big private landowners," and to its redistribution to poor and middle peasants and to "hired hands, coolies, and toiling laborers."[1] This prescription for revolution seems quite straightforward, but it masked a fluid indeterminacy and violence that ripped apart communities and shattered lives.

Land revolution or, as it is usually called, *land reform* was time-consuming. It could take up to six months for party leaders to break through peasants' passivity and suspicion to prepare them for revolutionary activity. Implicit in the reform was that power flowed from the people in what came to be called the *mass line*. Mao believed that too many past errors originated in top-down decision making by arrogant officials who paid little heed to on-the-ground realities. As a strong populist, he believed that the masses had more practical expertise and moral authority than even party cadres. Mass meetings had to decide every step of the land reform process, which for the first time brought the rural wretched poor into the political process. To carry out the land reform, committees were formed: A confiscation committee conducted a census, categorized the population, and charted the amount and quality of the landholdings. A land committee managed the land distribution: a mass meeting decided whether to allot equal portions for all or allot less than a full share to children or the elderly. Since soil quality was taken into account, the amount redistributed had to be adjusted so that those receiving poorer-quality land obtained proportionally more. When redistribution was complete, an inspection team investigated complaints and worked to solve attendant problems.

The trickiest problem in the reform process was categorizing peasants into their most appropriate socioeconomic group. What were the dividing lines between landlords, rich peasants, middle peasants, and poor peasants? If one were classified as a landlord, the future would definitely not be bright. The rich peasant status was also one not to be envied. The middle and poor peasant categories were definitely the places to be, for these peasants would almost certainly be allotted more land. Category boundaries between landlord and rich peasant, and between rich peasant and middle peasant, varied according to local conditions. In some counties, for example, rich peasants were better off and in others worse off. No objective standards existed for land reform categories; they were all and always relative—to the locality, its economic situation, and the attitudes and approaches of those managing the land reform process. Even more unsettling, the standards could be reevaluated at any time, with a person being moved from one category to another. The process inevitably stirred up old bitterness and animosity that flared into wars of words or fists. The fluidity and frequent reassessments of class rankings and the eruption of violent class struggle confused and alienated too many people, turning them into enemies. For that reason, the land reform experiment was discontinued, but it was revived in the 1940s and 1950s.

Identities: Mao Zedong (1893–1976): An Autobiography of a Son

I was born in the village of Shaoshan, in Xiangtan county, Hunan province, in 1893. . . .

My father was a poor peasant and while still young was obliged to join the army because of heavy debts. He was a soldier for many years. Later on he returned to the village where I was born, and by saving carefully and gathering together a little money through small trading and other enterprise, he managed to buy back his land. . . .

My father wanted me to begin keeping the family books as soon as I had learned a few characters. He wanted me to learn to use the abacus. As my father insisted upon this I began to work at those accounts at night. He was a severe taskmaster. He hated to see me idle, and if there were no books to be kept he put me to work at farm tasks. He was a hot-tempered man and frequently beat both me and my brothers. He gave us no money whatever and the most meager food. On the fifteenth day of every month he made a concession to his laborers and gave them eggs with their rice but never meat. To me he gave neither eggs or meat. . . .

There were two "parties" in the family. One was my father, the Ruling Power. The Opposition was made up of myself, my mother, my brothers, and sometimes even the laborer. In the "united front" of the Opposition, however, there was a difference of opinion. My mother advocated a policy of indirect attack. She criticized any overt display of emotion and attempts at open rebellion against the Ruling Power. She said it was not the Chinese way.

But when I was thirteen, I discovered a powerful argument of my own for debating with my father on his own ground by quoting the classics. My father's favorite accusations against me were of unfilial conduct and laziness. I quoted, in exchange, passages from the Classics saying that the elder must be kind and affectionate. Against his charge that I was lazy, I used the rebuttal that older people should do more work than younger, that my father was over three times as old as myself and therefore should do more work. And I declared [that] when I was his age I would be much more energetic. . . .

My dissatisfaction increased. The dialectical struggle in our family was constantly developing. One incident I especially remember. When I was about thirteen my father invited many guests to his home, and while they were present a dispute arose between the two of us. My father denounced me before the whole group, calling me lazy and useless. This infuriated me. I cursed him and left the house. My mother ran after me and tried to persuade me to return. My father also pursued me, cursing at the same that he commanded me to come back. I reached the edge of the pond and threatened to jump in if he came any nearer. In this situation demands and counter-demands were presented for cessation of the civil war. My father insisted that I apologize and *koutou* as a sign of submission. I agreed to give a one-knee koutou if he would promise not to beat me. Thus, the war ended, and from it I learned that when I defended my rights by open rebellion my father relented, but when I remained meek and submissive he only cursed and beat me more.

Reflecting on this, I think that in the end the strictness of my father defeated him. I learned to hate him, and we created a real united front against him. At the same time it probably benefited me. It made me most diligent in my work; it made me keep my books carefully, so that he should have no basis for criticizing me. . . .

From Mao's interview with journalist Edgar Snow in Red Star Over China *(1937).*

Long Marchers   Communists on the Long March cross the Jiajin Mountain, the first snow-covered mountain they crossed. Edgar Snow reported that five of the eighteen mountain ranges they traversed were perennially covered in snow.

In Nanjing, Jiang watched the Communist activity with a jaundiced eye. In 1930 he launched the first extermination campaign against the Jiangxi Soviet; over the next four years, he undertook four more. All failed until the last one, primarily because of bad military strategy, until the fifth in autumn 1933, when Jiang's forces totaled a million men and Jiang finally learned the lesson of the failed attempts: not to overextend his lines. In August 1934, in the face of defeat, the CCP began to plan the evacuation of their base. At the time, Mao was chair of the Chinese Soviet Republic's government but was not a member of the party's military decision-making hierarchy. In mid-October, about eighty-six thousand (including thirty-five women) broke out of the base to the southwest and began a 368-day forced march of about six thousand miles. This was the fabled Long March, "an Odyssey unequaled in modern times."[2] The marchers faced bombing attacks from Jiang's air force and harassment from Tibetan troops. Journalist Edgar Snow described the almost superhuman quality of the trek:

> Out of a total of 368 days en route, 235 were consumed in marches by day, and 18 in marches by night. Of the 100 days of halts—many of which were devoted to skirmishes—56 days were spent in northwestern [Sichuan], leaving only 44 days of rest over a distance of about 5,000 miles, or an average of one halt for every 114 miles of marching. The mean daily stage covered was . . . nearly 24 miles—a phenomenal pace for a great army and its transport to average over some of the most hazardous terrain on earth.
>
> Altogether [they] crossed 18 mountain ranges, five of which were perennially snow-capped, and they crossed 24 rivers. They passed through 12 different provinces, occupied 62 cities, and broke through enveloping armies of ten different provincial warlords, besides defeating, eluding, or outmaneuvering the [Nationalist forces]. They entered and successfully crossed six different aboriginal districts. . . .[3]

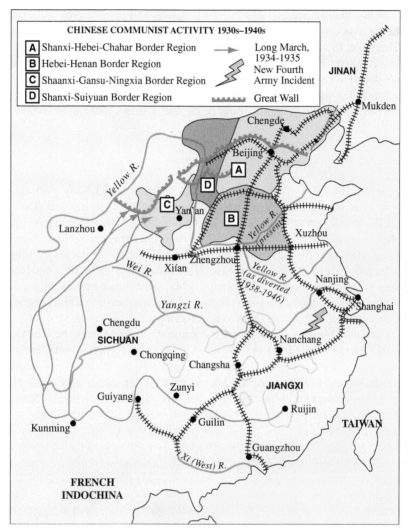

CHINESE COMMUNIST ACTIVITY 1930s–1940s

A Shanxi-Hebei-Chahar Border Region

B Hebei-Henan Border Region

C Shaanxi-Gansu-Ningxia Border Region

D Shanxi-Suiyuan Border Region

→ Long March, 1934-1935

New Fourth Army Incident

Great Wall

Map 13-1   The Long March and Communist Bases in North China.

In the mountains, they suffered from altitude sickness and frostbite. In the even worse marshlands, quicksandlike bogs swallowed people alive; they had to sleep standing up lest they sank into the saturated ground. Hunger, exhaustion, and illness were continual companions. It is not surprising that only eight thousand reached their destination.

Along the Long March in January 1935, at a meeting in Zunyi in Guizhou province, Mao emerged as one of the five most important party leaders. He still had rivals; indeed, there was a split among the marchers in early fall 1935. Mao took his Long Marchers north to Yan'an, in Shaanxi province, with a view to establishing a new base area on the borders of three northwestern provinces. In party history the Long March is hailed as a victory; until the late 1990s, the political leadership of the CCP and the government of the People's Republic was dominated by veterans of this extraordinary military trek. In reality, the Long March was necessitated by a great defeat. It has been identified as a victory, in part, from the survival, if only of less than 10 percent, of such brutal natural and human forces. Most important, it produced among the survivors an unquestionable sense of mission and dedication: while others had died, they had survived. Therefore, to atone for the deaths of their comrades, they had to commit their lives to the revolution to assure victory. For Mao, who emerged as the leader on the march, the experience strengthened his "already deeply ingrained voluntaristic faith that men with the proper will, spirit, and revolutionary consciousness could conquer all material obstacles and mold historical reality. . . ."[4] And it gave him a further sense of destiny: he and he alone would be the one to lead China out of its miserable past into a future bright with hope.

THE COMMUNISTS AT YAN'AN, 1937–1945

The Long Marchers' arrival at Yan'an in late 1935 did nothing to end Jiang's efforts to wipe out the Communists. It was his desire to keep them isolated that led to the Xi'an incident (December 1936) and the formation of the anti-Japanese united front. That front did not work effectively. Though nominally under Guomindang control, the main Communist Eighth Route Army was able to maneuver for its own ends by using the warfare to expand its own power in North China. Jiang reacted by reinstituting the military and economic blockade of Mao's Yan'an base. Thus already moribund, the united front emphatically ended in the New Fourth Army incident in January 1941, when, after months of military skirmishing, Nationalist troops turned on Communist forces in that army in southeastern China, massacring three thousand and killing many more after taking them to prison camps.

During the war years, Mao's place in the CCP became strong and secure: he was named chairman of the party's Central Committee in May 1943. He spent time setting forth his own theoretical vision as the new party orthodoxy, one that emphasized Chinese particularities, not standard Soviet ideology. Marxism-Leninism, he contended, had to be tailored to Chinese realities; one such reality was making the peasants equal partners with the proletariat in the vanguard of the revolution. Dogmatic as Mao could be, at this stage of his career he called for flexibility and pragmatism in forging the revolution:

> [T]he arrow of Marxism-Leninism must be used to hit the target of the Chinese revolution. . . . We must tell [those who regard Marxism-Leninism as religious dogma] openly, "Your dogma is of no use," or to use an impolite phrase, "Your dogma is less useful than excrement." We see that dog excrement can fertilize the fields, and man's can feed the dog. And dogmas? They can't fertilize fields; nor can they feed a dog. Of what use are they?[5]

At Yan'an, Mao launched two policies that became party hallmarks into the 1970s. The first was a *rectification* campaign that dealt with quality control of party membership and party cohesion. From 1937 to 1940, an estimated one hundred thousand immigrants flocked to Yan'an, helping to swell party membership from forty thousand to some eight hundred thousand. The rectification campaign, launched in February 1942—the first of many under Communist rule—was an effort to inculcate in new members (many of them intellectuals and students who had come from coastal cities) a uniformity of spirit and focus about the party's mission.

In the rectification process, cadres participated in small-group sessions studying documents Mao selected; they had to write out detailed self-criticisms; they were often criticized in mass meetings; and they had to confess their errors. If this last step was difficult or impossible, cadres might be isolated and various psychological pressures used against them. In the end, cadres and intellectuals were often sent to the countryside to live with and learn from peasants, to break down the barriers between urban elites and peasants, and to help begin to decentralize various party and government functions.

Mao believed in the power of human beings to change their thoughts and their lives; rectification was an important tool. Even so, the fact that there are various descriptions of this process, ranging from innocuous to frightening, reflects its controversial nature. From *rectification* (changing one's ways) to *reeducation* (a goal firmly in line with traditional Chinese moral training) to *thought reform* (implied authoritarianism) to *brainwashing* (inhuman destroyer of individuality), whichever view one takes of the process colors its meaning. In the end, the process grew out of the radical logic of those who were certain that they possessed the Truth.

The motive force of the revolution during the anti-Japanese war was the party's mass mobilization. Its most important vehicle was class struggle, used both in base areas and in guerrilla zones to reduce rents, taxes, and interest. Peasant associations, organized by party work teams to directly challenge village elites, "fundamentally changed rural power relations."[6] A second wave of mass organizing focused on women's and workers' associations as part of mobilizing the population for war. The timing of these efforts varied from place to place. In some areas of North China they were well underway by 1939 and 1940; in others they did not start until 1943 and 1944. Reforms began in Central China only in 1941. Class struggle became almost tangible in the *struggle meeting,* the "most intense, condensed form of peasant mobilization."[7] These often violent meetings were launched in the North against local despots by 1942 but did not occur in Central China until autumn 1943. Party cadres chose targets and encouraged the expression of latent peasant anger against village bosses and landlords. These staged events became pivotal in shattering mass apathy and passivity and disrupting whatever solidarity had existed among targets and community.

The secret of Communist revolutionary success varied from place to place, from time to time, and from tactic to tactic. Communist cadres had to understand all aspects of the locale—the natural environment; the social, economic, and political structures; and particular needs and grievances—and then build networks and coalitions with local leaders, mobilize local inhabitants, and carry out pragmatic, flexible policies. These efforts were frequently unsuccessful; leftist excesses and rightist betrayal were common; many times contingencies, not strategies, gave the Communists their success.

A second policy initiative that charted the Communists' direction throughout much of the twentieth century focused on the meaning and function of art and literature in a socialist society. The party's stance was outlined at a forum in May 1942. Art and literature were "powerful weapons for uniting and educating the people . . ., as well as [helping] the people wage the struggle against the enemy with one heart and one mind."[8] Art and literature served the *people*—defined as workers, peasants, and soldiers, not the petit bourgeoisie, students, or intellectuals. Above all, they served the revolutionary cause:

> *In the world today all culture, all art and literature belong to definite classes and follow definite political lines. There is in fact no such thing as art for art's sake, art which stands above classes or art which runs parallel to or remains independent of politics. Proletarian art and literature are part of the whole cause of the proletarian revolution. . . . Therefore, the Party's artistic and literary activity occupies a definite and assigned position in the Party's total revolutionary work and is subordinated to the prescribed revolutionary task of the Party in any given revolutionary period.*[9]

Thus, artists and writers had to tailor their work to make it politically correct by fitting in with every shift in direction of the party's policies; their creativity was straitjacketed. They had to give up their own consciousness and take on the consciousness of the masses.

When the author Ding Ling criticized Yan'an culture for its sexism and male dominance, she was sent to the countryside. Many writers who had criticized aspects of Yan'an society withdrew their criticisms in the rectification effort. One who did not was the writer Wang Shiwei, who had written essays on the

Source: Excerpt from an Essay by Wang Shiwei

Wang's essay set forth the realities of daily life and personal relationships in the years at Yan' an, noting the inequalities between leaders and subordinates. For his audacity, he was, in effect, tried and convicted. In an action that was more the exception than the rule in handling dissidents, he was executed in 1947. What would your verdict be: was Wang simply displaying "petty bourgeois emotion" or was he correct to point out what was happening?

During the New Year holiday I was walking home in the dark one evening from a friend's place. Ahead of me were two women comrades talking in animated whispers. We were some way apart so I quietly moved closer to hear what they were saying.

"He keeps on talking about other people's petty-bourgeois egalitarianism, but the truth is that he thinks he is something special. He always looks after his own interests. As for the comrades underneath him, he doesn't care whether they are sick or well, he doesn't even care if they die, he hardly gives a damn! . . . .

"Crows are black wherever they are. Even Comrade XXX acts like that"

"You're right! All this bullshit about loving your own class. They don't even show ordinary human sympathy! You often see people pretending to smile and be friendly, but it's all on the surface, it doesn't mean anything. And if you offend them, they glare at you, pull their rank and start lecturing you."

"It's not only the big shots who act that way, the small fry are just the same. Our section leader XXX crawls when he's talking to his superiors, but he behaves very arrogantly towards us. Often comrades have been ill and he hasn't even dropped in to see how they are. But when an eagle stole one of his chickens, you should have seen the fuss he made! After that every time he saw an eagle he'd start screaming and throwing clods of earth at it—the self-seeking bastard!"

There was a long silence. In one way, I admired the comrade's sharp tongue. But I also felt depressed. . . .

. . . At present there is no noodle soup for sick comrades to eat and young students only get two meals of thin congee a day (when they are asked whether they have had enough to eat, Party members are expected to lead the rest in a chorus of "Yes, we're full"). Relatively healthy "big shots" get far more than they need to eat and drink, with the result that their subordinates look upon them as a race apart, and not only do not love them but even . . . this makes me most uneasy. But perhaps it is a "petty bourgeois emotion" to always be talking about "love" and "warmth." I await your verdict.

Source: Quoted in R. Keith Schoppa, Twentieth Century China: A History in Documents *(New York: Oxford University Press, 2004), 102, 104.*

lack of equity between Yan'an elites and nonelites. For this the party made him an object lesson, putting him on trial in struggle meetings and executing him in 1947.

At the end of World War II, there were nineteen Communist base areas spread across northern China, with Communist units in Anhui and Jiangsu. Communist regimes stretched over a roughly 250,000-square-mile area. Mao claimed that there were 1.2 million CCP members by the close of the war. Communist military forces had increased almost tenfold from the beginning of the war, from 92,000 in the Eighth and New Fourth Armies in 1937 to 910,000 in 1945. The war against Japan gave the Communist movement breathing room and time to expand its support through its nationalistic appeal in fighting the Japanese, its policy of mass mobilization, and the military etiquette ("respect the masses") that it inculcated in and enforced on the Eighth Route Army.

Mutual Toasts   In Chongqing, where they held talks, Jiang and Mao toasted each other on October 10, 1945. For all their smiles, their talks came to nothing and civil war was not far way.

THE CIVIL WAR

When World War II ended, the relationship between the Guomindang regime and the CCP was bitter; a civil war loomed. Worried about a warring China, a destroyed Japan, and a strong Soviet Union to its north, the United States, openly aiding Jiang, tried to broker an agreement between the two sides. But that did not work, primarily because neither side wanted a coalition government and both were obstinately inflexible.

In 1947 China turned quickly to full-scale civil war, one of the largest wars of modern times. The struggle between the Guomindang and the CCP was ultimately decided on the battlefield, but underlying problems with Jiang's rule were probably more significant in determining why he was defeated. Foremost were the wrenching economic problems. Rampant inflation during and after the war was fueled by shortages of consumer goods, business restrictions, corruption, speculation, and hoarding

Bank Panic   With inflation run amok and banks closing, people were desperate to retrieve their money before all was lost. This crush developed at a bank in Shanghai in 1948. The economic catastrophe gutted popular support for Jiang's government.

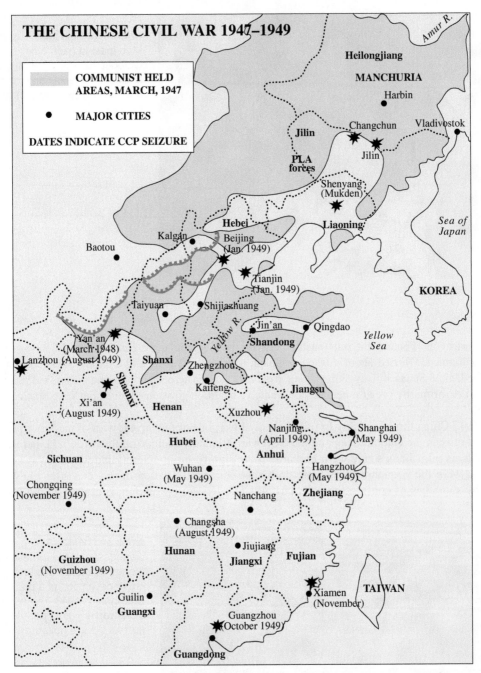

Map 13-2   The Chinese Civil War, 1947–1949.

Source: A Speech Before an Assassination

Poet and scholar Wen Yiduo, who taught literature at South-West United University in Kunming and was a member of the Democratic League, gave the following address on July 15, 1946, at a memorial service for Li Gongpu, a prominent Democratic League official who had been gunned down by Jiang Jieshi's agents a few days earlier. Minutes after he spoke, Wen himself was assassinated by Jiang's thugs. What was Wen's main point in his address?

A few days ago, as we are all aware, one of the most despicable and shameful events of history occurred here in Kunming. What crime did Mr. Li Gongpu commit that would cause him to be murdered in such a vicious way? He merely used his pen to write a few articles, he used his mouth to speak out, and what he said and wrote was nothing more than what any Chinese with a conscience would say. We all have pens and mouths. If there is a reason for it, why not speak out? Why should people be beaten, killed, or, even worse, killed in a devious way?

Are there any special agents here today? Stand up! If you are men, stand up! Come forward and speak? Why did you kill Mr. Li? You kill people but refuse to admit it and even circulate false rumors that the murder happened because of some sexual scandal or as the result of Communists killing other Communists. Shameless! Shameless! This is the shamelessness of the Guomindang, but the glory belongs to Mr. Li. . . .

Do you really think that if you hurt a few or kill a few, that you can intimidate the whole people? In fact, you cannot beat all the people or kill all of the people. For every Li Gongpu you kill, hundreds of millions of Li Gongpu will stand up! In the future you will lose the support of hundreds of millions of people.

The reactionaries believe that they can reduce the number of people participating in the democratic movement and destroy its power through the terror of assassination. But left me tell you our power is great.

The power of the people will win and truth will live forever. Throughout history, all who have opposed the people have been destroyed by the people! Didn't Hitler and Mussolini fall before the people? Chang Kai-shek, you are so rabid, so reactionary, turn the pages of history, how many days do you think you have left? You're finished! It is over for you!

Bright days are coming for us. Look, the light is before us. Just as Mr. Li said as he was dying. "Daybreak is coming!" Now is that darkest moment before dawn. We have the power to break through this darkness and attain the light!

To attain democracy and peace, we must pay a price. We are not afraid of making sacrifices. Each of us should be like Mr. Li. When we step through the door, we must be prepared never to return.

Source: Quoted in R. Keith Schoppa, Twentieth Century China: A History in Documents *(New York: Oxford University Press, 2004), 124–125.*

that eroded people's livelihoods. By 1945 the government's revenue covered only one-third of its expenditures; to make up the shortfall, it simply printed more money. The exchange rate between Chinese dollars and U.S. dollars rose from seven thousand to one in January 1947 to forty-five thousand to one in August 1947. Prices in July 1948 were *three million* times higher than in July 1937. This outrageous inflation lost Jiang the support of city dwellers—businessmen, salaried classes, intellectuals, workers, and those in the countryside. It was a total economic collapse; the very fabric of rural society was unraveling.

Jiang's political regime was inflexible, incompetent, and corrupt. He refused to open up the party to non-Communist political groups. Here is the evaluation of a political journalist:

> *The [Guomindang's] tyrannical style is causing deep hatred among liberal elements . . . .; the government officials by indulging in corrupt practices and creating every kind of obstruction have caused extreme dissatisfaction in business and industrial circles; and the violent rise in prices . . . and the continuation of civil war is causing sounds of resentment to be heard everywhere. . . .*[10]

During the war, Jiang's huge advantage in numbers of men and war materiel was quickly lost. Bad military strategy brought defeat upon defeat. The Manchurian campaign ended in November 1948 with a smashing victory of the People's Liberation Army (PLA), commanded by Lin Biao. The battle for Central China was lost by January 1949 at the battle of Huai-hai, mostly due to Jiang's faulty strategy. Costly it certainly was: Jiang lost almost half a million men and almost all of his mechanized troops. Beiping fell on January 31, 1949, and the capital, Nanjing, in April. In December the Guomindang government fled to Taiwan.

On the winning Communists: in the civil war, as in the Sino-Japanese War, the secret of Communist success was understanding the particular local situation and acting pragmatically and flexibly. In the military struggle, PLA commanders "appl[ied] a strategy that elevated flexibility in the field to the highest art of defensive warfare."[11] The Communists emerged as the superior military strategists in both offensive and defensive warfare. The Communist Eighth Route Army went all out to win the hearts and minds of the Chinese peasants, and in many cases they did. In contrast, the Guomindang secret police goons who assassinated and terrorized those who dissented from the Guomindang line alienated tens of thousands for every victim they shot. The corrupt Guomindang elite, living the good life while those around them were suffering from the depredations of war, was revoltingly scandalous.

THE PEOPLE'S REPUBLIC: SUCCESSES, 1949–1957

Mao Zedong stood in triumph on the Gate of Heavenly Peace to announce the establishment of the People's Republic of China (PRC) on October 1, 1949. He had been able to capture and symbolize the idealism and hope of the masses as success had bred success and led him to victory. To the new party, state, and military bureaucracies he brought "an operational set of principles and practices . . . [that might be] labeled the 'Yan'an complex'" because they were developed during the years at Yan'an.[12] For the first decades of the PRC these included the essential nature of ideology in keeping cadres in line with the aims of the party leaders; the importance of the mass line and, in the same vein, decentralized rule; a disdain of specialists and a preference for officials who could serve in a variety of areas; and witch hunts, false accusations, and confessions exacted in any way possible from those considered enemies within the Communist movement.

Because Mao Zedong dominated the PRC from its founding until his death in 1976, his ideas about and approaches to governing have special significance. Populism and voluntarism dominated Mao's worldview—"that properly motivated people could overcome virtually any material odds to accomplish their goals," exercising willpower to change their world.[13] Traditional Chinese social thought, in contrast, had assumed a world where forces of fate, nature, society, and birth dominated humans and taught that one must accept one's fate with resignation. Mao's revolutionary romanticism and strong populist faith proclaimed that people could transcend their fate. Through a number of large-scale construction projects and a wide variety of forceful changes produced by the Communist regime in its first eight years, Mao brought this new view of human capabilities into Chinese life. In implementing practical policies, Mao used the mass line and mass campaigns to mobilize the willpower of the people. The problem is that sometimes Mao's revolutionary romanticism had a way of soaring out of control, with insufficient grounding in reality.

If Mao placed great faith in the people, he had nothing but hatred and distrust for intellectuals. His strong anti-intellectualism was directed against scholars, writers, and journalists but also against scientists, engineers, and doctors—in a word, *experts*. Mao attributed the problems of late imperial China to intellectuals (degreeholders) who ran the government. Intellectuals had none of the practical sense of the people, yet they gloried in their presumed superiority, putting on airs and demeaning the masses. Mao thought that they constantly raised nit-picking objections to his programs and policies. His opposition to intellectuals seriously and negatively affected developments in the PRC. Although the First Five-Year Plan (see below), shaped and executed with Soviet support, did follow the Soviet model and emphasize technical expertise, Mao subsequently moved away from that practice. In the twenty years from 1957 to 1976 he frequently demonized intellectuals, attacking them viciously and creating, as it were, an intellectual scorched earth policy that dangerously weakened China.

Another of Mao's preeminent concerns was the crucial nature of ideology. To be ideologically correct (or, in the slang of the time, properly *red* or Communist) was absolutely essential, for it was ideological correctness that would carry the revolution to a successful conclusion. Ideological correctness was *Mao Zedong Thought,* an evolving body of thought, often emphasizing practice, not simply theoretical ideas. During his life, Mao was the producer, interpreter, and keeper of the ideological canon.

Mao's thinking on *class* contributed greatly to Mao Zedong Thought. The central process of class and revolution was class struggle, which Mao believed would mark society until Communism was attained. Mao further taught, in what might be called *ideo-biology,* that class status could be determined by political attitudes and that unless attitudes changed, class status would be passed on almost genetically to succeeding generations. Once a landlord, always a landlord; once a capitalist, always a capitalist. As one scholar suggests, Mao really created castes—"social orders with permanent, hereditary status that sharply [shaped] one's life experiences and prospects."[14] A person from a bad class became a public enemy of the people, defined primarily as workers and peasants.

The first eight years of the PRC are generally viewed as the most successful period of Communist rule under Mao's control. The debilitating economic inflation was broken with price controls, balanced budgets, austerity measures, and currency reform. The new regime began the rigorous task of reconstruction following decades of war and turmoil. The government expelled most foreigners and confiscated their property. The PLA fought the U.S. army to a standoff in Korea. Most important, Communists were able to launch aspects of their revolution across the nation.

Land Reform

The heart of the Chinese revolution—land reform—had been tried in the 1930s and in North China from 1946 to 1948. According to Liu Shaoqi, the second-ranking Chinese leader in 1949, land reform's goal was "to free the rural productive forces from the shackles of the landlords' feudal land-ownership system, so as to develop agricultural production and open the way for new China's industrialization."[15] The process involved destroying the old agricultural system through class struggle and building a new system based on collective rural production. However, applying the concept of class struggle across the board was problematic, given the ecological and social variety of the Chinese countryside. In the North, tenancy rates in the 1930s were only about 10 to 15 percent, but in the South and Southwest they were much higher (56 percent in Sichuan), and absentee landlords exploited tenants. The timing of the revolutionary process also varied. Land reform in the North took place mostly before and during the civil war, while in the South it happened after the establishment of the PRC. Therefore, in its approach to land reform, the party had to consider many variables. It was time- and space-specific.

Execution of a Landowner
A soldier executes a bound landowner in northern Xinjiang province during the land reform campaign.

Mobilizing peasants in rural villages by setting up mass organizations was usually slow and difficult. Cadres from outside the community had tough problems. They had to possess networking skills, and they had to begin their work by cultivating social ties in the community. Only by first winning the trust of local people could they begin to build grassroots networks, and only after they had constructed these networks could they begin their various programs of action. The local people generally had no sense of class sentiments. In many areas of the South and East, tenants rented land from a landlord in their own lineage. Given the all-important kin and native place networks, villagers did not easily understand what feudal class structures were or what exploitation meant. Party organizers also had to break down the social psychological barrier between peasants and local elites. In traditional times, peasants knew their place, masters at playing their social role as subordinates. The Communists worked to mobilize peasants to aggressively attack those who had held power over them; to get them to do so was a formidable task.

Once local organizing reached a revolutionary threshold, struggle meetings brought the local populace together to attack landlords and former village bullies. Struggle meetings were often violent and always volatile and unpredictable. Long-term bitternesses was given free rein to explode in anger. There were frequent violent outbursts: an estimated one to two million landlords were killed—either in the heat of struggle or by execution. An estimated 88 percent of rural households had completed the *land to the tiller* movement by summer 1952, when almost 43 percent of China's arable land was confiscated and then redistributed to about 60 percent of the rural masses.

But land reform, the purpose of which was greater production, could not stop at the land to the tiller stage, in which land was broken up into small parcels. Needed were large-scale farms that would allow the use of machines—tractors, seeders, combines, bailers—to make farming more efficient. Policymakers saw collectivization—bringing farmers together in cooperative units—as the key to modernizing agriculture. To ease the difficulties of moving into collectives, the government planned a gradual phased process. The first step, mutual aid teams (MATs), brought peasants together to share labor, farm animals, and tools. Peasants continued to own their own land, implements, and farm animals. Ten or fewer cooperating households made up a typical MAT, in many areas members of the same lineage. By 1956, 92 percent of all peasant households were MAT members.

In the next stage of collectivization, semisocialist lower-level agricultural producers' cooperatives (APCs) were created, composed of about three to five MATs or thirty to fifty households. Members

Source: A Struggle Meeting

China's most important female writer, Ding Ling, won the 1951 Stalin Prize for Literature for her novel of rural revolution, The Sun Shines Over the Sanggan River, *written in 1948. In this passage we see peasants, long socially submerged to landlord and village elites, break out of their timidity and fear and verbally and physically assault the local despot Schemer Qian. What does it take for the peasants to get up enough nerve to attack Qian?*

Then three or four militiamen took Schemer Qian up to the platform. He was wearing a lined gown of gray silk and white trousers, his hands tied behind him. His head was slightly lowered, and his small beady eyes were screwed up, searching the crowd. . . .

For thousands of years the local despots had had power. They had oppressed generation after generation of peasants, and the peasants had lowed their necks under the yoke. Now abruptly they were confronted with this power standing before them with bound hands, and they felt bewildered, at a loss. Some who were particularly intimidated by his malevolent look recalled the days when they could only submit, and now, exposed to this blast, wavered again. So for the time being they were silent.

All this time Schemer Qian, standing on the stage gnawing his lips, was glancing round, wanting to quell these yokels, unwilling to admit defeat. . . .

At this point a man suddenly leapt out from the crowd. He had thick eyebrows and sparkling eyes. Rushing up to Schemer Qian, he cursed him: "You murderer! You trampled our village under your feet! You killed people from behind the scenes for money. Today we're going to settle all old scores, and do a thorough job of it. Do you hear that? Do you still want to frighten people? It's no use! There's no place for you to stand on this stage! Kneel down! Kneel to all the villagers!" He pushed Qian hard, while the crowd echoed, "Kneel down! Kneel down!" . . .

Peasants surged up to the stage shouting wildly: "Kill him!" "A life for our lives!"

A group of villagers rushed to beat him. It was not clear who started, but one struck the first blow and others fought to get at him.

One feeling animated them all—vengeance! They wanted vengeance. They wanted to give vent to their hatred, the sufferings of the oppressed since their ancestors' times, the hatred of thousands of years; all this resentment they directed against him. They would have liked to tear him with their teeth. . . .

"Bah! Killing's too good for him. Let's make him beg for death. Let's humble him for a few days, how about it?" Old Dong's face was red with excitement. He had started life as a hired laborer. Now that he saw peasants just like himself daring to speak out and act boldly, his heart was racing wildly with happiness.

Source: Quoted in R. Keith Schoppa, Twentieth Century China: A History in Documents *(New York: Oxford University Press, 2004), 145–46.*

contributed land, draft animals, and equipment as capital shares to the cooperative and received a dividend, after wages were deducted, for their contribution. The establishment of lower-level APCs was highly variable, occurring in some areas by 1951 and in others not until 1955. By that time, considerable local resistance had begun to rise. Nevertheless, the party-state repeatedly demonstrated a *great leap* mentality. In the context of the perceived general success of collectivization through the lower-level APC stage, with Mao forging the path, the leadership decided to push full steam ahead to establish upper-level APCs—at a time when only 15 percent of peasant households were members of lower-level APCs. Frantic organizing in the last months of 1955 led to a skyrocketing membership in lower-level APCs of over 80 percent of peasant households in January 1956; at this time, roughly 8 percent of the peasants had not reached the MAT stage. The steps in the land reform process also varied from locality to locality. A tragic aspect of these APC decisions and efforts is that the party leaders abandoned the strategy of pragmatism and flexibility that had brought them political and military victory.

Higher-level APCs, more revolutionary than their lower-level predecessors, comprised two to three hundred households. The collective owned the land, ending private ownership. Compensation was based strictly on labor. By the end of 1956, almost 88 percent of peasant households were at least nominal members. Some peasants considered the higher-level APC a negative turning point in their relationship to the party-state and in their day-to-day relationships with the rural cadres who, in many cases, had forced this formation on the people. The state now attempted to institute direct agricultural planning through marketing restraints, quotas, and rations that increasingly constrained farmers' actions. Peasants lost control over their lives to rural cadres.

Revolution in the Family

The Marriage Law of 1950 struck at the very heart of the traditional family system, abolishing the old "arbitrary and compulsory arrangements and the superiority of man over woman." The new system was based "on equal rights for both sexes, and on the protection of the lawful interests of women and children."[16] Arranged marriages, child betrothals, polygamy, and the selling of women into marriage were forbidden. Women could initiate divorce proceedings. Infanticide was prohibited. Equal rights were given to women, a revolutionary concept in the context of traditional Chinese gender relationships. The law allowed single women, divorcees, and widows to own land in their own names for the first time ever. However, though the laws were on the books, they were not always followed in practice. The right to divorce created disorder when hundreds of thousands of women in unhappy marriages tried to do so. The numbers of murders and suicides stemming from the issue of divorce soared into the tens of thousands.

Urban Revolution

As in land reform, the revolution's urban phase targeted class enemies. In 1951 and 1952, the party attacked purveyors of what it called *non-Communist bourgeois values*. Targets of the Three-Anti Campaign were party cadres, government bureaucrats, and factory managers; the goals: to eliminate waste, corruption, and mismanagement. Targets of the Five-Anti Campaign were the national bourgeoisie—industrialists and big businessmen—for corruption, including bribery and tax evasion.

Communist Chinese Leaders, 1957 These were the men at the top of the Chinese party-state. The four men fully pictured are, from left to right, Zhou Enlai, Zhu De, Mao Zedong, and Liu Shaoqi.

Source: Marriage Law of 1950

With the announcement of the Marriage Law a mere seven months after the establishment of the PRC, the new government (on paper at least) recognized the equality of men and women. It gave women rights they had never had and protected children as well. What is the one situation in which a woman could not divorce her husband without his approval?

CHAPTER 1: GENERAL PRINCIPLES

ARTICLE 1:   The feudal marriage system which is based on arbitrary and compulsory arrangement and the superiority of man over woman and ignores the children's interests shall be abolished.

The New Democratic marriage system, which is based on the free choice of partners, on monogamy, on equal rights for both sexes, and on the protection of the lawful interests of women and children, shall be put into effect.

ARTICLE 2:   Bigamy, concubinage, child betrothal, interference with the remarriage of widows, and the exaction of money or gifts in connection with marriages, shall be prohibited.

CHAPTER 2: THE MARRIAGE CONTRACT

ARTICLE 3:   Marriage shall be based upon the complete willingness of the two partners. Neither party shall use compulsion and no third party shall be allowed to interfere.

ARTICLE 4:   A marriage can be contracted only after the man has reached 20 years of age and the woman 18 years of age.

CHAPTER 3: RIGHTS AND DUTIES OF HUSBAND AND WIFE

ARTICLE 7:   Husband and wife are companions living together and shall enjoy equal status in the home.

ARTICLE 8:   Husband and wife are in duty bound to love, respect, assist, and look after each other, to live in harmony, to engage in productive work, to care for the children, and to strive jointly for the welfare of the family and for the building up of the new society.

ARTICLE 10:   Both husband and wife shall have equal rights in the possession and management of family property.

ARTICLE 11:   Both husband and wife shall have the right to use his or her own family name.

ARTICLE 12:   Both husband and wife shall have the right to inherit each other's property.

CHAPTER 5: DIVORCE

ARTICLE 17:   Divorce shall be granted when husband and wife both desire it. In the event of either the husband or the wife alone insisting upon divorce, it may be granted only when mediation by the district people's government and the judicial organ has failed to bring about reconciliation. . . .

ARTICLE 18:   The husband shall not apply for a divorce when his wife is with child. He may apply for divorce only one year after the birth of a child. In the case of a woman applying for divorce, this restriction does not apply.

ARTICLE 19:   The consent of a member of the revolutionary army on active service who maintains correspondence with his or her family must first be obtained before his or her spouse can apply for divorce.

Source: Quoted in R. Keith Schoppa, Twentieth Century China: A History in Documents *(New York: Oxford University Press, 2004), 142–44.*

Like the Guomindang regime in the late 1920s and early 1930s, the Communist regime sought to sink its roots deeply into Chinese society. While the Guomindang attempt had not been successful, the Communist *danwei* (unit) was a very effective arm of the state. By the early 1960s, every person was assigned to a *unit*: if he was employed, at his place of work; for students, at school; for the unemployed or retirees, in the neighborhood. The party-state used the *danwei* for surveillance and to enforce control, political conformity, and ideological correctness at the lowest level of the polity. One had to get permission from one's *danwei* to get married or divorced, to have a child, or to change a job. The *danwei* controlled housing, gave out ration coupons, oversaw birth control, mediated disputes, and supplied burial funds. They were also the basic building blocks of mass campaigns.

The First Five-Year Plan

In 1953, the government announced its First Five-Year Plan to focus on heavy industry, the goal being to lay a foundation for subsequent industrial and economic development. Using the Soviet model for state-controlled development, the effort was headquartered in Manchuria, with its many industrial plants held for years by the government (the Japanese, the Nationalists, and now the Communists), and the area was close to the Soviet Union. Thousands of Soviet engineers and technical advisors came to teach Soviet methods during these years. The Chinese followed their Soviet patrons to the letter, and the advances were remarkable: most of the goals set forth in the plan (e.g., production of steel, machine tools, truck units) were substantially exceeded. Economic growth was 8.9 percent annually, with agricultural output rising 3.8 percent annually and industrial growth climbing an impressive 18.7 percent per year. This amazing record is underscored by data showing that the lives of Chinese were substantially better. Life expectancy, a good measure of the health and economic conditions of a country, rose from thirty-six years in 1950 to fifty-seven years in 1957, an amazing increase. Wages for workers were up by a third; and for peasants, income was up by a fifth. It was indeed a stellar beginning.

THE WAR IN KOREA, 1950–1953

Less than fourteen months into its existence, the PRC entered the Korean War to stave off a perceived threat from UN forces led by the United States. This was a terrible time for Mao to enter a major war, with the PRC being relatively new and with many problems waiting to be solved. China had wanted to end the civil war by dealing with Taiwan, but the United States demonstrated its hostility to the PRC when it sent the U.S. Seventh Fleet into the Taiwan Strait to prevent Mao from acting. China saw the United States as the world's foremost imperialist nation, now again intervening in the Chinese civil war; Zhou Enlai called it *armed aggression*.

After their postwar occupation by the Soviet Union and the United States, the two Koreas had faced each other with fiery nationalistic hostility. In June 1950 North Korea invaded South Korea, its troops marching all the way down the peninsula to a small perimeter held by the South Koreans around Pusan. After the United States prodded the UN to enter the war, UN troops landed at Inch'ŏn the coast near Seoul in September, forcing northern forces to beat a hasty retreat back across the thirty-eighth parallel. UN forces continued marching toward to the Yalu River, the border with China—changing their policy goal from *containing* the northern regime to *liberating* it. Even before the Inch'ŏn landing, China warned that it would intervene if UN forces invaded North Korea. Commanding General Douglas MacArthur had made increasingly belligerent statements about the artificiality of the border between China and North Korea ("they are all Communists"), about bombing sites in China ("take out all the industrial cities"), and about "unleashing" Jiang Jieshi against the mainland.

The PRC clearly felt that its own security was threatened by the UN actions. In a massive commitment, Chinese troops, totaling seven hundred thousand, entered the war in November. The early

Chinese campaigns were successful, with UN forces driven far south of the thirty-eighth parallel in late January 1951. But the war became a stalemate, though an armistice was not reached until mid-1953. About one million Chinese soldiers were killed. On the other hand, the PRC had fought the strongest power in the world to a draw, a reality that provided a huge psychological victory and helped legitimize the PRC regime.

At home, the Chinese government rallied the masses to the war's support; communities, for example, contributed money for the construction of planes and for other war materiel. From early 1951 to 1953, the party whipped up hatred for the United States through its "Resist America, Aid Korea" campaign and its targeting of *counter-revolutionaries*, especially former Guomindang members. Estimated executions of perhaps up to half a million suspects made it a particularly bloody time.

THE HUNDRED FLOWERS MOVEMENT AND THE ANTIRIGHTIST CAMPAIGN

In 1957, the early PRC successes began to turn sour: from this time until Mao's death in 1976, the party-state unleashed a series of tragedies, each more catastrophic than the one before. In 1957 the party called on intellectuals to critique the party-state and its policies in the Hundred Flowers Movement ("let a hundred flowers bloom"). Mao and others apparently believed that the party-state was strong enough to take some criticism, and that the criticism would, in any case, be minor and therefore tolerable. Though hesitant in the beginning, after persistent prodding by the party and government leaders, intellectuals began to voice their criticisms: the flowers bloomed for five weeks in May and June 1957. Criticisms of basic party policy and of the party itself were brutally frank. Criticism spread quickly to other groups, including farmers and urban workers. By mid-May students around the country were putting up critical posters on campus walls. This one is from a poster at Qinghua University in Beijing:

> . . .*Chairman Mao . . . that son of a bitch! A million shames on him! . . . Our pens can never defeat Mao Zedong's Party guards and his imperial army. When he wants to kill you, he doesn't have to do it himself. He can mobilize your wife and children to denounce you and then kill you with their own hands! Is this a rational society? This is class struggle, Mao Zedong style!*[17]

The party moved to tear out the blooming flowers by their roots, stopping the movement it had started. Noisily proclaiming a nationwide "anti-Communist plot," it announced a campaign against so-called rightists. Within the next few months, between four hundred thousand and seven hundred thousand intellectuals lost their careers and titles, were jailed, or were sent to labor camps or to do heavy labor in the countryside. Some committed suicide. Most were not rehabilitated until 1979, many of them posthumously. Mao had burned his bridges to China's intellectuals, in effect discarding them as useless in the development of a modern socialist China; the chasm between the party and intellectuals was both deep and gaping.

THE GREAT LEAP FORWARD (AND BACKWARD)

Mao believed that a mobilized populace was the key both to leaping over the mistakes of other developing states and to leaping forward into the developed future. The relative ease of collectivization thus far had given Mao a sense that it could now be carried to its logical conclusion. Thus, in 1958 the party launched the Great Leap Forward, a utopian campaign designed in part to establish communes in which Chinese life and labor would be militarized. A Politburo resolution in August 1958 called the people's communes "the basic social units of Communist society" and called for "actively us[ing] the form of people's

Adoration   Here, during the Great Leap Forward, a crowd adoringly surrounds Mao (raising his cap) and Zhou Enlai (to Mao's right). Despite the troubles of the Great Leap and its aftermath, the Great Famine, the cult of Mao continued to grow.

communes to explore the practical . . . transition to communism."[18] The commune on average was made up of about 5,500 households—approximately twenty-five times bigger than higher-level APCs. It became the locality's main governmental unit and form of socioeconomic organization.[19] With astonishing speed, by the end of December 1958, 99.1 percent of all rural families had become commune members. Private garden plots and private ownership of livestock were forbidden. Authorities adopted a distribution system in which earnings were paid on a per capita basis, not on the basis of labor contributions. Thus, differences between incomes were greatly reduced.

Two commune structures best epitomized the Great Leap: the backyard steel furnace and the commune mess hall. Rooted in Mao's idealistic populism was the sense that if the people had a participatory stake in production, their energies would be released and production would increase dramatically. While industry had generally not been located in the countryside, Mao believed that communes should develop local industries like steel making, in which people could participate and contribute their productive capacities. Communes built their own steel furnaces—at least one million dotted the Chinese landscape. Fueling them led to widespread deforestation. People contributed iron tools and implements, window frames, pots and pans for the making of pig iron. But because of faulty manufacturing techniques, the products cracked easily; useful iron implements, tools, and utensils had been turned into something totally useless. In terms of economic development, it was ridiculous: the expense of setting up the furnaces and the need for huge numbers of people to operate them surpassed by far any contribution to China's steel industry.

Perhaps no change made a greater impact on people's daily lives than the commune mess hall. Though not meant to be a direct blow to family cohesion, it probably undermined to a degree the closeness of the family unit. From the standpoint of agricultural production, mess halls were efficient; they gave each commune member more time for work or study, raised labor productivity about 30 percent, and released millions of women from domestic chores. The construction of mess halls was widespread and a major undertaking.[20] Other commune institutions, like nurseries and kindergartens, also tended to erode family cohesion. The state impinged more deeply on people's lives than ever before, directly penetrating family life by replacing traditional family practices with government services. This was also the first time that rural women achieved their own economic identity; an estimated 90 percent performed farm labor in 1958 and 1959.

The people's communes were the culmination of the militarization of Chinese society, a trend gradually developing since the first years of the twentieth century. The commune workforce was organized into military units called *brigades* (sometimes *companies*), which were further divided into *production teams* or *platoons*. Overseeing brigades were management districts, usually denoted *battalions*. The use of military terminology underscores the militarization of labor even as it suggests the degree of regimentation imposed on the people by the party-state. Establishment of the commune militia further enhanced militarization. Able-bodied citizens ages fifteen to fifty were in the ordinary militia and sixteen- to thirty-year-olds were in the so-called hard-core militia. By January 1959, 220 million men and women were serving as militia members.

It was clear by the end of 1958 that the Great Leap had fallen flat on its face. The utter failure of the steel-making experiment and its ripple effect on the economy at large was compounded by a deepening agricultural tragedy. Though the 1958 harvest was dismal, grain production estimates had been grossly inflated in the competition between communes to produce more and more. These inflated statistics were passed up the chain of command, and there were few attempts, if any, to verify their validity. By December 1958 projections showed a doubling of the 1957 harvest, clearly an impossibility. The party-state assessed taxes on the basis of the projections, as a result taking most of the grain produced. As little grain was left for the masses, people in the countryside began to go hungry. The tragedy was compounded by widespread mismanagement in the too hastily organized communes. Mao's positions on the Great Leap and the fear of some party leaders that a disaster might be approaching led them to compel Mao to relinquish the post of PRC president to Liu Shaoqi in December 1958. But that was about the only time Mao was challenged. He had created an ongoing situation that saw honest questioning and disagreement as a betrayal of the revolution. Only Mao understood and could properly interpret what was revolutionary and what was not. Even before the formal Mao cult of the 1960s was created, he had so traumatized the Chinese polity that few people would raise questions or speak against him or his positions.

At a conference in July 1959, rancor over the Great Leap began to tear apart the *political consensus* of the leadership group that had formed at Yan'an. This meeting set the stage for the national tragedy of the Cultural Revolution that would dominate the 1960s and 1970s. The major clash pitted Mao against Defense Minister Peng Dehuai. In a letter to Mao that the chairman made public, Peng charged that the Leap was not working, that the huge grain harvest figures were not credible, and that he was concerned about the direction of policies. Mao attacked Peng for going beyond the limits of permissible criticism and claimed that he was a counterrevolutionary rightist. Peng, the heroic commander during the Korean War, was dismissed from his post. Mao made it less likely than ever that oppositional viewpoints would be taken as anything but treachery and, worse, counterrevolutionary activity.

THE GREAT FAMINE, 1959–1961

The Great Leap, party-state ignorance, bad agricultural policies (like plowing too deeply), and natural disasters conspired to produce one of the world's worst twentieth-century tragedies: a deadly famine that affected over 60 percent of China's farmland. Grain output, at 200 million tons in 1958, dropped to 170 million in 1959 and to 144 million in 1960—a 28 percent decline in two years. Per capita food production would not reach its pre-1957 level until the early 1970s. Rural areas were more affected than cities, though all suffered. An estimated thirty million people died. People were not allowed to move to other areas in search of food. Most knew only what was happening in their own areas and did not understand the famine's extent; with its authoritarian powers, the government had tremendous control over news and information. Starving people ate rice husks, corncobs, weeds, grass, tree bark, even earth in an effort to remain alive. A Chinese economist noted that the Great Leap exacted a "high price in blood."[21]

As scandalous as creating such a situation was the fact that the government did little to respond to the crisis, the worst since the PRC came to power. The party seemed paralyzed, distributing almost no relief funds. It almost disbelieved what was happening, at the least not wanting to believe it. Whatever the motive, it appeared callous, even worse than Jiang Jieshi's reactions to the Henan famine. From 1958 to 1962, relief came to about 0.8 yuan per commune resident at a time when a kilogram of rice cost between 2 and 4 yuan.

THE SINO-SOVIET SPLIT

In early 1950, after Mao announced that in foreign affairs China was "leaning to one side"—that of the Soviet Union—he concluded a security treaty with Stalin. That treaty and the presence of thousands of Soviet technical advisors attest to the initial closeness of the two Communist nations. But Mao had never been close to the Kremlin and had ridden to power without the Soviet Union's active support. Then came the Great Leap, in which the Chinese broke with the Soviet model. The Soviets had given China huge amounts of development aid. To see the Chinese situation go so drastically awry when they left the Soviet path to follow the developmental road of mass mobilization angered Moscow. Furthermore, the Soviet Union saw itself as the world's Communist leader and the patron of developing Communist states. The Chinese actions were like a slap in the face. However, the crux of the matter for the Chinese was that national interests trumped shared ideology. The Chinese leadership was put off by what they considered Khrushchev's weakness and his announced policy of *peaceful coexistence* in April 1957 in the face of the actions of Western states.

In August 1958 a crisis over Taiwan further soured Sino-Soviet relations. Without consulting Khrushchev, the PRC launched a massive bombardment of the offshore island of Quemoy. But Mao clearly miscalculated the response of the United States, which had signed a mutual security treaty with Taiwan in 1954 and which dispatched the U.S. Seventh Fleet to convoy Nationalist supply ships to the island. In September, the United States called for *mutual deescalation* and Beijing stepped back, symbolically shelling the island only on even-numbered days. Khrushchev was bitterly angry since, under the 1950 security treaty, Mao had an obligation to inform Moscow beforehand. For Khrushchev, Mao, in initiating the Taiwan Strait crisis and the Great Leap Forward, had been guilty of huge miscalculations. Because of the Taiwan Strait crisis, Khrushchev canceled a nuclear weapons technology offer—an act that infuriated Mao and the Chinese government.

Other irritants in the Sino-Soviet relationship included conflicting national policies regarding India and Mao's cavalier attitude toward nuclear war (it would destroy capitalism, so it was not all bad). In April 1960, Beijing proclaimed that China had replaced the Soviet Union as the leader of the Communist world. In mid-July, as starvation was spreading in China, Khrushchev suddenly recalled all Soviet scientists, engineers, and industrial advisors in China. They were ordered to take with them all blueprints and materials; no fewer than 257 scientific and technical projects were canceled. The short-term effects on the PRC were severe, especially in light of the economic crisis and the institutional turmoil into which the Great Leap had thrown the party and state. As divorces go, this was one particularly hostile and bitter. No reconciliation would take place for almost thirty years.

THE GREAT PROLETARIAN CULTURAL REVOLUTION, 1966–1976

The cataclysm of the Great Leap Forward created a bitter split in party leadership. A number of leaders, including President Liu Shaoqi and CCP General Secretary Deng Xiaoping, began to see Mao's policies as antithetical to the goal of building a modern socialist state. As recovery from the disasters of the late 1950s began, a dispute between the Maoist line, with its fundamentalist approach, and the Liu-Deng line, with its pragmatic approach, began to fester. Though the two-line approach covers a more complex reality, it highlights the most essential differences in understanding subsequent developments.

Mao was not particularly upset about the Great Leap's failure. If people were properly motivated by moral incentives and revolutionary goals *(his* goals), he did not doubt that they would use all their energies unstintingly to achieve those goals. Mao thought that people (as opposed to *enemies of the people*) were by nature good. They also had more innate abilities and more common sense than intellectuals. He remained hostile to bureaucratized party cadres and to experts of any stripe. Ideological correctness trumped factual knowledge; it was better, in other words, to be red than expert. Perpetual revolution through perpetual class struggle was necessary because enemies of the people would rear their ugly class heads to challenge the people.

In contrast, Liu Shaoqi and Deng Xiaoping believed that the Great Leap was an unmitigated disaster that simply could not be repeated. They argued that people were most motivated by material incentives—rewards, bonuses, and higher wages—when they excelled or produced more than others. They were convinced that these incentives would be stronger than moral encouragement, suasion, and propaganda. Mao reviled such policies because they smelled of *revisionism,* that is, revising Marxism by sneaking in capitalist elements. In the debate over redness versus expertise, Liu and Deng championed expertise. Getting the job done right was the test of whether the method was right or wrong. An ignorant person, however red, could not do a good job. Deng put it simply: "It doesn't matter if the cat is white or black, so long as it catches rats."[22] More pragmatic than Mao's approach, the Liu-Deng line valued knowledge of technology and science as well as organizational and procedural approaches that emphasized logical and efficient routines. It also valued political stability, a prerequisite for building a modern socialist nation.

When Mao began a *Socialist Education Campaign* in 1962 to refocus the party on the value of class struggle, Liu and Deng made sure that the local work was carried on by party work teams rather than by masses at the grassroots level, as Mao had wanted. Mao saw his rectification program changing into a tool that revisionists could use to reassert party control in the countryside and became convinced that the Chinese revolution was in danger. Seeing himself and the revolution as one, he felt compelled to destroy the party that he had spent his life building but that now, in his estimation, had gone tragically wrong.

Between 1964 and 1966, Mao forged a coalition to help him take on the party. Most important was the PLA under his strong supporter Lin Biao; second was a group of ultraradicals called the *Gang of Four,* key among whom was Mao's wife, Jiang Qing; third were groups of the urban masses who saw themselves as increasingly disadvantaged: high school and college students with shrinking opportunities for upward mobility and workers stuck with low wages and no pension or medical benefits. Mao cultivated these groups.

On August 5, 1966, at a Central Committee meeting, Mao wrote a big-character poster of his own titled "Bombard the Headquarters"—the CCP itself—launching one of the most bizarre and spectacular events of the twentieth century. It was a struggle over the direction of the revolution—pragmatic reform undertaken gradually by experts and regularized bureaucrats or revolutionary turmoil created by young Red Guards in a never-ending revolution fueled by class struggle. It was also in part a personal power struggle and Mao's quest for revolutionary immortality.

In August, rebellious student groups reorganized themselves as Red Guards. Shouting slogans like "It is justified to rebel," a million youths crowded Tiananmen Square to see Mao at sunrise atop the Gate of

Heavenly Peace. Eight such rallies were held between then and the end of November; a total of thirteen million students came as if on pilgrimage (or, as they more commonly said, on their own Long March) to see their *Great Helmsman,* their *Red Sun,* their *Supreme Commander.* Mao directed them to destroy the four *olds:* old ideas, habits, customs, and culture. They were soldiers in the war against party and state leadership, the vanguard in the class struggle. Mao announced that his successor would be Lin Biao. He made no secret of the fact that the two main targets of the Cultural Revolution were Liu Shaoqi and Deng Xiaoping.

Utter chaos followed utter confusion. Red Guards rampaged throughout China, seeking out and destroying anything representative of the feudal past and the bourgeois present. Their actions ranged from amusing to criminal. Shop names and street names were changed to make them sound more revolutionary. People with long hair were seized and had it cut off. More destructively, Red Guards ransacked homes and pillaged museums and libraries, indiscriminately trashing books and newspapers, the notes and writings of scholars, religious art, and recordings of Western music. Red Guards tortured and beat people, especially teachers, principals, intellectuals, and those with bourgeois backgrounds—sometimes to death. A female Red Guard reported that her middle-school classmates beat to death an elderly former businessman—a murder in which one of the killers was the victim's own granddaughter. The humiliation and degradation that Red Guards inflicted drove many to suicide. The most well-known likely such victim was the famous novelist Lao She. Liu and Deng began to be strongly criticized and subjected to humiliating struggle meetings; in the summer of 1967 they were put under house arrest.

In an increasingly polarized atmosphere, Red Guard units around the country fought rival groups of Red Guards, farmers and workers (who resented them), and conservative mass organizations. China tottered on the brink of anarchy. In one episode in July 1967, Beijing had to send air and naval forces to restore order in the city of Wuhan. Bloody, and destructive battles erupted all over the country between the PLA and revolutionary groups who were seizing weapons from military bases. The turmoil spread briefly into the international arena when rebels took over the Foreign Ministry in Beijing for two weeks, seizing and burning the British diplomatic compound. In early September, Mao ordered the PLA to restore order. That was not so easy. In mid-1968, more bloody violence erupted in Beijing and in five provinces between competing rebel groups. This violent phase of the Cultural Revolution came to an end with the meeting of the Ninth Party Congress in April 1969.

Red Guard Demonstration
These Red Guards, demonstrating in front of the Soviet embassy in Beijing, use cymbals and drums to add to the cacophony of their sloganeering during the Cultural Revolution. Note the "little red book" held by a group in the foreground.

Source: Cultural Revolution Violence at Qinghua University

Red Guard units struggled with other Red Guard units at Qinghua University, the most prestigious university of science and technology in China. As struggles developed on the campus, the two key factions were called 4s and the Regiment, with the latter tending to be the more extreme and led by the superradical Kuai Dafu. This account appears in William Hinton's book Hundred Day War, *which first appeared as the July–August 1972 issue of* Monthly Review.

Unwilling to call off the attack, Kuai transferred his ambush contingent to the Bathhouse, leaving only twenty stalwarts to block the road against the 4s uncommitted troops. When they saw this opening, the 4s pushed forward with a formidable contingent of spear bearers behind a "tank." The tank was made out of a tractor welded over with steel plate. When the twenty Regiment fighters saw this monster coming, they formed a line across the road, but what could they do with spears against its steel plate? As the tank came close, they broke ranks and fled, only to be charged by the 4s' spearmen, who turned the retreat into a rout. One of the Regiment fighters, run through by a spear, bled to death.

To stop the 4s who were advancing from the south, Kuai ordered his "Flag" bow-and-arrow team into the fray. They fired a hail of arrows point blank at the opposition, killing one and wounding several.

The tank, invulnerable to arrows, kept going, but a little further down the road the Regiment defenders had buried what looked like a mine. "If you come any further, you'll be blown up," they shouted to the tank driver.

Not knowing whether the mine was real or not, the tank driver hesitated. Several Regiment fighters took advantage of this pause to rush forward and set the tank on fire with Molotov cocktails. Its crew had to abandon it before it blew up. One of them was so badly burned that three years later his face had still not healed.

With their tank out of action, with its crew scorched, with one man dead from an arrow and several other wounded, the 4s' main force gave up the assault and retreated into an old dormitory building to the west that had long been one of their strongholds. There they took up defensive positions in the basement.

At this point Kuai became desperate. So many had been wounded and several were already dead or dying on both sides, yet nothing had been won. Far from taking power, it looked as if the Regiment might even have to retreat. Kuai ordered his "rods" to pour gasoline on the Bathhouse. Molotov cocktails were quickly made and thrown against the gas-soaked walls. Flames shot up around the building. The 4s were trapped inside.

The defenders had had nothing to eat or drink since the night before. With their throats parched and their clothes scorched, they called out that they wanted to surrender. But Kuai would not listen. Instead of putting out the fire, he ordered more fuel. When the Haitien fire department arrived, he tried to prevent the firemen from going anywhere near the building.

This angered the peasants who had gathered from far and near to watch the battle.

"Don't burn people to death! How can you go to such extremes! Put up a ladder! Let the students out!" they shouted.

Finally Kuai relented.

As the scorched and suffocating 4s crawled down the rescue ladder, they were arrested as prisoners of war. The 4s lost a major fighting force—over thirty of their best people, the main troops of the Generator Building fighting team.

Source: Quoted in R. Keith Schoppa, Twentieth Century China: A History in Documents *(New York: Oxford University Press, 2004), 149–51.*

An estimated four hundred thousand to five hundred thousand Chinese were killed in these three years. Countless numbers of intellectuals, teachers, and professionals were persecuted. About three million party cadres and government officials were purged. Others endured beatings, torture, and even death. The best known was Liu Shaoqi, former president of the PRC and a Communist leader since 1923. Denounced as a "renegade, traitor, and scab hiding in the Party, a lackey of imperialism, modern revisionism, and the Guomindang reactionaries," he was expelled from the party, tortured, and beaten by Red Guards; he died of pneumonia without medical care.[23]

The Cultural Revolution's second phase (1969–1976) was marked by continual factional disunity, tension, and political struggle, though no longer against a backdrop of national anarchy. The conclusion of the violent phase was followed by a substantial migration of people from cities to the countryside. Over four million high school and university students (many former Red Guards) were sent to the countryside to live with farmers and undergo reeducation, an experience that prevented many from attending college and helped create a lost generation of disillusioned, cynical, and even antisocial adults. They had lost faith in the moralistic rhetoric of Mao and, above all, in the value and validity of the Communist political system. Up to three million party cadres and bureaucrats were also sent to the countryside for productive labor and political study—more accurately, hard labor and indoctrination.

The factional struggle was mostly about who would succeed Mao, who was ill with amyotrophic lateral sclerosis (Lou Gehrig's disease). The most mysterious incident involved Lin Biao, one of Mao's strongest supporters and named Mao's successor in 1966. Whatever the motive and the events surrounding the still mysterious event, Lin plotted Mao's assassination in 1971. When the plan went awry, Lin attempted to flee to the Soviet Union, but his plane crashed. Part of the motive may have been Lin's disgruntlement about the growing thaw in China's relations with the United States that brought President Richard Nixon to China in early 1972.

The year 1976 was traumatic for the Chinese nation. In the background was the scheming of the Gang of Four to seize the helm from the Great Helmsman. The deaths of Premier Zhou Enlai in January and Zhu De, founder of the Red Army, in July marked the passing of two giants in Chinese history. In July a devastating earthquake destroyed the city of Tangshan, near Tianjin, killing up to 660,000 people. On September 9, Mao died. Less than a month later, the Gang of Four was arrested. The 1981 death sentence of Mao's wife was commuted to life in prison, but she committed suicide in 1991.

Mao in Retrospect

In summer 1981 the CCP adopted a party resolution on Mao's legacy, noting that Mao's contributions far transcended his mistakes. Specifically, it pointed to his success in the revolutionary struggle against the Guomindang and in the socialist transformation's economic successes in the first years of the PRC. But the resolution also criticized Mao strongly for the extent of the 1957 antirightist campaign; for his leftist proclivities and mistakes in the Great Leap Forward; for his disregard of Leninist principles by sponsoring a personality cult and his "personal arbitrariness"; and for his leftist error in planning and conducting the Cultural Revolution. In the end, it said that "chief responsibility for the grave left error of the Cultural Revolution, an error comprehensive in magnitude and protracted in duration, does indeed lie with Comrade Mao Zedong."[24]

Perhaps it was the economic expert Chen Yun who best captured Mao's historical role: "Had Chairman Mao died in 1956, there would have been no doubt that he was a great leader of the Chinese people. . . . Had he died in 1966, his meritorious achievements would have been somewhat tarnished, but his overall record was still very good. Since he actually died in 1976, there is nothing we can do about it."[25]

CHRONOLOGY

1931	Establishment of the Chinese Soviet Republic (Jiangxi Soviet)
1930–1934	Jiang Jieshi's five extermination campaigns
1934–1935	Long March
1935	Zunyi meeting recognizes Mao's leadership
1942	Rectification movement (February)
	Yan'an Forum on Art and Literature (May)
1947–1949	Civil war
1949	Establishment of the PRC
1949–1956	Land reform
1950	Marriage Law
1950–1953	War in Korea
1953–1957	First Five-Year Plan
1957	Hundred Flowers Movement (May–June)
	Anti-rightist campaign
1958–1960	Great Leap Forward
1959–1961	Great famine
1960	Sino-Soviet split
1966–1976	Great Proletarian Cultural Revolution
1976	Death of Zhou Enlai (January)
	Death of Zhu De (July)
	Death of Mao (September 9)
	Arrest of the Gang of Four (October)

SUGGESTED READINGS

Ding Ling. *The Sun Shines Over the Sanggan River*. Translated by Yang Hsien-yi and Gladys Yang. Beijing Foreign Languages Press, 1954. This Stalin Prize–winning novel focuses on land reform in North China.

Li Zhisui. *The Private Life of Chairman Mao*. New York: Random House, 1994. Controversial and fascinating, this is a thoroughly critical view of the public and private life of Mao by the doctor who treated him and eventually embalmed him.

Ma Bo. *Blood Red Sunset: A Memoir of the Chinese Cultural Revolution*. Translated by Howard Goldblatt. New York: Viking, 1995. This is a harrowing and horrifying memoir of a young man whose chosen mission sent him into the Mongolian grasslands during the Cultural Revolution.

Saich, Tony. *The Rise to Power of the Chinese Communist Party*. Armonk, NY.: ME. Sharpe, 1996. This is a masterful analysis containing documents of the CCP from its founding until 1949; in its breadth and coverage it is unsurpassed.

Wou, Odoric. *Mobilizing the Masses: Building Revolution in Henan*. Stanford, CA: Stanford University Press, 1994. The empirical richness and analytical care of this study underscore the complex and diverse possibilities of revolutionary change.

CHAPTER FOURTEEN

The Phoenix:
Japan, 1945–1973

The Japanese Surrender The Japanese surrender delegation on board the U.S.S. *Missouri* in Tokyo Bay on September 2, 1945.

By the early summer of 1945, more than 40 percent of Japan's most important industrial cities had been devastated, one-third of its buildings destroyed, and thirteen million people made homeless. The destruction reached 90 percent in mid-sized cities like Toyama on the Sea of Japan and Aomori on the northern tip of Honshu. Coupled with the bombing campaign was an Allied effort to destroy Japan's merchant fleet. One-quarter to one-third of Japan's wealth was wiped out, leaving a defeated and demoralized country whose resurrection seemed unlikely, at least for many decades. What remained were "endless vistas of urban rubble."[1] But economic statistics show the phoenixlike quality of Japan in the aftermath of its disastrous war. Between 1950 and 1973, Japan's GNP (gross national product: total value of goods and services) soared at an average annual rate of 10 percent. By 1968, Japan had the third highest GNP in the world after the United States and the Soviet Union. Consumers crowded appliance stores to purchase washing machines, electric rice cookers, and air conditioners; and by 1963, over 80 percent of Japanese homes had televisions. The almost miraculous transformation of the Japanese economy and society can be analyzed in two chunks of time, the American occupation (1945–1952) and the *economic miracle* (1952–1973).

THE OCCUPATION

On September 29, 1945, all major Japanese newspapers printed a photograph of General Douglas MacArthur, Supreme Commander of the Allied Powers (SCAP), standing alongside and towering over Emperor Hirohito, the emperor dressed in a cutaway in contrast to MacArthur's more casual dress. The Home Ministry had ordered the photograph suppressed, but an infuriated MacArthur by fiat ended all restrictive laws on newspapers and films, and the major newspapers published it. The photograph "conveyed the subordinate position of the Japanese state and people with shocking force to the entire population."[2]

MacArthur and Hirohito   General Douglas MacArthur and Emperor Hirohito pose in the U.S. embassy in Tokyo, 1945.

The occupation has been called the "third turn [or turning point] in Japanese history" following the sixth-century wave of borrowing from China and the Meiji Restoration.[3] Though in name an Allied occupation, in truth it was American. MacArthur, an aloof, imperious, cocksure man, was a larger-than-life character to many Japanese, and many admired his personal characteristics. Indeed, one history textbook has as a heading "MacArthur as Shogun."[4] To carry out the daily tasks of the occupation, there were 430,000 U.S. troops stationed in Japan by November 1945.

The first tasks of SCAP (an acronym that refers to the entire occupation regime, not only to MacArthur) were demilitarizing, demobilizing, and repatriating Japanese who remained overseas. On September 2, 1945, the day of the Japanese surrender, SCAP issued its Directive No. 1, which ordered the demobilization of all Japanese forces; the Imperial General Headquarters was abolished about two weeks later. About 3.7 million soldiers (and some 3.2 million civilians) had to be repatriated, a task finished by the end of 1948. For many the homecoming was bleak. Many Japanese saw the veterans as losers who had let the nation down or, worse, as accounts of wartime atrocities began to appear, as despicable. Hear one veteran: "My house was burned, my wife and children missing. What little money I had was quickly consumed by high prices, and I was a pitiful figure. Not a single person gave me a kind word. Rather, they cast hostile glances my way."[5]

Part of demilitarizing was bringing to trial those who had played crucial roles in Japan's war machine. The Tokyo War Crimes Trials opened on May 3, 1946; charges continue to reverberate that this was, in fact, *victors' justice* and that only losing countries are charged with war crimes (the U.S. firebombing and nuclear bombing were not considered despite their nature). Be that as it may, 6 military leaders (including Tōjō Hideki) and 1 diplomat/civilian official were hanged in December 1948; 17 were sentenced to life in prison. Out of about 5,700 prosecuted Class B and C war criminals (for actions like atrocities against prisoners of war), 4,420 were convicted and 948 executed. In addition, about 200,000 men in the military, government, or business who had been involved in the war were purged. Many would emerge again; as one historian noted, "the bureaucracy that had sustained the militarist regime was on the whole kept intact. . . ."[6] From the end of the war down to the present, Japanese leaders have found it difficult to accept culpability for the war. The government of Shidehara Kijurō in November 1945, for instance, declared that "the Great East Asia War was an unavoidable war of self-defence under military and economic pressures from the United States, Britain, and others."[7] Sentences of all war criminals were commuted in 1957.

While the trials occurred and the work of the occupation proceeded, the Japanese people struggled with their bleak lives. Many lived in shantytown huts thrown together from trash, debris, and paper amid devastated cities; in 1948, 3.7 million families still had no shelter of their own. They were living on an average of 1,200 calories a day, relying on "barley and potatoes . . . , mixed ground acorns and sawdust with flour when making dumplings and bread, and got what protein they could from worms, grasshoppers, rats, and frogs."[8] They faced epidemics of the most deadly diseases—cholera, typhoid fever, diphtheria, and others—without sufficient medicines to stem the tide. Corruption was rampant as people took advantage of others to make their own lives more livable. In this nightmare, many turned to drink, joined gangs or the underworld, or became prostitutes. It was a far cry from the lives of Americans involved in the occupation who were setting out to change Japanese lives in ways almost beyond comprehension.

Indeed, SCAP's laundry list of reforms constituted a revolution in all but name. Chief of these was the new constitution, written by a committee of Americans in SCAP. No member of the twenty-four-person committee was a Japanese specialist; none had had any prior experience drafting a constitution. Further, MacArthur gave the committee a mere six days to produce the document—which attempted to democratize Japanese life and deal with perceived problems and weaknesses in the Meiji Constitution. The emperor had already renounced his divinity at SCAP's request on January 1, 1946, an act making it most unlikely that nefarious leaders would ever again be able to manipulate the imperial position for their own purposes. The Constitution of 1947 (sometimes called the *Shōwa Constitution* after Emperor Hirohito's reign name) placed sovereignty in the people. The emperor is a symbol of the state who holds his position by the will of the people; he has no power to govern. Further, the powerful bodies whose purpose was to support the imperial position were abolished. The two-house Diet, which had failed to solidify its political centrality in the 1920s, was made the highest organ and the sole lawmaking body in the state. The cabinet, led by the prime minister, was collectively responsible to the Diet. An independent judiciary was established, with the Supreme Court given the duty to review legislation or cases appealed from lower courts.

The constitution's Bill of Rights underscored its "made-in-the-USA" character. It specified freedoms of speech, assembly, and religion; guaranteed a free public education; assured the right to work, organize, and bargain collectively; and outlawed discrimination based on gender, race, creed, social status, or family origin. Especially noteworthy was that the constitution explicitly guaranteed women equality in marriage, divorce, property, and inheritance. Ironically, with this equal rights specification for women, Americans wrote something into the Japanese constitution that they would reject for their own in the 1980s.

Perhaps most surprising was the constitution's "no-war" Article 9:

> *Aspiring sincerely to an international peace based on justice and order, the Japanese people forever renounce war as a sovereign right of the nation and the threat or use of force as a means of settling international disputes.*
> *In order to accomplish the aim of the preceding paragraph, land, sea, and air forces, as well as all other war potential, will never be maintained. The right of belligerency of the State will not be recognized.*[9]

With the coming of the Cold War, the Communist victory in mainland China, and the Korean War, Article 9 began to look as unrealistic as it was. The United States encouraged Japan to build a force for dealing with issues at home and handling natural disasters; one month after North Korea invaded South Korea, the National

Source: From the 1947 Constitution

These "chapters" offer revolutionary changes from the Meiji Constitution, dramatically shifting the locus of sovereignty, the role of the emperor, the state's relation to war, and setting forth people's rights. What were the specific changes? You may want to refer to the excerpt from the Meiji Constitution in Chapter 7.

CHAPTER I THE EMPEROR

ARTICLE 1. The Emperor shall be the symbol of the State and of the unity of the people, deriving his position from the will of the people with whom resides sovereign power.

CHAPTER II RENUNCIATION OF WAR

ARTICLE 9. Aspiring sincerely to an international peace based on justice and order, the Japanese people forever renounce war as a sovereign right of the nation and the threat or use of force as a means of settling international disputes.

In order to accomplish the aim of the preceding paragraph, land, sea, and air forces, as well as other war potential, will never be maintained. The right of belligerency of the state will not be recognized.

CHAPTER III RIGHTS AND DUTIES OF THE PEOPLE

ARTICLE 13. All of the people shall be respected as individuals. Their right to life, liberty, and the pursuit of happiness shall, to the extent that it does not interfere with the public welfare, be the supreme consideration in legislation and in other governmental affairs.

ARTICLE 14. All of the people are equal under the law, and there shall be no discrimination in political, economic, or social relations because of race, creed, sex, social status, or family origin. . . .

ARTICLE 15. The people have the inalienable right to choose their public officials and to dismiss them.

All public officials are servants of the whole community and not any group thereof.

Universal adult suffrage is guaranteed with regard to the election of public officials. . . .

ARTICLE 19. Freedom of thought and conscience shall not be violated.

ARTICLE 20. Freedom of religion is guaranteed to all. No religious organization shall receive any privileges from the state, nor exercise any political authority. . . .

ARTICLE 21. Freedom of assembly and association as well as speech, press, and all other forms of expression, are guaranteed.

No censorship shall be maintained, nor shall the secrecy of any means of communication be violated.

ARTICLE 22. Every person shall have freedom to choose and change his residence and to choose his occupation to the extent that it does not interfere with the public welfare.

Freedom of all persons to move to a foreign country and to divest themselves of their nationality shall be inviolate.

ARTICLE 23. Academic freedom is guaranteed.

ARTICLE 24. Marriage shall be based only on the mutual consent of both sexes, and it shall be maintained through mutual cooperation with equal rights of husband and wife as a basis.

With regard to the choice of spouse, property rights, inheritance, choice of domicile, divorce, and other matters pertaining to marriage and the family laws shall be enacted from the standpoint of individual dignity and the essential equality of the sexes.

ARTICLE 25. All people shall have the right to maintain the minimum standards of wholesome and cultured living.

In all spheres of life, the state shall use its endeavors for the promotion and extension of social welfare and security, and of public health.

> *ARTICLE 26.* All people shall have the right to receive an equal education correspondent to their ability, as provided by law. . .
> *ARTICLE 27.* All people shall have the right and obligation to work.
>
> Standards for wages, hours, rest and other working conditions shall be fixed by law.
> Children shall not be exploited.
> *ARTICLE 28.* The right of workers to organize and to bargain and act collectively is guaranteed.

Source: David J. Lu, Japan: A Documentary History *(Armonk, NY: M. E. Sharpe, 1996), 472–73.*

Police Reserve was set up with seventy-five thousand men. It was expanded in 1952 and became the Self-Defense Force in 1954, consisting essentially of Japanese ground and maritime military forces.

Five other major initiatives under the occupation focused on land reform, zaibatsu busting, labor, education, and local government. Many Japanese charged with carrying out these initiatives shared SCAP's conviction that Japan had moved to aggressive war because its government was much too centralized, with insufficient participation of the people. The key was to break up the centralized structures in order to shift power to the grassroots.

Land reform broke the power of landlords and created small landowners who had been tenants in the past. Roughly 70 percent of Japanese farmers rented some land. Though Japan did not have large landholders, 46 percent of all land was farmed by tenants. The immediate prewar rural landscape was dotted with landlord-tenant disputes that numbered between three and six thousand per year. Dealing with the issue, then, had both economic and social stability objectives. The Land Reform Law of 1946 banned absentee landlordism: such landlords had to sell all their land to the government. Landlords who resided in the community where their property was located could keep 1 hectare (2.47 acres) and sell the government the rest. The government then sold it to former tenants, the price to be repaid within thirty years at an interest rate of 3.2 percent. Land reform was completed by August 1950; at that time, the proportion of farmers who were solely tenants was about 5 percent, down from about 28 percent in 1941. As one writer noted, "Land reform was more than an economic matter. Old values of submissiveness, self-abnegation, and holism in the context of the family and the local community were much weakened."[10]

If land reform was successful, zaibatsu dissolution on the model of U.S. trust busting was less so, but it was not a complete failure. SCAP's idea was to break up the large industrial combines—which were also linked with Japan's march to war—so that the "little guy" could get in on the economic action. SCAP itself ordered the dissolution of the Mitsui and Mitsubishi trading companies in 1947 and in early 1948 broke up eighteen more companies, redistributing their factories. As a result, in some industries—iron and steel, shipbuilding, beer brewing, and others—concentration was substantially reduced. Competition became livelier as firms like Toyota and Honda, which had not been zaibatsu before the war, emerged and became giants. But many of the zaibatsu, like Mitsui and Mitsubishi, revived after the occupation, structured as *enterprise groups (keiretsu).*

MacArthur had at first pushed labor rights, again with a view to giving more power to the people. When wartime restrictions on labor activity ended in the opening days of the occupation, the number of union members soared. The number of prewar union members had peaked in 1936 at 420,000 (7 percent of the labor force). By the end of 1946 there were 5 million union members; by 1949, 7 million (47 percent of the labor force). Labor disputes became more and more common in an economy beset by inflation and general poverty as unions became increasingly aggressive. When unions called for a general strike on February 1, 1947, with the goal of destroying the government of Prime Minister Yoshida Shigeru, SCAP banned it. Relations between SCAP and labor became rocky. What emerged over time through struggles over the purpose of unions—whether for economic goals or political ends (as in the 1947 strike call)—was the

Source: MacArthur's Comments on Article 9

The no-war article of the 1947 constitution was controversial. Here Douglas MacArthur, head of SCAP, comments in his memoirs on its inclusion in the constitution. From whom did the idea for such a change in policy come? What was MacArthur's attitude toward it?

It has frequently been charged, even by those who should be better informed, that the "no war" clause was forced upon the government by my personal fiat. This is not true, as the following facts will show: Long before work was completed on the new document by Dr. Matsumoto, I had an appointment with Prime Minister Shidehara, who wished to thank me for making what was then a new drug in Japan, penicillin, available in aiding in his recovery from severe illness. He arrived at my office at noon on January 24 and thanked me for the penicillin, but I noticed he then seemed somewhat embarrassed and hesitant. I asked him what was troubling him, that as prime minister he could speak with greatest frankness, either by way of complaint or suggestion. He replied that he hesitated to do so because of my profession as a soldier. I assured him soldiers were not as unresponsive or inflexible as they are sometimes pictured—that at bottom most of them were quite human.

He then proposed that when the new constitution became final that it include the so-called no-war clause. He also wanted it to prohibit any military establishment for Japan—any military establishment whatsoever. Two things would thus be accomplished. The old military party would be deprived of any instrument through which they could someday seize power, and the rest of the world would know that Japan never intended to wage war again. He added that Japan was a poor country and could not really afford to pour money into armaments anyway. Whatever resources the nation had left should go to bolstering the economy.

I had thought that my long years of experience had rendered me practically immune to surprise or unusual excitement, but this took my breath away. I could not have agreed more. For years I have believed that war should be abolished as an outmoded means of resolving disputes between nations. Probably no living man has seen as much of war and its destruction as I had. A participant or observer in six wars, a veteran of twenty campaigns, the survivor of hundreds of battlefields, I have fought with or against the soldiers of practically every country in the world, and my abhorrence reached its height with the perfection of the atom bomb.

When I spoke in this vein, it was Shidehara's turn to be surprised. His amazement was so great that he seemed overwhelmed as he left the office. Tears ran down his face, and he turned back to me and said. "The world will laugh and mock us as impracticable visionaries, but a hundred years from now we will be called prophets. . . ."

There were attacks made on this article of the constitution, especially by the cynics who said that it was against the basic nature of man. I defended it, and advocated that it be adopted. Not only was I convinced that it was the most moral of ideas, but I knew that it was exactly what the Allies wanted at that time for Japan. They had said so at Potsdam and they had said so afterward. Indeed, my directive read, "Japan is not to have an Army, Navy, Air Force, Secret Police organization, or civil aviation." And now this had been accomplished by the Japanese themselves, not by the conquering powers.

Source: David J. Lu, Japan: A Documentary History *(Armonk, NY: M. E. Sharpe, 1996), 480–81.*

Source: Excerpt from the SCAP Directive on Land Reform

This 1945 directive tried to democratize the land system by giving land to former tenant farmers. According to SCAP, what were the problems of the old land system? What steps were to be taken in the agricultural world that went beyond redistribution of land?

In order that the Imperial Japanese Government shall remove economic obstacles to the revival and strengthening of democratic tendencies, establish respect for the dignity of man, and destroy the economic bondage that has enslaved the Japanese farmer to centuries of feudal oppressions, the Japanese Imperial Government is directed to take measures to ensure that those who till the soil of Japan shall have a more equal opportunity to enjoy the fruits of their labor.

The purpose of this order is to exterminate those pernicious ills that have long blighted the agrarian structure of a land where almost half the total population is engaged in husbandry.

The Japanese Imperial Government is therefore ordered to submit to this Headquarters on or before 15 March 1946 a program of rural land reform. This program shall contain plans for:

a. Transfer of land from absentee landowners to land operators.
b. Provisions for purchase of farm lands from non-operating owners at equitable rates.
c. Provisions for tenant purchase of land at annual installments commensurate with tenant income.
d. Provisions for reasonable protection of former tenants against reversion to their tenancy status. Such necessary safeguards should include:

(1) Access to long- and short-term credit at reasonable interest rates.
(2) Measures to protect the farmer against exploitation by processors and distributors.
(3) Measures to stabilize prices of agricultural produce.
(4) Plans for the diffusion of technical and other information of assistance to the agrarian population.
(5) A program to foster and encourage an agricultural cooperative movement free of domination by nonagricultural interests and dedicated to the economic and cultural advancement of the Japanese farmer.

e. The Japanese Imperial Government is requested to submit, in addition to the above, such other proposals it deems necessary to guarantee to agriculture a share of the national income commensurate with its contribution.

Source: David J. Lu, Japan: A Documentary History *(Armonk, NY: M. E. Sharpe, 1996), 491–92.*

development of *enterprise unions*, formed by workers in one company and focusing on issues that were primarily economic rather than political.

SCAP believed that the Japanese educational system was too centralized, as well as a faithful conduit of Japanese militarism and military values. To crush these values, SCAP issued a series of educational directives: to expunge the ideology of supernationalism from school textbooks; to screen teachers; to insist on the separation of the state from Shinto and do away with Shinto influences in education; and to ban the teaching of ethics, national history, and geography (it was thought that these had fueled Japan's aggressive militarism). For SCAP, the crowning achievement in education was its imposition of the American model. Education was transferred from a central government ministry to locally elected boards of education so that localities could control and manage education. But educational overhaul was one of the least successful of SCAP's reforms, for it flew directly in the face of longtime Japanese practices. By the time of the San Francisco conference (1951) where the peace treaty was signed, Japanese educational authorities had already begun to backtrack; some of the traditional subjects, including Confucian ethics, were making their way back to the classroom. The Ministry of Education also began to reclaim its old power of managing national education, including censoring textbooks. Finally, the Japanese would not accept the idea of locally elected school boards—which over time came to be appointed and were clearly subordinated to the Home Ministry in Tokyo.

SCAP revamped local government in the hope that it would serve "as a bulwark against a revival of the pre-war system of central control and supervision."[11] Over the kicking and screaming of the Home Ministry, which had traditionally overseen local governments and the police, SCAP gave local powers to *elected* prefectural governors and urban mayors. Elections clearly took central control away from Tokyo. In addition, the Police Law of 1947 created a small national police force and prefectural police forces that were independent of Tokyo. At the same time, the once powerful Home Ministry was abolished, replaced by the ministries of Local Autonomy, Health and Welfare, Construction, and Labor.

The flurry of reforms might have continued had not the Cold War broken out. American policymakers looked warily at the growing turmoil on the Asian continent—the war in China, tensions on the Korean peninsula, a muscle-flexing Soviet Union, and a devastated Japan—almost as an invitation to the Soviets to take advantage of the situation. The United States came to believe that under the circumstances, Japan had to be strengthened and the sometimes destabilizing reforms reversed. First and foremost, Japan needed economic recovery; reformism was transformed into reconstructionism. In this *reverse course*, reforms were slowed or halted, and plans to dissolve more zaibatsu subsidiary companies were stopped. SCAP pressed the Japanese government to revise the labor laws so that public employees would not be allowed to strike. In 1950, with SCAP encouragement, the Japanese government initiated the Red Purge to break the back of the Japan Communist Party—after MacArthur's freeing of Communist political prisoners in the early days of the occupation. About thirteen thousand alleged Communist Party members lost their jobs because "their political activities were impeding the goals of the occupation."[12] Indicative of the increasingly conservative bent of the occupation, some of those who had been purged for their wartime activities were now depurged.

The economy during the occupation was poor. Inflation was rampant and production in ravaged industries was slow to revive, a situation worsened by severe coal shortages:

> *For several years, millions of people faced starvation. Thousands actually starved to death. By the spring of 1946 poor harvests and a paralyzed rationing system had produced a serious urban food crisis. The average household spent 68 percent of its income on food in 1946. The average height and weight of elementary school children decreased until 1948.*[13]

Japan's economy was saved not by the American financiers who became Tokyo's fiscal advisors but by the Korean War—a "gift of the gods," in the words of Japanese Prime Minister Yoshida. The war meant a flood of orders from the American military to Japanese industries. From 1951 to 1953, war supplies and material comprised about 60 percent of Japan's exports. Japanese companies began to earn profits for the first time since the war, and invested them in new factories and equipment. Japan's GNP expanded at double-digit rates.

With the rebounding economic reforms becoming solidified, and with the war crisis in Korea, the United States moved to end the occupation. It had to provide assurances to the nations in Southeast Asia traumatized by Japan's wartime actions that it would act decisively to prevent the reemergence of the Japanese military. The United States also had to deal with some countries' calls for war reparation—which was jettisoned as part of the reverse course. Once these issues were resolved, diplomats from forty-eight countries met in San Francisco in September 1951 to sign the peace treaty ending the war. Two countries were notably absent: the Soviet Union, which refused to sign the treaty, and China, which was not invited because the United States and Great Britain could not agree on the real capital of China—Beijing or Taibei.

The peace treaty, the ending of the occupation, and the U.S.-Japanese security treaty took effect in April 1952. The security treaty, which put Japan under the U.S. nuclear umbrella, pledged to protect Japan against external aggression. American "land, air, and sea forces" were to continue to be stationed "in and about Japan."[14] In a throwback to the old unequal treaty days, the agreement gave U.S. servicemen who committed crimes outside military bases the right of extraterritoriality: that is, they would be tried in American courts. In addition, an historian has noted that "[w]ith the Security Treaty . . . Japan was incorporated into the Pax Americana, and this prevented her from pursuing an independent foreign policy."[15]

JAPANESE POLITICAL DEVELOPMENTS, 1952–1973: "THE MORE THINGS CHANGE . . ."

The Yoshida Years, 1948–1954

For all the trauma of war and occupation, in the Japanese political world it is the *continuity* between prewar and postoccupation events that is most noteworthy. Japanese democracy, before it was hijacked by the military in the 1930s, was caught between moderate reform impulses and Japanese political realities and processes: particularly decision making by consensus, parties largely divorced from the masses, and conservative leaders who inched forward, eschewing bold moves that might isolate them from their peers. The result was decision making and policy adoption that moved at a glacial pace.

During the occupation, prewar political parties reemerged. The Seiyūkai, the party founded by the Meiji oligarchs, became the Japan Liberal Party; its main prewar opponent, the Minseitō, was transformed into the Japanese Progressive Party and later into the Democratic Party. These parties were joined for the first time by two left-wing parties, which formed after MacArthur's early-occupation freeing of all Japanese political prisoners: the Japan Socialist Party and the Japan Communist Party (which could for the first time operate openly). The first three prime ministers still operating under the Meiji Constitution clearly displayed the conservatism of Japanese postwar governments, even though, between 1945 and 1948, the new leftist parties enjoyed surging support. The first prime minister, Higashi Kuni Naruhiko (August–October 1945), was a relative of the emperor. The second was Shidehara Kijurō (October 1945–April 1946), who had served as foreign minister in the 1920s and embraced the diplomacy of international cooperation. The third, and most famous, was Yoshida Shigeru (May 1946–May 1947), a prewar diplomat and avid supporter of the Japanese empire, who served as foreign minister in the first two postwar cabinets.

The first election after the adoption of the new constitution in 1947 went to the Japan Socialist Party, which won by a plurality and had to form a coalition with the Democratic Party. The Socialist Party won mainly because of economic troubles, especially runaway inflation, and strong support from trade unions, which flexed their muscles in the heady days before the reverse course. But its victory was a flash in the pan. The Socialists ruled for only eight months; their power crumbled because of bitter factionalism (a problem that dogged all parties of the left into the 2000s) and because of opposition by SCAP when the reverse course became policy.

Yoshida Shigeru, of the Liberal Party, picked up the pieces, serving as prime minister between October 1948 and December 1954. Yoshida had won a "liberal" tag during the occupation period because he had distanced himself from the military during the war. In essence, however, he was close to being a monarchist (and was only marginally a democrat), having married the daughter of one of the emperor's closest advisors. His prescription for ending Japan's trouble was not reform but simply returning to the goals and values of the premilitarist state, principally building a modern nation-state. In his relations with SCAP, he was cooperative yet hard-nosed, shrewdly maneuvering to secure Japan's interests when many of SCAP's moves were in America's interests. He saw early on that national recovery might best be achieved with a three-way union between his conservative party, the top ranks of the bureaucracy, and big business. In 1949 his government established the Ministry of International Trade and Industry (MITI), which would manage and guide the process leading to Japan's economic miracle. He concentrated on promoting cooperation between bureaucracy and industry.

Yoshida followed a determinedly conservative path. Under his leadership, over 10,000 men who had played significant roles in the war, plus 3,250 army and navy officers, were depurged. Ostensibly this was done to build the National Police Reserve (NPR) that Yoshida set up on MacArthur's urging. Significantly, the decision to create the NPR was not debated or even taken up in the Diet; it was established by government decree. In 1952, when the NPR became the National Security Force, the number of soldiers was raised to 110,000, many of them new depurgees. As in the 1930s, most of the men in this force had agricultural backgrounds and most had been in the Imperial Army. In the elections of 1952, hundreds of former purged politicians returned to national politics. For some it was almost as if the occupation, with its demilitarization, was a dream from which they had awoken.

Certainly the repression of the left was a carbon copy of its treatment before the war. The left included labor. In 1950 a federation of anti-Communist unions was formed—the General Council of Trade Unions of Japan (Sōhyō); initially, even MacArthur supported this organization. But it became a bitter opponent of the U.S.-Japanese security treaty and grew aggressive in the early 1950s in *workplace struggles* where workers sought a voice in issues dealing with mine and factory and nationwide wage campaigns. Yoshida, passionately anti-Communist, tended to see the unions as radical; when labor had tried to unseat him in the foiled 1947 general strike, he had described union leaders as "a gang of unruly, insolent rebels."[16] To deal with radicals, Yoshida's government in 1952 strengthened the Subversive Activities Law. In 1954, Yoshida turned back an occupation reform by recentralizing the police system. His successor, Hatoyama Ichirō continued the backtracking from occupation reforms by recentralizing the education system.

By 1954, Yoshida's star was falling. He had antagonized many, some simply with his high-handed style. The left was understandably hostile, but he was also lambasted more and more by men from his own party. He was attacked for accepting *subordinate independence* when he signed the security treaty: dissenters claimed that it violated Japanese neutrality, betrayed Japanese sovereignty, and made Japan a lightning rod for U.S. enemies. In spring 1954 a Japanese fishing boat was hit by radioactive fallout from a U.S. atomic bomb test near Bikini Atoll in the South Pacific; one Japanese man died as a result. Over thirty million Japanese signed petitions calling for a halt to all atomic tests, and a wave of anti-Americanism swept over the country. Yoshida, who was seen as close to the United States, lost political support.

In addition, Yoshida's government was implicated in an early 1954 shipping scandal in which dozens of people were accused of accepting bribes from shipping firms to pass legislation favorable to those firms. (Two later prime ministers also took bribes: Ikeda Hayato [1960–1964] and Satō Eisaku [1964–1972].) Yoshida resigned in December 1954. Most historians assert that Yoshida laid a solid foundation on which the phoenix of Japan could rise. As one scholar noted: "he introduced . . . the 'conservative establishment line' that became the fundamental framework for the Japanese political system. It rested on two pillars: Japanese dependence on the United States for its military security [and] strong emphasis on economic development while downplaying constitutional reform."[17]

Conservatism and Polarization, 1954–1960

Two of Yoshida's key opponents in the Liberal Party—Hatoyama and Kishi Nobusuke—were "intent on demolishing the pacifist and democratic post-war structure which MacArthur, with Yoshida's passive cooperation, had built up."[18] They had a rocky time, governing in a period of political instability brought on by a clash between conservative and leftist forces over a number of issues. Hatoyama (1954–1956) was determined to undo as many parts of the occupation structures as possible. He had strong "turn-the-clock-back" goals: to raise the status of the emperor to head of state; to curtail civil liberties with a constitutional amendment that would give the government emergency powers in a crisis; and to abolish Article 9. The controversy over the no-war clause had heated up when MacArthur leaned on Yoshida to set up the Self-Defense Force. Many of the depurged, now in positions of power, believed that the day was not far off when the country might be able to rearm, if only for a sense of national worth. In 1956 Hatoyama urged the Diet to establish an advisory commission on the constitution, with a view to making some of the changes he wanted. The Diet concurred, though the Japan Socialist Party boycotted the process.

The problem was that ratifying an amendment required a two-thirds majority in the Diet. Even though Japan's two largest parties, the Liberal and Democratic parties, had joined in late 1955 to form the Liberal-Democratic Party (LDP), even at its high point in controlling the Diet it would have had insufficient numbers. The LDP remained the ruling party from 1955 to 1993, making Japan for almost four decades a one-party state—at best, with several minority parties, a one-and-a-half-party state. Given its record, the party was clearly neither liberal nor democratic. It was evident that the United States much preferred a solidly conservative party as a strong fortress against the Soviet Union. The LDP quickly established itself as the voice of big business, big industry, and farmers.

Both Yoshida and Hatoyama tried to heal some of the foreign relations ruptures created by the war. Yoshida concluded a peace treaty in 1952 with Jiang Jieshi's government on Taiwan; it had no relations with the Communist regime in Beijing, both because of its strong anti-Communist position and because the United States did not recognize that regime. In 1956 Hatoyama, against much opposition within his party, set out to conclude a peace treaty with the Soviet Union. He was able only to arrange a joint declaration that normalized relations between the two countries (and as of 2007, they still had not signed a peace treaty ending the war). Japan sat on the sidelines when important Asian issues were taken up at the Geneva conference in 1954 that dealt with problems in Southeast Asia or the first Afro-Asian conference the same year in Bandung. In contrast to the prewar years, "the Japanese government was conscious of being able to exert very little, if any direct influence"; such was the depth of distrust and hostility left by the war.[19]

Kishi Nobusuke (see Identities) had served in Tōjō Hideki's wartime cabinet and had been labeled a Class A war criminal, spending more than three years in prison. He was released in late 1948, depurged in 1952, elected to the Diet in 1953, became head of the LDP, and was named prime minister in 1957—a meteoric rise. Kishi had a reputation as an effective administrator; from his wartime experience as minister of commerce, he had connections to the arenas of finance and heavy industry. From Chōshū, he was seen by his allies as "representing a traditional heritage of stalwart patriotism."[20] Kishi is best remembered for the 1960 crisis he ignited over the revision of the U.S.-Japanese security treaty; the violence that erupted in that spring and summer was the greatest in postwar Japan.

In many ways, Kishi had provoked the Japanese people with his pointedly ultraconservative policy initiatives—priming the pump, as it were, for a convulsive explosion. His first political act, introducing legislation to give police more power in handling demonstrations, caused such opposition that it was dropped. But he continued to show his political colors. He introduced a bill to permanently prevent miners and electric power industry workers from striking, and he prohibited certain classes of civil servants from unionizing. He also made it clear that he wanted to slash the power of the Japan Teachers Union and Sōhyō. These actions pitted him squarely against blue-collar and middle-class citizens. But his order to the Ministry of Education (so recently recentralized) to reintroduce the teaching of ethics in schools brought back memories of prewar patriotic indoctrination and upset many people. Nor did he reassure people when, in a report to the House of Councilors, he said that "Japan should be permitted to use nuclear weapons within the limits of the right of self-defence."[21]

According to its original terms, the security treaty expired in 1960. Kishi wanted to renew it but with a clearer stipulation of Japan's sovereignty. Many leftist groups—the Japan Socialist Party, Sōhyō, the Japan Communist Party, and the radical student organization Zengakuren—opposed the renewal of the treaty on the principle that whereas Yoshida had been constrained by the United States and by the circumstances in the

Identities: Kishi Nobusuke (1896–1987):
Greater Asianist, Class A War Criminal, Prime Minister

Son of a prefectural official of samurai stock in the former domain of Chōshū, Kishi Nobusuke was adopted by a rich uncle, giving up his birth name of Satō (his biological brother was Satō Eisaku, prime minister from 1964 to 1972). In 1920 he graduated from Tokyo Imperial University, where he was an admirer of Kita Ikki and an acquaintance of Ōkawa Shūmei, an ultrarightist theoretician. Kishi joined the Ministry of Commerce and Industry and worked his way up to the top. In 1936 he was sent to Manchukuo, where he became the industrial czar. He developed personal ties to commanders of the Guandong Army, becoming closest to Tōjō Hideki; they were linked together "through a huge political fund derived from the opium trade carried out secretly by some of the Manchukuo officials."[1]

Kishi served as vice-minister of commerce and industry in 1939–1940. When Tōjō organized his first cabinet in 1941, he named Kishi the minister of trade and industry, ordering him to increase industrial production for the war effort by strengthening governmental controls and to help establish the control of the Greater East Asia Co-Prosperity Sphere. In November 1943 the Ministry of Munitions was formed, primarily to manage more rapid production of planes; Kishi was vice-minister under Tōjō, who served as minister. His tasks ranged from munitions to slave labor. In the summer of 1944, when Saipan fell and made possible the American bombing of Japanese cities, Kishi came to believe that ending the war would be necessary because Japanese war production would be halted by the bombing campaign. He left the cabinet.

He was imprisoned as a Class A war criminal for over three years, during which time he spelled out in his diary his thoughts about being released or, alternatively, executed, but he was convinced that Japan had fought "a just war." He was never convicted and was released in late 1948. However, he was not cleared to enter the public sphere until he was depurged in April 1952. In 1953 he was elected to a seat in the House of Representatives and played a pivotal role in organizing the Japan Democratic Party, which merged in 1955 with the Liberal Party. "It was Kishi who was to transform Japanese politics under the occupation into the politics of an independent Japan, and to achieve the unity of conservative forces based largely on the strength of wartime bureaucrats."[2]

In 1957 he became prime minister. He focused on trying to make Japan a more equal partner of the United States and had visions of Japan emerging as the leading nation in Asia, an extension of his prewar Greater Asianism. As a rightist, he also worked to strengthen the state's police powers and to amend the constitution. In the security treaty crisis of 1960, Kishi emerged as a man not strongly committed to democratic methods and procedures. The furor over his actions in the dead of night to force the Diet's passage of the treaty led quickly to his resignation in June. He continued to serve in the House of Representatives. His son-in-law, Abe Shintaro, served as minister of foreign affairs under Nakasone Yasuhiro from 1982 to 1986, and his grandson, Abe Shinzō, became prime minister in September 2006.

---

[1] *Chushichi Tsuzuki*, The Pursuit of Power in Modern Japan 1825–1995 *(Oxford: Oxford University Press, 2000), 387.*

[2] *Ibid., 388.*

1950s to agree to the treaty, Kishi on his own was seeking to make subordinate independence permanent. He signed the revised treaty in Washington, D.C., in January 1960, but it had to be ratified by the Diet. From the perspective of Japan, the revised treaty was a substantial improvement over the original. Whereas the original treaty had given Japan no say about how American bases in Japan were to be used, the revision specified that prior consultations would occur between the two countries if there were significant changes in the deployment of U.S. forces or armaments. The initial treaty gave the United States the right to intervene in any large-scale internal Japanese unrest, but the revision omitted that proviso in the name of upholding Japanese national sovereignty. In addition, the revision should have quieted fears that this would become a permanent arrangement by limiting the term of the treaty to ten years. But the temper of the times was strained; any treaty would have been an emotional target, for it ignited "the basic anxieties of the whole nation."[22]

Source: Security Treaty Concerns

This statement was drawn up at the formation of the People's Council for Preventing Revision of the Security Treaty in 1959. What are the main reasons that the group did not want a security treaty between the United States and Japan?

Through the Japan–U.S. security treaty and accompanying administrative and mutual security agreements, Japan has allowed American troops to be stationed on Japanese soil and provided military bases for them.

During this period, the Korean War and conflicts over the Taiwan strait occurred. These bases have thus become American outputs, and Japan has become a participant in these conflicts.

We are heavily burdened with fear when we see these bases, which were once maintained for the purpose of protecting us, being transformed into military outposts for attack.

When we protested against Sunakawa and other military bases, the Japanese government mobilized its police forces and let their sticks rain over farmers, workers, and students who were guarding their own land. The government willingly sacrificed the demands and interests of the Japanese people in order to follow faithfully the policy of the United States.

Through these variegated experiences, we have learned that the Japan–U.S. security treaty has obligated Japan to "restrict her independence and become a participant in conflicts without the knowledge of her people." Realization of that cold reality has been the motivating force in our continuing fight for its repeal.

Now the government is attempting to revise this treaty. The revision is not for the purpose of its repeal, but for the purpose of strengthening its provisions. With this revision, Japan will be obligated to engage in joint defense and will be asked to expand and strengthen the Self-Defense Forces and to begin her own nuclear armament. Japan may become an ally of South Korea and Taiwan and willingly supply military bases for attacking China and the Soviet Union. It means denial of our constitution and destruction of the bases of peace and democracy. These are serious matters, which will impact adversely on the destiny and future of Japan and of her people.

Let us not forget that irresponsible militarism and military alliances once led us into a path of war against China and other nations of Asia. It was done against the will of our people and forced us to suffer great miseries.

The path that the Kishi Cabinet is about to take is too similar to the path that we once trod.

We unequivocally oppose the revision of the security treaty, which will only endanger peace and democracy in Japan and destroy the lives of her people.

Source: David J. Lu, Japan: A Documentary History (Armonk, NY: M. E. Sharpe, 1996), 514–15.

Security Treaty Crisis
Street demonstrations protesting the renewed security treaty between the United States and Japan. The protests against Prime Minister Kishi's government and Eisenhower's planned visit to Tokyo led to violent demonstrations and eventually to Kishi's ouster.

Kishi chose May 19 for the Diet to take up the treaty so that it would be a done deal before a state visit from U.S. President Dwight D. Eisenhower. Boisterous, determined demonstrators took to the streets in April. Then on May 1, an American spy plane was shot down over the Soviet Union. Antitreaty forces became shriller, pointing out that the presence of U.S. military bases might suck Japan into war. Kishi, determined to see the treaty through the House of Representatives, was faced with a Socialist attempt to block any action by staging a mass sit-down to prevent the House speaker from reaching the podium to conduct business. Eventually five hundred police entered the Diet, literally carried every Socialist member out, and carried the speaker sideways "[l]ike a human ramrod" to the podium, where he called for a quick vote.[23] With the Socialists boycotting the session because of what had happened, the treaty's passage was assured.

But all hell broke loose. The key newspaper *Asahi Shimbun* headlined "The LDP and Government's Undemocratic Act,"[24] and the demonstrations increased in size and intensity. When Eisenhower's press secretary came to prepare for the state visit, he had to be rescued from demonstrators at the airport by a U.S. military helicopter; Eisenhower's visit had to be canceled. In the largest uproar on June 15, tens of thousands of demonstrators battled five thousand police; a female student was crushed to death. The treaty went into effect June 20; three days later Kishi announced his resignation, and the demonstrations petered out. But national nerves were on edge. In October, they shattered even more with the assassination of the head of the Japanese Socialist Party, Asanuma Inejirō, who was stabbed to death by an ultrarightist youth during a televised speech. It seemed to many déjà vu from the 1930s.

While the treaty drama was playing itself out, the biggest labor strike in postwar Japanese history was unfolding at Mitsui's Miike mine in Kyushu. The coal mining industry was on the skids as Japanese industrialists saw oil as the key resource for industrial modernization. Miners were uneasy about their jobs. In January 1959 Mitsui announced layoffs; negotiations led nowhere. When the company announced a lockout, the miners' union responded with a strike. Another union formed and was recognized by Mitsui. In March and July violent struggles between miners from the old and new unions erupted, leading to at least one death and over 1,700 injuries. Thousands of labor sympathizers and treaty protesters came to provide support for the striking miners. The government dispatched 15,000 police troops to keep order. The 313-day strike ended with the company and the union accepting the conclusion of a conciliation board that the company's plan to lay off workers fit into the company's efforts to "rationalize" its operations. It was, in short, a defeat for labor.

自由民主党 浅...

日本社会党 ...稲次郎氏

民主社会党 西尾末広氏

Assassination   The assassination of Asanuma Inejirō, leader of Japan's Socialist Party, on a public stage in Tokyo on October 12, 1960, stirred unhappy memories of the political assassinations of the 1930s. Asanuma's assassin was a seventeen-year-old ultranationalist who committed suicide less than a month later.

THE ERA OF GOOD FEELINGS: IKEDA'S PLAN

The tumultuous year of 1960 was soon only a bad memory, overshadowed by the policies of the new prime minister, Ikeda Hayato (1960–1964). Ikeda had served in the Finance Ministry from 1925 to 1948. Elected to the Diet in 1949, he spent the years up to 1960 heading the Finance Ministry and MITI. With his obvious expertise in finance and industry, it is not surprising that his major contribution came in the economic arena. Obviously aware of the extreme politicization of issues in the late 1950s, Ikeda set out to take an apolitical path that was inclusive in its approach to possible opponents. Deemphasizing political and diplomatic issues, Ikeda initiated an *income-doubling* plan—to double GNP per person within a decade. The plan established specific goals for investment in key industries; promoted cooperation between companies, even calling for company mergers; and pledged active government guidance for private investments. Public investment went to bolster the crucial infrastructure of roads and harbors. Ikeda also lowered taxes and interest rates.

The income-doubling plan appealed to the public and was the most popular program ever introduced by an LDP government. It was remarkably successful, achieving its goal in only seven years. In the first half of the 1960s, annual GNP growth reached 10 percent and the value of exports rose an annual 15 percent. Whereas earlier Japan had exported predominantly to Asian nations, by the early 1960s its exports to Europe and North America had increased markedly. France's President Charles De Gaulle pointed to Japan's growing wealth from exports by calling Ikeda "that transistor salesman."[25] In 1964, Japan became a member of two international economic organizations, the International Monetary Fund (IMF) and the Organization for Economic Cooperation and Development (OECD). (It had been a member of the General Agreement on Trade and Tariffs [GATT] since 1955.) Japan's participation in these international bodies "marked an 'official' recognition of Japan's new economic status."[26] (For a discussion of specific elements of the economic "miracle" from the early 1950s to the 1970s, see below.)

Ikeda's success came not only from his economic policy but also from his whole governing approach. He kept a low profile in the Diet to avoid overly politicizing situations. Though Sōhyō opposed his income-doubling plan, Ikeda met with its head, practicing the politics of accommodation rather than confrontation. As part of his inclusive strategy, he sponsored environmental legislation, largely in response to increasingly active citizens' movements.

Ikeda pointedly avoided controversial issues. For example, several developments during his tenure could have led to big trouble. In 1962, the Self Defense Force purchased surface-to-air missiles. Any moves toward greater militarization could have set off protests: this did not. Nor did the announcement at about the same time of a U.S. plan to bring a nuclear-powered submarine into a Japanese harbor. Further, the public was concerned with inflation in 1963 and 1964 and the nation's most important coal mines, for many years in deep economic distress, were shut down. These actions too did not trigger protests. The clearest sign of change was that the final report of the Commission on the Constitution, set up by Hatoyama, was submitted without fanfare and filed away in mid-1964. The "Commission's missions were fact-finding, deliberation, and reporting, and did not include the recommendation of extensive revision as some of its critics maintained from the start and as some of its members argued hotly in its later deliberations."[27] The Ikeda years brought both "calm and normalcy."[28]

For the general international community and for Japanese across the country, two symbols of Ikeda's era of good feelings stand out: the Tokyo Olympics and the opening of the Shinkansen, the high-speed bullet train, both in 1964. Japan had been slated to hold the Olympics in 1940, but the world was at war and the games were canceled. The selection of Tokyo in 1964 "symbolized full acceptance of Japan into the international community"[29] and showcased the increasingly modern nation. Hosting the games provided great impetus for further economic development: huge investments helped build two new expressway systems and the bullet train. Several ironies conjured up the past: the Olympics were held in an area that had housed the American military during the occupation, and the torch bearer who ignited the Olympic flame had been born in Hiroshima prefecture on August 6, 1945, the day the atomic bomb was dropped. When the bullet train was opened, it cut the travel time between Tokyo and Osaka from more than eight hours to three hours and ten minutes, traveling at two hundred miles per hour (by 2000 the Shinkansen covered most of Honshu and part of the southern island of Kyushu and traveled at three hundred miles per hour). The bullet train was a stunning example of Japan's technological success and brought observers from around the world to study it. For the Japanese, it "brought . . . a profound change in travel patterns, business practices, and lifestyles of common people."[30]

After the rocky security treaty episode, Ikeda also wanted to repair Japan's relationship with the United States. By this time, trade problems were causing tensions to rise. The United States began to pressure Japan to liberalize its restrictions on imports, to stop giving Japanese firms export subsidies, and to modify its system of exchange controls. In response to these problems, Ikeda traveled to the United States in 1961. The two nations agreed to set up a Joint Committee on Japan-U.S. Trade and Economic Relations to deal with the issues.

SATŌ EISAKU (1964–1972): ECONOMIC GROWTH AND HEALING THE SCARS OF WAR

Ikeda withdrew from government in 1964 due to ill health. His successor, Satō Eisaku, served as prime minister for a longer term than any prime minister under both the Meiji and Shōwa constitutions. He was the brother of Kishi Nobusuke (Kishi had been adopted into another family, hence the surname difference) and shared some of Kishi's attitudes even as he continued to carry out Ikeda's economic policies. Like Kishi, he was hawkish on labor matters. In one episode, he appeared to be ready to reintroduce mythic elements from Japan's past into the body politic. In 1966 he pushed a bill to commemorate the anniversary of the accession to the throne by the mythical first emperor, Jimmu. Attempting to revive the Shinto myth brought forth a hue and cry from non-LDP Diet members; the bill passed when the government decided to call the anniversary the Day to Commemorate the Founding of the State. Celebrated first on February 11, 1967, it has, as one writer noted, "become the day not to unite but to divide the nation." Troubling also was Satō's 1930s-sounding statement that the day should celebrate "community consciousness as a race."[31]

Like Ikeda, Satō had headed the Finance Ministry and MITI, so his experience in government and business had put him in a good position to manage what turned out to be a record-breaking eight years. It was under Satō that Japan's GNP became the third largest in the world. From the early 1950s until 1972, Japan's annual GNP growth rate was 9.3 percent (West Germany's at the time was 5.5 percent). By the

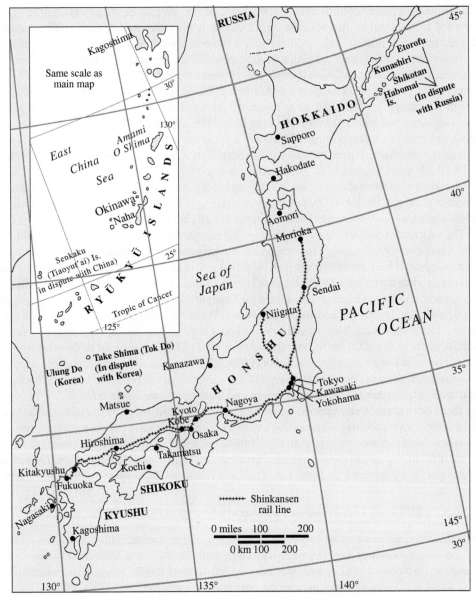

Map 14-1   Postimperial Japan with Bullet Train Lines.

end of Satōs term of office, "Japan co uld lay claim to being an advanced industrial nation, with a level of per capita income half that of the United States and ahead of those of some European countries."[32]

It is in foreign relations that Satō is probably best remembered. No country had harder feelings against Japan than Korea. The postwar occupation of the northern sector of the peninsula by the Soviet Union and the southern sector by the United States had frozen because of the Cold War, so that by 1950,

Opening the Olympics   In the 1964 Tokyo Olympics, Japan stepped back onto the international stage after the disasters of the war years. Fittingly, holding the Olympic torch was Yoshinori Sakai, who was born at Hiroshima on August 6, 1945, when the atomic bomb was dropped on the city.

when the Korean War erupted (see Chapter 15), there were two separate countries. From the early 1960s on, the United States had pushed its two Northeast Asia allies, Japan and the Republic of Korea (South Korea), to normalize their relations. Trade had brought the two economically close: South Korean imports from Japan totaled $162 million in 1963, fully 30 percent of all of Korea's imports. There were also other financial connections: between 1961 and 1965, Japanese companies supplied 67 percent of South Korea's ruling party's budget. In April 1965, the two countries signed a peace treaty normalizing diplomatic relations. The agreement was controversial in Korea "because it ended the possibility of future claims against Japan"—like those of comfort women.[33] As part of the normalization, Japan gave South Korea a direct grant of $300 million plus loans of $200 million; private Japanese firms invested $300 million in South Korean enterprises. Relations between Japan and North Korea as of 2007 had not yet been normalized.

Satō was determined to regain Okinawa for Japan. Lost in the vicious fighting from April to June 1945, with a staggering loss of life, Okinawa had become a pivotal military base for the United States and, more importantly, a staging area for its war in Vietnam. For Japan it was an ongoing reminder of World War II and the shattering of the Japanese nation. Satō reportedly said in 1965 that "until the restitution of Okinawa is realized, our 'post-war' will continue."[34] Negotiations between Japan and the United States began in early 1970, though discussions had been proceeding for years. The United States got Japan to agree that its military bases would remain in Okinawa and that in an emergency the United States might bring in nuclear weapons, two concessions that Okinawans found hard to accept. Be that as it may, Okinawa reverted to Japanese control in 1972.

Okinawa was not the only sticking point between Japan and the United States; there was also Japan's rapidly accelerating tendency to "shift from protection and obedience to competition and confrontation" with the United States.[35] Trade tensions were constant, and there was an ongoing possibility that misunderstandings in that arena would complicate overall relations. In a 1969 meeting, Satō discussed putting voluntary restraints on the textiles that Japan exported to the United States. U.S. negotiators understood

Source: The Shinkansen (Bullet Train)

This is an excerpt from a 1964 memoir (When We Built the Shinkansen) *by the chief engineer of the Shinkansen, Fujishima Shigeru. What attitudes about Japan and modernization are evident here?*

. . . When we started building the Shinkansen, we did not even question that it had to be an electric train. The technology of using alternate current that we introduced in 1957 became very useful. . . .

Each advance we make in our technological development becomes a building block for the next step. For our technology to come to its fruition, we need a clear-cut and justly determined direction. Without it, everything will be in vain.

Technicians in the railways share a common dream. That is speed. How to build a train that can be operated safely while obtaining a high speed? In this sense, the notion of the Shinkansen was not born overnight. After the war when the National Railways restarted its operations, some of us engineers began to talk about our shared dream.

It looks almost comical now when we look back to the time when we had our test run be-

tween the two stations of Mishima and Numazu. When the speedometer registered 120 kilometers per hour, those senior members who were gazing intently at the speedometer suddenly burst into a chorus of "Banzai." In the National Railways, senior colleagues are always there to share their joys with younger technicians and give them encouragement. . . .

In Japan, to a degree we can do almost everything with things we have within our borders. We have enough technological abilities in our related industries. If we have a problem, we can ask them for help, and they will do their best to respond. We speak of the National Railways' technology. But in the final analysis, it is the industrial capability of the country that has made it possible for us to create the Shinkansen. I think that is the reason people from overseas speak so highly of the Shinkansen.

Source: David J. Lu, Japan: A Documentary History *(Armonk, NY: M. E. Sharpe, 1996), 534–35.*

that Satō had vowed to initiate such restraints. When the Japanese did not do so, the Nixon administration was upset, continuing to apply pressure until 1971, when voluntary restraints were introduced.

The United States, in turn, upset the Japanese with what were referred to as *Nixon shocks.* The first shock was Nixon's July 1971 announcement of his upcoming trip to the People's Republic of China. The United States neither consulted with nor informed Japan, omissions that flabbergasted the Japanese—who had always thought that they should have a relationship with the Beijing government but had deferred because of their alliance with the United States. The second shock came a month later, when Nixon announced that he was devaluing the dollar against the yen, ending its fixed convertibility to gold, and placing surcharges on certain Japanese imports. This action roiled Japan's financial markets and caused severe monetary inflation—the first downturn since the rise of Japan's economic phoenix.

WHY THE ECONOMIC "MIRACLE"?

One analyst has suggested that Japan's economic advances from 1953 to 1973 were "more like a thoroughly well-organized expedition than like a miracle; more like the performance of a well-trained team in an athletic contest than like that of a conjurer."[36] What were the secrets of Japan's success? First, it is crucial to see that Japan's postwar phoenixlike economic flowering was not a sudden development. From the Meiji period on, Japan had enjoyed economic successes and built on them. Between the two world wars, Japan's industrial output soared 600 percent (at the same time, the U.S. increase was 66 percent).[37] The

The Bullet Train The bullet train (Shinkansen), a symbol of Japan's technological expertise and postwar modernization and renewal, streaks by Mount Fuji.

1930s saw rapid growth in industries that served as a base for further industrial growth: metals, engineering, and chemicals.

World War II itself may have contributed to Japan's postwar boom. One scholar has even referred to the war in this context as the "useful war."[38] It obviously spurred science and engineering for Japanese needing war materiel and equipment. During the war, many small and medium-sized businesses were organized, helping to create what has been called a *dual structured* economy: government guided the large industrial and business stratum that sat atop a stratum of smaller, less efficient, often family-owned businesses. The war was useful in other ways as well. The widespread destruction made it necessary in many cases to start all over; that meant that the new buildings would house up-to-date equipment and utilize the most modern approaches. Further, the demolition of the Japanese empire (which Japan had relied on for resources, labor, and markets) meant that Japan had to, and had the opportunity to, develop new markets and marketing strategies. Freed from the old system, Japan could launch new projects more boldly.

Japan's occupation and its relationship to the United States also contributed to its rapid industrial and economic development. Through the United States, Japan had access to advanced technology and received considerable financial and technical support. The special procurements of the U.S. military during the Korean War jump-started an economy that, if not floundering, was at best sluggish. The United States provided Japan with a wide open market, first in textiles, later in electronics and automobiles. In addition, the United States assisted Japan in the international economic sphere, sponsoring Japan for GATT membership in the mid-1950s and convincing non-Communist countries to open up their markets to Japanese exports. Finally, and perhaps most important, the U.S. pledge to protect Japan after the inclusion of Article 9 in its constitution meant that Japan was not burdened by the need to spend inordinate sums for military defense.

But by far the most important reasons for Japan's economic success were the nature, goals, and functioning of the Japanese system, known from the 1950s to the 1980s as *Japan, Inc.* First was the structure and nature of the economy. Since the 1930s and the gearing up for war, the system has been called "laissez faire in a box."[39] In it, the government played a key role in directing or administratively guiding industry. Government ministries were involved in this effort during the 1930s and 1940s; after 1949, the strong central MITI focused on specific industries to support and direct. When economic emphases and goals shifted, MITI targeted different industries. Government, industry, and business, rather than being strange bedfellows, were intimately involved and mutually supportive. This system has been described in many ways; perhaps one of the best is to see Japan as a "plan-rational as opposed to a market-rational state."[40] Apart from MITI planning, other government policies helped to engineer success: they obstructed foreign imports, implemented high tariffs, and enacted complex rules and regulations, thereby protecting Japanese industry.

Since 1960, cooperation between the Japanese workforce and management has also been key. From 1960 to 1980, scholars have noted how the transformation of Japanese agriculture provided a growing labor force for business and industry. During this period, the farm population dropped from about 36 percent of the national total to only 6 percent: many people left farming altogether, while others cut back on farming and supplemented their income with businesses. Workers were generally well educated (over 90 percent of Japanese graduated from high school and 40 percent from colleges and universities). They were skilled, disciplined, and extraordinarily hard-working—motivated by an ardent work ethic. From the 1960s on, management-labor relations were generally harmonious, with workers showing commitment and loyalty to their firms, which bestowed on them lifetime employment, a wage system based on seniority, and benefits through company unions. Workers took on the identity of their firms. One writer claims that "the single most important ingredient in Japan's success is the Japanese attitude toward work. The individual worker brings to his job a set of attitudes [conformity, group loyalty, and a sense of national uniqueness] and expectations that make him the perfect company man."[41]

Other management and operational factors contributed to Japan's success as well. Many firms functioned as keiretsu, a group of firms networked together; they were a later generation of the prewar zaibatsu. Most of them were centered on a bank. A keiretsu "include[d] a trust bank, an insurance company, an international trade firm, a real estate entity, and manufacturing firms, especially steelmaking, shipbuilding, electrical manufacturing, coal mining, automaking, beer brewing, and precision equipment making."[42] The keiretsu provided a venue for cooperation between firms and coordinated business planning and execution.

Japan's lifeline was its exports. Japanese companies, while relying on the government for guidance and support of various kinds, also used approaches and methods that made Japanese products desired around the world. Important was the emphasis on *quality control* (QC). Before the war and into the 1950s, Japanese products had had a reputation for shoddiness. During the occupation, an American consultant from the U.S. Bureau of the Budget, W. Edward Deming, introduced to the Japanese the idea and process of QC. It became a byword in Japanese industry and changed the perception of Japanese goods, giving them a reputation for quality workmanship.

To further increase the success of their products, Japanese firms adopted the most advanced and innovative technology, and they invested heavily in research and development. In the early 1980s, 6 percent of Japanese sales were plowed into research and development (as opposed to 1 percent in the United States at the time), allowing Japanese firms to make much greater use of automation in manufacturing. They were also ready to undertake long-term planning and were willing to accept lower profits in the present to gain greater profits in the future.

For investment monies, Japan had relied on the extraordinary savings rate of its people. In 1990, for example, the savings per household in Japan totaled $71,016; in the United States, by contrast, they were $28,125 (slightly less than 40 percent of Japan's). Reasons offered for these high saving rates included cultural factors (thrift), the bonus system (in which the firm shares its profits with its workers), insufficient social security, expensive housing, and costly education.

Finally, linked to business in Japan is a deep sense of public service. This may have grown out of the Hōtoku and Shingaku movements of the Tokugawa period (see Chapter 5), when one's occupational position was seen as a service to society and the state. "In contrast to U.S. businesspeople who tend[ed] to regard property rights as sacred, Japanese businesspeople consider[ed] property rights to be secondary to social needs and regard[ed] business companies as public entities that must meet social needs."[43] Statistics underscore the difference between the two countries in this regard: in 1982, the CEO of Toyota made $1.3 million, while Ford's CEO collected $7.3 million; and in 1990, the typical Japanese executive made about six times what the average Japanese employee earned, while the U.S. executive made about ninety-three times more than his or her U.S. employee.

THE NEW ACTIVISM

By the late 1960s and early 1970s, the bleakness of the occupation period and its aftermath had ended. Whether one was among the most financially successful, called by one writer the "new rich," or in the middle class as a *salaryman* (white collar worker), or a blue-collar worker, everyone had his or her version of the "good life."[44]

In the late 1950s, it was said, everyone wanted to have the three s's—a senpuki, sentaku, *and* suihanki *(electric household fan, electric washing machine, and electric rice cooker). A few years later consumer desires turned to three k's—*ka, kura, *and* kara terebi *(car, home air conditioner, and color television—while a more chic triad of j's—jewels, jet vacations overseas, and a* jutaku *(a splendid modern house)—set the tone for the 1970s.[45]*

Source: The Lifestyle of the Salaryman and His Family

As Japan's economy expanded amid Ikeda's income-doubling plan of the early 1960s, the salaryman (white-color employee) became a focus of sociological study in contemporary Japanese society. Here the U.S. scholar Ezra Vogel describes the daily life of a salaryman's family in the Tokyo suburb of Mamachi.

In addition to the frugal use of double-duty household facilities and to obtaining free services from go-betweens and friends, various customs serve to conserve possessions. Shoes are not worn inside the house since they bring in dirt and mar the floors. Only stockinged feet or bare feet are permitted on the straw mats which are swept every day. These mats can be re-covered once every year or two, but even a replacement is not expensive. Covers are used for all items of furniture including the cushions one sits on. The most valuable dolls are kept in glass cases and may be preserved for more than one generation. Television sets, electric toasters, and other appliances come with covers which are carefully placed over the equipment when not in use. Machines are not discarded so long as they can be repaired. Even paperback books come with extra covers, and hardback book are sold with a protecting cardboard box as well as a thin paper cover. At home and even for neighborhood shopping, the wife wears a white apron which covers not only the skirt as in the West but her blouse and sleeves as well. The child going to nursery school wears an apron as part of the uniform so that his regular clothes will not get dirty. Children of grade school age wear shorts and long stockings even in thirty for forty degree winter weather. While the families regard this simply as a custom, the wearing of shorts does make it possible to avoid worry about patched knees. Even though the women save by doing their own sewing, it is considered embarrassing to wear in public anything that is patched. Nylon hose, however, are mended, since this mending does not show. Old clothes are worn at home, and clothes which are beyond repair are cut up and sewn to make washcloths, hot pads, and rags. . . .

Younger children may protest about wearing hand-me-downs but the pattern is still fairly widespread, particularly in families which cannot easily afford to buy new clothes. It is perfectly permissible to wear the same clothes for several days in succession, and school uniforms make it possible for a child with only one or two suits to be well dressed throughout the school year. These frugal practices make it possible to conserve resources and live on little income, in a manner not too different from that of a few decades ago in the United States, and in Europe today.

Source: Ezra Vogel, Japan's New Middle Class *(Berkeley: University of California Press, 1968), 80–81.*

Mishima Yukio One of the mid-twentieth-century's most popular authors, Mishima Yukio, was an ultranationalist who despaired of Japan's political and economic direction after the war. He set up his own militia and won the right to train with Japan's Self-Defense Force. He committed seppuku in the office of a general at military headquarters on November 25, 1970, an act that shocked the nation.

During the occupation and its aftermath, people necessarily focused on their own and their family's survival and well-being. With the new affluence of the late 1960s and the 1970s, they had the time and interest to address and protest about pressing social, environmental, and political issues. Student demonstrations over college- and university-related issues (tuition, admissions policies, and the roles of faculty) exploded in 1968 at 115 institutions and then subsided. When the U.S.-Japanese security treaty came up for renewal in 1970, Japanese leaders were nervous about possible unrest, especially because of the widespread opposition of many Japanese to the Vietnam War. In 1965 a coalition of about 500 grassroots citizens' groups joined in the Citizen's Federation: Peace to Vietnam (*Beheiren*); it was dissolved in 1974 after the U.S. military left Vietnam. But between 1967 and 1970, an estimated 18 million people joined anti–Vietnam War protests. As for protests against the automatic extension of the security treaty, an estimated 770,000 people participated in the largest demonstration.[46]

But it was not only "big-ticket" political issues that caused people to lobby or protest. The rapid postwar industrialization had wreaked havoc on the environment and then on people in affected areas: polluted water produced tragic chemical poisoning episodes, and smog-filled air led to asthma outbreaks. The quality of water and air were the most obvious targets for protestors, who demanded that these issues be addressed to better the quality of life for the Japanese populace (for details on the pollution issue, see Chapter 20). Student activists joined farmers in a long protest over the construction of Narita airport from 1969 until 1978, when the airport, some forty miles east of Tokyo, finally opened. At issue were highhanded government efforts to force farmers to sell their land for the airport. In another airport story, protest demonstrators in Okinawa were able to block construction of an airport that would have destroyed an endangered species of coral.

Many citizen action and consumer groups were formed by housewives, who protested rising food prices, traffic congestion, inadequate disposal of garbage, the building of nuclear power plants near residential areas, and incidents around U.S. military bases. These groups called for monitoring of product safety and better public housing. In all these cases, citizens took the lead in addressing issues that the government in Tokyo had ignored. The new activism suggested a maturing of Japanese democracy and was a positive force amid widespread Japanese consumerism.

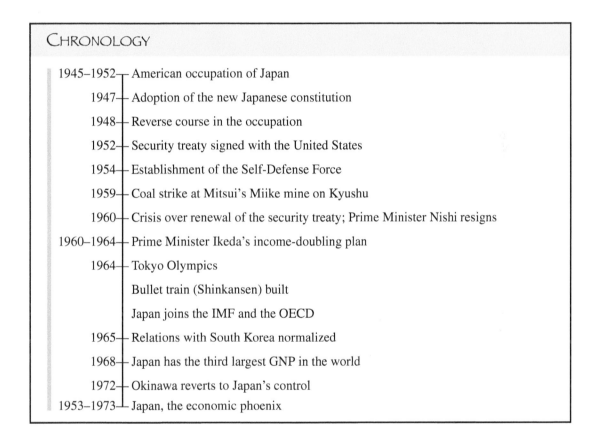

CHRONOLOGY

1945–1952	American occupation of Japan
1947	Adoption of the new Japanese constitution
1948	Reverse course in the occupation
1952	Security treaty signed with the United States
1954	Establishment of the Self-Defense Force
1959	Coal strike at Mitsui's Miike mine on Kyushu
1960	Crisis over renewal of the security treaty; Prime Minister Nishi resigns
1960–1964	Prime Minister Ikeda's income-doubling plan
1964	Tokyo Olympics
	Bullet train (Shinkansen) built
	Japan joins the IMF and the OECD
1965	Relations with South Korea normalized
1968	Japan has the third largest GNP in the world
1972	Okinawa reverts to Japan's control
1953–1973	Japan, the economic phoenix

SUGGESTED READINGS

Dore, Ronald. *Shinohata: A Portrait of a Japanese Village.* London: Allen Lane, 1978. Based on the author's visits to this village near Tokyo from the 1950s to the 1970s, this book showcases customs, social and political structures, and daily life as it describes the impact of rapid economic change on rural life.

Dower, John. *Embracing Defeat: Japan in the Wake of World War II.* New York: W.W. Norton, 2000. A well-written study of Japan's evolution under the American occupation, depicting the general mix of American innovation and Japanese tradition, with all their procedural contradictions and ironies.

Johnson, Chalmers. *MITI and the Japanese Miracle: The Growth of Industrial Policy, 1925–1975.* Stanford, CA: Stanford University Press, 1985. A cogent view of the management of Japan's industrial boom overseen and guided by this cabinet ministry, using what the author calls a "plan-rational" approach.

Mishima Yukio. *The Sea of Fertility*. New York: Alfred A Knopf, 1972–1974. Mishima's magnum opus, this fascinating tetralogy traces the history of Japan from the author's perspective from the early Taishō period to 1970. Its components are *Spring Snow* (early Taishō period), *Runaway Horses* (the 1930s), *The Temple of Dawn* (1950s and 1960s), and *The Decay of the Angel* (1970).

Vogel, Ezra. *Japan's New Middle Class: The Salaryman and His Family in a Tokyo Suburb*. Berkeley: University of California Press, 1963. Based on fieldwork from 1958 to 1960, this is an interesting and informative study of family and community life and values in the suburb of Mamachi.

CHAPTER FIFTEEN

The Korean Tragedy:
War and Identity, 1945–1979

Japanese defeat in August 1945 meant Korean liberation. Among the Koreans, jubilation was mixed with explosions of hatred and anger at what Japanese rule had done to the country and its people. A Korean recalled the time:

> *I remember the bonfires. . . . Many Shinto shrines quickly became objects of that anger. Crowds rushed up the steps, past the [t]orii gates, carrying axes and ropes. They tore down the wooden shrines, hacked them to pieces, and right there on the wide courtyards, they burned them to the ground.*[1]

THE KOREAN PEOPLE'S REPUBLIC AND ITS DEMISE

At war's end, the Koreans moved to establish their first free and independent government since the 1870s. In 1944, a famous left-wing nationalist, Yŏ Un-hyŏng, organized an underground Alliance for Korean Independence. When the Japanese asked him in mid-August 1945 to set up a political body to maintain order after their defeat, Yŏ established the Committee for the Preparation of Korean Independence. This committee formed branches (*people's committees*) throughout the country, from provincial capitals to small villages. On September 6, several hundred people from the capital and the provincial committees met in Seoul to form the Korean People's Republic (KPR) and to call for major social reforms. They wanted to have a free Korean government in operation before the American occupation forces landed, "both to show that Koreans could run their own affairs and to forestall either a prolonged American tutelage or the installation in power of other Koreans who might gain American favor."[2]

Source: People's Committees and Polarization

When people's committees began to be formed in the closing days of World War II, they were seen in many areas as an expression of grassroots democracy. This anecdote says otherwise and points to the deep polarization that developed under the Japanese regime. Kim Sŏng-su, referred to here, was a famous nationalist entrepreneur, educator, and newspaperman. What happened to this young man? What was he accused of when he chose to stop attending meetings?

Right after the surrender, some friends of mine who were Communists came up to me and said that a People's Committee was being set up, and invited me to join. At that time no one thought there was anything wrong with their being Communists—we were all the same during the Japanese occupation—we were all working for independence. I guess they wanted my name because I had some following among veterans [Koreans who had served in the Japanese Army]. It sounded like a good idea to form the committees, so I went to a couple of the meetings. They got many other people to attend the same way. Then, when they started denouncing landlords and making false charges against prominent people like Kim Sŏng-su, I decided that this was not something I wanted to be associated with, so I stopped going. Then my former "friends" came to me and tried to convince me that I should continue attending. When I refused, they drew a gun on me and told me they would shoot me if I didn't. However, I knew that they would be afraid to shoot me because my friends among the veterans knew who they were and would retaliate, so I told them to go ahead and shoot. After that, they went away and spread rumors about how I was cooperating with landlords and pro-Japanese.

Source: Joungwon Alexander Kim, Divided Korea: The Politics of Development, 1945–1972 *(Cambridge, MA: Harvard University Press, 1976), 50.*

A look at the backgrounds of the leaders elected by the September 6 assembly offers insights into the nature of this indigenous Korean leadership. Of the sixty-two (out of eighty-seven) leaders on whom we have data, thirty-nine (63 percent) had been imprisoned by the Japanese for political crimes. Only a few had collaborated. Between 1945 and 1948, the crucial consideration in judging Korean identity was the role a person had played under Japanese rule: did he collaborate or resist? The answer to that question sometimes led to assassinations and, at the least, to being politically persona non grata. Further, figures show that KPR participants belonged to two distinct generations whose life experiences led to different political approaches and outlooks. "The average age of nationalists and rightists was sixty-six, while that of leftists and communists was forty-seven. This striking difference clearly delineates the tendency of young Korean patriots in the 1920s and 1930s to turn to communism as a remedy for their country's predicament."[3]

The people's committees proliferated across the peninsula, "mark[ing] a period of rural participation unmatched in Korean history before or since."[4] This widespread political activism underscored the apparent readiness of Koreans at every social and economic level to take control of their public lives in order to deal effectively with longtime grievances. The platform of one people's committee in South Kyŏngsang province on the peninsula's southeast tip revealed their vision of a social and political revolution: Japanese-held property would be returned to Koreans; workers would control factories and farmers the land; and men and women would have equal rights. It was a strikingly auspicious beginning to life liberated from the Japanese.

LAYING THE GROUNDWORK FOR DISASTER, 1945–1948

But it was not to be. Just as the machinations of China, Japan, and Russia had prevented Korea from operating as a free and independent state in the late nineteenth and early twentieth centuries, in the late 1940s the Soviet Union and the United States, as occupying powers, once again subjected Korea to outside control. But it was even worse, for now Korea was divided, and the one nation it had been for a millennium was no more. As one historian has noted, "There was no historical justification for Korea's division: if any East Asian country should have been divided it was Japan (like Germany, an aggressor). Instead Korea, China, and Vietnam were all divided in the aftermath of World War II."[5] Further, there was no internal logical rationale for choosing the thirty-eighth parallel as the dividing line between the occupiers to the north (the Soviet Union) and to the south (the United States). Two army colonels, given half an hour to choose the dividing line, selected the thirty-eighth parallel so that Seoul would be in the southern zone. The Soviets did not contest the decision.

Although no one could foresee that the line would become the permanent boundary between two separate Korean states, its placement was a bane to the Koreans. The northern zone had 55 percent of the peninsula's land area and a population of about 9.5 million; the southern zone had 45 percent of the land area but a population of 15.9 million. The south produced 63 percent of the country's food grains and contained almost all of the peninsula's light industry but only 24 percent of its heavy industry. Electric power plants on the Yalu River in the north produced 99.5 percent of the country's electricity; without sufficient power in the south, many factories had to be shut down. Further, all the chemical fertilizer production was in the north. Without fertilizers, agricultural production in the south declined steeply, resulting in food shortages.

When the Soviet occupation of the north began in August 1945, military authorities recognized the legality of the KPR and the people's committees and began to work with them. American forces under General John Reed Hodge, hero of the war's Okinawa campaign, landed at Inch'ŏn on September 8. Like bulls in a china shop, they made insensitive and costly blunders early on, announcing that seventy thousand Japanese personnel—generally hated by Koreans—would stay on temporarily to facilitate the transition to the occupation. Open Korean resentment and anger led Hodge to remove the Japanese governor-general on September 12; however, incredibly, as late as January 1946, there were still about sixty Japanese personnel serving in important positions.

U.S. occupation forces aimed to reinforce the status quo and steer away from reform. Hodge established the United States Army Military Government in Korea (USAMGIK) as the southern zone's sole government. "Within one week Americans in Seoul, who had never met a Korean, decided that they knew which Korean political leaders they liked"[6]—conservative figures from the newly formed Korean Democratic Party, whose base consisted of wealthy landowners. They refused to recognize and indeed outlawed the leftist-coalition KPR and the people's committees, labeling them Communist front organizations. USAMGIK began systematically to suppress the people's committees, stimulating a tidal wave of opposition among the Koreans, who rose in rebellion in four provinces in the fall of 1946. Yŏ Un-hyŏng, founder of the KPR (see Identities), was flabbergasted by the U.S. policy. He stated:

> *Everything should be decided by general popular election. . . . I am not afraid of Communists. But I do not think that the theory of the extreme left is right. Those who think that the "People's Republic" is Red, are like first grade primary students. If we are divided we cannot build our nation. But if we unite, we can.*[7]

His voice went unheard by the United States.

Identities: Yŏ Un-hyŏng (1885–1947): Nationalist, Populist, Favorite of the Korean People

Born in a small town near Seoul in 1885, the son of a poor yangban, Yŏ studied at an English-language school popular with many young Koreans interested in progressive reforms at the turn of the twentieth century. He spent the years 1914 to 1930 in Shanghai. One of the leaders of the New Korea Youth Organization (NKYO) in Shanghai in 1918, Yŏ heard an unofficial representative of Woodrow Wilson speak about national self-determination at the Pan Pacific Conference and became excited about the possibility of Korean self-determination. During the March First Movement, the NKYO, through an office in the French concession, was instrumental in reporting developments in Korea to the Chinese and foreign news offices. Yŏ helped to establish the Korean Provisional Government in Shanghai in April 1919.

Like many other young Korean nationalists, Yŏ was attracted by the success of the Russian Revolution. In 1922 he and Kim Kyu-sik, a provisional government minister who had been sent to Paris in 1919 to lobby for Korea at the Versailles Conference, traveled to Moscow to attend the Congress of the Toilers of the East. On his return to China, he helped convene the National Representative Conference in Shanghai, an attempt to unify anti-Japanese Koreans scattered among China, Manchuria, Siberia, and the United States. Although 113 delegates representing 61 organizations attended, they did not become unified. During the mid-1920s, Yŏ met both Sun Yixian and Mao Zedong and propagandized for the Chinese Nationalists during the Northern Expedition. In 1929, Japanese agents in Shanghai seized him for anti-Japanese activities and spirited him off to a Taejon prison. Following his three-year imprisonment, he became the editor of the *Chungang Ilbo (Central Daily)* in Seoul.

At war's end, he was, according to one historian, "the closest thing that Korea had to a populist, in his role as an educated man who was also a favorite of the common people."[1] Handsome and articulate, he was a charismatic figure; with his "dashing white hair and mustache, he gained the nickname 'the Silver Axe.'"[2] A Western writer described him this way: "What an amazing Korean he was . . . grey fedora, grey tweed overcoat, grey flannel trousers, well-taylored [sic] tweed coat, blue shirt with clean collar and neatly tied foreinhand [sic] looking for all the world as tho' he were headed off for a date at the Greenwich Country Club."[3] His political views were a combination of "Christianity, democracy, and socialism."[4] Though favorable to the left, he never joined the Communist Party.[5] Under the U.S. occupation, he worked tirelessly to bring the left and right together and to end any north-south division. His founding of the KPR stained him Communist red in the eyes of the American military, who

also claimed that he had collaborated with the Japanese. Though, over time, occupation commanders came to see him more as a moderate leftist who could be worked with, Yŏ was never able to put together the left-right coalition he sought to deal with the problems of the occupation. Because of his efforts to work with the left, rightists distrusted and worked to destroy him. In March 1947 they attacked his home with grenades, causing great damage. On July 19, 1947, "a hot, dusty day," he was assassinated by a rightist who was never caught. Yŏ's death was a serious blow to the hope of wedding left and right to form a unified nation-state. Although the search was continued by Kim Kyu-sik and later under UN auspices, it ended in the tragedy of war and what (at least as of 2007) seemed a permanent division.

---

[1] Bruce Cumings, *"Conclusion: Liberation and Reconciliation in Korea,"* Korea Under the American Military Government, 1945–1948, *ed. Bonnie B. C. Oh (Westport, CT: Praeger, 2002), 156.*

[2] *Joungwon Alexander Kim,* Divided Korea: The Politics of Development, 1945–1972 *(Cambridge, MA: Harvard University Press, 1976), 44.*

[3] *Bruce Cumings,* The Origins of the Korean War, *Vol. 1 (Princeton, NJ: Princeton University Press, 1981), 535n.*

[4] *Bruce Cumings,* Korea's Place in the Sun *(New York: W. W. Norton, 2005), 191.*

[5] *This is the position of Cumings,* Korea's Place in the Sun, *191. Kim,* Divided Korea, *43, claims that Yo joined the Korean Communist Party, formed in Shanghai.*

While southern people's committees were being squashed, in October 1945, the military governments in both zones introduced two protégés who would play crucial political roles in the years ahead. The Soviet occupation introduced Kim Il-sung (1912–1994), a Soviet army captain and a hero among anti-Japanese guerrillas in Manchuria—such a thorn in the Japanese side, in fact, that they had put a price on his head. The United States put forward Syngman Rhee (Yi Sŭng-man, 1875–1965), a longtime prominent nationalist who had lived in the United States for many years; he was promoted by the U.S. Central Intelligence Agency (CIA) over State Department reservations. Within a very short time, both men emerged as the leading political stars in their respective zones of occupation.

EMERGENCE OF THE STATES OF NORTH KOREA AND SOUTH KOREA

Ominously, the military regimes in the north and south quickly moved in sharply divergent directions. The Soviet occupiers were politically savvy: they stayed in the background, letting Korean leaders run the show and making sure that they had been heavily involved in the anti-Japanese resistance. By February 1946, a provisional government headed by Kim Il-sung was operating. After purging those who collaborated with the Japanese, authorities undertook a vigorous program of radical reforms. In March the regime launched land reform: Japanese-held land and most of the lands of five thousand Korean landlords were confiscated and distributed to landless tenant farmers.[8] The regime nationalized key industries: by August 1946 about 90 percent of industries were state-owned. The government also sponsored labor reforms: an eight-hour workday, higher salaries, equal pay for men and women, and social security insurance. Efforts to ensure women's equality included outlawing female infanticide, prostitution, and concubinage. In many ways, the reform program reflected the spirit of KPR ideals and appealed to reformers and non-Communist leftists in general.

In the south, USAMGIK adopted rightist policies, treating the legacy of collaboration as if it did not exist. It built an army and a police force composed mostly of men who had formerly worked with the Japanese. In an interview, Yŏ Un-hyŏng, the leading figure in the establishment of the KPR and a tireless worker to bring left and right together (see Identities), argued that much of the growing animosity of Koreans in the south against the United States was due to "the American retention of the colonial police."[9] In February 1946, Syngman Rhee set up the Representative Democratic Council, considered by USAMGIK the first step toward a provisional government. No land reform was undertaken in the south until March 1948; then it involved only former Japanese-held land (less than 20 percent of the total land) and did not deal with serious problems of landlordism, primarily because the Koreans on whom the United States relied included many large landholders—in the words of one scholar, "like the old yangban aristocracy."[10] When a general strike of railroad workers in the fall of 1946 led to widespread insurrection in much of the south, the U.S. army, supporting Korean police and army troops, suppressed it. USAMGIK frowned on labor unions and strikes, instantly and invariably attributing them to Communist activity. On Cheju Island off the southern coast, the people's committee had developed into a de facto government; Seoul's attempts to suppress it produced widespread guerrilla warfare against government forces. The southern regime's quashing of the movement destroyed about 60 percent of the island's villages (230 of 400) and left tens of thousands of islanders dead.

When both armies of occupation set out to do their work, there were no plans for the emergence of separate states. The United States and the Soviet Union had agreed in December 1945 that a five-year four-power trusteeship should be set up (the other trustees being China and Great Britain), with both countries joining in a commission to oversee the formation of a unified provisional Korean government. Koreans generally opposed a trusteeship, wondering why they should spend yet more time under foreign rule. The joint U.S.-Soviet commission made no headway in its 1946 and 1947 meetings, a situation increasingly worsened by the rapidly developing Cold War. More serious, policies and events in the two occupation zones pushed them further and further apart; in the south, the establishment of an interim national assembly made a two-state peninsula more likely. In 1947 the United States took the Korean issue to the UN, which established a commission to oversee elections to form an independent Korean government. When the Soviet Union, which had opposed the measure in the UN, refused to let the commission into its northern zone, the UN gave a tragic go-ahead to hold elections only in the south. Kim Il-sung's regime denounced the decision as an American attempt "to cut through the middle, chop off the arms and legs of our homogeneous nation and tramp down our beautiful land with iron boots of imperialism."[11]

In the elections held in May 1948, 95.5 percent of registered voters voted. While some have seen this as a great victory for democracy, others have pointed out that Koreans were required to vote or they would lose their food rations.[12] The Republic of Korea (ROK) was inaugurated on August 15, 1948, with Syngman Rhee as president. As fiercely anti-Communist as he was nationalistic, Rhee suppressed all opposition, calling it Communist-inspired or -led; his autocratic regime, according to U.S. records, held 21,458 political prisoners in December 1947 and up to 30,000 by late 1949. Four-fifths of all court cases were brought against "Communists." Rhee was a strong, obstinate leader, no ventriloquist's dummy for the United States.

If Rhee struck out at leftists in general, the regime of Kim Il-sung struck with a vengeance against rightists. His party, the North Korean Workers' Party, dominated the political scene, even though a number of factions contended for power. Kim's natural power base was the Korean People's Army, established in February 1948. He became premier of the Democratic People's Republic of Korea (DPRK) on September 9, 1948, and moved to build a totalitarian state whose watchwords were *control* and *surveillance*. United as one country since 676 CE, Korea was now divided into two nations.

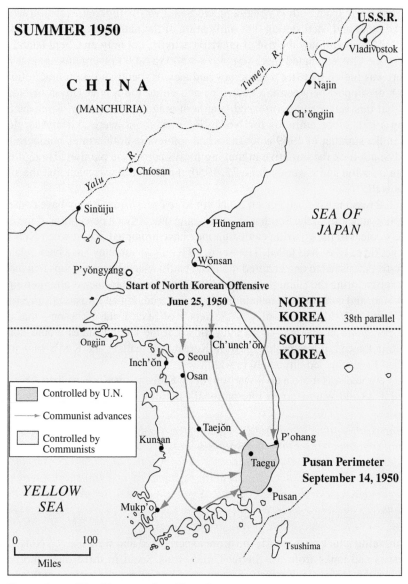

Map 15-1   The Korean Conflict, Summer 1950.

Even before the establishment of the Communist state, the regime had moved against all political freedom. Freedom of the press was dead by December 1946; all political opposition was banned; clandestine networks informed authorities on the actions and loyalty of citizens; and people with questionable backgrounds (capitalists, landlords, those who had worked with the Japanese, and those from the south) were under continuous surveillance. The Soviet Union withdrew its troops in late 1948.

THE KOREAN WAR, 1950–1953

From the start of the occupation in 1945, an increasingly malevolent polarization had colored the peninsular regimes deep red and stark white, especially after the 1948 establishment of the two states. "The unification rhetoric from both P'yŏngyang and Seoul was belligerent, each threatening to march and take over the other and each stating that unification of the nation must be achieved."[13] Beginning in November 1948, the South saw the rise of guerrilla activity, not only on Cheju Island but also on the peninsula, where the CIA estimated that there were 3,500 to 6,000 insurgents against Rhee's government. This effort was fueled by Rhee's autocracy and lack of social and economic reforms. There was no provable link or support between the guerrillas and either the Soviet Union or North Korea; evidence showed that this was a southern-based, southern-manned insurgency. Rhee successfully put it down by spring 1950. More ominous for North-South relations were skirmishes along the thirty-eighth parallel in the summer of 1949 at a time when soldiers in both armies numbered over 100,000. Both North and South took the initiative in making forays across the parallel. Though eventually Kim would launch an invasion and a war on June 25, 1950, the situation was such that the south was spoiling for a war as well.

Many potential reasons have been given for North Korea's invasion. It may have come, in part, out of fear of a preemptive attack from the South and, at the same time, from a perception of the South's military weakness. Rhee's defeat of the guerrilla campaign may have prompted action when Kim saw that southern attempts to get rid of Rhee had failed. The timing of Kim's action may have been related to the return of some seventy-five thousand to one hundred thousand battle-tested Korean troops that had fought for the Chinese Communists during the Chinese civil war. The North may have acted after getting endorsements from Stalin and Mao, and perhaps even help in planning and readying an invasion from Stalin. Perhaps the North took the January 1950 remarks of U.S. Secretary of State Dean Acheson—that did not include Korea in the U.S. *defense perimeter*—as an indication that the United States would not intervene in a Korean war. But, in the end, it was probably North Korean nationalism and Kim's wish to unite and preside over a unified Korea that led ultimately to war.

The war that erupted was more a civil war fought by Koreans for Koreans than it was, as the United States perceived it, a Cold War effort by international Communism on the march. The tragedy was that

> [a]n American's understanding of communism . . . held little relevance for under-
> standing communism in Korea . . . [which] was a specifically Korean communism.
> Its adherents could scarcely be distinguished from nationalists and conservatives in
> their belief in the uniqueness of the Korean race and its traditions and the necessity
> to preserve both, or in their understanding that a unique Korea required unique
> solutions.[14]

After the lightning attack on June 25, the more experienced and well-trained North Korean troops, with fighter planes and tanks from the Soviet Union, took Seoul in three days and drove the South Korean army down the peninsula. By early August, they had seized the entire South except for an area

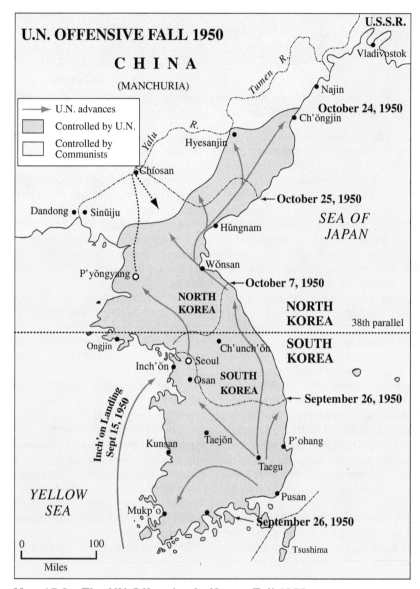

Map 15-2 The UN Offensive in Korea, Fall 1950.

around the southeastern port of Pusan, which became known as the *Pusan perimeter*. The United States acted quickly and in the beginning unilaterally, deciding to support Rhee's Korea with troops and sending the U.S. Seventh Fleet into the Taiwan Straits to prevent both Mao and Jiang from taking advantage of the crisis to reopen a hot civil war of their own. Having gained UN support, U.S. forces landed at Inch'ŏn near Seoul on September 15, forcing the North Korean army to retreat in a rout across the thirty-eighth parallel. Prompted by the United States, UN forces crossed the parallel, pursuing

Source: A Korean Housewife's Story

The plight of refugees fleeing during the North Korean invasion was tragic. Because much of the war was fought up and down the Korean peninsula, refugees were on the move almost continually in 1950 and 1951. What were the experiences of this Seoul housewife and her family?

The North Koreans attacked on June 25, early in the morning. I was home and first heard the news on the radio. At that time most people had very little money or food, because it was near the end of the month, but we knew we still had to leave before the North Koreans arrived in Seoul. Fortunately, every day I had saved a handful of rice, so we had some food to take with us on our journey to the South.

Together with my sister and her family, we crossed the Han River on a boat, with my husband carrying the bag of rice. Unfortunately, my sister was not a very healthy person, and she had several small children, so we could only walk about ten miles a day. We walked for about fifteen days to Hong Song, a city about seventy miles south of Seoul near the West Coast. We chose Hong Song because this is where my husband's family lived. There were many others trying to escape the North Koreans, and some became so weak from lack of food they dropped out along the way and died. We saw many dead people on the way to Hong Song. Because we had some rice, we were okay. We even had some rice left over when we finally arrived in Hong Song.

Everything seemed so peaceful when we entered the city, and we were quite hopeful. We lived with my husband's family, and everything seemed to be okay. Then, after we had been in Hong Song only about two days, the North Koreans arrived, and our lives were changed forever.

Because he loved his country so much, in Hong Song my husband belonged to a local patriotic society. He received no pay, but sometimes gave the local police information on those who supported the North Koreans. The North Koreans, however, regularly arrested and put in jail anyone they suspected of supporting South Korea.

Unfortunately, one day my husband . . . was seized by the North Korean police, who brutally beat him up. When the friend of my husband's brother learned what happened, he came to our house and took my husband to the police station.

That night my husband never came home. I went to see my husband's brother to see if he knew what happened. Together, we went down to the police station and found my husband so badly beaten he was near death. His clothes were so soaked in blood they stuck to his skin when removed. When the head policeman, the friend of my husband's brother, learned what happened he made sure my husband received medical attention. Then he permitted my husband to go home. Without his help, I'm quite sure my husband would have died.

Source: Richard Peters and Xiaobing Li, Voices from the Korean War *(Lexington: The University Press of Kentucky, 2004), 206–8.*

the North's army to the Yalu River, changing their policy goals from containing Communism to liberating North Korea.

As we have seen (Chapter 13), China looked in fear at the U.S.-led armies approaching its Manchurian frontier. Beijing had warned the United States well before the Inch'ŏn landing that any move into North Korea by UN forces would bring a Chinese military response. Feeling its security threatened, in November the PRC sent seven hundred thousand troops into Korea, successfully pushing UN forces far

MacArthur Strides Ashore
General Douglas MacArthur walks with naval and marine commanders after the Inch'ŏn landing.

south of the thirty-eighth parallel in January 1951. The war stalemated around the thirty-eighth parallel, though fighting continued until an armistice was reached at P'anmunjŏm on July 27, 1953. From 1951 until the armistice, one of the most serious and controversial issues at the peace talks was whether prisoners could choose *not* to be sent back to their home countries. Eventually, as the following chart shows, nonrepatriation became an option.

Repatriated and Nonrepatriated Prisoners of War[15]		
	Repatriated	Nonrepatriated
China	5,640	14,704
N. Korea	70,183	7,900
S. Korea	7, 862	335
U.S.	3,597	23

For the Koreans the war was an almost unbelievable tragedy. In the North the estimated killed, wounded, and missing totaled 1.5 million. Aerial bombing, which included the use of napalm, had leveled most cities, towns, villages, and farm homes and had destroyed huge irrigation dams, creating floods that swept away whole villages and their people and destroyed everything in their path. In the South the toll was estimated at 1.3 million, a third of all houses were destroyed, and almost 50 percent of industrial capacity was obliterated. Widespread guerrilla warfare made it a *people's war;* antiguerrilla *free fire zones,* where anything that moved was considered a legitimate target, were announced for territory south of Wŏnsan on the Sea of Japan. A Hungarian correspondent reported that "Everything which moved in North Korea was a military target; peasants in the field often were machine-gunned by pilots. . . ."[16]

Source: A Chinese Captain's Memories

When China entered the Korean War in November 1950, the People's Republic had existed for less than fourteen months. The war was a huge military commitment that China could ill afford to make, but its leaders feared UN forces might attack China. Here a Chinese captain relates the problems Chinese soldiers faced while fighting in northern Korea. What were these problems?

We had our own problems. First, we were unable to pursue retreating UN troops because of our unmotorized infantry and lack of supplies. The Twenty-sixth Army delayed their movement because they had to wait for their food and ammunition. We had thought we could collect grain from the local Korean people and ammunition from retreated enemy positions. We were wrong. The Chosin Reservoir area was very lightly populated and could not feed a large force with more than one hundred thousand men.

Second, the Ninth Army Group from South China was not prepared for a cold winter battle in North Korea. The Ninth had more than forty thousand casualties (out of one hundred thousand frontline troops) during its first battle (from November 17 to December 21, 1950). One half of the casualties were from frostbite. For the next three months, the entire Ninth Army Group became a giant field hospital for its wounded and severe frostbite soldiers. The army group was virtually disabled and unable to fight a major engagement until the late spring of 1951.

Third, as the CPVF [Chinese People's Volunteer Force] began to strike south, the tactics of "divide, encircle, and destroy" began to lose effectiveness. Although successful at first, the UN forces rapidly adjusted to these tactics. Also, as our supply lines became extended, the damage to our logistical efforts caused by UN air strikes became increasingly heavy.

For all of these reasons, the Ninth Army Group managed to drive the X Corps south of the 38th Parallel, but it fell short of the original plan of annihilating two divisions of X Corps. By the end of 1950, the badly depleted army group was ordered to return to the Chinese–North Korean border for its replenishment and reorganization.

Source: Richard Peters and Xiaobing Li, Voices from the Korean War *(Lexington: The University Press of Kentucky, 2004), 124.*

Open racism (primarily among U.S. troops) toward Koreans likely contributed to the horrifying war atrocities. U.S. troops called Koreans *gooks* and "never spoke of the enemy as though they were people, but as one might speak of apes."[17] Such attitudes helped promote indiscriminate killing. A *New York Times* reporter noted that "fear of infiltrators led to the slaughter of hundreds of South Korean civilians, women as well as men, by some U.S. troops...."[18] A sense of the lesser value of Koreans' lives, or at least insensitivity about killing large numbers of them, reached the top levels of the military. UN Commander Douglas MacArthur early on toyed with the notion of using tactical atomic weapons to stop either the Soviet Union or China from intervening in the war. "I see here a unique use for the atomic bomb—to strike a blocking blow—which would require a six months repair job. Sweeten up my B-29 force...."[19]

The historian Carter Eckert has summed up well the nature of the war experience:

> *the terror of alien armies and incendiary bombing; the separation of families, often to be permanent; the frantic flight to refugee camps up and down the peninsula; the sub-*

American Soldiers in North Korea
Bundled-up American soldiers rest in the snow. Bitter North Korean winter was as much of a challenge as Chinese and North Korean forces. Frostbite and its complications were constant threats. See the Source on p. 376.

sequent struggle for survival in a swirling mass of similarly displaced and desperate people; the fear of reprisal from one side or the other, or from a neighbor taking advantage of the chaos or politics to settle an old score. The war . . . left its scars on an entire generation of survivors, a legacy of fear and insecurity that continues even now to affect the two Koreas both in their internal development and in their relations with each other.[20]

THE DEMOCRATIC PEOPLE'S REPUBLIC OF KOREA (DPRK), 1953–1979

The "Supreme Brain of the Nation"

Kim Il-sung, born to Christian parents in P'yŏngyang, was in a sense an overseas Korean, for his original base had been Manchuria; he had no established political support on the Korean peninsula. For that reason (because the Soviet occupiers were suspicious of Korea's Koreans) and for his military renown, Kim became Moscow's man in P'yŏngyang early on. In what seemed typical Korean political cultural patterns, Kim's faction was challenged by other Communist factions: a North Korean domestic faction, a South Korean faction, a Soviet-Korean faction (Koreans with Soviet citizenship), and a Yan'an faction that had been with Mao in his base area. Kim spent the five years after the Korean War armistice getting rid of these factional rivals. The first was relatively easy: Kim called Pak Hŏn-yŏng and his South Korean Communist associates U.S. spies who were responsible for the North's disasters during the war and had them executed in 1955. Purges of the leaders of the other factions succeeded in eliminating Kim's competition by 1958 (the head of the Soviet faction was intimidated into committing suicide).

Many of Kim's policies and approaches grew directly out of a crucial Korean historical memory: subjection and humiliation by outside powers. After the war and with the reality of a still divided Korean

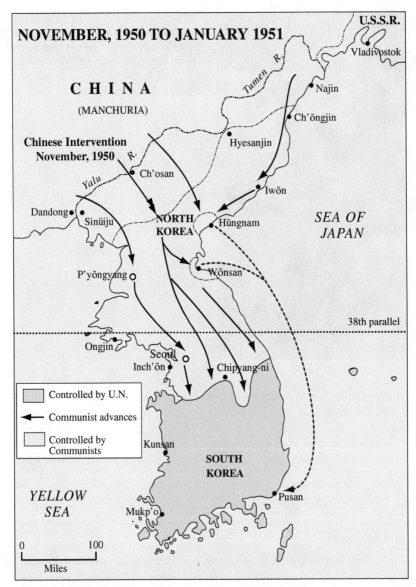

Map 15-3   Korea: The Chinese Advance, 1950–1951.

peninsula, Kim was determined to act independently. He wrapped up that proposition in the quasi-ideology of *juche,* a blend of nationalism and self-reliance; it served as the opposite to *sadaejuŭi,* a word meaning "serving and relying on a foreign power." Kim first talked about *juche* in a speech in December 1955, calling for the DPRK to cease imitating the Soviet Union. Here is a fuller explanation provided several decades later:

I say to our officials: if a man takes to flunkeyism (sadaejuŭi) he will become a fool; if a nation falls into flunkeyism, this nation will go to ruin; and if a party adopts flunkeyism, it will make a mess of the revolution. Once there were poets who worshipped

Guarding Chinese Soldiers
American marines guard Chinese prisoners of war (POWs), who are sitting on rocks in the bleak mountains of North Korea. The POW issue became a political hot potato after talks between the two sides began in 1951.

Pushkin and musicians who adored Tschaikovsky. . . . Flunkeyism was so rampant that some artists drew foreign landscapes instead of our beautiful mountains and rivers. . . . [But] Koreans do not like European artistic works.

Koreans must, he concluded, "hold fast to independence."[21]

Thus, one of Kim's chief concerns in the 1950s and 1960s was to avoid being pulled closely into the orbit of either Beijing or Moscow (he was fluent in both Chinese and Russian). In the mid-1960s animosity rose between the Soviet Union and North Korea. The DPRK's go-it-alone policy irritated Moscow, which pointedly criticized P'yŏngyang's sponsoring an Asian Economic Seminar. In response, the official newspaper of the Korean Workers' Party ranted: "What a slighting attitude of contempt and arrogance this is. What overbearing, insolent, and shameless nonsense it is! These are the words that can be used only by the great-power chauvinists who are in the habit of thinking that they are entitled to decide and order everything. . . ."[22] Even if such attacks and charges of Soviet revisionism brought *juche* satisfaction, they also meant having to pay in full for purchases of Soviet military equipment. Relations blew cold and hot with both China and the Soviet Union; during China's Cultural Revolution, P'yŏngyang railed against Chinese Communist dogmatism.

Beginning in the 1940s, Kim and those around him began to build him into a figure of mythic proportions. Listen to one of his guerrillas in 1946: "The sublime good fortune of our guerrilla detachment was to have at our center *the Great Sun.* Our general commander, great leader, sagacious teacher, and intimate friend was none other than General Kim Il-sung."[23] And that was just the beginning. Until his death in 1994, Kim was called *our father, the great sun of the people, the man of good heart, the Great Son of the Nation, the kindred king of human love,* and *the supreme brain of the nation.* A special medical institute was set up in P'yŏngyang to focus solely on Kim's aging process, and "a special toilet with built-in monitoring equipment . . . instantly analyzed whatever the Great Leader eliminated for any sign of health problems."[24] Kim's photograph adorned the wall of every home, shop, and office in the DPRK; beginning in the 1960s, every North Korean adult was required to wear a badge with Kim's likeness. The anniversaries of the deaths of Kim's father, son, uncle, and maternal grandfather came to be celebrated in solemn commemorations. Kim was so revered by the North

Source: Kim Il-sung's Illustrious Heritage

Kim's ascendance to godlike status was assisted by articles like this one in a North Korean publication. This genealogy was clear evidence that Kim was the "legitimate successor" to a "revolutionary family lineage." Though the authenticity of the claims cannot be judged, what experience does every predecessor except Kim's great-grandfather have?

The family of Comrade Kim Il Sung is a patriotic and revolutionary family that have fought from generation to generation for the independence of the country and the freedom and liberation of the people against foreign aggressors.

His great-grandfather Mr. Kim Ung U was a patriot who led the battle for sinking the pirate ship "General Sherman" dispatched by the U.S. aggressors as a feeler for their aggression of our country in 1866.

His grandfather Mr. Kim Bo Hyon and his grandmother Mrs. Li Bo Ik, too, were patriots who, backing the revolutionary struggle of their sons and grandsons, remained profoundly true to their national principles without yielding to the harsh repression and persecution by the Japanese imperialists and fought tenaciously against the aggressors.

His father Mr. Kim Hyong Jik was a pioneer and outstanding leader of the national-liberation movement in our country. He had a strong patriotic anti-Japanese spirit and extraordinary talents and noble qualities....

Mrs. Kang Ban Sok, mother of Comrade Kim Il Sung, was also endowed with remarkable talents, a kind heart and strong character, and she was an anti-Japanese revolutionary fighter who fought unyieldingly against the foes....

Mr. Kim Hyong Gwon, uncle of Comrade Kim Il Sung, too, was an ardent revolutionary fighter and staunch Communist who joined in the revolutionary struggle in his early years for the restoration of the fatherland....

The two younger brothers of Comrade Kim Il Sung were also Communists who took part in the anti-Japanese struggle in their early years and fought stoutly.

His younger brother Comrade Kim Chol Ju was an indefatigable revolutionary fighter who ... died a heroic death in 1935 fighting in arms against Japanese imperialism.

His cousin Comrade Kim Won Ju, too....

Mr. Kang Don Uk, grandfather of Comrade Kim Il Sung on the mother's side, and Mr. Kang Jin Sok, his uncle on the mother's side, were also anti-Japanese fighters who fought fiercely for the restoration of the fatherland.

Source: Joungwon Alexander Kim, Divided Korea: The Politics of Development, 1945–1972 *(Cambridge, MA: Harvard University Press, 1976), 318–19.*

Korean people that even the butts of cigarettes that he once smoked were on display in a P'yŏngyang museum. When Kim traveled by car, all other traffic was forbidden. He lived in at least five luxurious palaces and countless guesthouses. For his sixtieth birthday (a milestone in Korean society), a ninety-two-room Museum of the Revolution was opened to exalt him, and a sixty-six-foot-high bronze statue painted in gold was unveiled. By the time of his death, there were some thirty-four thousand monuments to him in the country; benches on which he had sat were covered in glass. In what seems a throwback to the Korean monarchical system, Kim groomed his son, Kim Jong-il, to succeed him in the 1960s and 1970s. After he was made heir apparent with key appointments to government, party, and military posts at the Sixth Congress of the Workers' Party in 1980, Kim Jong-il was referred to as the *party center*—which later became the *glorious party center*. For some, this escalation in exaltation must have been a particularly unsettling form of déjà vu.

Economic Developments

At the end of the Korean War, 75 percent of North Koreans were farmers, each of whom had been granted 2.5 acres of land in the prewar land-to-the-tiller reform. Rural destruction during the war and the decision of many in the countryside to move to rehabilitated cities after the war gave Kim's regime the opportunity to further transform the North Korean countryside. As in China's land reform effort, land to the tiller was not the goal; rather, the objective was to collectivize land into cooperatives, larger farms that might make mechanization possible, with the ultimate goal of increasing production. Some cooperatives, state farms, and tractor stations were established as early as November 1954, but then the push for collectivization intensified. By the end of 1957, 95 percent of North Korean farmers had been organized into collectives. The number of cooperatives in 1962 reached 3,800, with each cooperative averaging 300 farm households. Each family could have a small vegetable garden, fruit trees, and chickens; other than that, the families were dependent on what they received from serving the cooperative. Foreign visitors to the DPRK in the mid-1970s reported that most farms were mechanized and irrigated. As late as the mid-1970s, the DPRK was self-sufficient in agriculture, thereby achieving the goal of *juche*.

Economically, *juche* demanded a "conscious withdrawal from the capitalist world system and serious attempt to construct an independent self-contained economy."[25] Early on the policy seemed to work. Until the mid-1960s the North Korean economy outperformed that of South Korea; from 1954 to 1965, industry soared about 25 percent a year; from 1965 to roughly 1975, it continued at a torrid if lesser pace of 14 percent annually. Indeed, as late as the early 1980s, the DPRK's production of steel, machine tools, coal, electricity, and fertilizer was greater than or equal to that of South Korea—and with the North's having only half of the population of the South. But in the end, economic isolation became an obstacle to industrial growth as the country was closed to more highly developed economies (the United States closed itself off from the DPRK by its half-century economic blockade from 1950 to 2000). The country's expansion in the 1950s and early 1960s stemmed primarily from the postwar reconstruction.

Kim Il-sung Kim Il-sung (1912–1994) waves at a rally before an address given on North Korea's "Liberation Day." Kim's godlike status did not diminish after his death.

Constructing its policies in terms of multiple-year plans, Kim's regime oversaw positive developments until the early 1970s, when the economy began to slow. Planning problems, mismanagement, misallocation of resources, political favoritism, and infrastructural transportation weaknesses all served first as drags and then, in the late 1970s, as powerful negatives. Perhaps contributing to the growing problems was Kim's sponsorship in the late 1960s of the *Flying Horse* movement. Ancient legends told of a flying horse that could leap three hundred miles at a time. With obvious similarities to China's Great Leap Forward, the Flying Horse movement's purpose was to speed development throughout the economy. As in China, though not to the same dire extent, the movement in the end "produced chaos in all sectors of the North Korean economy."[26]

By the late 1970s, severe economic strains began showing. Large trade deficits (from 1973 to 1975 totaling $1,376 million) occurred along with increasing foreign debts: the total foreign debt in 1975 came to $2.12 billion; to Japanese firms alone, the DPRK owed $350 million. It then nonchalantly defaulted on its debts to Japan and Western European countries. The nation's money problems were underscored by scandals unprecedented in the history of diplomacy. In October 1976, DPRK diplomats in Denmark, Norway, Sweden, and Finland allegedly participated in smuggling and black market activities in order to stash some cash. It is probably the case, as one scholar put it, that "Kim Il-sung and his associates had an attitude of contempt of world public opinion, policies, or agreements between nations."[27]

Emphasizing and Expanding the Military

Early in his regime, Kim had decided that the government should focus on rebuilding heavy industry. National attention to consumer goods had much lower priority. To satisfy consumers, the government decided that food and consumer goods should be provided at the local level: food by provinces and consumer goods by counties. While the first Seven-Year Plan (1961–1967) was to have targeted light industry and agriculture, those budgeted monies were used to launch a thorough military buildup. Some specialists have pointed to the 1961 military coup of Park Chung-hee in Seoul and the 1962 Cuban missile crisis as stimulating the DPRK's race to militarize. The dramatic rise in the defense budget underscored the decision to modernize: in 1961, 2.6 percent of the budget went to the military; by 1968 it had soared to 32.4 percent. What has been called *total militarization* produced "the most militarized country on the face of the earth."[28]

Militarization aimed at arming the whole people, fortifying the country, modernizing weaponry, and preparing each soldier to become part of the nucleus of a rapidly expandable force that could invade the South once U.S. forces withdrew from the peninsula. Much of North Korea's foreign debt (on which it largely defaulted) came from hundreds of millions of dollars in loans from banking syndicates in Japan, the United States, and the European Union for the express purpose of importing equipment to produce war materiel. By the 1970s, the DPRK had committed itself to a continual program of military strengthening. By the end of the 1970s, it had 650,000 troops, twice as many tanks and artillery pieces as South Korea, and modern weapons including mortars, rocket launchers, and Scud-B and surface-to-surface missiles. Further, in the 1960s and 1970s, the DPRK began to use nuclear energy. In 1962 it got a small (likely four-megawatt) nuclear reactor from the Soviet Union for research purposes (a reactor converts uranium into plutonium). In 1977, P'yŏngyang placed it under the oversight of the UN's International Atomic Energy Agency (IAEA). In the late 1970s, North Korea began to build a thirty-megawatt reactor that was operational by 1987. It is not likely that P'yŏngyang toyed with building nuclear devices as deterrents until the 1990s (see Chapter 19). All in all, according to the Kim dynasty, the chief purpose of the state was "to build up the military for the mission of unification."[29]

THE REPUBLIC OF KOREA (ROK): AUTOCRATS, 1953–1979

Longtime nationalist Syngman Rhee was above all bitterly anti-Communist; sure of his indispensability to the Korean nation, he hung the Communist tag on any political opposition. Obstinate, unpredictable, and petulant, Rhee, according to one historian, represented what was a modal personality for "elderly Korean

Syngman Rhee and Ngo Dinh Diem   ROK President Syngman Rhee (1875–1965), left, on a state visit to the Republic of Vietnam, speaking with President Ngo Dinh Diem (1910–1963). Both were ultraconservative nationalists who did not easily accept American advice and pressure.

men of responsibility," who would show on the same day "ineffable charm and outrageous crudity— an icy Confucian demeanor of utter self-control and dignity at one point, giving way to a show of raging insanity or puerile inanity."[30] An example of Rhee's vengeful autocracy was his treatment of Cho Pong-am, his first agriculture minister, whom the president saw as a political threat because he had won 2.2 million votes as the candidate of the Progressive Party in 1956. In 1958, Rhee had Cho and other Progressive Party leaders arrested on trumped-up charges of espionage, executing Cho, despite worldwide outrage in 1959. At the same time, Rhee tried to toughen the National Security Law by mandating a five-year prison sentence for spreading false information to benefit the enemy. This was the law that—even without this new wrinkle—led to the arrest of 188,621 people in the first year after it was enacted.

In the election of 1960, Rhee claimed that he had received 90 percent of the vote. Election fraud was widespread: ballot boxes were stuffed or simply disappeared from communities where opposition to Rhee was strong. Student protests erupted in Masan on the southern coast. In this episode and others, the United States always sided with the autocrats rather than with the demonstrators, here allowing Korean marines to suppress the demonstrations. Things might have settled down had the body of a middle school student floating in Masan harbor not been discovered. Mass demonstrations started anew and spread to Seoul, where on April 19 palace guards fired into a huge demonstration, killing 115 students and injuring almost 1,000. Street protests exploded, with protestors screaming that Rhee must resign. At the urging of the United States, the eighty-five-year-old Rhee left for exile in Hawaii on April 29. This *April Revolution* thus removed Autocrat No. 1.

The new regime, organized by the opposition Democratic Party, was indeed democratic. Its hallmarks were a bicameral legislature that truly debated issues, a cabinet responsible to the National Assembly, and reduced presidential powers. But within a year, student pressure to push for unification with the DPRK, economic poverty in the countryside, and regime dependency on the United States (in contrast to Rhee's frequent defiance of the United States) fomented a military coup on May 16, 1961. The United States did nothing to oppose the coup, which ended constitutional government. For two years a junta of thirty military leaders controlled the government, abolished the National Assembly, and prohibited all political activity. From the junta emerged Autocrat No. 2: Park Chung-hee.

The Years of Park Chung-hee (1961–1979)

Park, the son of a farmer near Taegu, volunteered for the Japanese army in 1940 after three years of primary school teaching. As required, Park took a Japanese name (Masao Takagi), though many Koreans refused to do so; he proudly received a gold watch from Hirohito for his military services. He was a 1946 graduate of the Korean Military Academy. In the eyes of one Western journalist, "Park left his mark on South Korea to a greater extent than any other person in modern times."[31]

A survey of the years of his presidency shows two remarkable trends that define his rule, one amazingly positive and the other horrifyingly negative. The positive result first: the burgeoning of the South Korean economy. In the 1950s South Korea was mired in abject poverty, with a scarcity of goods; some U.S. officials believed that the ROK would never become an economically viable state. Because of its anti-Communist fears, the goal of the United States was to help move South Korea into a position where it could support itself and become a member of the international economic community. Much of this effort involved direct aid. It was no drop in the bucket: between 1945 and 1976, U.S. economic assistance totaled $600 per year for every South Korean man, woman, and child. In 1957 alone, the ROK received $383 million in economic assistance (its domestic revenue was $456 million) and $400 million in military aid.[32]

One secret of the ROK's initial success was, as one historian put it, "sucking the American teat for all it was worth."[33] But there were other reasons why the desperately poor and underdeveloped nation became an economic powerhouse. Some were related to culture and history. The traditional Confucian prizing of education translated into compulsory schooling that, in turn, produced an educated workforce. Further, the historical heritage of a powerful bureaucracy in control of the state was a natural lead-in to economic development directed by the state. During the junta's control in the early 1960s, Park had set up the Economic Planning Board (EPB), which functioned much like MITI in Japan—as an economic nerve center that planned, allocated, and directed the economy and economic development in multiple-year economic programs. Economic development was fueled by what is known as *import substitution industrialization;* the rationale was that a developing country should attempt to substitute local products for imported ones, in effect promoting high exports and minimizing imports in order to increase national wealth.

If Korea had its own MITI-like body coordinating economic stages and development, it also had zaibatsu-like conglomerates or chaebol, massive firms that were founded by families—with almost 70 percent of them still managed by those families in the first years of the twenty-first century. They were some of the most well-known South Korean firms: Hyundai, Samsung, and Daewoo. All three made the Fortune 500 list in the mid-1990s; in 2005 Samsung Electronics ranked thirty-ninth, with profits of $9,419.5 million, and Hyundai ranked ninety-second, with profits of $1,472.6 million.[34]

The Park administration was not above using high-powered tactics to bolster economic development. During the period of the junta, for example, the regime ordered twenty-seven entrepreneurs to cough up $37 million, which the Park regime claimed was their accumulation of "illicit wealth."[35] If they did not, the government threatened to seize their factories. An increasingly powerful tool of the government was the Korean Central Intelligence Agency (KCIA); indeed, the KCIA could in many ways be seen as the controlling agency of the government. Established in 1961, it originally had 3,000 employees; by 1964, it employed 370,000. Headed by Kim Chong-p'il, the husband of Park's niece, the KCIA was involved in numerous schemes to bring in big bucks. Scandal after scandal involving KCIA financial and commercial wrongdoing eventually came to light: "the importation by the [K]CIA of 1,642 Datsun automobiles from Japan, duty-free (the normal duty on automobiles was 110 percent) and their resale, at twice the import price . . . ; the importation of 880 pinball machines from Japan duty-free; the manipulation of the Korean stock market; and the construction of the Walker Hill Resort," an entertainment center to serve (and take money from) American soldiers.[36]

In the 1960s, South Korea's international relationships also spurred the economy. Any kind of relationship with Japan at this point in Korean history would have been difficult, but as Japanese trade with Korea heated up (by 1963 imports from Japan comprised 30 percent of Korea's total imports), Korean leaders and American officials talked about the importance of normalizing relations with Japan. This was accomplished in 1965. As part of the normalization, Japan gave the ROK a direct grant of $300 million, with additional loans totaling $200 million; private Japanese firms pledged another $300 million. The treaty was initially very unpopular with the South Koreans, but it was a great economic boon. The only downside was that as a final settlement, it did not allow any future claims against Japan (for example, from former comfort women during World War II).

The other economic bonanza was Korea's involvement in the U.S. war in Vietnam. The United States paid the ROK to send soldiers, a sum that for the years 1965 to 1970 totaled over $900 million. The number of Korean forces varied, with more sent to South Vietnam as the war continued. In March 1966, there were close to 23,000; at the end of 1969, 47,872; and two divisions remained at the end of the war in 1973. South Koreans killed and wounded in Vietnam totaled 12,000. The war brought significant profits to the Korean economy, with many Korean companies—especially construction firms—negotiating contracts with the U.S. army. The most famous chaebol, Hyundai, for example, was an important contractor for U.S. troops. In addition, the ROK's ten top chaebol made almost $22 billion in profits in Middle East construction from 1974 to 1979, with Hyundai alone pulling in over $6 billion.

In the early 1970s, Park inaugurated a new system called *Yushin,* or *revitalizing reforms,* the main goal of which "was to hemorrhage as much capital as possible into the heavy industrialization program."[37] Specifically, Park designed his *Heavy and Chemical Industries Promotion Plan* to expand six strategic industries: iron and steel, shipbuilding, chemicals, electronics, nonferrous metals, and machinery. This heavy-handed program was opposed by the EPB and Korean economists, for it replaced private initiative in the economy by government decision making and promoted greater autocracy.

> *The political economy of this bifurcated financial system was illiberal, undemocratic, and statist. . . . Every bank in the nation was owned and controlled by the state; bankers were bureaucrats and not entrepreneurs, they thought in terms of GNP and not profit. . . .*[38]

In many ways a visionary, Park took gigantic risks, plunging into steelmaking when Americans and economists from the World Bank argued that the ROK could never build and operate an integrated steel mill and refused to approve its financing. In a declaration of independence, Park went ahead and built the world's largest steel mill to serve as the base for Korea's heavy industry. In addition, he was the primary booster of the construction of the Seoul-to-Pusan expressway, also frowned on by experts.

The results for the South Korean economy were nothing less than spectacular. The ROK's GNP, adjusted for inflation, tripled in each decade after 1961, "condensing a century of growth into three decades."[39] Whereas over 40 percent of all households were below the poverty level in 1965, less than 10 percent were in that predicament in 1980. When Park pulled off his coup in 1961, per capita annual income was below $100; in 1979 it was over $1,000 and in 1997 it was over $10,000. For this reason, in a poll by a Seoul newspaper in March 1995, over two-thirds of South Koreans said that Park was the ROK's greatest president, the man whose policies created the "miracle on the Han [river]."

But in the realms of democracy and human rights, Park's record is bleak. Even before his program of *Yushin,* Park had shown his autocracy. With the junta in control, civilian and military purges, newspaper closings, and arbitrary arrests were common. The United States had to apply considerable pressure on Park to hold elections. When they were held in the fall of 1963, Park barely won. Constantly threatening to abolish the National Assembly and to reinstate martial law, Park riled students who demonstrated against his regime. He put the country under martial law in the summer of 1964, but things settled down and the late 1960s were fairly quiet.

Park Chung-hee Coming to power as part of an army junta in 1961, Park (1917–1979) became a strongman dictator by the late 1960s, maintaining that position until his assassination in October 1979. He is given credit for the ROK's successful economic modernization and for normalizing relations with Japan in 1965.

Then came *Yushin*. The political counterpart to Park's big push to heavy industrialization was a crushing blow to supporters of democracy. The *Yushin* constitution, approved by public referendum in November 1972, put no limits on Park's tenure as president; in effect, it created a legal dictatorship. It gave Park the power both to name and remove the cabinet and the prime minister. He could appoint one-third of the National Assembly, temporarily or permanently end all civil liberties, and issue decrees at any time. What accounts for this draconian turn?

Analysts suggest that the international situation may have played a role in moving Park in this direction. The United States, on which South Korea depended in the international community, took a number of steps that shook up the ROK regime. Richard Nixon's overtures to China and his trip there in February 1972 were unnerving enough, but then the United States lost its war with Vietnam and withdrew. If Seoul was the Korean equivalent of Saigon, ultimately how firm was the U.S. commitment to South Korea?—a question made even more urgent by Nixon's announcement that the United States was withdrawing a complete division of American troops from South Korea, reducing troop levels from sixty-two thousand to forty-two thousand. "If Richard Nixon was declaring his independence of America's Cold War commitments in the region, Park would declare Korean independence in politics, economics—and national security."[40] As part of this independence South Korea also embarked on a highly secret nuclear program, which Washington quickly squelched. Park also initiated talks with North Korea, another expression of independence from the United States. On July 4, 1972, North and South Korea announced that both regimes had made a commitment to peaceful reunification.

Some have speculated that *Yushin* may have been adopted because Park had nearly lost the 1971 election to opposition leader Kim Dae-jung and wanted to make his position untouchable by using electoral politics. Kim's near success was attributable to his adeptness at mass politics and to the fact that Kim's home base, the Chŏlla provinces in southwestern Korea, had been largely left out of economic development. A historian traveling there in 1972 noted that the "roads were still mostly hard-packed dirt . . . thatch-roofed homes were sunk in conspicuous deprivation, and old Japanese-style city halls and railroad stations were unchanged from the colonial era."[41] Park continued to ignore that area; in his early 1970s push for heavy industry, five of the six industries were located in his home province, Kyŏngsang, while the Chŏllas had only one. It was in the southwest, so often in the Korean past the site of rebellions and disturbances, that trouble would soon erupt.

Source: The Park Regime

Bruce Cumings, a leading American scholar of Korea, remembers his own experiences in Korea in 1971, and analyzes Park and his relationship to students and people in general. How does he depict the government's handling of student demonstrations? What point does Cumings make about Korea and Japan? What were some aspects of Yushin?

One day in mid-October 1971 I was studying on the campus of Korea University, the most prestigious private university in Seoul. The regime issued a "garrison decree," and suddenly armored columns of tanks burst through the campus gates and began spraying tear gas everywhere. Troops set up bivouac tents in the middle of the campus. I escaped with a woman professor who showed me how to climb a back fence onto the roof of a gas station; we descended to terra firma on a ladder. Having been gassed by American police during antiwar demonstrations in the period 1969–71, I can assure the reader that the Korean variety was a far more virulent kind of "pepper gas," excruciating to the eyes and nostrils. By the 1980s the whole process had become mechanized; as students would gather on the streets, Black Marias the size of tanks (but armored vans in fact) would roar into their midst, spewing out tear gas through yawning holes in their sides.

A month after the occupation of Korea University came emergency measures justified in terms of national security . . . and a year later came martial law, thousands of arrests, and the proclamation of Park's famous "Yushin system." "Yushin" is the Korean pronunciation of the Japanese *issin,* used by the Meiji leaders in

1868. Not for the last time, Seoul's rulers made their incessant anti-Japanese bombast look empty and silly by taking yet another model from their former colonial ruler; . . . Park sought to use Japanese values and practices to make a big happy family of the workplace, and he justified his deactivation of the National Assembly in terms of "organic cooperation" between the executive and the legislature. Few Koreans bought this rhetoric, however, even if many foreigners did.

The changes were nonetheless deep and definitive. Park had his scribes write a new constitution removing all limits on his tenure in office and giving him powers to appoint and dismiss the cabinet and even the prime minister, to designate one-third of the National Assembly (reducing it to a rubber stamp and a cringing bunch of myrmidons), to suspend or destroy civil liberties, and to issue decrees for whatever powers the Yushin framers forgot to include. Meanwhile, the National Security Law and the anticommunist law remained in place; still, emergency decrees flew out of Blue House like bats at dusk in the early 1970s. One 1973 decree declared all work stoppages to be illegal, and the infamous no. 9 in 1974 more or less made any criticism of the regime a violation of national security.

Source: Bruce Cumings, Korea's Place in the Sun *(New York: W. W. Norton, 2005), 362–63.*

Finally, some have suggested that Park chose *Yushin* because business in the early 1970s was rocky. A spate of businesses went bankrupt in 1969 to 1971, and many more were on the edge. In line with the harsh and often capricious decision making of *Yushin,* the government announced in August 1971 that there would be a moratorium on paying company debts owed to bond holders; this was great news for belabored businesses but a shock of the worst kind for investors.

By the *Yushin* period, the KCIA had become "a complete rogue institution"—Park's agent in detaining, arresting, and imprisoning anyone who disagreed with his policies or obstructed them. Once a suspect was arrested, torture was the norm; among the techniques were electric torture machines, water torture, and the Korean barbecue, in which victims were "strung up by their wrists and ankles and spread-eagled over a flame."[42] As Park's agent, the KCIA took on his political opponents. Kim Dae-jung, who had given Park the election scare in 1971, had been in Japan when Park declared martial law. He stayed there, continuing to lambast the Park regime. In August 1973 KCIA agents abducted Kim, anesthetized him, and returned him by ship to Korea. The United States put pressure on Park, saying that "there would be grave consequences for relations with the United States if Kim did not turn up alive."[43] Kim was released but placed almost immediately under house arrest.

The KCIA also played a pivotal role in restructuring labor organizations. In August 1961, it appointed a committee that set up twelve industrial unions and established a new countrywide labor federation. This was completely a top-down process, unlike the usual formation of unions and labor organizations. This KCIA effort was directed not at reform but at control. When a rash of strikes broke out in 1969 and 1970, the KCIA stepped in quickly to break them or, in a few cases, to mediate the dispute. Labor reforms were sorely needed, given the use of child labor, wretched factory conditions, and low pay. Exploitation of factory workers was the apparent reason for the self-immolation of a textile worker in November 1970. Workers began to form independent unions. When the Park regime used an iron fist to repress them, some Korean churches became sanctuaries. Liberal Christian ministers tried to make workers aware of their rights even as they condemned the Park regime for its autocracy.

An episode involving female textile workers of the YH Trading Company in August 1979 revealed the plight of workers and the brutality of the government in dealing with labor disputes. On August 7 the factory owner dismissed his 170 workers, closed the factory, and fled to the United States with the company's assets. Police evicted and beat up the workers. With the help of Kim Young-sam, head of an opposition political party, the women took refuge at party headquarters. A thousand police stormed the headquarters, killing one worker and injuring many others. Sympathy for the workers swept the country.

About two months later, on October 26, in a bizarre turn of events, Park Chung-hee, whose wife had been killed in an assassination attempt on Park in 1974, was himself assassinated. The killer was none other than the director of the KCIA, Kim Chae-gyu, with whom Park and the chief of presidential security, Cha Chi-chul, were having dinner. They had disagreed on how to handle a series of street demonstrations in the southeast—harsh repression or conciliation—with Park and Cha supporting the former and Kim, the latter. It appeared that Kim's main target was Cha, who was rumored to wield great influence over Park's decisions. Kim killed them both, though why he shot Park is unknown. In any event, the autocrat and the architect of the Korean economic miracle was gone.

RELATIONS BETWEEN NORTH AND SOUTH

For both North Korea and South Korea, unification was the prime objective; both countries from 1948 on made proposals on how to accomplish this. In August 1960, for example, Kim Il-sung suggested a confederation of the two countries, joined by a supreme committee composed of representatives from both countries.

That same month the post-Rhee prime minister, Chang Myŏn, called for unification through general elections supervised by the UN.

The early 1970s saw a flurry of proposals, as well as personal visits and talks, between representatives of the two regimes. In a speech to the Workers' Party's Fifth Congress in November 1970, Kim spelled out his position:

> *The basic task of the revolution is to drive the U.S. imperialist forces out of South Korea and eliminate their colonial domination . . . .*
> *To unify the divided fatherland is the greatest national task for the entire Korean people at the present stage and the most pressing task the solution of which brooks not a moment's delay.*[44]

In early August 1971, at a large rally in P'yŏngyang to honor Cambodia's Norodom Sihanouk, Kim abandoned the position he had taken up to that point and declared that "we are ready to establish contact at any time with all political parties, including the [ruling] Democratic Republican Party, and all social organizations and individual personages in South Korea."[45] Within less than a week, the South Korean Red Cross responded with a proposal to oversee an effort to reunite families separated by the demilitarized zone (DMZ). Two days later, the North Korean Red Cross agreed. This was the first agreement ever reached by the two countries, and the rapidity with which it was accomplished indicated the surging desire, if not yet for unification, at least for closer ties between the two Koreas.

During initial talks, each regime tried to portray itself in the best possible light. At the first meeting in P'yŏngyang, "[p]eople along the route had lined up to greet the visitors dressed in their Sunday best; shops in the capital had been specially stocked for the occasion, and public buildings illuminated." When the delegation from the North came to Seoul, they were lodged in a hotel on a mountain overlooking the city. "Businesses in the city's tall buildings were asked to leave their lights on to present a more impressive view." And when they were taken for a drive on the Seoul-to-Pusan expressway, "Seoulites were asked to drive their cars on the highway even if they had no place to go."[46] Unfortunately, no agreement was forthcoming; the two Red Cross organizations met off and on for ten years, but there were never any positive results.

In May 1972 Park secretly dispatched the head of the KCIA, Yi Hu-rak, to P'yŏngyang for direct government-to-government talks with Kim Il-sung and his brother Kim Yŏng-ju. Yi's aide kept a record of the exchanges between Yi and Kim Il-sung, which revealed the shared antipathy of North and South to outside powers. After the North Korean deputy premier visited Seoul, the DPRK and ROK issued a joint statement that stunned the world:

> *First, unification shall be achieved through independent efforts without being subject to external imposition or interference.*
> *Second, unification shall be achieved through peaceful means, and not through use of force against one another.*
> *Third, a great national unity, as a homogeneous people shall be sought first, transcending differences in ideas, ideologies, and systems.*[47]

Both sides declared that they would stop "slandering and defaming each other," a South-North Coordinating Committee was set up, and a direct telephone line between Seoul and P'yŏngyang was put into operation.[48] Kim Il-sung saw this dialogue as a way to wean the South Korean regime away from the United States and Japan and to bring about the withdrawal of U.S. troops. However, in 1973, the North unilaterally suspended the talks for a period; and for the rest of the decade, though talks occurred occasionally, they achieved no results.

Despite their occasionally positive rhetoric, both Koreas remained hostile, especially the North to the United States. Twice in the 1970s, the DPRK attempted to gain Soviet and Chinese support for a new invasion of the South, the first time in 1975 after the fall of South Vietnam and the second in 1979 after Park Chung-hee's assassination. Both times it failed. The North Koreans caused almost seven thousand incidents along the DMZ from 1953 to 1969; from 1970 to 1977, the incidents totaled almost thirty-three thousand. The North attempted to dig three tunnels under the DMZ in 1974, 1975, and 1978. In addition to the action at the DMZ, there were a number of more serious incidents. In January 1968 about thirty North Korean commandos were sent to assassinate President Park; two years later came another such attempt. On January 23, 1968, the North Koreans captured the *U.S.S. Pueblo*, an intelligence-gathering ship, on the high seas near the city of Wŏnsan; they held the crew of eighty-two for eleven months before releasing them. Today the *Pueblo* is a tourist attraction in P'yŏngyang, though the North in August 2005 offered to return it if relations between the United States and the DPRK were normalized. In the summer of 1976, North Korean soldiers attacked and killed two American soldiers as they were trimming trees at P'anmunjŏm in the DMZ. The situation on the peninsula remained tense and volatile.

CHRONOLOGY

1945 — Formation of the Korean People's Republic, unrecognized and aborted

1945–1948 — Emergence of Syngman Rhee in the U.S.-occupied South and Kim Il-sung in the Soviet Union–occupied North

1948 — Rhee becomes president of the ROK after a UN mandate for elections (August);

Kim becomes premier of the DPRK (September)

1950 — North Korea invades the South (June)

Inch'ŏn landing (September)

China enters the war (November)

1953 — Armistice (July)

1958 — Kim eliminates all factional rivals

1960 — Rhee ousted

1961 — Military junta seizes control in the South; emergence of Park Chung-hee

Establishment of the KCIA

1965 — South Korea normalizes relations with Japan

1972 — Referendum to ratify Park's *Yushin* (revitalizing reforms) and new constitution giving Park a legal dictatorship

1973 — KCIA agents abduct dissident Kim Dae-jung from Japan

1979 — Park assassinated

SUGGESTED READINGS

Anh Junghyo. *Silver Stallion*. New York: Soho Press, 1990. This novel, by one of South Korea's best-known authors, is set in a remote village during the Korean War and is described by a reviewer as "a blackly comic drama of culture shock."

Anh Junghyo. *White Badge*. New York: Soho Press, 1989. A novel depicting the Korean soldiers who fought in the Vietnam War, it is also a reflection on South Korean development and the role of the United States in it.

Oberdorfer, Don. *The Two Koreas*. New York: Basic Books, 2001. Subtitled *A Contemporary History,* this is a clearly written account of both Koreas from the 1960s to the present by an award-winning journalist.

Stueck, William. *Rethinking the Korean War*. Princeton, NJ: Princeton University Press, 2002. The author of several books on the Korean War, Stueck here offers "an up-to-date synthesis" of the major issues of the war, its origins, course, and meaning.

Suh Dae-sook. *Kim Il Sung: The North Korean Leader*. New York: Columbia University Press, 1988. Published six years before Kim's death, this book, offers insights not only into Kim's personality and his drives but also into North Korean policies and operations.

CHAPTER SIXTEEN

The Vietnam Wars, 1941–1975

During the period from 1941 (the year of the Japanese takeover and the founding of the Viet Minh by Ho Chi Minh) to March 1945, the Japanese allowed the Vichy French bureaucrats to continue to administer Vietnam. At this time, ironically, the French seemed more conciliatory; they granted Vietnamese more opportunities to participate in government and even did away with salary differentials between themselves and Vietnamese. Because France was cut off from Vietnam by the war, Vietnamese industries were more able to function on their own. The urban middle class generally enjoyed prosperity and the number of students increased by 55 percent, from 450,000 in 1939 to 700,000 in 1944. However, this relatively good time was but the prelude to three decades of destructive, bloody war.

THE VIET MINH AND THE AUGUST REVOLUTION

Vietnamese revolutionary politics from 1941 to 1945 were complicated—"constantly shifting configurations of alliances and truces, temporary cooperation, and betrayals."[1] The Viet Minh jockeyed for advantage with the VNQDD (the Vietnamese Nationalist Party) and the Greater Vietnam People's Rule Party (Dai Viet), which cooperated with the Japanese, expecting them to eliminate French control. In reunification conferences sponsored by the Chinese Nationalist government in 1943 and 1944 in the Chinese city of Liuzhou, representatives of the various parties and factions tried to thrash out their differences. The upshot was a power shift to the Communists and their front, the Viet Minh, who continued to stress their primary identity as nationalists. Indeed, in an open letter to Vietnamese, noted for its "unabashed patriotism," Ho Chi Minh in June 1941 appealed to "[a]ll Vietnamese who loved their country . . . to contribute whatever they had the most of, be it money, physical strength, or talent."[2] There was not a word about class struggle or Marxism.

Part of the appeal of the Viet Minh was the character of Ho Chi Minh, whom most people viewed as soft-spoken and pragmatically flexible. Truong Nhu Tang, who would later become a leader in the National Liberation Front in the 1960s, met Ho Chi Minh in Paris when Tang was a student there in 1946. Tang noted that "Ho exuded a combination of inner strength and personal generosity that struck me with something like a physical blow. He looked directly at me, and at the others, with a magnetic expression of intensity and warmth." Later Ho invited Tang and another student to afternoon tea, after which Tang swooned that he "had been won by [Ho's] simplicity, his charm, and his familiarity."[3] Ho insisted that people call him by the familiar name *Bac Ho* (*Uncle Ho*). Two other key Viet Minh leaders, frequently in Ho's company, were Pham Van Dong and Vo Nguyen Giap, who in December 1944 directed a small force in the northern Vietnamese highlands in ambush attacks and in stirring up political agitation.

On March 9, 1945, the Japanese, on the verge of defeat in the Pacific war, overthrew the French and imprisoned almost all French troops. The Japanese named Bao Dai the chief of state; but the government that he headed, while composed of people with some ability, was incompetent in dealing with the great problems it faced, the largest of which was a devastating famine. Neither the French before the overthrow nor the Japanese nor the Bao Dai government seemed to be able to move rice supplies from the south to the north. At least one million people in the north died in the summer of 1945. The Viet Minh endeared themselves to many in the north by seizing rice stocks from the rich and distributing grain to those who were starving. This peasant support provided them with a political advantage they never lost.

By August 1945, there was no effective functioning government in Vietnam. The Viet Minh spent the summer preparing for what would become known as the *August Revolution*, establishing a regime that could finally achieve national independence. They also actively assisted the U.S. military. When he was in China in early 1945, Ho Chi Minh had visited the U.S. Office of Strategic Services (OSS, the forerunner of the CIA) in Kunming. The OSS offered "small arms and explosives sufficient to equip 100 guerrillas"[4] and the training of a nucleus of 200 in "using automatic weapons, demolition equipment, [and] infiltrating and exfiltrating [sic] into various dangerous areas."[5] In return the Viet Minh supplied intelligence on

Source: Ho Chi Minh

This description of Ho Chi Minh is from Jean Sainteny, the principal French negotiator with Ho in Paris in 1945 and 1946. Sainteny says that at their first meeting, he recognized that Ho "was a personality of the first class." From Sainteny's verbal portrait, what particularly stands out about Ho's personality?

At first sight there was nothing exceptional in his appearance. Of medium height, rather short in fact, thin, and seemingly fragile, there was something about him that was secretive and shy. Contrary to what his Vietnamese biographers say, his hair had not turned white in the Chinese prisons; it was still brownish, as was his goatee, which, with his high and bulging forehead, made him look more like the typical Annamese scholars one sees in the Latin Quarter of Paris than a fighting chief or a party leader. His most striking features were his eyes—lively, alert, and burning with extraordinary fervor; all of his energy seemed to be concentrated in those eyes. As for the rest, he was usually dressed in the uniform now attributed to Mao, but Ho's uniform was rather shabby, and the tunic was rarely buttoned up to the neck. On his feet he wore the Yunnan cord-soled canvas slippers, and his socks always more or less sagged down over his ankles. Obviously he paid no attention whatsoever to his appearance.

Source: Jean Sainteny, Ho Chi Minh and His Vision *(Chicago: Cowles, 1972), 51–52.*

Japanese forces to the U.S. 14th Air Force. From all accounts, the working relationship between the Viet Minh and U.S. forces was close. In the spring and summer of 1945, Giap strengthened the Viet Minh position for action at the end of the war by establishing guerrilla bases with revolutionary regimes in six provinces around the Red River delta.

When the Japanese surrender came on August 15, the Viet Minh were ready. They declared Vietnam's independence. On August 16, a provisional government was established, with Ho sworn in as president the next day. On August 19 Viet Minh forces marched into Hanoi without military action; Bao Dai resigned, voicing the belief of many Vietnamese that "the government of Ho Chi Minh had the support of the Americans."[6] On August 28, Nationalist Chinese troops crossed the border into Vietnam, as planned, to accept the surrender of the Japanese in the northern sector of the country; Britain temporarily took over in the south.

On September 2 in Hanoi's Ba Dinh Square, Ho Chi Minh announced to the crowd of about half a million the establishment of the Democratic Republic of Vietnam (DRV) and read the Declaration of Independence. It began, "[a]ll men are created equal; they are endowed by their Creator with certain inalienable Rights; among these are Life, Liberty, and the pursuit of Happiness. This immortal statement was made in the Declaration of Independence of the United States of America in 1776."[7] In Giap's address after the reading of the declaration, he stated, in the presence of OSS officers who were there to celebrate the occasion, "The United States of America . . . has paid the greatest contributions to the Vietnamese fight against fascist Japan, our enemy, and so the great American Republic is a good friend of ours."[8] At that point the good will between Vietnamese and Americans was almost tangible.

But the new regime faced gigantic problems in both the south and the north. When the Japanese gave up direct rule, a United National Front, a coalition of Cao Dai, Hoa Hao, Dai Viet, and Trotskyites, held power in the south for a week. A Provisional Executive Committee headed by southern Viet Minh leaders tried to take the reins of power. The British occupiers, however, would not even give them the time of day. The commander, General Douglas Gracey, said later, "They came to see me and said 'welcome' and all that sort of thing. It was an unpleasant situation and I promptly kicked them out."[9] He believed without a second thought that the French should return as the colonial power very soon and made the immediate situation worse by releasing all the French troops that the Japanese had imprisoned in their coup of March 1945. These troops promptly seized all public buildings in Saigon and threw out the Provisional Executive Committee. When the Vietnamese retaliated, violence escalated between the French and Vietnamese in the early fall of 1945. In the end, "Saigon became a beleaguered French city; the Mekong delta, a battlefield."[10]

In the north, the occupying Chinese force of one hundred fifty thousand vied for the little rice that was available and, even worse, robbed and looted the Vietnamese. The Red River delta, having experienced a terrible famine, now suffered through floods and a cholera epidemic. Ho, for all of his personal popularity, "had little with which to work: no rice stocks, a bankrupt treasury, no bureaucracy, no foreign recognition of his nation, and no one experienced in running a nation."[11] Rampant inflation, strikes, and demonstrations further worsened the situation.

The French schemed from the beginning to return to power in the north. In early 1946, they maneuvered to obtain Chinese approval of this reoccupation in return for France's giving up its concessions in China. While Chinese troops were withdrawing from the north, Ho negotiated as best he could with the French, but he held no strong cards in his hand that would change the French determination to hold on to Vietnam. In March 1946, Ho and the French seemed to have reached an agreement. Ho allowed the French to maintain forces in the north temporarily; in turn, the French recognized the DRV as a free state, though it remained part of "the Indochinese Federation and of the French Union."[12] Many Vietnamese opposed the agreement. Nevertheless, Ho traveled to Paris at the end of May to work out the details. He was met by a letter from disgruntled Vietnamese living in France: "You have signed an agreement accepting autonomy for Vietnam, not its independence . . . we are now full of anger and ashamed at having chosen you as our leader. . . . You have backslid, you have betrayed your own ideals."[13]

Talks that were renewed in July broke down in early September, when it became clear that the French would not let southern Vietnam (Cochinchina) become part of the DRV. Frustrated and losing hope, Ho left France in September. Tensions between Vietnamese and French quickly ratcheted up. In August the French insisted on controlling the port of Haiphong; when the Viet Minh refused, the French sent in tanks and armored vehicles to seize public buildings. The French ordered all Viet Minh to leave Haiphong; when they refused, the French bombarded the city on November 23, killing many Vietnamese; in the words of a French soldier, "all the Vietnamese neighborhoods were wiped out."[14] In mid-December, General Giap issued a call to arms as the Viet Minh attacked the French, seriously wounding Jean Sainteny, the chief French negotiator. On December 20, Ho Chi Minh called on Vietnamese to fight to the end. The first Vietnam War had begun.

THE FRENCH WAR, 1946–1954

Ho predicted that the war would be "the war of the tiger and elephant. The tiger could not meet the elephant in an equal contest, so he would lay in wait for it, drop on his back from the jungle, and rip its flesh with his claws. Eventually the elephant would bleed to death."[15] It was an accurate prediction of both Vietnam wars. The French cause was not economic; by 1950 the costs of the war were greater than all of the French investments in Indochina. The French fought the war for political and psychological reasons: they needed Indochina to maintain the "grandeur" of the French empire and perhaps especially out of fear of a sort of domino theory: if one piece of their empire broke away, then all French colonies would also spin out of the French orbit.

For the Vietnamese, the motive for fighting was expressed by a Viet Minh soldier:

> *The French were physically large and they had many weapons. But we Vietnamese had something which we could use as a weapon against them, and that was our morale, our courage. We were determined to fight the French until the end because the French came here to steal our land and oppress us. That was how I felt.*[16]

One of Ho Chi Minh's oft-repeated slogans also expressed the Vietnamese motive in the context of French imperialism: "Nothing is more precious than independence and liberty."[17]

Early on in the fighting, the French determined that their role would be more palatable, especially to Vietnamese who opposed the Viet Minh, if they had a Vietnamese regime that was an ally. In June 1946 Georges d'Argenlieu, high commissioner for Indochina, set up the Republic of Cochinchina as a foil against the Viet Minh and called on the former emperor, Bao Dai, to become its leader. This *Bao Dai solution*—putting a Vietnamese face on the French effort to maintain control over Vietnam—was implemented in April 1949, when, after years of negotiation, Bao Dai returned to lead the State of Vietnam as part of the French Union.

Events outside Vietnam in 1949 and 1950 considerably changed the meaning of this colonial war. In October 1949, the Communist victors in the Chinese civil war announced the establishment of the People's Republic of China. The PRC immediately became an ally and a source of weaponry and equipment for the Viet Minh; furthermore, the Viet Minh now had a "'sanctuary' where they could refit and retrain their troops with full impunity in Chinese Communist training camps."[18] About nine months later, North Korea invaded South Korea, igniting a three-year war with the UN (read, the United States). For the United States, the Communist victory in China and Communist aggression in Korea put the war in Vietnam into the automatic category of Communist expansion. If there had been any perception in the minds of U.S. policymakers that the Vietnamese war was about imperialism and nationalism, it was now gone forever. Vietnam became another test case of international Communism's efforts to take over the world. U.S. policymakers believed that the French were the bulwark against Communism in Vietnam. In May 1950, the United States sent $10 million in direct aid to the French; by the end of that year, it had sent aid worth $150 million in tanks, planes, ammunition, fuel, and napalm. By 1954, the United States was paying roughly 78 percent of the costs of the French war in Vietnam.

This war, like the one the United States would fight later, was not a war of lines and fronts but, in the main, a guerrilla war of points: ambushes, sniper attacks, booby traps, land mines—sudden explosions killing and maiming, then quiet until another explosion. There were also some larger-scale traditional set-tos. In 1950 Giap trapped an entire French army in Cao Bang province in northeastern Vietnam, a humiliating defeat for the French, who lost 6,000 soldiers, 450 trucks, and enough artillery pieces, mortars, and guns to stock a Viet Minh division. In the words of the journalist Bernard Fall, it "doomed all French chances of full victory" because it meant that the French could no longer insert themselves between the Viet Minh and China.[19] Vietnam north of the Red River was forever out of French hands.

Another "meat-grinder" battle came west of Hanoi at Hoa Binh from November 1951 to February 1952. There the French commander, Jean de Lattre de Tassigny, emboldened by more U.S. military aid, chose to initiate a battle on the main Viet Minh road between the Viet Minh's tightly controlled territory to the northeast of the Red River delta and the southern delta. Unprepared for the number of Viet Minh soldiers that Giap was able to marshal against them, the French had to call for additional forces from bases in Laos and Cambodia, thus weakening those outposts. That necessity pointed to one of the main flaws of the French in the war: they never committed enough troops to win a predominantly guerrilla war. Though the Viet Minh perhaps sustained over ten times the number of casualties of the French in this battle, "their divisions gained firsthand experience in fighting the French and learned enemy strengths and weaknesses."[20] Further, the French hold on the town of Hoa Binh did nothing to stop the Viet Minh from continuing their drive into the Red River delta. Only in Cochinchina were the French successful; in central Vietnam, they were able to retain control over limited territory around the old imperial capital of Hue and the cities of Danang and Nha Trang.

For the French, Vietnam was like quicksand. Political and military realities militated against any success. During the war, the government in Paris was constantly unstable, changing approximately every three or four months. As defeat followed defeat, new military commanders were sent to try their hand: there were seven different French commanders before war's end. A critical problem in giving the war some sense of direction was defining clearly what the French hoped to gain. The words of French Captain Jean Pouget ring ominously in this regard:

> *When General Navarre [the seventh commander, who came in mid-1953] arrived, he opened a file right away and on that file I wrote "War Goals." We looked for what to tell the troops. Well, until the end this file remained practically empty. We could never express concretely our war goals.*[21]

The French had been unabashedly overconfident when the war began, dismissing the Viet Minh as "the barefoot army." But the guerrilla war was like some Sisyphean nightmare: the French "pacified" an area, left it, and it slipped almost immediately back to Viet Minh control. The French controlled the cities, the Viet Minh the countryside. The French controlled the day, the Viet Minh the night. Under such frustrating and deadly conditions, troop morale was bad, and officers were being lost faster than new ones could be trained. As with the Bao Dai solution, the army began to try to put a more Vietnamese face on the military by building up the army of the State of Vietnam in a policy known as *le jaunissement* (yellowing). Meanwhile, the French at home soured on the war that they called the *dirty war,* frustrated by the lives and money that were, it seemed, being thrown away with little thought.

France faced different problems in different areas of Vietnam. Most of the fighting with the Viet Minh came in the north, where the French were almost continually bested. In the early 1950s the DRV made it clear that it was part of the international Communist community and looked to its longtime cultural model, China, for direction. In the early 1950s, two hundred thousand copies of forty-seven key Chinese Communist writings were published. Following the CCP model, the DRV conducted its own rectification campaign in 1952 and 1953, putting some sixteen thousand party cadres through reeducation in order to "purify" both party and government. In the central and extreme southern parts of the north, militant Catholic groups with their own militias staved off both the French and the Viet Minh.

In the south the political situation was chaotic, with a hodgepodge of groups, many of which were practically states unto themselves. Bao Dai had ruled the south since 1949 but in name only. The Cao Dai sect flexed its muscles with its own militias, courts, schools, and social welfare programs. South of Saigon lay Hoa Hao headquarters, with its own flag and with lands protected "by fiercely wielded machetes and rifles."[22] In addition, there was a gang of river pirates, the Binh Xuyen, who had branched out, heading, incongruously enough, the Saigon police department and organized crime and vice. As diverse as the social, political, and religious landscape was, Bao Dai legitimately claimed that all groups were cooperating against the Viet Minh. One once and future key southern figure, Ngo Dinh Diem, had worked tirelessly to achieve leadership for Bao Dai but had refused to serve as his prime minister. Diem had left Vietnam in August 1950 for a four-year sojourn in Japan, the United States, Rome, Belgium, and Paris. By late 1953 Bao Dai's government was in serious trouble, having antagonized many groups with proposed reforms; consequently, the government stalemated.

Though no one knew it in 1953, the war was moving to a dramatic climax. Vo Nguyen Giap's strategy in the spring of that year was to invade Laos and, with the help of Communist Pathet Lao troops, take Laos, then seize Cambodia, and eventually join those forces to attack Saigon—truly an Indochinese strategy. The

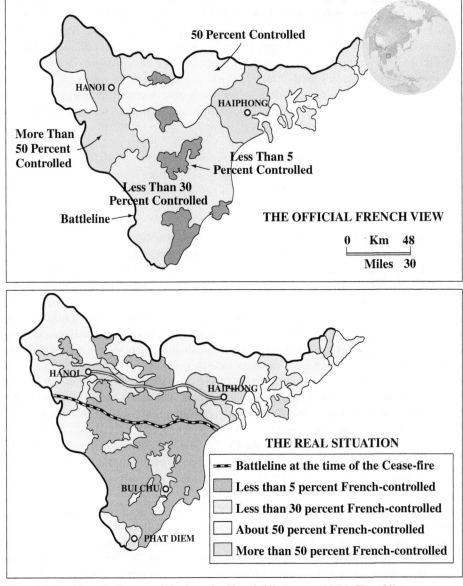

50 Percent Controlled

HANOI ○

HAIPHONG ○

**More Than
50 Percent
Controlled**

**Less Than 5
Percent Controlled**

**Less Than 30
Percent Controlled**

Battleline

THE OFFICIAL FRENCH VIEW

0   Km   48

Miles   30

HANOI ○

HAIPHONG ○

THE REAL SITUATION

▬▬▬ **Battleline at the time of the Cease-fire**

▨ **Less than 5 percent French-controlled**

☐ **Less than 30 percent French-controlled**

☐ **About 50 percent French-controlled**

▨ **More than 50 percent French-controlled**

BUI CHU ○

○ PHAT DIEM

Map 16-1   Revolutionary Warfare in North Vietnam, 1953: Two Views.

French, however, stopped the Viet Minh from seizing the Plain of Jars in northern Laos. That defeat did not end Giap's plans to take Laos; in fact, in December 1953 and January 1954, he won most of southern and central Laos. However, a battle on the invasion route into Laos at the village of Dienbienphu ended the war.

The Battle of Dienbienphu, one of the great battles of the twentieth century, began when French planes dropped 2,200 paratroopers into the area of the village completely surrounded by high hills. General Henri Navarre believed that he could lure the Viet Minh to the area and defeat them in a more conventional battle.

Ho Chi Minh and Vietnam Workers' Party Politburo Members   Under a straw-covered shelter, North Vietnam's President Ho Chi Minh discusses the opening of the Dienbienphu campaign with members of the party's politburo. General Vo Nguyen Giap is on the far right.

Navarre made several strategic blunders. He estimated that Giap would not be able to send more than one division and could not get artillery up the mountains to attack the French on the plain. These predictions, like others throughout the war, were based on overconfidence and almost out-of-hand negation of Viet Minh capabilities; one of the French soldiers captured at Dienbienphu disdainfully dismissed the Viet Minh as "red termites."[23] In essence, Navarre ceded the hills to the Viet Minh and did not even try to camouflage French artillery positions, making them easy targets for Viet Minh artillery.

In the end, Giap sent four divisions of troops. In the hills surrounding the plain, the Viet Minh had 49,500 combat troops and 31,500 support personnel; in addition, there were 23,000 maintaining supply lines to the Chinese border. (The French side had only 10,814 men, one-third of whom were Vietnamese from the State of Vietnam.) The artillery—which brought far greater firepower than the French possessed—was dragged and inched up the hills, with men shoving boards under the wheels of caissons after an inch or two of forward progress to prevent them from rolling back. A song sung at the time reveals the motives of those who participated in what was a gargantuan task:

> *The mountains are steep, but the determination in our hearts is higher than mountains.*
> *The chasms are deep and dark, but what chasm is as deep as our hatred?*
> *How do we sing, two three how [sic], the fowl are about to crow on the mountain tops.*
> *Pulling our artillery across mountain passes, before the early dawn.*[24]

Dienbienphu was a nightmare for the French. From the beginning of the battle on March 13, 1954, the Viet Minh artillery blasted the French day and night from the heights; artillery shells destroyed the airstrip, on which the French depended for getting supplies, on the second day. The Viet Minh initially utilized (under Chinese advice) human wave assault attacks; within four days, they completely controlled the perimeter. "The French command staff was shocked. Colonel de Castries [the commander] became withdrawn, uncommunicative. On the second night the artillery commander committed suicide, saying, 'I am completely dishonored.'"[25] Giap then changed tactics, stopping the artillery attacks and the human wave assaults and instead digging trenches and tunnels to tighten the noose around the French.

Then the rainy season came early, and the drenching downpours caused French shelters and dugouts to collapse. There was no clean water. "Medical supplies ran out. No planes could land to evacuate the wounded. Men who were wounded in the trenches sunk under the yard-high mud to die."[26] At this desperate impasse, the French asked the United States to intervene. Washington and Paris discussed air strikes to relieve the French and even the use of tactical nuclear weapons. Some in the Eisenhower administration were ready to act, but the president would not implement such a policy without British support. The British refused, for on April 26 an international conference was opening in Geneva, Switzerland, to deal with the crises in Indochina and Korea. The United States did not act. Dienbienphu fell on May 7, the day before the conference took up the Indochina crisis. The Dienbienphu toll: French—1,500 dead, 4,000 wounded, and some 10,000 taken prisoner (many of whom died in Viet Minh camps); Viet Minh—8,000 dead, 15,000 wounded. But the larger toll from the eight years of war is staggering. For the French and their Indochinese allies, there were 189,162 killed or missing and 156,968 wounded. The estimated Viet Minh toll was probably three times higher, and perhaps as many as 25,000 civilians had been killed.

THE GENEVA ACCORDS, 1954

At the time of their military victory, it is estimated that the Viet Minh held up to 80 percent of the territory in Vietnam; they went to the Geneva Conference warily, fearing diplomatic loss of what they had won on the battlefield. Indeed, that is what happened. China and the Soviet Union both stressed the importance of Viet Minh compromise; with the U.S. actions in Korea in stark memory, China was especially fearful of U.S. intervention should the Viet Minh be inflexible. As a result, the Viet Minh did not become rulers in their own country: the Geneva Accords of July 1954 temporarily split Vietnam into two zones, north and south of the seventeenth parallel. This was not a permanent division into two countries; the two zones were to be reunified following nationwide elections in the summer of 1956. The cease-fire, other details of the accords, and the elections were to be overseen by an International Control Commission composed of representatives from Canada, India, and Poland. Neither zone was allowed to increase the number of its armaments or military bases, nor could either zone adhere to military alliances. The United States, acting contrary to the Geneva Accords, which it and South Vietnam did not sign, made South Vietnam by special protocol a country linked to the Southeast Asia Treaty Organization (SEATO).

THE REPUBLIC OF VIETNAM, 1954–1968

Ngo Dinh Diem and "Nation-Building"

But the promise of reunifying elections was never fulfilled. As the French left Vietnam, the Bao Dai government appointed Ngo Dinh Diem prime minister. Diem had served as provincial governor in the 1920s and as minister of the interior under Bao Dai in the 1930s. He was a devout, conservative, and ascetic Catholic who had spent two years at Maryknoll Junior Seminary in Lakewood, New Jersey, meeting and cultivating prominent individuals like Supreme Court Justice William O. Douglas, Francis Cardinal Spellman, and John F. Kennedy. Indeed, part of Bao Dai's interest in Diem for his government came from what he perceived as Diem's American connections. From the viewpoint of the United States, terrified of the spread of Communism during the Red Scare of the Joseph McCarthy era, finding someone who could stabilize southern Vietnam to keep it properly anti-Communist was essential. Diem became the Americans' man in Saigon. The United States therefore set out to build a new nation, the pre-Dienbienphu State of Vietnam becoming the Republic of Vietnam and the temporary seventeenth parallel zone divider becoming a hard-and-fast boundary between two countries. It was no small order.

Ngo Dinh Diem Comes to Washington President Dwight Eisenhower and Secretary of State John Foster Dulles greet President Diem at Washington's National Airport on a 1957 visit. They touted him as the "miracle man of Asia."

Diem essentially had no power base in Vietnam and lacked the charismatic political personality to help build one. The United States sent CIA operatives to create paramilitary units to destabilize Ho's regime in the north and to undertake a propaganda campaign to encourage northern Catholics to move south during the three-hundred-day free movement period specified in the Geneva Accords. Over eight hundred thousand did so, many moved by the U.S. navy and resettled with $282 million in support from the U.S. government—providing Diem with something of a political base. But Diem showed considerable early ability at establishing his control. In March 1955, the three southern "states unto themselves"—Cao Dai, Hoa Hao, and Binh Xuyen—joined in an ultimatum calling for the establishment of a new government; they were not ready to play under Diem's rules. Diem succeeded in bribing the religious sects and in 1955–1956 defeating their militias. In May 1955, encouraged by the United States, five loyal army battalions moved against the Binh Xuyen in Cholon, the Chinese sector of Saigon, with tanks. Though much of Cholon was destroyed and many ethnic Chinese were killed, Diem ended Binh Xuyen's reign.

The United States was ever more determined to support Diem, who, emboldened, called for a national referendum on whether to retain the monarchy under Bao Dai or establish a republic with Diem as president. After the October 1955 referendum, Diem announced that he had received 98.2 percent of the votes, obviously a fraud (in many places, he received more votes than there were registered voters). Diem established not a democracy but a dictatorship, one supported by U.S. leaders who came to see Diem as the indispensable man in preserving "democracy" in the Republic of Vietnam. Diem announced that he was canceling the nationwide elections called for in the Geneva Accords; the United States supported him. Indeed, "if Diem served as a mandarin under the aegis of the United States, he was a puppet who frequently pulled his own strings."[27] In the late 1950s, the United States supplied Diem with almost $300 million annually in economic and military assistance. "Without American support, Diem would never have survived. With it, he seemed to have done the impossible. Washington held him up as the model of anti-communism, the miracle man of Asia."[28]

But Diem alienated large segments of South Vietnamese society. The Viet Minh veterans who had remained in the South were angered by Diem's refusal to hold nationwide elections and uncertain about how to respond. Fearful of U.S. intervention and needing time to industrialize and gain economic stability, the North initially advised them to use peaceful means to try to gain power. Farmers were upset; Diem had allowed former landlords who had abandoned their land during the war to return and take it back from peasants who had farmed it. The United States pushed for land reform that would limit landholdings and fix a rent ceiling, but although Diem talked about it, he never implemented it. The fact that he even considered it alienated the landlords; that he did nothing antagonized the peasants (15 percent of the population owned three-quarters of the land in the South in 1961). Diem's decision to abolish elected village councils embittered those in the countryside. He also antagonized the ethnic Montagnards by trying to impose Vietnamese culture on them, something the French had never attempted.

Diem's regime became increasingly authoritarian. It censored the press and attempted to place controls on Buddhists. It banned contraceptive use, dancing, and sentimental songs. "Divorces, passport applications, promotions and reassignments of military commanders and civil servants, and property transfers involving foreigners all required Diem's personal approval. . . ."[29]

The Insurgency: The National Liberation Front

It is little wonder that, beginning in 1958–1959, an anti-Diem insurgency began to grow. Led by the Viet Minh, it was a coalition of the disaffected and disgruntled: former Cao Dai, Hoa Hao, and Binh Xuyen adherents, peasants, students, and intellectuals. In December 1960 they came together in the National Liberation Front (NLF), supported by Hanoi. Leaders in the North came to believe that a military insurgency might be the only way to reunify the nation and that it had greater potential for success, given Diem's miserable record. Thus, Hanoi committed itself to resuming armed struggle in the South, a position formalized at the Third Party Congress of the Vietnam Workers' Party (the name of the Communist organ in Hanoi) in September 1960, "assign[ing] liberation of the south equal priority with consolidation in the north."[30] The level of violence in the South rose dramatically; whereas in 1958 about 700 local government officials were assassinated, in 1960 the number reached 2,500.

Diem's regime dubbed the NLF's partisans *Viet Cong* (a derogatory term for Vietnamese Communists). To protect farmers (including the Montagnards), the regime adopted the Agroville (1959) and Strategic Hamlet (1962) programs, which forcibly relocated farmers in fortified settlements to protect them from the Viet Cong. The relocated population deeply resented this uprooting from their ancestral homes; when the Viet Cong began to target these fortified settlements for attack, their resentment turned to hostility against the regime.

Diem's reaction to dissent and the insurgency was to throw suspects into prison and introduce terrorism into the increasingly combustible situation. In May 1959 he had the National Assembly pass Law 10/59, which "created special military tribunals to arrest any individual 'who commits or intends to commit crimes . . . against the State.' Equipped with portable guillotines, the tribunals rendered one of three verdicts: innocent, life in prison, and death."[31] Many of those who staffed the tribunals were members of the increasingly hated secret police, headed by Diem's brother Ngo Dinh Nhu, the gray eminence of the regime. Nhu was head of the Vietnamese Special Forces, in effect his own private army, and his pet programs were the Agroville and Strategic Hamlet fiascos. The Diem regime reported that there were twenty thousand political prisoners by 1956, and over the years the numbers grew to hundreds of thousands.

Opposition to Diem and his policies seemed omnipresent. When eighteen prominent South Vietnamese leaders issued a statement detailing and protesting government abuses in April 1960, they were immediately arrested. Coup attempts occurred in November 1960 and February 1962. The United States sent increasing numbers of military advisors to the South from 1961 on and repeatedly told Diem to undertake reforms, but he sat on his hands. The United States had little leverage with him. As the Viet Cong presence, threat, and terror against its opponents grew and the overall political situation deteriorated, the United States made renewed efforts to strengthen the Army of the Republic of Vietnam (ARVN), by sending even more military advisors to train them.

In 1963, Diem and Nhu went too far. On May 8, Buddhists in Hue protested an order forbidding them to display flags in honor of the Buddha; government troops fired, killing nine demonstrators. Demonstrations then spread across the country. On June 11 a Buddhist monk burned himself to death on a street in Saigon, triggering what amounted to an uprising of Buddhists, students, and disaffected urban residents. Douglas Pike, an American analyst, noted that he could see "the whole fabric of Vietnamese society coming apart."[32] In Washington, the view was just as bleak. Diem and Nhu in a sense dug their own graves by continuing to persecute the Buddhists, raiding and ransacking pagodas and arresting monks. When key figures in Diem's army plotted a coup, the United States supported the effort. The overthrow of the Diem regime on November 1, 1963, ended, unhappily for America's sense of moral rectitude, with Diem's and Nhu's murders. Though Diem had been an obstreperous ally, his voice from beyond the grave might well have warned, *"après moi le deluge."*

Changing Civil War into an American War

After Diem's murder (and that of John Kennedy three weeks later), there seemed to be no way to restore stability to South Vietnam. Coup after coup brought in a series of military figures, none of whom were able to govern effectively; there were seven changes of government in 1964. Against that backdrop the war escalated. On August 2, a U.S. intelligence-gathering ship, the *U.S.S. Maddox,* was attacked by North Vietnamese torpedo boats in the Gulf of Tonkin. Two days later, reports (later found to be erroneous) came that the North Vietnamese had struck again at the *Maddox* and another ship, the *Turner Joy.* President Lyndon B. Johnson ordered retaliatory strikes on North Vietnam, the first bombing of the North in the war. They destroyed 90 percent of the oil storage facilities at Vinh and twenty-five patrol boats. More ominously, the U.S. Congress passed the Tonkin Gulf Resolution, which gave the Johnson administration the go-ahead "to take all necessary steps including the use of force to assist any member or protocol state of the Southeast Asia Collective Defense Treaty requesting assistance in defense of its freedom."[33] The resolution was a blank check allowing the U.S. administration to do whatever it pleased in dealing with the war.

Six months later, in February 1965, the United States began a campaign of continuous bombing of the North to try to force the North to come to terms. The campaign expanded each year—from 25,000 sorties in 1965 to 79,000 in 1966 to 108,000 in 1969. Early on, the bombers hit military bases and facilities

Helicopters Over Rice Paddies U.S. helicopters in action in South Vietnam in February 1966. The helicopter provided rapid mobility for troop movement and medical evacuation.

Spraying Agent Orange   In order to defoliate dense jungle, U.S. planes sprayed eighty million liters of poisonous chemicals, including forty-five million liters of Agent Orange, a defoliant containing dioxins, which accumulate in the body to cause cancers. Agent Orange was sprayed over 10 percent of the country. Birth defects were a common result.

and infiltration routes into the South. In 1966 the targets were industries and transportation facilities, and the bombing area stretched farther to the North. In 1967 the missions zeroed in on power plants, steel mills, and sites around Hanoi and Haiphong. The United States had destroyed most of its targets by 1967, but in the end the bombing had no demonstrable effects on the war, with the possible exception of strengthening the North Vietnamese determination to resist. Indeed, as bombing grew heavier, the rate of infiltration into the South increased, from 35,000 soldiers in 1965 to an estimated 90,000 in 1967. Each B-52 mission cost the United States $30,000; overall it lost 950 planes costing about $6 billion. The bombing both crippled and redirected North Vietnam's efforts to develop a modern industrial economy. Under the slogan "The mother factory gives birth to many child factories," almost all factories that employed more than 100 workers were divided into many "small-production agencies" and then scattered throughout nonindustrialized provinces where there was less of a possibility that they would be destroyed in the bombing.[34]

The bombing was devastating to the North. Even U.S. government officials admitted that there were likely a thousand civilian casualties each month, even though the bombing was not directed at the civilian population. And as in the Korean War, racial prejudice among U.S. forces in the South was overt or just beneath the surface of everyday life. The Vietnam War was the third war the United States had fought in Asia in three decades in which all women were called *mama-san, san* being only Japanese: in effect, it was a way of saying that all Asians were alike and denying their cultural differences.

Soldiers referred to Vietnamese—friends and enemies alike—as "gooks," "slopes," "slant-eyes," or "dinks." Many just gave up trying to separate friendly from unfriendly Vietnamese and considered them all as enemies. Some Americans used a modified Wild West analogy, mouthing such sentiments as "The only good gook is a dead gook." In the minds of many soldiers, the Vietnamese had become some subhuman species— repulsive, duplicitous, and deadly.[35]

These attitudes produced many killings, even massacres, of civilians, the most horrifying being the massacre of over five hundred civilians and the rape of at least twenty women at the village of My Lai on March 16, 1968.[36] Racism appeared perhaps most overtly in comments made by General William Westmoreland, the U.S. commander from 1964 to 1968, who said, "Vietnam reminds me of the development of a child": it is clear that "if adults of lower races are like children, then they may be treated as such— subdued, disciplined, and managed. . . ."[37] But the most telling comment was: "Well, the Oriental does not put the same high price [on life] as the Westerner. Life is plentiful. Life is cheap in the Orient. And as the philosophy of the Orient expresses it, life is not important."[38]

By 1965, the leadership situation in the Saigon government had stabilized under two military men, Nguyen Cao Ky (1965–1967) and Nguyen Van Thieu (1967–1975). Ky became premier about three months after the United States upped the ante and began sending U.S. combat troops in March. By the end of the year there were 200,000 troops in South Vietnam; that number swelled to 543,400 in April 1969 before troop withdrawals began.

THE DEMOCRATIC REPUBLIC OF VIETNAM, 1954–1968

Even though there was an ongoing war, it did not embroil all, nor did it become an obsessive problem until the 1960s. Hanoi was trying to pull off a revolution, the core of which, as in China, was land reform. In order to keep as many non-Communist supporters for the Viet Minh as possible, land reform was moderate in the beginning. Only landlords who supported the French had their land confiscated, and for Viet Minh supporters, land reform only entailed rent reduction. Starting in 1953, however, the state moved to a more radical phase, beginning land confiscation and redistribution in Thai Nguyen province north of the Red River. In two provinces south of the Red River delta, Thanh Hoa and Ninh Binh, land reform turned brutal and violent. The longtime Communist leader Truong Chinh, a zealot who revealed his inflexibility by denouncing his own father over land reform issues, headed the campaign. Thousands defected from the Viet Minh, whose leaders halted the radical land reform until after the war and the three hundred days of civilian movement across the seventeenth parallel ended. Ho Chi Minh dismissed Chinh, who was forced to admit his "left-wing deviationism."

In the land reform, over 2 million acres of land were confiscated and redistributed to 2,104,000 peasant families. But, as in China, the ultimate goal of land reform was not giving land to individual farmers but increasing agricultural production by setting up cooperatives to achieve greater efficiency. Collectivization began almost immediately after land reform was completed. By 1960, over 68 percent of all farmland and 85 percent of peasant families had been brought into cooperatives. The Vietnamese cooperatives were different from those in China, which were multifunctional and very large. In Vietnam they focused on one or two socioeconomic roles and were usually limited in size to the population of a village; sometimes a village had more than one cooperative.

In prosecuting the war, the North Vietnamese received assistance from both the Soviet Union and China; this support was stepped up when the U.S. bombing became more severe. Until January 1968, the Soviet Union provided 1.8 million rubles in aid, with about 60 percent earmarked for military materiel— primarily tanks, fighter planes, and surface-to-air missiles. In addition, Moscow sent three thousand technicians who, among other tasks, manned antiaircraft batteries and surface-to-air missile sites. The Chinese, who had had advisors at Dienbienphu, let it be known that, as in Korea, they would send in Chinese forces if the United States invaded North Vietnam. Beijing sent many supplies: vehicles, small arms, ammunition, uniforms, shoes, and rice. It also dispatched 320,000 engineering and artillery troops who helped build highways, bridges, and railroads to facilitate the transport of supplies from China.

Source: The Views of a North Vietnamese Army Draftee

The views of Nguyen Van Hung, a draftee from Hai Duong province, just to the west of Haiphong, reveal that not all North Vietnamese soldiers were enthusiastic about fighting in the South. What is his attitude toward the government in Hanoi and to serving in the army? Does it change over time? Why?

I was twenty-eight years old when I received my draft notice. My father had been a deputy village chief under the French regime, so I was classified as what was called a "middle farmer element." This was an undesirable classification, and of course my father had worked with the French. So even though he died when I was four I still had this bad classification. In addition I was an only son, and the head of my own family as well. By law I should have been exempt from service, but by 1967 there was such an emergency in the South that the authorities were taking everyone they could between eighteen and thirty-five. It didn't matter if you were a good element or a bad. So in April 1968 I found myself in the army. . . .

When I got the draft notice I knew I was destined to go South. And I knew the chances of coming back were very slim. About a hundred guys from my village had gone, starting in 1962, and none had returned. Their parents and wives were waiting for them up to their eyes in fear. But nobody had gotten any news. The govern-ment was very explicit about it. They said, "The trip has no deadline for return. When your mission is accomplished you'll come back." Uncle Ho had declared, "Your duty is to fight for five years or even ten or twenty years." So it was clear to me that the whole business was going to be long and dangerous. I was really agitated when I left for the army.

I especially resented the government's callousness about my family situation. After I received my draft notice, my wife began crying at night. She wanted me to petition against being called up. I knew that wasn't possible. So I had to swallow my bitterness and convince her that sooner or later my fate would be set, so I'd better go. It hurt to see my baby and wife left alone. But I didn't dare say anything openly.

But once I was at the training camp, I began to understand that the fight for the South had to be done. Actually I must say that I already believed the Americans were a hundred times crueler than the French.

Source: David Chanoff and Doan Van Toai, "Vietnam": A Portrait of Its People at War (London: I. B. Tauris, 1996), 48.

In addition, in 1965, Chinese, Soviet, and North Korean engineers and advisors worked on improving the Ho Chi Minh Trail for truck transport. The trail was a network of roads that led from North Vietnam through eastern Laos into South Vietnam on which men and supplies from the North made it into South Vietnam. Started as a footpath in 1955, by 1971 it had "fourteen major relay stations in Laos and three in South Vietnam. Each station, with attached transportation and engineering battalions, served as . . . storage facility, supply depot, truck park and workshop. Soviet . . . trucks, with a capacity of five to six tons, traveled day and night on all-weather roads."[39]

WAR, 1968–1975

At the Fourteenth Plenum of North Vietnam's Central Committee in late 1967, Hanoi's leaders committed themselves to launching a general offensive in the South. It was planned to coincide with the Lunar New Year, Tet, the most important holiday festival in Vietnam. It was massive and ambitious: units of the NLF

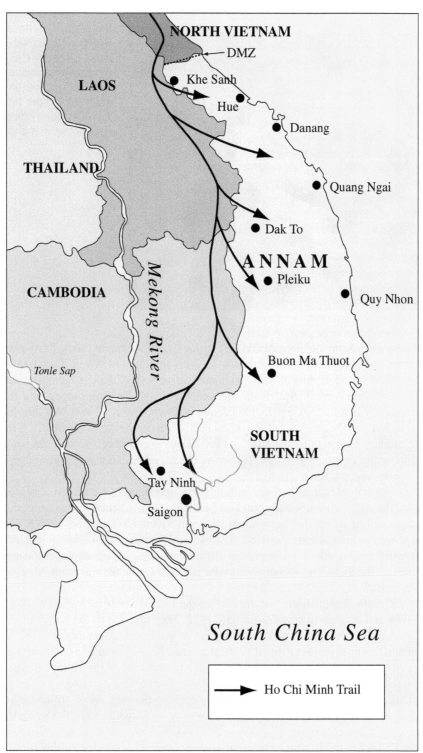

Map 16-2   The Ho Chi Minh Trail.

Summary Execution   The South Vietnam National police chief, Brigadier General Nguyen Ngoc Loan, executes an alleged Viet Cong officer on February 1, 1968, during the Tet offensive. The Viet Cong officer was caught carrying a pistol.

and the North's People's Army of Vietnam (PAVN) struck five of six major cities, thirty-six of forty-four provincial capitals, and sixty-four district capitals. Targeted in Saigon was U.S. Commander Westmoreland's headquarters, the headquarters of South Vietnam's general staff, the U.S. embassy, the Presidential Palace, and Tan Son Nhut Airport. Americans had spent late 1967 hearing propaganda about the great progress American forces were making (Lyndon Johnson, December 22, 1967: "All the challenges have been met. The enemy is not beaten but he knows that he has met his master in the field."[40]) In this context, such a massive military campaign by the NLF and PAVN was astonishing; Washington was in "a state of 'troubled confusion and uncertainty.'"[41] In this sense, the Tet offensive was a psychological victory for the North Vietnamese and the NLF.

In truth, however, it marked a military defeat for the two opponents of the United States. South Vietnam did not collapse, the ARVN did not collapse, and South Vietnam's general population did not rally to the northern cause, all of which had been hopes of North Vietnam's strategists. PAVN and NLF battle deaths may have been as high as forty thousand. The biggest loser was the NLF: they had led all the major attacks, and they suffered huge loss of life and the disruption of their organizational infrastructure. For the remainder of the war the Viet Cong was never a major factor in battle; the war from this point on was run completely by the North.

The shock and disillusionment that Tet created for the United States led to peace talks that began in Paris in May 1968 and eventually bore fruit in late 1972. They also led to the policy of Vietnamization adopted by President Richard Nixon in 1969, a reprise of the French *jaunissement*. The U.S. policy of withdrawal did not, however, call for a direct or rapid exodus. Nixon began a secret bombing campaign of Cambodia in 1969, which ultimately paved the way for the success of the Khmer Rouge (Cambodian Communists) and their holocaust of the Cambodian people. The bombing was kept a secret for four years. In spring 1970, the United States invaded Cambodia to find the elusive Central Office for South Vietnam (COSVN), the alleged headquarters of the NLF, but it was never found. In 1971 the South Vietnamese invaded Laos.

In the early 1970s, South Vietnam's President Thieu solidified his control, calling for a number of reforms. He took a more enlightened view of Buddhists, peasants, and the ethnic Montagnards. He distributed

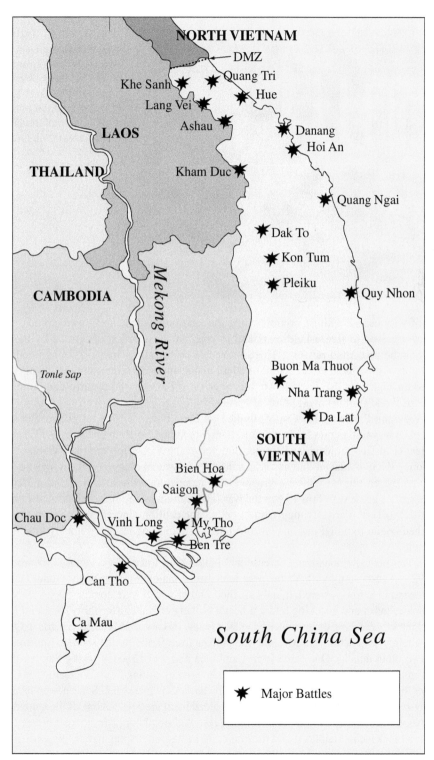

Map 16-3   The Tet Offensive, 1968.

Ho Chi Minh Mausoleum
This mausoleum sits on Ba Dinh Square, where, twenty-four years before his death, Ho Chi Minh had read Vietnam's Declaration of Independence and declared the founding of the DRV. It is visited annually by millions.
Source: Vision Photo Agency PacificStock.com.

land to about fifty thousand families, compensating the landlords whose lands were confiscated. In addition, he had laws passed to freeze land rents and to prohibit the eviction of tenants by their landlords. However, even as he mandated reforms, Thieu moved to dictatorship. In 1971 he rammed through the National Assembly a bill that in effect disqualified all major opposition forces in the October election. In 1972 he pushed through laws that forbade workers to go on strike, allowed the arrest and imprisonment of people without trial and shut down all political parties.

In North Vietnam, President Ho Chi Minh died on September 2, 1969, of congestive heart failure. One-man rule gave way to the joint leadership of Pham Van Dong, Vo Nguyen Giap, and Le Duan, the last longtime lieutenant of Ho Chi Minh and former director of the Viet Minh in South Vietnam. Dong oversaw foreign policy, Giap managed defense issues, and Duan was in charge on the domestic front, but all three had to sign off on crucial issues, a practice that hampered decisive action. After Ho Chi Minh's death, a heated debate arose over how to win the war. The erstwhile land reform leader and now chief theoretician for the Workers' Party, Truong Chinh, called for caution since "time was on their side": the United States had begun to withdraw, and North Vietnam should not act precipitously to stimulate a new U.S. commitment.[42]

Until 1972 this policy, emphasizing defense and building up forces for a victory drive, held sway. On March 30, 1972, however, the North Vietnamese launched a major invasion of the South at a time when ninety-five thousand U.S. troops were left, only six thousand of which were combat troops. Accompanied by two hundred Soviet tanks and attacking under a heavy artillery barrage, over thirty thousand PAVN troops moved south of the DMZ, taking the provincial capital, Quang Tri City, on May 1. The battle in Quang Tri was in many ways a feint: Giap hoped that it would draw forces from farther to the south to improve the chances of success in two other attacks. One came from Cambodia and was aimed at taking Saigon; the other was aimed at cities in the Central Highlands, with the ultimate goal of cutting South Vietnam in two. There were minor successes in the Central Highlands, but the ARVN, backed by massive U.S. air power, held and blunted the offensive by July. The cause of South Vietnam was aided by aggressive actions of the United States. During the offensive, on May 8, the Nixon administration resumed bombing of Hanoi and ordered, for the first time in the war, a blockade of Haiphong and the mining of its harbor, helping to take pressure off the ARVN.

The peace talks at Paris since May 1968 had borne no fruit. Throughout the talks, Hanoi's position continued to be that, for the war to end, U.S. troops had to be withdrawn; that the present South Vietnamese

Source: Ho Chi Minh's Last Will and Testament

It has been said that there were several drafts of this will and testament. What does Ho say about the American war? What is his legacy to the nation?

The war of resistance against American aggression may be prolonged. Our compatriots may have to consent to new sacrifices in property and human lives. No matter what, we must be resolved to combat the American aggressor until total victory is ours. *Our rivers and mountains and men will be here forever. The Yankees having been defeated, we will build up our country much finer than ever.*

No matter what the hardships and privations, in the end our people will surely conquer. The American imperialists will surely take to their heels. Our fatherland will surely be reunited. Our compatriots of the North and of the South will be reunited under the same roof. Our country will then have the distinction and honor of being a small nation that, through heroic combat, vanquished two great imperialisms—the French and the American—and brought a worthy contribution to the national liberation movement. . . .

As to personal affairs. Throughout my life I have served the fatherland, the revolution, and the people with all my heart and strength. Now that I am about to leave this world, I have nothing with which to reproach myself. I merely regret that I am unable to serve longer and better.

I hope there will be no great funeral ceremony after my death. I do not want to waste the time and money of the people.

Lastly, I bequeath my unlimited affection to all our people, to our party, to our armed forces, and to my young nephews and nieces.

Likewise, I address fraternal greetings to my comrades, friends, and the youth and children of the world.

My ultimate desire is that all our party and all our people, closely united in combat, will raise up a Vietnam that is peaceful, unified, independent, democratic, and prosperous. Thus we will make a worthy contribution to world revolution.

Source: Jean Sainteny, Ho Chi Minh and His Vision *(Chicago: Cowles, 1972), 168–70.*

government be dissolved and the ARVN disbanded; and that a coalition government including Communists be formed. After the blunting of the 1972 offensive, the North Vietnamese principal negotiator, Le Duc Tho, for the first time agreed that the Saigon regime might be allowed to remain and to negotiate a political settlement with the political arm of the NLF, the Provisional Revolutionary Government (PRG), established in 1969 as a rival of the Republic of Vietnam.

But when the United States and North Vietnam reached an agreement in October 1972, Thieu's government balked. It had not been properly briefed about the proposed agreement, and in an outrageous policy gaffe, the Americans had only an English-language translation of the agreement to present to the Saigon government. The South Vietnamese were especially incensed because the agreement allowed North Vietnamese troops to remain in the South and legitimized the PRG. Saigon refused to sign the agreement. Huang Duc Nha, aide to President Thieu, put it this way:

We said, "Well, you know there are still some substantial issues that are not resolved, and we are not going to sign it." And when we were threatened [with a] brutal reaction, we said, "Well we know what brutal reaction means. We accept that." At that time, it was a calculated move on our part. We said, "All right, if we were the U.S. side, they have two options: either do something drastic in South Vietnam, or bomb the North."[43]

Bach Mai Hospital   A funeral is held at the entrance to Bach Mai Hospital, which was hit in late 1972 by U.S. planes during the Christmas bombing. Note the poster on the left, with President Richard Nixon's face on the bomb.

As time passed, the North Vietnamese also seemed to have second thoughts. The American diplomat John Negroponte set forth their likely reactions to the U.S. inability to get South Vietnam to go along:

> *For a moment put yourself in the North Vietnamese shoes. They had gone through this entire negotiating process, [sic] they had reached agreement with us. They had even begun giving instructions to their cadre to prepare for a cease fire. Some of the North Vietnamese leaders might have begun to think that they had been the victims of the biggest con job in history and that we had simply led them down the garden path, and then we're going to welsh on the deal.*[44]

In these circumstances, Nixon exercised one of the options set forth by Huang Duc Nha: to bomb the North. Beginning on December 18, 1972, the United States unleashed the most intensive bombing campaign of the war. The thirty-six thousand tons of bombs dropped in the eleven-day *Christmas bombing*, were more than were dropped in the period between 1969 and 1971. Targets included power plants, rail yards, communication facilities, docks and shipping facilities, petroleum storage areas, bridges, highways, and military sites. Over 1,600 North Vietnamese civilians were killed, and large sections of Hanoi and Haiphong were laid waste. "The North Vietnamese believed that the raids were a deliberate act of terror."[45] World opinion was outraged.

When talks resumed, agreement came fairly quickly. The final agreement to end U.S. involvement in the war was essentially the same one that had been acceded to in October before the Christmas bombing. This time Washington gave Thieu an ultimatum—sign or else, the latter being the loss of any further U.S. support for his regime. Though Thieu never signed the Paris agreement, he indicated that he would not oppose it. Signed in Paris on January 27, 1973, the agreement provided for complete U.S. troop withdrawal and a return of prisoners of war within sixty days. The cease-fire was to be overseen by an International Commission of Control and Supervision made up of representatives from Canada, Hungary, Indonesia, and Poland. Elections were to be held in the South after negotiations between the Thieu government and the PRG. The U.S. phase of the war thus ended with one hundred fifty thousand North Vietnamese troops in the South and with recognition of the PRG.

Napalm This 1973 Pulitzer Prize–winning photograph shows terrified, screaming children who were victims of a U.S. aerial napalm attack on suspected Viet Cong hiding places on June 8, 1972.

THE END GAME

In October 1974, Le Duan, who had emerged as first among peers in government decision making, argued in an address before the Politburo that "The U.S. imperialists would find it very difficult to intervene directly. . . . They cannot save the Saigon regime from collapse."[46] The leadership's perception was that U.S. domestic problems and general opposition to continuing the war militated against any further U.S. action; the decision to launch the final offensive came rather easily. North Vietnam already had one hundred fifty thousand completely equipped troops in place in South Vietnam, along with a wealth of tanks and artillery pieces. The general in charge, Van Tien Dung (who replaced Giap in 1974), had overseen the infiltration of more troops into the South, a process, as he put it, of "strong ropes inching gradually, day by day, around the neck, arms, and legs of a demon, awaiting the order to jerk tight and bring the creature's life to an end."[47]

Dung used an attack on the province of Phuoc Long, along the Cambodian border some forty miles north of Saigon, as a test to see if the United States would intervene and if the ARVN could put up any resistance. The attack began on January 5, 1975, and led to a smashing victory. The United States sent no B-52s, and the one ARVN division that Thieu dispatched was no match for the two full PAVN divisions. Confident that they could move in for the kill, North Vietnamese leaders decided to cut South Vietnam in two by driving to the South China Sea from the Central Highlands. In early March they easily took the provincial capital of Ban Me Thuot. When that city fell, Thieu made the fateful decision to surrender the Central Highlands and pull ARVN troops back to protect the major cities of the South. But to avoid creating panic among the population, Thieu did not announce the withdrawal or his rationale for it. Rumors went wild, creating the very panic he had hoped to stifle, because people did not know what to believe. While Dung achieved more victories in the Central Highlands, hundreds of thousands of South Vietnamese along with thousands of ARVN troops poured south, fleeing the military clashes. North Vietnamese heavy artillery attacked these refugees. It is estimated that over one hundred thousand civilians and up to fifteen thousand ARVN soldiers died in this panicked flight.

Identities: Bui Tin (1924–):
The Vagaries of Revolution

It has been said that a revolution eats its own revolutionaries. Bui Tin is a case in point. Little is known about the first two decades of his life. He joined the Viet Minh in 1945 and served for a while as a bodyguard for Ho Chi Minh. He fought against the French in the Red River delta in the early 1950s and at Dienbienphu, becoming an important member of the Workers' Party and rising to the rank of colonel in the People's Army. In 1963 he was dispatched to South Vietnam to assess the situation there, traveling by foot down the Ho Chi Minh Trail. On his return in early 1964, he reported to the Hanoi leaders that the NLF needed more northern assistance. In 1973 he was the official spokesman for the North Vietnamese delegation sent to Saigon after the Paris Accords to arrange for the handling of U.S. prisoners of war.

Bui Tin became editor of the *People's Army Daily (Quan Doi Nhan Dan)*, and in the final offensive in 1975 he served as a war correspondent. He was on one of the tanks that broke through the fences around the presidential palace in Saigon on April 30, 1975; as the senior officer on hand, Bui Tin accepted the surrender of President Minh. Later he became deputy editor-in-chief of the party newspaper *People's Daily (Nhan Dan)*. Unfortunately, as a journalist, he began to rub some of the leaders of the Socialist Republic of Vietnam the wrong way. In spite of the government's great reluctance, he reported on the growing tensions between Vietnam and Cambodia in the run-up to Hanoi's overthrow of

Pol Pot's Cambodian regime. When that happened, Bui Tin was one of the first journalists to visit Phnom Penh. Colleagues reportedly said that "He was always in the right place at the right time."[1]

Frustrated by Hanoi's authoritarian policies and lack of material progress, Bui Tin journeyed to Paris in 1990, allegedly for medical treatment. Though his family remained in Vietnam, he went into self-imposed exile. His memoirs, *Snowdrop (Hao Xuyen Tuyet)* and *The Real Face (Mat That)*, were published in 1991 and 1993, respectively—both of which argued for major changes in Vietnam.

Bui Tin continued to lambast the Hanoi government from Paris, often broadcasting on the BBC. His lack of reverence for Ho Chi Minh infuriated the Hanoi leaders. When he argued that Ho made mistakes, including adopting the Stalinist economic and political models, they called him a traitor. Bui Tin also excoriated the Hanoi government for its press censorship and its "half-baked" economic reforms (see Chapter 17).[2]

In 1991 Bui Tin was stripped of his party membership. As if to underscore his characterization of the government's authoritarianism, his house in Vietnam was under constant surveillance; his family was forbidden to communicate with him; his daughter was forced to leave her position as an eye surgeon and to become an eyeglasses clerk; and his son-in-law was not allowed to accept a fellowship from Harvard University. The trajectories of Bui Tin's life reflect the roller-coaster ride of the Vietnamese revolution.

---

[1] *See http://www.tuvy.com/resource/books/f/following_ho_chi_minh.htm.*

[2] *This charge can be found at http://www.venguon.org/Post-doc/News/VNg_HanoiIndignant.html.*

Source: The Causes of the American Defeat

This analysis of the reasons for the U.S. defeat in its war with the Viet Cong and North Vietnamese comes from Truong Nhu Tang, a leader of the NLF. What is the heart of his argument? Is it compelling?

. . . At the same time, their military orientation deflected American attention away from the internal fissures in our own camp. The Eisenhower and Kennedy administrations had chosen to regard Ho Chi Minh as a tool of Chinese expansionism, ignoring the separate integrity and strength of Vietnamese national aspirations. Just so, the Johnson and Nixon administrations persisted in treating the NLF as part of a North Vietnamese monolith, casually shrugging aside the complex realities of the Vietnamese political world. As a result, the Americans were constantly trying to stamp out fires in their own front yard but never lighting any themselves in our garden. Kissinger was as maddened by this situation as his predecessors had been. More imaginative than they, he responded by striking back through the Soviets and Chinese, hopeful that our allies would eventually pressure us into moderation. But he never went for the jugular. Indeed, his strategic perspective prevented him from seeing where the jugular was.

In looking back at this period and at the negotiations that flowed out of it, some writers have taken pains to denigrate Henry Kissinger's abilities. If the purpose of observing history is to learn from it, such exercises are not only nonsensical but dangerously misleading. The flaw in Kissinger's thinking was in fact hardly personal. In considering the problem of Vietnam, he had inherited a conceptual framework from his American and French predecessors that he either could not or would not break out of. And it was this conceptual framework that led him to disaster. Along with their political forebears, both Nixon and Kissinger suffered from a fundamental inability to enter into the mental world of their enemy and so to formulate policies that would effectively frustrate the strategies arrayed against them, the strategies of a people's war.

Source: Truong Nhu Tang, A Viet Cong Memoir: An Inside Account of the Vietnam War and Its Aftermath *(New York: Vintage Books, 1986), 209, 213.*

When the final offensive was planned, North Vietnamese strategists believed that victory would come after a two-year campaign. But the rout of ARVN troops and the blunders of the Saigon government brought success much more quickly. In late March the PAVN began a huge offensive in the northern part of South Vietnam, attacking Quang Tri province and moving toward Hue. Thieu abandoned Hue, hoping to draw the line at Danang, fifty miles down the coast. PAVN forces took Hue on March 24, and their seemingly inexorable march led to the seizure of Danang on March 29. Thieu's plans crumbled into ashes: "South Vietnam was imploding."[48] The losses in the Central Highlands and the northern sector of the county had brought the deaths of one hundred fifty thousand ARVN troops and the loss of countless pieces of military equipment.

Thieu, who had isolated himself in the presidential palace, saw the inevitable and resigned on April 21. By that time, Saigon was surrounded on all sides by PAVN forces. On April 28, Thieu's longtime rival, Duong Van Minh, became South Vietnam's president. The United States completed its evacuation on April 30, transporting 7,100 U.S. and South Vietnamese personnel by helicopter to aircraft carriers off the coast and sending over 70,000 South Vietnamese via naval ships to other U.S. ships in the South China Sea.

North Vietnamese forces entered Saigon from six different directions that same day, completing the final offensive in only fifty-five days. Colonel Bui Tin (see Identities) accepted the surrender of President Minh. He later reflected on that day:

> *When I saw fear on the faces of Minh and the others present, I said, "The war has
> ended today, and all Vietnamese are victors. Only the American imperialists are van-
> quished. If you still have feelings for the nation and the people, consider today a
> happy one." That night, when I sprawled on the lawn of the Independence Palace with
> members of a communication unit, we all agreed it was the happiest day of our lives
> because it was a day of complete victory for the nation, because the war ended.*[49]

The war against the Americans and their South Vietnamese compatriots had ended; superior military strategy combined with a crumbling and demoralized ARVN and Thieu's disastrous regime had led to North Vietnam's victory. Losses were enormous. In 1995, Hanoi reported that 1.1 million PAVN and Viet Cong soldiers were killed and 600,000 wounded between 1954 and 1975; it estimated that 2 million civilians were killed (the U.S. estimate for northern civilians killed in its bombing campaigns was 30,000). For South Vietnam, the minimum number of ARVN killed was 110,357 and almost 500,000 wounded; civilian dead were estimated at 250,000. The United States suffered more than 58,000 deaths and more than 153,000 wounded.

Vietnam was once again united and independent, but domestic peace and material progress were not yet achieved. The economy was in ruins; over 50 percent of the population was left without homes, and at least 70 percent of the nation's industrial capacity had been blasted away in the bombing. The bitterness of three decades of war and 120 years of subjection to outsiders continued to linger, though in new guises.

Source: "A Tale of Two Soldiers"

This is a song written by Pham Duy (b. 1921), a popular folksinger and composer. Though he had joined the anti-French resistance, Duy left when he saw that it was dominated by the Communists. He left Vietnam in 1975 but returned to live in Ho Chi Minh City in 2005. What does this song say about Vietnam during the French and American wars?

There were two soldiers who lived in the same
village
Both loved the fatherland—Vietnam.
There were two soldiers who lived in the same
village
Both loved the fields and the earth of Vietnam.
There were two soldiers, both of one family,
Both of one race—Vietnam.
There were two soldiers, both of one family,
Both of one blood—Vietnam.

There were two soldiers who were of one heart,
Neither would let Vietnam be lost.
There were two soldiers, both advancing up a
road,
Determined to preserve Vietnam.

There were two soldiers who traveled a long
road,
Day and night, baked with sun and soaked with
dew.
There were two soldiers who traveled a long road,
Day and night they cherished their grudge.

There were two soldiers, both were heroes,
Both sought out and captured the enemy troops.
There were two soldiers, both were heroes,
Both went off to "wipe out the gang of common
enemies."

There were two soldiers who lay upon a field,
Both clasping rifles and waiting.
There were two soldiers who one rosy dawn
Killed each other for Vietnam
Killed each other for Vietnam.

Source: Neil Jamieson, Understanding Vietnam *(Berkeley: University of California Press, 1993), 321–22.*

CHRONOLOGY

1945	Japanese overthrow the French (March)
	Japanese surrender (August 15)
	Establishment of the DRV (September 2)
1946	French bombard Haiphong
1946–1954	The French war
1953–1960	Land reform in the North
1954	Battle of Dienbienphu
	Geneva Conference undoes Viet Minh victory
1955	Referendum makes Ngo Dinh Diem president of the Republic of Vietnam
1958–1959	Insurgency in the South against Diem
1960	Hanoi commits itself to resume armed struggle (September)
	NLF recognized by the North (December)
1963	Diem overthrown and killed
1964	Gulf of Tonkin incident
1965	U.S. Marines sent to South Vietnam (March)
1968	Tet offensive
1969	U.S. troop numbers reach 543,400 by April
	Death of Ho Chi Minh
1973	Paris Accords end the U.S. involvement in the war.
1975	North Vietnamese victory over the South

SUGGESTED READINGS

Chanoff, David, and Doan Van Toai, eds. *"Vietnam": A Portrait of Its People at War.* London: I. B. Tauris, 1996. This book of interviews with North Vietnamese and members of the Viet Cong dispels any idea that they necessarily shared similar attitudes and views; it underlines the diversity and complexity of that side of the war.

Elliott, Duong Van Mai. *The Sacred Willow: Four Generations in the Life of a Vietnamese Family.* New York: Oxford University Press, 1999. This haunting and heartbreaking story brings the struggles and experiences of the Vietnamese to life.

Fall, Bernard B. *Hell in a Very Small Place: The Siege of Dien Bien Phu*. Philadephia: J. B. Lippincott, 1967. This is the classic study of one of the most important battles of the twentieth century.

Truong Nhu Tang. *A Viet Cong Memoir: An Insider's Account of the Vietnam War and Its Aftermath*. New York: Vintage Books, 1986. This memoir of a top leader of the Vietcong changes the way people have generally thought about the Viet Cong, their goals, and their relationship to the North Vietnamese.

Woodside, Alexander. *Community and Revolution in Modern Vietnam*. Boston: Houghton Mifflin, 1976. This insightful and compelling analysis focuses on social organization in Vietnam's wars and revolution.

CHAPTER SEVENTEEN

Socialism with a Chinese and a Vietnamese Face, 1980s to the Present

Both China (since 1978) and Vietnam (since 1986) adopted capitalist measures to rev up the engine of economic development, a policy euphemistically called *socialism with a Chinese (or Vietnamese) face*. However, despite economic liberalization, both states continued to be politically authoritarian.

CHINA: REFORM AND REACTION

By late 1978, Deng Xiaoping had been reappointed to his old government positions. Deng had about eighteen years to remake China according to his vision—and remake it he certainly did. The chief goal was to realize the *Four Modernizations* in the arenas of agriculture, industry, national defense, and science and technology. At the Third Plenum in December 1978, the question of how to achieve the Four Modernizations was clarified. It "requires great growth in the productive forces and ... changes in all methods of management, actions, and thinking.... Socialist modernization is therefore a profound and extensive *revolution* [emphasis added]."[1] Such a revolution involved both China's internal or domestic situation and its relationship to the outside world.

The economic liberalization of the 1980s and 1990s began with the household responsibility system. It is notable that this reform started at the grassroots level when farmers in a poor area of Anhui province on their own initiative removed their land from commune control and began to farm it on their own. When Deng Xiaoping learned of this action he allowed it to stand, and when this return to pre-Communist farming practice increased production, the party-state decided to institutionalize it. Individual households leased land for fifty years; even though this was not private ownership, the land could be bought, sold, and inherited. Farmers could decide on their own how to farm. Once they met state grain quotas, they could sell their produce and/or commodities and keep the profits. The people's communes, in place for a quarter of a century, were gone: the commune became the township, the brigade the administrative village, and individual households the basic accounting and production units. The Mao years were seemingly sliced away.

The ability to keep profits was the crucial incentive prompting the rapid development of family farming and stimulating a surge in agricultural production—averaging 9 percent annually from 1978 to 1984. The possibility of improving their financial situation motivated farmers to plant cash crops that would bring higher prices; some farmers put money into food processing and other small-scale township and village enterprises. After the mid-1980s, prosperity in the countryside was maintained by the expansion of these enterprises, which by 1995 employed over 125 million workers.

Premier Deng Xiaoping and President Jimmy Carter
Deng and Carter, on a White House balcony overlooking the south lawn, wave to the crowds as their wives shake hands on Deng's visit to the United States early in 1979.

Source: The Reforms of Deng Xiaoping

In his capacity as special assistant to General Secretary Hu Yaobang, Ruan Ming helped direct agricultural reform in the early 1980s. In his memoir, published in 1992, he notes some of the consequences of the reform. What are the most important results?

The rapid spread of the family responsibility system in the countryside and disappearance of the People's Communes emancipated the peasants and the forces of agricultural production. The outlook of the rural population was fundamentally changed. As a first consequence, harvests were bountiful four years in a row, from 1980 to 1984. In five years' time, the total output of grain increased by 100 billion kilograms and cotton production by 3.8 million tons. The old problem of the nourishment and basic clothing of the Chinese peasants was at last resolved....

The second consequence of the rural reform was that the market economy made great strides in the countryside. The most profound economic change induced by reform was that it put an end to the combination of the self-reliant and semi-self-reliant natural economy that has dominated China for thousands of years and that was joined after 1953 to a barter economy under the protection of the state. But the Chinese economy was nevertheless entering a new era. Despite the many frustrations of the ten-year reform, the development of the rural commercial economy is irreversible. More than 65 percent of the rural economy was converted into a market economy. More than 100 million people formed

rural enterprises that produced one trillion yuan worth of merchandise.

Finally, the third consequence of rural reform: The farmers constitute the greatest force for reform in China and a powerful new independent force. Land reform in the early 1950s freed them the first time, as a class, from the landlords. In theory they were the masters of the country, but in reality they lived as prisoners of the People's Communes and state planning. This time, now that they are emancipated, they truly want to influence the nation's destiny.

Their power is first of all manifested in the economic realm: Rural merchandise has flooded the Chinese market, and some has even penetrated the global economy. The independent economic status of China's farmers has increased. At the same time, the emancipation of agricultural production forces has led more and more free rural people to quit the land to enter industry, commerce, and service areas or to install themselves in cities, where they have become the motivating factor behind urban reforms. That was the big picture of the great reform carried out from 1979 to 1980. The countryside had overwhelmed the cities.

Source: Quoted in R. Keith Schoppa, Twentieth Century China: A History in Documents *(New York: Oxford University Press, 2004), 162–63.*

With these changes, rural per capita income almost doubled from 1978 to 1984. Improved living standards for many farmers meant new homes, a better diet, and purchase of consumer goods. (See Chapter 20 for a discussion of the deeper social and cultural impacts of the reforms.) Others did not do well. The new system allowed farmers to rent out their land and to hire wage laborers to help on the farm. Those who worked essentially as subtenants and hired hands were among the poor. Most towns and villages in the countryside experienced greater economic inequality than previously; the reappearance of class divisions was usually rationalized by Deng's maxim that "some must get rich first."

In urban business and industry the *market model*—allowing the production and distribution of goods to be determined by the market rather than by central government planners—was adopted in late 1979. An industrial *responsibility system* replaced the old system whereby the state received all the profits. Now, after an enterprise paid the state a 55 percent tax on revenues, it could keep half of the profits after production costs were deducted (the state received the other half). Price controls on small consumer items were lifted, with prices allowed to float according to the market level. Individual enterprises operated autonomously (within broad state guidelines) and for profit. The late 1980s saw booming industrial production as well as higher inflation (up to 25 percent in early 1989). As the private sector grew, the urban economies of many cities were invigorated. Factory managers made business decisions, including hiring and firing their employees. The key word is *firing,* for up to this point, workers in PRC state enterprises (i.e., all enterprises) could never be fired; they held the *iron rice bowl,* a term for lifetime job security. Now that situation was changed: in the midst of general economic growth, workers had to be concerned about job security and financial benefits.

An estimated 100 to 130 million people from the countryside, now freed from restrictions binding them to their land, traveled to cities in the mid-1980s. Many of them did not have jobs. They were unattached to work or neighborhood units (which during the Maoist period had been the crucial institutions for local control). Many in this so-called floating population quickly became the wretched poor. The lucky ones found lodging in bleak shantytowns that grew up at the edges of cities; others lived on the streets, in parks, or in train stations. If these floaters found jobs, they were usually low-paying jobs that other workers refused—street vendor, prostitute, or hawker—with none of the welfare safety-net subsidies of people with urban residence certificates. The number of floaters grew from 70 million in 1993 to 140 million in 2003. They represented over 10 percent of the population and about 30 percent of the rural workforce. Statistics showed that 65 percent of the floaters were floating in their home province, while 35 percent crossed provincial boundaries. The faces of floaters were youthful, with 80 percent between the ages of fifteen and thirty-five.[2]

OPENING THE WINDOW TO THE WORLD

During the 1970s and 1980s China opened many windows to the world. The number of countries that established diplomatic relations with the country rose from 57 in 1970 to 137 in 1989. One of the most important diplomatic relationships was with the United States. The Taiwan question had loomed over this relationship since the United States had fostered close economic and political ties with the island in the 1950s and 1960s. The February 28, 1972, Shanghai Communiqué, negotiated during Nixon's visit, set down the general framework for relations between China and the United States. From the Chinese perspective, most important were the general foreign policy pledges and the U.S. statement on Taiwan. Both countries pledged not to seek hegemony in the region and to oppose other countries' attempts to do so. They agreed that trade, cultural, and scientific exchanges should be increased and that they should move to establish full diplomatic relations. On Taiwan:

> The United States acknowledges that all Chinese on either side of the Taiwan Strait maintain [that] there is but one China and that Taiwan is a part of China. The United States does not challenge that position. It reaffirms its interest in a peaceful settlement of the Taiwan question by the Chinese themselves. With this prospect in mind, it affirms the ultimate objective of the withdrawal of all U.S. forces and military installations from Taiwan. In the meantime, it will progressively reduce its forces and military installations on Taiwan as the tension in the area diminishes.[3]

Domestic problems in both countries delayed the start of full diplomatic relations until January 1979. To nurture the U.S.-China relationship, Deng visited the United States that winter. The diminutive (4′ 9″) leader was serenaded at the Kennedy Center in Washington, D.C. with the strains of "Getting to Know You." He donned a ten-gallon hat and ate barbecue at a Texas rodeo. It was a public relations coup. After the first corporate agreements in late 1978 with Coca-Cola and Boeing, U.S.-based firms greatly expanded their operations in Chinese investments and trade.

As China strode into the international arena, people-to-people contact increased. In the 1980s, large numbers of foreign tourists brought rapid growth in the tourist industry and ever-greater numbers of Chinese also traveled abroad. The number of students studying overseas rapidly increased, as did the number of foreign students coming to China. From 1979 to 1989, about eighty thousand Chinese students and scholars went to the United States alone, and the total number of student visas issued from 1983 to 1988 reached one hundred fifty thousand. The government sent students abroad to acquire advanced training in order to help achieve the Four Modernizations on their return. Even though some students stayed longer in their programs than the government had anticipated and some students chose to remain in the United States, the government was not deterred. As evidence of the brain drain, by 1989 eleven thousand students had become permanent residents in the United States.

All returning students and scholars had been exposed to new ideas and attitudes, which could be problematic. In addition, China's opening entailed more porous borders, with increasing numbers of foreign books and journals, as well as the presence of computers and other electronic media. Policymakers understood that an opened window might let in some mosquitoes and flies (bourgeois ideas) but self-assuredly noted that they could be quickly swatted and killed.

Opening also referred to expanding foreign trade and allowing foreign investment. Beginning with a handful of loans, credits, and joint ventures, opening eventually led to full foreign ownership and operation of Chinese enterprises. In many ways, this smacked of the pre-1949 domination of Chinese cities by Westerners, but now China was calling the shots, and its leaders saw foreign investment and know-how as the engines that could rev up that drive. In 1979 four special economic zones (SEZs) were opened on the southeast coast (the most famous being Shenzhen) to offer concessions to foreign investors; fifteen more were added in 1986. To lure foreign investment, the Chinese provided low tax rates, convenient transportation networks, new industrial plants, and a well-trained, cheap labor force. The zones brought huge economic benefits, including the infusion of foreign capital to underwrite the costs of industry and other modernization projects, helping to solve the problem of chronic shortfalls in foreign exchange, greater ease in keeping up with the advanced technology of the West and Japan, and work opportunities for Chinese.

The SEZs had a cascading impact and far-reaching implications beyond the zones. Foreigners willing to do business in China needed predictable, regularized economic conditions that included laws protecting property and governing contracts. In the early 1980s China essentially had no such laws, governing instead by fiat, government regulations, and the orders of individual officials. Thus, it was necessary to develop a legal system including laws, a court system, and lawyers. In 1980 China had only about 3,000 lawyers. Goals announced in 1993 called for 150,000 lawyers by 2000, but in March 2004 there were only 102,000 lawyers for a population of 1.3 billion.

In entering the international economic system, China aimed to join international economic organizations like the World Bank, the International Monetary Fund (IMF), and the Asian Development Bank, which provided low-interest loans and technical and economic advice. In 1980, the World Bank and the IMF expelled Taiwan in favor of the PRC. However, membership was a two-way street: it brought China great benefit, but it also meant that China had to follow international guidelines and be more forthright about the details of its economic realities.

POLITICAL AUTHORITARIANISM

While opening brought greater economic freedom and its various ripple effects, in the political realm repression was the icy name of the game. Occasionally in the 1980s and 1990s warm-ups occurred, but they were always followed by a return to even more frigid conditions. Party-state leaders varied in their attitudes toward political liberalization; some favored more political tolerance, while others championed repression

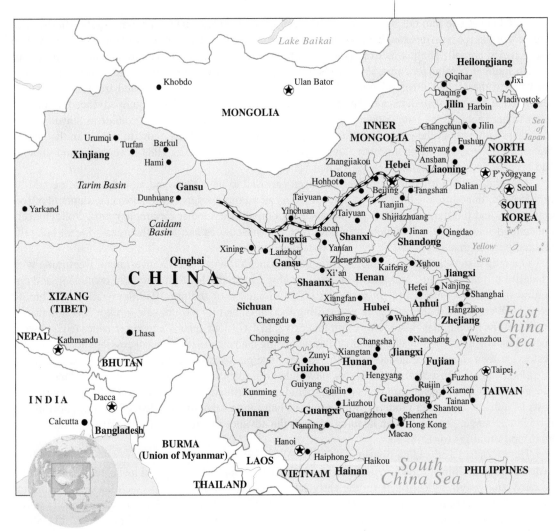

Map 17-1 The People's Republic of China.

to maintain order and stability. Factional struggle was as much a reality as struggle between the government and those in society pushing for greater political change.

Among those who were primarily economic reformers, the key figure was Zhao Ziyang, provincial reformer in Sichuan, who became premier in the early 1980s. The second of Deng's protégés, Hu Yaobang, was a political liberal. Having served for many years as head of the Communist Youth League and the Chinese Academy of Social Sciences, he became party general-secretary in the early 1980s. Zhao and Hu were opposed by antireform old Maoists. Whereas in the 1960s and 1970s the political context made these men leftists or radicals, the changing contexts of the 1980s and 1990s cast them as rightists or reactionaries.

Democracy Wall (1978–1979)

In November 1978, people began to place posters, essays, poetry, pamphlets, and mimeographed magazines with titles like *Explorations* and *Beijing Spring* on a stretch of wall along Chang'an Boulevard. Debates sprang up at the wall about a host of political and social issues; many participants were blue-collar workers with a high school education or less. Though Deng first gave the wall his blessing, other leaders perceived its combustible potential. At the very time that Democracy Wall began to flourish, hundreds of thousands of people sent to the countryside during the Cultural Revolution were returning to the cities with grievance petitions about their unjust sufferings. The CCP under Hu Yaobang called strongly for the reexamination of cases of "unjust persecution" in order to see if rehabilitation was in order. Over one hundred thousand came to Beijing and Shanghai alone. Given the potential for social turmoil, Democracy Wall's widening criticism of the party-state became another potentially disruptive element beyond party control. The memory of the Cultural Revolution's social violence and its impact on Chinese life was all too fresh; unleashing a new round, some leaders thought, would undercut any hope of achieving the Four Modernizations.

Then there came a call for a Fifth Modernization—democracy. Wei Jingsheng, a twenty-eight-year-old electrician who had served for four years with the PLA, created a poster with that title in December. In essays published in the journal *Explorations*, editor Wei challenged Deng with blistering criticism. "Does Deng Xiaoping want democracy? No, he does not. . . . If his idea of democracy is one that does not allow others to criticize those in power, then how is such a democracy different from Mao Zedong's tyranny. . . ?[4]

Source: Wei Jingsheng's Critique

In this excerpt from his essay, Wei Jingsheng, who emerged in 1979 as one of China's chief dissidents, pointedly attacked the policies of Deng Xiaoping. This essay was used by the prosecution in the government's case against him in 1979: the state argued that it was evidence of Wei's "counter-revolutionary agitation and propaganda" and his "incitement to overthrow the dictatorship of the proletariat." The essay was first published in the March 1979 issue of the journal Tansuo *[Explorations]. What are its essential points about Deng and democracy?*

Everyone in China knows that the Chinese social system is not democratic, and that this lack of democracy has severely stunted every aspect of the country's social development over the past thirty years. In the face of this hard fact, there are two choices before the Chinese people. Either to reform the social system if they want to develop their society and seek a swift increase in prosperity and economic resources; or, if they are content with a continuation of the Mao Zedong brand of proletarian dictatorship, then they cannot even talk of democracy, nor will they be able to realize the modernization of their lives and resources.

Where is China heading and in what sort of society do the people hope to live and work? The answer can be seen in the mood of the majority. It is this mood that brought about the present democratic movement. With the denial of Mao Zedong's style of dictatorship as its very prerequisite, the aim of this movement is to reform the social system and thereby enable the Chinese people to increase production and develop their lives to the full in a democratic social environment. This aim is not just the aim of a few isolated individuals but represents a whole trend in the development of Chinese society. . . .

Does Deng Xiaoping want democracy? No, he does not. He is unwilling to comprehend the misery of the common people. He is unwilling to allow the people to regain those powers usurped by ambitious careerists. He describes the struggle for democratic rights—a movement launched spontaneously by the people—as the actions of troublemakers who must be repressed. To resort to such measures to deal with people who criticize mistaken policies and demand social development shows that the government is very afraid of this popular movement. . . .

Source: Quoted in R. Keith Schoppa, Twentieth Century China: A History in Documents *(New York: Oxford University Press, 2004), 178.*

When the democracy movement began to spread across China, the other leaders convinced Deng that it could not be allowed to continue. The Beijing municipal government issued strict regulations limiting mass meetings and demonstrations. The *four cardinal principles* were issued, forbidding all activities opposed to socialism, the proletarian dictatorship, party leadership, or Marxism-Leninism-Mao Zedong Thought. Democracy Wall under Deng was no more viable than the Hundred Flowers under Mao. The upshot was that Wei, along with other activists, was arrested. He was charged with spying and "counterrevolutionary incitement" and sentenced to fifteen years in prison.[5] Most of his arrested colleagues were imprisoned for ten to fifteen years, often in solitary confinement. The end of Democracy Wall in 1979 at the beginning of the economic reforms was symbolic of the political repression that accompanied economic liberalization in the regimes of Deng and his successors, Jiang Zemin and Hu Jintao.

Antireformers attempted to strike out at the reforms in the 1981 Campaign against Bourgeois Liberalization, targeting certain writers, and the 1983 Campaign against Spiritual Pollution, attacking certain "polluting" practices (Western-style individualism, clothing, hairdos and facial hair; pornographic films; "decadent" music; and "feudal" superstitions and religion). The first effort died a quick death. The second was squelched by Hu Yaobang and Zhao Ziyang, who asserted that it was frightening foreigners who wanted to invest in China and that, if China was to continue to modernize, this sideshow had better stop.

Exit Hu Yaobang (1986–1987)

More serious practical problems for the reformers erupted in late 1986. The previous year had seen some campus unrest across the country over a wide range of issues on campuses and beyond. Increasing the possibility of an antireformist backlash, economic reforms had hit some snags: inflation was rising, and some people felt disgruntled at having been left behind amid the new prosperity. In the summer of 1986, party leaders began to debate the advisability of instituting greater political reforms, discussions that only sharpened the antagonism between the factions.

The most influential spokesman for basic political change was the astrophysicist Fang Lizhi, one of China's leading scientists. In an open session with students in November 1986, he declared, "I am here to tell you that the socialist movement, from Marx and Lenin to Stalin and Mao Zedong, has been a failure. I think that complete Westernization is the only way to modernize."[6] Fang encouraged students to take the struggle for democracy into their own hands. In December 1986, student demonstrations broke out and spread to one hundred fifty campuses in seventeen cities; demonstrators numbered in the tens of thousands. Students called for greater freedom, an end to party nepotism, and better university dormitories and cafeterias. They were met by repression.

The major casualty of the affair was Party General Secretary Hu Yaobang, one of Deng's chosen successors. A man of relatively liberal political views, he had called for conciliation in dealing with the students. Faced with a barrage of panicked shrieks from the conservatives about the dangers of bourgeois democracy, Deng decided that Hu had to go. The party line was that he had not been tough enough in combatting spiritual pollution and had not provided proper party leadership. Hu resigned in January 1987. Several prominent intellectuals, including Fang, were expelled from the party.

THE DEMOCRACY MOVEMENT (BEIJING SPRING, 1989)

These demonstrations were but the precursor to the so-called Democracy Movement in the spring of 1989. Between the student demonstrations and this movement, liberal reformers held sway, with many older conservative members of the Politburo retiring in the fall of 1987 at the Thirteenth Party Congress, where Zhao

Ziyang was confirmed as Hu's successor. In 1988, the economy was marked by rising inflation, declining wages, and rising unemployment. To complicate the economic picture, in spring 1988 the government began to deregulate the prices of certain retail items—eggs, meat, vegetables, and sugar, later joined by cigarettes and alcoholic beverages. Before each deregulation consumers tended to panic, going on buying sprees, fearful that without price controls inflation would go through the roof. People even used all their savings and money in their checking accounts to buy up items rumored to be deregulated next. Both Zhao and Deng had initially supported price deregulation but Deng backed away from it, leaving Zhao suddenly vulnerable. Coupled with economic woes were social problems. Labor unrest increased as 20 to 30 million workers in state enterprises were laid off. Urban unemployment in August 1988 was over 4 million, a situation worsened by the continuing influx of the floating population—which reached 1.1 million in Beijing alone.

Crime was increasing, especially the white-collar corruption of party bigwigs and cadres. The reforms stimulated corruption almost everywhere. To get rich, the thinking went, do whatever it takes. It was always difficult to draw the line between bribery and legitimate making of connections, which always entailed gift giving. Bribery, however, was only one of the tools of corruption, which included embezzlement, nepotism, smuggling, fraud, extortion, kickbacks, illegal business transactions, and stock manipulation.

Five decades of socialist rule had brought to power party leaders and state enterprise managers who monopolized the means of production, resources, education, and recruitment into the system. They often used their position and its resources for their own betterment, and they manipulated recruitment so that family members and connections could profit as well. For example, the son of senior party leader Hu Qiaomu, who directed an anticorruption campaign in 1986, was reportedly involved in "illicit activities, including providing pornographic videotapes for PLA sex parties and skimming off 3 million [yuan] in tuition fees to his privately operated correspondence law school."[7] When he was arrested, his father tearfully appealed to Deng Xiaoping to show mercy to his son, who got off with a slap on the wrist—all charges against him were dropped.

To help control corruption, Beijing developed hundreds of regulations; anticorruption bureaus and hotlines were set up so that people could report corruption. But these mechanisms did not work because they were all controlled by the party, which itself was rife with corruption. Any action against corrupt party members could have serious political repercussions for those in power. Jiang Zemin decided early on that he would not touch the families of first-generation revolutionaries, no matter how deeply they were involved in corruption. The public became increasingly indignant over the situation—even as they joined in petty graft and bribery. Beginning about 1998, however, the party began to crack down on serious corruption, imprisoning and executing major offenders. Still, corruption remained a serious political issue.

Among party leaders in the late 1980s there was clear dissatisfaction with Zhao Ziyang's economic policies. Premier Li Peng, for one, wanted to pour ice water on the overheated economy by slowing the pace of development. He and others seemed to win: at the end of 1988, price controls were slapped back on items ranging from eggs to shoes to washing machines. Some older conservatives who had left the Politburo hammered Zhao from the wings and pressed Deng to get rid of the economic reformer. In this volatile environment, liberal intellectuals including Fang Lizhi continued to push for democratic reforms. In January 1989, Fang sent Deng an open letter asking for the release of all political prisoners, including Democracy Wall victim/hero Wei; seventy-five scholars and writers sent letters supporting Fang.

A contingent event, the death of Hu Yaobang on April 15, brought many of these tensions to a head. Hu had supported the students in 1986 and remained the strongest voice for political reform. As with Zhou Enlai in 1976, commemoration of Hu became a pretext for political action. Students flocked to Tiananmen Square and took to the streets of cities all over the country. They called for democracy, an end to party nepotism and corruption, increased salaries and budgets for education, a reevaluation of Hu's 1986 role, rehabilitation of victims of the Campaign against Bourgeois Liberalization and the Campaign against Spiritual Pollution, and publication of the incomes of top leaders and their children.

Party leaders immediately denounced the demonstrations. Deng believed that if the government gave an inch, student demands would stretch a mile. He and the party branded student actions *turmoil*, a particularly strong condemnation that only stiffened the backs of student leaders, who seemed filled with a sense of destiny. Zhao, already in hot water with party leaders because of the economy, further alienated conservatives by calling for a more conciliatory approach to the students. Students formed autonomous organizations and participated in demonstrations. Between May 4 and May 19, over 1.5 million students in 500 colleges and universities from around the country demonstrated in support of Beijing students; by the end of May that number had risen to 3 million.

Flagging Beijing student commitment in early May was revived by a hunger strike staged at Tiananmen Square, which transformed the Democracy Movement into a moral crusade against an evil government, a crusade with the notable potential for martyrdom. For the hunger strikers, compromise became less possible as the rhetoric of moral superiority and outrage was heightened. The new reality created by the hunger strategy split student demonstrators into two camps mirroring the division in the government leadership. Some student leaders, like Wu'er Kaixi and Wang Dan were willing to seek a compromise, but others, like Chai Ling (see Identities), were moral zealots unwilling to budge an inch. Chai mused, "How can I tell them [her fellow students] that what we are actually hoping for is bloodshed, the moment when the government is ready to butcher the people brazenly? Only when the square is awash with blood will the people of China open their eyes. Only then will they really be united."[8] Several government initiatives to deal with the students failed because student radicals refused to compromise. The hunger strike also stimulated support from Beijing society at large—workers, teachers, police, doctors, nurses, and journalists.

The student occupation of Tiananmen Square deeply embarrassed the Chinese government when Mikhail Gorbachev arrived on May 15 to normalize relations between China and the Soviet Union. What was to have been a crowning glory for the aged Deng turned into bitter humiliation. Shortly after Gorbachev left on May 18, hard-liners led by Premier Li Peng removed Zhao from power, formally ousting him from the Politburo on May 24. On May 20, Premier Li imposed martial law: "The situation in [Beijing] is still worsening, and has already affected many other cities in the country.... This will lead to nationwide turmoil if no quick action is taken to turn and stabilize the situation. The nation's reform and opening to the outside world, and the fate and future of the People's Republic, are facing serious threat."[9] Units of the PLA were ordered to clear the streets of demonstrators. But when an estimated one to two million people blocked advancing troops to dissuade them from acting against the demonstrators, the government ordered the troops pulled back temporarily.

This massive and unprecedented display of people power brought a new group, industrial workers, more fully into the demonstrations. On April 20 they had formed the Beijing Workers Autonomous Federation. Concerned more with bread-and-butter issues than abstract issues of democracy, the federation nevertheless threw its support behind the students. With only two thousand members at the beginning of May, its membership shot up to twenty thousand after the declaration of martial law. Students in Tiananmen Square had little contact with the federation until, with student ranks beginning to thin at the end of May, they invited the federation to set up their headquarters at the square. The specter of the proletariat forming their own independent unions was especially frightening to the CCP's old guard.

For two weeks the stalemate between the people and the PLA continued. By June 3 party leaders had had enough, and they launched a crackdown in the early morning hours of June 4. As the PLA moved into the city from the west on Chang'an Boulevard, which ran along the north side of the square, many citizens who had blocked intersections with buses and other barricades were killed. Estimates of civilian fatalities have ranged from hundreds to thousands. In the square itself there were few, if any, casualties. As for the army, on one stretch of the boulevard over sixty PLA trucks and about fifty APCs were reportedly destroyed, with about another five hundred damaged; in this sector, 6 PLA soldiers were killed and over 1,100 were wounded.

The government's rationale for cracking down was fear of counterrevolution and anarchy. The leaders were certain that the movement had to be stopped. From the perspective of the people, the *People's*

Identities: Chai Ling (1966–):
Demagogue or Democrat?

Widely known for her role as chief commander of the students at Tiananmen Square in 1989, Chai Ling became controversial in the 1990s because of her depiction in the documentary film *The Gate of Heavenly Peace.* The film suggests that her uncompromising stance—accepting nothing less than the overthrow of the party-state—contributed in a major way to the tragic outcome of the Beijing Spring episode.

Born in 1966 to two military doctors, Chai from childhood was a take-charge person. Reportedly, when her parents were assigned to handle a six-month earthquake relief effort, they gave her primary responsibility at age ten to take care of two younger siblings and her grandmother. At sixteen, she was named one of two hundred outstanding students in the Communist Youth League. At Beijing University, she studied child psychology and was elected president of the student government; she graduated in 1987. She was enrolled in a master's program in developmental psychology at Beijing Normal University when the Democracy Movement began.

Chai became a leader at Tiananmen Square, known for her fiery rhetoric and the relentless pursuit of her goals. An originator of the idea of a hunger strike, she became the commander of that effort in the square and, along with other student leaders, met with lower-ranking government officials in mid-May. At the end of May, the stress of the situation led her to believe that other students might try to usurp her power; at one point apparently, students from the provinces tried to kidnap her and her then-husband, Feng Congde. She attacked as traitors students who advocated compromise or who wanted to leave the square and return to their campuses to continue the protests there.

After the crackdown, Chai left Beijing and spent the next ten months traveling around the country incognito, disguising herself as a rice farmer, a laborer, and a maid. Her escape from the PRC to Hong Kong was harrowing: she spent 105 hours lying in the "suffocating darkness of a nailed-shut crate ... hidden in the hold of a leaky boat," with only water and a piece of bread.[1] She made her way to France and then to the United States. Two Norwegians nominated her for the Nobel Peace Prize in 1990.

Chai received a master's degree in international affairs from Princeton University and spent the years 1993 to 1996 serving as a consultant at Bain, a global management consulting firm. After attending the Harvard Business School, she founded a software company, Jenzabar, with her second husband, Robert Maginn, where she served as vice-president and partner. Although she still talked about contributing to change in China, it is not likely that she or any of the other students from 1989 who left China will be able to return and become important players.

In any case, her chief interest in the early 2000s was business. She says, "T[he] creation of a company is no less stressful than running a hunger strike in Tiananmen Square." Whereas she talked about the square "awash with blood" as a goal in 1989, she used "blood" in a completely different way at the turn of the twenty-first century:

Never forget. Money is your master. When you are down to your last dime and you have a $250,000 payroll to meet, venture capitalists are your friends. But make no mistake. Their job is to get the last blood out of you. Even if no artery gets cut.[2]

[1] See http://www.alumni.hbs.edu/bulletin/1998/june/salute/ling.html.
[2] See http://www.jenzabar.net/news/pressroom/baseline.html.

The Goddess of Democracy   This thirty-foot-high statue was created by students at the Central Academy of Fine Arts using a metal frame, styrofoam, and papier-mâché. Here it confronts the picture of Mao head on.

Liberation Army had been mobilized for the first time against the people. Around the world there was shock and condemnation of a government that had resorted to brute force. Only later did it come to light that the students also had to share the blame by refusing to consider a compromise. Protest demonstrations against the violence erupted around the country, with deaths and injuries reported at least in Shanghai and Chengdu, the capital of Sichuan province.

The government enforced at least outward conformity to its rule with mass arrests and harsh repression. Thousands of cadres who had participated in or sympathized with the Democracy Movement were expelled from the party; intellectuals and political dissenters became targets. In the end, after trials for counterrevolutionary crimes in early 1991, thirty-one dissidents were convicted and sentenced for up to thirteen years in prison. Fang Lizhi and his wife, who had taken refuge in the U.S. embassy, were allowed to leave the country in June 1990.

The Aftermath: Sino-American Relations

The 1989 Beijing tragedy poisoned relations with the United States through the 1990s, jeopardizing the trading relationship as the U.S. Congress debated every year whether to bestow on the PRC *most favored nation status*.[10] The U.S. government carped about China's record on human rights, technology transfers, trade, and various strategic issues. Beijing's response to the frequent criticism was that the United States was trying to contain and isolate China as it tried to assert its own hegemony; a mid-1996 poll of Chinese college students found that 95.7 percent agreed with that proposition.

The Aftermath   Beijing citizens survey the damage on the morning of June 4, 1989, after the PLA put down the Democracy Movement. Most of the violence occurred on the main road leading to Tiananmen Square. Pictured are burned-out military vehicles torched by Beijing residents trying to halt the progress of the PLA.

U.S. policy toward Taiwan, the touchiest of all Chinese issues, was a constant irritant (see Chapter 20 for coverage of the Taiwan issue). U.S. sale of planes and other military hardware to Taiwan, and especially U.S. deployment of ships in the vicinity of military exercises off Taiwan in the spring of 1996, stirred up anti-American feelings. The U.S.-Japanese security agreement in 1996 was also seen as threatening because it put Taiwan in the "sphere of common defence [sic] interests" of the two countries. A spokesman for Jiang Zemin stated that "[t]his can absolutely not be accepted by the Chinese government and the Chinese people."[11] State visits by Jiang in 1997 and by President Bill Clinton in 1998 seemed to warm up the often-chilly relationship.

But in 1999 that thaw was replaced by a freeze, the worst since the establishment of diplomatic relations two decades earlier. Frequent China bashing in the U.S. Congress over a range of issues antagonized the Chinese. In May 1999, during the war in Kosovo, NATO planes bombed the Chinese embassy in Belgrade,

Presidents Jiang Zemin and Bill Clinton   Watched by admiring crowds, President Jiang escorts President Clinton to a welcoming ceremony in Tiananmen Square in 1998. Clinton's visit produced a frank exchange on human rights that was televised all over China.

destroying the building and killing several Chinese journalists. The United States called the bombing a mistake, attributing it to faulty maps. The Chinese sneered at what seemed to them a lame excuse. They argued that the bombing was intentional and that the United States, like a neo-imperialist bogeyman, was determined not to allow China to take its rightful place among the nations of the world. Chinese students reacted violently to the bombing, taking to the streets and attacking the U.S. embassy. Then, in April 2001, a U.S. EP-3 spy plane collided with a Chinese fighter jet along the Chinese coast. The U.S. plane landed safely, but the Chinese jet crashed. The incident strengthened the Chinese belief that the United States was trying to contain China. This chill in relations was relieved by the September 11 terrorist attacks in the United States. With its fears of Islamic separatism and terror, China became an ally of sorts with the United States in its war on terrorism.

ECONOMICS IN COMMAND

The crisis in the spring of 1989 did not end the wrangling between Chinese government reformers and conservatives, but they reached an implicit compromise: reform but go slowly. To succeed Zhao as the party general secretary, Deng chose the centrist Jiang Zemin, former mayor of Shanghai, who supported reforms yet also stressed the four cardinal principles. In April 1991, much to the chagrin of the conservatives, Jiang selected another former mayor of Shanghai, Zhu Rongji, well known for his commitment to reform, to head economic restructuring efforts. That autumn, conservatives' cries became ever shriller, bluntly charging that the "'reformist road' was actually the 'capitalist road.'"[12] Deng, who was eighty-seven years old and walked and talked with difficulty, grew increasingly angry. When a group of retired conservatives in December 1991 called for the restructuring of the SEZs because they "were capitalist in nature and had become hotbeds of peaceful evolution [rather than revolution through class struggle]," Deng acted dramatically to save his reform program. From January 18 to February 21, 1992, he traveled to the south to inspect two SEZs, Shenzhen and Zhuhai, and visit three cities—Wuhan, Guangzhou, and Shanghai. His goal was to point to the progress brought by reform and the policy of opening, thereby justifying his policies. Deng used the tour as an occasion for calling for even faster progress:

> *We should be bolder in carrying out reforms and opening up to the outside world and in making experimentations; we should not act like a woman with bound feet.... One just cannot blaze a trail, a new trail, and accomplish a new undertaking without the spirit of daring to break through, the spirit of taking a risk, and without some spirit and vigor.*[13]

The Fourteenth Party Congress, which met in October 1992, confirmed Deng's directions for rapid economic market reforms. It also swept into the Politburo seven strong supporters of Deng's program, while two of its most outspoken opponents died in 1993 and 1995.

After Deng's southern tour, state enterprises were given greater autonomy to deal with markets at home and abroad, as well as to issue stocks that could be bought and sold on stock exchanges in Shenzhen and Shanghai. Whereas at the beginning of the 1990s most foreign investment had come from overseas Chinese via Hong Kong and Taiwan, by the late 1990s multinational companies, including some from Japan and the United States, had begun to surpass the earlier investors.

Deng himself died on February 19, 1997. Perhaps an American scholar said it best: "Although Deng Xiaoping could claim a long revolutionary lineage, he will best be remembered as the father of Chinese capitalism."[14] Indeed, one of the keys of the reform period was the emphasis on material incentives over ideology. Deng's pragmatic openness to capitalistic innovations in order to build a modern socialist state was best symbolized by his verdict that "It doesn't matter if the cat is white or black so long as it catches

Source: Building a Spiritual Civilization

One offshoot of the reforms was the creation of a widespread mania to get rich, which produced corruption at all levels of society. Some believed that China had lost its moral standards. This radio report by CCP spokesman Shen Daren about a December 1990 meeting on "building a spiritual civilization" reveals this concern. How does he define spiritual civilization?

A four-day meeting on building spiritual civilization and antipornography work in the province ended in Nanjing on the afternoon of December 10. Shen Daren, secretary of the provincial CCP committee, delivered an important speech at the meeting.

He pointed out: The key to furthering the building of spiritual civilization and antipornography work lies in the full implementation of relevant policies. Shen Daren said: It is our unswerving principle to pay equal attention to persisting in building both socialist material and spiritual civilizations. When pursuing our socialist modernization drive, we must persist in making economic construction our central task and strive to develop social productive forces. Making economic construction our central task, however, does not mean we can be lax about building spiritual civilization. The building of spiritual civilization will guarantee that we take the correct direction in building material civilization. The development of material civilization requires spiritual and intellectual support from spiritual civilization....

First, we must formulate a good plan for building spiritual civilization and include it in the overall scheme of the Eighth Five-Year Plan [1991–95] and the ten-year strategy for economic and social development. Second, we must pay particular attention to doing well in ideological and moral education. Third, we should organize well the activities for launching the building of spiritual civilization among the masses, continue proven methods for activities, constantly enlarge the scope of activities, and improve the forms of activities. Fourth, we must continuously do a good job in antipornography work. Great efforts should be made to effect a thriving socialist culture.

Source: Quoted in R. Keith Schoppa, Twentieth Century China: A History in Documents *(New York: Oxford University Press, 2004), 173.*

rats." With that approach, his second most famous dictum—"To get rich is glorious"—carried the day. Even his lingering death (his last public appearance came in February 1994) helped perpetuate his program, for it allowed Jiang Zemin and the reformers time to gain firm control of the policymaking apparatus. The Fifteenth Party Congress, held seven months after his death, in September 1997, reconfirmed the party's commitment to Deng's vision. In March 1998, the reformer Zhu Rongji replaced the conservative Li Peng as premier.

At the beginning of the twenty-first century, the party-state redefined the party. In February 2000, Jiang Zemin publicly discussed what became known as the *three representations*. The CCP, he argued, should continue to lead China as long as it represented the "advanced forces of production, advanced culture, and the interests of the people."[15] In essence, with the first two representations, he opened up party membership to capitalists and technocrats—"advanced forces of production" in the reformist agenda— and intellectuals—"advanced culture." This was a historic break with Marxist doctrine and the Maoist past. Jiang promoted these ideas because of problems and challenges that the CCP had to face (see Chapter 20). There was nothing to suggest that the party-state would necessarily liberalize politically, but the public announcement of the three representations suggested that the party-state was reacting to challenges pragmatically. There were indications that this pragmatic face—and the fact that the party stood mainly for economic reform and nationalism, not dogma—had rehabilitated the party, at least in the minds of the younger generation. Whereas in 1990 only 1 percent of university students were CCP members, by 2003, 8 percent had joined. From 2000 to 2003, party membership rose from 61 to 67 million; of the members in 2000, 17.9 percent were college graduates, 4.5 times the number of CCP college graduates in 1982. The face of the party was changing.

At the Sixteenth National Party Congress in November 2002, Jiang retired as general secretary, having served for thirteen years. The new general secretary was Hu Jintao, handpicked by Deng and groomed by Jiang. Hu, head of the Communist Youth League in the 1980s and member of the Politburo Standing Committee since 1992, was an activist reformer, seventeen years younger than Jiang but not a political liberal. This new generation of leadership contained more experts in economics and finance than any in the past. The new Central Committee was composed of 356 members, 180 of whom were new faces. All but 5 of the members had at least a junior college degree.

The most daring of Jiang Zemin's economic proposals was partial privatization of state-owned enterprises (SOEs). These made up 40 percent of industrial output in 1997 and were critical in the areas of high technology and heavy industry (steel, mining, machine building, petrochemicals). Almost 70 percent of the SOEs were losing money and had to be subsidized by the state, a policy that depleted state coffers and did nothing to spur development and modernization. Partial privatization of these firms was daring for two reasons. First, by conventional definition, socialism (which all the reformers still claimed was the Chinese system) is a system in which the state owns and controls industry. If the state was now turning over most industry (with the exception of key industries) to private hands, where was the socialism that was allegedly the hallmark of the system? Second, the SOEs employed over 120 million workers. When they were privatized and profit became the bottom line, many workers would have to be fired (estimates were up to one third). Despite worries about the potential for serious social unrest in such a case, the Fifteenth Party Congress in September 1997 gave the go-ahead to privatization.

A drastic restructuring of the social and economic landscape ensued. After three years of this restructuring directed by Zhu Rongji, 52.5 percent of the SOEs had been turned around: they were out of financial trouble. The downside was that from 1997 to the end of 2001, 34 million jobs in the state sector were lost (30.8 percent of the total). Despite the rising unemployment and rising urban poverty rates, privatization continued. In 2002, the government approved dismantling of the State Power Corporation, breaking it up into a number of private power companies. In 2003, plans were announced for the privatization of television production. Privatization had immense economic, social, and political implications for the Chinese people and the Chinese state.

Beijing was proactive in trying to prevent social strife. In order to defuse growing rural unrest, it abolished land taxes as of January 1, 2006. This seemed an almost revolutionary step, since for 2,600 years the land tax had been the central levy on which the government relied. But the threat of unrest was all too real: in 2004, there were seventy-four thousand protests and riots in the countryside involving some three million people. In 2005 the number of protests shot up to eighty-seven thousand. Despite the abolition of the land tax, farmers were still burdened with many local taxes and levies. In order to make life easier for them, the government offered subsidies to farmers growing grain and more subsidies for buying better crop strains, agricultural machinery, and tools. It also stepped up the state's investment in rural and interior areas.

CHINESE INTERNATIONAL RELATIONS: AN OVERVIEW

In the absence of a strong functioning ideological component driving its actions at home or abroad, raising the flag of nationalism became a crucial aspect of China's relations with other nations. By 2000 the brain drain, which had been worrisome in the 1980s, was reversed. Pride in China and Chinese-ness, coupled

Source: A Farmer's Perspective

This account is from a sixty-three-year-old farmer who lives in a village in Guizhou province, one of China's poorest. He is married, and has two sons and three daughters. What is he most concerned about? What is his perspective on economic matters? What is his attitude toward the government?

We grow crops—wheat, rice, potatoes, tomatoes, kidney beans, red peppers, green vegetables and several fruit trees including trees growing apples, pears, peaches, and plums.

Of course we would like to own the land by ourselves. In my family, we have 5 mu (0.3335 hectares) in total to farm.

The environment is not as good as in cities—people here don't understand what this means. I think it's dirtier than in the town.

Taxation against farmers is heavy, but it is less than last year's after people complained to the government. The government cut some taxation like education fees this year.

I should say our lives have been improved a lot since the time of the Great Leap Forward. At that time, people couldn't even feed themselves fully; but now this is not a problem at all.

I think there is still a difference between city and countryside. Generally speaking, people in town are richer than in the countryside, but some people in the countryside also are rich.

URBANISATION

My children all have work in the town. They do things like house decorating or guarding building sites. Although their work is not regular, they can often find some work to do.

In my village, most young people go to town for work, which allows them to earn more money and make their lives better.

Of course there are changes—at least our lives are much better than before. Sometimes change also brings some bad things. In which way? For the moment I can't exactly remember.

I know about the coming Party congress, but don't feel it has much relevance to my life.

Source: http://www.news.bbc.co.uk/2/shared/spl/hi/asia_pac/02/china_party_congress/voices/html/zhao_jun.stm.

with China's image as a more pragmatic and less ideological state, had ended the problem. In the 1990s and early 2000s, China strode onto the world stage confidently, pragmatically, and with greater maturity than previously. It was increasingly seen as one of East Asia's and the world's key leaders. In 2001, at a meeting of the Association for Southeast Asian Nations (ASEAN) Plus 3 (China, Japan, and South Korea), Premier Zhu Rongji took the lead in negotiating an agreement to create a regional free trade zone of over 1.7 billion people by 2010. In December 2001, China joined 146 other nations in the World Trade Organization (WTO), the international body that regulates trade between nations. Joining the WTO was a symbolic coming of age. Also symbolically significant was China's winning the right to host the 2008 Summer Olympics. And in what one writer called "China's calling card as a great power," China launched its first manned space vehicle, Shenzhou 5, in October 2003.[16] In 2003, ranked third in the world in global research and development after the United States and Japan, China announced plans for a manned trip to the moon, a visit to Mars, and the launching of a space station.

For all the good news, China's erratic handling of the severe acute respiratory syndrome (SARS) epidemic that swept several areas in China in 2002–2003, and of an epidemic of acquired immune deficiency syndrome (AIDS) in Henan province, showed a disturbing pattern. The government first acted as if there were no problem and then tried to censor information about the disease and its victims. This imposed news blackout came from "fear of social panic and economic disaster," but to the rest of the world, it "made China seem foolish, if not dangerous, to outsiders."[17]

GREATER CHINA: ISSUES OF IDENTITY

With the regained colonies of Hong Kong and Macao, so long identified with Britain and Portugal, respectively, and of the autonomous regions of Tibet and Xinjiang (won for the Chinese empire in the eighteenth century), but unhappy with their current relationship with Beijing, issues of identity today in these areas are as important as they were for the Qianlong emperor in the eighteenth century.

Special Administrative Regions: Hong Kong and Macao

Hong Kong had historically been made up of three parts: Hong Kong island, ceded to Britain in 1842; the Kowloon peninsula, ceded to Britain in 1860; and the New Territories, leased for ninety-nine years in 1898. After a strong Chinese initiative, negotiations over the return of all three parts led to Britain's agreement to return Hong Kong to China. According to Hong Kong's Basic Law, the Chinese stipulated that for fifty years after that date, Hong Kong would retain a capitalist economy, becoming a *special administrative region* under the formula of *one country, two systems.* During that period English would remain the official language, Hong Kong residents would pay no taxes to China, and the city's economy would remain generally autonomous. Hong Kong's defense and foreign policy would fall under China's control. The transfer of the former crown colony went off without a hitch on July 1, 1997, but relations between Beijing and Hong Kong's Legislative Council continued to be prickly because of China's desire to control certain political processes and policies.

The small peninsula of Macao had been occupied in 1557 and controlled since then by Portugal with tacit Chinese consent. It was the Chinese territory held the longest by a foreign state, almost four and a half centuries. Less significant economically and strategically than Hong Kong, it was nevertheless of great symbolic importance. The territory reverted to Chinese control in December 1999.

Autonomous Regions: Tibet and Xinjiang

Tibet Autonomous Region.   The protectorate that China had established over Tibet in the eighteenth century remained into the twentieth century. By the late nineteenth century, however, given China's weakness, its hegemony over Tibet remained in theory but in actuality was a dead letter. China's political and military weakness continued into the early Republican period, meaning in effect that Tibet was on its own. All Chinese leaders, however, from Sun Yixian to Jiang Jieshi to Mao Zedong, claimed Tibet as part of the Chinese nation.

When the PRC was established in 1949, Beijing tried to negotiate a *peaceful liberation,* but the Tibetan government refused. As a result, PLA forces invaded Tibet in October 1950 and quickly defeated the weak Tibetan army. Tibet had no choice but to sign an agreement in May 1951 that stated: "the Tibet people shall return to the big family of the Motherland—the People's Republic of China."[18] Tibet thus recognized China's sovereignty; in exchange, China agreed to maintain the traditional political and economic system, including the Dalai Lama. China's generally moderate policies in the 1950s ended, however, with a Tibetan rebellion in 1959 that Beijing put down with considerable bloodshed. The Dalai Lama fled to India.

During the Cultural Revolution, Tibet experienced the same brutal chaos and trashing of traditional culture as China proper. Under Deng's reforms, however, China's policy again became more conciliatory, and from 1979 to 1981 the per capita income of Tibetan peasants rose 73 percent. Perhaps even more important, traditional customs and cultural practices emerged from the dustbin into which they had been discarded during the Cultural Revolution. China loosened other restrictions on Tibet. Issues of identity continually cropped up in their relationship.

Many Tibetans took advantage of the thaw by displaying photographs of the Dalai Lama and defying Chinese regulatory laws. These years also saw a large influx of Han Chinese, ranging from laborers to professionals to demobilized troops, who were encouraged by the Chinese government to settle in the country. In late September 1987, having tasted greater freedom, Tibetan monks demonstrated for independence. Their arrests and beatings brought demonstrations and confrontations between demonstrators and Chinese police. The Chinese declared martial law. As demonstrations continued in early 1989, the Chinese reasserted strong control over Tibetan religion and religious institutions.

In the early 2000s, what the future held for Tibet in the grip of China was unclear. The most destabilizing element in contemporary China-Tibet relations was economic development. In 1994, the Chinese opened the Lhasa Stock Exchange. Capital began to pour into the country and into enterprises, often headed by Chinese. Also worrisome to Tibetans was the huge influx of Han Chinese into Tibet as part of the economic development plan. This migration clearly had the political purpose of making Tibet a more integral part of China. A symbol of China's determination to do just that was the completion of the Qinghai-Tibet railway in October 2005. The world's highest railroad, reaching an elevation of 15,640 feet above sea level, was a marvelous engineering feat, given the altitude for working conditions. Passenger service started on July 1, 2006. "The trains [were] equipped with pressurized wagons and [were] serviced by doctors and nurses. Passengers [were] provided with oxygen masks."[19]

Xinjiang-Uighur Autonomous Region.   In the first years of the twenty-first century, the most potentially explosive autonomous region was Xinjiang. Oil- and mineral-rich, with the lowest population density in the country, Xinjiang contained millions of Muslims, many of whom had only feeble allegiance to Beijing. Tensions and animosities between Chinese authorities and local ethnic groups had festered for decades, and the threat of Muslim separatism remained real. A large confrontation came in April 1990, when Chinese troops tried to break up a rally of some two thousand Uighur separatists at a town near Kashgar. The Uighurs were rumored to have smuggled in weapons from Afghanistan to use in a *jihad*, or "holy war," to free Xinjiang from China. Dozens were killed and hundreds injured in the clashes. In the aftermath, the Chinese substantially upped the number of troops stationed in Kashgar, Urumqi (the provincial capital), and elsewhere in Xinjiang. Rumors abounded that secessionists wanted to establish an East Turkistani Republic that would incorporate Uighurs from China and Russia.

In the 1990s, there were a number of incidents called by the Chinese terrorist attacks but by the Uighurs acts to gain their freedom. Xinjiang leaders asked Beijing for more autonomy, but Jiang Zemin was determined not to give an inch to what were called *splittists*. As in Tibet, the government encouraged Han Chinese settlement of the area. In 2004 there were reports that Han Chinese developers had forced Uighurs from their land. The future of Chinese-Muslim relations seemed perilous.

China and the East Asian Region

Japan.   Relations with Japan, until the 1990s the East Asian economic giant, were mostly economic. In 1978 the two countries signed a peace treaty and long-term trade agreements, paving the way for Japan's assistance in China's economic development. In the early 1980s came a $10 billion industrial aid agreement. China and Japan jointly explored for oil in the North China Sea, and Japan invested heavily in the Liaodong peninsula in southern Manchuria.

In the early years of the twenty-first century, China's relations with Japan were strained by disputes over oil and gas exploration in the East China Sea and by issues of responsibility for acts committed by Japan during World War II. In the first, at stake were 200 million cubic meters of natural gas reserves in four oil and gas fields. Japan argued that China's drilling siphoned gas from Japanese territory, basing its position on the UN Convention of the Law of the Sea (which both countries had signed), which allowed coastal countries to claim economic zones up to 370 kilometers from their shores. China, on the other hand, based its claim on the 1958 Geneva Convention of the Continental Shelf, which allowed coastal countries to extend their borders to the edges of their undersea continental shelves. Three rounds of negotiations up to the fall of 2005 left the two nations at loggerheads. In September 2005, a Chinese naval destroyer aimed its guns at a Japanese Maritime Self-Defense Force surveillance plane. A Japanese diplomat stated, "It will be difficult for either Japan or China to compromise in this dispute, but failure to do so could create a very dangerous situation."[20]

Memories of World War II continued to be a festering wound since, in China's eyes, Japan seemed unwilling to accept categorically the responsibility for its actions. Prime ministerial visits to Yasukuni Shrine, where fourteen Class A Japanese war criminals are buried, brought Chinese street demonstrations. The history textbooks in both countries set forth the nationalistic perspectives of each, thus becoming an embittering irritant in their relationship. The 1991 visit of Japan's prime minister to Beijing was followed in 1992 by one from the Heisei emperor, the first ever by a Japanese emperor to China. Jiang Zemin, in turn, visited Tokyo in 1998 and Prime Minister Koizumi was in Beijing for talks in 2002, but the visits fostered no apparent good will.

The Koreas.   While China remained an ally of North Korea, its relationship with P'yŏngyang in the first years of the 2000s became testy over North Koreans fleeing to China and North Korea's continuing to flirt with nuclear weapons (see Chapter 19). Ironically, China's relationship with South Korea in the 1990s became closer than that with the North. Beijing and Seoul established diplomatic relations in 1992. Trade grew rapidly as South Korea invested heavily in Shandong province. In 2003, China surpassed the United States as the leading market for South Korean exports.

Dealing with the Soviet Union (Russia After 1991)

The hostility that produced the Sino-Soviet split in 1960 and military skirmishes in early 1969 did not begin to subside until the presidency of Mikhail Gorbachev. In 1985, expanded trade and cultural contacts began to relieve tensions, consulates were reopened in Shanghai and St. Petersburg, and China purchased Soviet aircraft. Gorbachev's trip to Beijing in May 1989, at the time of the Democracy Movement demonstrations, formally healed the three-decade rupture between the two countries. The Soviet Union's collapse in 1991 left an impotent Russia, but the long border they shared made Russia an important consideration in China's strategic thinking. In the early 2000s, the two nations seemed to be attuned to each other's needs. The Russians offered assistance in the Three Gorges Dam project on the Yangzi River. In 2000, the two countries announced that China had committed itself to purchase $15 billion in weapons from Russia over five years. They held joint naval exercises in 1999 and joint military exercises in 2004.

THE SOCIALIST REPUBLIC OF VIETNAM

In many ways, economic and political developments in Vietnam reflected Chinese patterns. Proponents of liberal economic reform battled it out with conservatives who demanded that the party-state be in firm control of every aspect of life. Factional struggles often led to political paralysis. In the 1960s, the factions debated which Communist model to follow. The pro-Soviet faction argued that the most important goal was reunification of the nation. As the war continued, they were challenged by those who argued that, war or no war, a Maoist-like policy of radical economic and social change had to be instituted in the north. Through purges the Maoists eventually won, with the installation of a Stalinist central-planning economic program.

The Socialist Republic of Vietnam was declared on July 2, 1976. One of the first issues was integrating the south into the new nation; the process was not smooth. Relations between the wartime NLF and the government of the DRV soured immediately after the military victory of north over south. From the perspective of the Viet Cong, the northerners acted like conquering heroes, treating the southerners as their inferior subjects. NLF leader Truong Nhu Tang wrote that peace "had brought with it not blessings but a new and even more insidious warfare, this time a warfare practiced by the liberators against their

Aerial View of Hanoi   These high-rise buildings are located on the west bank of the Red River, looking toward the skyline of Vietnam's capital in 1998. Especially noteworthy are the trees that line the streets and give the city, despite its nerve-rattling traffic, a more humane atmosphere.

own people ... the truth was that the problems [between Northerners and Southerners] had been precipitated by ideological ruthlessness and a contemptuous disregard for human dignity."[21]

From the perspective of the northerners, "the heterodoxy, the degree of individualism, and freedom of thought and expression to which the people of south Vietnam had grown accustomed, was anathema. The 'corrupted' culture of the south was an obstacle to progress."[22] The solution? Eradicate all the individualistic, Westernized books, movies, journals, songs, radio and television; replace them with the writings of Ho Chi Minh, Marx, and Lenin and accounts of the successes of the Vietnamese Communists; and, most important, reeducate the south Vietnamese populace. Over one million (about 5 percent) of the south Vietnamese intellectual and political elites were ordered to go to reeducation camps to be transformed into new socialist models. For many, the time at these camps, marked by hard physical labor and little food, meant physical and/or psychological breakdowns, even death.

In addition to reeducation, the Hanoi regime launched a massive relocation effort. Approximately one million people were moved from Ho Chi Minh City (formerly Saigon) and other cities in the south to *new economic zones,* with orders to cultivate unfarmed, ecologically marginal land primarily in mountain regions—efforts that had little chance of succeeding. In addition, about two hundred fifty thousand Montagnards were forcibly moved from their mountain homes to valleys to become productive farmers. By the late 1980s, about three million Vietnamese had been relocated. The other mass movement in the country had been an exodus, mostly of ethnic Chinese but also of middle-class Vietnamese, as *boat people* and as refugees fleeing into China. It is estimated that seven hundred thousand people fled.

The other trial for the south was the policy of agricultural collectivization. Most farmers in the south had run their own farms and were in no mood to cater to the ideologically correct approaches of the Hanoi regime. They reacted to the policy of collectivization in 1977–1978 with passive resistance, which only exacerbated a drop in production stemming from wretched weather, a dearth of chemical fertilizers, and government mismanagement. Since production was the name of the game for the government, its policies were counterproductive. It is estimated that no more than a quarter of farm households ever participated in collectives in the south.

As if the peacetime disruptions were not enough, Hanoi became involved in more war. Relations between Hanoi and the Communist Khmer Rouge in Cambodia, who had come to power in 1975, had become increasingly tense, with each country making incursions into the other. Vietnam was also fearful of Chinese intentions because of Beijing's support of the Khmer Rouge, a position China took, in part at least, because of Vietnam's cozy relationship with the Soviet Union. Then in December 1978, Vietnamese leaders dispatched PAVN troops, which occupied Cambodia and installed a pro-Hanoi Communist government in

Aerial View of Ho Chi Minh City   With a park in the foreground, new apartment buildings in Ho Chi Minh City reflect a city on the move. In contrast to the more staid Hanoi, the former Saigon seems rambunctious and, to a degree, chaotic.

Phnom Penh. The Chinese, allies of the Khmer Rouge regime and angered by Hanoi's moves, sent one hundred thousand PLA troops across the border into Vietnam in February 1979 to "teach Vietnam a lesson," condemning (in ideological buzzwords) "Vietnamese hegemonism abetted by Soviet social-imperialism."[23] In fact, it was the Chinese who were taught a lesson about the effectiveness of the Vietnamese military: stiff PAVN resistance forced a Chinese withdrawal in a little over two weeks. But meanwhile, the Chinese invasion had considerably damaged the infrastructure in the northern part of the country.

In the late 1970s and early 1980s, Vietnam survived mainly on foreign aid from the Soviet bloc. China's aid fell sharply in what was in effect a cold war after the brief hot one in 1979. By the mid-1980s, wars, disruption, bad weather, and resistance to Hanoi's leadership and policies meant that Vietnam was unable to produce enough rice to feed itself; it had to import 1.5 million tons of rice in 1986 to prevent starvation. This crisis, added to the fact that Vietnam by that time had one of the lowest per capita incomes in the world, led to a loosening of the Stalinist central-planning model.

At the Sixth Party Congress in December 1986, the government adopted a policy of *doi moi* (renovation), a shift to market socialism or *socialism with a Vietnamese face*. It diminished, though it did not end, the role of central planners in favor of reliance on market mechanisms. Agriculture was virtually decollectivized; private enterprises were encouraged and given considerable autonomy; and businesses in the south that had been nationalized in the late 1970s were returned to their owners. To encourage foreign investment, in essence the same as China's opening, Hanoi set up *export-processing zones* for foreign-owned companies. Some of these changes were adopted slowly and somewhat erratically, but the 1991 collapse of the Soviet Union, which had underwritten 23 to 30 percent of Vietnam's state budget during the late 1970s and 1980s, required Vietnam to move even faster toward economic liberalization.

Doi moi shaped Vietnam in the subsequent decades. The results were uneven: cities fared better than the countryside. "Hanoi went in just a few years from being a dusty and slow city, dimly lit at night, to a bustling, glitzy place, draped in neon and throbbing with commerce. However, just a few miles outside the city centre were villages that had seen few benefits of reform."[24] But the ripple effects of *doi moi* were felt far beyond the economy: capitalism and individualism infused a dynamism and direction that had been missing. "The wheels of life began to spin faster, and they meshed less often with the controlling gears of state."[25]

Overall, the years 1986 to 1997 saw marked progress. From 1993 to 1997, the economy grew at an annual average rate of 9 percent. A general Asian economic crisis in 1997 coupled with losses by state

Source: Vietnam's Strategy for Development, 2001–2010

These excerpts from the Ninth National Congress in 2001 set forth general and specific goals for the socioeconomic development of Vietnam for the decade. The Human Development Index was created in the early 1990s to measure well-being and quality of life. It includes three indicators: life expectancy, the adult literacy rate, and the country's gross domestic product. What is the government's stance on state enterprises and private enterprises?

1. **The overall goals are:**

   - to bring our country out of underdevelopment; improve noticeably the people's material, cultural and spiritual life; lay the foundations for making ours basically a modern-oriented industrialized country by 2020. To ensure that the human resource, scientific and technological capacities, infrastructure, and economic, defense and security potential be enhanced, the institutions of a socialist-oriented market economy be basically established and the standing of our country on the international arena be heightened

2. **The specific goals are:**

   - To ensure that by 2010, GDP will have at least doubled the 2000 level.
   - To raise substantially our country's Human Development Index (HDI).
   - To ensure our endogenous scientific and technological capacities in the application

of modern technologies, in approaching to the world standard, and developing on our own in a number of fields, particularly information, biological, new materials and automation technologies.
   - The infrastructures are to meet demand of socio-economic development, national defense and security, and to make a step forward.
   - The leading role of the state-economic sector is to be enhanced, governing key domains of the economy: state enterprise[s] are to be renewed and developed, ensuring production and business efficiency. The collective economic sector, the individual and small-owner economic sector, the private capitalist economic sector, the state capitalist economic sector and the foreign invested economic sector are all to develop vigorously and durably. The institutions of a socialist-oriented market economy are to be basically established and to operate smoothly and efficiently.

Source: http://www.vietnamembassy.org.uk/vndevelop.html.

firms led to a slackening of that rapid pace, but the growth from 1997 to 2004 was still 6.8 percent. These rates were second in the world only to China's.

But the speed and scope of the *doi moi* policy were hampered by the continuing debate about how far it should go. Some argued that the system should be liberalized so that market forces become the determining factor in the economy. But old-line party members opposed that policy, arguing that the party had to continue to dominate all decision making in every sphere of life. Whenever crises emerged and new decisions were required, the issues of how much and how fast flared anew. Challenges in the late 1980s, so soon after the adoption of *doi moi,* included severe inflation, famine in some rural areas, and high urban unemployment.

At the Seventh Party Congress in 1991, the new prime minister, Vo Van Kiet, called in almost revolutionary fashion for ending the Leninist concept of democratic centralism; adopting the rule of law for Vietnamese economic and political systems; giving private enterprise a level playing field; and appointing officials based on expertise rather than ideological correctness or factional alignment. Kiet's proposals touched off a bitter political battle in an atmosphere that one commentator called a "wild menagerie of personal fiefdoms, provincial power bases, ideological blocs, and competing financial interests."[26]

In China, the formative experience that produced the Communist leadership up to the late 1990s was the Long March; in Vietnam it was imprisonment in the colonial period and involvement in the 1945 revolution. Writings from prison, like Ho Chi Minh's *Prison Diary,* helped shape the party's identity: "glorifying suffering in prisons [was seen] as a badge of revolutionary honor."[27] In 1997, the long-held control of the party by men who had lived during the colonial period and experienced French prisons ended. The new leadership came of age under socialism; the prime minister, Phan Van Khai, had been Ho Chi Minh City's mayor in the 1980s. Whereas from the 1970s to the early 1990s the party's legitimacy was based on the war, the new leaders attempted to base their legitimacy on their management of the economy.

At the turn of the twenty-first century the party faced serious problems, including internal divisions, corruption, and a paucity of charismatic figures to ignite interest and garner support. In the late 1990s, 60 percent of the population was aged thirty or less, an age group that comprised only 11.6 percent of the party. Another problem was the regional north-south difference. Most of the party members lived in the

---

Source: Culture and Faith

In early October 2006, representatives of the twenty-one countries that make up Asia-Pacific Economic Cooperation (APEC) met in Indonesia to hold an Inter-Cultural and Faith Symposium. This excerpt from a speech by Tran Trong Toan, executive director of the APEC Secretariat, raises the question: "Why should APEC, a regional forum devoted to the goals of free and open trade and investment, concern itself with matters of culture and faith?" How does he answer this question?

The Asia-Pacific region is home to 59 per cent of the world's population and is proud to be one of the richest and most diverse regions in terms of history, religion and cultural traditions. The successful implementation of APEC's long-term and noble vision of building an Asia-Pacific community requires us to promote our region's unity in diversity. This is our greatest mission.

The question has been raised as to why should APEC, a regional forum devoted to the goals of free and open trade and investment, concern itself with matters of culture and faith?

The answer is three-fold:

Firstly, the key to doing business and expanding trade and investment in such a multi-cultural environment as the Asia-Pacific is to understand each other—our histories, cultural traditions, and yes, our sensitivities—in order to have a meeting of minds and feelings at all levels. Better mutual understanding will provide a more stable foundation for trade and business relationships.

Secondly, through improved mutual understanding among cultures, religions and faiths, we can promote increased trust, respect and sense of moderation and tolerance as advocated in the United Nations, thus helping to reduce extremist activities in order to ensure a safe and secure business environment in the region.

Thirdly, in view of the historical legacies and cultural diversity for the region, building a mutual understanding, and through it, mutual trust and respect is indispensable for the implementation of APEC's vision of an Asia-Pacific community based on the shared interest of stability, security and prosperity.

Source: http://www.apecsec.org.sg/apec/news_media/speeches/051006_ina_interculturalsympttt.html.

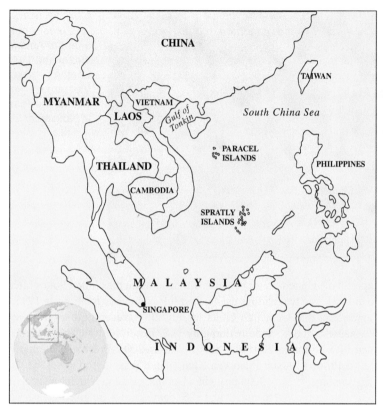

Map 17-2   Vietnam and the Disputed Islands.

north, mostly in and near Hanoi. Only 1.7 percent of the people in Ho Chi Minh City were party members. In contrast to China, party members in Vietnam were poorly educated. Fewer than 14 percent had a university degree, and almost 50 percent had no education beyond the age of fourteen.

The early 1990s saw Vietnam move toward international integration, signing trade agreements with Great Britain, France, Germany, Australia, Japan, and South Korea and the regional Association of Southeast Asian Nations (ASEAN). It became a full-fledged member of the latter organization in 1995. In April 1992, the National Assembly adopted a new constitution, confirming market reforms but calling for Communist Party guidance.

Vietnam also made peace with its longtime enemies: Cambodia, China, and the United States. Vietnam pulled its last troops out of Cambodia in 1989 and signed a peace agreement the same year. Relations with China had been on ice since the 1979 war; they were not helped by the strident claims of both to the oil-rich Spratly Islands in the South China Sea (which Vietnam calls the East Sea). The two skirmished over China's seizure of six atolls in 1988, leading to the death of eighty sailors and the loss of two ships. But the visit of Vietnam's prime minister and party general secretary in November 1991 led to the normalization of relations. Since then, ongoing state visits of government leaders have led to much better relations. Despite the rivalry over the islands, Chinese Politburo member Jia Qinglin, on a state visit to Hanoi in March 2006, said that their relations were "in one of the best times in history."[28]

Clinton in Hanoi   The first U.S. president to visit Vietnam after the American war in the 1960s and 1970s, President Clinton shakes hands with Vietnamese well-wishers after visiting the Temple of Literature in November 2000.

Bitter enmity against the United States began to diminish when the United States lifted its three-decade-long trade embargo in 1994. The two nations established full diplomatic relations in 1995. In July 1999 they approved a trade agreement that went into effect in July 2000, reducing export duties, opening up the United States to Vietnamese goods, and encouraging U.S. firms to invest in Vietnam. U.S.-Vietnamese bilateral trade totaled $1.5 billion in 2001 and $6.4 billion in 2004. President Clinton visited Vietnam in 2000, and in June 2005 Prime Minister Phan Van Khai visited Washington to set the "long-term relationship in the twenty-first century."[29] May 2006 brought a landmark deal in which trade barriers were removed, U.S. quotas on Vietnamese textiles were ended, and U.S. companies were given greater access to Vietnam's markets.

CHRONOLOGY

China

1978–1979	Democracy Wall
1979	Adoption of the market model in business and industry; setting up of the first SEZs
1979–1983	Abolition of people's communes; adoption of the responsibility system
1980s	Opening to the world
1987	Ouster of Hu Yaobang
1989	Death of Hu Yaobang, the catalyst of the Democracy Movement
	Normalization of relations with the Soviet Union
	Ouster of Zhao Ziyang
	Crackdown on the Democracy Movement (June 4)
1992	Deng Xiaoping visits Shenzhen and calls for rapid implementation of reforms
1997	Deng Xiaoping dies (February)

Reversion of Hong Kong to Chinese control (July)

Move to privatize SOEs (September)

1999 — NATO planes bomb the Chinese embassy in Belgrade (May)

Reversion of Macao to Chinese control (December)

2000 — Jiang Zemin's three representations

2001 — U.S. EP-3 spy plane collides with a Chinese fighter jet (April)

China joins the WTO (December)

2003 — China's first manned space vehicle launched

Vietnam

1976 — Socialist Republic of Vietnam declared

1977–1978 — Collectivization in the south

1970s–1980s — Massive relocations project

1978 — PAVN troops occupy Cambodia

1979 — Chinese invasion

1986 — Policy of *doi moi* (renovation) adopted (December)

1989 — Last PAVN troops withdrawn from Cambodia

1991 — Collapse of the Soviet Union ends all aid to Vietnam

Normalization of relations with China

1990s — Rapid economic growth

1995 — Vietnam became a member of ASEAN

Normalization of relations with the United States

SUGGESTED READINGS

Brook, Timothy. *Quelling the People: The Military Suppression of the Beijing Democracy Movement.* New York: Oxford University Press, 1992. A detailed narrative of the role of the PLA in crushing the Democracy Movement in June 1989.

Bui Tin. *Following Ho Chi Minh: Memoirs of a North Vietnam Colonel.* Honolulu: University of Hawaii Press, 1999. This memoir of a once powerful figure, who, disenchanted by the regime, now lives in exile, contains many interesting insights and commentary on some of the key figures in socialist Vietnam.

Dutton, Michael. *Streetlife China.* Cambridge: Cambridge University Press, 1998. Described as a "guided tour of the cultural landscape of contemporary China," this intriguing collection includes newspaper articles, interviews, an exploration of slang terms, social analysis, and sections on Mao memorabilia.

Templer, Michael. *Shadows and Wind: A View of Modern Vietnam*. New York: Penguin Books, 1999. A fast-paced, insightful look at contemporary Vietnam, its politics, society, and culture, and its successes and problems.

Zhang Liang, comp. *The Tiananmen Papers*. Edited by Andrew Nathan and Perry Link. New York: Public Affairs, 2001. Purported to consist of government documents and records of government meetings during the crisis of 1989, this book, in the words of a reviewer, is "an absolute must read for anyone interested in the politics" of the episode.

CHAPTER EIGHTEEN

Whither Japan?
From the 1970s to the Present

Ginza   This shopping and entertainment area in downtown Tokyo is one of the most exclusive and expensive shopping areas in all Japan. It also has the most expensive real estate on earth.

With the 1973 and 1979 oil crises the only minor breaks in the trajectory of Japan's postwar economic miracle, Japan's economy in the 1970s and 1980s soared, much as an airplane flies faster when pushed by a tailwind. From 1975 to 1991 the annual GNP rate of growth was a solid and consistent 4 to 5 percent. But then, suddenly, the bottom seemed to drop out as Japan's economy found itself in a tailspin. The Nikkei index of the Tokyo Stock Exchange fell from 40,000 in December 1989 to 20,000 in October 1990 to 14,000 by the summer of 1992. In 1993 the GNP growth was 1 percent, and in 1994 it was almost flat. In the context of past successes, this riches-to-rags story seemed positively un-Japanese.

Finally, there was a turnaround, though not a boisterous one; subdued expansion began in early 2002 and continued at least until 2007. Though modest, it was the second longest expansion in postwar Japan but also the feeblest (following a robust period from November 1965 to July 1970 and the *bubble* economy of December 1986 to February 1991). The annual average GDP growth rate was 2.4 percent, and the "recovery" was marked by very little job growth and mostly stagnant wages. While Japan's export record grew 55.7 percent during that time, personal consumption increased only 6.7 percent.

LDP Hegemony, 1972–1987

The fifteen years bookended by the prime ministerships of Tanaka Kakuei (1972–1974) and Nakasone Yasuhiro (1982–1987) were a period of almost unchallenged political domination by the LDP. Both were tough-minded men who left their marks, both good and bad, on the party.

Tanaka lacked the usual prime minister's background—graduate of Tokyo National University and career as a bureaucrat. He had received only an elementary school education and made a fortune in the construction industry. But he had an expansive vision of change, expressed in the title of his book published right before his election, *On the Reconstruction of the Japanese Archipelago*. He called for "redrawing the industrial map" by moving industries from the Pacific coast to remote areas of Japan and building a number of pivotal cities in the provinces. The move would be made possible by a Shinkansen (bullet train) network and by expressway construction financed by a new car tax. In addition, a public corporation would manage the building of bridges connecting Honshu to Shikoku. Tanaka's vision focused on reallocating resources and rebuilding nationally. Critics noted that his plan would simply spread pollution and scatter industries, inevitably producing duplication. After the publication of his book, land speculators went to targeted areas to buy up land and then make a killing; one critic noted that Tanaka's book became "the bible for land speculation in the Japanese Archipelago."[1]

Economic realities forced Tanaka to put his plans back on the shelf. In October 1973, during the Middle East war, oil-exporting countries raised oil prices 21 percent and cut production to those countries that favored Israel 5 to 30 percent. Since Japan imported 99.7 percent of its oil, this was a serious matter. The Tanaka administration, stung by the Arab decision, declared Japan to be opposed to Israel and dispatched Vice Premier Miki Takeo to the Middle East to plead for oil. The oil crisis made inflation much worse (in 1973 the price of oil was $2 a barrel; by 1981 it was $35 a barrel). In 1974, Japan slipped into an economic recession that lasted into 1976, its first since the war's end. In late 1974, Tanaka was attacked by an influential journal for "money politics," stating that he had been involved in extortions and shakedowns, using his own political support organizations to become richer. He resigned in December 1974. His one major achievement was his normalization of diplomatic relations with China in 1972, following the lead of the United States earlier that year.

Then in February 1976, in U.S. Senate hearings, it came to light that high-ranking Japanese officials had received a bribe from the Lockheed Corporation to purchase its Tri-Star aircraft. Tanaka was part of the bribery scheme and operation; some say he received as much as several million dollars. He was indicted, found guilty in 1983, and sentenced to four years in prison. He was still appealing that decision in 1985, when a stroke put him out of commission; he died in 1993. But from the time he was found guilty until his stroke, he was known as the *shadow shogun,* dominating the LDP from behind the scenes. His faction continued to dominate Japanese politics for almost a decade after 1985. The Tanaka years point to the constants of Japanese politics in the last quarter of the twentieth century: money, corruption, and factional rivalry. Since the LDP was in such firm control, the interplay between its factions was the main political story.

In the thirty-two years after Tanaka's resignation, Japan had sixteen prime ministers, each serving an average of only two years. On the whole, most of these men have been described as colorless, with ineffective, feeble governments. Factional strife was fierce. The government of Prime Minister Miki (1974–1976) was a coalition of four LDP factions. The government of Ōhira Masayoshi (1978–1980) was fatally wounded when three other factional leaders demanded his resignation over an unpopular consumer tax he proposed. Of the four prime ministers between Tanaka and Nakasone, three—Miki, Fukuda Takeo (1976–1978), and Suzuki Zenkō (1980–1982)—were conservative and nationalistic; all went to the Yasukuni Shrine to revere the Japanese war dead.

There are also other indications of the conservative nationalism of these administrations. Fukuda's government oversaw passage of a law by which an era's name would be associated with the reign of the emperor. This would "keep Japan provincial, self-centred [sic], and emperor-oriented, not only in counting calendar years but also in recording her history. Officially an era name was to be preferred to the international calendar year."[2] Thus, 1980 would be called Shōwa 55, the first year of Shōwa being 1926. Though the Education Ministry had overseen textbook content since the late 1950s, this role became controversial in the Suzuki years when Japanese history textbooks were censored to downplay the role of Japan's aggression in World War II. The word *aggression* was actually altered to *advance.* Even mention of the Nanjing massacre and the violence that accompanied Japan's crushing of the Korean independence movement was minimized.

One other constant in the administrations of the late 1970s and early 1980s was Japan's relationship with the United States. Beginning as early as 1965, Japan's trade with the United States showed exports exceeding imports. In the 1970s, "a flood of Japanese products to the United States began to overwhelm the flow of American exports to Japan."[3] By the mid-1980s, annual U.S. trade deficits with Japan were generally about $50 billion. Japan imported food, raw materials, and oil and exported finished manufactured products. Increasingly, American companies failed to match Japanese prices and workmanship; many American firms simply folded. Whereas, for example, in 1955 twenty-seven U.S. companies produced televisions, in the 1980s Zenith was the sole remaining American company to do so.

In the late 1970s and 1980s, the American car-buying public seemed to be captivated by Japanese automobiles, purchasing cars from Toyota, Honda, Nissan, Subaru, and Mazda. In 1980 the Japanese produced more cars and more tons of steel than the United States, becoming the world's top exporter of cars and steel. The U.S. response, as the top automobile companies, General Motors and Ford, suffered was to complain about a variety of unfair Japanese practices, especially *dumping* products abroad below cost simply to increase their market share and then in various ways keeping the Japanese market largely closed to American goods. The solution was to hammer out agreements whereby the Japanese would "voluntarily" limit their sales to the United States. These agreements were preferable to tariffs slapped on finished products, for that might bring on a trade war. Such agreements applied to steel (1969, 1978), textiles (1972), color televisions (1977), and cars (1981 to 1993).

In 1982, after a run of lackluster prime ministers, Nakasone was an entirely different sort: a fervent, outspoken nationalist who was anything but bland. He wanted to revise the constitution: years earlier, he had reportedly told Yoshida Shigeru that "as long as the current Constitution exists, the state of unconditional surrender persists."[4] He put his money where his priorities were: his first budget raised the defense line 6.8 percent; in previous administrations, annual increases had averaged 1.4 percent. Nakasone told a *Washington Post* reporter that he was primed to "make the Japanese archipelago an unsinkable aircraft carrier."[5]

Like his contemporaries, Margaret Thatcher in Great Britain and Ronald Reagan in the United States, Nakasone wanted to reduce government control and privatize the work of government agencies and institutions. Nippon Telephone and Telegraph and Japan Tobacco were privatized in 1985. Two years later, the Japan National Railway was privatized and broken up into six firms. This action had dual goals: to save money by eliminating government subsidies and to break the back of the railway union, which had been one of the most militant. The new private railway companies closed money-losing rural lines and concentrated on lines between cities that brought greater profit. The Nakasone administration also sold government-owned lands, some in the best areas of major cities.

One of Nakasone's goals was to make Japan a greater force in international relations and to strengthen its relationship with the United States. In 1982, Japan agreed in joint strategy sessions with the United States that Japanese ships would patrol the sea lanes for up to a thousand miles from Japan's shores, an area that extended "from Japan to the central Pacific and the Philippines."[6] Nakasone visited South Korea in 1983, pledging to maintain close relations with Seoul. He strongly supported U.S. President Reagan in his

Burakumin Children
Though they look like typical Japanese schoolchildren, these children are from a traditional outcast group of people whose occupations are considered tainted with death or ritual impurity—butchers, leather workers, executioners, and undertakers. Traditionally they were discriminated against by other Japanese and only relatively recently began to fight for their rights.

confrontation with the Soviets. In part to deal with the perceived Soviet threat and in part to neutralize Americans who claimed that Japan was getting a free ride in terms of defense and therefore could more easily keep its economic powerhouse thriving, Nakasone increased military spending. In 1980 Japan was eighth in the world in military spending after the United States, the Soviet Union, China, Saudi Arabia, Britain, France, and West Germany. By 1987, the last year of Nakasone's leadership, Japan ranked sixth in the world, and in 1990 it had moved up to third. One writer states that during Nakasone's terms as prime minister, "Japan may be said to have secured full international acknowledgement of the attainment of the country's postwar goal of equality with the most influential and powerful Western nations."[7]

The great trade imbalance between Japan and the United States continued to be a source of tension. In the 1980s, the United States was purchasing about one-third of Japan's entire export trade. In an effort

Source: A Critique of Contemporary Japanese Lifestyles

This critique of Japanese life in the 1990s by Nakano Koji (b. 1925), a professor of German literature, is taken from a small book he wrote in 1992. Called Thoughts on Enjoyment of the Simple Life *[Seihin no Shisō], it called for a return to a simple life. What specifically does Nakano criticize about contemporary Japan?*

We became a nation of seekers of efficiency and productivity first only in the past half century. We sought a better life because we lost everything in the war. To a certain extent we can justify our present-day pursuit of materialism, when we know that its origin was in the lack of possession we experienced through the ruins of war. But we are beginning to realize that is not what life is about.

Japan has become an economic superpower. But it does not translate into the Japanese people having a better life or having leisure. We are a nation of workaholics, and we continue to work very hard. We live in tiny houses, commute a long distance in overcrowded trains, and work late. And as you are aware, we even have a special term, *karōshi,* for death resulting from overwork.

It is true that today we have more material possessions. Our markets are as abundant as any in the European Community countries. Yet, no matter how much the production of goods becomes abundant, it does not bring about happiness in life. We are now beginning to realize that to obtain happiness, we need a new principle or way of life that is not attached to material possessions.

Actually, we are beginning to realize also that as long as we are enslaved to material possessions, being entrapped in a cycle of buying, possessing, consuming, and throwing away, we cannot have fulfillment in our inner selves. We also know that to live together on this earth with other peoples, we cannot have unlimited production of material goods and consuming them unnecessarily. We know we have to protect our environment and resources. True richness, in other words, inner fulfillment, can come only from our willingness to limit our possessive urges and from our regaining the freedom of nonpossession. Many of us are now returning to basics and are questioning what is needed and not needed to gain happiness in our daily living.

In Japan there used to be a beautiful philosophy called *seihin,* or contentment in the simplicity of life. There was even a paradoxical thought that by restraining possessive urges to the absolute minimum, one could make a quantum jump in inner freedom. Let us now return to that subject.

Source: David J. Lu, Japan: A Documentary History *(Armonk, NY: M. E. Sharpe, 1996), 587–88.*

to prevent the United States from raising tariffs to keep Japanese goods out, financial decision makers from the so-called Group of Five nations (Japan, the United States, Great Britain, France, and West Germany) met at the Plaza Hotel in New York City in September 1985. They decided that to promote Japanese imports, the overvalued dollar should be lowered and the value of the yen raised: "exchange rates should better reflect fundamental economic conditions than has been the case before."[8] They also asked the Japanese government to sponsor policies and projects that would boost domestic demand. Though, after the Plaza Accord, the trade gap was narrowed slightly in yen, in dollars it increased substantially. The greatest impact came with the sharp rise in the value of the yen: by the end of 1986, Japan controlled 60 percent of the world's capital assets; of the ten largest banks in the world, eight were Japanese.

Statistically, Japan had become one of the richest countries in the world. By 1987, its trade surplus was about $100 billion. The government encouraged companies to invest overseas; by 1987, Japan had built up assets abroad of over $132 billion, almost 40 percent of which were in North America. The Japanese invested in U.S. treasury bills, in effect financing the galloping U.S. budget deficit in those years. With land and apartment buildings came some high-profile purchases. By the early 1980s, the Japanese had bought almost every resort hotel on Waikiki Beach in Hawaii. In 1989, they bought New York City's Rockefeller Center and CBS Records. The Sony Corporation purchased Columbia Pictures. In 1990, the Japanese bought the famed Pebble Beach golf course. The Nakasone years ended with Japan flying high.

JAPAN AND THE UNITED STATES: TRADE, MUTUAL PERCEPTIONS, AND CULTURAL CLASH

There was considerable resentment in the U.S. press and in Congress about the Japanese "takeovers" of traditional American institutions. There was also great disgruntlement that despite very low tariffs in Japan, the voluntary agreements, and the Plaza Accord, the United States was unable to crack the Japanese market. Americans began to feel that the Japanese system was rigged against them and any other outsiders trying to do business in Japan, and they started to talk about *structural impediments* that made it impossible to succeed in the Japanese market. Americans complained that Japan's retail distribution system kept foreign goods out: " [b]efore consumer products reach[ed] the buyer, they travel[ed] through a labyrinthine network of wholesalers and middlemen and finally end[ed] up in tiny neighborhood stores—'mom-and-pop' stores in the United States, but 'papa-mama' in Japan."[9] These tiny stores made up over 50 percent of all retail stores in Japan (compared to 3 percent of retail stores in the United States). This retail culture, built over many years, was strengthened by personal, familial, and educational connections—often close friendships. These networks were difficult, if not impossible, for outsiders to break into. To circle the wagons even more, the Japanese government in the 1970s passed laws protecting these small retailers from the new competition of larger stores. Thus, Americans charged that government and business were working to keep foreign businesses and goods out of Japan.

Americans also charged that collusion between government and big business and industry cut off meaningful competition. Targeted here were industrial groups or keiretsu, which commonly included twenty or more major companies that managed up to one hundred or more subsidiaries. The groups cohered through legal ties of interlocking directorships and personal connections. Thus, heads of keiretsu frequently met in conferences that set prices and apportioned the work on particular projects among the involved keiretsu. "Without a relaxation of *keiretsu* links, Japanese firms . . . invariably [bought] from each other rather than from foreign companies, Americans insist[ed]. 'Sweetheart' deals [would] continue to be preferred over the competitive bidding of the free market-place."[10]

Further, Americans argued that the Japanese system was biased in favor of corporate investment over the living standards of Japanese citizens. They pointed out that two-thirds of all Japanese homes in 1990 were still unconnected to sewers; sewage trucks regularly came to homes to pump out their cesspools. "The Japanese . . . joke[d] that their country 'ha[d] a first-class economy and a third class standard of living' (some threw in 'a second-class political system' to the mix)."[11]

One commodity that was the subject of many trade talks was rice. The Tokyo government forbade the importation of almost all rice, a prohibition that galled American rice growers, who produced rice much more cheaply than Japanese farmers, primarily because of the scale of operation. Most Japanese rice farms were like garden plots, often on mountain terraces, while U.S. rice farms were usually several hundred acres. A Japanese farmer spent up to 320 hours per year to grow one acre of rice, while in California it took only 6 hours per year to do the same. Rice grown in Japan therefore cost five or six times its price on the world market, and the government paid for it. Because there were similar situations involving other foodstuffs, Japanese consumers spent about a third of their income on food, more than twice what Americans paid.

Why was this inefficient system allowed to continue? The most important reason was political. Through what amounts to a very generous subsidy, the LDP got solid support from the Japanese farmers. To let in cheap rice would undercut Japanese farmers, who bristled at the possibility. Japanese also argued that cultural issues were significant in policymaking concerning rice. (See Chapter 1 for a discussion of Japanese ideas and attitudes about the culture of rice.) An American commentator had observations on this issue:

> *When they think of rice, even today's urbanized Japanese think of their devoted uncle or grandmother stooped over in the fields. . . . When the first Japanese settlers moved to Hokkaido, a hundred years ago, it was a land of wheat and barley but no rice. On their deathbeds, Professor Hemmi Kenzo, of Tokyo University, has said, the lone pioneers would ask their children to place a few grains of rice in a bamboo tube and shake it, "so the parent could at least hear the sound of rice once more before he or she died."*[12]

Though the ban on importing rice remained, in 1993, because of a very poor rice harvest, rice was imported but sold at the Japanese price—six times that of other nations. In a 1989 conference on world trade, Japan agreed to allow 4 percent of its rice to be imported by 1995, eventually to be raised to 8 percent.

The Japanese were nonplussed and irritated by American reactions. They pointed out that Japan's tariff rates were some of the lowest in the world. American goods and fast food chains were ubiquitous in the country. Moreover, Japan was a large importer of American commodities, in 1990 importing 20.5 percent of all U.S. agricultural exports. To put the trade problem in perspective they pointed out that each Japanese consumer on average purchased $361 worth of American products per year, while each American consumer bought Japanese goods valued at $378 per year.

The Japanese tended to blame Americans for their trade problem. Americans, they averred, often failed because they did not learn either the Japanese language or the Japanese culture. The classic Japanese question to Americans, especially those upset over the importation of Japanese cars, was: "Why . . . did Detroit never design a right-hand-drive car for the Japanese consumer if it was serious about breaking into that market?"[13] Since so many of the obstacles to American business success related to Japan's basic group-centered culture, the Japanese were stunned that Americans could be so arrogant as to insist that this culture be changed for them.

The Japanese, in addition, tended to castigate the United States and its culture, both business and otherwise. They saw Americans as pleasure seeking, irresponsible, indolent, and concerned only about the quick fix. Some Japanese saw American society as too heterogeneous to work together effectively for national goals. American businesses, in Japanese eyes, looked only for the immediate profit, and they paid their CEOs outrageous salaries and retirement packages. American workers, according to the Japanese, had neither a strong sense of commitment to their company nor pride in and satisfaction from work. A popular 1989 book by the head of Sony Corporation and an LDP Diet member, *The Japan That Can Say "No,"* set forth the conviction of many Japanese that their nation should not be a pushover for the United States, but that in their dealings they should be able to firmly say "no."

Source: The Japan That Can Say "No"

An instant best-seller when it was published in 1989, The Japan That Can Say "No," *written by Sony chairman Morita Akio and novelist-politician Ishihara Shintarō, was, on one level, a plea for Japan to be taken more seriously by the United States. What did the authors foresee would happen to U.S.-Japanese relations?*

The United States has not sufficiently appreciated Japan and even taken us all that seriously, because since 1945, we have been under Uncle Sam's thumb. Today, Americans may feel that Japan is getting out of hand. My own view is that Japan should not immediately disassociate itself from the U.S. security system. For our sake and that of the whole Pacific region, the special Tokyo–Washington relationship must be preserved. A breakup could destroy the budding new developments in that region. Japan should play an expanded role in the post-Cold War world order. Effective use of our economic power—technology, management skills, and financial resources—at our own initiative can be the key to stable progress. . . .

As the tempestuous twentieth century draws to a close, I would like to add a postscript to modernism. Caucasians deserve much credit in the creation of modern civilization, but they were not the only agents of change. Historian Arnold J. Toynbee concluded that we had simply imitated the West. Regrettably, some Japanese agree with the British scholar's interpretation and are delighted at this "high praise." This sad lot does not understand history. What to superficial observers seems like the instantaneous aping of Western ways was actually the fruition of innumerable cultural advances over the course of many centuries. . . .

. . . Over the next few years, Japan-bashing in the United States will become even more virulent. Although I see the bilateral relationship as the dominant force in the next century, before we reach that level of cooperation, U.S. policy toward Japan will approximate the stance against the Soviet Union at the height of the Cold War.

First, Americans will argue that Japan is different and therefore a threat. Next, a "collective security system" will be created to block Japan's economic expansion. Then protectionist measures and sanctions against Japanese products will follow one after the other. An alliance is already being formed against Japan. Finally, there will be a witch hunt directed at everything Japanese. We must be prepared for stormy days ahead.

If we try to bend with the wind, making concessions and patchwork compromises as usual, the tempest will abate for a while, only to recur with even greater force. We must not flinch in the face of pressure. The only way to withstand foreign demands is to hold our ground courageously. No more temporizing. When justified, we must keep saying no and be undaunted by the reaction, however furious. A prolonged standoff forces both sides to find areas of agreement. That is the best way to resolve disputes, not unilateral concessions by Japan, which leave the other party unaware of how we really feel. Our lack of assertiveness in the past has led to disparaging epithets like "the faceless people."

Source: David J. Lu, Japan: A Documentary History *(Armonk, NY: M. E. Sharpe, 1996), 558, 559, 561.*

THE NEW AFFLUENCE

Through the 1970s and 1980s, Japanese experienced increasing economic affluence. Though all did not approve of the consumerism that flourished, all benefited to some degree (see Chapter 20 for further treatment of consumerism). The new rich (successful businessmen and company leaders, to name only two such groups) lived in plush, modern two-story homes, drove BMWs, took vacations abroad, wore the most fashionable name-brand clothes, and frequently ate at trendy restaurants.[14] At the other end of the salary scale were blue-collar workers and white-collar businessmen at smaller companies, or perhaps young couples just beginning their careers, who lived in tiny apartments with a floor space of four or five hundred square feet. If they owned a car, it would probably have been built in Japan, and any vacations would probably be taken in Japan.

Between these groups was the urban middle class. In the closing days of the U.S. occupation, 38 percent of Japanese lived in cities; by 1972, the percentage reached 72. In 2000, almost 50 percent of all Japanese lived within a thirty-mile radius of Japan's three largest cities—Tokyo, Osaka, and Nagoya. The man of the middle-class family was likely to be a *sarari-man* or salaryman, a white-collar office worker for a large corporation. It was often said that salarymen owed as much loyalty to their companies as samurai formerly did to their lords. They were expected to work long hours, and once the workday was over, they went to drink together and let off steam. In the 1970s and 1980s they were assured of

The Japanese Bow   Japanese businessmen exchange bows. A bow in Japan has many functions. It can show respect; it can be a simple greeting or an act of thanking or apologizing. How deeply one bows depends on the status or age of the person to whom one is bowing; the bow should be deeper if the other person is older or of higher status.

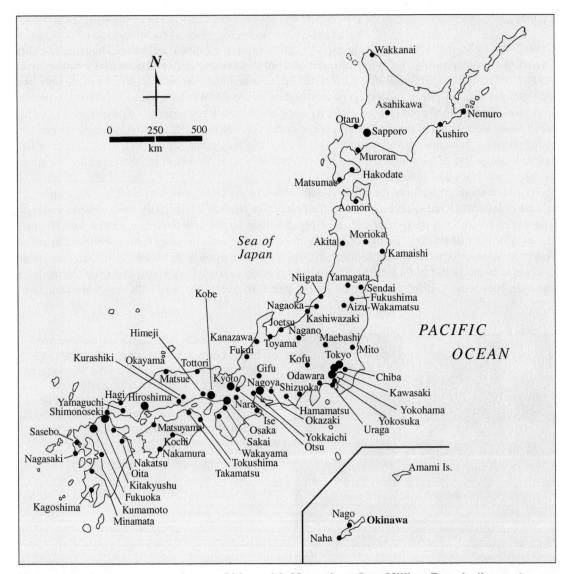

Map 18-1　Contemporary Japan: Cities with More than One Million People (largest dotted cities).

lifetime employment, were provided all benefits, and could vacation at company resorts. They lived in rather modest suburban houses or modern condominiums. Their wives were expected to stay home to raise their children, manage the family finances, and oversee the children's education—a role that wives saw as fulfilling and/or frustrating. Many Japanese saw the life of the salaryman and his family as ideal, for it was a position that was "within the range of realistic hopes and modern enough to be worthy of their highest aspirations."[15]

In Japan's countryside, whereas in 1950 at least 50 percent of all Japanese were involved in farming, in 1990 just 3 to 5 percent did so. Mechanization made planting, transplanting, plowing, and harvesting

Shopping   Throngs of shoppers crowd Takeshita Street in the Harajuku area of Tokyo, the center of Japan's most extreme teenage cultures and fashion styles. In this area are trendy shops, used-clothing stores, boutiques, crepe stands, and fast food restaurants.

much less backbreaking. It also reduced the time needed to finish farm tasks, so many farmers took part-time jobs in towns and cities. Indeed, in many families, farm work was taken over by the women of the home. Mechanization was a major force in the rapid rise of farm incomes from 1960 on. "[B]y 1990 only one in eight of Japan's farm families pursued agriculture on a full-time basis, and most rural families earned a whopping 70 percent of their incomes from nonfarm activities."[16]

Amid the new affluence in the 1980s, two popular art forms, *manga* and *anime,* moved into the cultural mainstream and, like other Japanese culinary and cultural items—sushi, packaged ramen noodles, karaoke, martial arts, and films—became hits abroad as well. *Manga,* literally "random (or whimsical) pictures," were comics or print cartoons that appeared, mainly in black and white, after World War II—probably inspired by printmaking in the Tokugawa. Often criticized as being too violent and too sexual, they were both a popular art form (with an emphasis on line rather than form) and a form of popular literature. Popular *manga* were sometimes turned into *anime* (short for *animation*). Just as their name suggests, *anime* were animated cartoons, sometimes hand drawn but more commonly created on computers. They were characterized by detailed backgrounds and stylized characters.

THE END OF THE SHŌWA ERA

There remained among many Japanese deep interest in and respect for the imperial family. In 1959, Crown Prince Akihito chose to marry Shoda Michiko, the daughter of a rich industrialist—not an aristocrat, which upset Empress Nagako. The wedding coverage on television prompted many people to purchase television sets, as they beamed to hear telecast announcers praise this modern love marriage. Akihito and his wife set new living patterns by choosing to rear their four children in their own home. Akihito, whose reign era was Heisei (meaning "achieving peace"), was an expert on fish and an accomplished cellist.

In January 1989 Emperor Hirohito, who had been on the throne since 1926, died of duodenal cancer; he had collapsed in September 1988, and his deathwatch was punctuated by daily media reports on his temperature, pulse, and the amount of blood vomited or anally bled. In death he took the name of his reign era, Emperor Shōwa ("Shining Peace"). Though this person who, for the first twenty years of his reign, was considered divine, the graphic reports on his illness (and obviously his death) made his humanity all too evident. His reign had been extraordinary, covering the turbulent 1930s, the Sino-Japanese War and the Pacific war, his renunciation of his divinity and the American occupation, and then the spectacular economic success of the postoccupation years. For many conservative Japanese, there was a desire in the funeral ceremonies to exalt the person of the emperor and the Chrysanthemum Throne. For moderate Japanese, the desire was to exalt the symbolic head of the Japanese constitutional regime; Hirohito was, after all, the first emperor to die after the adoption of the 1947 constitution, which had turned him into only a symbol of the state. He was an amateur marine biologist. For all of his doddering old age, he still remained a controversial figure: how much responsibility did he have for starting the war and executing it?

"From the instant of his death to the staging of his burial some forty days later, the state choreographed an elaborate dance representing constitutionality and mystery, Western modernity and Eastern tradition."[17] His father, the Taishō emperor had had a simple Shinto ceremony. For Hirohito, a Shinto ceremony for the imperial family were held behind a black curtain with a temporary *torii* (shrine gate). When that was completed, the curtain and torii were removed for the civil ceremony with 9,800 people present, called by the *Asahi Shimbun*, "the largest funeral in history."[18]

The Emperor's Funeral   The coffin of the Shōwa emperor in a royal litter arrives at the Shinjuku Imperial Garden preceded by court musicians playing a traditional funeral dirge and by Shinto priests.

Source: August in Japan

In this poignant prologue to her stunning book In the Realm of a Dying Emperor: Japan at Century's End, *anthropologist Norma Field raises the question of the Japanese memory of World War II. What does her last question mean?*

. . . The skies are brilliant, the air is heavy with the souls of the dead. The New Tokyo International Airport heaves with its own ghostly hordes straining for the beaches of Guam and Waikiki and the shops of San Francisco, Los Angeles, and New York, where everything is cheap, from paper napkins to Vuitton bags. Those who cannot participate in this rite of self-confirmation as members of the newly internationalized breed of Japanese may still join the exodus to the countryside that leaves Tokyo in a sun-blasted silence four or five days of the year. For this is O-bon: time to welcome the souls of ancestors, feast, and then encourage them to return whence they came so that the living can proceed with the business of the living. Less refreshed than their forebears, families struggle home, laden with gifts received in exchange for offerings dragged from Tokyo but a few days earlier. Increased efficiency in the dissemination and satisfaction of taste means that the goods traveling to and from the ancestral home are increasingly indistinguishable. Nature, for its part, gallops in flight from this meeting of city and countryside.

It isn't only folk custom that makes August the haunted month. First the sixth, then the ninth, and finally the fifteenth: Hiroshima, Nagasaki, and surrender. So many souls to be appeased. Television coverage of memorial rites in the two cities has declined precipitously since I was a child. In fact, second city Nagasaki barely makes it to the morning and evening news. Every year, however, in both cities there are still the black-clad representatives of the bereaved, the white-gloved officials, speeches, wreaths, and doves. A scant minority insist on calling August 15 the Anniversary of Defeat rather than, more reassuringly, the Anniversary of the End of the War. (Just across the Japan Sea, in Korea, August 15 is the Return of Light Day, marking the joyous dissolution of the Japanese Empire.) In 1988 a dying Hirohito officiated as usual in the ceremonies held at the giant hall for martial arts constructed for the Tokyo Olympics. He was flown in by helicopter from his summer villa to alight as a frail embodiment of the war, still nullifying all possibility of its discussion. The era closed with his life; does changing a name guarantee the obliteration of memory?

Source: Norma Field, In the Realm of a Dying Emperor: Japan at Century's End *(New York: Vintage Books, 1993), 5–6.*

Not all Japanese were willing to give the Shōwa emperor a free ride on the issue of the war. Even before his illness, Nagasaki Mayor Motoshima Hitoshi said (in December 1988):

> *Forty-three years have passed since the end of the war, and I think we have been able to reflect sufficiently on the nature of that war. . . . I think that the emperor does bear responsibility for the war.*[19]

For these remarks, Motoshima was verbally attacked and threatened; his family had to keep a full-time police guard. He was stabbed by right-wing zealots in 1990.

AFTER NAKASONE

Of the eleven prime ministers who served after the departure of Nakasone in 1987 until 2001, six had terms of two years, two of one year, and two of a few months. Only Prime Minister Koizumi Junichirō (2001–2006) equaled Nakasone's five-year tenure. One would not expect it to be a period of outstanding political accomplishments, and that is certainly the case. Indeed, politically, it was the bleakest period since the war.

Scandals

Scandals weakened the LDP, involving ministers and vice-ministers in the bureaucracy. A few months after he left office, a scandal involving Nakasone and other LDP leaders came to light. Shares of the Recruit-Cosmos Company (a business that began in the 1960s to market advertising in university newspapers) were distributed to influential LDP members before they were listed on the stock exchange. Nakasone received nineteen thousand shares, on which he could have made about 43 million yen if he had sold the shares when they were listed. In addition, Recruit planned to give 45 million yen to Nakasone's political coffers. This would have allowed recruit to name several appointees in the Ministry of Education to help benefit their business. Nakasone's successor, Takeshita Noburu, also received bribes. Takeshita had also made serious mistakes. He had a new sales tax passed, and he antagonized farmers by allowing the importation of foodstuffs. His approval rating fell almost off the charts—down to 4 percent. He resigned in May 1989. His successor, Uno Sōsuke, lasted only two months; he was ruined by the news not only that he kept a mistress but, even more upsetting, that he treated her badly when he broke off the affair.

The Sagawa Express Scandal erupted in 1992 after the party's new wheeler-dealer, a man named Kanemaru Shin, had taken charge of the Tanaka faction; behind the scenes, he pulled the strings of the next two prime ministers, Kaifu Toshiki (1989–1991) and Miyazawa Kiichi (1991–1993). In this scandal Kanemaru was reportedly cavorting around with underworld figures. Using money obtained from them, he bribed politicians to vote as they and he wanted. There were fervent calls for ending what looked like endemic corruption, but the LDP acted as though this was normal activity and undertook no reforms.

Economic Collapse

After the Plaza Accord in 1985, the government had taken various steps to encourage both investment and domestic consumption. The economy overheated. When average price-to-earnings ratios for stocks are rightly valued, they run between 20 and 30. The euphoria of the economic bubble sent Japan's price-to earnings ratio up to 80; brokers predicted that the Nikkei index might shoot up to 60,000, even 80,000. The bubble started to burst when financial officials decided to raise interest rates to cool the rampant speculation. In early January 1990, the stock market fell into a tailspin, dropping by 50 percent in ten months and even more after that. Banks had loaned to speculators who now could not repay their debts. Banks closed. Higher interest rates meant that real estate developers, already overextended, could not afford the steeper borrowing costs. Land values plummeted. Despite these serious problems, however, Japan still garnered huge trade surpluses. The GNP in 1990 and 1991 was still rising at a rate of 4 percent, so the underlying economy did not immediately reflect the financial chaos caused by the bursting of the economic bubble.

But in 1992, the results of the burst bubble spread to the broader economy; Japan fell into a recession marked by a fall in wholesale prices, industrial production, and construction starts. Then the stock market toppled again. More banks failed, and more became involved in corruption and scandal. In the Daiwa Bank scandal of July 1995, American branches of the bank were found to have hidden $1.1 billion in trading losses from authorities. In the Sumitomo Trading scandal of October 1996, a copper trader in England had secretly lost $2.1 billion. In the Jusen Bank scandal in 1996, seven home-loan corporations went bankrupt—with debts of up to 8 trillion yen; then they tried a cover-up by showing bank investigators three different sets of figures. One of the big four brokerage houses, Yamaichi Securities, declared bankruptcy; then $2 billion was found squirreled away in offshore accounts. Sometimes the scene became tawdry. In 1994, a Dai-Ichi Kangyo Bank official took an inspector from the Ministry of Finance as a "favor" to an evening at a "no-pants *shabu-shabu* [quick-cooked beef] restaurant" featuring waitresses in the nude from the waist down."[20]

There was a weak economic recovery in 1995 and 1996, though many debts had not been repaid. Official statements about loan repayment were usually questionable, since many bank directors were retired Ministry of Finance regulators. Then in 1997, Prime Minister Hashimoto Ryūtarō (1996–1998) took a foolish and costly step. In order to cut the large government deficit, he increased the consumption tax by two thirds, from 3 to 5 percent. This scared consumers, who cut back on their spending and stopped the developing recovery dead in its tracks. Calls for reforms poured forth, reforms that included getting the government out of the private economy and cutting down on government regulation of business.

The government took three major actions in the late 1990s to try to jump-start the economy. First, it developed a program to deregulate the financial markets, including banking, insurance, and securities. Second, it passed a Financial Revitalization law to try to restructure the banking system, still burdened with debt; it was not effective in dealing with the issues, however. Third, it decided to spend a lot of money, even though this would increase the deficit, to lift the country out of recession. Yet, progress was minuscule: from 1997 to 1998, real GDP dropped 2 percent; in 1999 and 2000, there was no real growth. And the deficits soared. "By the end of 2000 the sum of accumulated central and local government debt had surpassed 140 percent of GDP."[21] In 2001 an out-of-the-mold LDP leader, Koizumi Junichirō, became prime minister, speaking with candor and calling for "harsh economic medicine."[22] He helped engineer the economic recovery through "Reaganesque policies of deregulation, privatization, spending cuts, and tax breaks for the rich." [23]

Dysfunctional Japanese Politics

We have discussed the factionalism, corruption, and stalemates of Japanese politics, all of which reduced the effectiveness of the political system and its reputation in the eyes of its citizens. Unfortunately, several other chronic difficulties remained. One was that, except for a very few years, the government was led by one party, the LDP. There were periods when a flurry of other parties seemed to offer the promise of developing beyond what was called at best a *one and a half* party system—the half party being all the other parties waiting in the wings. These parties took the stage only once, from the summer of 1993 to January 1996, in the aftermath of scandal, corruption, and economic stagnation. During that time there was a coalition government including the LDP and members of the Clean Government Party (*Kōmeitō*, formed in the 1960s and based originally on the sect of Nichiren Buddhism), the Democratic Socialists, and several from the Japan Socialist Party (JSP).

The JSP had been buoyed briefly in 1986, when it had elected an able and charismatic woman, Doi Takako (see Identities), as its chair and had won 46 seats in the House of Councillors (the weaker of the two houses in the Diet), compared to 36 for the LDP. The JSP took its record high number of 136 seats in the Diet in 1990, mainly due to Doi's popularity. She was elected speaker of the house in the 1993 coalition government and continued when, in the 1994 elections, the coalition became one primarily of the LDP and the JSP—longtime ideological rivals. Many believed that Japan was on the brink of moving at last to a two-party system. But the LDP had too many connections to the sources of power and was able to regain sole control in 1996; in those elections the JSP (renamed the *Social Democratic Party of Japan*) experienced a catastrophic meltdown, its Diet seats falling from 70 to 15, eliminating it after decades as a political force. The LDP, for all of its problems, clung to power at least until 2007.

The seeming inability of the government to respond adequately to crises made many question its viability. In January 1995 a huge earthquake hit the Kobe region on the Inland Sea, leaving almost 6,400 people dead and at least 300,000 homeless. It was the *yakuza*, the organized crime syndicates, that were the first to respond, along with thousands of volunteers. "Meanwhile, government bureaucrats remained

Identities: Doi Takako (1928–):

The "Madonna Boom"

The most prominent woman in Japanese politics in the twentieth century, Doi Takako studied law at Dōshisha University, one of Japan's elite universities, in Kyoto. She served as a lecturer at Dōshisha for two decades. In 1969 she was elected to the Diet as a member of the JSP. Until 1980 she remained largely behind the scenes. "At first, she was less than popular with her predominantly male colleagues, who questioned her lack of femininity and her single status. . . . But standing at 170 cm [about 5' 6"] and armed with a husky voice and formidable debating skills, she was more than a match for her male counterparts."[1]

Doi first came to national attention in 1980, when she criticized the unequal treatment of women in Japan. In 1986 she became the first woman to lead a major party, the JSP. A so-called Madonna Boom swept through Japan, bringing more and more women into the political world. Doi's goal as party leader was to make the JSP more mainstream, steering it away from doctrinaire positions.

In 1989, she led the JSP's opposition to the LDP proposal for a new 3 percent sales tax; she and the JSP lost. But in the February 1990 elections, the LDP lost the majority of its upper house seats to the JSP for the first time ever. Since the House of Councilors is the weaker house of the Diet and cannot veto a budget passed by the House of Representative, the LDP remained in control. Doi still appropriately remarked, "The mountain has moved."

In the summer of 1993, in the wake of the Sagawa Express scandal and the economic collapse, a vote of no confidence over the LDP's inability even to propose needed reforms passed

when opposition parties including the JSP were joined by maverick LDP members. The LDP lost a majority of seats. Two new reform parties joined the JSP and the Clean Government Party in a coalition, the first non-LDP government since 1947. Doi became speaker of the House of Representatives, where she served until 1996. However, the coalition collapsed, and in the 1996 elections the LDP returned to power.

Doi renamed the JSP the Social Democratic Party in 1996, hoping to moderate the emphasis on socialism in an effort to achieve wider appeal. Ironically, the party's membership began to move into some of the new reform parties. Whereas in the 1990 elections the JSP had won 24.4 percent of the votes, by 2000 its vote totals had fallen to 3.8 percent. Doi herself was at least partially responsible for the decline. Despite her efforts to put a more moderate face on the party, her own comments upset many Japanese. In 1987, in North Korea for Kim Il-sung's birthday, Doi announced that "We JSP members respect the glorious successes of the DPRK under the great leader Kim Il-sung." In 2003, responding to the abduction of Japanese citizens by the North Korean government, Doi lost much support by telling the families of the abductees on national television to just "get over it."[2]

In the 2003 election after that remark, Doi lost her seat but was able to remain in the Diet through the proportional representation system. But in the September 2005 elections she lost that seat as well. Like a meteor, Doi had burned brightly briefly, but her public leadership career was quickly snuffed out.

---

[1] See http://www.japan-zone.com/modern/doi_takako.shtml.

[2] See http://www.en.wikipedia.org/wiki/Takako_Doi.

entwined in red tape, not even allowing aid from the outside world to enter the country, treating aid goods like import commodities required to meet rigid standards set by the government."[24]

In March 1995, members of a new religious cult, Aum Shinrikyō, released sarin, a deadly nerve gas, on two subway lines in Tokyo. Twelve people were killed and more than 5,500 were injured. The sect, organized by a disgruntled blind former yoga teacher, was composed mostly of elites, graduates from the best universities and professionals, who followed blindly the orders of the sect's head—the goal, to hasten an anticipated apocalypse. What shocked the public, beyond the act itself, was that even though the sect had been involved in earlier crimes, the police had done nothing to prevent it from getting the chemicals and illegal arms. In this case, however, the government got good marks for its effective response—acting forcefully but not overreacting.

Then in 1996 came the shocking revelation that in the early 1980s, after the discovery of the AIDS virus, Japan's Ministry of Health and Welfare had chosen not to ban the production of unheated blood for transfusions after it became known that heating the blood would kill the virus. Part of the reason was that the only producers of heated blood were American drug companies. A 1983 decision that "emergency imports of heat-treated products [would] be allowed" was withdrawn "because it would 'deal a blow' to Japan's marketers of untreated blood products."[25] Although the government finally agreed to import heated blood from the United States, it continued to use the Japanese-produced unheated blood without issuing any warnings to hemophiliacs. When some hemophiliacs as early as 1984 were found to have been infected with human immunodeficiency virus (HIV) from untreated blood, this was concealed from the public. In the late 1980s, 40 percent of Japanese hemophiliacs tested positive for the virus. The head of the Ministry of Health and Welfare's Pharmaceutical Affairs Bureau at the time and two colleagues were found guilty of professional negligence and given short prison sentences. The whole affair shook the confidence of the Japanese people in their government, whose bureaucrats were charged with regulating private industry for the health and safety of the populace.

THE PROCESS OF POLITICAL DECISION-MAKING

Japan's dependence on consensus decision-making, while advantageous in some ways, on the whole handicapped effective political action, especially at times of crisis. Consensus decision-making generally occurred during many meetings: decision makers often began discussing pertinent issues in very vague, general, and uncommitted ways until a sense of shared agreement emerged. The advantages of this system were obvious.

Source: Postmortem on the Kobe Earthquake

The Japanese government was severely criticized for its dilatory response to the Kobe earthquake. Here Matsushina Yusuke, the highest commander of the Self-Defense Force on the scene, describes some of the problems in getting help and relief to the area's people. According to Matsushina, what were the chief problems?

Another suggestion concerns the national government's readiness for crisis management. The National Land Agency sponsors a conference on measures to be taken in the event of an earthquake to which the Defense Agency is invited as an observer, just to sit there and watch. This has very little meaning to it. The Self-Defense Forces have the organization and ability to engage in rescue operations. They must include us actively in future planning.

On the matter of the Defense Agency director's "order for action," the Kobe earthquake provides us many valuable lessons. Along with local self-governing bodies, the Defense Agency director has the right to issue such an order. The line of command in such an instance is from the Defense Agency director to area commanders of Ground, Maritime and Air Self-Defense Forces.

For example, if the Central Area wants to borrow helicopters or water-supply wagons from the Hokkaido Area or Kyushu Area, each area commander must make that request to the Defense Agency director through the chief of staff of the Ground Self-Defense Force. Unless the director orders the area commander of Hokkaido to lend that water-supply wagon, no action can be taken. Staff officers of the three services in Tokyo coordinate the actual transfer.

At the time of the Kobe earthquake, I made a request to the director that helicopters, water-supply wagons, kitchen wagons, and rescue equipment be sent from other area commands. The Defense Bureau within the Self-Defense Agency handled the clerical matter. They had to circulate papers around all the bureaus within the agency before they could get the approval of the Director. In each of the bureaus, several officers were responsible for approving the papers. It took time. To make matters worse, some people were not familiar with the equipment we were requesting. As for the director, he had to be at the Diet while it was in session. On the matter of water-supply wagons, it took anywhere from thirteen to fifteen hours before the necessary papers from the chief of staff reached the desk of the director. And we did not have ferries from Hokkaido contracted in advance. It took four to five days for us to borrow water-supply wagons from Hokkaido....

Source: David J. Lu, Japan: A Documentary History *(Armonk, NY: M. E. Sharpe, 1996), 580–81.*

Decisions made this way gave each member of the group a sense of participation. Consensus also made it harder for someone who had helped to make the decision, especially if it turned out to be wrong, to suggest later that he had disagreed all along. Finally, consensus made carrying out the decision easier because the participants understood the issues thoroughly and had committed themselves to implementation.

The disadvantages, however, weighed heavily on the process. Consensus decision-making was extraordinarily time-consuming, often requiring meeting after meeting. Often opposing views emerged that were difficult to ignore or reconcile; a thoroughly convinced—or obstinate—minority could hold out for weeks and ultimately obstruct any decision or greatly delay it. In particularly difficult cases, where consensus seemed almost impossible, a façade of consensus had to be reached—a vague and almost noncommittal decision that, in the end, stymied action and led to greater confusion. Finally, in a sense, if everyone decided, in the end no one decided. The system tended to encourage *mutual irresponsibility:* because the decision was made by consensus, if things went badly, everyone tended to be evasive when faced with the responsibility.

The shocking political statistic was that 90 percent of all bills passed the Diet unanimously. The time spent reaching these consensuses was almost unimaginable; it was little wonder that action in the

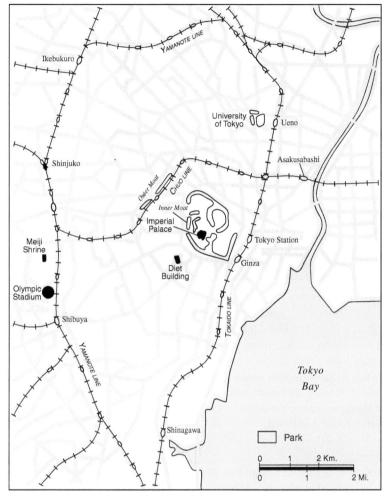

Map 18-2 Contemporary Tokyo.

Diet was glacial. This reality also pointed to the downside of party factionalism. The administration of Miki Takeo in the 1970s was, as we have seen, a coalition of four LDP factions. In building consensus for bills, there first had to be a consensus within each of the factions before they dealt with the other political parties in the Diet. The health of Japanese democracy seemed questionable in the early twenty-first century.

JAPAN IN THE WORLD

As the sixtieth anniversary of the end of World War II came and went, there was considerable talk in Japan and among some U.S. policymakers about whether Article 9, the no-war clause in the Japanese constitution, should be abolished. The arguments? First, for a country with immense economic power not to have more military power is neither normal nor prudent. Second, though the United States was still committed to preserving the security of Japan, U.S. military involvement in many areas of the world meant that if push came to shove, the United States might not have the power to do so. Third, the threat of the rogue state of North Korea and a strengthened China required Japan to be more prepared militarily.

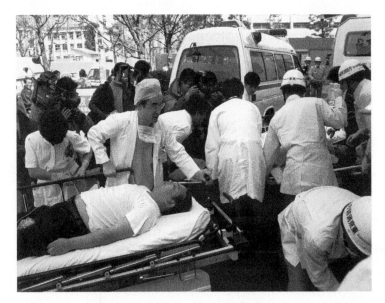

Poison Gas Attack Two months after the Kobe earthquake, on March 20, 1995, the Aum Shinrikyō ("Supreme Truth") cult released deadly sarin gas in the Tokyo subway system. A dozen people died and more than 5,500 others were sickened.

In 1992, Prime Minister Miyazawa shepherded the International Peace Cooperation Law through the Diet; it allowed troops from the Self-Defense Force to be used in peacekeeping operations. The first troops were sent three months later to serve with UN forces in Cambodia. In 2004 six hundred Self-Defense Force soldiers were sent to Iraq, the first time since World War II that Japanese troops were sent into a war zone; their withdrawal was announced in June 2006. Restrictions were eased on the Japanese military, which was allowed to cooperate with the United States in establishing a missile defense system. The Self-Defense Force worked in the opening years of the twenty-first century to structure a more mobile force with multifunctional capabilities.

The United States

Japan, despite its wealth, continued to function as a subordinate to the United States in international relations. Some have compared Japan's role under Pax Americana to its role in China's old Confucian-inspired tributary system. As the Cold War ended and a new age of terrorism began, the United States wanted Japan to play a greater political and diplomatic role. But the memory of World War II remained strong for many Japanese, who, when pressured to play a greater role, took refuge in the no-war clause of the constitution. In the 1991 Persian Gulf War, Japan sent $13 billion in cash, though it had no say in how the war was conducted; the United States wanted it to play a more active military role. Against strong opposition, the Japanese government did send minesweepers to the Persian Gulf. But on other war-related issues, such as organizing rescue missions for refugees, a consensus could not be reached.

Friendly relations continued, as evidenced by joint security and scientific efforts like the 2003 agreement to proceed with the Integrated Ocean Drilling Program. But the trade issues did not disappear. In December 2003, Japan placed a ban on U.S. beef when one case of mad cow disease was found in a U.S. herd. That ban was lifted in December 2005 but reimposed in January 2006; the second ban was lifted in June 2006. American farmers and ranchers were upset about the bans and, in the second case, pressured the U.S. government to apply sanctions if purchases did not begin by the end of August. These episodes always gave rise to talk of a trade war. In 2005 the Japanese ban on the importation of U.S. apples was lifted. U.S. disgruntlement with the nonagricultural Japanese market appeared in 2006 talks about easing Japan's strict regulations for approving and pricing pharmaceuticals imported from the United States.

Source: Relocating the Japanese Capital

There has been debate about moving the Japanese capital since at least the 1960s, but nothing more. This report, written in 1966 by the head of the Sendai branch of the Japan Association of Corporate Executives, specifies criteria for relocating the capital, which many see as an impetus for reform, and possibly shrinking the size of government. What are his criteria and what kinds of priorities do they suggest?

The final report of the Commission to Investigate Relocation of the National Diet and Other Organizations was issued in December 1995. This report deals with the issues of relocating the Diet and major administrative and judicial functions to local areas. I would like to add my voice in support, as a concerned citizen from outside the capital zone.

Nine criteria are selected in identifying the location of a new capital. They are:

1. The new capital must be located in such a way that imbalance will not be created in the access to it from different regions of the country.
2. It must be located at a site not less than 60 kilometers and not more than 300 kilometers from Tokyo.
3. It must be located within forty minutes commuting distance from an international airport.
4. It must be possible to obtain quickly and smoothly the land needed for building a new capital.
5. Areas that are likely to be devastated by serious earthquakes and other calamities must be avoided.
6. Due consideration must be given to maintenance of normal urban living even in case of emergencies caused by natural calamities.
7. Places that are mountainous or with precipitous topography must be avoided.
8. Avoid areas where the emergence of a new urban area with a population of six hundred thousand people may cause water shortage.
9. A proper distance must be maintained from those major urban centers designated as administratively designated cities.

Most people seem to be interested only in these nine criteria. The media generally discuss the competition that exists between the three prime candidates for the site of the new capital, namely, Northern Kantō, Tohokū, and Tōkai regions. People outside these regions may be less interested, but the matter is of concern to everyone regardless of from which region he comes. Relocation of the capital is a bold move to restructure Japanese politics and administration for the twenty-first century and beyond. It is accompanied by an attempt to redefine the respective roles of the central and local governments.

Source: David J. Lu, Japan: A Documentary History *(Armonk, NY: M. E. Sharpe, 1996), 582–83.*

One noneconomic problem between the United States and Japan at the turn of the century concerned U.S. military bases on Okinawa. Beginning in 1990, the governor of Okinawa called for a reduction in these bases. The Japanese government undertook no such initiative and indeed supported a U.S. Pentagon report in early 1995 that stressed the need to keep three-quarters of its one hundred thousand men stationed in Japan on Okinawa, its armed forces and the continuation of the U.S.-Japan security treaty being crucial to the security of the region. In September 1995, however, a U.S. serviceman stationed on Okinawa raped a twelve-year-old schoolgirl. The governor then announced that he would refuse to sign documents required for the Tokyo government to keep U.S. forces on the island; his intent was to bring the matter of U.S. bases to Japanese courts. Though he was defeated, his actions, plus his almost unanimous support from the Okinawans, put pressure on the Tokyo government to respond and at least talk about moving some American troops out of Okinawa. It took until 1997 for the Diet to decide to maintain the status quo and keep the troops in place, an action that alienated the Okinawans.

China

The commercial relationship between Japan and China continued to thrive up to the turn of the twenty-first century (see Chapters 17 and 20 for more extended treatment of Sino-Japanese relations). By 1993 China had become one of Japan's biggest trading partners, with import-export trade valued at $37.8 billion (compared to the U.S.-Japan trade valued at $160.5 billion). But tension began to appear in 2001, when Japan raised tariffs on items like shiitake mushrooms, scallions, and rushes for tatami mats; China retaliated by raising tariffs on cars, mobile phones, and air conditioners imported from Japan. The tensions over trade—as with the United States—were omnipresent.

The Koreas

Perhaps even more delicate and complex than Japan's relationship with China was its relationship with the Koreas. Japan's relationship with North Korea was icy for two main reasons. P'yŏngyang's 1998 firing of a long-range missile (part of a failed effort to put a satellite into orbit) that flew over Japan before landing in the Pacific Ocean did not endear North Korea to Japan. Coupled with North Korea's flirting with nuclear weapons in the first years of the twenty-first century, the 1998 episode made Japanese fearful about North Korean intentions. The North's launching of seven missiles that landed in the Sea of Japan in early July 2006 touched off a Japanese proposal for sanctions again P'yŏngyang in the U.N. North Korea's underground testing of a nuclear weapon in October 2006 only increased Japan's anxiety.

The other ongoing dispute concerned bizarre North Korean abductions of Japanese citizens in the 1970s and 1980s. Such abductions had been rumored for years. Japan began to raise the issue with the North in 1991, but the P'yŏngyang government categorically denied all the allegations. At a summit meeting in September 2002, Kim Jong-il admitted, however, that sixteen Japanese citizens had been kidnapped; five were returned to Japan a month later. Another summit in May 2004 led to promises that five members of victims' families would be repatriated and that North Korea would launch investigations to see if any more of the abducted individuals remained alive. The reasons for these kidnappings were unknown. Some suggested that the purpose was identity theft for North Korean government agents; others believed that it was to coerce the abductees into teaching North Korean agents to act as Japanese. Still others believed that the kidnappings were executed by the *Yodo-go* group, which was responsible for hijacking a Japan Airlines plane on March 31, 1970. Whatever the explanation, the kidnappings and the still unsatisfactory North Korean response left a bad taste in the mouths of Japanese.

As with China, Tokyo's relationship with South Korea was primarily economic. By 1990 South Korea was Japan's third largest trading partner. In 2003 the two launched official talks to establish a bilateral Free Trade Agreement, but negotiations deadlocked in November 2004 over issues related to the agricultural and fisheries trade. Worsening their relations in the early 2000s were Japan's textbook censorship of its role in World War II, Koizumi's visits to the Yasukuni Shrine, and a dispute over a group of islets known as *Takeshima* in Japan and *Dokdo* in Korea. They were uninhabited, but the waters around them were rich for fishing. The islands were claimed by Japan's Shimane prefecture in 1905, but they have been controlled by South Korea since the end of the Korean War. In February 2005, Shimane prefecture approved a provincial bill establishing Takeshima Day. Matters were not helped when Japan's ambassador to Seoul declared that Tokyo had sovereignty over the islands. South Korea's President Roh Moo-hyun warned:

> *Now, the South Korean government has no choice but to sternly deal with Japan's attempt to justify its history of aggression and colonialism and revive regional hegemony. . . . There could be a hard diplomatic war. . . that may reduce exchanges in various sectors and cause economic difficulty. . . .*[26]

For their part, the Japanese made it clear that they would not return to the bilateral trade talks until the political situation became more amicable.

Southeast Asia

Another area where wartime memories were raw was Southeast Asia. Japan's first foray into Southeast Asia after its rapid economic modernization involved Prime Minister Tanaka in 1974. Anti-Japanese mobs met Tanaka in Thailand and Indonesia, burning Japanese embassy flags and Japanese cars. This reaction was in response not only to what Japan had done in the war, but also to perceived Japanese arrogance in its growing economic power in the region. In 1977 Prime Minister Fukuda Takeo, speaking at a Manila meeting of the Association of Southeast Asian Nations (ASEAN), announced what some have called the *Fukuda doctrine*—that Japan would work to build relations with Southeast Asia based on "heart-to-heart" communication and would cooperate with the other nations in the region as an equal partner. After that, Japanese leaders met many times with ASEAN leaders. In 1991, Japan replaced the United States as the world's largest donor of development aid, with about 60 percent going to Asia. Prime Minister Miyazawa, in a 1991 Bangkok speech, predicted that, "The Asian economic zone will outdo the North American economic zone and [the] European economic zone at the beginning of the 21st century, and assume a very crucial role in the world."[27]

The Soviet Union (Russia after 1991)

With the Soviet Union and Russia, trade was of little concern. In 1992, for example, 0.3 percent of Japanese exports went to Russia and Japan imported 1 percent from Russia. The crucial issue in Japan-Russian relations was the dispute over four islands that arc from Hokkaido northeast to the Kurile Islands. At the end of World War II, Russia received Sakhalin Island and the Kuriles and claimed that all four islands were part of the Kuriles. Most observers said that the northernmost islands probably belonged to the Kuriles but that the southern two seemed extensions of Hokkaido. By an agreement in 1956, the Soviet Union agreed to give back the southern two islands after a formal peace treaty ending the war. But in 1960 the Soviet regime said that there could be no peace treaty until all foreign troops (read: those of the United States) were removed from Okinawa and Japan—the Cold War obviously coming into play. In the early twenty-first century, Russian President Vladimir Putin offered to revive the 1956 offer but Tokyo refused, saying that was not enough. In disputed waters in this struggle over fishing rights between 1994 and 2005, the Russians seized thirty Japanese fishing boats and over two hundred Japanese crew members; the incidents produced some injuries. On August 16, 2006, Russian boats fired at a Japanese fishing boat and killed a Japanese fisherman—the first fatality in the disagreement since October 1956. Each side in this incident argued that the boat was in its own territorial waters. As of mid-2007, Japan and Russia still had not signed a peace treaty concluding World War II.

The Middle East

Japan was dependent on Middle East oil. Its skittishness in the Gulf War stemmed from the uncomfortable fact that in 1988, Japan imported 57 percent of its oil from Persian Gulf states and that amount was rising steadily. In 2003, Japan imported 78 percent of its oil from that region. For comparison's sake, in 2003 Japan imported 4.2 barrels of oil per day from the Middle East, while the numbers for the United States and Western Europe were 2.5 and 2.6, respectively. Japan obviously wanted to keep as low a profile as possible except for its oil purchases. If oil supplies were sharply reduced or cut off, Japan would be in dire straits.

Europe

Most European nations had unfavorable trade balances with Japan. Japan's warmest partners in Europe were Germany and the United Kingdom. France, in contrast, did not allow the Japanese easy access to its market and was quicker to retaliate in trade conflicts. Perhaps the French attitude was epitomized by the racist remarks of Edith Cresson, prime minister of France in 1991: The "Japanese [were] short yellow people who stay[ed] up all night thinking of ways to screw the Americans and Europeans"; she also stated that Japan had "an absolute determination to conquer the world."[28] A statement this bitter might have been more understandable in 1941 than in 1991, but it revealed the burden under which Japan labored, a burden of history and of the perception of Japanese actions in the contemporary world.

CHRONOLOGY

1972	Normalization of relations with China
1973	Oil crisis during the Middle East war
1980s	Serious trade disputes between Japan and the United States
1989	Hirohito dies
1990–1992	The Japanese economic bubble bursts; recovery drags on for over a decade
1993–1996	LDP temporarily loses power to a coalition
1995	Kobe earthquake (January)
	Sarin gas attack in the Tokyo subway (March)
2001–2006	Tensions with China over trade and undersea natural gas drilling
2004–2006	Japanese forces in Iraq, first postwar involvement in a war zone
2006 (Sept.)	New Prime Minister, Abe Shinzō determined to strike no war clause from 1947 Constitution

---

SUGGESTED READINGS

Armacost, Michael. *Friends or Rivals?* New York: Columbia University Press, 1996. Written by a former U.S. ambassador to Japan, this analysis provides a compelling study of the implications of U.S.-Japan relations at the end of the Cold War.

Bernstein, Gail Lee. *Haruko's World: A Japanese Farm Woman and Her Community.* Stanford, CA: Stanford University Press, 1983. An account through the eyes of a farm woman in Ehime prefecture in the mid-1970s, bringing to life her concerns, emotions, and family life.

Field, Norma. *In the Realm of a Dying Emperor: Japan at Century's End.* New York: Vintage Books, 1993. This stunning book focuses on the period of the death of the Shōwa emperor by looking at political dissenters, including the mayor of Nagasaki.

Kaplan, David, and Andrew Marshall. *The Cult at the End of the World: The Incredible Story of Aum.* London: Arrow, Open Market Edition, 1997. This book, dealing with the perpetrators of the 1995 nerve gas attack in the Tokyo subway, raises social issues in contemporary Japan.

Kerr, Alex. *Dogs and Demons: Tales from the Dark Side of Japan.* New York: Hill and Wang, 2001. A well-written, insightful survey of contemporary problems in Japanese politics and society.

CHAPTER NINETEEN

A "Democracy" in the South, a "Hermit Kingdom" in the North: *Korea, 1980s to the Present*

In the quarter century after 1980, both Koreas went through troubled times, and the unification of the peninsula seemed to be more remote than ever. The South did break out of the darkness of authoritarian government in the later 1980s and became a functioning democracy, while the North remained in the icy grip of totalitarian control. Both Koreas experienced tensions with other countries over a wide range of issues.

THE SOUTH

Sunday, Bloody Sunday

On Sunday, May 18, 1980, paratroopers from the army of the ROK entered the southwestern city of Kwangju and began bayoneting and clubbing its citizens. The brutality was unleashed after the soldiers were told that Communists were taking over the city. It was all part of a plan by Chun Doo-hwan, who had served Park Chung-hee as head of the Defense Security Command, to conduct a coup and seize complete power. Chun had headed the investigation of Park's assassination, and his actions in the months after Park's death were a dead giveaway that his aim was total control of the country.

His first step was to seize military power. On December 12, 1979, supported by his close friend Roh Tae-woo, head of the army's Ninth Division (Seoul's capital garrison), Chun forced out of power the army's chief of staff and over three dozen high-ranking officers. This came four days after the release of hundreds of political prisoners, including the dissident Kim Dae-jung, by the civilian government leader. Chun had undoubtedly determined that such action was inimical to his potential leadership. In April 1980 he took over the KCIA, the most powerful government organ—an action that brought student protests calling for an end to martial law, the abolition of Park's *Yushin* system, and Chun's resignation. On May 15, seventy thousand to one hundred thousand students took to the streets of Seoul. Warned by the opposition leaders Kim Young-sam and Kim Dae-jung that they might precipitate a military crackdown, the students called off a demonstration slated for the next day.

But Chun had had enough. On May 17 he declared martial law throughout the country, abolished the National Assembly, shut down all colleges and universities, prohibited labor strikes, and banned all political activity. Then came Sunday, bloody Sunday. Chun's paratroopers struck at Kwangju largely because it was the home base of Kim Dae-jung, who was arrested that day. Kwangju's citizens reacted by fighting back. From May 19 to 22, about 200,000 of them launched a full-scale revolt, occupying government offices and police stations and seizing military armories. It was "the largest and severest regional disturbance in the history of the Republic after 1950."[1] On May 27 Chun sent in frontline troops (an action okayed by General John Wickham, commander of the U.S. forces in South Korea), who brutally suppressed the uprising. The government's official death count was 200, but most sources agreed the total might have reached 2,300. In the aftermath, strong anti-American anger arose among Korean students and residents of Cholla province. Not only had Wickham agreed to send the troops, an action that one historian said "made hash of [President] Carter's human rights policies," but the U.S. government also did not respond to calls of citizen's committees in Kwangju for mediation of the dispute.[2] One creative student poster put Chun's head on Mount Rushmore, with Jimmy Carter "down below guarding the ramparts with an M-16."[3]

After the Kwangju episode, still officially tagged as a Communist-inspired rebellion, the government tried Kim Dae-jung for sedition related to the episode and sentenced him to death. At this point, the United States did pressure the Chun regime not to carry out the sentence; ultimately, it was reduced to twenty years in prison. Chun's actions at Kwangju were, however, to cost him dearly: even though he took complete power, people never awarded him the legitimacy he needed. While Park had come to power in 1961 with little bloodshed, Chun's ascent involved violent episodes in the military confrontation of December 1979 and the May 1980 Kwangju killings (called a massacre by those opposed to Chun).

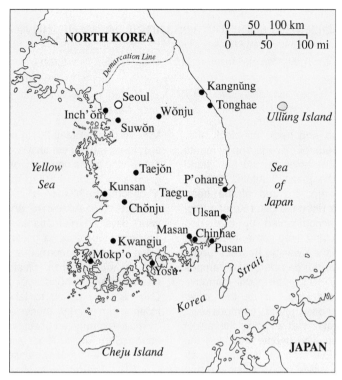

Map 19-1   Contemporary South Korea.

Chun's "Fifth Republic," 1981–1987

Chun tried to establish some legitimacy by condemning past corruption and promising economic growth, the pursuit of high ideals, and the promotion of justice. But the realities belied these efforts. He had a "widespread reputation for dullness, obstinacy, and arrogance, and his family. . . continued to be implicated in financial scandal."[4] While he undertook very minor reforms (abolishing a curfew enforced since the Korean War and moderating dress codes for students), he continued to emphasize Park's *Yushin* policy of economic development over political development, building his strongly loyalist and centralized Democratic Justice Party. He was, in the words of one scholar, "the most unpopular leader in postwar Korean history."[5] Even so, he was the first head of state to be invited to the Reagan White House in February 1981—from the perspective of many South Korean rubbing salt in wounds, from the perspective of the Reagan administration keeping relations with Seoul warm "lest the North try to fish in troubled waters."[6] Chun had spent a year in American military schools; though he had only a marginal command of English, he felt that he knew and understood the United States. Reagan sold Chun thirty-six F-16 fighter jets and, reversing the policy of Carter, who had begun to withdraw American troops from the South, sent four thousand more troops.

Chun, described by an American journalist as "a very simple man who [saw] pictures in black and white," struck with a vengeance against opponents.[7] He banned the political activities of almost nine thousand officials and politicians. He ordered about thirty-seven thousand students, teachers, journalists, and labor leaders to *purification camps* deep in the mountains to be inculcated with ideologically correct thought; the camps were exercises in brutality where beatings and subsequent deaths were not infrequent. Though Chun's administration initially oversaw political stability and (after 1983) a return to solid economic

Source: Commemorating the Kwangju Massacre

The American anthropologist Linda Lewis notes with some irony the change over time in the commemoration of the tragic events in Kwangju in May 1980. Most of this account describes her 1995 visit. What changes did she find from 1995 to 2000? What does this say about South Korean society?

. . . Looking down and back, for block after block, I saw hundreds of citizens and students marching down Kŭmnamno toward the sound stage set up by the plaza fountain. Carrying funeralesque banners, pictures of the dead wrapped with black ribbon, a giant Korean flag, with floats and accompanied by costumed dancers and musicians, they came, reenacting in song and dance the Kwangju People's Uprising story. The parade depicted now famous scenes from May 1980—the local narrative brought to life, stretching out on the street below, familiar episodes retold, memorialized, and celebrated. Later that evening the street would be crammed with people watching the open air Uprising Eve program (Chŏnyaje); afterward, students milled about, singing and dancing around bonfires until midnight. We walked around enthralled. Never had I imagined May in Kwangju would be like this, and I knew right then I wanted to study the 5.18 memorialization process.

In 1995 the relatively quiet fifteenth anniversary commemoration was more like a civic festival than the protest demonstration I had envisioned. In fact, that year it extended for ten days, from May 16 through May 26. In addition to the main events—the Eve Fest on May 17 and the memorial service at the cemetery on May 18—the program also included "Keep the Spirit Alive" and "Prosecute the Murderers" rallies; "Holy Sites Pilgrimage," "Anti-American," and "Democratic Drivers'" days; an international symposium and an academic workshop; a political cartoon display, video showings, performances of a psychodrama, and a *kŭt* (shaman ritual); and Protestant, Catholic, and Chŏndokyŏ religious services. Citizens were asked to take part by burning incense and piling up stones at the cemetery and by mailing preprinted postcards to President Kim Young Sam urging legal action against those responsible for the May massacre. . . .

. . . The militant, oppositional tone that made the fifteenth anniversary events seem like a kind of political Mardi Gras was banished; by 2000, the increasing commodification of the Kwangju Uprising was underscored by the appearance of a cute little cartoon May 18 mascot, Nuxee, whose smiling visage adorned key chains, T-shirts, and postcards available for purchase by visiting schoolchildren in the 5.18 Democratization Cemetery gift shop.

Source: http://www.uhpress.hawaii.edu/books/lewis_intro.pdf.

growth, by 1986 his tenure was destabilized by student protests and by violent clashes between students and workers and police. The protestors and Chun's political opposition called for a constitutional amendment that would mandate presidential election by a direct vote. In January 1987, the death of a student under interrogation led to investigations that uncovered what had been rumored for years—that political prisoners in the Republic were often tortured.

All hell broke loose in mid-June 1987, when Chun made it known that his party's presidential candidate was his old comrade-in-arms Roh Tae-woo. Demonstrations turned into violent street fighting in major cities around the country; students were joined by members of the rising but disaffected middle class. Roh himself took the wind out of the protestors' sails with an announcement on June 29 that the presidential elections scheduled for December would be by direct vote. He also announced an eight-point plan for reform, including lifting press restrictions, promoting political parties, restoring the civil rights of Kim Dae-jung and others, and upholding human rights. After many years of keeping a tight lid on labor organizing and the right to strike, the government took the lid off. The result was not only a huge increase in union membership (up by 64 percent) but also more than three thousand labor disputes and strikes (most involving wage rates) from July through October 1987. Roh persuaded the retiring Chun Doo-hwan to sign on to the reforms. Although the reasons behind Roh's abrupt about-face are not fully known, specialists suggested likely motivations. One was a sense that support for the students in Korean society was widespread; another was pressure from the United States not to resort to a military solution to end the unrest. Possibly the most important reason was South Korea's hosting of the Olympic Games in the summer of 1988. The unrest of 1986 and 1987, if not dealt with effectively, had the potential for continuing and thereby disrupting the games. South Korean authorities saw the Olympics as a coming of age where the rest of the world would see modern Korea firsthand.

The Presidency of Roh Tae-woo (1988–1993)

Students and opposition political leaders wanted a direct presidential election because they believed that military rule would be ended and civilian rule restored. The irony was that in the December elections, Chun's handpicked general and ally, Roh Tae-woo, was elected with 35.9 percent of the vote when the two most important opposition leaders, Kim Young-sam and Kim Dae-jung, split the vote. In the election, voting was almost completely regional, with the candidates' home bases going strongly for their respective native sons: the southwest went for Kim Dae-jung (giving him between 80 and 90 percent of the vote), the southeast supported Kim Young-sam, and Roh won the center. As one Korean professor noted: "each candidate was like a Chinese warlord occupying his own solid territory."[8]

Despite Roh's reform agenda, his regime remained repressive. Called by a journalist "a man of environment and situation," he seemed to be aware of more complexity in governing choices than Chun.[9] He presided over a successful Olympics (September 17–October 2, 1988) in which 160 nations participated, though 24 did not yet have diplomatic relations with South Korea. Roh's accomplishments were in the main foreign policy successes. His agenda was to emphasize his *northern policy*, by which he hoped to develop a positive and stable relationship with P'yŏngyang (see below). He normalized relationships with the Soviet Union in 1991 and with China in 1992, as well as with other former Communist states in Eastern Europe—actions that antagonized Kim Il-sung's regime even as Roh was trying to win it over. Both Koreas entered the UN in 1991. However, Roh struck out with new force against dissidents; under the National Security Law (on the books since the late 1940s), he arrested, for example, an average of 3.3 per day in 1989. He also quickly suppressed labor strikes in the name of economic growth.

Opening Ceremony of the 1988 Seoul Olympics   The 1988 summer Olympics was, in a sense, a coming-of-age affair for South Korea. Here participants march in the opening parade of nations at the Olympic stadium track, led by a Korean woman in traditional dress.

The Presidency of Kim Young-sam (1993–1998)

The return to civilian government for the first time since 1961 came with the election of Kim Young-sam in late 1992. He was able to defeat Kim Dae-jung, now a bitter foe (they had worked together from the 1970s to the mid-1980s), by merging his party in 1990 with the Democratic Justice Party, the party of Chun and Roh. His election totals brought him only a bit more than 40 percent of the votes, a fact that led some to predict another military coup if his administration stumbled badly.

One of Kim's chief goals as president was to destroy the rampant corruption in Korean politics and business. Six months after he became president, the *real name* bank deposit law passed the National Assembly; no longer could people use fictitious names on bank accounts or deposit money in other people's accounts to hide it. By January 1996, moreover, interest earned on bank accounts would be taxed. This law revealed that Roh Tae-woo had been placing money that he had amassed in other people's accounts. When confronted, Roh admitted that he had built up a "governing fund" of $625 million and had taken $212 million of it when he left office (this figure was later revised upward). In a public opinion poll, Roh had the dubious distinction of being labeled "the most loathsome politician" in the country.[10]

When Chun Doo-hwan, whose family had frequently been called corrupt, was investigated, the findings were even more egregious: his personal funds totaled $1.8 billion, with $265 million taken when he left office. In addition, he had 6.1 billion won (the Korean currency) stashed in apple boxes in a Seoul warehouse. In an act that would forever stand as the hallmark of his presidency, Kim not only decided to bring the two former presidents to trial for corruption, but also sought and got from the National Assembly the right to try them for treason and insurrection in the December 1979 "night of the colonels" and the Kwangju massacre of May 1980. During the trial (March to August 1996), Roh was apologetic though Chun remained defiant, even starting a hunger strike. In the end, both were found guilty. Chun was sentenced to death (later commuted to life imprisonment), and Roh received 22½; years (later commuted to 17 years). In early 1998, both were pardoned by incoming president Kim Dae-jung. Kim Young-sam's bold action against the two former presidents was, some saw, "a fine moment for Korean democracy; [it] vindicated the masses of Koreans who had fought for democratic rule over the past fifty years."[11]

Unfortunately, not all was bright in Kim's presidency. The National Security Law had not been repealed, and Kim, the former dissident, used it against dissidents, though not on the scale of Chun and Roh. Kim's 1990 alliance with the party of Chun and Roh (and other staunch right-wingers) made him continually wary of actions that might antagonize these allies. It is said, for example, that after Kim Il-sung's death in July 1994, in order to assuage the right wing of his party, Kim Young-sam kept up such a constant barrage of malicious attacks on the deceased North Korean leader that North-South relations sharply deteriorated. Kim was a strident anti-Communist: in 1993, during talks between the United States and North Korea over the light water reactor plan (see below), he charged that North Korea was leading the United States on. In his political struggle with Kim Dae-jung, he attacked Kim for being pro-Communist. Yet, in his inaugural address he indicated that he was ready to meet the North Korean leader anywhere and any time.

By 1997, Kim's anticorruption crusade was marred by rumors of his own corruption: that he may have taken millions in illegal campaign funds in the 1992 election and that top aides accepted bribes from businessmen; his own son was indicted for bribery and tax evasion. Finally, in 1997, South Korea faced a serious labor crisis precipitated by government action; then the country fell into the most severe economic crisis since the early 1950s.

Economic Crisis of the Late 1990s

The economic heyday of the ROK came during the Park Chung-hee years (1961–1979). The Korean model of development, like that of Japan, was one of strong state-business coordination, specifically a tight nexus between government, large banks, and conglomerates (chaebol). As an indication of these

Campus Struggle   The reunification of the two Koreas was a controversial and polarizing issue. Here South Korean police, armed with riot gear, battle students demonstrating for unification on the campus of Yonsei University in Seoul.

close ties, in the Park years the government customarily guaranteed chaebol international loans. In the early 1980s the economy dipped slightly; Japan came to the rescue with $4 billion to alleviate the debt crisis and, with the United States, offered advice. Chun, in turn, opened Korean markets to Japanese and American banks and insurance companies and to certain American agricultural products. The late 1980s saw a refired economy, with economic growth rising to 12 percent per year. In these years the chaebol became even stronger and the link between them and government ever tighter: the government provided easy credit and low interest rates for the chaebol. "It was top-down economic government directives and regulations rather than a decentralized market system that dominated, all under the rubric of a slogan calling for economic development."[12] This approach brought positive results when the economy was expanding.

After 1987, when labor organizations were legalized, labor had to be considered in any economic equation; its power was especially robust in heavy industries—steel, automobiles, chemical, and shipbuilding—and it achieved moderate wage gains in the early 1990s. In December 1996, President Kim, noting that the ROK had "come of age as an advanced economy," took the country into the Organization of Economic Cooperation and Development, a group of thirty countries committed to democracy and a market economy.[13] Before joining the organization, Kim abolished the Economic Planning Board, which had directed and shaped Korea's economy since the Park years. At this point, problems developed. One reason was that changing from a government-led economic development model to a market-based model could not be done overnight. Even worse, the economic deregulation was not effectively supervised. Largely hidden to this point was the reality that over the years of economic advances, the close government-business ties had led to festering corruption, and many mercantile banks owned by chaebol and insurance companies had made extremely risky loans.

Still in bed with business, the government was pressed by business, increasingly in debt, to cut labor costs. Therefore, in December 1996, Kim sponsored and the National Assembly passed a labor law that recognized only the state-controlled Korean Federation of Trade Unions and, in effect, made illegal the independent Korean Confederation of Trade Unions, with half a million members. The pro-business law also stipulated that businesses had the right to lay off workers and to hire scabs to replace strikers. Since there was no unemployment compensation for Korean workers, hundreds of thousands of workers were left in the lurch. In January 1997 they came out in force, clogging Seoul's streets for weeks, creating, for all practical purposes, a general strike. Kim and the government ate humble pie and withdrew the law.

Laborers and Students Rally The 1997 economic crisis reverberated across Korean society. In this rally on December 27 at a Seoul park, workers and students shout slogans, demanding that the government take responsibility for the crisis and act to solve it.

But that same month, one of the largest chaebol, Hanbo Steel, went bankrupt; in the following months six more of the top thirty chaebol followed suit. A crisis quickly developed when a large number of short-term international loans came due for many key Korean firms. In this crisis, "a seminal event in the country's history," the government, which through the years had catered to business, seemed impotent.[14] Part of the reason was Kim Young-sam's lame-duck status, in the last year of his presidency and saddled with the corruption of his son, who had been indicted for bribery. Another was the turnover in ministerial leadership: because cabinet posts had become a reward for party members during Kim's presidency, it was common for ministers to serve less than a year so that other "deserving" party members could be rewarded; the result was a lack of experience and cohesiveness in policy development. In addition, major reforms were opposed by labor unions and the political opposition.

The government approached the IMF, seeking a bailout. The IMF offered $57 billion on the conditions that the government "tighten its fiscal and monetary policies," begin a market-oriented reform of its business and industry, and allow more foreign investment and the importation of foreign products. The ceiling on foreign investment was to be raised from 26 to 50 percent. The IMF also specified that the labor market had to be made more flexible (i.e., that workers could readily be fired). These were stiff conditions whose implementation led to a severe recession and created considerable anti-IMF and anti-U.S. feeling (U.S. government financial leaders had played a key role in setting down the terms). The chairman of the U.S. Federal Reserve Board, Alan Greenspan, crowed: the result of the Asian crisis (it affected other Asian countries as well) was "a worldwide move toward 'the Western form of free market capitalism.'"[15] The new president, Kim Dae-jung (see Identities), adopted the reforms as if he had created them.

Identities: Kim Dae-jung (1925–):
The Face of Korea's Struggle for Democracy

In 2000, Kim Dae-jung was awarded the Nobel Peace Prize, the first Korean ever to win this award and only the fourth East Asian since the prize was created in 1901 (the others were Le Duc Tho [1973], Satō Eisaku [1974], and the Dalai Lama [1989]). A Roman Catholic, Kim said that he revered Abraham Lincoln for his sense of forgiveness and reconciliation; Kim himself was a great reconciler in his efforts to bring North and South Korea together.

His career until 1987 was marked by continual persecution, imprisonment, and house arrest. Three days after his first election to the National Assembly in 1961, Park Chung-hee's coup dissolved the assembly. A public speech he made in 1969 attacking Park's plan for constitutional revision (in what came to be known as *Yushin*) brought him acclaim for his courage. As a presidential candidate vying with Park in 1971 he received 46 percent of the vote, an accomplishment that made Park angry and vengeful. After his presidential loss came the first of five attempts on his life (a truck plowed into his car), leaving him with a permanent leg injury. Park's vindictiveness also led to the KCIA's brutal kidnapping of Kim in Japan in 1973.

On the fifty-seventh anniversary of the March First Movement (in 1976), Kim joined other leaders in celebrating the *Independence Day for Democratization;* as a result, he was sentenced to five years in prison. Released after Park's assassination, he was rearrested in the wake of the Kwangju massacre and sentenced to death for treason but released two years later, going into exile in the United States. Returning to Korea in 1985, he was immediately placed under house arrest. Finally, in June 1987 he was cleared of all charges, and his civil and political rights were restored. Defeated in the presidential elections of 1987 and 1992, he was elected president of the ROK in 1997 with 40.3 percent of the vote (notably less than he received against Park). The election, however, was historic: the first peaceful transition from the ruling party to the opposition party in Korean history. Kim's record was perhaps the strongest overall in the Republic: engineering recovery from the economic crisis, undertaking democratic reforms and restructuring, and beginning a bold initiative in 2000 to engage with the North with a view to eventual reunification.

Some, however, suggested that he was a better opposition leader and dissident than a president. While his innate self-confidence (sometimes bordering on arrogance) aided him as an opposition leader, it was not always an asset in a leader. Some believed as well that he relied on too small a clique of advisors, which contributed to the perception of an imperial presidency. In his last years as president, Kim had to deal with the fact that two of his three sons were convicted for corruption and imprisoned. Many Koreans blamed Kim for not having raised his sons properly; Kim did accept responsibility for their actions.

Ultimately, his great initiative resulting in the summit conference of 2000 died in the face of the North's drive for nuclear weapons and missile technology. On the whole, his presidency was bittersweet. Whatever the ultimate historical verdict, his career was illustrious for his vigorous and principled support of democratic ideals and his determination not to be beaten down by political tyrants and their oppression.

The Presidency of Kim Dae-jung (1998–2003)

It is no small irony that Kim Dae-jung, who had railed about the government-business nexus, came to power in the middle of the severe economic crisis. As one commentator aptly analyzed it, "The 1997 crisis was a reflection of weakened state autonomy."[16] Kim's important accomplishment as president was to restore that autonomy. The continual economic loser throughout the history of the ROK had been labor. Though Kim was not especially in the labor camp, he was more sympathetic to it than previous leaders. In early 1998, he called together leaders of labor, business, and government to devise "fair and equitable policies" to carry out the IMF's terms.[17] Through hard bargaining, Kim persuaded labor to accept huge layoffs (raising the unemployment rate from 2 to 6 percent) in return for official recognition of the legality of labor unions and the right of labor to engage in politics and run candidates for election. This was a milestone in the emergence of labor as a legitimate force in Korean society.

The tough nut to crack in the economic crisis was the power of the chaebol, and in the end, Kim did not wholly succeed. He did not set out to break them up, which, given their power, was probably impossible. He did attempt to address the problems noted by the IMF by applying various pressures to loosen the connection between chaebol, big banks, and government, well aware of the "moral hazard" of corruption spawned by what had become an unholy alliance.[18] Kim was helped in the short term by the bankruptcies and dismantlement of seven powerful chaebol. But any further regulation was blocked by the business community and the bitterly contentious political opposition. As of 2004, during his successor's presidency, problems remained: "excessively high debt levels, a heavy reliance on short-term debt, the lack of transparency [openness in dealings and record keeping], weak corporate governance, and corporate structures dominated by individual families rather than professional business managers."[19]

In the 1970s and 1980s, because of his role as leader of the political opposition and the foremost dissident, Kim had suffered almost continuous government repression and persecution. In the 1980s the government's Agency for National Security Planning had brought to trial hundreds of dissidents under the National Security Law, many on trumped-up or exaggerated charges. In the 1997 elections, the agency even tried to tar Kim with the brush of pro-Communism. Its bureaucracy of seventy thousand was dominated by the Park-Chun-Roh strain of regional Korean politics: only three of the seventy highest officials and one of the thirty-five section chiefs were from Kim's native southwest.[20] Kim took the agency on. He slashed its domestic operations by 50 percent, focusing its actions on dealing with security vis-à-vis North Korea, reduced its staff by 10 percent, and fired some of its most powerful officials.

Kim's greatest contribution, for which he won the Nobel Prize in 2000, was his gutsy initiatives regarding North Korea (see below); they were continually opposed by the vocal political opposition and most newspapers, which charged that Kim was giving everything and receiving nothing in return. Not one to duck a battle, Kim decided in 2001 to have the government investigate twenty-three newspapers after allegations of their tax evasion; in the highly politicized atmosphere where each action seemed to escalate tension, this action gave rise to charges of a political vendetta.[21]

Another quiet contribution that had immense political impact was Kim's choice of Roh Moo-hyun to succeed him. Roh, the son of a peach and chicken farmer, was out of the mainstream of Korean political elites, a human rights attorney who spent the 1980s defending student and labor activists. He had served in the National Assembly from 1988 to 1993 and was reelected in 1998. The only bureaucratic position he held was that of minister of Maritime Affairs and Fisheries from August 2000 to April 2001. Two of his campaign pledges in the 2002 presidential elections were to settle labor conflicts and to rein in the regional rivalries dominating South Korean politics. Bitterly opposed by the old ruling party and its elites, Roh's victory with Kim Dae-jung's support meant that they "achieved a thorough political transition away from the elites who [had] dominated the Republic of Korea since 1948."[22]

The old elites did not play dead, however: in March 2004, they impeached Roh for breaking a minor elections law. The Constitutional Court ruled in May that although Roh did break the law, the offense was not serious enough to justify his removal from office. On the whole, Roh's presidency fell on hard times, with continual attacks by the political opposition and plummeting public opinion polls (which showed 70 to 80 percent disapproval in 2006). He could not move ahead on his agenda, and well into 2006 he was mired in the same struggles that Kim Dae-jung had had with the conservative press.[23]

THE NORTH

Kim Il-sung had fashioned what his biographer called "'a peculiar brand of oriental despotism' rather than communism."[24] A diplomat who had spent several years in P'yŏngyang noted that "Once said by Kim, it is said forever. Nobody is allowed to change anything; the smallest sign of deviation means the system has developed a dangerous crack."[25] The system and life he produced for his people, for all its brutal authoritarianism, was not especially bleak on the surface. Korean specialist Bruce Cumings commented on P'yŏngyang when he visited it in 1987:

> [People who expected the worst] were ill prepared for the wide tree-lined boulevards of P'yŏngyang, swept squeaky clean and traversed by determined, disciplined urban commuters held in close check by traffic women in tight uniforms, pirouetting with military discipline and a smile, atop platforms at each intersection. They had not expected a population living in modern high-rise buildings, hustling out in the morning like Japanese "salarymen" to a waiting subway or electric bus.[26]

But beneath the surface, Cumings noted that North Korea was "the most militarized country on the face of the earth." He said it best and most chillingly:

> This is a garrison state with one in twenty citizens in the military, compulsory military service for everyone, an army one million strong, millions more in militias, enormous military bases and arsenals built deep underground, subterranean subway stations with gigantic blast doors recessed into the walls, round-the-clock vigils for trouble along the DMZ, a dictator who sleeps in a different place every night for security reasons, and twenty-two million citizens each with a personal reliability rating.[27]

Kim Il-sung said in 1979 that the North Koreans had a per capita income of $1,900 and, by the late 1980s, over $2,500; whether this was true or not, the bottom began to drop out of the economy in the early 1990s. In the first years of the twenty-first century, Western analysts put per capita income at about $1,000. The decline began in earnest in 1991 with the collapse of the Soviet Union, until then North Korea's "major trading partner and a generous provider of agricultural and other subsidies."[28] Whereas in 1990 Soviet exports to North Korea totaled $1.97 billion, in 1991 they had fallen to $0.58 billion; in 1993 they were equal to one-tenth of the total that P'yŏngyang had received before the Soviet Union's fall. China upped its contribution, but not nearly enough to make up for what was now forever gone. Tellingly, in 1991 the government initiated a campaign entitled "Let's eat only two meals a day." Food shortages began to be noted in 1993.

Then suddenly, on July 8, 1994, the Great Sun died of a massive heart attack. Once news of his death was broadcast (thirty-six hours after it had occurred), there was a mass outpouring of what seemed genuinely intense grief followed by a hundred-day mourning period. Heir apparent since 1980, the *party center* and *Dear Leader* Kim Jong-il observed the traditional three-year mourning period before taking the role of *maximum leader*. But after "the death of Kim Il-sung, the North...faced one terrible crisis after another."[29]

Source: Life in a Police State

This 2003 news story from the Washington Post *details the misery and uncertainties of living in North Korea and confronting the equally tragic options of a political prisoner's camp or exile. What did Han do to incur the wrath of the government? Who did Han think might have informed on him? What does that say about life in North Korea?*

. . . Han, a Communist Party official in North Korea, was walking home from work when he heard he was in trouble. He had smuggled a radio back from China after an official trip. He listened to it late at night, huddled with earphones on and shades drawn, to hear music that brought him a whisper of sanity and took him away from the horrors of his day.

Now, someone had found it, or someone had told.

"It could have been my children who said something outside. It could have been my friend; one knew," said Han, 39, who spoke on condition he be identified only by his surname.

"If a farmer or laborer had a radio, he could have been released," Han said, "But I was an official. In my case, it would have been torture and a life sentence in a political prisoners' camp."

At that moment, he made a choice faced by thousands who flee North Korea: He left his family to try to save his own life. He went straight to the Chinese border on that July day in 1997 and waded across the river, abandoning his wife and sons, then ages 4 and 2, and spent the next three years on the run in China, until missionaries helped get him to Seoul.

Since he left, he has had no contact with his wife and sons. "I think of them every day," he said recently in Seoul. "I try to forget it," he added slowly. "But they are my family."

Source: http://www.washingtonpost.com/as2/wp-dyn/A41966-2003Oct3?language=printer.

A seemingly endless string of natural disasters catastrophically exacerbated the food shortages apparent after 1991. Summer floods in 1995 forced evacuation of half a million Koreans, especially from the northern part of the country, and eventually slashed the production of grain by almost 2 million tons, around 30 percent of what was needed to feed the population. The next year, flooding hit the southern part of the country, an area that customarily produced up to 60 percent of the grain needed for the people. In 1997, the problem was a serious drought in the middle of the growing season, cutting the production of grain by 700,000 tons to 1.9 million tons. The winter of 1998 saw exceptionally light snowfall that extended the drought into the summer of that year.

On all sides there was breakdown. "[T]he economy in effect collapsed, with the country's gross national product more than halved, most of its factories either cannibalized or operating at less than 30 percent capacity, and an increasing number of people . . . either falling into a slow-motion famine cum triage mode . . . or defecting to China as food refugees."[30] To make matters worse, there was evidence that food assistance that was reaching the country was being hoarded by the military, so that many Koreans who were in desperate straits received no help. Indeed, the military received at least 25 percent of the country's annual budget.

Because of the general economic collapse, plus the floods and droughts, between 1995 and 1998, pharmaceutical production dropped 60 percent—increasing even more the mortality created by natural disaster, starvation, and malnutrition. Electric power shortages meant, for example, that fertilizer plants,

Map 19-2   Contemporary North Korea.

essential for agricultural production, operated on a greatly reduced schedule, leading to an obvious short-age. Western analysts believe that between 1995 and 2000 the most likely number of famine-related deaths in North Korea ranged from six hundred thousand to one million.[31] In mid-2000, reportedly 62 per-cent of North Koreans were chronically malnourished; 16 percent suffered from acute malnutrition, as did 30 percent of children between the ages of one and two.

In July 2006, two major storms flooded sixty-five thousand acres of prime farmland, destroying the harvest. Though the government put the dead and missing at around three hundred, some reports said that the number was closer to ten thousand; about twenty thousand families were made homeless. North Korea, however, initially turned down offers of help from the South Korean Red Cross and the UN's World Food Program. Several months before, dozens of foreign aid workers had been expelled because North Korea said that it "did not need outside support."[32] Amid fears of another famine, the government did finally accept aid. In early 2005 almost three hundred thousand North Korean refugees flocked into China to escape famine under the P'yŏngyang regime.

The Impact of Famine
These North Korean kindergartners stare out of their school window, emaciated and malnourished during the devastating famine of 1997. Though outside aid was accepted, it was received somewhat grudgingly because of the *juche* (self-reliant) approach of the government.

Source: Let Them Eat Grass

This news story from the BBC New World Edition on June 20, 2002, covers a famine in what seemed to be a continuing reality in North Korea: one famine after another, with consequent malnutrition and starvation. Problems in dealing with the famines ranged from P'yŏngyang's reluctance to accept outside aid to insufficient aid. In this case, the UN's World Food Program was forced to cut its food aid because of insufficient donations. What were the social impacts of this situation?

North Koreans are turning to grass and seaweed as means of sustenance in the face of a severe shortage of food aid in the impoverished country.

A representative of the UN's World Food Programme, who has just returned from a visit to North Korea, said people were abandoning work and school to forage for sustenance.

"You see people of all ages going up into the hillsides with bags and sacks and coming back down with grasses. You see women on the seashores scavenging for edible seaweeds," said WFP's Gerald Bourke.

The agency has been forced to suspend cereal rations to more than one million people until at least August because of a lack of international donations.

"Teachers say attendance at school is down because children are out collecting wild foods," said Mr. Bourke, adding that teachers themselves were also taking time off for the same purpose.

He said that he had asked a class of third graders, in the eastern coastal city of Kimchaek, how many had tasted meat in the last month.

"There were 25 pupils and only three of them had had meat in the last month," said Mr. Bourke.

"The basic staple at present is maize. Very occasionally an egg, a little bit of vegetable and that's it. No meat, no rice, no food. Very little protein."

Source: http://www.news.bbc.co.uk/2/hi/asia-pacific/2055658.stm.

Youth Rally for the "Dear Leader"   About fifty thousand youth rallied in P'yŏngyang on February 11, 2003, to celebrate the birthday of Kim Jong-il (b. 1941). The enthusiastic students pledged their loyalty to Kim in his approach of giving the nation's military the highest priority.

The *juche* mindset was evident in the government's attitude and roles during the famine. It did not want to accept outside aid, but critical circumstances demanded it. Even so, government officials did not want representatives from the organizations dispensing aid to monitor its distribution. They grudgingly admitted some monitors but restricted their access. In the summer of 1998, after a slightly improved harvest but with famine conditions still prevailing, P'yŏngyang told the Paris branch of Doctors without Borders (who were planning to provide medical care) "that the emergency was over and the organization should switch its aid operation from health care to supplying pharmaceutical raw materials to its factories."[33]

The man at the top of what seemed to be a disintegrating state and society, Kim Jong-il, "grew up in privilege from his teenage years, had never served a day in the military until he was named supreme commander of the People's Army in December 1991, wore his hair in an artsy pompadour, and was notably uncomfortable amid the roar of the crowd."[34] A 1964 graduate of Kim Il-sung University, he became a specialist on film, art, and theater in his work for the Central Committee of the Workers Party. Stories of his hard drinking and womanizing abounded. Almost as a forerunner of the Japanese kidnappings of the 1980s, he ordered the kidnapping in 1978 of a Korean actress and her former husband, a film director from Hong Kong, because he "absolutely needed" them "to improve P'yŏngyang's unprofessional film industry."[35]

For all of his reported quirkiness, Kim's power in the government lay in his military leadership, for it was military power that became "not only...the last trump card, displaying power in the fierce diplomatic and ideological stand-off with imperialism, but also as a necessary and sufficient condition for the success of socialist and self-supporting economic development." His title as head of state was *chair of the national defense commission.* "My power," Kim asserted in an interview, "comes from the military...."[36] In mid-2001 the North Korean regime called attention to its policy of "resolving all problems in revolution and construction in accordance with the military-first principle."[37]

RELATIONS BETWEEN NORTH AND SOUTH KOREA FROM THE 1980S ON

This reliance on the military and military techniques led to terrorism in the mid-1980s. On October 9, 1983, during a presidential visit by South Korea's Chun Doo-hwan and a high-level official delegation to Rangoon, Burma, a powerful bomb placed on the roof of the Martyr's Mausoleum, where President Chun was to lay a wreath, was detonated by a North Korean army major. Seventeen South Korean officials were killed, including a number of cabinet officers and two presidential secretaries, one an important foreign policy advisor and the other a key planner of the country's economic development. It was a huge and demoralizing loss. Chun avoided death by being stuck in traffic. Though some in the

Seoul government advised bombing the North in return, Chun refused to retaliate. Though much about the bombing remains a mystery, Kim Jong-il was rumored to have been responsible for it, even though it occurred when his father was in Beijing for talks on approaches to take for a diplomatic breakthrough with the United States.

Kim Jong-il was also allegedly responsible for the terrorist bomb attack that blew up Korean Airlines flight 858 on its November 29, 1987, run from Abu Dhabi to Seoul, killing all 115 passengers. The North Korean terrorists, posing as Japanese tourists, had begun the flight in Baghdad and disembarked in Abu Dhabi, leaving a time bomb hidden in a hollowed-out portable radio. One of the terrorists, a twenty-five-year-old woman, was captured and taken to South Korea, where she was tried and sentenced to death but was eventually pardoned. She reportedly believed that her deed "was for national unification, which was a great purpose and aspiration of the nation." She went on to say that Kim Jong-il initiated the terrorist attack: "I thought about it as a military order, to be accepted without question."[38]

Elected president of South Korea the next month, Roh Tae-woo, who pardoned the terrorist, set out to better relationships with the North. His *north policy* (*Nordpolitik*) reportedly developed with the 1988 Olympics in mind: undertaking such an initiative would make it easier for Communist nations to attend the games. In July 1988, Roh announced a program that included exchanges between the North and South at all levels and the promotion of trade and humanitarian contacts. P'yŏngyang responded coldly, calling it a maneuver to "permanently split the country."[39] Roh's goal was to seek political and business contact with the North. With the latter in mind, he encouraged the Hyundai conglomerate founder, Chŏng Chu-yŏng, to tour the Diamond Mountains near North Korea's east coast with a view to opening a joint venture with the North to promote tourism. Both sides had agreed to allow families to cross the DMZ to visit both North and South, but the two governments fell into bitter arguments and there were no exchanges. For the first time, talks between prime ministers were held, initially in Seoul in September 1990 and a month later in P'yŏngyang.

The biggest accomplishment of Roh's north policy came in December 1991 with the signing of an Agreement on Reconciliation, Nonaggression, Cooperation, and Exchange: it called for both sides to recognize the other's political system and pledged to end "mutual vilification and confrontation"; it guaranteed nonaggression, promised cooperation and exchange in many areas, and pledged free travel for the millions of Korean families separated by the war. Finally, both countries promised to work to transform the armistice, which had ended the war, into a full-fledged, lasting peace. Both countries also agreed in writing that they would work to keep both Koreas free of nuclear weapons. But for all the fanfare, the 1991 agreement, like the one in 1972, was a dead letter, never put into operation.

The Hyundai initiative in the Diamond Mountains did get off the ground in 1998, when the North Korean government approved it. In 2002 the 8,200-acre site, surrounded by barbed wire and guards, was organized as a separately administered tourist region. Though Hyundai lost money on the operation, a land route to the site was opened in 2003. In June 2005, Hyundai announced that the one millionth South Korean visit had taken place. The tourist region allowed P'yŏngyang to obtain hard currency: the official currency was the U.S. dollar, and the North Korean government as of early 2004 had reportedly profited to the tune of $480 million.[40]

The Kim Young-sam years started with considerable expectation of improved relations. Indeed, an unprecedented summit meeting between him and Kim Il-sung was planned for July 25, 1994. But Kim Il-sung died three weeks before the summit was to have occurred. After his death, Kim, largely for domestic South Korean consumption, felt compelled to denounce the North bitterly, and on the whole, relations with the North generally "went south."

When Kim Dae-jung became president in 1998, he was determined to continue Roh Tae-woo's initiatives with the North; he argued that a better relationship would result from engaging the North instead of condemning it. In what became known as his *"Sunshine Policy,"* Kim first proposed a summit meeting with Kim Jong-il to "discuss issues of mutual cooperation, peaceful co-existence, and co-prosperity." First issued in a Berlin speech, the proposal called for South Korean assistance to the North:

[working to expand] the North's "social infrastructure, including highways, harbors, railroads and electric and communications facilities." He proposed business-related treaties on investment guarantees and prevention of double taxation. To deal with the underlying causes of the North's famine, he proposed "comprehensive reforms in the delivery of quality fertilizers, agricultural equipment, irrigations systems, and other elements of a structural nature" with the assistance of the South.[41]

The icing on the cake was remarks Kim made a month earlier: "I believe [Kim Jong-il] is a man of good judgment, equipped with great knowledge."[42]

Kim was attacked by the political opposition; no South Korean leader had ever endorsed Kim Jong-il in such a positive fashion. His whole Sunshine Policy was viewed by the political opposition, newspapers, and business as enormously suspect; allegations of his pro-Communism appeared everywhere. But Kim Dae-jung was not deterred. In March 2000, P'yŏngyang responded positively. As a result, the two governments in secret sent representatives to Shanghai to discuss the details. In April, they agreed that a summit was appropriate—to be held in P'yŏngyang on June 12–14 (it was actually held on June 13–15).

It was a moment to be savored, certainly unlike anything that had been seen since the division of Korea. On national television, Koreans watched the South Korean delegation land at the North Korean capital. "Meeting them on a red carpet laid on the tarmac was Kim Jong-il . . . who greeted Kim Dae-jung with a warm two-handed handshake and words of welcome. . . . En route to a state guest house, the two leaders occasionally held hands in a gesture of friendship as they chatted."[43] The summit resulted in a joint declaration with five major points. The two governments vowed to solve the problem of unification on their own "through the joint efforts of the Korean people, who are the masters of the country"—a clear slap at the United States and perhaps Japan. The goal of reunification, the second point specified, would be preceded by a *federation* (the North's proposed word) or a *confederation* (the word supported by the South). Both countries, further, agreed to deal quickly with humanitarian issues (like family visits). They pledged to build mutual confidence through economic cooperation and exchanges in many areas. Finally, they agreed to meet soon to carry out the provisions of the declaration.

The immediate aftermath appeared hopeful. In the months following the June summit, ministers from both countries met four times to establish cooperation and exchanges. In addition, there were discussions involving Red Cross representatives from both countries, talks between defense ministers, and a working-level

Sunshine and Embraces   South Korean President Kim Dae-jung (b. 1925) hugs North Korean President Kim Jong-il at the P'yŏngyang airport. Kim Dae-jung was leaving North Korea after a visit to further his Sunshine Policy of working with the North.

military discussion. Emotional reunification of one hundred separated families on both sides and the promise of more buoyed national feelings. The two countries agreed to revive the main North-South railway by repairing the line between Seoul and Sinŭiji, on the Yellow Sea at the mouth of the Yalu River. The marching together of athletes from the two Koreas under one peninsular flag at the Sydney Olympics in September 2000 symbolized the dramatic change in the relationship.

But it was not to continue. In February 2001 the two sides could not agree on further visits of separated families. P'yŏngyang announced that it would not participate in an already scheduled ministerial meeting. In May, North Korea ended its efforts to rebuild the North-South railway. The earlier plan had been for Kim Jong-il to go to Seoul for a summit meeting to reciprocate Kim Dae-jung's P'yŏngyang visit, but that plan was aborted. Speculation on reasons for this decision generally focused on the presidency of George W. Bush, who had placed North Korea in his self-created *axis of evil;* Kim Jong-il stopped plans to visit the South, the thinking went, because he expected little gain from this trip due to Bush's attitude and policy.[44] Kim Dae-jung's bold initiative failed in the end, but he was awarded the Nobel Peace Prize for his efforts. The citation that included some of Kim's other contributions read: "For his work for democracy and human rights in South Korea and in East Asia in general, and for peace and reconciliation in North Korea in particular."[45] Roh Moo-hyun, taking office in 2003, was committed to keeping open the lines of communication with P'yŏngyang even after North Korea's government announced in October 2002 that it would actively pursue a nuclear weapons program. Though Roh believed that this action would not promote Northeast Asian peace or stability, he and other South Korean officials continued to display a moderate attitude toward the North.

NORTH KOREA, THE UNITED STATES, JAPAN, AND NUCLEAR WEAPONS

In the 1990s and the first years of the twenty-first century, North Korea's flirtation with nuclear weapons and missile technology, except for a brief interlude during the presidency of Bill Clinton, kept U.S.-North Korea and Japan-North Korea relations in the deep freeze. Ironically, it was the United States that had introduced nuclear weapons into the Korean peninsula in January 1958, and a Pentagon document from 1967 made it clear that the United States would not hesitate to use them if war with the North came: "The twelve ROKA and two U.S. divisions in South Korea had . . . keyed their defense plans almost entirely to the early use of nuclear weapons."[46] U.S. nuclear weapons remained in South Korea until President George Bush withdrew them in 1991.

The Soviet Union provided North Korea with a small nuclear reactor (probably with a four-megawatt capacity) for research in 1962; it was placed under the safeguard of the UN's International Atomic Energy Agency (IAEA) in 1977. In 1987, a larger reactor (thirty-megawatt capacity) was completed at Yŏngbyon, sixty miles north of P'yŏngyang. American spy satellites in 1989 picked up a two to three-month shutdown of the reactor while North Koreans withdrew fuel rods and added new fuel. North Korea signed the IAEA safeguard agreement in January 1992.

What specialist Bruce Cumings calls "the most dangerous crisis involving Washington and P'yŏngyang since the Korean War" played itself out from January 1993 to October 1994, a period, he says, "when another Korean War nearly began."[47] In January, newly elected President Bill Clinton said that he planned to proceed with the Team Spirit Games (which former President Bush had suspended in 1992 but reinstated for 1993). These were very large joint military exercises initiated in the Reagan administration, involving as many as two hundred thousand American and South Korean soldiers. North Korea, fearful of U.S. attacks, always became unnerved during the games. North Korea was horrified by the February 1993 announcement of General Lee Butler, chief of the U.S. Strategic Command, "that he was retargeting strategic nuclear weapons (i.e., hydrogen bombs) meant for the former Soviet Union on North Korea (among other places)."[48]

On March 12, North Korea, in the face of what it perceived to be increasing threats to its security, announced plans to withdraw from the Nuclear Non-Proliferation Treaty (NPT). However, after the Team Spirit Games ended, the North acceded to U.S. calls for high-level talks; P'yŏngyang then resumed its responsibilities under the NPT. Thrown into the mix at this time was the demand of the IAEA to search what it said was a nuclear waste dump but which North Korea claimed was an off-limits military site. The North also believed that the IAEA was working hand in glove with the United States and would forward any information it discovered or received to Washington. P'yŏngyang then ratcheted up U.S. anxieties when it launched a medium-range SCUD missile that hit its target in the Sea of Japan in June 1993. P'yŏngyang played a smart game of extracting concessions from both the IAEA and the United States with its confrontations, hyperbolic rhetoric, and negotiations.

In July 1993, North Korea suggested that its current nuclear facilities would be dismantled and replaced by light-water reactors—which were less conducive to the production of weapons. The United States was willing to talk and consider the proposal and presented a deal to P'yŏngyang in November 1993, but the North put it on hold. With things in limbo, the Clinton administration considered military contingencies. On December 10, 1993, Clinton received USFK-OpPlan 502716, a plan that noted "four main consequences of another Korean War":

> *(1) Seoul and its adjacent areas with 40 percent of the South Korean population would be immediately in a sea of fire under a lethal barrage from some 8,400 long-range artillery pieces and 2,400 rocket launchers of the North deployed along the front line; (2) the war would be a high-intensity conflict lasting 82 to 112 days; (3) it would produce tens of thousands of American casualties and far more among South Koreans; and (4) radioactive pollution could escape in the direction of Japan and Hawaii, positioned directly to the east of the Korean peninsula.*[49]

Such possibilities made war unthinkable. But in June 1994, the North Koreans took an action that created a crisis and made it imperative that the United States respond. They shut down their reactor, withdrew about eight thousand fuel rods, and deposited them in cooling ponds. The removal of spent fuel rods enabled the harvesting of more weapons-grade plutonium, and the plutonium thus gained probably would have yielded material for two nuclear bombs.

Former President Jimmy Carter, aware of the dangerous situation, went to P'yŏngyang for direct talks with Kim Il-sung. He got Kim to agree to a deal: if the North froze its reactors (kept the spent fuel rods in the cooling ponds), the United States, Japan, and South Korea would give the North light-water reactors to provide electric power. This was basically the deal that the North had put on hold in the fall of 1993. Diplomatic negotiations began on July 8, the day of Kim's death. The deal was approved in October 1994 and included granting loans and credits to P'yŏngyang for purchase of the reactors. In any event, because of the workup time for building the reactors, the arrangements could not be completed until 2008 at the earliest. In the meantime, the United States pledged to provide heating oil for electric power. The problems seemed to have been solved by Carter's deft diplomacy.

Alas (a word that could be used in almost every sentence dealing with U.S.-North Korea relations), this was not to be. In August 1998 came reports that North Korea had launched a long-range missile that flew over Japan and landed in the Pacific Ocean. It now appears that those reports (sensationalized by the American media) were erroneous: P'yŏngyang had actually tried to launch a satellite as part of the fiftieth anniversary of the establishment of the DPRK.[50] Because of the ongoing tensions between the two countries, the Clinton administration conducted a thorough analysis of its Korea policy. In June 1999, former Secretary of Defense William Perry was dispatched to P'yŏngyang for talks. His report in the fall called for engagement with the North rather than condemnation and confrontation. Engagement, according to Perry, meant strengthening diplomatic relationships with Kim Jong-il's government, recognizing that reunification might be many years away; it entailed granting ample aid to P'yŏngyang; it meant lifting the embargo against the North in effect since 1950. In June 2000, the Clinton administration eased sanctions against North Korea and generally lifted the embargo. Imports were allowed from the North; direct personal and commercial transactions were permitted between citizens of both countries; restrictions on investments were lessened; and commercial planes and ships carrying U.S. goods could land in North Korea. The 1994 Agreed Framework also called on the United States "to provide formal assurance to the DPRK that the U.S. would not threaten the use of nuclear weapons."[51] In return, the DPRK would hold to the 1994 agreement, stop its missile program, and halt its sale of missiles (begun in 1985) to countries like Iran, Syria, and Yemen. Some believe that these talks and Clinton's approach created the right atmosphere for the Kim-Kim summit in the summer of 2000. Time ran out, however, for the Clinton administration to complete the negotiations.

In his 2002 State of the Union address following the 9/11 attacks, President George W. Bush targeted North Korea as part of his so-called axis of evil. His administration cast off the policy of engagement and returned to the iciness of condemnation and isolation: it had, in fact, no high-level contact with the North until October 2002. In those talks, the Bush envoy accused the North Koreans of operating a nuclear program. Bush's attitude toward the North came through in his talks with Kim Dae-jung in 2001 when he called "Kim Jong-il a 'pygmy'" and told an American reporter "that he 'loathed' Kim and wanted to 'topple' his regime."[52] His administration characterized North Korea as "a Stalinist criminal nation that [had] recently starved two million of its own citizens and that is known as 'Missiles 'R' Us' because its principal source of income came from the sale of missiles...."[53] Bush's policy, personal attitudes, and approaches frightened Kim Jong-il and his advisors, who were cited by a journalist as not so much Communists as "extreme nationalists."[54]

Neither country fulfilled its pledges under the 1994 Agreed Framework. The United States did not move to establish diplomatic relations with North Korea and never gave more than oblique assurances that the United States would not attack the North. Instead, U.S. Secretary of Defense Donald Rumsfeld in December 2002 said, "The United States military has the might to counter threats from North Korea and Iraq simultaneously. We are perfectly capable of doing that which is necessary."[55]

Especially unnerved by the tough U.S. stand on Iraq and fearful that it might be next on the list to be attacked, the DPRK in December 2002 declared that it would indeed reoperate the nuclear plant and would begin to construct two more plants, one with a fifty-megawatt and the other with a two hundred-megawatt capability. It withdrew from the NNP and expelled all the IAEA inspectors, actions that flew in the face of the 1994 Agreed Framework, directly contravening its central elements. The apparent achievements of the Clinton years were wiped out.

The Bush administration belittled Clinton's efforts as attempts to "shower Kim Jong-il with 'flowers and chocolates.'" A spokesman said that officials in the "Democratic administration went to P'yŏngyang with offers of light-water reactors, 'a basketball signed by Michael Jordan, and many other inducements for the dear leader to try to agree not to develop nuclear weapons—and it failed.'"[56] The Bush White House placed its hopes in the belief that isolation would eventually cause the Kim regime to collapse.

In August 2003, China sponsored three-party talks between North Korea, the United States, and China that evolved into six-party talks, adding Russia, Japan, and South Korea. The meetings, held between August 2003 and December 2006, led nowhere. In Round 3 of the talks (in June 2004), the U.S. position was that the North had to "fully disclose its nuclear activities, submit to inspections, and pledge to begin eliminating its nuclear program after a 'preparatory period' of three months." In return, the North "would receive shipments of heavy fuel oil to meet its energy needs," and the United States would give a "provisional security guarantee."[57] North Korea wanted head-to-head talks with the United States alone, but the Bush administration flatly refused, saying that to give in to that demand was like rewarding the North Koreans for their bad behavior.

This attitude did nothing to make North Korean actions more palatable. In May 2005, P'yŏngyang announced that it had removed more spent fuel rods from a reactor: that meant harvesting of more weapons-grade plutonium. The North claimed to have at least one nuclear weapon. At the time, the head of the IAEA said that he thought that the DPRK had enough plutonium to make six bombs.

On July 5, 2006, North Korea broke the only remaining one of its 1994 pledges, launching seven missiles (one, a long-range ballistic missile) toward the Sea of Japan. The UN Security Council imposed limited sanctions on P'yŏngyang for its missile launchings: it condemned the DPRK for the missile tests and barred any further testing; and it declared that no UN member state could sell North Korea technology or materials related to missiles or weapons of mass destruction. Then, in October 2006, P'yŏngyang announced that it had successfully tested a nuclear weapon underground, an action that probably produced considerable nationalistic pride among many North Koreans even as it created a new, more dangerous world. In response, the United States pushed a resolution through the UN Security Council imposing a cluster of bans, including "the interception of [North Korean] vessels on the high seas."[58]

Countries in the region were obviously extremely unnerved by North Korea's missile and nuclear testing and considered imposing their own sanctions. South Korea stopped sending additional rice and fertilizer to P'yŏngyang and talked about ending the Hyundai-initiated trips to the Diamond Mountains and an industrial site at Kaesong. Japan, which has been in the line of fire in the missile tests and was the only nation ever to suffer an atomic attack, worried about security issues. Japan and North Korea continued to hold talks on diplomatic normalization, but the security issues and resolution of the issue of the North Korean abductions of Japanese (see Chapter 18) prevented Japan from moving closer to establishing diplomatic relations.

CHRONOLOGY

North Korea

1980s	Terrorist attacks on the South, allegedly under Kim Jong-il's auspices
1994	Death of Kim Il-sung; succeeded by his son, Kim Jong-il
	North Korea and the United States come close to war
1995–2000	Floods and economic collapse cause malnutrition and starvation
1998	Hyundai initiative at the Diamond Mountain begins
2000	First summit between the North and South
2006	P'yŏngyang launches ballistic missiles (July)
	P'yŏngyang tests a nuclear weapon (Oct.)

South Korea

1980	Kwangju rebellion and massacre
1988	Seoul summer Olympic Games
1996	Former presidents Chun Doo-hwan and Roh Tae-wu tried for corruption, and for treason and insurrection in connection with the 1980s unrest
1997	Serious economic crisis
2000	Kim Dae-jung launches his Sunshine Policy and meets Kim Jong-il in P'yŏngyang

SUGGESTED READING

Abelmann, Nancy. *The Melodrama of Mobility: Women, Talk, and Class in Contemporary South Korea.* Honolulu: University of Hawaii Press, 2003. Based on this anthropologist's account of the lives of eight middle-class women, this book offers fresh insights into social experiences in modern South Korea.

Lintner, Bertil. *Great Leader, Dear Leader: Demystifying North Korea Under the Kim Clan.* Chiang Mai, Thailand: Silkworm Books, 2005. This insightful book covers a range of contemporary issues concerning North Korea, its leadership, and its international relations.

McCormack, Gavan. *Target North Korea: Pushing North Korea to the Brink of Nuclear Catastrophe.* New York: Nation Books, 2004. This book cogently analyzes the historical background and development of North Korean attitudes and behavior.

Park, Chung-shin. *Protestantism and Politics in Korea.* Seattle: University of Washington Press, 2003. Since at least 25 percent of South Koreans today consider themselves Christian, this is a book well worth reading. Its strength is in its elucidation of "the interaction of Christian ideology and Korean society."

Steinberg, David I. *Korean Attitudes Toward the United States: Changing Dynamics.* Armonk, NY: M. E. Sharpe, 2005. This book of essays covers various dimensions of the growing anti-American sentiment in the ROK.

CHAPTER TWENTY

Contemporary East Asian Identities:
Commonalities and Differences

This book has probed the political, economic, social, and cultural identities of East Asian states from traditional times through their evolution and revolutions to the present. While Chapter 1 looked at commonalities in traditional East Asia, this one examines common or similar problems, situations, and strategies that identified them in the early twenty-first century, among them consumerism and the culture of consumption; environmental degradation; family and gender relations; and the nature and import of their political cultures, all stoked by nationalism.

CONSUMERISM AND THE CULTURE OF CONSUMPTION

China

In the 1990s, China experienced an economic boom unprecedented perhaps in the entire world. From 1991 to 1997 its GDP rose at an annual average rate of 11 percent. In the first years of the new century, while countries around the world stumbled through hard economic times, China prospered. Between 1980 and 2000, the size of the Chinese economy quadrupled. Indeed, as one journalist put it, "The explosion of wealth in China may prove to be the most important trend in the world during this age."[1] The country's economic reforms had lifted millions of Chinese out of poverty and restored pride in the nation. In 2006, China had the fourth largest economy in the world.

The reforms made it likely to get rich if one mastered the system. The average real wages of urban workers more than doubled from 1978 to 1990 and went up another 50 percent from 1990 to 1994. With improving living standards, people ate better; wore better and more varied clothing; and bought the consumer items that became all the rage: colored television sets, stereos, electric fans, refrigerators, sewing machines. In the 1990s the list expanded to include air conditioners, high-tech sound systems, and motorcycles. Perhaps nothing better showcased the new consumerism than the construction of shopping malls: four hundred to five hundred were built by 2004, the year that the largest shopping mall in the world was constructed in Beijing. The Golden Resources Shopping Mall, an Art Deco structure of glass and steel, contained over 1,000 shops, a skating rink, a restaurant space that would fill two football fields, and 230 escalators; one could purchase anything there, from "goat-leather motorcycle jackets, Italian bathroom sinks [and] handmade violins [to] grandfather clocks, colonial style desks, Jaguars, [and] diapers."[2] With Deng's blessing on getting rich, the period was one of vibrant capitalism in the cities where money called all the shots. In 2000, I was refused a base for my research because I did not offer the proposed base institution enough money.

Pudong at Twilight Across the Huangpu River from the Bund is the new city of Pudong, with its high-rises and many futuristic buildings here in the financial district. At the center is the Oriental Pearl TV tower, with an illuminated circular pod and a tower that juts upward from it.

The government announced the goal of an all-around *xiaokang* society by 2020. *Xiaokang* means "well off," essentially middle class. Reaching that goal might be difficult, though some of the most developed cities, like Shenzhen, near Hong Kong, had increasing numbers of people in the first years of the century who could be called middle class. By that time, the culture of consumption had produced a widening gap between those rolling in yuan and those with insufficient money to live adequately. The wealth gap was evident in cities where the urban poor walked past glitzy department stores and specialty shops. The reforms also produced a regional wealth gap that in time had the potential to produce social instability and unrest. People on the coast and in big cities benefited most from the reforms, while those in the interior and the countryside were largely left behind; yet, they could see on television the much wealthier coastal and urban areas, a sight that brought resentment and jealousy. It is estimated that between 60 and 70 percent of China's population were left out of the economic boom. In 2005 the per capita net income of farmers was 3,255 yuan ($405), while that of urban residents was 10,493 yuan ($1,304). The richest 10 percent of the people held 45 percent of the wealth in China; the poorest 10 percent held only 1.4 percent. The disposable income of the richest 10 percent was 11.8 times that of the poorest 10 percent.

Many resented the impact of the reforms: putting a price on everything—essentially the commodification of essential aspects of social life under the philosophy of getting rich. It seemed tawdry and immoral compared to the self-giving patriotism of Maoism. One cadre, who had once supported widespread reform, mused in 1993 that with the reforms "the level of morality has dropped drastically. Girls think nothing of coming from villages for a short stint as a prostitute and then going home proud of the money they take back."[3] The glories of getting rich obviously had trade-offs.

Taiwan

As in other East Asian states, the expansion of exports was the engine that drove Taiwan's rapid economic growth and industrialization in the 1960s and 1970s, when consumerism became ingrained in society. The percentage of GNP from foreign trade skyrocketed from 23 percent in 1952–1953 to 88 percent in 1988. Export processing zones, with their electronic and electrical appliance industries and cheap labor (workers earned 15 percent of the wages of comparable workers in the United States and 20 percent of those in Japan), were the cornerstones of this economic success. American and Japanese investment boosted these industries. In the 1970s Taiwan moved into the machine tool and transportation equipment industries, and

Final Moments In dealing with crime, the Chinese regime has often favored execution. Here six men, charged with the possession and sale of drugs, were taken in trucks to a public rally in Shenzhen. There their appeals were rejected, and they were sentenced to death. They were immediately taken elsewhere and executed.

in the 1980s it made great strides in the computer/information technology industry. Supporting the expansion was a government commitment to fostering research and development.

As for the culture of consumption, it was estimated that 70 percent of the population was consumer-oriented. If shopping malls can be taken as a measure of consumerism, Taiwan was an enthusiastic participant in the culture of consumption. In 1994 a Shopping Center Development Council was founded "to facilitate mall development." Its website contended that "the Taiwanese consumer has [matured] and has come to demand the latest trends and the best products the international community has to offer."[4] A 1992 film, *Rebels of the Neon God*, cast a jaundiced eye on Taiwan's reputation as a shopping mecca, depicting the young "generation drowning in the imported values of the modern metropolis and American-style individualism and hence in conflict with old values. . . ."[5] In the film, advertisements, the quintessential indicator of consumerism, on "excess signage dominate[d] Taibei streets to the extent that the buildings they [hung] on [were] barely visible."[6]

The economic miracle seemed to disappear in the early twenty-first century. Although foreign trade continued to flourish, economic troubles abounded. They stemmed from political stalemate (see below), from the global economic recession, and from the effects of bad debts in the banking system. From March to December 2000, the Taiwan stock market fell more than 50 percent. In the recession of 2001, the first year of negative growth ever recorded in Taiwan, imports and exports shrank by over 20 percent. For many workers this meant stagnant or even falling wages as many manufacturing jobs were outsourced to the PRC. Wealth inequality tended to grow. A reporter noted that the average income of the seven hundred thousand poorest households fell from 2000 to 2006 to a very low New Taiwan (NT) dollar of 36,000 per year ($1,116), while the average income of the seven hundred thousand wealthiest households was NT 1,740,000 per year ($53,920).

Vietnam

The reform policy of *doi moi*, adopted in 1986, brought many changes to Vietnam. The key was economic development, with its attendant social change. In 2005 the country saw its sixth consecutive year of rapid economic expansion, with the economy growing 6.9 to 8.4 percent per year. Significantly, driving the economy most strongly was domestic demand. When asked in a poll to name the most important factor in family happiness, 33.2 percent of respondents answered "home appliances"; sex was named by just 27 percent. Industry and the service sectors led the way. The growth of industry in the early years of the century was spurred on by cheap labor and substantially improved infrastructure. Exports remained strong, with 40 percent in 2005 in the form of light manufactured goods. The service sector expanded by over 8 percent that year, fueled by the roles of finance and the four T's: tourism, trade, telecommunications, and transport. Expensive Japanese motorbikes and even automobiles were much-sought-after items, with auto sales up 37 percent in 2002 from 2001.

The state explicitly promoted private enterprise even as it restructured state enterprises to make them more productive. In some instances, state enterprises were merged or sold. These trends accelerated the movement to a market-based economy. While 14,400 new private enterprises were registered in 2000, the number shot up to 38,100 in 2005. Indeed, after the early 1990s, the main source of jobs was the private sector. The high rate of poverty, the bane of Vietnam in the 1970s and 1980s, fell rapidly—from 58 percent of the population in 1993 to 19.4 percent in 2004. Even so, there was a vast disparity between rich and poor; the rich earned roughly 12.5 times more than the worst off. In October 2006, the government made it clear that one of its goals was to gradually eliminate the wealth gap, especially among ethnic groups, particularly Montagnards, and those in remote areas.

Probably the greatest impediment to economic development was the Communist Party's unwillingness to give up absolute control over all arenas of life. It was a telltale sign that Prime Minister Phan Van Khai, in a June 2005 interview, noted, in looking ahead to the Communist Party Congress in 2006, that on the agenda was further debate about the pace and scope of reforms. That was indeed the case, though at the meeting there was no definitive conclusion.

Economic reforms had varying effects on the populace, apart from the rising consumerism. To seek new jobs, people left the countryside in droves, increasing the population of cities, where many lived in slums with few services: inadequate water (despite abundant rainfall), poor drainage and sanitation, and mostly unpaved streets. In Ho Chi Minh City, as many as three hundred thousand people lived in these slums.

Japan

Japan's tremendous postwar economic success and its reviving economy in the early twenty-first century led to a "mass society" where most people were "reasonably well-to-do, well educated, and proud of their values and lifestyle." They lived in a nation in "an era of prosperity, internal stability, and international peace unprecedented in its modern history."[7] In the 1970s and 1980s, various polls showed that over 90 percent of all Japanese considered themselves middle class. In contrast to Chinese and Vietnamese, Japanese saw themselves as a one-class nation marked by social homogeneity.

Yet, such a standardized picture masked the reality of the lives of many Japanese. If the desired lifestyle was that of the salaryman (see Chapter 18), then less than 25 percent of all Japanese workers had achieved it. Just over half of all high school graduates went on to college. The lives of farmers, though much improved, did not match the standardized picture—nor did the lives of outcast *burakumin*, the preyed-on Ainu, or the discriminated-against Koreans. There were disparities of wealth by region,

The Nonconformers   While conformity to the group still prevails in Japanese culture, there are always individuals who choose to go their own way. The outlandish hairstyles and hostile expressions on their faces suggest teenage rebelliousness.

with high growth rates in intensively industrial areas, and also between rich and poor. In April 2006, Prime Minister Koizumi argued that "a certain degree of class disparity [was] a healthy thing in a modern society."[8]

By contrast, social criticism of well-to-do Japanese abounded, arguing that their lives were devoid of meaning and purpose. Critics contended that the "expensive tennis lessons, hundred dollar melons, top-of-the-line automobiles that were driven only on Sunday, and memberships in exclusive golf clubs that ran into the tens of thousands of dollars" of the new rich indicated bored, empty lives.[9] An American writer noted that in a French restaurant in Tokyo, "[d]essert consisted of chocolate mousse. The waiter reappeared with 'some kind of grinder, and instead of cinnamon or flaked chocolate he began decorating my mousse with shavings of pure gold."[10] Some argued that the culture of consumption had brought spiritual bankruptcy. There was an abrupt rise in teenage prostitution called *subsidized friendship*. Advertising through commercial voice mail, a teenage girl solicited interested men, willing to engage "in sex simply because she wanted 100,000-yen designer handbags and other brand name luxuries that she could not afford from her family allowance."[11]

Part of the critique of the new middle class was an idealization of families living downtown (*shitamachi*)—that is, areas of small shopkeepers and craftsmen who maintained relationships with their neighbors and thus (ideally) the idea and substance of community. Another aspect of this craving for meaning was to look back to the past, when theoretically traditional personal relationships were most highly valued. As in any form of nostalgia, memory romanticized the past, making it sweeter than it actually was.

The Koreas

North Korea.   North Korea clearly had no problem with consumerism, since there were few goods to be purchased. But social inequality was apparent. Social elites consisted of party elites, who had a relatively high standard of living and access to some consumer goods. Party members utilized their social status to send their sons and daughters to universities. By contrast, whereas upper- and middle-class people occasionally had beef and pork, the ordinary people had only dog meat. Party members might have detached houses; ordinary people had apartments with only one or two rooms. The irony was that though socialism calls for social equality, the political system in the North fostered deep inequality.

South Korea.   With the eleventh largest economy in the world in 2006, South Korea was a huge economic success story: it had a number of world-class companies and was proud of its prosperous upper middle class. But in contrast, its middle class was shrinking (by close to 5 percent) and its lower class was soaring. "In 1995, the bottom 10 percent of the population earned 41 percent of the national income average. By 2003, that number had fallen to 34 percent. Those living in poverty (earning less than U.S. $1,360 per month) in the same time period had more than doubled—from 7 to 15 percent of the total population." In contrast, "the income of the top 10 percent of South Koreans rose from 199 percent of the national average in 1995 to 225 percent in 2003."[12]

Some people saw the gap between the haves and have-nots. The haves were employees of important exporting companies and full-time workers who were union members and had done well after the 1997 IMF crisis. The have-nots were those who worked in small companies producing for the domestic market and part-time workers, who made up 37 percent of the workforce in 2004 (compared to 27 percent in 2001). Part-timers generally earned less than 65 percent of the wages of full-timers and had very few health benefits. The society and economy became more polarized. Another marker of growing social inequality was housing. Fully 40 percent of all Korean families and 50 percent of those in Seoul did not own their own homes. The more housing costs rose, the more likely they would sharply demarcate social classes.[13]

ENVIRONMENTAL CRISES

The identity of a people is reflected in their relationship to the environment—whether they are heedful of protecting and preserving it or not. Presumably, as I posited in Chapter 1, the tendency of East Asians to see the world and life as holistic would have promoted great concern for the environment. But as in other modernizing areas of the world, East Asian development produced environmental degradation, which, in the end, reshaped people's lives and identities. The magnitude and finality of the environmental crises made them key issues that had to be faced.

In China, the post-1980 reforms produced serious environmental problems that the government was aware of but seemed little equipped to handle. Sixteen of the world's twenty most polluted cities were in China: the air in Beijing was sixteen times more polluted than the air in New York City. In five of the seven major river systems in China, 70 percent of the water was thoroughly polluted, and reportedly 90 percent of the water flowing through cities was undrinkable. Soil erosion worsened as a result of deforestation. Land usage was another huge concern. From the mid-1970s to 2006, the net loss of arable land was almost a million acres each year—the result of taking land for economic development projects and also turning it into pastureland, even golf courses. Whereas in 1973 arable land per capita was 1.6 mu (about a quarter of an acre), in 2030 it was projected to be 0.83 mu (just over a tenth of an acre). Because of China's burgeoning population land shrinkage was a grave concern. If population growth continued, a conservative prediction suggested it would top 1.5 billion by 2015; the population would then be three times larger than it was when the PRC was established. The grimmest figures suggested that in 2015 the total amount of grain needed to feed China's populace would be about 50 percent more than the total harvest in the mid-1990s. In addition, there was a perilous water shortage: in 1997 this affected half of all Chinese cities and in 2006 two-thirds. One problem was the distribution of water supplies: southern China had 75 percent of the water supply for about a third of the land, while northern China had relatively little water.

China's attitude to the environment was that it could be manipulated for development purposes; the best example was the Three Gorges Dam on the Yangzi River, which environmentalists had opposed almost from day one. The dam will become the largest in the world, 1.5 miles wide and more than 600 feet high; when completed in 2009, it will create a reservoir 525 feet deep stretching for 375 miles. Its supporters have argued that it will provide flood protection and electricity for Middle Yangzi provinces like Hunan and Hubei. But its opponents have noted that 1.3 million people who live west of the dam site—mostly in Sichuan province—will have their homes, towns, and croplands inundated and will have to be resettled, an extraordinary expense.

Taiwan also experienced extreme environmental pollution in its rush to economic prosperity. In the mid-1990s "in all of Taiwan, less than 1 percent of human excrement receive[d] even primary sewage treatment; in Taibei City the figure was less than 3 percent. Not surprisingly, Taiwan had among the highest incidence of hepatitis B in the world."[14] The most toxic pollutants were hazardous wastes: pesticides, caustic chemicals, and radioactive wastes. Air pollution—"the ugly brown pall"—was caused by an eye-watering mix of industrial pollution, motor vehicle emissions, aerosols, and burning waste. Noise pollution in cities, with noise levels of about eighty decibels, came in the form of constant horn honking. As in the PRC the amount of land available for farming was declining at an alarming rate; even worse, close to half of the land under cultivation was considered marginal. Soil erosion was a serious problem. As in the PRC as well, there was a potentially serious water shortage.

Vietnam suffered from the same environmental problems as the PRC and Taiwan. Compounding the degeneration, at least 10 percent of its land and forests had been destroyed in the war by napalm, land mines, and defoliants like Agent Orange. To counter the loss of forests, the government launched a massive reforestation project that seemed to begin to reverse the destructive trend. Industrial production grew most rapidly in SOEs, which tended to have bad environmental impacts given the lack of adequate controls, poor treatment of wastewater, and airborne emissions. Some corrective policies were adopted, but the crucial issue became effective enforcement. Water in downstream sections of major rivers, as well as in urban lakes and canals, was seriously contaminated with sewage.

During the war, the United States sprayed a total of 80 million liters of poisonous chemicals, including 45 million liters of Agent Orange, a defoliant laced with dioxins that accumulate in the body to cause cancers. Agent Orange was sprayed over 10 percent of Vietnam (and secretly in parts of Cambodia). A late 1990s Canadian study showed that dioxin levels where Agent Orange was sprayed were thirteen times higher than average in the soil and twenty times higher in human fat. A Japanese study found that in sprayed areas, children were three times more likely to be born with mental disabilities, cleft palates, or extra fingers and toes. Residents of the Agent Orange hotspot of Bien Hoa, close to Ho Chi Minh City, had dioxin concentrations more than two hundred times the norm. Nguyen Trong Nhan, a former president of the Vietnamese Red Cross, called the use of Agent Orange a war crime. A spokesman for an American group, the Fund for Reconciliation and Development, noted that the United States had provided funds for clearing mines it had placed in Vietnam and stated that "we think the U.S. should do the same with Agent Orange."[15]

From 2003 to 2006, Vietnam, like other Southeast Asian countries, sporadically battled bird flu, a virus that some scientists predicted might mutate into a form that could spread by human-to-human contact and thus threaten a worldwide pandemic. From January 2004 to September 2005, forty-four Vietnamese died. To stop the disease from spreading, the first strategy was to kill millions of chickens and other poultry. But in the fall of 2005, a vaccination program was undertaken for sixty million chickens and waterfowl; it was a huge undertaking since bird flu was endemic in both the Red River delta in the north and the Mekong delta in the south. Other strategies to fight the disease included disinfecting contaminated markets and other sites, disseminating information, thorough training, and quality control and enforcement of poultry transport regulations. In late 2005 and much of 2006 it seemed that the problem had been solved—no human deaths and no animal cases; but in September 2006, the death of one hundred ducks in the south's Ben Tre province put authorities back on alert that in this global public health problem "Vietnam was at the front line."[16]

In addition to industrial pollution and the pollutants common in all the developing countries of East Asia, Japan's most famous pollution case, the Minamata scandal, dating from the 1950s, was concluded only in 1995. In Minamata Bay near Kumamoto on Kyushu, the Chisso Corporation's fertilizer plant discharged methyl mercury into the bay. Between four and five hundred people died after eating contaminated fish. From 1953, when Minamata disease became known, until almost the end of the twentieth century,

Vietnamese Farm Scene   This farmer herds a small flock of ducks into rice paddies in Hoa Lu, near Hanoi. Ducks in Vietnam have been carriers and victims of avian flu.

government and industry did everything they could to prevent petitioners from bringing the case to court. Initially they hired gangsters to frighten and intimidate victims who wanted their grievances addressed. Doctors who were involved in searching for the source of the illness saw their research money dry up.

In 1967 some of the victims filed lawsuits, confronting the government's biggest weapon—delay. Not until 1973 did one group of Minamata plaintiffs win some compensation. In another suit filed in 1982 by fifty-nine more plaintiffs, the court ruled in 1994 that it "could find no negligence on the part of either the national government or Kumamoto Prefecture for failing to stop Chisso from discharging mercury into the bay."[17] The judge ordered relatively small damages paid. However, it was not until 1995 that two thousand plaintiffs won a settlement through mediation.[18] General antipollution legislation was eventually passed, but the key to Japan's environmental successes was the pressure from activist citizens and professionals.

The most critical environmental problem in North Korea was the "degradation of forest reserves. Forests covered 74 percent of North Korea, but almost all are steep slopes." The major problems included "a doubling of firewood consumption, wild fires, insect attacks associated with drought, and conversion of forest to farmland" (in an effort to work toward agricultural self-sufficiency).[19] But there were also severe potential water shortages, as well as mostly untreated wastewater and sewage. Dependent on coal (and expected to increase coal production 500 percent by 2020), North Korea experienced continually worsening air pollution. Finally, the inability to feed the people came in part from the fall in major crop yields in the 1990s because of "land degradation caused by loss of forests, droughts, floods and tidal waves, acidification due to over-use of chemicals, as well as shortages of fertilizers, farm machinery, and oil."[20]

In South Korea, air pollution was the environmental culprit. Industry-produced sulfur dioxide and suspended particulates were the first problems, eventually reduced substantially by high environmental standards and strict government enforcement. Later problems were increased carbon emissions and automobile exhaust; large diesel buses and trucks were responsible for 40 percent of the latter. South Korea's total energy-related carbon emissions rose from 35.1 million metric tons in 1980 to 120.8 million metric tons in 2001. In that year, in fact, South Korea ranked eighth in the world in carbon emissions, which were predicted to increase 3 percent a year through 2020. Beginning in April 2003, the Seoul government attempted to deal with the problem by increasing environmental standards and offering financial incentives to industry.

A crucial question facing the countries of East Asia, all exhibiting nationalistic spirit, was whether that nationalism could be overcome to achieve cooperative solutions to transnational problems like bird flu, AIDS, and environmental disasters. Initial signs were encouraging. In 1993, North and South Korea, Japan, China, Russia, and Mongolia formed the Northeast Asia Sub-regional Program of Environmental Cooperation to reduce pollution, monitor the environment, and increase energy efficiency. In 1994, South Korea, Japan, Russia, and China established the Northwest Pacific Action Plan to focus on ocean pollution. In 2000, with the South Korean Environmental Minister Kim Myong Cha heralding the "century of the environment," Japan, China, and South Korea agreed to study the problems of acid rain and air pollution and to jointly run an environmental data center.

THE FAMILY AND GENDER RELATIONS

In all countries of East Asia except North Korea, capitalism and its consequent focus on consumption brought fundamental changes to family structure and relations. In North Korea, changes in family and gender relationships came not from economic development but from the political and military constraints of the state.

China

In the PRC, families and the role of women have been changed by two factors: population policy and economic reforms. In the 1960s and early 1970s, families often had five or six children. In the mid-1970s the government began to dispense birth control devices and increase population control propaganda. The population had to be controlled for China to modernize and raise its people's living standards. In 1980 Hua Guofeng, exiting as CCP chairman, pushed for a one-child-per-family policy except among ethnic minorities. This call prompted a new marriage law that raised the marriage age for men to twenty-two (from twenty) and for women to twenty (from eighteen).

When 1981 statistics revealed that about 6 million "one-child" families had another baby and that over 1.5 million families with five children or more had another baby, the government instituted a more draconian population control policy. If a woman had one child, she had to have an intrauterine device implanted; and if a couple had more than one child, the wife or husband had to be sterilized. Birth control cadres had to meet sterilization quotas and, if necessary, force even late-term abortions. Families who had more than one child lost various welfare and medical benefits and might be fined; in the rural areas, they might even lose their land. Such policies enforced the international image of a totalitarian state intruding into the most personal decisions.

Despite this rigorous birth control program, rapid population growth continued. In part this came from the difficulties of enforcement. As a gesture to farmers, who under the economic reforms could likely increase their profits with more children working in the fields, rural couples were permitted to have more than one child. Even in urban areas, however, the one-child law was difficult to enforce. In the early 1990s, about one-third of all births were second children and close to one-sixth were third children. This situation was worsened by the freedom of movement brought by the reforms, which greatly reduced the controls of *danwei*. The future outlook was grim. In the 1990s, China added 125 million people to its population, the equivalent of adding a contemporary Japan.

Scholars have also noted other social and cultural problems raised by the population control policies. The one-child-per-family policy played havoc with the traditional custom of the son's caring for aging parents. If that one child was female, she would be married off, leaving no one to carry out the traditional role and perhaps leaving her parents in a precarious social and economic position. For this reason, reports of female infanticide surfaced in some areas. With ultrasound technology available for checking the gender of the fetus, a rash of postultrasound abortions of female fetuses also occurred. The government quickly forbade abortion for gender control. Nevertheless, statistics showed that the number of male births was significantly greater than the number of female births (114 to 100), pointing to future social problems once the surplus male population reached marriage age.

Perhaps most significant, if the one-child-per-family policy was generally successful, it would ultimately create a cultural revolution, changing the concept of the family. Gone with the family planning clinic would be the old ideal (however different in reality) of the extended family. There would be no siblings, no aunts, no uncles, and no cousins. Parents doted on their single child. If the child were a son, he became the only way that the family line could be extended. Some commentators noted that this pampering had produced a generation of so-called little emperors or, perhaps more appropriately, little meatballs, the first generation of fat children that China had ever seen.

The economic reforms gave women diverse opportunities that had many implications for family life. It is difficult to generalize: "[a]ge, education, geographic location, residence (rural or urban), enterprise ownership form, type of industry, skills, capital and network resources [were] all important variables that intersected with gender in differentiating women in the turbulent social and economic transformations that were reshaping China."[21] Women who were praised as excellent students had many different venues for work. Since the state had begun to deemphasize class, feminist thought emerged to question gender inequality.

Taiwan

In Taiwan too, education allowed women to emerge as never before. Women often started to enter the workforce before marriage, thereby gaining independence from their families. After marriage, their wages and salaries put them more on par with their husbands, so that they often participated more in decision making than women in traditional marriages. Work after marriage also generally meant smaller families. It was not only economically that women advanced. A more educated woman was more aware of her legal rights (vis-à-vis men) and her political rights and opportunities in general; she was also more likely to participate in social causes.

The person most responsible for raising the issue of women's consciousness in Taiwan was Lu Hsiu-lien (Annette Lu), who was elected vice-president of the Republic of China in 2000 and 2004. Educated at Harvard Law School, she inaugurated Taiwan's feminist movement with essays she wrote in the early 1970s. Her major work, *New Feminism,* was published in 1974. Both a history of women's movements around the world and an account of the traditional role of women in China, the book argued that the real glass ceiling for women was not economic oppression but the patriarchal ideas that persisted in society.

The women's movement did not remain in the realm of the elites or the activists. From the mid-1970s to the mid-1990s, no fewer than ninety-six popular magazines were published for women; they discussed women's roles, family issues, and sexuality. Often the double standard was evident in talking about husbands and wives, whether it concerned who did the housework when both spouses worked or the permissibility of extramarital affairs for husbands but never wives. In the last decades of the twentieth century, premarital sex was more common than ever before: a 1984 report of the Taiwan Family Planning Institute claimed that "34.4 percent of newlyweds had had sex before marriage, and, of these, 77 percent of the women were pregnant at the time of marriage."[22] Even though divorce was possible, the divorce rate was very low. Why? Children were part of the husband's family line; therefore, divorced women were hardly ever given custody of the children. Divorce might mean that a woman would never see her children again. If a woman initiated a divorce, she would probably not be given alimony.

Vietnam

Especially in cities, the nuclear family replaced the three-generation family; in Hanoi in 1995, 66 percent of all families were nuclear. The number of newlywed couples who lived separately from their families rose. In some cases, rural families sent children to cities to find work to supplement the family income, in effect breaking up the traditional family. In cities, young people often joined others from their native place to form surrogate families. In the reform period, dual-income families became more common. The vast majority of women worked full time outside the home, but traditional gender models held sway at home, where men worked, on average, only forty-eight minutes a day and women worked three hours and nine minutes. Women did become more vocal at home and beyond. In the former case, greater female assertiveness perhaps contributed to the rising divorce rate; in the latter, by 1997, 26.7 percent of the National Assembly were women (compared with 16.3 percent of women in the U.S. Congress in 2007). Most commentators said that the acknowledged high rates of domestic violence were unfortunately common in the doi moi period.

Japan

Changes in family and gender relations in Japan came both from economic development and from changes wrought, as in the PRC, by demographic realities. Whereas in the 1920s over 30 percent of Japanese households included three or more generations, in 1985, only 15 percent did so. By the mid-1980s, 61 percent of families were nuclear and 18 percent consisted of a single person. Certain social critics suggested that these changes alone connoted some diminution of traditional values.

The role of women was an important barometer of family issues. The traditional pattern had been for women to quit work, marry, and raise children. A 1992 government poll revealed that 94 percent of Japanese women would follow that pattern, but importantly, there was increasing uncertainty about whether that pattern would persist. Demographic realities came to the fore. Japan was rapidly becoming a "gray society."[23] In 2000 slightly more than 10 percent of the population was sixty-five years of age or older. It was predicted

Source: Vietnam's Soaring Population

In contrast to Japan and South Korea, whose low birthrates may mean a diminishing population, Vietnam has the opposite problem: a rapidly increasing population. According to this article in the English-language Vietnam News *(dated November 2, 2006), what are the dimensions of the problem? What is the related concern?*

. . . Viet Nam's population is increasing by the average size of a province or over one million people each year, says a population expert.

Nguyen Dinh Cu, head of the National Economics University's Population Research and Social Affairs Institute, also reveals that the country's population density is six to seven times higher than the standard world density.

Cu confirms that Viet Nam, a country with a very large population, is growing rapidly, adding up to more than one million people annually. The figure is equal to the average size of a province, he elaborates.

According to the General Statistics Office, Viet Nam is the 13th most populous country in the world with 252 people residing in one square kilometre. The ideal figure put forward by population experts of the United Nations is between 30 to 40 people per square kilometre for ensuring a harmonious life.

People born in the years after 1975 account for about 63 percent of the population, while people aged 60 years and above make up nine percent, Cu says, pointing to increasing gender imbalance with people showing preference in having male children.

As per the 1999 census, the general sex ratio in the country was about 96 males for every 100 females. But boys were increasingly outnumbering girls in the 0 to 4 age group.

While the Hong (Red) River Delta claimed the highest regional imbalance in sex ratio with 116 males for 100 females in the country, the provinces of An Giang, Kien Giang and Kon Tum had extraordinary ratios at 128, 125 and 124 males, respectively, for every 100 females.

If the situation is not addressed urgently, the country may suffer from serious population imbalance, Cu says. Also, population is not evenly distributed and the emigrant problem is making the situation more unstable, Cu says.

Source: http://www.vietnamnews.vnanet.vn/showarticle.php?num=02POP021106.

in 2025 this would rise to 27 percent (30 million). This trend had several implications for women. One was in keeping with the traditional role of women as not working outside the household: in 1990 one of every fifteen such women provided home care for the elderly; that number was expected to rise by 2025 to one of every two.

But there were also countervailing pressures. From the 1980s on, the birthrate in Japan fell (in 1999 it was only 1.34 per woman). If there was no change in the birthrate—and no large number of immigrants—it was predicted that the Japanese population had peaked and would begin to fall all the way from 125 million to 55 million. When that prediction was coupled with the reality that the Japanese had the longest life expectancy in the world (in 2006, 81.04 years) and fewer people to support social security services, the tax burden promised to be severe. In 1990 each retired person was supported by 5.8 working-age (fifteen to sixty-four) people. It was predicted that in 2025 there would be only 2.3 people to support each retired person. This suggested that women had to work outside the home in order to pay taxes to support the elderly. Old patterns and identities were indeed in question.

In terms of spousal relations, whereas in the early 1960s 50 percent of all marriages were love marriages, by the mid-1990s, the percentage had risen to 75. That would seem to suggest that traditional attitudes like those of a farmer two hundred miles southwest of Tokyo were dying out. When "asked if he loved his wife of thirty-two years," he answered, "Yeah, so-so, I guess. She's like air and water. You couldn't live without it, but most of the time you're not conscious of its existence."[24] And yet, the divorce rate rose 100 percent between 1970 and 1995. In 2000, twenty-four marriages out of every hundred in Japan ended in divorce, compared to thirty-two in France, forty-two in Germany, and fifty-five in the United States.

The Koreas

Because of the closed nature of North Korea, reliable statistics on family structure and processes are not available. Certain general patterns of families, who have remained the basic social unit, have been reported. Because of work and military service, marriage for both men and women in their late twenties and early thirties was common. Traditional arranged marriages had generally disappeared. Sons were still prized, for economic reasons and for continuing the family name. Family size was generally small—four to five. Divorce was discouraged, though a woman could divorce without her husband's consent; he, however, had to get his wife's okay. Aging parents often lived with their youngest son rather than their oldest. Lengthy military obligations meant that an estimated 80 percent of farm workers and over 90 percent of workers in light industry were women (who were expected to work outside the home). The state provided nurseries for child care when both parents worked.

In South Korea, traditional family life had certain characteristics: the family was the most enduring social structure; there was a strong bond between mother and child; and between husband and wife there was weak emotional dependency. But in the last decade or so, there have been marked changes in family life. Patriarchal authority lessened and the gender division of labor became more indistinct. Among the thirty countries belonging to the OECD, South Korea had the second highest divorce rate. Both men and women began to delay marriage: the average age for men in 1995 was thirty; for women it was twenty-six.

Polls taken by the Ministry of Health in Seoul showed that 70 percent of women preferred a career to marriage, while 70 percent of men believed that marriage was necessary. Between 2000 and 2005, the proportion of women between the ages of twenty-five and thirty-four who were single rose from 25.5 to 37.9 percent, while the proportion who were married dropped from 73 to 60.3 percent. At the same time, the number of single-person households increased 42.5 percent. Commentators suggested that the trends propelling women to careerism were materialism, hedonism, and feminism. In any case, in part because of this situation, South Korea had the lowest fertility rate in the world; in 2005 it was 1.08 per woman. This issue caused serious concern. Japan, which also had a very low fertility rate (in 2005, 1.25), and South Korea held working meetings on the subject in late 2006.

POLITICAL CULTURE AT THE BEGINNING OF A NEW MILLENIUM

A strong feeling of nationalism was a hallmark of all East Asian nations in the first decade of the 2000s. One important question for the future was: how would each country's people express this nationalism at a time when all of them were still developing their modern identities in a fuller sense? How did their emerging identities reflect, reject, or incorporate their past?

China

The early twenty-first century for China was a heady time to revel in the new nationalism. CCP membership—70.8 million—was at an all-time high, and the party itself, largely because of China's economic success, seemed to be riding high. And yet, Communism as an ideology was dead. The charade of socialism with a Chinese face could only be played for so long. With democracy a watchword since the May Fourth Movement, there were inklings that China might move gingerly in that direction.

Like the household responsibility system, elected villager committees began as an initiative by villagers themselves in two counties in Guangxi province in late 1980 and early 1981. Village elders, former cadres, and community-minded villagers formed them, without the knowledge of local authorities, to address political problems that were growing out of the household responsibility system. County administrators reported this development to their prefectural superiors, who recommended that villager committees be established throughout the region. In December 1982, villager committees to manage neighborhood issues were written into the national constitution as elected mass organizations of self-government. In November 1987, the provisional local self-government law allowed villagers to elect villager committees and village heads in multicandidate elections. In some places, county and township officials on their own introduced voting. In others, villagers who had heard about the law pressured townships to let them nominate and vote for committee members.

From the beginning, many local administrators harbored doubts about the role of villager committees, fearing that they might become uncontrollable. Many local officials did all they could to delay or rig elections. Tactics included conducting elections with very little warning, demanding that party members vote for handpicked nominees, banning unapproved candidates from making campaign speeches, annulling elections if the "wrong" candidates won, and insisting that voting be conducted by a show of hands. By the late 1990s, the use of elections had spread to 60 percent of China's villages in almost every province. Rural people were quick to recognize that elections provided a way to target corrupt, arrogant, and incompetent cadres. When they were deprived of their vote, they fought back, lodging complaints at higher levels.

With the passage of a revised local self-government law in November 1998, self-government shed its trial status and reached a new level. It named two groups to be the formal decision-making body of a village: the villager committee and the villager assembly (the supreme decision-making body of village government). Since as many as four hundred to six hundred persons might attend villager assemblies, the government established a representative assembly of roughly twenty-five to forty members to serve as the permanent organ when the villager assembly was not in session.

The self-government law clarified many election procedures. All villager committee candidates had to be directly nominated by villagers (in the villager assemblies), more candidates than positions were required, and voting had to be done in secret. At least fifteen days before the election, an appointed election committee had to register village residents who were at least eighteen years old. Voting was done in three ways: mass voting, where voters went to a central polling place in the early morning, voted, and remained there until the end of the count; individual voting throughout the day; and voting via the roving ballot box, carried around the village to people who could not go to the polling station. One of the most democratically advanced provinces by 2000 was coastal Fujian, advanced in the sense that it had nomination by villagers in general; its candidates for the representative assembly were selected by direct primary; a secret ballot and a voting booth were required; and there was an open public count of the votes.

The reform efforts and these local changes raised the ultimate question: where was China's soul? A year before the 1989 turmoil, a six-part television documentary, *River Elegy (Heshang)*, asked where China was headed as it neared the twenty-first century. Using vivid imagery, especially that of the Yellow River, the film caustically criticized the "dogmatic chauvinism inherent in classical Confucianism and revolutionary Maoism alike" and waxed enthusiastic over modern Western ideas, values, and institutions.[25] It advocated leaving behind the *Yellow River civilization* and moving into the *Azure Ocean civilization*, promoting full-steam-ahead Westernization in what some called the new culture wars of the 1990s. Not surprisingly, the party's central propaganda department banned the film. "*Nothing* [was] guiding people—not Marxism, not Confucianism, not religion."[26] The sense that even a higher standard of living could not substitute for lives without substantive values led to widespread disillusionment. No consensus developed on what values should be upheld as the guiding principles.

Then in late 2006, the publication of new junior high school and senior high school history textbooks brought more questions about where China might be headed. Though initially these textbooks were for use only in Shanghai, the city's leadership in educational trends frequently made choices the

Whither China? Modern advertising (showing cute babies and a young woman undressing) is contrasted to the wizened old man and the poverty of the streets in the special economic zone of Shenzhen in 1993.

national standard. The history textbooks clearly were moving away from China's own history. They omitted discussion of dynasties, ethnic rivalries, imperialism, and the Communist revolution, preferring to look to the future and focusing on economic growth, political stability, innovation, foreign trade, and social harmony. "Mao, the Long March, colonial repression of China and the Rape of Nanjing [were] taught only in a compressed history curriculum in junior high."[27] The senior high school textbook mentioned Mao only once—"as part of a lesson on the custom of lowering flags to half-staff at state funerals, like Mao's, in 1976." Socialism was the subject of only one of fifty-two chapters, with less coverage than the Industrial Revolution.

Some critics believed that the textbooks reflected the political thinking of former leader Jiang Zemin and current leader Hu Jintao. Jiang's three representations did much to deemphasize the importance of class in viewing Chinese society, while Hu stressed the phrase *harmonious society* (sharply reminiscent of Confucius's goal) as the objective in a state marked by stability, prosperity, and unity.

One of the scholars who wrote the new textbooks argued that they "do not come from someone's political slogan"; instead, they "make the study of history more mainstream and prepare our students for a new era." But others were not so sanguine. One Shanghai teacher said bluntly, "The junior high textbook castrates history, while the senior high school textbook eliminates it entirely." For a culture whose hallmark had always been seeing the past as a framework for moving into the future, these developments seemed ominous—an effort to diminish and obscure crucial aspects of the Chinese historical identity. It was problematic whether the country could achieve long-term stability without that identity.

Source: A "Harmonious Society"

China's president and CCP chairman, Hu Jintao, has called for the construction of a "harmonious society." What aspects of Chinese society does this Asia Times online *article (dated October 11, 2006) call attention to as being unharmonious?*

. . . The Chinese Communist Party's policymaking Central Committee began its annual plenary session on Sunday. A major focus of the four-day session is to set policy principles to implement President Hu Jintao's signature concept of building a "harmonious society". . . .

On the other hand, the theme of this plenum strongly suggests there now are so many acutely "unharmonious" factors in Chinese society that the party policymakers have to spend their annual gathering to ponder possible solutions. For if society were quite harmonious, the party elite would devote their precious time to other more urgent issues.

Indeed, social problems, such as the widening wealth gap and social injustices, have piled up to such an extent that if the CCP were to fail to address them properly, its very legitimacy would be questioned and challenged. . . .

And there are good reasons for the CCP elite to be deeply concerned. The wealth gap has caused increasingly serious social differentiation, threatening social stability.

A survey by the National Bureau of Statistics last year showed that 10% of urban residents commanded 45% of the total wealth in Chinese cities, while the bottom 10% shared only 2% of the total wealth. . . .

The wealth gap between urban and rural areas is also expanding. In 2005, average per capita income of urban residents was 3.22 times that of farmers. Wealth disparity between regions is widening too. Per capita GDP in the richest province in coastal eastern China now is 10 times that in the poorest province in western China. The income gap among workers in various industries is also growing. . . .

One of the major causes for rapidly expanding wealth disparity is social injustice, which is also a major source of growing public discontent. Many people have gained their wealth not through their own enterprise but through their connections with officialdom. . . .

Therefore collusion between entrepreneurs and officials is running wild. One of the most notorious shortcuts for some to become rich quickly has been to collude with officials to speculate on land lots for construction. The parcels are taken away from farmers with minimal compensations and then sold at high prices. Land acquisition has become such a problem that most of the nearly 90,000 mass demonstrations (those involving more than 100 protesters) in 2004 were triggered by unjust land requisition.

Entrepreneur-official collusion has also been rampant in coal-mining. With the protection of local officials, private coal-mine owners simply ignored safety regulations to cut production costs. As a result, thousands of miners are killed in accidents.

Source: http://www.atimes.com/atimes/China/HJ11Ad01.html.

Taiwan

The political scene in Taiwan and its shaping political culture were something of a roller coaster after 1945. When the Chinese took control of Taiwan after World War II, they treated the Taiwanese as second-class citizens. Japanese economic and educational policies had helped create an able Taiwanese elite, but Guomindang officials wanted to control every aspect of the economy and monopolize all political positions. Relationships between mainlanders and Taiwanese deteriorated. A street incident in Taibei in February 1947 escalated into fighting and a bloody purge in which an estimated ten thousand Taiwanese were killed—a whole generation of potential Taiwanese leaders wiped out. When Jiang Jieshi retreated to Taiwan in 1949, authoritarian rule resulted in the arrest and killing of tens of thousands of people, Taiwanese and mainlander alike, all accused of being Communists.

Not until the 1970s were Taiwanese appointed to party posts at the county and municipal levels in an effort to buy them off in what has been called *Taiwanization*. Efforts of dissenting Taiwanese led to one episode of repression after another. Jiang's son, Jiang Jingguo, became president in 1978 amid growing opposition protests.

On December 10, 1979, protestors held a rally in the southern port of Gaoxiong (Kaohsiung). The government sent in hired thugs to attack the police and blame the violence on the protestors. Jiang cracked down with arrest and imprisonment of the protestors. One scholar called the Gaoxiong incident "a pivotal event in modern Taiwanese history" for it fueled a more robust democratic movement.[28] In the early 1980s, advocates of other causes—environmentalism, women's rights, workers' rights, veterans' welfare, and consumer rights—took to the streets. Jiang, aware of the changing times, courageously initiated reforms in 1986 that, in retrospect, marked the "transition from authoritarian rule to some kind of participatory democracy."[29] In September 1986, opposition leaders announced the establishment of the Democratic Progressive Party (DPP). Jiang's government accepted an evolution to greater democracy by abolishing martial law (in place since 1947) and removing the ban on the formation of new parties. Taibei lifted all travel restrictions to the PRC, enabling thousands of people to visit their homes for the first time since 1949.

Jiang died in January 1988. His chosen successor was an American-educated native Taiwanese, Lee Tenghui, who had served as Jiang's vice-president since 1984. Lee hastened the Taiwanization of the political system, naming sixteen Taiwanese (40 percent of the total) to the party's central committee. Conservative manipulations to derail democratic reforms and deny Lee the presidency brought a huge reaction from university students, who emulated the 1989 Democracy Movement in the PRC. In mid-March 1990, they occupied the grounds of Taibei's Jiang Jieshi Memorial, made demands, and even went on hunger strikes. Lee fulfilled his promise to the students at that time that he would sponsor a conference to discuss the issues of democracy. He did so, bringing together political and academic leaders (June 28–July 4), and he viewed their recommendations as a mandate to democratize and undertake constitutional reform.

In 1991 the provisions that had given the president the right to rule under emergency conditions and had been the basis for the Guomindang dictatorship were abolished. From that point on, two-thirds of the legislative National Assembly and the Legislative Yuan were composed of representatives elected from Taiwan and one-third from among overseas Chinese, an original idea of Sun Yixian. The constitution was changed in 1994. Presidents were to be elected directly by voters, and terms of legislators were set at four years. The provincial governor and the mayors of Taibei and Gaoxiong were also to be elected directly by the people.

On March 18, 2000, the Guomindang, the party of Sun Yixian and Jiang Jieshi, went down to a smashing political defeat in the presidential election. Little more than thirteen years after the first legal two-party election in Taiwan, the rebel DPP won, sending the Guomindang into shock and disarray. The former mayor of Taibei, Chen Shui-bian, who had been jailed in 1986 for opposition to the government, was elected president. He was reelected in 2004, though the years of his presidency had few successes, for the Guomindang threw continual roadblocks in his way. In June 2006 the Guomindang failed to oust him through recall after Chen was tainted by corruption in his family; however, though he remained in office, commentators thought that the episode had made him a lame duck.[30] Democracy seemed to hang by a thin thread.

Source: The Disappointment over Chen Shuibian

When Chen Shuibian swept the Guomindang out of power in 2000, many people hoped that he would undertake policies to benefit all Taiwanese. However, everything went downhill after that election. What does this editorial in the English-language newspaper The China Post *(dated October 4, 2006) say about Chen's policies and the predicament in which he found himself?*

Taiwan's governing party celebrated its 20th anniversary last Thursday amid sinking popular support in the wake of corruption scandals surrounding President Chen Shui-bian.

The Democratic Progressive Party (DPP) swept to power in 2000 on a campaign promise to eradicate corruption.

Now, only six years after Chen was elected president, the DPP's popularity has plunged as Chen himself faces mounting pressure to resign over allegations of corruption by himself, his wife, in-laws and others in his inner circle.

For nearly a year, approval ratings for both the president and the ruling party sank to the teens, with no indication that they would ever pick up. And more than 60 percent of the people thought Chen should voluntarily resign since the thresholds for his recall or impeachment are too high to cross. Even a show of people power on Sept. 15, the famous "besiege the city" march by an estimated 360,000 protesters, failed to impress the battered president.

The U.S. Taiwan's mentor and protector, has openly put Chen to a "test" of his "leadership, dependability and statesmanship" to fulfill his repeated commitments not to unilaterally change the status quo.

At rallies marking the DPP's birthday, Chen, defying warnings from both Washington and Beijing against any move to change the island's Constitution and alter its territorial definitions, reiterated his "impossible missions" to push for a new charter as well as U.N. membership under the name of "Taiwan."

Chen's China-provoking rhetoric was an obvious attempt to please fundamentalist pro-independence voters, who account for only 20 percent of the population.

The DPP has no major achievements to speak of and no other cards to play except the old trick of raising tensions in the Taiwan Strait. It has to rely on its core pro-independence voters for support in the December mayoral polls for Taipei and Kaohsung. A defeat in the southern stronghold would deal a crushing blow to both Chen and the ruling party.

On the eve of the party's anniversary, a group of young DPP members openly declared that Chen is no longer a trusted and respected leader and not fit to rule.

Several heavyweight DPP lawmakers have also criticized Chen for failing to address public grievances about the party and its commitment to its long cherished ideals. They called on the party to distance itself from Chen by quickly naming a presidential candidate for the 2008 race. Many DPP members favor Premier Su Tseng-chang. But the president has other plans.

Source: http://www.chinapost.com.tw/editorial.

At stake throughout these years was not only the identity of political rule in Taiwan but also the identity of the state. Was the government headquartered in Taibei the Republic of China temporarily in exile? Or should the regime more appropriately be known as the Republic of Taiwan? Until 2000 the identity was always determined by the mainland Guomindang, which held all political and military power. Chen changed that situation in 2000, but the issue of political identity remained acutely sensitive.

Deng Xiaoping announced in 1979 that the PRC would no longer use the phrase "liberate Taiwan," would accept the reality of Taiwan's existence, and would support the one country, two systems' approach (used in Hong Kong) for PRC-Taiwan relations. President Lee in May 1991 announced the end of civil war from Taiwan's perspective, an end to the *Period of Mobilization for the Suppression of the Communist Rebellion,* and an acceptance of the Beijing regime. In his speech marking the reversion of Macao to China in 1999, Jiang Zemin indicated that it was time to deal with the Taiwan question; he supported Deng's one country, two systems model. Until the presidency of Chen Shuibian, Taiwan publicly agreed with the one-China formulation. The heart of the problem was that the PRC and Taiwan could not agree on the most basic question—which China was in the formula? The position of many Taiwanese, especially the DPP, was that reunification would not occur; there was one China and one Taiwan, or two Chinas; independence for Taiwan would ratify the reality that had developed in fact, if not in name, since 1949. Taiwan was a separate nation; it should be named the Republic of Taiwan. This position was anathema to PRC leaders.

Despite Beijing's instinctively suspicious reaction, Taiwan's President Lee set out to strengthen ties to the mainland. He lifted restrictions on Taiwanese businessmen, who could now participate directly in the PRC's economic development through investments. Representatives from both governments held talks on emigration, fishing rights, and direct air links between the two. Though there were several episodes relating to Taiwan's status when Lee's speech or actions riled Beijing's leadership, Lee continued to acknowledge that there was only one China. But mainland-island relations during Chen's presidency were especially tense. Beijing was well aware of Chen's 1993 statement on democracy: "[D]emocracy is the process and independence is the goal."[31] From 2000 to 2007, there was an almost total political and rhetorical impasse between Taibei and Beijing. Practical dealings continued with various exchanges (communication, transportation, shipping, trade) agreed to in the late 1980s and early 1990s. Cross-strait talks that took off with much fanfare in 1993–1994 remained in the deep freeze.

Taiwan was a nation-state in fact but not in name. Ousted from the UN in 1971, and with countless nations breaking diplomatic relations with it to embrace the PRC, Taiwan was almost an international pariah. It was repeatedly denied reentrance to the UN and admittance to the World Health Organization. The United States, one of Taiwan's closest allies and the one most helpful in creating the island's modern economic miracle, severed diplomatic relations with Taibei in January 1979, when it established relations with Beijing. Three months later, the U.S. Congress passed the Taiwan Relations Act, which, in effect, accorded Taiwan "treatment equivalent to [that of] a sovereign state." Relations between the two were handled by the Taibei Economic and Cultural Representative Office in Washington, D.C., and the American Institute in Taiwan, essentially functioning as embassies. The Taiwan Relations Act also made strong commitments to Taiwan, stating that PRC efforts to take Taiwan by "other than peaceful means" would be "of grave concern to the United States, which continued to send "defensive" weapons to Taibei, ranging from F-16 fighter planes to a long-range radar system to detect ballistic and cruise missiles.[32]

Vietnam

In early 2007, two salient features of Vietnam's political culture emerged. The first was a growing sense that the Hanoi government was not meeting the needs of the people. An Internet blog in June 2006 set forth the specifics quite graphically:

At the time of the last general election a little boy said to his father, "Do you know what the party, government, trade unions and people are doing—because everyone in school is talking about it?"

The father was amazed that children were asking such serious questions. He thought of explaining the issues, but was afraid the child would be confused and wouldn't understand.

He answered, "The party is the father who linked the family together. The government is the mother who carries out policy given by the father and deals with relations with neighbors and relatives. The trade unions are the grandmother; and the people look up to the father to feed them when they're hungry and cover them when they're cold. The people are you and your sister."

A few days later a man came to visit the family. The child was playing in the playground naked. The man asked, "Hey, boy, where are your pants, parents, and grandma?"

The boy answered immediately: "The party and government are hugging each other on the bed; the trade union is having a short nap; and the people are hungry and have nothing to wear."[33]

In what forms this disgruntlement would be expressed was difficult to know, but its presence seemed real.

Another reality that continued to be important in Vietnam's political culture was the dichotomy between north and south. Visits to Hanoi and Ho Chi Minh City in 2006 dramatized the differences between the two areas. The tree-lined streets of the capital, the colonial architecture, and its many lakes lent it a certain civility despite the traffic-choked streets and the constant din of honking horns. There was a sense of continuation from the past. Vietnamese themselves often mentioned Ho Chi Minh City as part of the frontier, brought under continuous Vietnamese control little more than two centuries ago. The city was spread out, under construction, on the make, with building rubble and trash heaps everywhere. The more severe north, the more laid back yet rambunctious south: their separation from 1954 to 1975 probably reflected the present cultural divide.

Postwar politics was dominated by northerners who tried to achieved some balance with southern leaders. The new leadership generation that came to power in late June 2006 represented the south in the state structure more than ever before. The new premier, Nguyen Tan Dung, from Ca Mau province in the south, had served as first deputy premier from 1997 to 2006. At fifty-six, he was postwar Vietnam's youngest premier, the first leader to be born after the August Revolution in 1945. The new president, Nguyen Minh Triet, had been the Communist Party leader in Ho Chi Minh City; trained as a mathematician, he was very popular with the foreign business community. To bring the north into the power mix, the National Assembly choose Hanoi's party head, Nguyen Phu Trong, as its chairman. This leadership troika plus the National Assembly appeared to be thoroughly committed to the reform agenda as the nation hosted the November 2006 Asia-Pacific Economic Cooperation (APEC) summit.

Japan

Japan's political identity, and its relationship to Japanese traditions and the more immediate past, were much talked about at the turn of the twenty-first century. Prime Minister Nakasone Yasuhiro argued that Japan "must advance rapidly as an international state and from this standpoint, it is extremely important to re-evaluate and re-establish Japanese 'identity.'"[34] He supported the 1987 establishment of the International Center for the Study of Japanese Culture at Kyoto, set up to probe the uniqueness of Japanese-ness and to assert Japanese identity in an increasingly internationalized world. This was part

The Ubiquitous Peace Sign
The coming of peace after the disaster of World War II was so welcome that the habit of flashing the peace sign when photographs were taken became the rule, especially among children and youths, such as the three here standing on the street in front of a McDonald's.

of the effort to unpack "theories of Japan," or *Nihonjinron,* continuing what has been part of the Japanese tradition from the eighteenth century (Atsutane and Norinaga) to the 1930s thought of Pan-Asianists like Kita Ikki. These thinkers described the cohesiveness and special nature of the Japanese people, and some, like important leaders of the International Center, even spoke of Japan's core being the emperor (see Identities). Clearly, given the conservative nature of Japanese political rule, the resurrection of such rhetoric and worldview was disquieting to non-Japanese. Yet scholars, both Japanese and Western, pointed out that much that constitutes *Nihonjinron* was, or at least bordered on, the ridiculous.

> *Writers pointed to traits ranging from toilet functions and nose picking to Japan's version of pinball, called pachinko, as emblematic aspects of a unique Japanese culture. One [Japanese] defended import restrictions on beef on the grounds that the unique structure of Japanese intestines could not tolerate imported sirloin. Another defended the domestic sporting goods industry by claiming that the special character of Japanese snow ruled out importing foreign skis.*[35]

Nakasone was an unapologetic defender of Japan's role in the Pacific war. Speaking in 1983, he mused that the international community saw the war as arising from Japan's invasion of China; but, he continued, "to a great many [Japanese] soldiers and officers . . . it was a war for the emancipation of Asia. Many fought and died believing it was a sacred war."[36] In 1984, he became the first prime minister to attend New Year's worship at the Yasukuni Shrine with all the members of his cabinet. The visit brought the ire of the Chinese and Korean governments. Yet, conservative leaders saw it as a statement about the identity of Japan and being Japanese, however that appeared to the rest of the world. Prime Minister Koizumi visited the shrine annually. In August 2006, he dismissed Chinese and Korean outrage at this shrine visit as "immature." The periodic controversies when the Ministry of Education, in its textbooks, pointedly downplayed or rationalized the nature of Japan's actions did not quiet East Asian fears.

The frequent question in the early twenty-first century was: where is Japan headed? Perhaps the largest problem with Japan's standing in East Asia was its image. Despite apologies by some officials for

Identities: Prince Hisahito (2006-):
Decision Deferred

On September 6, 2006, a son was born to the brother of the crown prince of Japan, the first male birth in the royal line since 1965. It was a major development because Japan had been faced with the possibility that a woman might ascend the Chrysanthemum Throne. Crown Prince Naruhito (b. 1960) would likely succeed his father, Emperor Akihito (b. 1933), the 125th emperor in the unbroken imperial line. The only other male available until Hisahito's birth was his father, Akishino, a brother to Naruhito.

As early as May 2001, Prime Minister Koizumi Junichiro- indicated his willingness to change the 1947 Imperial House Law, which allowed only male imperial successors. Tensions mounted because Naruhito and his wife were unable to produce a son. While a majority of Japanese favored amending the law, a majority of the LDP did not. Then, when Akishino's wife, Princess Kiko, became pregnant, all talk of changing the House Law was put on hold. The cesarean birth prompted celebrations—and relief that important, perhaps wrenching, issues for the Japanese nation and its imperial system could be avoided. Any such debate would certainly have raised serious questions about the function of the Japanese monarchy in the twenty-first century.

But for many in Japan, most assuredly many women, the birth was not necessarily an occasion for jubilant celebration; reporters noted that in some quarters the birth (and consequently the easy way for politicians to duck social issues relating to women and their roles) was greeted with consternation, chagrin, even bitterness. It meant that crucial decisions about the monarchy would lie dormant and that the court would remain in the throes of traditions that some Japanese believed distanced it from the people.

Beyond the court, as Professor Machiko Osawa of Japan's Women's University said, the episode raised issues about the roles of women in Japanese society. "This birth and the issues around it come as a real awakening. Women have a role in this society, but it's not publicly recognized or acknowledged."[1]

---

[1] *http://www.iht.com/articles/2006/09/07/news/japan.php.*

Japan's wartime actions on the continent and in the Pacific in the 1930s and 1940s, Japan was perceived as unwilling or unable to accept, once and for all, responsibility for its actions. Comfort women brought lawsuits against the Japanese government in 1991, and in 1999 victims of Japanese biological warfare (bubonic plague) followed suit. In 1995 Japan did set up an Asian Women's Fund, a semiprivate charity to collect contributions to aid the women forced into sexual slavery by the military. The Japanese High Court in July 2003 acknowledged for the first time that the government had not kept its promise to provide security for the comfort women; but when it was time to put their money where their mouth was, in the end (November 2004) neither the High Court nor the Tokyo District Court awarded the women any damages. In the biological warfare case brought by 180 Chinese, the Tokyo District Court found in August 2002 that any compensation was out of the question.

The legacy of the war was, then, an identity that Japan seemed hard pressed to overcome; it created among China, Japan, Korea, and Southeast Asia a lack of trust, making it hard for Japan to play an assertive

Source: A Concerned View of Prime Minister Abe Shinzō

This editorial in The China Post *raises some red flags about the political positions of new Japanese Prime Minister Abe Shinzō, who took office in late September 2006. What issues are of greatest concern from this viewpoint?*

As of Tuesday, Sept. 26, 2006, Shinzo Abe, 52, is Japan's new prime minister, the youngest since World War Two and the first to have been born after it.

His relatively young age and inexperience in pains of war dictate a new course for the "Land of the Rising Sun" where traditional values of the samurai still run deep and sense of humiliations of the defeat in the war and the unconditional surrender of 1945 have become unbearable to many conservative politicians, academics and artists.

Abe's election signals not only a generational change in Japanese politics but also the dawning of an assertive new Japan intent on taking its rightful place in the world by employing its economic clout to raise its political profile, and shaping the power balance in Asia in a way so that China does not dominate.

Under Abe, Japan is set to formally break out of its pacifist cocoon by revising its U.S.-imposed Constitution and eliminating the military proscription enshrined in Article 9—a goal high on his agenda.

Abe's perception of Japan's modern wars forms his basic political orientation. He does not hide his dislike of the war-renouncing Constitution, and views with disdain the core part of the Pre-amble of the Constitution, which he calls a degrading "signed deed of apology (wabi jomon)" from Japan to the Allied Powers.

Abe does not want to admit Japan's war responsibility. He refuses to clarify his position on the apology delivered by then Prime Minister Tomiichi Murayama on Aug. 15, 1995, the 50th anniversary of the end of WWII, for the damage and suffering Japan's colonial rule and aggression caused to the people of many countries, particularly those in Asia. Subsequent administrations, including Junichiro Koizumi's, issued similar statements, making it Japan's official stance on its wars of the 1930s and 1940s. Abe said judgments on such matters should be left to historians.

The new prime minister once derisively compared Japan's past diplomacy to performing "sumo to please foreign countries in a ring they made, abiding by their rules." Sumo wrestling is Japan's unique traditional sport dating back hundreds of years, but, alas, today the top wrestlers are non-Japanese.

Abe's nationalism and hawkishness may be attractive to a segment of the Japanese people. But it is unhealthy for Japan and will likely only rekindle nationalism in neighboring China, and North and South Korea, leading to a further deterioration in Japan's relations with them.

Source:http://www.chinapost.com.tw/editorial.

Tower of the *Juche* Idea   This tower, completed in 1982, is 170 meters (560 feet) tall; it is a four-sided tapering spire. It is said to contain the same number of stone blocks as there were days in Kim Il-sung's life. In front of it are three statues (one is blocked from view) that hold a hammer, sickle, and writing brush.

role in Asian security. Japan's relations with China and South Korea worsened when the continental nations blocked Japan's bid for a permanent seat on the UN Security Council in 2005.

North Korea

Since 1994, the DPRK had experienced the death of Kim Il-sung, an estimated two million deaths from famine in 1997–1998 and tens of thousands in the following years, and a foreign policy that was a cat-and-mouse game of brinkmanship. The godlike figure of Kim Il-sung was still paramount. The constitution was amended in 1998 to call him the *eternal president.* Indeed, beginning in the mid-1990s, both the Communist Party and the government newspaper described both Kims as God. One North Korean defector said about life in the North, "We are taught that the whole world worships Kim Il-sung."[37] On the third anniversary of his death, North Korea adopted a new calendar, the *juche* calendar, named for Kim's dogma of self-reliance, which had taken on an almost religious quality as the God's legacy. Year One was 1912, the date of Kim's birth; thus, 2000 became *juche* year 89. One of the most impressive sites in P'yŏngyang was the Tower of the Juche Idea, an obelisk about as tall as the Washington Monument. Kim's birthday, April 15, became the *Day of the Sun,* "the greatest festival for the Korean nation."[38] In school, a large percentage of each day was spent on ideological education through the compulsory eleventh grade.

At the same time, the P'yŏngyang government was transformed into a completely military regime. War was continuously thought about and talked about. A defector reported, "Everybody believes a war will break out sooner or later. A hundred percent want war to occur. . . . They're even prepared to die in a nuclear war. A hundred percent believe that North Korea would win, so they support war."[39] How sincerely they believe that and how much they are mouthing the government line is hard to determine. Many outsiders agree that until perhaps the 1990s most North Koreans believed their government, though it is likely that the stresses of that decade eroded some support and raised questions about the state. The continuing stress and deprivation undoubtedly took a psychic toll on many North Koreans. In the face of the grim economic situation the government held firmly to the *juche* ideal, which in essence meant the struggle to survive.

The paucity of travel to North Korea was striking evidence of its isolation. According to travel schedules in March 2006, there were only seven flights in and out of the country each week: three to Beijing, two to Shenyang, and one each to Bangkok and Vladivostok. Train service was approximately four times a week to Beijing; one train to Russia was no longer used. There had been unscheduled cargo passenger ship travel from Wŏnsan to Niigata, Japan, but it was suspended when P'yŏngyang began testing missiles. Finally, "a bus is theoretically available from Dandong (China) across the Yalu River to Siniǔju [sic], but it's not easy to find [and] has no schedule. . . ."[40]

South Korea

In contrast, the ROK "is connected to the world . . . [f]rom rock music to high fashion; it is "traffic-choked [and] neon-lit."[41] With high-rise cities and cross-country expressways, South Korea was a land (in 2001) of ten million licensed drivers out of a population of forty-three million. Some three million foreign tourists entered the country each year, and two million South Koreans traveled abroad.

Since the end of World War II, South Korea's political and international identity has been that of an ally of the United States, which at various times saw itself as the patron of the ROK. With U.S. troops continuing to remain in the South, that long-time arrangement still seemed, on the surface, to be intact. But in fact, in the first years of the twenty-first century, more South Koreans saw the United States as a bigger threat to their national survival than North Korea. The South's relationship with its northern neighbor is its other main issue of identity. A poll by the Pew Research Center in December 2002 found that 44 percent of South Koreans had a negative or unfavorable view of the United States, and a Korean Gallup poll put it at 53.7 percent. The anti-American sentiment had "moved into the mainstream" of Korean society.[42]

The ROK-U.S. alliance, built on political, economic, and security issues, basically unraveled. Until democracy was established in 1987, the U.S. policy objective in the ROK remained political stability. The United States repeatedly allied itself with and offered support to those it believed could best bring stability—first the strongman Syngman Rhee, then the military tyrants Park Chung-hee and Chun Doo-hwan. U.S. actions at the time of the Kwangju crisis in 1980 stuck in the craw of South Koreans—when, instead of acting to promote democracy, the United States agreed to make it easy for Chun Doo-hwan to crush the demonstrators. This led Koreans to conclude that "Washington's relationship with the dictatorship of Chun was far cozier than with the democratic administrations of Kim Dae-jung and Roh Moo-hyun."[43] Corroborating that conclusion was George W. Bush's administration's deeply negative attitudes toward Kim and Roh—calling Kim's Sunshine Policy appeasement and casting a jaundiced eye on Roh because of his career as a human rights lawyer. And in the 1997 financial crisis, the United States insisted that the IMF impose stringent conditions on South Korea before the bailout. Many South Koreans believed that the United States did not act as a longtime friend but instead took advantage of South Korea's pain to increase its own economic profitability.

During the Cold War, South Korea was under the U.S. security umbrella. Beginning in 1994, however, things began to change rapidly. In the crisis between the United States and North Korea, when war seemed imminent, President Clinton did not even consult with South Korean leaders about policy at a time when, if war had come, South Koreans would have paid a terrible price. Further, they were chagrined when President Bush placed North Korea in the axis of evil at the very time Kim Dae-jung was cultivating the North with his Sunshine Policy. The Bush administration refused to talk with Kim Jong-il, considering

South Korean Soldiers Patrol the DMZ
Occasionally, incidents occur along the DMZ separating the two Koreas. Here, in April 1996, soldiers of the ROK patrolled the border after Seoul put its military on its highest state of alert since 1981 after North Korea sent armed soldiers into the village of P'anmunjŏm, where negotiations infrequently take place.

him a terrorist. Countries in the region (Japan, China, and South Korea) wanted negotiations so that problems could be handled peacefully. But as one scholar pointed out, the United States wanted "moral clarity"; she quoted George W. Bush's commencement address at West Point in 2002:

> *Containment is not possible when unbalanced dictators with weapons of mass destruction can deliver those weapons on missiles or secretly provide them to terrorist allies. . . . Because the war on terror will require resolve and patience, it will also require firm moral purpose. . . . Moral truth is the same in every culture, in every time, and in every place.*[44]

The last sentence, if nothing else, suggested a regrettable lack of understanding of other cultures, an unhappy situation in a world where moral truth can and does differ under different philosophies and social systems. In any event, juxtaposing that closed moral certitude with the 2003 U.S. invasion of Iraq, South Koreans began to think that the United States, far from bringing security, instead had brought greater insecurity to the peninsula. They feared that a United States turned global bully might start a disastrous second Korean War.

One event that took on great symbolic importance for many South Koreans occurred on June 13, 2002, when two U.S. soldiers ran over and killed two young Korean girls with their truck. Because extraterritoriality for American troops had existed since they first arrived in 1945, the sergeants were tried not in a Korean court but in an American military court. They were exonerated on all charges, including that of criminal negligence. South Koreans were outraged. Some saw more than a little racism at work; indeed, Korean perceptions of American racism were an additional source of anti-Americanism.[45] In 1999 the Associated Press published accounts of the murders of hundreds of innocent Korean civilians by American soldiers in July 1950 at No Gun Ri. South Koreans began to call it "Korea's Mylai" (Mylai was the South Vietnamese hamlet where American marines killed almost five hundred people in March 1968). South Koreans called for compensation to the families of the slain; the American refusal led to more charges of racism.

Political trends since the establishment of democracy include the rather rapid formation, disappearance, and merger of political parties. Generally parties were formed not around substantive issues but on the basis of regionalism, a hallmark of the political scene since the time of Park Chung-hee. Since the early to mid-1990s, legislation passed by the National Assembly created local assemblies and mandated the popular election of most local officials. These laws thus created a sense of local autonomy, encouraging greater political consciousness and activism at the local level. This was especially the case in areas around U.S. military bases, where local activists have in a sense challenged the monopoly of the Seoul government in handling the alliance that still exists, however strained, between the two countries. Adding more liveliness to the local and national scene was the growth of nongovernmental organizations (NGOs) that functioned like interest and advocacy groups and focused on a wide array of issues, among them the environment, women's rights, corporate corruption, and the rights of the disabled. The NGOs became adept at joining in coalitions and facilitated their work through the use of the Internet. South Korea has one of the highest rates of Internet usage in the world.

The six nations of East Asia entered the twenty-first century all having faced (and still facing) their culture's dialogues, struggles, and accommodations in shaping their modern existential identities. Each country found itself at various social, political, and cultural crossroads, with the necessity of confronting crucial questions about its directions for the future. Whatever paths to the future were chosen would be felt the world over.

SUGGESTED READINGS

Bestor, Theodore C. *Tsukiji: The Fish Market at the Center of the World.* Berkeley: University of California Press, 2004. This ingenious book opens up important social, economic, political issues in Japan while delving (in the words of a reviewer) "into the concrete ordinariness of human life in a specific time and place."

Johnson, Ian. *Wild Grass: Three Stories of Change in Modern China.* New York: Pantheon, 2004. These tales explore the social tensions in human terms touched off by the economic reforms.

Luong, Hy V., ed. *Postwar Vietnam: Dynamics of a Reforming Society.* Lanham, MD: Rowman and Littlefield, 2003. Nine very fine essays analyze the social transformation sweeping Vietnam in the 1990s and 2000s.

McVeigh, Brian J. *Nationalisms of Japan: Managing and Mystifying Identity.* Lanham, MD: Rowman and Littlefield, 2004. The author shows that there are a variety of nationalisms in turn-of-the-century Japan.

Yan, Yunxiang. *Private Life Under Socialism: Love, Intimacy, and Family Change in a Chinese Village, 1949–1999.* Stanford, CA: Stanford University Press, 2003. One reviewer says it all: "Overall, this is one of the best accounts of social change in contemporary China ever written."

Endnotes

CHAPTER 1

[1]Benjamin Schwartz, *In Search of Wealth and Power: Yen Fu and the West* (New York: Harper and Row, 1969), 2.

[2]See Edward T. Hall, *Beyond Culture* (Garden City, NY: Anchor Press/Doubleday, 1976), 74–101.

[3]*The Baltimore Sun,* August 23, 2005, Section A, 5.

[4]Quoted in Robert J. Smith, *Japanese Society* (Cambridge: Cambridge University Press, 1983), 112.

[5]Jonathan R. Herman, "Talkin' 'Bout My Parents' Generation: Translating Confucian Ethics and Family Values," *Education about Asia* 8, no. 2 (Fall 2003): 12.

[6]Ibid.

[7]"Philosophy and the Early Chinese World View: An Interview with Roger Ames," *Education about Asia* 9, no. 2 (Fall 2004): 29.

[8]Neil L. Jamieson, *Understanding Vietnam* (Berkeley: University of California Press, 1993), 40.

[9]Ibid., 17.

[10]G. B. Sansom, *Japan, A Short Cultural History* (New York: D. Appleton-Century, 1943), 115.

[11]*The Analects of Confucius,* trans. Simon Leys (New York: W. W. Norton, 1997), 63.

[12]Quoted in Fei Xiaotong, *From the Soil: The Foundations of Chinese Society,* trans. Gary Hamilton and Wang Zheng (Berkeley: University of California Press, 1992), 79.

[13]Jamieson, *Understanding Vietnam,* 35.

[14]Ibid., 16.

[15]Schwartz, *In Search of Wealth and Power,* 243.

[16]Fox Butterfield, *China: Alive in the Bitter Sea* (London: Coronet Books, 1983), 74–75.

[17]Russell J. Dalton, Pham Minh Hac, Pham Thanh Nghi, and Nhu-Ngoc T. Ong, "Social Relations and Social Capital in Vietnam: Findings from the 2001 World Values Survey," in *Human Values and Social Change,* ed. Ronald Inglehart (Leiden: Brill, 2003), 143.

[18]Fei, *From the Soil,* 78–79.

[19]Jamieson, *Understanding Vietnam,* 37.

[20]Bruce Cumings, *Korea's Place in the Sun: A Modern History* (New York: W. W. Norton, 1997), 62.

[21]Jonathan D. Spence, *The Search for Modern China* (New York: W.W. Norton, 1999), 124. County magistrates served as detective, judge, and jury in law cases.

[22]Stevie Eveland, "Summer Research: Religion and Risk-taking" (December 16, 2004). http:/ /www. bucknell.edu/News_Events/ More_News/December_2004/Lorson_Boyatzis_research. html.

[23]Frederick W. Mote, *Intellectual Foundations of China* (New York: Alfred A. Knopf, 1989), 15.

[24]Quoted in Jacqueline M. Piper, *Rice in South-East Asia: Cultures and Landscapes* (Kuala Lumpur: Oxford University Press, 1993), 13–14.

[25]Ibid., 46.

[26]Because of an efficient night soil collecting system and other routine methods of sanitation, early modern Japan had far fewer epidemics than Europe or the United States. See *The Cambridge History of Japan, Vol. 4, Early Modern Japan,* ed. John Whitney Hall and James McClain (Cambridge: Cambridge University Press, 1991), 697–98.

[27]This account comes from Nold Egenter, "Japanese Rice Culture: The Misunderstood Philosophy of the Agrarian Past": http:// www. home. worldcom. ch/~negenter/ 473bTx_E01.html.

[28]Emiko Ohnuki-Tierney, "Rice as Self: Japanese Identities through Time," *Education about Asia* 9, no. 3 (Winter 2004): 4–5.

[29]For this discussion, I am following the line of presentation in David Jones, "Navigating Our Way through the Analects," *Education about Asia* 5, no. 2 (Fall 2000): 4–13. Quotations come from this essay.

[30]Ibid., 6.

[31]Ibid., 10.

[32]William J. Duiker, *Vietnam, Nation in Revolution* (Boulder, CO: Westview Press, 1983), 119.

[33]Andrew C. Nahm, *Korea, Tradition and Transformation: A History of the Korean People* (Seoul: Hollym Corporation, 1988), 95.

[34]Martin Collcut, "The Legacy of Confucianism in Japan" in *The East Asian Region: Confucian Heritage and Its Modern Adaptation,* ed. Gilbert Rozman (Princeton, NJ: Princeton University Press, 1991), 114.

[35]William Theodore De Bary, Wing-Tsit Chan, and Burton Wilson, eds., *Sources of Chinese Tradition,* Vol. 1 (New York: Columbia University Press, 1960), 57.

[36]Ibid., 52.

[37]Sebastian de Grazia, ed., *Masters of Chinese Political Thought* (New York: Viking, 1973), 249.

[38]De Bary et al., *Sources of Chinese Tradition,* 61–62.

[39]Richard J. Smith, *China's Cultural Heritage* (Boulder, CO: Westview Press, 1983), 172.

[40]Tanizaki Jun'ichiro, *In Praise of Shadows,* trans. Thomas J. Harper and Edward Seidensticker (Stony Creek, CT: Leete's Island Books, 1977), 30.

[41]Jamieson, *Understanding Vietnam,* 11.

[42]Nahm, *Korea, Tradition, and Transformation,* 68.

CHAPTER 2

[1]Quoted in Frederic Wakeman, Jr., *The Great Enterprise* (Berkeley: University of California Press, 1985), 1:209.

[2]Dorothy Ko, *Teachers of the Inner Chambers* (Stanford, CA: Stanford University Press, 1994), 150.

[3]Wakeman, *The Great Enterprise,* 648–50.

[4]Quoted in Evelyn S. Rawski, *The Last Emperors* (Berkeley: University of California Press, 1998), 208.

[5]Ibid., 301.

[6]Jonathan Spence, *The Search for Modern China* (New York: W. W. Norton, 1990), 94. These figures come from Ho Ping-ti, *Studies on the Population of China, 1368–1953* (Cambridge, MA: Harvard University Press, 1959), 281.

[7]Susan Naquin and Evelyn S. Rawski, *Chinese Society in the Eighteenth Century* (New Haven, CT: Yale University Press, 1987), 223.

[8]Philip A. Kuhn, *Soulstealers: The Chinese Sorcery Scare of 1768* (Cambridge, MA: Harvard University Press, 1990), 39.

[9]Pamela K. Crossley, *Orphan Warriors: Three Manchu Generations and the End of the Qing World* (Princeton, NJ: Princeton University Press, 1990), 21.

[10]Rawski, *The Last Emperors,* 21.

[11]R. Kent Guy, *The Emperor's Four Treasuries* (Cambridge, MA: Harvard University Press, 1987), 35.

[12]John King Fairbank, *Trade and Diplomacy on the China Coast* (Cambridge, MA: Harvard University Press, 1954), 19.

[13]Quoted in Jonathan D. Spence, *The Chan's Great Continent* (New York: W. W. Norton, 1998), 53.

[14]Jane Kate Leonard, *Controlling from Afar: The Daoguang Emperor's Management of the Grand Canal Crisis, 1824–1826* (Ann Arbor: University of Michigan Press, 1996), 195.

[15]Arthur W. Hummel, *Eminent Chinese of the Ch'ing Period* (Washington, DC: U.S. Government Printing Office, 1945), 575.

[16]Quoted in Peter Ward Fay, *The Opium War, 1840–1842* (Chapel Hill: University of North Carolina Press, 1975), 9.

[17]Ibid., 154.

[18]Jonathan Spence, "Opium Smoking in Ch'ing China," in *Conflict and Control in Late Imperial China,* ed. Frederic Wakeman, Jr., and Carolyn Grant (Berkeley: University of California Press, 1975), 151. A chest usually contained 133 English pounds.

[19]Chang Hsin-pao, *Commissioner Lin and the Opium War* (Cambridge, MA: Harvard University Press, 1964), 39.

[20]"Lin Zexu's Moral Advice to Queen Victoria, 1839," in *China's Response to the West,* ed. Ssu-yu Teng and John K. Fairbank (Cambridge, MA: Harvard University Press, 1954), 25.

[21]The phrase is Immanuel C. Y. Hsu's in *The Rise of Modern China* (New York: Oxford University Press, 1970), 228.

[22]Fay, *The Opium War,* 268.

[23]Paraphrased in John K. Fairbank, Edwin O. Reischauer, and Albert M. Craig, *East Asia, The Modern Transformation* (Boston: Houghton Mifflin, 1965), 142.

[24]Stuart Creighton Miller, "Ends and Means: Missionary Justification of Force in Nineteenth Century China," in *The Missionary Enterprise in China and America,* ed. John K. Fairbank (Cambridge, MA: Harvard University Press, 1974), 252.

[25]Ibid., 255.

[26]Paul Cohen, *China and Christianity* (Cambridge, MA: Harvard University Press, 1963), 49.

CHAPTER 3

[1]"Zeng Guofan: A Proclamation against the Bandits of Guangdong and Guangxi, 1854," in *The Search for Modern China: A Documentary Collection,* ed. Pei-kai Cheng and Michael Lestz with Jonathan Spence (New York: W. W. Norton, 1999), 147–48.

[2]Frederic Wakeman, *The Fall of Imperial China* (New York: Free Press, 1975), 170.

[3]Philip A. Kuhn, "The Taiping Rebellion," in *The Cambridge History of China, Volume 10: Late Ch'ing, 1800–1911, Part 1,* ed. John Fairbank (Cambridge: Cambridge University Press, 1978), 317.

[4]Quoted in Kwang-ching Lin and Richard Smith, "The Military Challenge: The North-West and the Coast," in *The Cambridge History of China, Volume II: Late Ch'ing, Part 2,* ed. John Fairbank and Kwang-ching Liu (Cambridge: Cambridge University Press, 1980), 228.

[5]Immanuel C. Y. Hsu, *The Rise of Modern China* (Oxford: Oxford University Press, 1970), 163.

[6]Fairbank and Liu, eds., *The Cambridge History of China, Volume 11: Late Ch'ing, Part 2,* 88.

[7]Quoted in Lloyd E. Eastman, *Throne and Mandarins* (Cambridge, MA: Harvard University Press, 1967), 38.

[8]Ibid., 33.

[9]This phrase was used by the governor-general of Yunnan-Guizhou. It is cited in Lloyd E. Eastman, "Ch'ing-I and Chinese Policy Formation During the Nineteenth Century," *Journal of Asian Studies* 24, no. 4 (August 1965): 602.

[10]Ibid.

[11]John K. Fairbank, Edwin O. Reischauer, and Albert M. Craig, eds., *East Asia: Tradition and Transformation* (Boston: Houghton Mifflin, 1973), 613.

[12]R. Keith Schoppa, *Revolution and Its Past,* 2nd ed. (Upper Saddle River, NJ: Pearson Prentice Hall, 2006), 96.

[13]Immanuel C. Y. Hsu, "Late Ch'ing Foreign Relations, 1866–1905," in *The Cambridge History of China, Volume 11, Late Ch'ing, 1800–1911, Part 2,* ed. John Fairbank and Liu Kwang-ching, 115.

[14]Hao Chang, "Intellectual Change and the Reform Movement, 1890–1898," in *The Cambridge History of China, Volume II, Late Ching, 1800–1911, Part 2,* 290.

[15]Jonathan Spence, *The Gate of Heavenly Peace* (New York: Viking Penguin, 1981), 329.

[16]Hao Chang, "Intellectual Change and the Reform Movement," 337.

[17]Joseph Esherick, *The Origins of the Boxer Uprising* (Berkeley: University of California Press, 1987), 125.

[18]Paul Cohen, *History in Three Keys: The Boxers as Event, Experience, and Myth* (New York: Columbia University Press, 1997), 34.

[19]Ibid., 89.

[20]John K. Fairbank, Edwin O. Reischauer, and Albert M. Craig, *East Asia: The Modern Transformation* (Boston: Houghton Mifflin, 1971), 397, 400.

[21]Stuart Creighton Miller, "Ends and Means: Missionary Justification of Force in Nineteenth Century China," in *The Missionary Enterprise in China and America,* ed. John K. Fairbank (Cambridge, MA: Harvard University Press, 1974), 279–80.

[22]Quoted in Esherick, *The Origins of the Boxer Uprising,* 310.

CHAPTER 4

[1]Communications in government and official business continued to use Chinese characters into the twentieth century.

[2]www.humnet.ucla.edu/humnet/ealc/faculty/dutton/TSsite.html.

[3]"The Tay Son Rebellion," http://www.reference.allrefer.com/country-guide-study/vietnam/vietnam24.html.

[4]John K. Fairbank, Edwin O. Reischauer, and Albert M. Craig, *East Asia, Tradition and Transformation* (Boston: Houghton Mifflin, 1973), 275.

[5]The phrase is from Joseph Buttinger, *The Smaller Dragon, A Political History of Vietnam* (New York: Frederick A. Praeger, 1958), 274.

[6]Ibid., *The Smaller Dragon,* 352.

[7]Professor James Huffman noted the similarity of Tu Duc's reactions to domestic rebels and the French and Jiang Jieshi's reactions to the Communists and Japanese in the 1930s. Personal communication.

[8]Buttinger, The Smaller Dragon, 384.

[9]William J. Duiker, *Vietnam, Nation in Revolution* (Boulder, CO: Westview Press, 1983), 29.

[10]Joseph Buttinger, *Vietnam: A Dragon Embattled* (New York: Frederick A. Praeger, 1967), 42–43.

[11]Neil Jamieson, *Understanding Vietnam* (Berkeley: University of California Press, 1993), 62.

[12]The phrase is Jamieson's in ibid., 28.

[13]Ibid., 67.

[14]William J. Duiker, *The Rise of Nationalism in Vietnam, 1900–1941* (Ithaca, NY: Cornell University Press, 1976), 115.

[15]Jamieson, *Understanding Vietnam,* 83.

[16]See, for example, Duiker, *The Rise of Nationalism in Vietnam, 1900–1941,* 126–27.

[17]Ibid., 140.

[18]Ibid., 142.

[19]Alexander B. Woodside, *Community and Revolution in Modern Vietnam* (Boston: Houghton Mifflin, 1976), 2.

[20]See David G. Marr, *Vietnamese Tradition on Trial, 1920–1945* (Berkeley: University of California Press, 1981), 43.

[21]Woodside, *Community and Revolution in Modern Vietnam,* 211–12.

[22]David G. Marr, *Vietnamese Tradition on Trial, 1920–1945,* 17.

[23]Quoted in Marr, *Vietnamese Tradition on Trial,* 18.

[24]The Saigon commentator was Tran Huy Lieu. Marr, *Vietnamese Tradition on Trial,* 19.

CHAPTER 5

[1]Ivan Morris, *The World of the Shining Prince* (Baltimore: Penguin, 1969), 24.

[2]G. B. Sansom, *Japan: A Short Cultural History* (New York: D. Appleton-Century, 1943), 286.

[3]Quoted in Robert Bellah, *Tokugawa Religion* (New York: Free Press, 1957), 91.

[4]Sansom, *Japan,* 500.

[5]Bellah, *Tokugawa Religion,* 90.

[6]Harold Bolitho, "The Domain," in *The Cambridge History of Japan, Vol. 4, Early Modern Japan,* ed. John Whitney Hall (Cambridge: Cambridge University Press, 1991), 221.

[7]Jurgis Elisonas, "Christianity and the Daimyo," in ibid., 367.

[8]Helen M. Hopper, *Fukuzawa Yukichi: From Samurai to Capitalist* (New York: Pearson-Longman, 2005), 4.

[9]John Whitney Hall, "The Castle Town and Japan's Modern Urbanization," in *Studies in the Institutional History of Early Modern Japan,* ed. John W. Hall and Marius B. Jansen (Princeton, NJ: Princeton University Press, 1968), 185.

[10]Sansom, *Japan,* 474.

[11]Louis G. Perez, *Daily Life in Early Modern Japan* (Westport, CT: Greenwood Press, 2002), 287.

[12]Oliver Statler, *Japanese Inn* (New York: Random House, 1961), 159, quoted in Perez, *Daily Life in Early Modern Japan,* 260.

[13]The preceding quotations in this paragraph all come from Sansom, *Japan,* 467.

[14]Thomas C. Smith, "The Japanese Village in the Seventeenth Century," in *Studies in the Institutional History of Early Modern Japan,* ed. John W. Hall and Marius B. Jansen (Princeton, NJ: Princeton University Press, 1968), 274.

[15]Ryusaku Tsunoda, William Theodore De Bary, and Donald Keene, comps., *Sources of Japanese Tradition, Volume I* (New York: Columbia University Press, 1965), 461.

[16]Ibid., *Volume II* (New York: Columbia University Press, 1965), 18.

[17]Ibid., 39.

[18]The quotations are from Ronald P. Dore, *Education in Tokugawa Japan* (Ann Arbor, MI: Center for Japanese Studies, 1992), 294.

[19]Bellah, *Tokugawa Religion,* 13–15.

[20]Ibid., 115.

[21]Ibid., 127–28.

[22]Ibid., 128.

[23]Ibid., 155.

CHAPTER 6

[1]Harold Bolitho, "The Tempō Crisis," in *The Cambridge History of Japan, Vol. 5, The Nineteenth Century,* ed. Marius B. Jansen (Cambridge: Cambridge University Press, 1989), 119.

[2]Cited in James L McClain, *Japan, A Modern History* (New York: W. W. Norton, 2002), 122.

[3]The Japanese scholar is Aoki Koji, quoted in Bolitho, "The Tempō Crisis," 121.

[4]Ibid., 133.

[5]Ibid., 139.

[6]Quoted in John Hunter Boyle, *Modern Japan: The American Nexus* (Ft. Worth, TX: Harcourt Brace Jovanovich, 1993), 59.

[7]Ibid., 60–61.

[8]Joan Didion, *The White Album* (New York: Simon and Schuster, 1979), 11, quoted in George M. Wilson, *Patriots and Redeemers in Japan* (Chicago: University of Chicago Press, 1992), 47.

[9]This section is based on the fascinating analysis of Wilson in *Patriots and Redeemers,* 43–117.

[10]Wilson, *Patriots and Redeemers,* 44.

[11]Ibid., 50.

[12]McClain, *Japan,* 149.

[13]Wilson, *Patriots and Redeemers,* 53.

[14]Ibid., 58.

[15]Ibid., 62.

[16]The phrase is Wilson's, ibid., 64.

[17]Ibid., 68.

[18]Marius B. Jansen, "Japan in the Early Nineteenth Century," in Marius Jansen, ed., *The Cambridge History of Japan, Vol. 5, The Nineteenth Century* (Cambridge: Cambridge University Press, 1989), 114.

[19]H. D. Harootunian, *Toward Restoration: The Growth of Political Consciousness in Tokugawa Japan* (Berkeley: University of California Press, 1970), 98–99.

[20]H. D. Harootunian, "Late Tokugawa Culture and Thought," in *The Cambridge History of Japan, Vol. 5, The Nineteenth Century,* 187.

[21]Conrad Totman, "Political Reconciliation in the Tokugawa Bakufu: Abe Masahiro and Tokugawa Nariaki, 1844–1852," in *Personality in Japanese History,* ed. Albert M. Craig and Donald H. Shively (Ann Arbor, MI: Center for Japanese Studies, 1995 reprint), 183.

[22]Bolitho, "The Tempō Crisis," 150.

[23]Harootunian, *Toward Restoration,* 198.

[24]Ibid., 193.

[25]The word is Harootunian's in *Toward Restoration,* 88.

[26]Harris wrote later that he did not want this kind of treaty, that he saw tariff and extraterritoriality clauses as unjust, but that he knew that only this kind of treaty would satisfy Congress. Personal communication from Professor James Huffman.

[27]W. G. Beasley, *The Meiji Restoration* (Stanford, CA: Stanford University Press, 1972), 112.

[28]Ibid., 115.

[29]W. G. Beasley, *The Meiji Restoration* (Stanford, CA: Stanford University Press, 1972), 138.

[30]Marius B. Jansen, "Introduction" in *The Cambridge History of Japan, Vol. 5, The Nineteenth Century,* 19.

[31]John K. Fairbank, Edwin O. Reischauer, and Albert M. Craig, *East Asia: Tradition and Transformation* (Boston: Houghton Mifflin, 1973), 499.

[32]The phrase is Marius Jansen's in "The Meiji Restoration" in *The Cambridge History of Japan, Vol. 5, The Nineteenth Century,* 363.

[33]In Japan's early history (through the eighth century), emperors generally did rule.

[34]Jansen, "The Meiji Restoration," 365.

CHAPTER 7

[1]Donald Keene, *Emperor of Japan: Meiji and His World, 1852–1912* (New York: Columbia University Press, 2002), 716.

[2]Ibid., 140.

[3]Ibid., 139.

[4]Peter Duus, *Modern Japan,* 2nd ed. (Boston: Houghton Mifflin, 1998), 94.

[5]I am indebted for this point to Professor James Huffman.

[6]Duus, *Modern Japan,* 92.

[7]Helen M. Hopper, *Fukuzawa Yukichi: From Samurai to Capitalist* (New York: Pearson Longman, 2005), 30.

[8]John Hunter Boyle, *Modern Japan: The American Nexus* (New York: Harcourt Brace Jovanovich, 1993), 90.

[9]Eiichi Kiyooka, trans., *The Autobiography of Fukuzawa Yukichi* (New York: Columbia University Press, 1968), 114, 116.

[10]Ibid., 134.

[11]Hugh Borton, *Japan's Modern Century* (New York: Ronald Press, 1955), 87.

[12]Ibid., 97.

[13]Stephen Vlastos, "Opposition Movements in Early Meiji Japan," in *The Cambridge History of Japan, Vol. 5, The Nineteenth Century* ed. Marius B. Jansen (Cambridge: Cambridge University Press, 1989), 411.

[14]W. G. Beasley, "Meiji Political Institutions," in *The Cambridge History of Japan, Vol. 5, The Nineteenth Century,* 657.

[15]A third party, the Constitutional Imperial Party, was pro-government. Itagaki and Ōkuma had founded their parties in 1881 and 1882, respectively; both had been relatively inactive until the Diet was established.

[16]Andrew Gordon, *A Modern History of Japan* (New York: Oxford University Press, 2003), 84.

[17]The language is from Article 3 of Chapter 1 of the constitution. See Gary D. Allinson, *The Columbia Guide to Modern Japanese History* (New York: Columbia University Press, 1999), 229.

[18]Keene, *Emperor of Japan,* 331, 344.

[19]Beasley, "Meiji Political Institution," 648–49.

[20]Keene, *Emperor of Japan,* 789, n. 3.

[21]These phrases are from Kenneth B. Pyle, *The Making of Modern Japan* (Lexington, MA: D. C. Heath, 1978), 122.

[22]Allinson, *The Columbia Guide to Modern Japanese History,* 16.

[23]John K. Fairbank, Edwin O. Reischauer, and Albert M. Craig, *East Asia: Tradition and Transformation* (Boston: Houghton Mifflin, 1973), 522.

[24]Kenneth B. Pyle, "Meiji Conservatism," in *The Cambridge History of Japan, Vol. 5, The Nineteenth Century,* 684.

[25]Quoted in Keene, *Emperor of Japan,* 392.

[26]Ibid., 394.

[27]The phrase is Keene's translation in ibid., 193.

[28]Hirakawa Sukehiro, "Japan's Turn to the West," in *The Cambridge History of Japan, Vol. 5, The Nineteenth Century,* 497.

[29]Borton, *Japan's Modern Century,* 211–12.

[30]Peter Duus, *The Abacus and the Sword* (Berkeley: University of California Press, 1998), 398.

[31]Ibid., 403.

[32]Ibid., 407.

[33]Ibid., 409.

[34]Quoted in Borton, *Japan's Modern Century,* 236.

[35]Boyle, *Modern Japan,* 140.

[36]Keene, *Emperor of Japan,* 646.

[37]Quoted in Boyle, *Modern Japan,* 145.

CHAPTER 8

[1]The phrase is Andrew Nahm's in *Korea: Tradition and Transformation* (Elizabeth, NJ: Hollym, 1991), 17.

[2]Bruce Cumings, *Korea's Place in the Sun* (New York: W. W. Norton, 1997), 49–50.

[3]Edward J. Shultz, "Top Ten Things to Know about Korea in the 21st Century," *Education about Asia* 7, no. 3 (Winter 2002): 8.

[4]Cumings, *Korea's Place in the Sun,* 57.

[5]Ibid, 56.

[6]The phrase is from Carter J. Eckert, Ki-Baik Lee, Young Lew, Michael Robinson, and Edward Wagner, *Korea: Old and New—A History* (Cambridge, MA: Harvard Korean Institute, 1990), 185.

[7]Cumings, *Korea's Place in the Sun,* 65.

[8]Nahm, *Korea,* 95.

[9]Ibid., 117.

[10]Ibid., 125.

[11]JaHyun Kim Haboush, trans., *The Memoirs of Lady Hyegyong: The Autobiographical Writings of a Crown Princess of Eighteenth Century Korea* (Berkeley: University of California Press, 1996), 282.

[12]Ibid., 2.

[13]Marius Jansen, *Japan and China: From War to Peace, 1894–1972* (Chicago: Rand McNally, 1975), 107.

[14]Ibid., 105.

[15]Quoted in Chong-sik Lee, *The Politics of Korean Nationalism* (Berkeley: University of California Press, 1965), 10.

[16]Ibid., 21.

[17]Ching Young Choe, *The Rule of the Taewŏn'gun, 1864–1873: Restoration in Korea* (Cambridge, MA: Harvard University Press, 1972), 28.

[18]Cumings, *Korea's Place in the Sun,* 100.

[19]Nahm, *Korea,* 153.

[20]Cumings, *Korea's Place in the Sun,* 105.

[21]Quoted in Wanne J. Joe, *A Cultural History of Modern Korea* (Seoul: Hollym, 2000), 196.

[22]Jansen, *Japan and China,* 116.

[23]Vipan Chandra, *Imperialism, Resistance, and Reform in Late Nineteenth Century Korea: Enlightenment and the Independence Club* (Berkeley, CA: Institute of East Asian Studies, 1988), 91.

[24]Joe, *A Cultural History of Modern Korea,* 288.

[25]Quoted in Nahm, *Korea,* 208.

[26]Quoted in Joe, *A Cultural History of Modern Korea,* 355–56.

[27]Quoted in Nahm, *Korea,* 205.

[28]Ibid., 534.

[29]Quoted in Lee, *The Politics of Korean Nationalism,* 73.

[30]Ibid., 74.

[31]Quoted in Joe, *A Cultural History of Modern Korea,* 359–60.

CHAPTER 9

[1]See Susan Mann, *Precious Records* (Stanford, CA: Stanford University Press, 1997), 226.

[2]See the similar evaluation in Edward J. M. Rhoads, *Manchu & Han: Ethnic Relations and Political Power in Late Qing and Early Republican China, 1861–1928* (Seattle: University of Washington Press, 2000), 285.

[3]See the excerpt "Zou Rong on Revolution, 1903," in *The Search for Modern China, A Documentary Collection,* ed. Pei-kai Cheng and Michael Lestz with Jonathan Spence (New York: W. W. Norton, 1999), 197–202.

[4]In fighting in the area between Nanjing and Shanghai, for example, revolutionary troops walked alongside the British-owned Shanghai-Nanjing railroad rather than ride or seize the train for their use, for they dared not risk damaging British property. Given such realities, it is not surprising that the revolutionaries turned to Yuan.

[5]Lu Hsun, "A Madman's Diary," in *Selected Stories of Lu Hsun* (Beijing: Foreign Languages Press, 1972), 10.

[6]Lu Hsun, "Preface to the First Collection of Short Stories, 'Call to Arms,'" in ibid., 5.

[7]Ssu-yu Teng and John K. Fairbank, eds., *China's Response to the West* (Cambridge, MA: Harvard University Press, 1954), 240.

[8]Quoted in Chow Tse-tsung, *The May Fourth Movement* (Stanford, CA: Stanford University Press, 1960), 184.

[9]See Ding Ling, "Miss Sophie's Diary," in *Miss Sophie and Other Stories* (Beijing: Panda Books, 1985).

[10]R. Keith Schoppa, *Blood Road: The Mystery of Shen Dingyi in Revolutionary China* (Berkeley: University of California Press, 1995), 108.

[11]Leo Ou-fan Lee, "Literary Trends I: The Quest for Modernity, 1895–1927," in *The Cambridge History of China, Vol. 12, Republican China, 1912–1949, Part 1,* ed. John K. Fairbank (Cambridge: Cambridge University Press, 1983), 467.

[12]Quoted in Chow, *The May Fourth Movement,* 106–7.

[13]John K. Fairbank, Edwin O. Reischauer, and Albert M. Craig, *East Asia: The Modern Transformation* (Boston: Houghton Mifflin, 1965), 669.

[14]C. Martin Wilbur and Julie Lien-ying How, *Missionaries of Revolution* (Cambridge, MA: Harvard University Press, 1989), 44.

[15]Jiang did not begin to work with Sun until 1921; many others were closer to Sun than Jiang.

[16]Wilbur and How, *Missionaries of Revolution,* 124.

[17]The first major effort of the Communists to organize unions was a tragic disaster. In the fall of 1922, workers, demanding better pay and union recognition, struck various railroads and mines in North China. After authorities forbade them to meet, Beijing-Hankou railway workers called a general strike in February 1923. Warlord Wu Peifu violently broke the strike, killing thirty-five workers and injuring many.

[18]Quoted in C. Martin Wilbur, *The Nationalist Revolution in China, 1923–1928* (Cambridge, MA: Harvard University Press, 1983), 131.

[19]Lloyd Eastman, *The Abortive Revolution: China Under Nationalist Rule* (Cambridge, MA: Harvard University Press, 1974), 67.

[20]Ibid., 1.

CHAPTER 10

[1]Akira Iriye, *Japan and the Wider World* (New York: Longman, 1997), 23.

[2]Ibid., 33–34.

[3]The phrase is Andrew Gordon's in *A Modern History of Japan* (New York: Oxford University Press, 2003), 166.

[4]Peter Duus, *Modern Japan* (Boston: Houghton Mifflin, 1998), 189.

[5]Chushichi Tsuzuki, *The Pursuit of Power in Modern Japan* (Oxford: Oxford University Press, 2000), 193.

[6]John Hunter Boyle, *Modern Japan, The American Nexus* (Fort Worth, TX: Harcourt Brace Jovanovich College Publishers, 1993), 159.

[7]Mikiso Hane, *Peasant, Rebels, and Outcasts: The Underside of Modern Japan* (New York: Pantheon Books, 1982), 34–35.

[8]Quoted in Gordon, *A Modern History of Japan,* 145–46.

[9]Quoted in Hane, *Peasants, Rebels, and Outcasts,* 182.

[10]Hugh Borton, *Japan's Modern Century* (New York: Ronald Press, 1955), 233.

[11]Quoted in Ikuhiko Hata, "Continental Expansion, 1905–1941" in *The Cambridge History of Japan, Vol. 6, The Twentieth Century,* ed. Peter Duus (Cambridge: Cambridge University Press, 1988), 279.

[12]Daniel L. Smith, "Robert Lansing, 1915–1920," in *An Uncertain Tradition: American Secretaries of State in the Twentieth Century,* ed. Norman A. Graebner (New York: McGraw-Hill, 1961), 115.

[13]Quoted in Tsuzuki, *The Pursuit of Power in Modern Japan,* 232.

[14]W. G. Beasley, *Japanese Imperialism, 1894–1945* (Oxford: Clarendon Press, 1987), 177.

[15]Ryusaku Tsunoda, William Theodore DeBary, and Donald Keene, eds., *Sources of Japanese Tradition, Vol. II* (New York: Columbia University Press, 1965), 39.

[16]Ibid., 204.

[17]Marius B. Jansen, *Japan and China: From War to Peace, 1894–1972* (Chicago: Rand McNally College Publishing, 1975), 345.

[18]Ben-Ami Shillony, *Revolt in Japan: The Young Officers and the February 26, 1936 Incident* (Princeton, NJ: Princeton University Press, 1973), 60.

[19]Jansen, *Japan and China,* 338–39.

[20]Shillony, *Revolt in Japan,* 61.

[21]Ibid., 36.

[22]Jansen, *Japan and China,* 348.

[23]Ibid., 390.

[24]Shillony, *Revolt in Japan,* 64.

[25]This is Jansen's verdict in *Japan and China,* 391.

[26]George M. Wilson, *Radical Nationalist in Japan: Kita Ikki, 1883–1937* (Cambridge, MA: Harvard University Press, 1969), 123.

[27]James L. McClain, *Japan, A Modern History* (New York: W. W. Norton, 2002), 426.

[28]Ibid., 469.

[29]Gordon, *A Modern History of Japan,* 199.

[30]McClain, *Japan,* 427.

[31]Ibid., 460.

[32]Beasley, *Japanese Imperialism,* 182.

[33]Ibid.

[34]Ibid., 200.

[35]Lloyd Eastman, *The Abortive Revolution* (Cambridge, MA: Harvard University Press, 1974), 91.

[36]Parks Coble, *Facing Japan* (Cambridge, MA: Harvard University Press, 1991), 212.

[37]The five were Hebei, Shandong, Shanxi, Chahar, and Suiyuan.

[38]James B. Crowley, *Japan's Quest for Autonomy* (Princeton, NJ: Princeton University Press, 1966), 338–39.

[39]Quoted in Lyman Van Slyke, "Nationalist China during the Sino-Japanese War, 1937–1945," in *Cambridge History of China, Vol 13, Republican China, 1912–1949, Part 2*, ed. John K. Fairbank and Albert Feuerwerker (Cambridge: Cambridge University Press, 1986), 550.

CHAPTER 11

[1]David G. Marr, *Vietnamese Tradition on Trial, 1920–1945* (Berkeley: University of California Press, 1981), 61.

[2]Ibid., 65.

[3]Quoted in Alexander B. Woodside, *Community and Revolution in Modern Vietnam* (Boston: Houghton Mifflin, 1976), 125.

[4]Quoted in Neil Jamieson, *Understanding Vietnam* (Berkeley: University of California Press, 1993), 159–60.

[5]The phrase is William Duiker's in *The Rise of Nationalism in Vietnam, 1900–1941* (Ithaca, NY: Cornell University Press, 1976), 159.

[6]Quoted in Oscar Chapuis, *The Last Emperors of Vietnam* (Westport, CT: Greenview Press, 2000), 109.

[7]Duiker, *The Rise of Nationalism in Vietnam,* 165.

[8]Pham Quynh, "Letter ouverte a son Excellence le Ministre des Colonies," in *Nam Phong,* no. 166 (October 1931), quoted in ibid., 168.

[9]Tai, Hue-Tam Ho, *Millenarianism and Peasant Politics in Vietnam* (Cambridge, MA: Harvard University Press, 1983), 86.

[10]Ibid.

[11]The phrase is Alexander Woodside's in *Community and Revolution in Modern Vietnam,* 186.

[12]Tai, *Millenarianism and Peasant Politics in Vietnam,* 117.

[13]Quoted in ibid., 123.

[14]Duiker, *The Rise of Nationalism in Vietnam,* 205.

[15]Quoted in Marr, *Vietnamese Tradition on Trial,* 382.

[16]Quoted in Chong-sik Lee, *The Politics of Korean Nationalism* (Berkeley: University of California Press, 1965), 78.

[17]Andre Schmid, *Korea Between Empires, 1895–1919* (New York: Columbia University Press, 2002), 44.

[18]Bruce Cumings, *Korea's Place in the Sun* (New York: W. W. Norton, 1997), 146.

[19]Lee, *The Politics of Korean Nationalism,* 76.

[20]F. A. McKenzie, *The Tragedy of Korea* (London: Hodder and Stoughton, 1908), 151, quoted in ibid., 83.

[21]This is the title of a book of interviews of Koreans who lived under the Japanese occupation: Hildi Kang, *Under the Black Umbrella: Voices from Colonial Korea, 1910–1945* (Ithaca, NY: Cornell University Press, 2001).

[22]Carter Eckert, *Offspring of Empire: The Koch'ang Kims and the Colonial Origins of Korean Capitalism, 1876–1945* (Seattle: University of Washington Press, 1991), xii.

[23]Quoted in James L McClain, *Japan, A Modern History* (New York: W. W. Norton, 2002), 463.

[24]Cumings, *Korea's Place in the Sun*, 139ff.

[25]Andrew Nahm, *Korea, Tradition and Transformation* (Elizabeth, NJ: Hollym, 1991), 224.

[26]Ibid., 226.

[27]Cumings, *Korea's Place in the Sun*, 152.

[28]Lee, *The Politics of Korean Nationalism*, 104.

[29]Ibid., 106.

[30]Quoted in F.A. McKenzie, *Korea's Fight for Freedom* (Seoul: Yonsei University Press, 1969), 247–48. On the Internet, see www.geocities.com/Tokyo/Towers/5067/k-sun.htm.

[31]Ibid.

[32]These figures are taken from Lee, *The Politics of Korean Nationalism*, 115–18. They come from figures released by the Japanese-run government in Seoul.

[33]Carter J. Eckert, Ki-Baik Lee, Young Lew, Michael Robinson, and Edward Wagner, *Korea Old and New—A History* (Cambridge, MA: Harvard University Press, 1990), 283.

[34]Cumings, *Korea's Place in the Sun*, 182.

[35]Kang, *Under the Black Umbrella*, 115.

[36]Ibid., 113.

[37]Ibid., 114.

[38]Eckert et al., *Korea Old and New*, 316.

[39]Kang, *Under the Black Umbrella*, 117–18.

[40]Eckert et al., *Korea Old and New*, 318.

[41]Cumings, *Korea's Place in the Sun*, 166.

[42]Ibid., 170.

[43]The phrase is in Harry Lamley, "Taiwan Under Japanese Rule, 1895–1945," in *Taiwan: A New History*, ed. Murray Rubinstein (Armonk, NY: M. E. Sharpe, 1999), 204.

[44]Sung-sheng Yvonne Chang, "Taiwanese New Literature and the Colonial Context," in ibid., 262–63.

[45]Ibid., 267.

CHAPTER 12

[1]Frank Gibney, ed., *Sensō: The Japanese Remember the Pacific War* (Armonk, NY: M. E. Sharpe, 1995), 79–80.

[2]Quoted in John Hunter Boyle, *Modern Japan: The American Nexus* (Fort Worth, TX: Harcourt Brace Jovanovich, 1993), 185, 191.

[3]Alvin D. Coox, "The Pacific War," in *The Cambridge History of Japan, Vol. 6, The Twentieth Century*, ed. Peter Duus (Cambridge: Cambridge University Press, 1988), 323.

[4]Ibid., 320.

[5]Quoted in Dun J. Li, ed., *The Road to Communism: China since 1912* (New York: Van Nostrand Reinhold, 1969), 208.

[6]James L. McClain, *Japan, A Modern History* (New York: W. W. Norton, 2002), 449.

[7]Mark Eykholt, "Aggression, Victimization, and Chinese Historiography of the Nanjing Massacre," in *The Nanjing Massacre in History and Historiography*, ed. Joshua Fogel (Berkeley: University of California Press, 2000), 16–17.

[8]For the activities of Unit 731, see Sheldon H. Harris, *Factories of Death: Japanese Biological Warfare, 1932–1945, and the American Cover-Up* (London: Routledge, 1994).

[9]Lyman Van Slyke, "The Chinese Communist Movement during the Sino-Japanese War, 1937–1945," in *Cambridge History of China, Vol. 13, Republican China 1912–1949, Part 2*, ed. John K. Fairbank and Albert Feuerwerker (Cambridge: Cambridge University Press, 1986), 627.

[10]Theodore H. White and Annalee Jacoby, *Thunder Out of China* (New York: William Sloane Associates, 1946), 132.

[11]Lloyd E. Eastman, "Nationalist China during the Sino-Japanese War, 1937–1945," in *Cambridge History of China, Vol. 13, Part 2*, 572.

[12]White and Jacoby, *Thunder Out of China*, 133.

[13]Ibid., 138.

[14]Taken from Eastman, "Nationalist China," 585.

[15]White and Jacoby, *Thunder Out of China*, 173–74.

[16]Ibid., 177.

[17]Quotations are found in Eastman, "Nationalist China," 580.

[18]"Joint Declaration of the Assembly of Great East Asiatic Nations, 1943," in David J. Lu, *Japan: A Documentary History* (Armonk NY: M. E. Sharpe, 1997), 423–24.

[19]Boyle, *Modern Japan*, 282–83.

[20]Andrew Gordon, *A Modern History of Japan* (New York: Oxford University Press, 2003), 212.

[21]McClain, *Japan,* 484.

[22]Gordon, *A Modern History of Japan,* 216.

[23]Ibid., 212.

[24]McClain, *Japan,* 508.

[25]Carter J. Eckert, Ki-Baik Lee, Young Lew, Michael Robinson, and Edward Wagner, *Korea Old and New—A History* (Cambridge, MA: Harvard Korean Institute, 1990), 323.

[26]Quoted in Bruce Cumings, *Korea's Place in the Sun* (New York: W. W. Norton, 1997), 180.

[27]Ibid., 179.

[28]See the film *The Fog of War,* Sony Pictures Classics, 2004.

[29]Quoted in Boyle, *Modern Japan,* 260.

[30]Ibid.

[31]Ibid., 261.

[32]"The Potsdam Declaration, 1945," in Lu, *Japan,* 453–55.

[33]Boyle, *Modern Japan,* 288.

[34]"Imperial Rescript on Surrender, 1945," in Lu, *Japan,* 457–58.

Chapter 13

[1]"Land Law of the Soviet Republic (November 1931)," in *The Rise to Power of the Chinese Communist Party,* ed. Tony Saich (Armonk, NY: M. E. Sharpe, 1996), 556.

[2]Edgar Snow, *Red Star Over China* (New York: Modern Library, 1938), 177.

[3]Ibid., 216.

[4]Maurice Meissner, "Yenan Communism," in *Modern East Asia: Essays in Interpretation,* ed. James Crowley (New York: Harcourt, Brace, and World, 1979), 271.

[5]Saich, *Rise to Power,* 1066–1067.

[6]Ch'en Yung-fa, *Making Revolution: The Communist Movement in Eastern and Central China, 1937–1945* (Berkeley: University of California Press, 1986), 221.

[7]Ibid., 220.

[8]Saich, *Rise to Power,* 1123.

[9]Quoted in J. Mason Gentzler, ed., *Changing China* (New York: Praeger, 1977), 232.

[10]Quoted in Suzanne Pepper, "The KMT [GMD] Conflict, 1945–1949," in *The Cambridge History of China, Vol. 13, Republican China. 1912–1949, Part 2,* ed. John K. Fairbank and Albert Feuerwerker (Cambridge: Cambridge University Press, 1986), 738.

[11]Ibid., 781.

[12]Kenneth Lieberthal, *Governing China* (New York: W. W. Norton, 1995), 51. At each territorial-administrative level (Center [or nation], province, prefecture, city, county, and township) there was a full range of both party and state organs. A small party committee generally held power at each level. At the Center, the committee was called the *Politburo,* chaired by the chair of the party and generally composed of 14 to 24 members. When the Politburo was not meeting, its Standing Committee, made up of five or six of the most powerful leaders in the country, held power. The party's Central Committee (ranging in size from about 100 up until 1966 to almost 300 in the 1980s and 1990s) mainly ratified decisions already made by the Politburo. The Central Committee's full meetings, called *plenums,* were numbered in the order in which they met following meetings of the Party Congress, a body composed of as many as 1,500 people. For example, the 8th Party Congress met in 1956, but the 11th Plenum of the 8th Party Congress met in 1966. The state or government, like the party, had organs at each territorial-administrative level. The most important government body after 1954 was the State Council, headed by the premier. Theoretically, the party made policy and the state executed it. Because of the complementary nature of party and state, the ruling structure in the PRC was often referred to as the *party-state.* The military (the PLA) had bureaucratic rank just like the State Council. It was *outside* the jurisdiction of the state and answered to a *party* body, the Military Affairs Commission. The military's highest priority was to protect the party, not the state.

[13]Ibid., 63.

[14]Ibid., 75.

[15]Quoted in Edwin Moise, *Land Reform in China and North Vietnam* (Chapel Hill: University of North Carolina Press, 1983), 106.

[16]"The Marriage Law of the People's Republic of China, May 1, 1950," reprinted in J. Mason Gentzler, *Changing China* (New York: Praeger, 1977), 268.

[17]Gregor Benton and Alan Hunter, eds., *Wild Lily, Prairie Fire* (Princeton, NJ: Princeton University Press, 1995), 100–101.

[18]Allen W. Whiting, "The Sino-Soviet Split," in *The Cambridge History of China, Vol. 14, The People's Republic of China, Part I: The Emergence of Revolutionary China, 1949–1965,* ed. Roderick MacFarquhar and John K. Fairbank, (Cambridge: Cambridge University Press, 1987), 500.

[19]It was charged with agricultural production; the development and fostering of industry and commerce; the provision of health care, police and social services, and education; and the collection of taxes.

[20]In the average-sized county of Xiaoshan in Zhejiang province, 2,726 mess halls were constructed between 1958 and 1962.

[21]The economist was Sun Yefang. Cited in Thomas P. Bernstein, "Stalinism, Famine, and Chinese Peasants," *Theory and Society* 13, no. 3 (May 1984): 343.

[22]Richard Baum, *Burying Mao: Chinese Politics in the Age of Deng Xiaoping* (Princeton, NJ: Princeton University Press, 1994), 29.

[23]Harry Harding, "The Chinese State in Crisis," in *The Cambridge History of China, Vol 15, The People's Republic of China, Part II: Revolutions within the Chinese Revolution,* ed. Roderick MacFarquhar and John Fairbank (Cambridge: Cambridge University Press, 1991), 226.

[24]Maurice Meisner, *Mao's China and After* (New York: Free Press, 1999), 463–64.

[25]*Ming Bao*, January 15, 1979, p. 1, cited in Roger Garside, *Coming Alive: China After Mao* (New York: McGraw-Hill, 1982), 190.

CHAPTER 14

[1]John Dower, *Embracing Defeat: Japan in the Wake of World War II* (New York: W. W. Norton, 2000), 46.

[2]Andrew Gordon, *A Modern History of Japan* (New York: Oxford University Press, 2003), 233.

[3]Theodore Cohen, *Remaking Japan* (New York: Free Press, 1987), xv, 1–2, quoted in Chushichi Tsuzuki, *The Pursuit of Power in Modern Japan, 1825–1995* (New York: Oxford University Press. 2000), 332.

[4]John Hunter Boyle, *Modern Japan: the American Nexus* (Fort Worth, TX: Harcourt Brace Jovanovich, 1993), 314.

[5]James L. McClain, *Japan, A Modern History* (New York: W. W. Norton, 2002), 532.

[6]Tsuzuki, *Pursuit of Power,* 334.

[7]Ibid., 343.

[8]McClain, *Japan,* 530.

[9]Quoted in David J. Lu, *Japan, A Documentary History* (Armonk, NY: M. E. Sharpe, 1997), 472.

[10]Quoted in Tsuzuki, *Pursuit of Power,* 357.

[11]Ibid., 354.

[12]Gordon, *A Modern History of Japan,* 239.

[13]Ibid., 229.

[14]Quoted in Lu, *Japan,* 500.

[15]Tsuzuki, *Pursuit of Power,* 376.

[16]Ibid., 360.

[17]Michio Muramatsu, "Bringing Politics Back into Japan," in *Shōwa: The Japan of Hirohito,* ed. Carol Gluck and Stephen Graubard (New York: W. W. Norton, 1992), 146.

[18]Tsuzuki, *Pursuit of Power,* 383.

[19]Sydney Giffard, *Japan among the Powers, 1890–1990* (New Haven, CT: Yale University Press, 1994), 155.

[20]Ibid., 156.

[21]Tsuzuki, *Pursuit of Power,* 392.

[22]The phrase is from George Packard, *Protest in Tokyo* (Princeton, NJ: Princeton University Press, 1966), 32, quoted in Tsuzuki, *Pursuit of Power,* 393.

[23]Giffard, *Japan among the Powers,* 161.

[24]Gordon, *A Modern History of Japan,* 250.

[25]Peter Duus, "Introduction," in *The Cambridge History of Japan, Vol. 6, The Twentieth Century,* ed. Peter Duus (Cambridge: Cambridge University Press, 1988), 17.

[26]John M. Maki, "Review Article: The Documents of Japan's Commission on the Constitution," *Journal of Asian Studies* 24, no. 3 (May 1965): 475–76.

[27]Haruhiro Fukui, "Postwar Politics, 1945–1973," in *The Cambridge History of Japan,* Vol. 6, 187.

[28]Yoshikuni Igarashi, "The 1964 Olympics and Historical Redemption" (abstract of a paper presented at the 1997 Association for Asian Studies convention). Available at: http://www.aasianst.org/abts/1997abst/Japan/j141.htm.

[29]Lu, *Japan,* 531.

[30]Tsuzuki, *Pursuit of Power,* 406.

[31]Edward J. Lincoln, "The Shōwa Economic Experience," in Gluck and Graubard, *The Japan of Hirohito,* 193.

[32]Bruce Cumings, *Korea's Place in the Sun* (New York: W. W. Norton, 1997), 320.

[33]Tsuzuki, *Pursuit of Power,* 409.

[34]Shinichi Kitaoka, "Diplomacy and the Military in Shōwa Japan," in Gluck and Graubard, *The Japan of Hirohito,* 169.

[35]Giffard, *Japan among the Powers,* 163.

[36]Mikiso Hane, *Eastern Phoenix: Japan Since 1945* (Boulder, CO: Westview Press, 1996), 108.

[37]John Dower, "The Useful War," in Gluck and Graubard, *The Japan of Hirohito,* 49–70.

[38]Ibid., 65.

[39]Ibid.

[40]Jared Taylor, *Shadows of the Rising Sun* (New York: Quill, 1983), 171, quoted in Hane, *Eastern Phoenix,* 115.

[41]Gary D. Allinson, *The Columbia Guide to Modern Japanese History* (New York: Columbia University Press, 1999), 153.

[42]Hane, *Eastern Phoenix,* 110.

[43]The phrases are from McClain, *Japan,* 582–87.

[44]Ibid., 590.

[45]The security treaty, still in effect in 2007, has not been amended or revised since 1960.

CHAPTER 15

[1]Hildi Kang, ed., *Under the Black Umbrella: Voices from Colonial Korea, 1910–1945* (Ithaca, NY: Cornell University Press, 2001), 147.

[2]Bruce Cumings, *The Origins of the Korean War: Liberation and the Emergence of Separate Regimes, 1945–1947* (Princeton, NJ: Princeton University Press, 1981), 84.

[3]Ibid., 85.

[4]Ibid., 267.

[5]Bruce Cumings, *Korea's Place in the Sun* (New York: W. W. Norton, 2005), 186.

[6]Ibid., 192.

[7]Jeon Sang Sook, "U.S. Korean Policy and the Moderates During the U.S. Military Government Era," in *Korea Under the American Military Government*, ed. Bonnie B. C. Oh (Westport, CT: Praeger, 2002), 91.

[8]If a landlord had not collaborated with the Japanese, he might keep 12.25 acres of land.

[9]Cumings, *Korea's Place in the Sun*, 208.

[10]Ibid., 215.

[11]Andrew Nahm, *Korea: Tradition and Transformation: A History of the Korean People* (Elizabeth, NJ: Hollym, 1988), 358.

[12]The phrase is in Nahm, *Korea: Tradition and Transformation,* 363. The food rations information is in Cumings, *Korea's Place in the Sun,* 212.

[13]Nahm, *Korea: Tradition and Transformation,* 370.

[14]Cumings, *The Origins of the Korean War*, p. 86.

[15]Internet: http://www.korea50,army.mil/history/factsheets/pow.shtml.

[16]Cumings, *Korea's Place in the Sun,* 297.

[17]Ibid., 271.

[18]Ibid., 271–72.

[19]Ibid., 272.

[20]Carter Eckert, Ki-Baik Lee, Young Lew, Michael Robinson, and Edward Wagner, *Korea Old and New—A History* (Cambridge, MA: Harvard Korean Institute, 1990), 345–46.

[21]Cumings, *Korea's Place in the Sun*, 413–14.

[22]Joungwon Alexander Kim, *Divided Korea: The Politics of Development, 1945–1972* (Cambridge, MA: Harvard University Press, 1976), 296–97.

[23]Quoted in Cumings. *Korea's Place in the Sun*, 417.

[24]Don Oberdorfer, *The Two Koreas: A Contemporary History* (New York: Basic Books, 2001), 18.

[25]Ibid., 429.

[26]Kenneth B. Lee, *Korea and East Asia: The Story of a Phoenix* (Westport, CT: Praeger, 1997), 214.

[27]Ibid., 211.

[28]The first phrase is from Hy-sang Lee, *North Korea: A Strange Socialist Fortress* (Westport, CT: Praeger, 2001), 3; the other quotation is from Cumings, *Korea's Place in the Sun*, 406.

[29]Hy-sang Lee, *North Korea: A Strange Socialist Fortress,* 5.

[30]Cumings, *Korea's Place in the Sun*, 346.

[31]Oberdorfer, *The Two Koreas,* 31.

[32]In addition, the United States footed the bill of $300 million for its soldiers stationed in Korea.

[33]Cumings, *Korea's Place in the Sun*, 304.

[34]Internet: http://www.money.cnn.com/magazines/fortune/fortune500.

[35]Illicit wealth included "profiteering from preferential access to government contracts and loans, and misallocation of foreign funds." This was highly controversial. See Steven Haggard, Byung-kook Kim, and Chung-In Moon, "The Transition to Export-led Growth in South Korea, 1954–1966." *The Journal of Asian Studies* 50, no. 4 (November 1991): 858–59.

[36]Joungwon Kim, *Divided Korea,* 240–41.

[37]Cumings, *Korea's Place in the Sun,* 316.

[38]Jung-en Woo, *Race to the Swift: State and Finance in the Industrialization of Korea* (New York: Columbia University Press, 1991), 159.

[39]Oberdorfer, *The Two Koreas,* 37.

[40]Cumings, *Korea's Place in the Sun,* 364.

[41]Ibid., 367.

[42]Oberdorfer, *The Two Koreas,* 41.

[43]Ibid., 43.

[44]Joungwon Kim, *Divided Korea,* 321–22.

[45]Oberdorfer, *The Two Koreas,* 12.

[46]Ibid., 28.

[47]Ibid., 24.

[48]Kenneth Lee, *Korea and East Asia,* 244.

CHAPTER 16

[1]Neil Jamieson, *Understanding Vietnam* (Berkeley: University of California Press, 1993), 180.

[2]David G. Marr, *Vietnamese Tradition on Trial, 1920–1945* (Berkeley: University of California Press, 1981), 401.

[3]Truong Nhu Tang, *A Viet Cong Memoir* (New York: Vintage Books, 1985), 12, 16.

[4]Spencer C. Tucker, ed., *Encyclopedia of the Vietnam War: A Political, Social, and Military History,* entry: "Deer Mission" (New York: Oxford University Press, 2000), 95

[5]The speaker is Archimedes Patti of the OSS. See "Roots of a War" from *Vietnam, A Television History* (Boston: WGBH Transcripts, 1983), 14.

[6]Ibid.

[7]Robert J. McMahon, ed., *Major Problems in the History of the Vietnam War* (Lexington, MA: D. C. Heath, 1990), 35.

[8]Quoted in Jamieson, *Understanding Vietnam,* 196.

[9]Ibid., 198.

[10]Ibid., 199.

[11]Tucker, *Encyclopedia of the Vietnam War,* entry: "Vietnam, Democratic Republic of: 1945–1954," 446.

[12]Quoted in ibid., entry: Document: "Preliminary Franco-Viet Minh Convention (6 March 1946)," 502.

[13]Quoted in Jean Sainteny, *Ho Chi Minh and His Vietnam* (Chicago: Cowles, 1972), 73.

[14]"The First Vietnam War (1946–1954)" from *Vietnam, A Television History,* 2.

[15]Quoted in Tucker, *Encyclopedia of the Vietnam War,* entry: "Indo-China War (1946–1954)," 188.

[16]"The First Vietnam War (1946–1954)" from *Vietnam, A Television History,* 11.

[17]Tang, *A Viet Cong Memoir,* 15.

[18]Bernard B. Fall, *Street without Joy* (Harrisburg, PA: Stackpole, 1961), 32.

[19]Ibid.

[20]Tucker, *Encyclopedia of the Vietnam War,* entry: "Battle of Hoa Binh," 177.

[21]"The First Vietnam War (1946–1954)" from *Vietnam, A Television History,* 9.

[22]This description is Jamieson's in *Understanding Vietnam,* 215.

[23]"The First Vietnam War (1946–1954)" from *Vietnam, A Television History,* 15.

[24]Jamieson, *Understanding Vietnam,* 227.

[25]"The First Vietnam War (1946–1954)" from *Vietnam, A Television History,* 12.

[26]Ibid., 13.

[27]Patrick J. Hearden, *The Tragedy of Vietnam* (New York: Pearson Longman, 2005), 59.

[28]"American's Mandarin (1954–1963)" from *Vietnam, A Television History,* 7.

[29]Jamieson, *Understanding Vietnam,* 236.

[30]George C. Herring, *America's Longest War* (Boston: McGraw-Hill, 2002), 82.

[31]James S. Olson and Randy Roberts, *Where the Domino Fell: America and Vietnam, 1945–1990* (New York: St. Martin's Press, 1991), 68.

[32]Quoted in Frances Fitzgerald, *Fire in the Lake* (Boston: Little, Brown, 1972), 134.

[33]Ibid., 232.

[34]Alexander B. Woodside, *Community and Revolution in Modern Vietnam* (Boston: Houghton Mifflin, 1976), 263.

[35]James S. Olson and Randy Roberts, *My Lai: A Brief History with Documents* (Boston: Bedford Books, 1998), 8.

[36]*Baltimore Sun,* August 6, 2006, 16a.

[37]Westmoreland's quotation is from the film *Hearts and Minds;* the explanation is available on the Internet: http://www.sjgarchive.org/library/text/ontogeny/p0126.htm.

[38]The statement is from *Hearts and Minds;* See the Internet: http://www.homepage.newschool.edu/~wilder/ArgumentbyIrony.html.

[39]Tucker, *Encyclopedia of the Vietnam War,* entry: "Ho Chi Minh Trail," 176.

[40]"Tet, 1968" from *Vietnam, A Television History,* 4.

[41]Townsend Hoopes, *The Limits of Intervention (*New York: David McKay, 1970), 145, quoted in Herring, *America's Longest War,* 233.

[42]The quoted phrase is from Olson and Roberts, *Where the Domino Fell,* 225–26.

[43]"Peace Is at Hand (1968–1973)" from *Vietnam, A Television History,* 16.

[44]Ibid., 14.

[45]Ibid., 18.

[46]Olson and Roberts, *Where the Domino Fell,* 258.

[47]Tucker, *Encyclopedia of the Vietnam War,* entry: "Van Tien Dung," 439.

[48]Olson and Roberts, *Where the Domino Fell,* 261.

[49]Ibid., 19.

CHAPTER 17

[1]"Quarterly Documentation," *China Quarterly* 77 (March 1979): 168.

[2]Internet: http://www.english.peopledaily.com.cn/200507/27/eng20050727_198605.jtml.

[3]Jonathan D. Pollack, "The Opening to America," in *The Cambridge History of China, Vol. 15, The People's Republic, Part 2: Revolutions within the Chinese Revolution, 1966–1982,* ed. Roderick MacFarquhar and John K. Fairbank (Cambridge: Cambridge University Press, 1991), 423–24.

[4]Wei Jingsheng, "Democracy or a New Dictatorship?" *Explorations* (March 1979), reprinted in Gregor Benton and Alan Hunter, eds., *Wild Lily, Prairie Fire* (Princeton, NJ: Princeton University Press, 1995), 182.

[5]The specific charge of spying was that he had turned over information to a foreign journalist about the just finished debacle of China's invasion of Vietnam.

[6]Richard Baum, *Burying Mao: Chinese Politics in the Age of Deng Xiaoping* (Princeton, NJ: Princeton University Press, 1994), 201.

[7]Ibid., 176.

[8]Quoted in Geremie Barmé, *In the Red* (New York: Columbia University Press, 1999), 329.

[9]"Li Peng's Announcement of Martial Law, May 20, 1989," in Pei-kai Cheng and Michael Lestz with Jonathan Spence, *The Search for Modern China: A Documentary Collection* (New York: W. W. Norton, 1999), 497.

[10]The most favored nation status would permit China to trade at the normal tariff level enjoyed by U.S. trading partners.

[11]Elizabeth J. Perry, "China in 1992: An Experiment in New-Authoritarianism," *Asian Survey* 33 (January 1993): 18.

[12]Baum, *Burying Mao,* 339.

[13]"Main Points of Deng Xiaoping's Talks in Wuchang, Shenzhen, Zhuhai, and Shanghai from January 18 to February 21, 1992" in *China Since Tiananmen,* ed. Lawrence R. Sullivan (Armonk, NY: M. E. Sharpe, 1995), 151.

[14]Maurice Meisner, *Mao's China and After* (New York: Free Press, 1999), 521.

[15]Li Cheng, "China in 2000: A Year of Strategic Rethinking," *Asian Survey* 41. no. 1 (January–February 2001): 84.

[16]Richard Kraus, "China in 2003: From SARS to Spaceships," *Asian Survey* 44, no. 1 (January–February 2004): 154.

[17]Ibid., 148.

[18]Melvyn C. Goldstein, *A History of Modern Tibet, 1913–1951* (Berkeley: University of California Press, 1989), 765.

[19]*The Straits Times* (Singapore), June 29, 2006, 7.

[20]Internet: http://www.uofaweb.ualberta.ca/chinainstitute/nav03=44057&nav02=43872&nav01=43092.

[21]Truong Nhu Tang, *A Viet Cong Memoir* (New York: Vintage Books, 1986), 289.

[22]Neil L. Jamieson, *Understanding Vietnam* (Berkeley: University of California Press, 1993), 360.

[23]Steven J. Hood, *Dragons Entangled: Indochina and the China-Vietnam War* (Armonk, NY: M. E. Sharpe, 1992), 50.

[24]Robert Templer, *Shadows and Wind: A View of Modern Vietnam* (New York: Penguin, 1999), 4.

[25]Ibid.

[26]Ibid., 90.

[27]Ibid., 117.

[28]People's Daily Online: http://www.english.people.com.cn/200603/22/eng2006032_252443.html.

[29]Internet:http://www.washingtonpost.com/nipdyn/content/2005/06/16/AR2005061601756_5.html.

CHAPTER 18

[1]Quoted in Chushichi Tsuzuki, *The Pursuit of Power in Modern Japan, 1825–1995* (Oxford: Oxford University Press, 2000), 424.
[2]Ibid., 430.
[3]Andrew Gordon, *A Modern History of Japan* (New York: Oxford University Press, 2003), 292.
[4]Mikiso Hane, *Eastern Phoenix, Japan since 1945* (Boulder, CO: Westview Press, 1996), 55.
[5]Tsuzuki, *The Pursuit of Power,* 432.
[6]Akira Iriye, *Japan and the Wider World* (London: Longman, 1997), 180.
[7]Sydney Giffard, *Japan among the Powers, 1890–1990* (New Haven, CT: Yale University Press, 1994), 191.
[8]"The Plaza Accord," in David J. Liu, *Japan, A Documentary History* (Armonk, NY: M. E. Sharpe, 1997), 557.
[9]John Hunter Boyle, *Modern Japan: The American Nexus* (Fort Worth, TX: Harcourt Brace Jovanovich College Publishers, 1993), 400.
[10]Ibid., 402.
[11]Ibid., 392
[12]The commentator is James Fallows, quoted in ibid., 397.
[13]Ibid., 385.
[14]The term *new rich* and the general description of these groups come from James L. McClain, *Japan, A Modern History* (New York: W. W. Norton, 2002), 582–87.
[15]Ezra Vogel, *Japan's New Middle Class* (Berkeley: University of California Press, 1968), 268.
[16]McClain, *Japan,* 589.
[17]Norma Field, *In the Realm of a Dying Emperor* (New York: Vintage House, 1993), 20.
[18]Tsuzuki, *The Pursuit of Power,* 449.
[19]Field, *In the Realm of a Dying Emperor,* 178.
[20]Alex Kerr, *Dogs and Demons: Tales from the Dark Side of Japan* (New York: Hill and Wang, 2001), 142.
[21]Gordon, *A Modern History of Japan,* 326.
[22]Ibid., 323.
[23]Internet:http://www.nytimes.com/2006/04/16/world/asia/16japan.html?ex=1302840000&en=146ba57.
[24]Hane, *Eastern Phoenix,* 126.
[25]Internet: http://www.ed.wikipedia.org/wiki/ HIV-tainted_blood_scandal_(Japan).
[26]Internet: http://www.pinr.com/report.php?ac=view_report&report_id=286&language_id=1.
[27]Giffard, *Japan among the Powers,* 195.
[28]Quoted in Hane, *Eastern Phoenix,* 94.

CHAPTER 19

[1]Andrew C. Nahm, *Korea, Tradition and Transformation* (Elizabeth, NJ: Hollym, 1991), 467.
[2]The phrase is from Bruce Cumings, *Korea's Place in the Sun* (New York: W. W. Norton, 2005), 382.
[3]Ibid., 386.
[4]Carter Eckert, Ki-Baik Lee, Young Lew, Michael Robinson, and Edward Wagner, *Korea Old and New: A History* (Cambridge, MA: Korean Harvard Institute, 1990), 377.
[5]Cumings, *Korea's Place in the Sun,* 385.
[6]Ibid., 383.
[7]The description is from Don Oberdorfer, *The Two Koreas: A Contemporary History* (New York: Basic Books, 2001), 174.
[8]Ibid., 178.
[9]Ibid., 174.
[10]Ibid., 379.
[11]Cumings, *Korea's Place in the Sun,* 395.
[12]Uk Heo and Sunwoong Kim, "Financial Crisis in South Korea: Failure of the Government-Led Development Paradigm," *Asian Survey* 40, no. 3 (May–June 2000): 494.
[13]Cumings, *Korea's Place in the Sun,* 334.
[14]The phrase appears in Mark E. Manyin, "South Korea-U.S. Economic Relations: Cooperation, Friction, and Future Prospects," in the Congressional Research Service's *Report for Congress* (July 1, 2004), CRS-3. Internet: http://www. RL30566.pdf.
[15]Cumings, *Korea's Place in the Sun,* 336.
[16]Young-Kwan Yoon, "South Korea in 1999: Overcoming Cold War Legacies," *Asian Survey* 40, no. 1 (January–February 2000): 167.
[17]Cumings, *Korea's Place in the Sun,* 398.
[18]Yoon, "South Korea in 1999," 167.

[19]Manyin, "South Korea-U.S. Economic Relations," CRS-6.

[20]See the analysis of Cumings, *Korea's Place in the Sun,* 400.

[21]See Yoon-Chool Ha, "South Korea in 2001: Frustration and Continuing Uncertainty," *Asia Survey* 42, no. 1 (January–February 2002): 59–60.

[22]Cumings, *Korea's Place in the Sun,* 401.

[23]Yoav Cerralbo, "The President vs. the Dailies: Korea's Number 1 Boxing Match," *The Seoul Times* (July 31, 2006). Internet: http://www.theseoultimes.com/ST/?url=/ST/db/read.php?idx=1162.

[24]Quoted in Oberdorfer, *The Two Koreas,* 21.

[25]Ibid., 22.

[26]Cumings, *Korea's Place in the Sun,* 405.

[27]Ibid., 406.

[28]Daniel Goodkind and Loraine West, "The North Korean Famine and Its Demographic Impact, *Population and Development Review* 27, no. 2 (June 2001): 220.

[29]Cumings, *Korea's Place in the Sun,* 442.

[30]Samuel S. Kim, "North Korea in 1999: Bringing the Grand *Chollina* March Back In," *Asian Survey* 40, no. 1 (January–February 2000): 151.

[31]Goodkind and West, "The North Korean Famine," 234.

[32]*The Guardian*, August 4, 2006: Internet: http://www.guardian.co.uk/korea/article/0.,1836986,00.html?gusrc=rs.

[33]Hy-Sang Lee, *North Korea: A Strange Socialist Fortress* (Westport, CT: Praeger, 2001), 196.

[34]Oberdorfer, *The Two Koreas,* 346.

[35]Ibid., 348. The couple worked with Kim in making films in North Korea before their escape to Vienna in 1986.

[36]Samuel S. Kim, "Surviving through High Hopes of Summit Diplomacy," *Asian Survey* 41, no. 1 (January–February 2001): 26.

[37]Yinhay Ahn, "North Korea in 2001: At a Crossroads," *Asian Survey* 42, no. 1 (January–February 2002): 47.

[38]Oberdorfer, *The Two Koreas,* 185.

[39]Ibid., 186.

[40]Internet: http//www.washingtontimes.com/world/20040219-094837-2967r.htm.

[41]Oberdorfer, *The Two Koreas,* 427.

[42]Ibid.

[43]Ibid., 430.

[44]See, for example. Ha, "South Korea in 2001," 57. Also see the http://english.chosun.com/w21data/html/news/200607/200607310026.html.

[45]See http://www.nobelprize.org/nobel_prizes/peace/laureates/2000/

[46]Cumings, *Korea's Place in the Sun,* 493–94.

[47]Ibid., 479, 488.

[48]Ibid., 489.

[49]Hy-Sang Lee, *North Korea: A Strange Socialist Fortress* (Westport, CT: Praeger, 2001), 184.

[50]See http://www.wisconsinproject.org/countries.nkorea/bm98.html.

[51]Eric Hundman, "Engage the 'axis of evil'": see http://www.sin.ethz.ch/news/sw/ details.cfm? ID=16469.

[52]Cumings, *Korea's Place in the Sun,* 504.

[53]Internet: http://www.chinapost.com.tw/editorial/detail.asp?ID=85856&GRP=i.

[54]Bertil Lintner, *Great Leader, Dear Leader: Demystifying North Korea Under the Kim Clan* (Chiang Mai, Thailand: Silkworm Books, 2005), 194.

[55]Dianne E. Rennack, "North Korea: Economic Sanctions" *Report for Congress*. Internet: http://www.fas.org/man/crs/RL31696.pdf.

[56]Internet: http://www.hindu.com/thehindu/holnus/003200607111014.htm.

[57]B. C. Koh, "Six-Party Talks: Round 3": Internet:http://www.nautilus.org/fora/security/0426A_ KOH.html.

[58]Internet: http://www.wsws.org/articles/2006/dec2006/kore-d28.shtml.

CHAPTER 20

[1]Nicholas D. Kristof and Sheryl Wudunn, *China Wakes* (New York: Random House, 1994), 14.

[2]"China's Supersized Mall," *Christian Science Monitor* online: http://www.csmonitor.com/2004/1124/p01s03-woap.html.

[3]Cited in Charlotte Ikels, *The Return of the God of Wealth* (Stanford: Stanford University Press, 1996), 269.

[4]Internet: http://www.icsc.org/about/affiliates_taiwan.php.

[5]Internet: http://www.vanguardonline.f9.co.uk/0612tw4.htm.

[6]Internet: http://www.moviemartyr.com/1992/**rebels**ofthe**neongod**.htm.

[7]James L. McClain, *Japan, A Modern History* (New York: W. W. Norton, 2002), 591.

[8]Internet: http://www.washtimes.com/world/20060427-101330-4859r_page2.htm.

[9]McClain, *Japan,* 595.

[10]Quoted in Sheldon Garon, *Molding Japanese Minds* (Princeton, NJ: Princeton University Press, 1997), 321–32.

[11]McClain, *Japan,* 622.

[12]This data comes from the Newsweek International Online edition: http://www.msnbc.msn.com/id/10854742/site/newsweek.

[13]Internet: http://www.keywords.oxus.net/archives/category/education/inequalityinKorea.

[14]Jack F. Williams, "Paying the Price of Economic Development: Environmental Degradation," in *The Other Taiwan: 1945 to the Present,* ed. Murray A. Rubinstein (Armonk, NY: M. E. Sharpe, 1994), 241.

[15]"The Legacy of Agent Orange": http://www.news.bbc.co.uk/2/hi/asia-pacific/4494347.stm.

[16]Internet: http://www.enn.com/today.html?id=8830.

[17]Alex Kerr, *Dogs and Demons: Tales from the Dark Side of Japan* (New York: Hill and Wang, 2001), 57.

[18]It is said that overall in Japan plaintiffs with lawsuits against the state win a mere 5 percent of the cases.

[19]Alex Kirby, "North Korea's Environmental Crisis," BBC News online: http://www.news.bbc.co.uk/2/hi/science/nature/83598966:stm.

[20]Ibid.

[21]Wang Zheng, "Gender, Employment, and Women's Resistance," in Elizabeth J. Perry and Mark Selden, *Chinese Society: Change, Conflict, and Resistance,* 2nd ed. (London: RoutledgeCurzon, 2003), 178.

[22]Catherine S. Farris, "The Social Discourse on Women's Roles in Taiwan: A Textual Analysis," in Rubinstein, *The Other Taiwan,* 320.

[23]McClain, *Japan,* 613.

[24]Ibid., 617–18.

[25]Richard Baum, *Burying Mao: Chinese Politics in the Age of Deng Xiaoping* (Princeton, NJ: Princeton University Press, 1994), 231–32.

[26]Ikels, *The Return of the God of Wealth,* 269.

[27]Joseph Kahn, "Where's Mao? Chinese Revise History Books," *The New York Times,* September 1, 2006, Internet: http://www.nytime.com/2006/09/01/world/asia/01china.html?ex=1314763200&en=abf86c087b22be74&ei=5088&partner=rssnyt&emc=rss.

[28]Murray A. Rubinstein, "Political Taiwanization and Pragmatic Diplomacy: The Eras of Chiang Ching-kuo and Lee Teng-hui, 1971–1994," in *Taiwan: A New History,* ed. Murray A. Rubinstein (Armonk, NY: M. E. Sharpe, 1999), 441.

[29]Hung-mao Tien, "Taiwan's Evolution Toward Democracy: A Historical Perspective," in *Taiwan, Beyond the Economic Miracle,* ed. Denis Fred Simon and Michael Y. M. Kau (Armonk, NY: M. E. Sharpe, 1992), 9.

[30]See *The Straits Times* (Singapore), June 28, 2006, 7, and June 29, 2006, 6.

[30]Ibid., 162.

[32]Quoted in Gary Klintworth, *New Taiwan, New China: Taiwan's Changing Role in the Asia-Pacific Region* (New York: St. Martin's Press, 1995), 63.

[33]This was reported by the travel guide Nguyen Minh Thang in late June 2006.

[34]Quoted in Chushichi Tsuzuki, *The Pursuit of Power in Modern Japan, 1825–1995* (Oxford: Oxford University Press, 2006), 439.

[35]Andrew Gordon, *A Modern History of Japan* (New York: Oxford University Press, 2003), 300–301.

[36]Tsuzuki, *The Pursuit of Power in Modern Japan,* 441.

[37]Ibid.

[38]Hy-sang Lee, *North Korea: A Strange Socialist Fortress* (Westport, CT: Praeger, 2001), 220.

[39]Nicholas Kristof "The Hermit Nuclear Kingdom," *New York Review of Books* (February 10, 2005); Internet: http://www.nybooks.com/articles/17721.

[40]Internet: http://www.wikitravel.or/en/North_Korea#By_train.

[41]Don Oberdorfer. *The Two Koreas* (New York: Basic Books, 2001), 235–36.

[42]Mark Manyin, "South Korean Politics and Rising Anti-Americanism: Implications for U.S. Policy toward North Korea," Report for Congress; Internet: http://www.27530.pdf. Manyin argues that sharp critics of the United States tend to be under the age of fifty; he divides them into three groups: radical leftists, who have traditionally been anti-American; nationalists, who resent the intrusion of the United States into Korean life; and individuals who still support the Cold War alliance between Seoul and Washington but who oppose U.S. policy on specific issues.

[43]The phrase is from Meredith Woo-Cumings, "South Korean Anti-Americanism," Japan Policy Research Institute Working Paper, Number 93 (July 2003). Internet: http://www.jpri.org/publications/workingpapers/wp93.html.

[44]Ibid.

[45]Quoted in Woo-Cumings, "South Korean Anti-Americanism."

[46]For an analysis of perceptions of racism, see James I. Matray, "Why South Koreans Think of the United States as a Global Bully," History News Network. Internet: http://www.hnn.us/articles/3740.html.

Phonetic Spellings of Chinese, Japanese, Korean, and Vietnamese Words

CHINESE PEOPLE

Pinyin	Phonetic	Pinyin	Phonetic
Bei Dao	bay dow	Liu Shaoqi	lee-o shaow chee
Cai Yuanpei	tsigh you-en pay	Lu Hsiu-lien	loo she-o lee-en
Chai Ling	chigh leeng	Lu Xun	lu shwun
Chen Duxiu	chun doo-sheeoh	Mao Zedong	mao dzi dung
Chen Shuibian	chun shway bee-en	Peng Dehuai	pung duh why
Cixi, Empress Dowager	tsi-she	Qianlong emperor	chee-en lung
Daoguang emperor	dow gwahng	Qing dynasty	ching
Deng Xiaoping	dung she-ow peeng	Qiu Jin	chee-oh jeen
Fang Lizhi	fahng lee-jer	Song Jiaoren	soong jee-ow ren
Fei Xiaotong	fay shee-ow tohng	Sun Yixian	sun yee shee-en
Feng Yuxiang	fung you shee-ahng	Tongzhi emperor	tonhg jer
Guangxu emperor	gwahng shu	Wang Dan	wahng dahn
Hong Xiuquan	hung she-o chew-on	Wang Jingwei	wahng jeeng way
Hu Qiaomu	who chee-ow moo	Wu'er Kaixi	woo-er khigh she
Hu Shi	who sher	Wei Jingsheng	way jeeng shung
Hu Yaobang	who yao bahng	Yongzheng emperor	yohng jeng
Hua Guofeng	hwah gwo fung	Yu Xian	you shee-en
Jiang Jieshi	jee-ahng jee-eh sher	Yuan Shikai	yu-en sher khigh
Jiang Zemin	jee-ahng dzi-mean	Zeng Guofan	dzung guo-fahn
Jiangqing emperor	jee-ahng ching	Zhang Xueliang	jahng shueh leeahng
Kang Youwei	kahng you way	Zhang Zhidong	jahng jer-dung
Kangxi emperor	kahng she	Zhang Zongchang	jahng dzung chahng
Kong Fuzi	kohng foo-zeh	Zhang Zuolin	jahng dzwo lin
Lee Tenghui	lee tongue-hway	Zhao Ziyang	jao dzi yahng
Li Dazhao	lee dah jao	Zhou Enlai	jo en lai
Li Hongzhang	lee hung jahng	Zhu De	joo duh
Li Peng	lee pung	Zhu Rongji	joo rong jee
Liang Qichao	lee-ahng chee chow	Zou Rong	dzoh ruong
Lin Biao	lin bee-ow	Zuo Zongtong	dzwo dzung tahng
Lin Zexu	lin dzi-shu		

CHINESE PLACES

Pinyin	Phonetic	Pinyin	Phonetic
Changsha	chahng sha	Macao	meh cow
Chengdu	chung doo	Nanjing	nahn jing
Chongqing	chong ching	Ningbo	neeng bwo
Dagu forts	dah goo	Qiantang	chee-en tahng
Dalian	dah lee-en	Qinghai	ching high
Fujian	foo jee-en	Qingdao	ching dao
Fuzhou	foo joe	Shaanxi	shen she
Gansu	gahn su	Shandong	shahn dung
Gaoxiong	gow see-ohng	Shanxi	shahn she
Guangzhou	gwahng jo	Shenzhen	shun jun
Guilin	gway lin	Sichuan	si chew-an
Hainan	high nahn	Taibei	tigh bay
Hangzhou	hahng jo	Tianjin	tee-en jeen
Hankou	hahn co	Urumqi	you room chee
Hebei	huh bay .	Wuchang	woo chahng
Henan	huh nahn	Xi'an	she ahn
Hubei	who bay	Xiamen	she-ah mun
Hunan	who nahn	Xinjiang	sheen jee-ahng
Jiangsu	jeeahng su	Yan'an	yen ahn
Jiangxi	jeeahng she	Zhejiang	juh jeeahng
Jiaozhou bay	jee-ow jo	Zhili	jer lee
Liaodong	lee-ow dung	Zhuhai	joo high
Liuqui islands	lee-oo chee-oo	Zunyi	dzwun ee

JAPANESE PEOPLE

Romanization	*Phonetic*
Abe Masahiro	ah-bay mah-sah-he-roe
Abe Shinzō	ah-bay shin-zoe
Aizawa Seishisai	ah-ee-zah-wah say-ee-she-sah-ee
Aizawa Saburō	ah-ee-zah-waw sah-buu-roe
Akihito, emperor	ah-kee-he-toe
Amaterasu	ah-mah-tay-rahss
Arai Hakuseki	ah-rah-ee ha-kuu-say-kee
Asanuma Inejirō	ah-sah-nuu-mah ee-nay-jee-roe
Ashikaga shogunate	ah-she-kah-gah
Bashō	bah-show
Chikamatsu Monzaemon	chee-kah-mah-t'sue moan-zah-eh-moan
Doi Takako	doe-ee tah-kah-koe
Dōshikai	doe-she-kah-ee
Fukuda Takeo	fuu-kuu-dah tah-kay-oh
Fukuzawa Yukichi	fuu-kuu-zah-wah you-kee-chi
Genroku period	gen-roe-kuu
Hamaguchi Osachi	hah-mah-goo-chi oh-sah-chee
Hara Kei	hah-rah kay-ee
Hashimoto Ryūtarō	hah-she-moe-toe ryuu-tah-roe
Hatoyama Haruko	hah-toe-yah-mah hah-ruu-koh
Hirata Atsutane	he-rah-tah ah-t'sue-tah-nay
Hirohito	he-roe-he-toe
Hōtoku movement	hoe-toe-kuu
Hotta Masayoshi	hoet-tah mah-say-yoe-she
Ii Naosuke	ee ee nah-oh-skay
Ikeda Hayato	ee-kay-dah hah-yah-toe
Inoue Kaoru	ee-no-uu-eh kah-oh-ruu
Inukai Tsuyoshi	ee-nuu-ka-ee t'sue-yoe-she
Itagaki Taisuke	ee-tah-gah-kee tie-skay
Itō Hirobumi	ee-toe he-roe-buu-mee
Iwakura Tomomi	ee-wah-kuu-rah toe-moe-mee
Kaifu Toshiki	kah-ee-fuu toe-she-kee
Katsura Tarō	kah-t'sue-rah tah-roe
Kenseikai	ken-say-ee-kah-ee
Kido Kōin	kee-doe koe-een
Kishi Nobusuke	kee-she no-buu-skay
Kita Ikki	kee-tah eek-kee
Koizumi Junichirō	koe-ee-zuu-me june-ee-chee-roe
Konoe Fumimaro	koe-no-eh fuu-me-mah-roe
Meiji emperor	may-ee-jee
Miki Takeo	me-kee tah-kay-oh
Minobe Tatsukichi	me-no-bay tah-t'sue-kee-chee

JAPANESE PEOPLE (*Continued*)

Romanization	Phonetic
Minseitō party	mean-say-toe
Miyazawa Kiichi	me-yah-zah-wah kee-ee-chee
Mori Ōgai	moe-ree oh-gah-ee
Motoori Norinaga	moe-toe—oh-ree no-ree-nah-gah
Nagata Tetsuzan	nah-gah-tah tay-t'sue-zan
Nakasone Yasuhiro	nah-kah-so-nay yah-suu-he-roe
Ninomiya Sontoku	nee-no-me-yah sewn-toe-kuu
Oda Nobunaga	oh-dah no-buu-nah-gah
Ōkubō Toshimichi	oh-kuu-boe toe-she-me-chee
Ōkuma Shigenobu	oh-kuu-mah she-gay-no-buu
Ōshio Heihachirō	oh-she-oh hay-hah-chee-roe
Rai San'yō	rah-ee sahn-yoe
Saikaku	sah-ee-kah-kuu
Saigō Takamori	sah-ee-go tah-kah-moe-ree
Sakamoto Ryōma	sah-kah-moe-toe ryoe-mah
Satō Eisaku	sah-toe eh-ee-sah-kuu
Seiyūkai	say-you-kah-ee
Shibusawa Eiichi	she-buu-sah-wah eh-ee-chee
Shimazu Nariakira	she-mah-zuu nah-ree-ah-kee-rah
Shidehara Kijūrō	she-day-hah-rah kee-juu-roe
Shingaku movement	sheen-gah-kuu
Prince Shōtoku	show-toe-kuu
Shōwa emperor	show-wah
Suzuki Zenkō	sue-zuu-kee zen-koe
Taishō emperor	tie-show
Takeshita Noburu	tah-kesh-ta no-buu-ruu
Tanaka Kakuei	tah-nah-kah kah-kuu-eh-ee
Tanizaki Jun'ichirō	tah-nee-zah-kee june-ee-chee-roh
Tōjō Hideki	toe-joe he-day-kee
Tokugawa Ieyasu	toe-kuu-gah-wah ee-eh-yah-su
Tokugawa Nariaki	toe-kuu-gah-wah nah-ree-ah-kee
Toyotomi Hideyoshi	toe-yoe-toe-me he-day-yoe-she
Tsuda Umeko	t'sue-dah uu-may-koe
Yamagata Aritomo	yah-mah-gah-tah ah-ree-toe-moe
Yanaihara Tadao	yah-nah-ee-hah-rah tah-dah-oh
Yoshida Shigeru	yoe-she-dah she-gay-ruu
Yoshida Shōin	yoe-she-dah show-een
Yoshino Sakuzō	yoe-she-no sah-kuu-zoe

JAPANESE PLACES

Romanization	Phonetic	Romanization	Phonetic
Aomori	ah-oh-moe-ree	Mito	me-toe
Chōshū	choe-shuu	Minamata Bay	me-nah-mah-tah
Deshima	day-she-mah	Nagasaki	nah-gah-sah-kee
Edo	eh-doe	Nagoya	nah-goyah
Fukuoka	fuu-kuu-oh-kah	Nikko	neek-koe
Funai	fuu-na-ee	Osaka	oh-sah-kah
Hakodate	hah-koh-dah-tay	Ryūkyū islands	ryuu-kee'yu
Hiroshima	he-roe-she-mah	Satsuma	sah-t'sue-mah
Hizen	hee-zen	Sekigahara	say-kee-gah-ha-rah
Hokkaido	hoek-kah-ee-doe	Shikoku	she-koe-kuu
Honshu	hone-shuu	Shimane	she-mah-nay
Ise	ee-say	Shimoda	she-moe-dah
Kagoshima	kah-go-she-mah	Shimonoseki	she-moe-no-say-kee
Kanagawa	kah-nah-gah-wah	Takeshima	tah-kay-she-mah
Karatsu	kah-rah-t'sue	Tosa	toe-sah
Kobe	koh-bay	Toyama	toe-yah-mah
Kumamoto	kuu-mah-moe-toe	Tsushima	t'sue-she-mah
Kyoto	k'yoe-toe	Usuki	uu-sue-kee
Kyushu	kee'yu-shu	Utsonimiya	uu-t'sue-no-me-yah
Mikawa	me-kah-wah	Wakayama	wah-kah-yah-mah

KOREAN PEOPLE

Romanization	Phonetic	Romanization	Phonetic
An Chang-ho	ahn chahng-hoe	Kim Yŏng-ju	gim yuhng-joo
Chang Myŏn	chang myuhn	Kim Young-sam	gim young-sahm
Chŏng Yag-yong	juhng yahg-yong	Kojong, king	goh-jong
Ch'oe Che-u	chay jay-oo	Min Yŏng-hwan	men yuhng-hwahn
Ch'oe Ik-hyŏn	chay lik-hyuhn	Pak Hŏn-yŏng	bahk huhn-yuhng
Ch'ŏlchong, king	chuhl-jong	Pak Yŏng-hyo	bahk yuhng-hyo
Ch'ŏndogyo	chuhn-doe-gyo	Park Chung-hee	bahk juhng-hee
Chŏng Chu-yŏng	juhng joo-yuhng	Roh Moo-hyun	roh moo-hyuhn
Chŏngjo, king	juhng-joe	Roh Tae-woo	roh tay-oo
Chun Doo-hwan	juhn joo-hwahn	Sado, Prince	sah-doh
Hyegyŏng, Lady	hyeh-gyuhng	Sŏ Chae-p'il	suh jay-pill
Hyŏn Sang-yun	hyuhn sahng-yoon	Taewŏn'gun	day-wuhn-goon
Kim Chae-gyu	gim jay-gyoo	Tonghak	dong-hahk
Kim Chong-p'il	gim jong-pill	Yi Sun-shin	ee soon-shiin
Kim Dae-jung	gim day-juhng	Yi Sŭng-man	ee suhng-mahn
Kim Il-sung	gim il-suhng	Yi Tong-hwi	ee dong-hwee
Kim Kyu-sik	gim gyoo-shik	Yŏ Unhyŏng	yuh oon-hyuhng
Kim Ok-kyun	gim ohg-gyoon	Yŏngjo, king	yuhng-joe

KOREAN PLACES

Romanization	Phonetic	Romanization	Phonetic
Cheju	jay-joo	Pusan	boo-sahn
Chŏlla	juhl-lah	P'yŏngyang	pyuhng-yahng
Ch'ungch'ŏng	choong-chuhng	Seoul	suh-ool
Inch'ŏn	een-chuhn	Taedong River	day-dong
Kangwha	Gahng-hwa	Tongnae	dong-lay
Kyŏngju	gyuhng-joo	Wŏnsan	wuhn-sahn
Kyŏngsang	gyuhng-sahng	Yongbyŏn	yuhng-byuhn
P'anmunjŏm	pahn-moon-juhm		

VIETNAMESE PEOPLE

Romanization	Phonetic	Romanization	Phonetic
Bao Dai	bao dye	Nguyen Anh	nwit'n ine
Bui Tin	bwee deen	Nguyen Cao Ky	nwit'n gao gee
Cao Dai	gao dye	Nguyen Minh Triet	nwit'n meen dree-et
Cuong De	geung day	Nguyen Phu Trong	nwit'n fuu droong
Dong Kinh Nghia Thuc	doong geen ngee-ya thuk	Nguyen Tan Dung	nwit'n done zuum
		Nguyen Thai Hoc	nwit'n tye hawp
Duong Van Minh	zeung van meen	Nguyen Van Thieu	nwit'n van tee-u
Duy Tan, emperor	zwee done	Nguyen Van Vinh	nwit'n van veen
Gia Long, emperor	za loong	Le dynasty	lay dynasty
Ham Nghi, emperor	ham ngee	Pham Dinh Phung	fam deen fuum
Ho Chi Minh	hoo chee meen	Pham Quynh	fam gween
Hoa Hao	hwa hao	Pham Van Dong	fam van doong
Huang Duc Nha	hwang deuk nya	Phan Boi Chau	fan boy joe
Huynh Phu So	hween fuu soo	Phan Van Khai	fan van kye
Khai Dinh, emperor	kye deen	Quang Trung, emperor	gwang juum
Le Duc Tho	lay deuk thaw	Tay Son rebellion	day son
Le Duan	lay zwuan	Trinh	jeen
Minh Mang, emperor	meen mang	Truong Chinh	jeung jeen
Ngo Dinh Diem	ngoo deen zee-em	Tu Duc, emperor	de duk
Ngo Dinh Nhu	ngoo deen nyuu	Van Tien Dung	van dee-en zuum
Nguyen Ai Quoc	nwit'n ai gweuk	Vo Nguyen Giap	vaw ngwen zap
Nguyen An Ning	nwit'n an ning	Vo Van Kiet	vaw van gee-et

VIETNAMESE PLACES

Romanization	Phonetic	Romanization	Phonetic
Annam	an nam	My Tho	mee tho
Buon Ma Thuot	ban may twu-ot	Nghe An	ngay an
Ben Tre	ben jeh	Nghe-Tinh soviets	ngay deen soviets
Bien Hoa	bee-en hwa	Nha Trang	nya jang
Ca Mau	ca maw	Ninh Binh	neen been
Can Tho	kan tho	Pac Bo	back boo
Cao Bang	gao bang	Phuoc Long	fwu-ok loong
Cochinchina	koo cheen china	Poulo Condore	pwoo loo coon door
Danang	da nang	Quang Tri	gwang jee
Dienbienphu	dee-en bee-en fuu	Qui Nhon	gwee nyoon
Ha Tinh	ha deen	Saigon	sye gone
Haiphong	hye fong	Thai Nguyen	tye ngwit'n
Halong Bay	ha loong	Thanh Hoa	tang hwa
Hanoi	ha noo-ee	Tonkin	tawn keen
Ho Chi Minh City	hoo chee meen city	Vinh	veen
Hoa Binh	hwa been	Yen Bay	yen bye
Hue	hway		

Map Sources

Map 2-1: Felipe Fernández-Armesto, *The World: A History* (Upper Saddle River, NJ: Pearson Prentice Hall, 2007), 685.

Map 2-2: R. Keith Schoppa, *Revolution and Its Past: Identities and Change in Modern Chinese History* (Upper Saddle River, NJ: Pearson Prentice Hall, 2006), 56.

Map 3-1: Patricia Ebrey, Anne Walthall, and James B. Palais, *East Asia: A Cultural, Social, and Political History* (Boston: Houghton Mifflin, 2005), 380.

Map 3-2: R. Keith Schoppa, *Revolution and Its Past* (Upper Saddle River, NJ: Pearson Prentice Hall, 2006), 112.

Map 4-1: Alexander B. Woodside, (*Community and Revolution in Modern Vietnam* (Boston: Houghton Mifflin, 1976), frontispiece.

Map 4-2: Hue-Tam Ho Tai, *Millenarianism and Peasant Politics in Vietnam* (Cambridge, MA: Harvard University Press, 1983), 62.

Map 5-1: Tsuzuki Chūshichi, *Pursuit of Power in Modern Japan, 1825–1995* (Oxford: Oxford University Press, 2000), 484.

Map 5-2: John Whitney Hall, ed., *The Cambridge History of Japan, Vol. 4, Early Modern Japan* (Cambridge: Cambridge University Press, 1991), 543.

Map 6-1: Arthur Walworth, *Black Ships Off Japan: The Story of Commodore Perry's Expedition* (Hamdon, CT: Archon Books, 1966), 110.

Map 6-2: James L. McClain, *Japan, A Modern History* (New York: W. W. Norton, 2002), 139.

Map 7-1: Marius B. Jansen and Gilbert Rozman, eds., *Japan in Transition, from Tokugawa to Meiji* (Princeton, NJ: Princeton University Press, 1986), 327.

Map 7-2: James L. McClain, *Japan, A Modern History* (New York: W. W. Norton, 2002), 305.

Map 8-1: Andrew Nahm, *Korea, Tradition and Transformation* (Elizabeth, NJ: Hollym, 1991), 98.

Map 8-2: Carter J. Eckert, et. al., *Korea: Old and New—A History* (Seoul: Ilchokak, 1990), 219.

Map 9-1: R. Keith Schoppa, *Revolution and Its Past*. (Upper Saddle River, NJ: Pearson Prentice Hall, 2006), 195.

Map 9-2: Hans J. Van de Ven, *War and Nationalism in China, 1925–1945* (London: Routledge Curzon, 2003), 191.

Map 10-1: R. Keith Schoppa, *Revolution and Its Past* (Upper Saddle River, NJ: Pearson Prentice Hall, 2006), 95.

Map 10-2: R. Keith Schoppa, *Revolution and Its Past* (Upper Saddle River, NJ: Pearson Prentice Hall, 2006), 251.

Map 11-1: William Duiker, *The Rise of Nationalism in Vietnam, 1900–1941* (Ithaca, NY: Cornell University Press, 1976), frontispiece.

Map 11-2: Bruce Camings, *Korea's Place in the Sun* (New York: W. W. Norton, 1997), 144.

Map 11-3: Murray Rubinstein, ed., *Taiwan: A New History* (Armonk, NY: M. E. Sharpe, 1999), 226.

Map 12-1: Hans J. Van de Ven: *War and Nationalism in China, 1925–1945* (London: Routledge Curzon, 2003), 52.

Map 12-2: John Hunter Boyle, *Modern Japan, The American Nexus* (Fort Worth, TX: Harcourt Brace Jovanovich, 1993), 266.

Map 13-1: R. Keith Schoppa, *Revolution and Its Past* (Upper Saddle River, NJ: Pearson Prentice Hall, 2006), 225.

Map 13-2: R. Keith Schoppa, *Revolution and Its Past* (Upper Saddle River, NJ: Pearson Prentice Hall, 2006), 295.

Map 14-1: Marius Jansen, *The Making of Modern Japan* (Cambridge, MA: Belknap Press of Harvard University Press, 2002), 758.

Map 15-1: William Stueck, *Rethinking the Korean War* (Princeton, NJ: Princeton University Press, 2002), 63.

Map 15-2: William Stueck, *Rethinking the Korean War* (Princeton, NJ: Princeton University Press, 2002), 90.

Map 15-3: William Stueck, *Rethinking the Korean War* (Princeton, NJ: Princeton University Press, 2002), 120.

Map 16-1: Bernard B. Fall, *Street Without Joy* (Harrisburg, PA: Stackpole, 1961), 67.

Map 16-2: Stanley Karnow, *Vietnam: A History* (New York, Viking, 1983), 333.

Map 16-3: Stanley Karnow, *Vietnam: A History* (New York, Viking, 1983), 524.

Map 17-1: R. Keith Schoppa, *Revolution and Its Past* (Upper Saddle River, NJ: Pearson Prentice Hall, 2006), 402.

Map 17-2: Steven J. Hood, *Dragons Entangled: Indo-China and the China-Vietnam War* (Armonk, NY: M. E. Sharpe, 1992), 120.

Map 18-1: Chushichi Tsuzuki, *The Pursuit of Power in Modern Japan, 1825–1995* (Oxford: Oxford University Press, 2000), Map 4 (at end of book).

Map 18-2: Patricia Ebrey, Ann Walthall, and James B. Palais, *East Asia: A Cultural, Social and Political History* (Boston: Houghton Mifflin, 2005), 162.

Map 19-1: http://www.geography.about.com//library/cia/bicsouthkorea.htm.

Map 19-2: http://www.geography.about.com/library/cia/bicnorthkorea.htm.

Credits

p. 2 *photo*: Bill Hatcher/National Geographic Image Collection; p. 5 *Source*: Tale #23, p. 301 from *Myths and Legends from Korea* comp. James Huntley Grayson. © 2001. Reprinted by permission of Thomson Publishing Services on behalf of Taylor & Francis Books (UK); p. 6 *figure*: Figure 3, p. 5 from "The Vietnamese Public in Transition: The 2001 World Values Survey" by Russell J. Dalton and Nhu-Ngoc T. Ong. (Nov 1, 2001). Center for the Study of Democracy, Paper 01–09. © 2001 by the authors. Reprinted by permission of Russell J. Dalton; p. 7 *photo*: AP Wide World Photos; p. 9 *Source*: Excerpt from pp. 228–229 in *The Last Emperors: A Social History of Qing Imperial Institutions* by Evelyn Rawski. © 1998 by University of California Press. Reprinted by permission of Copyright Clearance Center on publisher's behalf; p. 11 *Source*: Excerpt from pp. 75–76 in *Understanding Vietnam* by Neil Jamieson. © 1993 by University of California Press. Reprinted by permission of Copyright Clearance Center on publisher's behalf; p. 13 *Source*: From p. 9 in *Folktales of China* ed. Wolfram Eberhard. © 1965. Reprinted by permission of University of Chicago Press; p. 14 *photo*: Evans/Getty Images Inc.—Hulton Archive Photos; p. 15 *photo*: Jean Paul Nacivet/eStock Photography LLC/© Jean Paul Nacivet/eStock Photography, LLC; p. 19 *photo*: Michael S. Yamashita/Corbis/Bettmann; p. 21 *photo*: Bruce Behnke/Danita Delimont Photography/© Bruce Behnke/DanitaDelimont.com; p. 27 *Source*: From p. 22 in *Daughter of Han* by Ida Pruitt. 1945 by Yale University Press. Reprinted by permission of publisher; p. 28 *Source*: Reprinted from p. 26 in *The Face of China: 1860–1912* by L. Carrington Goodrich and Nigel Cameron. © 1978. Published by Aperture Foundation; p. 29 *photo*: Bibliotheque Nationale de France; p. 31 *photo*: Karen Su/Danita Delimont Photography/© Keren Su/DanitaDelimont.com; p. 31 *photo*: The Art Archive/Picture Desk, Inc./Kobal Collection; p. 32 *photo*: The Cleveland Museum of Art/Giuseppe Castiglione, Italian (worked in China), Chinese, 1688–1766, "Inauguration Portraits of Emperor Qianlong, The Empress, and the Eleven Imperial Consorts," 1736. Handscroll, ink and color on silk, 52.9 × 688.3 cm. © The Cleveland Museum of Art, 2003. John L. Severance Fund, 1969.31; p. 36 *Source*: As published in *An Embassy to China: Being the Journal Kept by Lord Macartney During His Embassy to the Emperor Chi'oen-Lung, 1793–1794* ed. J. L. Cramner-Byng. Addison Wesley Longman, 1962; p. 37 *Source*: Excerpt from Changing China: *Readings in the History of China from the Opium War to Present*, ed. J. Mason Gentzler. © 1977. Reproduced with permission of Greenwood Publishing Group; p. 38 *Source*: Reprinted by permission of publisher from *Trade and Diplomacy on the China Coast: The Opening of Treaty Ports, 1842–1854* by John King Fairbank, p. 19, Cambridge, MA.: Harvard University Press, 1953 by The President and Fellows of Harvard College; p. 41 *photo*: Courtesy of the Library of Congress; p. 43 *photo*: Baldwin H. Ward/Corbis/Bettmann; p. 46 *photo*: Felice Beato/Getty Images Inc.—Hulton Archive Photos/George Eastman House/Felice Beato/Hulton Getty Collection/Archive Photos; p. 47 *Source*: Reprinted from p. 26 in *The Face of China: 1860–1912* by L. Carrington Goodrich and Nigel Cameron. © 1978. Published by Aperture Foundation; p. 53 *Source*: From pp. 119–120 from *God's Chinese Son: The Taiping Heavenly Kingdom of Hong Xiuquan* by Jonathan D. Spence. © 1996 by Jonathan D. Spence. Used by permission of W. W. Norton & Co. Inc.; p. 54 *Source*: From pp. 121–122 from *God's Chinese Son: The Taiping Heavenly Kingdom of Hong Xiuquan* by Jonathan D. Spence. © 1996 by Jonathan D. Spence. Used by permission of W. W. Norton & Co., Inc.; p. 56 *photo*: Art Resource/The New York Public Library Photographic Services/Collections of The New York Public Library, Astor, Lenox and Tilden Foundations/Art Resource, NY; p. 56 *photo*: CORBIS–NY/© CORBIS All Rights Reserved; p. 57 *Source*: Reprinted from p. 26 in *The Face of China: 1860–1912* by L. Carrington Goodrich and Nigel Cameron. © 1978. Published by Aperture Foundation; p. 59 *Source*: Excerpt from p. 1091 in "Blinkered Visions: Islamic Identity, Hui Ethnicity, and the Panthay Rebellion in Southwest China, 1856–1873" by David G. Atwill, *Journal of Asian Studies*, V 62, iss 4, 2003. © 2003 by Cambridge University Press. Reprinted by permission of publisher; p. 68 *photo*: French School, (19th century)/The Bridgeman Art Library International/Private Collection/The Bridgeman Art Library; p. 69 *Source*: Reprinted with permission of Scribner, an imprint of Simon & Schuster Adult Publishing Group, from *Modern China: From Mandarin to Commissar* by Dun J. Li. © 1978 by Dun J. Li. All rights reserved; p. 71 *photo*: Courtesy of the Freer Gallery of Art, Smithsonian Institution, Washington, D.C.; p. 72 *Source*: From p. 186 in *The Search for Modern China: A Documentary Collection* by Pei-kai Cheng, Michael Lestz and Jonathan Spence. © 1999 by W. W. Norton. Used by permission of W. W. Norton & Company, Inc; p. 73 *photo*: The Granger Collection; p. 74 *photo*: Corbis/Bettmann/© Bettmann/CORBIS All Rights Reserved; p. 75 *photo*: Keystone, Hamburg/Getty Images Inc.—Hulton Archive Photos; p. 79 *photo*: Keren Su/Getty Images Inc.—Stone Allstock; p. 82 *Source*: Adapted from Document 4, "Nguyen Hue's Address to the Army (1789)" from *Patterns of Vietnamese Response to Foreign Intervention: 1858–1900* trans. by Truong Buu Lam, Mono. Series No. 11, Southeast Asia Studies, Yale University. © 1967. Reprinted by permission of Professor Truong Buu Lam; p. 83 *Source*: As published on pp. 13–17 in *Minh-Mang* by Marcel Gaultier. Paris: Larose, 1935; p. 84 *photo*: Sami Sarkis/Getty Images, Inc.—Photodisc.; p. 86 *photo*: Tim Hall/Getty Images, Inc.—Photodisc.; p. 87 *photo*: Dufresne, Charles Georges (1876–1938)/The Bridgeman Art Library International/Private Collection/The Bridgeman Art Library; p. 90 *photo*: Keren Su/Danita Delimont Photography/© Keren Su/DanitaDelimont.com; p. 90 *Source*: Quoted in Nguyen Van Thai and Nguyen Vang Ming, *A Short History of Vietnam* (Saigon, 1958); p. 93 *Source*: Excerpt from p. 75 in *Community and Revolution in Modern Vietnam* by Alexander Barton Woodside. Houghton Mifflin College Division, 1976; p. 94 *Source*: Excerpt from p. 84 in

Index

Note: In the Index, acronyms are used for lengthy country names. Thus, PRC stands for the People's Republic of China, ROC stands for the Republic of China (located in Taiwan after 1949), DPRK is the Democratic People's Republic of Korea (North Korea), while ROK is the Republic of Korea (South Korea). Finally, DRV stands for the Democratic Republic of Vietnam (North Vietnam from 1954 to 1976), while SRV(Socialist Republic of Vietnam) is all of Vietnam from 1976 to the present. The United States becomes simply US without periods.